UNDERSTANDING CHURCH GROWTH

by
DONALD A. McGAVRAN

WILLIAM B. EERDMANS PUBLISHING COMPANY
GRAND RAPIDS, MICHIGAN

Library of Congress Cataloging in Publication Data:

McGavran, Donald Anderson, 1897–
Understanding church growth.

Bibliography: p. 461.
Includes index.
1. Church growth.   2. Sociology, Christian.
I. Title.
BV652.25.M293   1980   266   80-10923
ISBN 0-8028-1521-9

PREFACE TO THE REVISED EDITION

In the last two decades of the twentieth century the Church is hearing anew God's clarion call to bring the peoples of every continent to faith and obedience. Increasingly it is turning its vast resources toward evangelism and church growth. Small denominations, large denominations, Protestants, and Roman Catholics are focusing on the propagation of the Gospel at home and abroad. It is becoming crystal clear that there will be no great advance in righteousness, peace and justice until there are many more practicing Christians and believing churches in every segment of mankind.

Evangelization intends the redemption of individuals and the multiplication of Christ's churches. Concern for evangelism and church growth is an essential part of the Christian Faith and an irreplaceable part of the work of the Church. The Church is the Body of Christ and brings persons and nations to faith and obedience as it proclaims the Gospel effectively in every people and incorporates believers from every people in ongoing churches. Believing this, the Church girds for action.

However, engaged in many good activities, Christians often take the growth of the church for granted. They neither pray earnestly for it nor work systematically at it. They assume it will take place automatically as Christians study the Bible, do good to others, and worship God. As a result, in the midst of huge numbers of receptive men and women, many churches stop growing and become static enclaves of comfortable middle-class Christians. These feed the hungry, visit the sick, clothe the naked, build attractive houses of worship, train leaders, and influence society for good, but they do not grow. The dynamism of the Early Church does not dwell in them. Huge populations in Eurica and huger populations in Africasia remain undiscipled. They do not have the Son. They do not have eternal life. Church growth has been assumed and is, alas, not occurring.

This was the case in Christian Missions overseas in the mid-twentieth century. Tremendous resources were spent in mission work, often for very little growth of the Church. Where growth was impossible, this outcome was understandable, but sometimes little growth was unnecessary. Christians, pastors, and missionaries were coming out of the ripe fields empty-handed. During the decades following World War II, little or no growth also marked most denominations in the United States. Some biological and transfer growth did occur but conversion growth was spotty and slight. Whole denominations became static or actually declined. Pastors in America, like their brothers overseas, often led congregations which remained at about the same number of members for years, or even lost a few hundred.

Determined effort to understand church growth, to record where it was and was not happening, and to ascertain the causes for growth and decline first began overseas. God granted me unique opportunities to study such matters in many lands. The Church Growth Movement, therefore, between 1955 and 1970 was very largely concerned with growth of churches overseas. How can churches be more faithful to God? Are missions reaping as largely as they can? Are congregations in Africasia multiplying as God desires? How can missionaries engage in more effective evangelism? What factors accelerate and what retard church growth in new denominations? These were the questions asked. On such topics the global *Church Growth Bulletin* published hundreds of articles, authored by leaders of Christian thought in many lands. Career missionaries assembled in Church Growth Seminars, enrolled in the historic Institute of Church Growth in Eugene, Oregon, and later in the School of World Mission of Fuller Theological Seminary to study these matters. Courses of lectures on church growth were given, refined to fit aspects of growth which researches carried out by career missionaries had discovered, and given again. In 1967 the first draft of *Understanding Church Growth* was written. Mimeographed copies of the manuscript served as the basic text in church growth for three years. The book was published in 1970.

In 1971, as church growth writings began to circulate widely in the United States and *Understanding Church Growth* was read and studied by ministers, conviction began to form that growth was fully as much a

concern of American Churches as it was of missionary societies and Afericasian Churches. Drs. Peter Wagner, Ralph Winter, Winfield Arn, and
George Hunter played significant parts in the spread of that conviction.
The Southern Baptists, Nazarenes, and some other denominations have
devoted large resources to church growth. As a result, in America the
seventies have seen a veritable explosion of interest in the growth of the
Church. Interest is beginning in Scandinavia and England. Books and
articles pour from the presses. Hundreds of ministers assemble in church
growth seminars. Doctoral programs of church growth are taught in many
seminaries. Denominational headquarters make substantial annual allocations to stop the decline and initiate decades of increase.

As American leaders studied the 1970 *Understanding Church Growth*
(which they considered the basic book) they found its illustrations came
very largely from overseas. Some Americans, therefore, were tempted to
think that church growth principles did not apply to the United States.
Wiser men realized that they applied fully as much and asked me to revise
the 1970 edition so they would be easily seen to do so.

In addition, during the seventies (a decade rich in insights concerning
ways in which the Faith is communicated in the tremendously complex
mosaic of mankind) leading advocates of church growth had made major
contributions to the art. These, I felt, ought to be gathered up in one book.
The problem was how to determine which were major contributions and
which were needed popularizations and applications. Books on many,
many aspects of church growth had been published during the decade.
Hundreds of contributions had been made, far too numerous to be covered
in one book. In making the revision, therefore, it had to be my steady aim
to stick to the *germinal principles*.

Church growth is much wider and deeper than adding names to church
rolls. It delves into how persons and peoples become genuinely Christian
and revolutionize and bless the cultures and populations in the midst of
which God has placed them. Church growth arises in theology and biblical
faithfulness. It draws heavily on the social sciences because it always
occurs in societies. It continually seeks for instances in which God has
granted growth and then asks what are the *real* factors which He has
blessed to such increase. The Preface to the 1970 edition (which follows
immediately) stresses these wide essential emphases of church growth and
should be read before beginning the book.

This book is published with the prayer that it may be used of God
to aid in the urgent revitalization of His Church and the incorporation of
sufficient men and women in it so that major social advance may be

achieved in all nations. The long-range goal of church growth is the discipling of *panta ta ethne*, to the end that rivers of the water of eternal and abundant life flow fast and free, to every tongue and tribe and people in all the earth.

July 1, 1980   DONALD MCGAVRAN
                                         School of Mission
                                         Fuller Theological Seminary
                                         Pasadena, California

PREFACE TO THE 1970 EDITION

Discipling the nations, reconciling men of all races to God in Christ, bringing all nations to faith and obedience, and preaching the Gospel to the whole creation—in short, the missionary enterprise—has arrived at one of the hinges of history.

Vast reinterpretation of what mission essentially is in this rapidly changing world engages voices, pens, and minds. Many see only a small part of the total scene and ardently define what they think mission in that sector should be. Many of the problems of Europe and America—for the simple reasons that most Christian writers are provincial Europeans and Americans—occupy the center of the stage. "Mission" becomes what these Western writers think should be done. Furthermore, what the true Christian goals *are* is hotly debated. In this new day what does the Triune God demand? And do we understand what He demands on the basis of our reason or His revelation?

The theory and theology of mission is what is in dispute. As God carries out His mission in the world and the Church seeks to be found "about His business" what *should* be done? What priorities are correct? Among many good enterprises, which has preeminence? Which should come first and which—if any have to be—should be omitted? How is carrying out the will of God to be measured? What has really been accomplished as the Church has spread on new ground? Considerations of anthropology, sociology, theology, and organizational complexity pile up

ix

one on the other. Never was a clear mission theory more needed than today—a theory firmly rooted in biblical truth.

Understanding Church Growth has been written in the midst of this welter of opinion. It is speaking to this hinge of history. It has been formed against the confusion of means and ends so typical of today's missions. It is at once a book on mission theology, mission theory, and mission practice. These three do not exist in isolation, but as an integrated whole, theology influencing theory and practice, practice coloring theology and theory, and theory guiding both practice and theology.

This book is not by any means the last word on the subject. Rather, it is an attempt to take the reconciling of men to God in the Church of Jesus Christ seriously, in view of the empirical churches actually founded. It maintains throughout—and this is one of the stones in its theological foundation—that the establishment of churches (assemblies of baptized believers) is pleasing to God. Furthermore, it maintains throughout—and this is one of the stones in its anthropological foundation—that the size, number, ethnic and cultural composition, and relationship to the undiscipled are matters which, if the Christian is to be a good steward of God's grace, can be measured and *must be known*. I hope many other books about the establishment of churches—units of God's righteousness, peace, and forgiveness—will continue to be written.

Similar books should be made available to the Churches of Asia, Africa, and Latin America in the languages of those lands. This book in English will be read by highly educated nationals and missionaries from Europe and America. That is good, but not enough. The younger Churches are in grave danger of being misled by the very plethora of good things to do, the intensity of feeling in the older Churches about the problems of Europe and America, and the confusion in the theory, theology, and practice of mission. The fact that eighty percent and more of the activities of missions today are organized good deeds and social action takes the attention of many younger Churches off the propagation of the Gospel. They need to center their attention on the basic fact of the Gospel, that Jesus Christ died for all men and that "the Gospel...according to the commandment of the everlasting God, [has been] made known to all nations for the obedience of faith" (Rom. 16:25, 26). Till everyone has had a chance to respond to that good news, the mission must go forward.

The great campaigns of evangelism are urgent. They are one way in which the Gospel advances. But, as the pages of this book show abundantly, campaigns need to be carried on in such fashion that multitudes of new churches *are* established and multitudes of new converts *do* become reliable members of Christ's Body. Furthermore, many other ways to advance the Gospel are being and must be used. All of them, including evangelism, must be used in the light of feedback from the on-going mission enterprise, guided by the degree to which men and *ethne* are being brought to the obedience of the faith, and churches are being multiplied.

January 1, 1970   DONALD McGAVRAN
                                     School of Missions and
                                          Institute of Church Growth
                                     Fuller Theological Seminary
                                     Pasadena, California

CONTENTS

PREFACE TO THE REVISED EDITION   v
PREFACE TO THE 1970 EDITION   ix

PART I THEOLOGICAL CONSIDERATIONS

1. The Complex Faithfulness Which Is Church Growth   3
2. God's Will and Church Growth   23
3. Today's Task, Opportunity, and Imperative   41

PART II DISCERNING THE OUTLINES

4. The Marvelous Mosaic   59
5. A Universal Fog   76
6. The Facts Needed   93

PART III CAUSES OF CHURCH GROWTH

7. Discovering the Why of It   123
8. Sources to Search for Causes of Growth   144
9. Helps and Hindrances to Understanding   165
10. Revival and Church Growth   186

PART IV THE SOCIOLOGICAL FOUNDATION

11. Social Structure and Church Growth   207
12. Without Crossing Barriers   223
13. The Receptivity of Men and Societies   245

PART V SPECIAL KINDS OF CHURCH GROWTH

14. The Masses, the Classes, and Church Growth   269
15. Halting Due to Redemption and Lift   295
16. Discipling Urban Populations   314
17. People Movements   333
18. Kinds of People Movements and Their Care   354
19. Indigenous Church Principles and Growing Churches 373

PART VI ADMINISTERING FOR CHURCH GROWTH

20. Stream Across the Bridges   395
21. Set Goals   412
22. Make Hard, Bold Plans   434

EPILOGUE   458
BIBLIOGRAPHY   460
INDEX   468

NOTE ON UNUSUAL TERMS

Anyone who works in a specialized field for many years is apt to evolve words of his own for situations and concepts he is constantly dealing with. Some provide short cuts through otherwise cumbersome parlance. Others are more exact or carry more connotative freight. A few such terms seem so helpful that I allow myself to use them in writing, as I would in talking with serious students, instead of expressing the ideas in more conventional speech.

Most Americans are familiar with the awkwardness or impossibility of making an adjective or pronoun out of the words "United States," so that Canadians and Latin Americans alike are recurrently a bit annoyed at our preempting of "American" for ourselves (as if they were not of this hemisphere). While we, in turn, cannot help ourselves, confronted as we are by the plain perversity of language.

In church growth, one of the verbal difficulties is the lack of any single word for "Europe and North America." The combination has to be used repeatedly in speaking of Western Churches and their programs of evangelism at home and abroad. In my classes and books, I have come to use Eurica and its adjective Eurican for this. Even more unhandy is the lack of any term for all those areas of the earth—Africa, Latin America, Asia, and other smaller ones—where the younger Churches and the great un-Christianized populations of the world are located. "Africasia" for my purpose includes them all, in something less than the two or three lines it would require to convey the same idea in normal English (not to mention the occasional need, in a book about evangelism and missions, to refer to this dominant portion of the globe more than once in the same paragraph or even three or four times on a page).

Other terms I have found helpful, whose exact meaning will be apparent in the text, are homogeneous unit, a people in the sense of a tribe, lift, stoppage, overhang, winnable, classes and masses, and so on—not very many. To one who is not constantly discussing my subject they may seem at first strange, but their usefulness should be clear. Indeed, some broad ranges of fact have, I believe, gone too long unnoticed or imperfectly realized in the field of church growth, partly for lack of easy definitive terms to apply to them. As the science of missiology grows, more and more words will be used in specialized senses. Some new ones will be coined. They will facilitate exact thought.

In a further effort toward exact thinking, I capitalize the word *Church* when it means a denomination or the Church Universal or the Church in general. When the word means a congregation or is used as an adjective it appears thus: church.

I apologize to the reader for any inconvenience which these unusual terms or usages may cause him or for the jar to his sense of language, and only hope that he will not allow them to obscure the deeper sense of what, in this book, I am trying to convey.

D. McG.

PART I
THEOLOGICAL CONSIDERATIONS

1

THE COMPLEX FAITHFULNESS
WHICH IS CHURCH GROWTH

TREMENDOUS GROWTH is going on in the Christian Church today. For some observers this tends to be obscured by the world population explosion and the increasing percentage of non-Christians which that so far implies. I shall hope to show before the end of this volume that the potential of Christian church growth is not thereby overshadowed. Meanwhile, the fact is that the number of Christians is greater now than it has ever been. With the rise of the Free Churches and the expansion of the Church among non-Christian populations, multitudes of small congregations of less than a hundred members have been formed. Consequently the number of congregations is far greater than at any time in history.

The Church is even now expanding in many towns and cities in North America and overseas in numerous cultures and subcultures, languages and dialects, tribes, classes, and kindreds. Whereas in the year 1800 it was confined largely to Europe and the Americas, by the last years of the twentieth century it had spread to almost every country on earth.

Frequently a Church splits and both sections grow. The divisions of the Presbyterian Church in Korea in the 1950's were widely cited by pessimists as proof of dark days and degeneracy, but during the fifties the Presbyterian Church in Korea (all branches) more than doubled, erected hundreds of new church buildings, and in 1960 had far more influence in the land than in 1950. Superficial thinkers among the Roman Catholics in

3

Chile may bewail the fact that a tenth of their people have become Pentecostal Christians; but wiser heads among them no doubt praise God for the vitality and growth of the Pentecostal sections of the Church. Denominational pride often prevents us from seeing that when our branch of the Church loses members to a more vital branch, we are awakened and stimulated to greater effort, and the Church Universal prospers. Thus when George Fox in Cromwell's time multiplied meetings of Friends across England and these spread around the world, who can doubt that the Church Universal prospered? Or when reformers left the Syrian Orthodox Church in Kerala, India, about 1890 and established the Mar Thoma Syrian Church (which then grew from a few congregations to a denomination of 400,000 members in 1977), not only did the Church Universal prosper, but the sleepy Orthodox Syrian Church itself was moved to mission.

Sections of the Church, sometimes large, sometimes small, do of course at times face difficulties or new problems and enter a period of malaise. War, famine, pestilence, the spread of some debilitating theology, adjustment to radically new conditions, migration to new lands or cities, and totalitarian oppression are some of the factors that not only check church growth but may enervate the people of God for a time. The hand of Midian sometimes prevails against Israel—till God raises up Gideon. This evident truth must not, however, be allowed to obscure the worldwide growth of the Church. Just as non-Christian populations are prodigiously growing, so the mere excess of births over deaths in the Christian community vastly increases the number of those who count themselves Christians rather than Secularists, Marxists, Confucians, Buddhists, or followers of some other faith; while subsequent personal confession of Christ transforms hundreds of thousands of these every year into convinced Christians. To these additions from within must be added others from without, through the conversion of unbelievers living on the edge of innumerable existing congregations, intermarrying with their members, and counting themselves as already in some vague way "Christian." Hundreds of thousands of such conversions are constantly going on almost unnoticed. To this new total should be added the dramatic conversions of great numbers of non-Christians. Between 1936 and 1966, 120,000 Ethiopian pagans became baptized believers in the Church founded by the Sudan Interior Mission. During the two decades prior to 1966, 80,000 highlanders became Presbyterian Christians in Formosa. After India became independent in 1947, the Methodist Church in the Raichur Vikarabad area grew from 100,000 to 200,000. Between 1906 and 1980 the Nazarene Church in

America has grown enormously. Numerous other illustrations could easily be given.

Christians, preoccupied with domestic problems and denominational housekeeping, often fail to see the phenomenon of mighty church growth which God is continually bringing to pass on all six continents. Some persons, surprised at the extent of this growth, may even doubt its reality. But like Mt. Everest, it is there. It is going on all the time. And understanding it is an urgent task.

CHURCH GROWTH IS FAITHFULNESS TO GOD

Anyone who would comprehend the growth of Christian Churches must see it primarily as faithfulness to God. God desires it. The Christian, like his Master, is sent to seek and save the lost. Rather than gaining something for oneself, finding the lost is to become "your servant for Christ's sake." Church growth is humane action: the strong bearing the burdens of the weak and introducing to the hungry the bread by which man lives. Nevertheless, God's obedient servants seek church growth not as an exercise in humanity, but because the extension of the Church is pleasing to God. Church growth is faithfulness.

Only where Christians constrained by love obediently press on, telling men the good news of the Savior, does the Church spread and increase. Where there is no faithfulness in proclaiming Christ, there is no growth. There must also be obedience in hearing. Churches do not multiply and spread across a land or through a city unless among the multitudes who hear there are many who obey and—loving Christ more than father or mother—deny themselves, take up their cross daily, and follow Him.

Church growth follows where Christians show faithfulness in finding the lost. It is not enough to search for lost sheep. The Master Shepherd is not pleased with a token search; He wants His sheep found. The purpose is not to search, but to find. The goal is not to send powdered milk or kindly messages to the son in the far country. It is to see him walking in through the front door of his father's house. For church growth also requires obedience in being found. It never takes place among the indifferent or rebellious, save as they renounce their indifference and rebellion.

Church growth follows where the lost are not merely found but restored to normal life in the fold—though it may be a life they have never consciously known. Faithfulness in "folding and feeding"—which unfortunately has come to be called by such a dry, superficial term as follow-up—is essential to lasting church expansion. When existing Christians, marching obediently under the Lord's command and filled with His compassion, fold the wanderers and feed the flock, then churches multiply; but when they indolently permit men and women who have made costly decisions for Christ to drift back into the world, then indeed churches do not grow. Faithfulness in proclamation and finding is not enough. There must be faithful aftercare. Among the found, also, there must be fidelity in feeding on the Word.

The multiplication of churches nourished on the Bible and full of the Holy Spirit is a *sine qua non* in carrying out the purposes of God. Conversely, would-be disciples must be joyfully built into His Body—they must not wander alone in the wilderness. Because some Churches appear to give the empirical Church a value and authority beyond that which she accords to Jesus Christ, her Lord, some misguided Protestants speak as if the natural goal for man were a vague Kingdom of God toward which we all automatically proceed—as if the multiplying of Christian churches among all men were an unworthy aim. This is to misread Scripture and fly in the face of common sense. Though God's triumphant reign will not come till Christ returns in power, it is clear that in this era the more men love Christ and live "in Him" as part of His Body, the more goodness and truth will prevail in their communities. Righteousness and peace will surely spread as sound churches multiply throughout the three billion persons who now feel no allegiance to Jesus Christ.

Wholesome growth also means faithful obedience to God in developing churches so solid in their human matrix that they can grow, but also so separated and holy that they remain pleasing to God. It is true that churches can so divorce themselves from their neighbors that, sealed off and introverted, they cannot communicate the Gospel. These have disobeyed the Bible in taking themselves out of the world. Christians must remain in the world. Like their Master, they must become incarnate in the ignorant, filthy, and sinful villages and cities of the real world. They must become "slaves" in the families of mankind. To do this is difficult, and a still greater difficulty comes in being "in but not of the world." Yet that is the scriptural injunction. Christians must remain Christian. They must "come out and be separate"—separate enough to maintain a vivid life with Christ—not with a vague cosmic Christ, but with the Jesus Christ portrayed in the Gospels and Epistles. This is perhaps the most difficult faithfulness of all, but without it there is little growth. His churches, though solid with the world, must also be clearly His.

Church growth is no mere sociological process. To be sure, an agnostic from his self-limited cell would see it as merely the outcome of an interplay of anthropological, historical, economic, and political forces. The agnostic, believing in no transcendent Source of Truth, confines himself, for his understanding of reality, to evidences which filter into his mind through the grid of reason—at its present state of development and with all its fluctuating limitations. But I, the writer, am not an agnostic; I am a convinced Christian. I believe in God the Father Almighty, Maker of Heaven and Earth, and in Jesus Christ His Son. The Truth to which I am bound inheres in the ultimate stuff of the universe: the Word which was in the beginning with God, by whom all things were made, without whom was not anything made that was made—He is Truth, and to Him I give answer for everything I think and say and do.

I am not free to indulge my prejudices or to slight any of the evidence. I must take into account what comes in through the filter of my small reason and what comes to me through revelation and in every other way. All evidence must be weighed before the bar of Truth. Therefore I cannot consider church growth merely a sociological process. It is that, to be sure; but much more than that, it is what happens when there is faithfulness to the God and Father of our Lord Jesus Christ.

The spread of the Church throughout the world must not be thought of in merely human terms. We are not speaking about the multiplication of branches of an American organization; that would be cultural imperialism. As Cullmann says (1961:46), "The Church itself is an eschatological phenomenon . . . constituted by the Holy Spirit." It is part of the new order which began at the resurrection of Jesus Christ. Churches multiplying across the world in every nation demonstrate that a new era has begun. Like the Holy Spirit, they are an earnest of the triumphant reign of God, which in His good time He will bring in.

Church growth is basically a theological stance. God requires it. It looks to the Bible for direction as to what God wants done. It believes that Acts 4:12, John 14:6, and scores of similar passages are true. It holds that belief in Jesus Christ, understood according to the Scriptures, is necessary for salvation. Church growth rises in unshakeable theological conviction.

But since church growth has been born in an interdenominational milieu and taught to missionaries and ministers of many theological persuasions, and does not allow denominational differences to hide God's desire that His lost children be found and His churches be multiplied, therefore advocates of church growth have avoided voicing those of their own theological convictions which are not—at this time under these circumstances—either causing or preventing church growth. Naturally therefore to denominational theologians church growth looks inadequately theological. They consider it as method not theology. Baptismal regenerationists complain that church growth does not believe in baptism. Some Calvinists complain that church growth overlooks the sovereignty of God. Pentecostals tend to feel that church growth gives insufficient emphasis to the Holy Spirit. Those fighting for social justice like to say that church growth men teach cheap grace. Those interested in liturgy find that church growth says very little about liturgy.

To all such critics we reply, "The basic positions of church growth are profoundly biblical and theological; but are not a complete theology. Complete *your* theology by building these basic growth concepts as to the urgency and authority of evangelism into it. As you set forth church growth theory and theology for your congregations and your denomination use your own creedal statements, your own system. *Voice church growth theology in your patois.* Do not attack church growth as theologically inadequate. Make it adequate according to the doctrines emphasized by your Branch of the Church. The test as to whether you have done this or not is whether your congregations are stimulated to vibrant grateful growth such as New Testament churches exemplified."

THIS FAITHFULNESS IS COMPLEX

Very many kinds of church growth are found in the world today, each varying from people to people, from time to time, and from denomination to denomination. Understanding the nature of church growth is impossible unless the student apprehends the many different types and their various stages. Starting from the forms of growth in which he was reared and those he has seen where he has come to work, he must go on to recognize and remember scores of others. Only the unusual student, the specialist, can hope to be at home in the—literally—thousands of forms of church growth. For growth occurs in connection with many factors, and these combine and recombine in various parts of the world in almost astronomical variety.

The six following illustrations from the United States and other lands will reveal something of the tremendously complex process by which the Church multiplies congregations among the tongues and cultures of mankind, and how God brings about His beneficent reign among all who believe.

Church Growth in the Central Philippines

When the Japanese occupied the Philippines in 1942, the Rev. Leonardo G. Dia and his wife, refusing to collaborate with them, withdrew from the city of Cebu to the mountainous interior of the island and threw in their lot with three small neglected Presbyterian congregations. These had never had a resident pastor, let alone an able man like Mr. Dia. For the first few months the couple steadily visited the scattered homes of Christians, an arduous task in that mountainous country. They found the second-generation Christians friendly but largely ignorant of the Bible or of why they were Evangelicals. At Mr. Dia's urging, three small chapels of bamboo and thatch were built in well-hidden locations. Regular worship and instruction began. The pastor had R. H. Brown's book on the use of the Bible in personal evangelism in the Philippines, prepared years before by a Presbyterian missionary, which anchored the main Christian truths to about a hundred key passages in the New Testament. Instruction consisted in finding these in the Bible, explaining their meaning, and having the passages memorized. As fast as anyone learned all the passages with their references, and could explain what they meant, his name was written on the wall of his chapel (paper to write anything down being difficult to get in wartime). The competition stimulated everyone to learn.

As the congregations learned the passages, these Christians turned to each other in amazement, saying, "Our religion is true." Then they rushed out to persuade their loved ones and friends to become believers. In the first six months membership doubled. In the next year it doubled again. Other congregations were established.

This particular church growth was made possible by seven distinct factors which converged at the same moment. (1) Neglected Christians began to receive highly competent pastoring. (2) They received it from a minister-patriot who refused at the risk of his life to collaborate with the enemy. (3) He gave them not merely good preaching, house-to-house visitation, and the Bible (a vast knowledge) but a clear system which, within a small compass, made these neglected Christians masters of an outline of the Christian Way. (4) The second-generation Evangelicals were living in close contact with their nominally Roman Catholic relatives and friends. Once the Evangelicals had the Gospel they could communicate it. (5) The Evangelicals were largely literate, thanks to the American emphasis on schools in the Philippines. (6) The Roman Catholic priests, partly no doubt due to wartime confusion, did not bring instant persecution upon those who attended the Protestant chapels or became Evangelicals. (7) Mr. Dia was faithful in proclaiming Christ, finding the lost, feeding them, and building them into growing churches.

This particular kind of church growth—so conditioned by World War II, dependent on the Bible, closely connected with an ordained minister, naturally erupting from revived congregations, and geared in with literacy and other products of Western civilization—cannot take place in most parts of the world. Other kinds of growth can, but this particular kind will not.

In the United States

During the Civil War (1860-64) the Baptist Churches, like the Presbyterians and Methodists, split into two halves. Northern Baptists absolutely prohibited any traffic with slavery. Southern Baptists included many who owned slaves. The division continues till this day. Each denomination has its own Convention, its own associational rules and regulations.

Till the 1930s, it was understood by both Conventions that the Southern Baptists would work in the South and the Northern Baptists in the North. California was Northern Baptist territory. Southern Illinois, for a curious reason, while technically in the North was considered Southern Baptist territory. In short, a comity agreement was being observed. In 1930, there were only 12 Southern Baptist churches in the whole state of California. In that decade, observing that the Northern Baptists were not aggressively multiplying churches in California, the Southern Baptists (who were pouring into the state to take up land and jobs) said bluntly, "If you are not going to take advantage of the great opportunities for church growth in California, we will no longer consider the state as your territory. We will come in and multiply Southern Baptist churches." The Northern Baptists did not like it. They complained of the Southern Baptist "invasion," but could not stop it.

Growth took place in two ways. (1) Baptists moving to California from Georgia, the Carolinas, Texas, and other southern states, formed Southern Baptist congregations. Partly they did this on their own, and partly they did it actively assisted by the National Mission Board in Atlanta, Georgia. (2) In addition, Southern Baptist leaders frequently found an unchurched community and, whether there was a nucleus of Southerners there or not, established a new congregation. They did this not only among immigrant whites and native-born white Americans, but also among Japanese, Korean, Filipino, and Chinese immigrants.

As a result, the twelve congregations of 1934 in 1979 numbered more than a thousand. It is worth noting that none of the other mainline denominations—Methodists, Disciples, Presbyterians, Lutherans, or others—have displayed anything like this magnitude of growth. It was there to be had, but they did not get it. We shall speak later in this volume about receptivity and the need to recognize receptive populations; but Southern Baptist growth in California demonstrates that without the will to grow, without recognizing that effective evangelism is pleasing to God and is in fact commanded by Him, denominations do not grow as much as they should even in highly receptive populations. Unless a Church is faithful to God, it does not bring many sheaves out of ripe fields.

In South India

In 1840 the American Baptists started a mission at Nellore on the eastern coast of India. For twenty-five years they labored among the upper castes, winning less than a hundred converts.

In 1865 John Clough* and his wife came out as new missionaries. As they learned the language and studied the Bible to see what God would have them do, each independently came to the conclusion that, on the basis of I Corinthians 1:26-28, the policy followed rigorously by the older missionaries of seeking to win only the upper castes was displeasing to God (Clough 1915:133). The Madigas (Untouchables), known to be responsive to the Christian message, had been bypassed lest their baptism make it still more difficult for caste Hindus to become Christians. The Cloughs moved from Nellore, opened the station of Ongole, and began baptizing some remarkably earnest and spiritual Madiga leaders. By 1869, hundreds were being added to the Lord.

In 1877 a great famine swept that part of India. Many of the 3,000 baptized believers died of hunger. To save those he could from starvation, John Clough contracted to build three and a half miles of a canal which the government was putting through as famine relief work. He thus provided labor and food for 1,500 Christian men and women who had found it impossible to get work on sections of the canal where caste Hindus were foremen. Then, besieged by their starving non-Christian relatives and other Madigas, he put 1,500 pagan Madigas to work. In the famine camps along the canal, the Christians assembled in the evenings for worship and teaching. Pagan Madigas, too, heard the Word with joy and wonder, but were not baptized. Lest men become Christians for the loaves and fishes, Clough had stopped baptizing early in 1877.

As the canal was finished, the famine became more acute. Government and missions started other work projects and even distributed free food. A hundred thousand dollars passed through Clough's hands, and thousands of lives were saved.

After the crisis was over, requests for instruction and baptism poured in from the pagan relatives of the Christians. Clough and his helpers visited

*Rhymes with "how."

and preached in scores of villages. They taught, examined, and helped organize potential churches. Then on July 2, 3, and 4 of 1878, 3,536 believers were buried with their Lord in baptism. Within a few months over 6,000 others had followed them into the Church, making the total for that year 9,601, in a total membership of 12,806. Adherents were not counted but formed a much larger number (Clough 1915:284).

This kind of church growth differs enormously from the first two. Its conditioning factors—oppression, untouchability, burning conviction that the oppressed ought not to be denied salvation, a terrible famine, and a canal passing through the district—plus a missionary who was enough of an engineer to take a contract for part of the canal, devout enough to preach the Gospel to Untouchable laborers, wise enough to defer baptism till they had gone back to their villages, and courageous enough to baptize 9,601 in a single year. These particular factors may never again fall together. Other favorable elements will converge at a single time and place, but not these. Exactly this kind of church growth should not be expected to occur again.

The School Approach

A distinctive kind of church growth is found in Rhodesia and Zambia. This part of Africa was occupied by missions in the last third of the nineteenth century. The London Missionary Society began work there in 1859, the South African Dutch Reformed Church in 1872, the Anglicans in 1888, the English Methodists in 1891, and the American Methodists in 1898. Many other missions also have entered these lands.

The 1952 *World Christian Handbook* (pp. 195, 203) gives the membership of the thirty-four Protestant Churches or missions in this area for that year. Communicants totaled 125,266 and "places of worship," 3,883.

The degree of growth these figures indicate might at first glance be considered satisfactory. When it is remembered, however, that (1) a considerable fraction of the 125,266 full members were Europeans (out of a European population of 213,000 at least 35,000 were communicants); and (2) the total African population in 1950 was about 3,500,000, it is readily seen that the African communicants (about 90,000) comprised a mere 2.6 per cent of the African population.

Assuming 300 places where worship in English was carried on, the 90,000 vernacular-speaking African communicants were distributed in about 3,500 places of worship. Assuming about two hundred large African congregations with a total of possibly 30,000 communicants in towns, mission stations, and educational centers, this leaves 60,000 African communicants distributed in 3,300 places of worship. The average place of worship would have about 15 communicants.

What kind of church growth was this for the first hundred years of missionary labor in David Livingstone's land?

It was a special variety which I shall call "school-approach church growth." Missions carried on schools as an essential part of their evangelistic work. A chief once said to a missionary, "We adults are committed to our fetishes and to our tribal gods. We are polygamists. We cannot become Christians; but take our youth. Put them in schools. They will become Christians." It was government policy also to do all education through the missions. Only missions which promised to maintain schools and dispensaries were permitted to enter these countries, and were assigned territories of their own. Before 1950, almost the only way an African boy could get an education was to go to a mission school, where, as he was taught the Bible day after day by Christian teachers, he often became a Christian. Around mission stations and their far-flung schools many became Christians—as a result of schooling, employment in the church-mission establishment, genuine conversion, shrewd assessment of the advantages of being a Christian, commitment to the detribalized Western way of life, or for other reasons. The picture is one of many small congregations, led by teachers and convening in school buildings, while the pagan power structures of the tribe, composed of the mature men, remained intact. At the larger towns and mission stations, with their complexes of institutions and employment, a few score large congregations led by ministers met in church buildings.

In Rhodesia and Zambia the school approach produced this distinctive kind of church growth. It is a common variety in Africa south of the Sahara. For it to occur, a delicate balance of tensions in tribal society must make it possible for children of pagan parents to become Christians without seriously rupturing family relationships. In India, Latin America, and many other lands, church growth of this sort cannot occur. Minors cannot become Christians unless their parents lead the way into baptism.

When this kind of growth is continued long enough under favorable circumstances, it is complicated and obscured by second- and third-generation Christians and by dozens of people movements to the Christian faith. The latter (often called revivals) sweep sections of tribes into both (1) the mission-connected denominations, and (2) the independent African denominations whose theological bases are distributed all the way from the biblical to the syncretistic. People movements range from weak, quickly arrested Christward impulses affecting a few extended families, to powerful surges which do not stop until, over a span of years, they bring thousands of one tribe (or of several) to the Christian faith. In Southern Rhodesia and Zambia there have been few people movements into the mission-founded denominations. Those that have occurred have been weak and quickly arrested. Thus the school-approach pattern stands out clear.

The unformulated assumptions behind this approach have yet to be dug out of the letters, mission and government policies, allocations of mission budgets, and other sources so that we can see them clearly. Until this is done, one can only hazard a guess that the following considerations bulked large: (1) Tribal life is so pagan, illiterate, and evil as to be beyond redemption. (2) The goal of missions-cum-government is to break up the tribes and bring converts out into a modern, Christian post-tribal social order. (3) Polygamy is so entrenched in tribal life that it is impossible for most adults of the tribe to become Christian. (4) The correct way to Christianize, therefore, is through prolonged schooling. The argument was this: Many boys and girls will become Christian before their marriage. Many will remain Christian despite the pull of the tribe. The old generation will die off. Educated Christians will gradually control society. (5) The British Government will continue on indefinitely to the great advantage of the Africans. Over the centuries the old pagan order will gradually wither away and a Christian African population take its place. (6) The establishment of mission stations, dispensaries, hospitals, schools, and—in connection with them—churches is therefore the chief task of missions and the only sound way to proceed. (7) Sweeping Christianization of the tribes could take place only by impossible compromises with Christian conviction. (8) It is good to have 2 per cent of the population communicant, detribalized, and Christian; one may trust the gradual processes of history within a British Christian framework to extend the Christian pattern from the top downward until it embraces a large part of the population.

So long as the British framework remained, the school approach had much to commend it. It was not based on New Testament practices; but then African conditions between 1880 and 1950 were so very different from the New Testament world.

Since the British framework has collapsed, however, the case is far otherwise. Education is being rapidly taken over by the African states. Secularism, materialism, and Marxism bid for the allegiance of the educated, and no one can count on hundreds of years of peaceful evolution within any given system of government. Under today's conditions, the school approach has little to commend it. It is too slow, too vulnerable, too foreign, and too smug. Obviously the Churches must move ahead to win the masses of the population to Christian faith before they are captured by some of the great ideologies, religious or otherwise, that seek the allegiance of mankind.

In Rhodesia and Zambia this narrow kind of church growth, which during the years 1880-1950 was developed to fit one kind of government and social structure, must speedily be transformed into one that fits the political and social realities of the last fifth of the twentieth century in southeast Africa. Any policy that leaves Churches and missions satisfied with the glacial advance which is all the school approach *can* deliver, is suicidal. An evangelization which will multiply sound congregations in rapidly growing towns and cities is urgent. It is not enough for Churches and missions to "increase urban work." Urban work (mark the vague word "work") which fails to convert multitudes of non-Christians and to plant a host of new churches in the cities is a deceptive measure. It gives the impression that what is necessary has been done, when as a matter of fact, invaluable resources are being expended without achieving the goal intended. When the right kind of evangelism is projected into this situation, it will produce a new kind of church growth.

The tribe also must be recognized and welcomed as a significant political and social entity in the new Africa. Even if a hundred years from now tribes should cease to exist, they are a powerful part of the contemporary scene. A mode of mission must be perfected which converts not only individuals but "individuals and societies." The adult power structures of most villages and wards must be made up of Christian men. The mature men who control each ward and village should not be complacently left pagan, in the expectation that in time they will die off. The tribes must come to have as much consciousness of being Christian as the Scottish clans once had. This will require a type of church growth very different from that generated by the school approach.

Nothing will redeem the citizens of these two African countries but new kinds of church growth which leave sound, self-propagating congregations in all kralls, compounds, wards, and clusters of houses—whatever they may be called. A simplistic view which imagines that the Church will grow in Rhodesia and Zambia according to the present pattern is not merely useless: it is dangerous. The complex nature of the faithfulness which is church growth cries aloud to be learned by church and mission leaders, not only in these two countries but in all nations south of the Sahara.

Iceland About A.D. 1000

The Saga of Burnt Nyal is a bloody tale of family feuds in one part of Iceland. It would have merely antiquarian interest, except that a few chapters recount how the natives turned from paganism to Christianity. Burnt Nyal is not history. The turning actually took many decades, as first one group of families and then another became Christian. Eric the Red, who settled Greenland about A.D. 1000, died a pagan, while his wife Thjodhild and son Leif, who discovered America, became Christian. Nevertheless, the events recounted are either the actual ones or the kind of happenings that did take place. (The saga, translated into English in 1861 by Sir George Dasent, is available from E. P. Dutton & Co.)

Icelanders were the farthest out of the seafaring communities along the shores of Denmark, Norway, the Orkney and Shetland Islands, and Iceland. They lived by fishing, raising animals (ponies are frequently mentioned), and raiding villages in more favored lands. They were a hard-bitten, savage, and ruthless lot, who kept slaves and thought little of killing them. Constant feuds between extended families killed off the weaklings. Female infanticide was practiced—probably to keep the community from being burdened with surplus women.

Into the saga comes passing mention of Kolskegg, who went to Denmark and bound himself to Forkbeard, the Danish king. He was there baptized, then fared south to Micklegarth (Constantinople), took service with the Emperor, and married a Christian lady (Dasent, 1861 ed., 1960:142).

Then the islanders heard that

> there had been a change of rulers in Norway . . . and a change of faith. They had cast off the old faith and King Olaf had in addition baptized the western lands, Shetland, the Orkneys, and the Faroe Isles. . . . Many men said it was a strange and wicked thing to throw off the old faith; but Njal said, "It seems to me as though this new faith must be much better and he will be happy who follows this rather than the other; and if those men come hither who preach this faith, then I will back them well." That same harvest a ship came out into the fiords [of Iceland] at Gautawick. The captain Thangbrand was sent by King Olaf to preach the faith. Along with him came that man of Iceland whose name was Gudlief—a great manslayer and one of the strongest of men (Dasent, 1861 ed., 1960:176).

As these traveled from fiord to fiord, some accepted and some refused Christianity. Thorkell, an Icelander, spoke vigorously against the faith and challenged Thangbrand to single combat. The end of it was that Thangbrand slew Thorkell. A typical sentence of the saga reads, "Then Hildir the Old and all his household took upon them the new faith."

After many families and lineages became Christian, the islandwide Thing, where rough justice was meted out and feuds adjudicated, was convened at the Hill of Laws. Men rode to the Thing that year in battle array, because it seemed likely that pagans would fight Christians to determine which faith would hold Iceland. Both sides went to the Hill of Laws. Christians and heathen declared themselves "out of the other's laws." A great tumult arose. At the critical moment the Christian spokesman turned to the pagan witch doctor, Thorgeir, priest of Lightwater, and "gave him three marks of silver to utter what the law should be."

> Thorgeir lay all that day on the ground and spread a cloak over his head, so that no man spoke with him. . . . The day after, men went to the Hill of Laws and Thorgeir spoke thus: "It seems to me as though matters were come to a deadlock, for if there is a sundering of the laws, we shall never be able to live in the land. So I will ask both Christian men and heathen whether they will hold to these laws which I utter." They all said they would. . . . "This is the beginning of our laws," he said, "that all men shall be Christians and believe in one God . . . but leave all idol worship, not expose children to perish, and not eat horseflesh. It shall be outlawry if such things, done openly, are proved against any man; but if these things are done by stealth, then it shall be blameless."
>
> But all heathendom was done away with within a few years' space, so that those things were not allowed to be done either by stealth or openly (Dasent, 1861 ed., 1960:184).

This unique kind of church growth, so questionable and repugnant to Christians today, was not unusual in northern Europe a thousand years ago. It will never occur again. The special conditions which produced it have ceased to exist. All must regret the savagery, illiteracy, and isolation which made knowledge of the Bible and the Savior so scarce in the Dark Ages in Europe that only a low form of Christianity could develop; but thinking men must rejoice that those rough peoples did decide to "follow the new faith." They took the one essential step by which later advances in Christian living could be made by the Wycliffes, Knoxes, Luthers, Foxes, Wesleys, Careys, Hauges, and others. Icelandic church growth a thousand years ago was a part of the complex faithfulness which pleases God.

Urban Latin America

In 1964 the Evangelical church leaders in Aracaju, Brazil, in conjunction with the missionaries, planned a city-wide, year-long evangelistic campaign. They divided the city into sections and assigned one to each congregation. They organized cells in each to pray for revival and ingathering. Ministers preached on the lostness of unbelievers and the blessedness of those who repent of their sins and accept Jesus Christ as Lord and Savior. Joint open-air services were held. Those to whom God had granted special effectiveness as evangelists were invited in from other cities. The program progressed from congregational assemblies to gatherings of all the Evangelicals in each ward. Hundreds of thousands of tracts and Bible portions were distributed. Processions wound their way through the streets of the city. Christians two by two called on all houses in the urban area, inviting people to meetings and offering to teach them the way of the Lord.

All the Evangelical Churches, from the Assemblies of God to the United Presbyterian, cooperated in this campaign. A sense of expectation arose in congregation after congregation. Men and women, boys and girls, were won to Christian faith from week to week and joined in winning their neighbors and friends. Sins were confessed. Restitution for wrongs was made. Broken families were reunited. Instruction classes for inquirers and catechumens were opened in every church. When the campaign ended and inquirers had been instructed and baptized, it was found that the membership of the Evangelical Churches had more than doubled, from 1,200 to 2,400 baptized believers.

This church growth is more akin to North American patterns than some others described. Americans feel that this is more real and more spiritual than what occurred in Ongole or Rhodesia. That it is more spiritual may be doubted, but certainly it is different. Growth of this particular variety is possible only in certain circumstances. The general public must already consider itself Christian in some fashion. It must believe the Bible is its own Scripture, and read tracts and Bible portions and hear sermons and witness with that in mind. Opposition from leaders of the majority community must be mild or even nonexistent. Numerous existing Evangelicals must live in close contact with their unconverted neighbors and kinsmen. The existing congregations and denominations must be indigenous enough to appear thoroughly national, yet have enough missionary aid to finance a city-wide campaign. The churches must have missionary and national leaders who believe that accepting the Lord Jesus is the most important thing any man can do. Leaders who *as their paramount duty* are promoting social reconstruction, or engaging in dialogue with other religions, would wreck any such campaign and prevent the Church doubling in twelve months.

These six summarized cases of church growth indicate in bare outline the complexity of the process by which God is pleased to multiply His churches. As seams of coal cropping out in a few ravines point to vast deposits, so such cases point to a phenomenon of vital significance to the Church. And as the extraction and use of coal becomes a branch of knowledge to which men devote their entire lives, so—on a quite different plane—understanding church growth and applying that understanding to the evangelization of the world should become the life work of a large number of churchmen. As the humble treasure of the earth has contributed to the welfare of men, so the hidden fire, which in the providence of God emerges as church growth, contributes significantly—and may contribute still very much more—to the better world which, despite all modern discouragements, we see coming into being. When the Church plants congregations in the many cultures of America or any other nation, it multiplies credible witnesses who can readily be understood by the men of those cultures. Church growth will lead to saving faith in Jesus Christ the "ten thousand times ten thousand and thousands of thousands" whom Christ is redeeming from "every kindred, and tongue, and people, and nation."

A Schematic Look at the Complexity of Church Growth

The limitless intricacy of church growth may be further understood by locating each Church at its proper place on the following five lines of distribution, or axes.

A. DEPENDENCE VERSUS INDEPENDENCE
B. INDIVIDUAL VERSUS GROUP CONVERSION
C. PROPORTION OF TOTAL POPULATION
D. SPEED OF GROWTH
E. INDIGENEITY

On Axis *A* the "most dependent Churches" will be placed at the far left and the "most independent Churches" at the far right. All others are placed in between according to their degree of independence.

A DEPENDENCE VERSUS INDEPENDENCE					
1	2	3	4	5	6

To qualify for position 1, a Church would be heavily dependent, spiritually and materially, on its founding mission. To qualify for position 6, it would receive no missionary aid from abroad, carry on all its domestic labors effectively, and propagate Christianity inside and outside its own language area.

Similarly Churches can be located, according to their characteristics, on the other four axes whose two ends are defined.

B INDIVIDUAL VERSUS GROUP CONVERSION

1 Church has arisen by pure individual decision.	Church has arisen by pure group decision.	6

C PROPORTION OF TOTAL POPULATION

1 Church forms 1% or less of class or tribe concerned.	Church forms 90% or more of class or tribe concerned.	6

D SPEED OF GROWTH

1 Church has grown at less than 10% per decade.	Church has grown at more than 200% per decade.	6

E INDIGENEITY

1 Church has been formed in mold of foreign founder.	Church has been formed in indigenous mold.	6

If on the following axes the Iceland (A.D. 1000), Ongole (1900), Rhodesian (1952), Aracaju (1964), and Californian (1970) Churches be represented by their initial letters, something like the following distribution will be obtained. The pattern from top to bottom for each Church should be observed, remembering that reality would require, to reflect the complexity of conditions, *many more axes.* Five lines of distribution allow only highly simplified patterns to emerge. However, if hundreds of other Churches were charted according to even these five variables, the number of patterns would already be very large. The zigzag diagram from Ongole (O) indicates the possibilities.

Exact dates for these Churches (1000, 1900, 1952, 1964, and 1934) are necessary because each Church changes with the years. Its illustration on these axes can be calculated only for a specific time. The changing fortunes of each Church from decade to decade add to the complexity of possible patterns of growth.

Axis **A**   DEPENDENCE VS. INDEPENDENCE

O	R	A	I

Axis **B**   INDIVIDUAL VS. GROUP CONVERSION

R	A	O	I

Axis **C**   PROPORTION OF TOTAL POPULATION

A	R O		I

Axis **D**   SPEED OF GROWTH

R	A O		I

Axis **E**   INDIGENEITY

R	O A		I

Starting with Axis A, note that the Rhodesian and Ongole Churches were highly dependent, though the former had risen from individual conversion and the latter by group conversion (Axis B).

Observing Axis E, note that group conversion did not make the Ongole Church highly indigenous, though it did redeem it from the extreme position of the Rhodesian Church.

As to the location of the Iceland Church on all five lines, one may judge that extreme isolation in A.D. 1000 probably had more to do with its consistent position to the right than any other factor.

In the coming century, as Christianity spreads throughout the myriad cultures of Eurica and Afericasia, many factors varying from place to place and time to time will combine to give each Church a unique growth pattern and to locate it at a particular place on each axis. Among these will be the ways in which congregations first arise; theological and ecclesiological convictions (and muscle) of the founding Churches and missions; degree of opposition; speed of growth; odor of cultural dissimilarity exuded by the founders; familiar fragrance diffused by the growing Church; economic condition of the first Christians; intensity of their faith and prayer life; their certainty of Christ and faithfulness to the Bible—all these and many other elements.

The thousands of individual cases, each different from all others, can be classified into a few dozen kinds or modes of growth. It is too early in the development of our knowledge of this field to attempt this, but patently some of the modes will be the following, though no doubt more tersely named. We shall recognize growth through

> Individual accessions from nominally Christian populations (the common or garden variety in America).
> Individual accessions from non-Christian populations.
> Movements from peoples with high consciousness of community.
> Movements from peoples with low consciousness of community.
> Web movements in disintegrating societies.
> Missions laboring on new ground.
> Churches laboring among their own kin.

Under each of these modes will be listed many subvarieties. For example, movements from peoples with high consciousness of community would cover people movements from the castes of India, the tribes of many lands, and non-Christian ethnic minorities in most countries, such as the Chinese in London. Since the hundreds of castes in India differ greatly from each other socially, economically, racially, and linguistically, the people movements in this one great nation alone would number scores of subvarieties. Or again, under individual accessions from non-Christian populations would fall, as separate subvarieties, accessions from such groups as Secularists, Animists, high Buddhists, animistic Buddhists, high Hindus, Hinduistic animists, Koranic Moslems, animistic Moslems, hard-core Marxists, nominal Marxists, and many others.

SUMMARY

This glance at possible efforts to classify actual instances of church growth with a view to understanding their nature and real sources, should be sufficient to suggest the bewildering diversity that confronts us. As the Church contemplates the staggering complexity of mankind and observes that in each ethnic, linguistic, or cultural unit she has grown at a different rate and in a different way, she may well be frightened at the task to which God calls her: "Go, disciple *panta ta ethne*—the classes, tribes, lineages, and peoples of earth." This is why church multiplication must be seen as faithfulness. The Church, the Churches, and all Christians must faithfully press forward, beseeching men to be reconciled to God, discipling both their neighbors and the nations, and leaving the final outcome to God.

2

GOD'S WILL AND CHURCH GROWTH

CHURCH GROWTH must be carried on today in the parish and abroad in a kaleidoscopic world, with its divisions, hatreds, and wars—where Russia captures Kabul before hundreds of millions, and visions of world peace both elude and inspire men. In this world, men and women long attached to old faiths and loyalties are faced with new scientific truth, world civilization, dreams of abundant life, principles of democracy and communism, and the revolutionary revelation of God in Christ. Jolted out of old adjustments and social, political, economic, and religious patterns, they are searching for better, truer, and more satisfying ways of life. The population explosion is raising up countless multitudes, alike in new cities and old countrysides, who will be even more exposed to change than are their fathers.

In this world, mission must be what God desires. It is not a man-initiated activity but *missio Dei,* the mission of God, who Himself remains in charge of it. Hence the problems of mission should be viewed in the light of His revealed will. Being the kind of God He has shown Himself to be in Christ, what kind of mission does *He* desire? For that is what mission essentially and theologically is.

Mission defined as "God's program for man" is obviously many-sided. Each aspect of it can be called mission. Has God assigned any priority among these myriad good activities? For example, in His eyes does establishing equality of educational opportunity for all citizens of the

23

United States have a higher priority than beautifying the highways? We believe He has. His will in these matters can be learned from His revelation and is mandatory for Christians.

WHAT DOES GOD DESIRE?

It is not necessary to consider a thousand aspects of God's mission one by one. The live options today come conveniently grouped. Using "what God desires" as a compass to help us pick our way among the baffling good alternatives that confront the Church, let us look briefly at two of the easier groups of choices, first considering good works as against reconciling men to God in Christ.

As in the light of Christ we look at the world—its exploding knowledge, peoples, revolutions, physical needs, desperate spiritual hunger and nakedness, and enslavement to false gods and demonic ideologies—we realize that Christian mission must certainly engage in many labors. A multitude of excellent enterprises lie around us. So great is the number and so urgent the calls, that Christians can easily lose their way among them, seeing them all equally as mission. But in doing the good, they can fail of the best. In winning the preliminaries, they can lose the main game. They can be treating a troublesome itch, while the patient dies of cholera. The question of priorities cannot be avoided. In this fast-moving, cruel, and revolutionary era, when many activities are demanded, a right proportioning of effort among them is essential to sound policy. And "rightness"—a true and sound proportion in our labors—must be decided according to biblical principles in the light of God's revealed will.

Among other desires of God-in-Christ, He beyond question wills that persons be found—that is, be reconciled to Himself. Most cordially admitting that God has other purposes, we should remember that we serve a God *Who Finds Persons*. He has an overriding concern that men should be redeemed. However we understand the word, biblical witness is clear that men are "lost." The Finding God wants them *found*—that is, brought into a redemptive relationship to Jesus Christ where, baptized in His Name, they become part of His Household. He is not pleased when many findable sheep remain straggling on the mountain, shivering in the bitter wind. The more found, the better pleased is God.

Among other characteristics of mission, therefore, a chief and irreplaceable one must be this: that mission is a divine finding, vast and continuous. A chief and irreplaceable purpose of mission is church growth. Service is good, but it must never be substituted for finding. Our Lord did not rest content with feeding the hungry and healing the sick. He pressed on to give His life a ransom for many and to send out His followers to disciple all nations. Nor must service be so disproportionately emphasized at the expense of evangelism that findable persons are continually lost. In the proportioning of service and church planting, the degree of growth being achieved must always be taken into account. God's servants carry on mission in a fast-moving world and must constantly adjust the proportions of service and evangelism, as the Church grows from a few scattered cells to Churches forming substantial majorities of the population, so that *maximum finding occurs.*

Second, let us consider the Christianizing of the social order as against the multiplication of cells of Christians throughout "every kindred and tongue and people and nation."

Today the sinfulness of the social order offends thoughtful Christians everywhere, particularly where they are numerous and powerful. The great inequalities of wealth and poverty among the haves and have-nots, and the revolting treatment meted out to oppressed minorities, are clearly contrary to the will of the God and Father of our Lord Jesus Christ. Christians of all shades of theological opinion recognize this and, in varying measure, work to rectify it in the areas of their responsibility. They carry on a widespread war against these sub-Christian practices and are remarkably alike in their degree of involvement in them.

But they are dramatically different in the relative importance they attach to evangelism, and to Christianizing the social order. One school of thought assigns weight on the basis of immediate reason—what seems most urgent to them today as they and other men of good will, of every religion and no religion, look at the tragic human scene. The other school assigns importance on the basis of biblical principles in the light of the life, death, and resurrection of Jesus Christ. It maintains that Christianizing the social order is a fruit of new life in Christ and of church multiplication and must, therefore, receive a lower priority. Under some circumstances, to be sure, and for a limited time, Christianizing some aspect of the social order may legitimately be assigned a higher priority and receive greater attention than evangelism. Some Christian leaders under the circumstances prevailing in the sixties, and for a limited time, did well to turn from winning men to Christ to winning the civil rights battle. But as a rule, the multiplying of cells of reborn Christians continues to have the higher priority. But for the presence of millions of practicing American Christians of all races, the battle for civil rights could never have been mounted.

George Hunter in the March 1977 *Church Growth Bulletin* speaks powerfully to this point. He says, "I address those in the Church whose 'holy bag' is Christian social action—peace, food, reconciliation, justice. . . . Wherever, anywhere in the world over the last 19 centuries, when the Christian Movement has emphasized disciple-making, two things have happened. . . . We have made some new disciples and planted some churches and have had a social influence out of proportion to our numbers. But, whenever the Christian mission has neglected disciple-making and concentrated on the other facets of Christ's work, we have not made many disciples or planted many churches and have not had much social influence either! *Our social causes will not triumph unless we have great numbers of committed Christians.*"

May it not be concluded that until many cells of Christians exist in a given segment of society, its members cannot take adequate steps to bring about a just order? We shall examine, presently, why this is so.

God directs His people, facing these choices and remembering these priorities, to press ahead in "finding men" and engaging in social action. Congregations of Christians living in vital connection with their Head will manifest the fruits of the Spirit in individual and corporate life. Churches properly show their members what the Holy Spirit requires in community life today. Granting all this, nevertheless, the God Who Finds is not pleased when, to win battles on limited fronts, the basic need of lost human beings is minimized or neglected—to repent of their sins, believe on the Lord Jesus, and follow Him obediently into baptism and the Spirit-filled life.

SEARCH THEOLOGY AND A THEOLOGY OF HARVEST

Up to this point, mission has been widely defined as "God's total program for man," and we have considered the alternatives arising from that definition. Mission may now be defined much more meaningfully. Since God as revealed in the Bible has assigned the highest priority to bringing men into living relationship to Jesus Christ, we may define mission narrowly as *an enterprise devoted to proclaiming the Good News of Jesus Christ, and to persuading men to become His disciples and dependable members of His Church.* Even after establishing the priorities among good deeds, social action, and evangelism, the Church still has many baffling alternatives, and this definition is necessary if we are to discover among them the path desired by the God Who Finds.

God, who "became flesh and dwelt among us," is primarily concerned that men be saved, and His mission must also be so concerned.

Such mission in today's responsive world demands a theology of harvest which the New Testament is uniquely prepared to afford. Yet at this critical time many Christians are firmly committed to a theology of seed sowing, which might also be called a theology of search. It arose in the era of missions just ending. It maintains that in Christian mission the essential thing is not the finding, but going everywhere and preaching the Gospel— for which there is some excellent biblical authority.

Search theology framed its major beliefs under the impact of four chief factors, and cannot be understood except as we see the part these have played in its genesis.

First, it arose in the face of indifference at home and hostility abroad. At home, the Western Churches did not naturally engage in mission. The conversion of non-Christians of other lands seemed to the Church expensive, politically inexpedient, meddlesome, dangerous, and not the will of God. Denomination after denomination had to be roused by its prophets before it would engage in foreign missions. Missionary societies had to be organized on the fringe of the Churches—among the women, the devout, the specially concerned. Abroad, hostility faced Christian mission—both the hostility of Western traders who feared that missionaries would upset their business and that of cultures which regarded Christianity as the spearhead of an invading imperialism. Christian mission needed a theology which would undergird it during the long years when it was weak at home and hard beset abroad. Search theology did this. It strenuously denied that results had anything to do with mission. Search was God's will.

Second, of recent years, a vast relativism, based on the study of non-Christian religions, has enveloped the West and in a curious way buttressed search theology. It has aggressively attacked the doctrine that Christ is the full, final, once-for-all Revelation of God; also its corollary, that every Christian should proclaim Christ and persuade men to become His disciples and responsible members of His Church. This relativism is the more powerful—one might almost say, more insidious—for being the product of a fundamentally sympathetic impulse. In fifty years or less we have become heirs to a transformed world of communications, transportation, cultural interchange, and the validation of all kinds of formerly unfamiliar peoples, lands, national histories, literatures, and folk art, to name but a few strands in this drawing together of human interest and knowledge. At the same time, the endless hospitality of Western institutions of learning has given visitors from other lands the means to communicate more coherently both with the West and with other nationals around them (a hospitality which was never inversely available to Westerners). And, in becoming more able to talk to the West, they become real and actual to us, people of value.

The new, tender relativism among us, rightly anxious to defer, to heal, not to wound—eager to make up for past crude indifferences to which Westerners were sometimes a party—pauses in appreciation before the richness of non-Christian religions. It then wrongly concludes that there are many ways to God, that men are "saved" by the sincerity with which they follow whatever light they have.

Meanwhile sensitive Christians, shamed in recent generations by appalling displays of cruelty, discrimination, and lack of brotherhood in Western societies where Christians have been in control, hesitate to call any religion less worthy than their own. There is a certain reluctance to discuss the down-to-earth realities of mission and church growth. The egalitarian element in an attitude of religious relativism makes such reluctance at times almost *de rigueur* among those thinking people to whom the Bible has become mythic and Christianity itself merely the Judeo-Christian way of life. Relativism is one of the ways in which they express their revulsion from the whole human history of oppression and contempt for alien races and creeds.

To be sure, most committed and informed Christians themselves have not accepted relativism in any such terms; but its intellectual climate has enveloped them and their missionaries and has heavily influenced what they thought most worth doing. Those affected by relativism have also agreed to search theology. It is alright, they say, to look for men and proclaim Christ by word and deed (specially by kindly deed), but it is misguided to work for actual conversions. The era of planting churches, they hold, is definitely over. The aim of mission in friendly, cooperative relationships with other religions is to develop a new humanity, a new just and participatory society.

Today's vast relativism combined with contemporary passion to restructure society has deflected most Conciliar Churches and missions from evangelism and church multiplying. The documentary history of this crucial episode in Christian Mission is extensive. This brief reference to it merely illustrates how easy it is for search theology (or a theological position to the left of that) to be substituted for a theology of harvest.

The third chief factor whose impact resulted in "search" theology has been the enormous gap between the rapidly rising standard of living in the West and that of the masses in Africasia, which faced the missionary everywhere with a multitude of good things to do. Compared to the West in the twentieth century, the average of health, literacy, nutrition, comfort, production, cleanliness, enlightenment, and general helpfulness in Aferi-casia left much to be desired. The missionary was beset by requests for schools, hospitals, and agricultural demonstration centers. His Christian message was looked at askance, but his Western cultural adjuncts were much in demand. He could not produce many converts; but he could produce many hospital treatments and grant many school certificates. Against his will and in the face of his sincere protestations that his real task was discipling the nations, he was pushed into all kinds of philan-thropic work. These were defended as "a preparation for the Gospel," "a more effective way of preaching the Gospel," and on occasion "just as good as the Gospel."

Fourth, as it carried out mission, the Church in many fields faced very small growth in membership. It had to find a rationale for existence and continuance which did not depend on numbers of converts. Under such conditions it welcomed a theology of mission which proclaimed that "only search" was God's command. Results *should not* be taken into account.

Goaded by these four pressures, search theology fiercely attacked any emphasis on results. Not, be it marked, on results in terms of patients cured, pupils passed from one class in school to the next, tons of rice grown to the acre, government recognition, or popular acclaim. These were avidly sought. But results in terms of men won to Christ have become suspect across wide stretches of the Church. They are seldom expressly included as a goal of Christian mission. On rare occasions when they are, the speaker hurries on to say that he is not interested in numerical increase, of course, but rather in changed life. Missionary writers vie with one another in deprecating mere numbers. The shepherds, going out to search for lost sheep, meet at the gate to announce that they do not intend to notice particularly how many are found.

A typical news note reads like this: "Reverend John P. Everymission-ary and his colleagues are conducting a wide program of schools, clinics, hospitals, improved farming techniques, food crops, stock raising, and evangelism." With this kind of goal, the numbers of the "found" will usually be small. The main emphasis is not on reconciling men to God.

It must not be thought that search theology affects only overseas mis-sions. It also reduces the effectiveness of American pastors. They content themselves with being the church in their suburb, town, or city. If anyone wants to hear the Gospel, he can attend the morning service. They think the idea of a harvest of souls waiting to be reaped is too aggressive. It takes the Bible too literally. All the various factors which impel toward search theology are found in American congregations and seminaries, though perhaps in America they would more exactly be denominated a theology of maintenance. Under either name, they inculcate a lack of interest in fervent continuous evangelism.

IS GOD PLEASED WITH SEARCH THEOLOGY?

Is search theology true to God as revealed in Jesus Christ? Standing in His presence, let us ask the following three questions. Their concreteness may offend some, but we know of no better way to narrow the issue down to the essential question: Is *God* concerned that countable persons be won to Christ?

1. Theologically speaking should the number of people found bear any relation to the direction and intensity of the search?

2. Speaking with the utmost sincerity before God, do we feel that the number of sinners *obeying* the call to repentance and discipleship should or should not influence where and how that call is issued?

3. Is it more pleasing to God to proclaim Christ where men are reconciled to God than where they are not?

These questions focus attention on God's will in regard to the expansion of the Church in America and around the world. They are not concerned with whether church growth is expedient in our present cultural picture or otherwise humanly desirable. What does *God* command? That is the question.

Christians with a theology of search answer each of these three questions with a ringing "No!" They hold mission to be the proclamation of Christ by word and deed *everywhere,* whether men hear or not, whether they obey or not. God commanded Ezekiel saying, "Go to your people and say to them, 'Thus says the Lord' whether they hear or refuse to hear." Many hold that the mission of the Church is similarly to proclaim Christ. The Church is to pay no attention to the response; its duty is complete in proclamation. This position is neutral toward results—one may call it a neutralist position. To have an eye on results would be immodest toward God and coercive toward one's fellow man.

This understanding of mission is justified theologically in various ways. Some hold that, in this dispensation before the millennium, God is taking out of the Gentiles a limited number of people to be His Church. Nothing the Christian does can add to or subtract from His purposes. In the fullness of time the millennium will come; the Church and the Holy Spirit will be taken out of the world and then God will cause first the Jews and then the Gentiles to be reconciled to Himself. Hence mission today consists simply in preaching the Gospel to the whole creation. We cannot tell who will be saved and who will not.

Other Christians have studied psychology as well as the transforming social trends of our age. They realize that man easily rationalizes his conduct and assigns impeccable motives to immoral activities. They feel that "winning men to Christ" or "planting the Church" or "extending the Kingdom of God" is really an expression of imperialism, pride, or an unconscious, patronizing sense of superiority. The dilemma of the Christian, in other words, is that the Church is *his* Church. If he seeks to bring men into it, he is building up his own ego. He is naively bending men to his own purposes, using them to the aggrandizement of *his* religion. A recent writer objects to any evangelism on the ground that it is "a method of imposing the personal or corporate will of a few on others in the name of Christ." Such Christians affirm that mission is simply proclaiming Christ out of pure gratitude for what He has done for us. They say that the true Christian "proclaims Christ without seeking for any 'result' in the world of persons," hence without the danger of manipulating or in any way persuading people to become Christians. At evangelism of such a pure type none can take offense. To praise God by confessing Christ is a Christian's inalienable right. It proselytes no one, coerces no one. Yet the Holy Spirit can and does use this proclamation, centered entirely in God, to convict others of sin, call them to penitence, and add many a man and woman to the Churches.

Some of the plateaued and declining denominations in all six continents, but specially in North America and Europe, owe their stagnant condition to the inroads which the above reduced and twisted view of evangelism has produced in their leaders, both lay and clerical.

Still other Christians, depending heavily on the theology of "the Christ event," say that Christian mission is to proclaim the Lordship of Christ over all of life. Christ, the Center of history, has come. Mission is the announcing of this event by word and deed. Industrial life, political life, the organization man, primitive man, urban man, depersonalized man, modern man—Christ is Lord of us all. When Christians live knowing Him to be so, they are carrying on mission; but here again the Christian remembers that he is man, not God. He merely announces God's act in Christ. To persuade, to have an eye on numbers, would be presumptuous. God gathers into the Church whomever He will. The Christian is not concerned with results or numbers. Those are strictly in the hands of God.

Some Christians fear numbers because they see one soul as of infinite value. Christ died for each man, hence every soul is worth the entire effort of all mission from the day of Pentecost on. They argue that a church or a mission which over a period of fifty years leads fifty souls to the feet of Christ is as pleasing to God as one which in the same period wins fifty thousand and plants the Church firmly in an entire countryside. Persons evangelizing indifferent or resistant populations usually espouse a theology of search on this score.

Faced with the question, "Theologically speaking, should the numbers of those who can be effectively *found* have anything to do with the direction and intensity of the search?" these four varieties of Christians would answer, "No! The Gospel is to be proclaimed everywhere, and God will gather into His Church whom He will."

To the comparatively few Christians holding this neutralist position on the basis of a consistent search theology should be added the much larger number who "have a burden" for some population of non-Christians: a resistant Chinese clan, a Moslem city, Buddhist intellectuals—or secular Western man bored with the Christian faith. These many Christians also affirm that we are told to proclaim but not persuade. We search for lost sheep; the finding is not in our hand. We sow the seed; God in His good time gives the increase.

One has great sympathy with the purposes that inspire search theology, and with the limited truths it so often expresses. With Christ's second coming, what now appears impossible will be possible. The Gospel must be proclaimed to all men, both receivers and rejectors.Men should not be coerced or badgered into accepting it. Personality must be respected. All this is true. Nevertheless, with the most cordial acknowledgment of these things, we do not believe the neutralist position is *theologically* sound. It is out of harmony with the mainstream of Christian revelation. Christ's words and deeds contradict it. The apostles and the early Church would have repudiated it.

At base, the trouble is that mere search, detached witness—without the deep wish to convert, without wholehearted persuasion, and with what amounts to a fear of the numerical increase of Christians—is not biblically justified. *Mere search is not what God wants. God wants His lost children found.* Let us examine the evidence.

GOD'S PASSION TO FIND

Four kinds of biblical evidence nourish the conviction that God has a passion to find men.

1. Explicit statements of our Lord and His apostles are against the

neutralist position. Matthew records (9:37) that our Lord instructed His disciples to pray that God would send laborers into *His* harvest. Seeing the responsiveness of a particular population, our Lord recognized the need for reapers. The whitened fields were God's. Simply walking through them proclaiming Christ's lordship was not enough. God wanted the grain cut, bound into sheaves, and carried back into His barns.

In Matthew 10:14 (parallels in Mark, Luke, and Acts) He says, "If any will not receive you shake off the dust of your feet as you leave that town." Our Lord carefully instructed His disciples not to tarry with those who rejected the Gospel, but to hurry on to those who welcomed it. Acts 13:51 indicates that Barnabas and Saul knew of this instruction and followed it. It is a fair inference that this was the common practice of the New Testament Church. It did not badger and bother people who resisted the Good News, but hurried on to those who were ready to become believers. The duty of disciples was not fulfilled through extended proclamation to the stiff-necked. Christians besought those who could believe and enter eternal life.

These words of the Lord Jesus and this practice of the early Church are not applicable in all times and all populations; there are too many instances of decades of work among the unresponsive being followed by rapid growth of the Church. Yet this New Testament principle should be applied whenever a specific Church or mission faces a New Testament situation, i.e., where part of its hearers are responsive and part have set their faces like flint against the Gospel. There Christians must win the winnable while they are winnable. Recent immigrants from Mexico to the United States are a case in point. The New Testament example is entirely germane.

In the thirty-fourth chapter of Ezekiel, the prophet says some hard words about shepherds who substitute other activities for finding lost, scattered, and countable sheep and bringing them home. He is speaking theologically. *God* wants countable lost persons found. The shepherd with ninety-nine lost sheep who finds one and stays at home feeding or caring for it should not expect commendation. God will not be pleased by the excuse that His servant is doing something "more spiritual" than searching for strayed sheep. Nothing is more spiritual than the actual reconciliation of the lost to God.

The Great Commission itself is weighty evidence. On a very solemn occasion our Lord specifically commanded His followers to "disciple the nations." This is straightforward language. The New Testament knows nothing of the comfortable doctrine that a Christian can witness to Christ and yet not intend conversion. When Paul proclaimed Christ in Corinth, the record says, "he argued in the synagogue every Sabbath and persuaded Jews and Greeks." If we read these words in the light of Romans 9:1-3 we cannot imagine that Paul, while testifying that the Christ was Jesus, steered clear of persuading Jews to become Christians.

Indeed, any formula which limits the Christian to search, maintenance, or neutralist witness, whether out of respect for the sovereignty of God or fear of practicing religious imperialism, has an artificial ring to it. It fits a system, not the New Testament. In avoiding the manipulation of persons, it falls into the sin of passing by on the other side. It may enable Christians to continue witness to an unresponsive society, or to maintain a stagnant congregation in a growing city, but that does not make the formula pleasing to God or true to the New Testament Church.

2. Our Lord's parables often emphasize an actual finding. The woman does not merely search, but searches *till she finds* the lost coin. The shepherd does not make a token hunt and return empty-handed. He "goes after the one which was lost, *until he finds it.*"

At the great banquet, the Master did not commend the servant who brought news that the invited could not come. He did not say, "Continue inviting these indifferent persons until they accept." He said to His servant, "Bring in the poor, the maimed, the blind, and the lame." When there was yet room, He said again, "Go out into the highways and the hedges and compel [other] people to come in." Issuing the invitation was not the end: partaking of God's feast was. If one group would not accept the summons, then the servant was to find other men who would.

Parables should not be unduly pressed, but in the above three the meaning rests on objective finding. The purpose of witness is not the cultural improvement of the Christian, but that sinners be found. It very much distorts biblical witness and any possible way that early Christians could have understood it, to regard it as a spiritual exercise which is merely good for the Christian. In the Bible, witness is always a means for bringing back the lost. The primary question is not how the witness can maintain his own status as an obedient unselfish person; it is how the Christian can witness so that men are *in fact* reconciled to God in Christ.

There is no way for a Christian to avoid open search for the lost. The real Christian candidly avows that he desires men to become fellow disciples and is bending all his efforts to that end. Plain honesty requires it. The neutralist formula does not really enable us to avoid manipulating people. If, when Christ is proclaimed, the Holy Spirit does convert some persons, has the proclaimer not manipulated them? The fact is that man is an incurable persuader. Human life involves influencing others; we do it every day. It is better for the Christian to avow his great wish that others may know the profoundly vitalizing and freeing experience of Christ than to take shelter under some circumlocution.

The legitimacy of persuasion does not depend at all on the new course of conduct arising solely in the mind of the persuaded. Its rightness depends entirely on (a) whether the action proposed is good for the persuaded, and (b) whether he freely accepts it. The sleeping man in a burning building is a case in point. Is it legitimate to shake him, wake him, and persuade him to leave? Certainly—even, in fact, if the arouser risks his own life merely for the plaudits of men or because he is paid for it. His motives have nothing to do with the legitimacy of persuasion.

Strictly speaking it is not legitimate to force the awakened man to leave. If he wishes to stay on in the burning building, he should be free to do so. That firemen and police universally override such impulses to suicide can be favorably regarded only on the assumption that the persons concerned, when they come to themselves, will rejoice that they were rescued. Religious liberty is the ground from which we proceed. In the free persuasion and counterpersuasion which is life, men must not be forced, tricked, or bribed into doing what they do not wish to do—even if we are very sure it would be good for them. But religious liberty must never be made to mean that persuasion is in some way a violation of personality or an infringement of the sovereignty of God. Among God's own ways of persuading is this: that He persuades through our efforts.

Behind this facade of sudden sensitivity concerning persuasion, what is really at stake is the truth of the Christian religion. If there are many paths to God, then for Christians to induce others to follow their path may indeed be self-aggrandizement. But if Christ is the only real Savior, despite all the richness of other faiths in many respects, then persuading men to accept Him is not really open to the charge of selfishness, whatever the imperfections of the human agents of God's love.

3. Behind the specific passages and parables mentioned, however, lies still more weighty evidence. The revelation of God culminating in Christ tells us that God Himself is a searching, saving God. He found Israel in Egypt and bound her to Himself in the covenant at Sinai. He remained faithful to the covenant when Israel again and again was faithless. God wants men—multitudes of men—reconciled to Himself. He was in Christ reconciling *the world* to Himself.

Jesus Christ, our Lord, came to seek and save the lost. The lost are always persons. They always have countable bodies. As Scripture says,

"We have this treasure in earthen vessels"—vessels which can be numbered. Again, "that the life of Christ may be manifested in our mortal flesh"—flesh which is distributed among persons numerous as the sands of the sea. Our Lord would have rejected the thought that the number of those found has no bearing on the direction of the search. On the contrary His very mention of the joy in heaven over a single saved soul is but added testimony to the urgent importance of the many. A healthy realism pervades Jesus' teaching. He may well have limited His disciples at first to the lost sheep of the house of Israel precisely because only in Israel could enough be found and redeemed to begin the Church.

This finding is not primarily in the realm of man's temporal life. Our Lord did not despise the physical side of life. He healed men and fed them. Yet He often warned His disciples not to fear those who could destroy the body, but those "who can destroy both soul and body in hell." He counseled them to sell their possessions, and give alms, and to provide for themselves purses which do not grow old. He Himself turned from being a teacher of divine truths and a healer of men's bodies and minds to die for them on Calvary. He deliberately set His face to Jerusalem, knowing He would there meet death. No critical examination of the text shakes this cornerstone. The cross is the measure of God's desire for the eternal salvation of myriads yet uncounted by man, whose very hairs are numbered and known to a loving God; and of the priority of salvation over the comforts or even the necessities of temporal life.

To *God,* as He has thus revealed Himself, proclamation is not the main thing. The main thing is the salvation of persons. This is so obvious, it is almost embarrassing to state. Is it conceivable that God our Savior is more interested in the form than in actual saved men and women? Is He more pleased by "grateful witness to the fact of Christ"—or by lost sons and daughters welcomed to the Father's house? The proclamation of the Gospel is a means. It must not be confused with the end, which is that men—multitudes of them—be reconciled with God in Christ.

Scripture knows nothing of the modern cliche that numbers are unimportant, which arises to some extent from the way Free Churches—beginning as *small* movements—have broken away from the State Churches. The kernel of truth which has given rise to the cliche is that the validity and quality of a Church are not necessarily in direct ratio to its size. This truth correctly supports evangelistic efforts which are proclaiming Christ to resistant populations; but it must not be distorted. Stated in the form of a general proposition that "numbers are unimportant" it ceases to be true and becomes a cliche without biblical basis. The revelation of God throughout assumes that the numbers of the redeemed do count. It believes, for example, that as "grace extends to *more and more people,*" thanksgiving to the glory of God increases (II Cor. 4:15).

4. Finally we note that the New Testament Church went where men responded, believing this to be God's will.

For possibly fifteen years, witness was confined almost entirely to the Jews. "They spoke the word to none but Jews," During the years when Jews responded by becoming disciples of Christ, the Church multiplied itself among the Jews. This is often regarded as a grievous fault in the Early Church, but in the circumstances then prevailing it was, on the contrary, one of its great virtues. The Church won the winnable—while they could be won. If Peter on the day of Pentecost, in an effort to win the Gentiles, had required all would-be converts to practice inclusiveness in eating, marrying, worshiping, and proclaiming, and the apostles had immediately given as much attention to Gentiles living in Jerusalem and Judea as they did to Jews, very few Jews would have become Christian.

This may be why our Lord commanded the Gospel to be preached to all mankind "beginning with Jerusalem"—where men would respond, be baptized, and form churches.

After A.D. 48 the Church broke out from among the racial Jews—Hebrews born of Hebrews—and spread rapidly in the synagogue communities with their large numbers of Gentile converts and devout persons or sympathizers. Indeed, had the Church not multiplied enormously among the synagogues of the Roman world, their Gentile fringes would never have become Christian.

The apostles did not consciously plan this sequence. It happened, Luke tells us, under the direction of the Holy Spirit. And it has theological significance. The Early Church allowed the numbers baptized to determine the direction and intensity of its missions, in the case both of the Jews and of the Gentiles. The Early Church remembered, repeatedly related, and finally recorded those sayings of Jesus and the parables which we have mentioned (and others which we have not) which direct Christians to harvest ripe fields. That Church lived in the first bright light of the revelation of God in Christ and was vividly aware of the God Who Finds. Its Lord repeatedly said that He came to bring sinners to repentance; that those who had the Son had the Father and that those who did not have the Son did not have the Father. Convinced that persuading men to believe in Jesus as the Messiah was in harmony with the eternal nature of God, they went everywhere preaching the Gospel and beseeching their intimates and relatives to become disciples. With this understanding of God, how could they help but win those who could be won, as their highest privilege and duty?

The apostles believed in the sovereignty of God and emphasized that, while we are ambassadors, it is God who speaks through us. Yet they also emphasized their own responsibility and thoroughly identified themselves with the search. They recorded Jesus' words, "From now on you will be fishers of men." They firmly believed that Peter's sermon "cut people to the heart," and recorded that he instructed men to repent and be baptized. They did not trouble themselves with circumlocutions to the effect that man preaches the Word but God does the persuading. Though they believed that God was adding to the Church daily those who were being saved, and were quite sure that the Holy Spirit was acting in and through them, they never hesitated to speak as if men played a real part in conversion. Barnabas and Saul and Silas and Apollos and others "made disciples," "instructed people in the way of the Lord," "persuaded Greeks," "besought them to be reconciled to God," and "had unceasing anguish of heart and uttered deep prayers of the heart that they might be saved." Luke records that when Peter and John laid on hands, intending that the Holy Spirit should descend, the Holy Spirit did descend (Acts 8:15-18). The Early Church believed God had given the apostles the power of conferring the Holy Spirit and expected them to use it.

A VAST FINDING

In view of all this and much more evidence, must we not consider mission in intention *a vast and purposeful finding?* Is it possible to maintain that biblically only "search" is the thing, motives are what matter, and the finding of multitudes of persons is something rather shabbily mechanical and "success ridden"? Can we believe it theologically tenable to be uninterested in the numbers of the redeemed? Is taking seriously "numbers which the Lord adds to the Church"—is this "submitting to the tyranny of statistics"?

Does not the biblical evidence rather indicate that in the sight of the God Who Finds, numbers of the redeemed are important? God Himself desires that multitudes be reconciled to Himself in the Church of Christ. Indeed, God commands an ardent searching for the lost *in order to find them.* The Church which our Savior bought with His blood is made up of saved sinners engaged in beseeching others to be reconciled to God. The congregation which is not engaged in proclaiming Christ to men and persuading them to become His disciples and responsible members of His

Church, may be a religious club, but it is not the Body of Jesus Christ. His Body is filled with His Spirit and engaged in finding lost men.

The God Who Finds is now and always will be in charge of His mission. He intends today that His banquet hall be filled. If one group refuses, then another must be persuaded. If its members are insufficient, then still others must be found to come and feast at His table.

Hence mission is always properly concerned that its labors be guided by considerations of where men are in fact being found.

Fields white to harvest and long lines of laborers bringing sheaves out of certain ones of them have theological significance. Christians do not go into white fields of their own will: God sends them in. They do not bring out sheaves for their own profit; they carry them to the Master's storehouse. God gives the growth. God ripens the grain. God rewards the workmen. Before *God,* then (to revert to my earlier questions), the number of sinners obeying the call to repentance and discipleship *should* influence where and how that call is issued. Certainly it is more pleasing to God to proclaim Christ where men are reconciled to Him than where they are not. Thus speaks a theology of harvest.

In the revolutionary churning up of the world in which we live, fantastic increase of churches is obviously the will of God. He it is who shakes the foundations. Since He is the Father Almighty and not some blind Force or cosmic Urge, inherent in His action must be some good purpose. What purpose is more in line with His intent to save men than to marshal, discipline, strengthen, and multiply His churches until every man on earth has had the chance to hear the Gospel from his own kinsmen, who speak his own language and whose word is unobstructed by cultural barriers? In many regions, missionaries must start the process; but it is clear that the Gospel cannot be proclaimed to every creature, belief cannot become a real option to every person, until churches exist in all groupings of men, city and country, high caste and low caste, educated and illiterate, throughout the earth. Thus speaks a theology of harvest.

SEARCHING AND FINDING AND THE CROSS

Is then the theology of search false? By no means; but it is partial. It is true for some men and some populations. It is false only in so far as it claims to be the sole theology of evangelism and applicable to all men.

As we confront the indifferent or the hostile, we must remember that God yearns for the salvation of all His children. He searches even when

He does not find. Our Lord stands at the door and knocks, but enters only if the door is opened. Yes, God is a Searcher and commands searching.

As we look at those who respond and are found, however—and their name is legion—we must remember that God finds. It should be easy for us who have been found to remember this: He not only searched, but He also found. God searches until He finds. He searches where He finds. He reconciles men to Himself. He has appointed us shepherds. He commands us to find and save the lost.

Theology of mission, remembering that God is One, must look equally to the God Who Searches and the God Who Finds. It is not theologically permissible for the Christian's true intention to be "only search"; though sometimes, with some populations, the outcome is—alas—no more than this. The cross comforts the Christian when, contrary to his deepest desires, this is the result. He is united with Christ on the cross when the outcome is only search. But if "only search" does not put the Christian on the cross, does not humiliate, frustrate, and crucify him, then he is not one with Christ. For Christ came to find and save the lost. And so must Christ's Church.

3

TODAY'S TASK, OPPORTUNITY, AND IMPERATIVE

THE TASK

IT IS difficult to speak about today's task when hundreds of tasks lie before the Church and God calls her to every one of them. Internal tasks abound—raising church budgets, helping Christians grow in grace, holding educated youth, erecting new buildings, training lay leaders, teaching the Bible, and many more. External tasks abound—building brotherhood in the midst of racial strife, giving underprivileged youth a chance, working for peace and justice, reaching unevangelized men and women with the Gospel, establishing new churches in suitable locations, and scores of others. The calls from across the seas were never more numerous or clamant. Great numbers of persons die each year of hunger and malnutrition. Yet there are still refugees to house, illiterates to teach, the sick to heal—and *three billion who have never heard the name of Christ* to flood with knowledge of their Savior.

In spite of all, the thesis of this chapter is that—for the welfare of the world, for the good of mankind—according to the Bible, one task is paramount. Today's supreme task is effective multiplication of churches in the receptive societies of earth.

The other good and urgent things to do, far from contradicting this thesis, reinforce it. The many tasks that lie at hand should be done—there can be no two opinions about that. Preaching good sermons, teaching illiterates to read, working at planned parenthood or the world's food supply, administering churches skillfully, applying Christianity to all of life, using mass media of communication, and hundreds of other activities are not sinful. They are good. Some are urgent.

But are they all of equal importance? Even if the mission of the Church is defined as everything she does outside her four walls, are all these activities of equal value? Does mission consist in a large number of parallel thrusts between which Christians may not discriminate? Does it make no difference which comes first, or which is omitted?

If a man stands upon this planet with no other guidance than to follow what seems reasonable to him, in the Bible or out of it, then if there is any mission at all it consists in countless parallel thrusts, each having no more authority than that of the man who advocates it. If he is a man of genius or has seized control of some powerful Christian organization or apparatus, his project will achieve temporary importance. To enhance this and persuade other men, he may quote such random verses of Scripture as support his purposes. Soon, however, others who also hold his position on "guidance" will come to power and quote other Bible verses which support *their* thrusts in mission, since it depends on what seems reasonable to man. The guidance becomes confusion.

In contradistinction to such chaos, Christians accept the authority of the Bible in its total impact and, believing that God's revelation in Christ and the Bible establishes guidelines for all men, find sure guidance concerning the relative importance of various courses of conduct. They are not left to human wisdom, with some maintaining that man is a responsible being and some that he is an automaton. They do not have to wonder whether the highest good is ethical achievement or being in Christ. Their path is illumined by God's revelation. Such Christians can and should draw the distinction between root and fruit, and base their policies in mission upon it. Those who prepare mission budgets and spend mission funds should never be in doubt as to the ultimate outcome they desire, the ultimate goal to which God directs them. They will carry on innumerable activities; they will take innumerable steps. But they should be certain what that ultimate goal is. The Church does not vacillate between sending missionaries to preach the Gospel when that is popular and distributing "the pill" when that is "in." In her supreme duty, led by the Holy Spirit, the Church obediently engages in God's mission according to Scripture.

We must not oversimplify the situation, as if Christians could do one task and leave all others undone. They can and should do many tasks together. When Nehemiah built the wall, some carried stone, some brought water, some mixed mortar, and some laid the stones in place. All were controlled, however, by the overriding purpose—all were building the wall. The supreme aim guided the entire enterprise. Stones and mortar arrived at the wall in the right proportions at the right time to guarantee maximum wall-building.

In mission today many tasks must be carried on together; yet the multiplicity of good activities must contribute to, and not crowd out, maximum reconciliation of men to God in the Church of Jesus Christ. God desires that men be saved in this sense: that through faith they live in Christ and through obedience they are baptized in His name and live as responsible members of His Body. God therefore commands those of His household to go and "make disciples of all nations." Fulfilling this command is the supreme purpose which should guide the entire mission, establish its priorities, and coordinate all its activities.

The Church today faces deep cleavage among her members at just this point. Some are so deeply impressed by the physical needs of man—and who can deny their urgency?—that meeting these needs becomes for them the highest present purpose of God and the Church.

In 1977, my *Conciliar Evangelical Debate: The Crucial Documents 1964-76* presented the writings of 15 spokesmen of the Conciliar and 15 of the Evangelical Wing of the Church. Sharply differing opinions as to ends and means mark the volume. In the rough and tumble of vigorous disagreement, the writers spoke of the basic questions of evangelism and mission. The convictions of major thinkers were weighed in the balance of reason and revelation and, when found adequate, embraced and, when found wanting, rejected.

In 1979 Dr. Harvey Hoekstra, then president of the Reformed Church in America, published his well-researched book *The WCC and the Demise of Evangelism,* showing how the leaders of the Conciliar Churches and Mission Boards, following the theory and theology of "New Mission," had all but abandoned evangelism as they sought to minister to the physical needs of mankind and to rectify the basic injustices of the global social order.

Deeply as I sympathize with the problem and long as I have ministered to desperate physical needs—for years I superintended a leprosy home— I cannot ally myself on this point with those who put social action first. On the contrary, my conviction is that the salvation granted to those who believe on Jesus Christ is still the supreme need of man, and all other human good flows from that prior reconciliation to God.

The Lord Jesus put it succinctly when He said, "Seek first the kingdom of God and His righteousness and all these things shall be added to you." He spoke of food and clothing, the simplest necessities of life, but the passage will bear much added freight: safety, health, education, comfort, production—even justice, peace, and brotherhood. As we try to help men to achieve these, the longest first step we can lead them to take is to believe in Christ as Lord and Savior and become dependable members of His Church. Enormous liberation of the human spirit and extension of righteousness among men will become possible as sound churches of Christ are multiplied among the three billion who now yield Him no allegiance. Such liberated persons and congregations will become in their own cultures and communities the most effective and permanent sources of "good works" as well as of true cooperation toward solving the bitter practical problems of the world.

Some earnest Christians, who readily grant the above, nevertheless reject multiplication of churches as today's chief task because they pin their hopes on quality rather than quantity. What use, they ask, to make more Christians unless they are *better* Christians? Throughout much of Africasia they affirm that education of Christians is more important than evangelism. In America they assert that brotherhood or church unity is more important than church extension.

No doubt the Church must win on both educational and brotherhood fronts. Both are important sectors of the ceaseless battle against the powers of darkness. Christians should be able to read the Bible, and should speed the spread of the marvelous learning God has granted us in our age. Race pride, too, which refuses equal opportunity to people of other groups and customs, and seems to doubt that God is the Father of all mankind, must be very firmly rejected.

But we must not throw out the baby with the bath. As C. S. Lewis, I believe, once said, you *cannot* (my italics) have the brotherhood of man without the fatherhood of God. Nothing can advance learning and brotherhood more in the long run than for men of every tribe and tongue and kindred and nation to become disciples of Christ in whom there is no Jew or Greek.

Furthermore, we must inspect closely this attractive plea for quality. As soon as we separate quality from the deepest passion of our Lord—to seek and save the lost—it ceases to be Christian quality. No amount of sophistication can change this very simple fact. To fight for brotherhood is good; but to proclaim that brotherhood is more important than salvation is misguided. If in Africasia we rear Christians who shine with a high polish, speak beautiful English, have an advanced education, but care nothing whatever about their unconverted kinsmen being reconciled to God, then their vaunted quality as Christians is ashes. Even if we produce Christians who live as full brothers with men of other races, but do not burn with desire that those others may have eternal life, their "quality" is certainly in doubt.

Any who seriously plead for this kind of quality are in effect advocating works righteousness and substituting ethical achievement, the fruit of the Spirit, for the Gospel. Christians, when true to the Scriptures and to Christ, reject such legalism and insist that ethical achievement *grows out of life in Christ* and must not be made a prerequisite for faith in Him.

On a practical plane, church leaders have continually to choose between pressing tasks, all good. They would do well to listen to Dr. Ralph Winter, who writes,

> I used to be an expert in the gadgets and the gimmicks—the various means and types of ministries common to most missions. Recently it has become steadily clearer to me that the most important activity of all is the implanting of churches. The care, feeding and reproduction of congregations is the central activity to which all the gimmicks and means must be bent.

The Chief Task: Often Left Undone

Christian mission should take serious account of the many Africasian Churches marked by slight growth. Specialists in carrying water abound, but there are few masons. Tons of mortar arrive, but few stones. The wall does not go up. Slight church growth characterizes many whole denominations, both liberal and conservative. Worse, the lack of growth is taken as natural and unavoidable.

In the state of Sinaloa in the west of Mexico, the Congregational Church, now the United Church of Christ, has been at work for over half a century. During all these years its dedicated missionaries have labored earnestly, yet in 1962 it had only "300 members in 9 small static churches" (McGavran, 1963:45).

Scores of denominations both large and small in North America have plateaued or declined. For example, three large denominations—the United Presbyterians, the United Church of Christ, and the United Methodists—lost 10 to 12 per cent of their membership between 1965 and 1975. The Oregon Yearly Meetings of Friends is a typical small denomination. In 1961 the average figure for church membership, Sunday School membership, and Sunday morning attendance in its sixty-one congregations was 5,300. In 1968 the average figure was 5,400 (Willcuts: 27).

In Taiwan, where the Presbyterian Church has registered great growth, trebling in twelve years from 57,407 in 1952 to 176,255 in 1964 (Taiwan

Presbyterians, Synodical Office 1966:76, 80), and the Baptists who came over from the mainland in 1948 with a few hundred numbered 21,783 in 1967 (Coxill, 1968:181), the Methodists in 1967—despite the fact that Methodist Chiang Kai Shek and Madame Chiang were ardent Christians—numbered only 4,553. The Methodist Church in Taiwan demonstrates that it is quite possible to miss church growth in receptive populations.

In Chile, where Pentecostal denominations in the last forty years have grown from nothing to a total communicant membership of 360,000, one North American mission with thirty missionaries, at work for about 30 years, in 1965 counted less than 300 Chilean Christians in its congregations. It believes that Chile has "an almost Islamic population."

The secretary of a large conservative missionary society said recently, "We have spent $3,000,000 in Japan in the last thirty years; and our churches there now have less than 500 full members."

My interest in church growth was first roused when Pickett's survey showed that 134 mission stations in mid-India (where I was a missionary) had experienced an average church growth of only 12 per cent per decade, or about 1 per cent per year (Pickett, 1956:ix). The ten stations of my own mission, the India Mission of the Disciples of Christ, were not significantly different from the other 124. They had a staff of over 75 missionaries and a "great work"—but had been notably unsuccessful in planting churches. In the town of Harda where my wife and I with six other missionaries worked from 1924 to 1930, not one baptism from outside the church occurred between 1918 and 1954, a period of thirty-six years.

Lack of church growth is part of my own experience. I present these few instances as typical of much mission effort. The churches and missions cited are not more blameworthy than others; indeed, I hesitate to call them blameworthy at all. They do good work. They pour out life. They bear witness to Christ. They teach and heal men, distribute powdered milk, and demonstrate improved agricultural methods. But they do all these things, and much more, while their churches grow, if at all, by baptizing their own children. It may be truly said that the ambiguous cliche "splendid church and mission work, whether the Church grows or not" characterizes most churches and missions today—in America and elsewhere.

It is not fair to take examples from brief periods of nongrowth. Even rapidly growing Churches have occasional plateaus. So it is specially instructive to consider the following century-long graph of growth of the combined membership of four notable Churches in Jamaica.

In 1850 the Baptist, Methodist, Moravian, and Presbyterian Churches in Jamaica had a total membership of 54,000 communicants or full members (see the left bottom corner of the graph). During the next hundred years the memberships increased to 60,000—that is, over a full century, during which they were continuously assisted by missionaries and funds from England, they added a total of only 6,000 members, or 15 members per year per denomination!

Meanwhile, the population of the island rose from 400,000 to 1,400,000. The communicants of these four denominations formed 13 per cent of the island population in 1850 and 4 per cent in 1950 (McGavran, 1962:20).

Since Jamaica was an advanced field, where missions turned authority over to the Churches between 1840 and 1880, its record in church growth is a sober warning to those who like to believe that when nationals are in charge of Africasian Churches, all will be well.

These cases of little growth have been taken from lands where the Church *can* grow, as proved by the fact that some branches are growing. They are significant because in populations where the Church *can* grow, some missions and missionaries, Churches and ministers, engaged in witness for Christ and "many good works," nevertheless seem content with little or no growth. Faced with a general population in which some segments are accepting Christ, they try to propagate the Gospel either among gospel rejectors or by methods which obviously are not blessed of God to the increase of the Church. This is the predicament of a considerable portion of the Church today, in England, America, and elsewhere.

FIGURE 1. CHURCH GROWTH IN JAMAICA

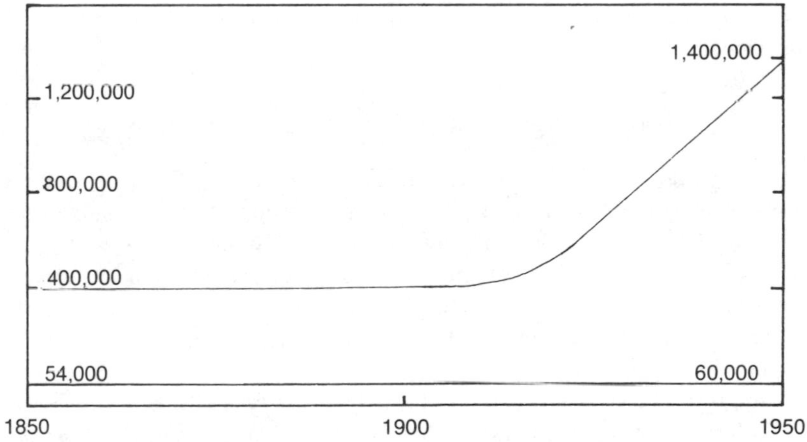

| 1850 | 1900 | 1950 |

Illustrations of lack of growth in receptive populations could be multiplied indefinitely. Most missionary societies, both conservative and liberal, if they would chart accurately the growth of the Africasian Churches they assist, would find many cases of small growth. For example, leaders of the Foursquare Gospel Church—a vigorous Church of the Pentecostal family—recently had occasion to study the development of ten of its younger Churches. They found one greatly growing Church of 25,000, three moderately growing Churches of around 10,000, and six static Churches of less than 2,000 each.

In a few cases, nongrowth or slight growth is irremediable. It can be truly ascribed to the hard, rebellious hearts of those to whom the Gospel is proclaimed. Resistance is too high, hostility too great, for men to obey or even "hear" the Gospel. There are counties and cities in almost every nation in which Christians can preach, teach, and heal for decades with practically no one accepting Christ. Such resistant populations exist. Procedures in these cases will be discussed later. Remembering our Lord's command that the Gospel must be preached to every creature, the Church should not bypass these.

In most cases, however, the situation is remediable. Arrested growth can be ascribed to faulty procedures. Sometimes, when a shepherd returns empty-handed, it is because the sheep refuse to be found and flee at his approach. Sometimes, however, empty-handedness becomes a habit and is caused by peering into ravines where there are no sheep, resolutely neglecting those who long to be found in favor of those who refuse to be. Sometimes it is a question of sticking for decades to methods which have proved ineffective. Suffice it to say that lack of church growth is an unnecessary trait, or experience, of many branches of the Church and many missionary societies.

TODAY'S OPPORTUNITY: RECEPTIVE POPULATIONS

The urgency of church growth is heightened by the fact that the Church now faces a most responsive world. Together with many little-growing Churches, some are growing moderately, and a few with great vigor. Together with lack of growth in far too many instances goes an amazing amount of real, sometimes spectacular growth in other cases. When it is realized that much of the standstill is unnecessary and can be replaced by a steady, healthy increase among those who have become new creatures in Christ, the extent of today's opportunity can be better assessed.

North America is commonly held to be a difficult field. Indifference to Christ marks its secular pluralistic populations. Denominations decline. Church growth is most unlikely. Why strive for it? Thus it appears to the leaders of static Churches. Yet in this very land, the General Conference Baptists grew from 40,000 in 1940 to 125,000 in 1978. The fact is that ripe harvests abound in North America—but men with scythes are needed. Conviction that the Lord of the harvest has sent them in to work is essential if the fields are to be reaped.

Overseas, comparison with conditions a hundred years ago heightens appreciation of today's responsiveness. Then a chief goal of most missions was to get into closed lands and manage to stay there. Dread diseases killed off many Westerners. Non-Christian rulers and governments with the power of life and death considered missionaries the advance agents of Western imperialism and often prohibited entry as long as they could. When the missionaries got in, it was to encounter incredible difficulties.

Today in countless areas all this has changed. Danger to health has been dramatically reduced. Missionaries come and go, harassed by nothing more than delays and paper work. It is true that some countries present hindrances to mission—China, India, Egypt, Russia—but by contrast with earlier days the world is full of mission opportunities and eager populations, with relatively little risk to life and limb. Six-month journeys on foot are rare. Missionaries arrive by jet to find large and flourishing Churches glad to receive them. If they know where to look and want to evangelize the people whom God has prepared, they can generally find hundreds or thousands who, like the common people in the day of our Lord, will hear the Gospel gladly and obey it.

The responsiveness of peoples to the Gospel is sometimes obscured by adjustment to the postcolonial era. Inside Afericasian Churches, transfer of authority to nationals has been painful in many cases. Friction between church and mission leaders has not been pleasant for either side. Outside the Churches, newly independent nations have sometimes treated missionaries from Eurica as Euricans once treated Afericasians. Entry has been denied. Missionaries have been sent home. Yet all this, which gains headlines, is more than balanced by the great cordiality with which most missionaries are treated in the fields where they work. The incontrovertible fact that the number of missionaries working abroad was never larger than it is today is a tremendous testimonial to open doors.

Probably a greater cause for pessimism concerning church growth in Afericasia lies in domestic conditions in Europe and, to a lesser extent, in America. European powers have seen their empires fade away. Public and private worship has declined. The disaster and disruption of two world wars have torn the Church. The inability of state Churches to evangelize their own nominal members, and their determination to prevent Free Churches from doing so (lest they multiply "sects" in the land), have denied them the greatest single source of renewal. The new religion of secularism, arrayed in beautiful Christian clothing which it did not make, has seemed particularly attractive. All these factors have contributed to a feeling that the advance of the Church is no longer a tenable hope for intelligent men.

The failure of nerve at home cast a black pall across the estimate of things abroad. Avant-garde Eurican Christians came to feel that the Church ought to renounce a "sociological triumphalism" and espouse the "humble and much more Christian role" of servant in the house of common humanity. Inevitably such feelings in Eurica obscured the spiritual hunger of millions in both Eurica and Afericasia and their readiness for change. Responsiveness to the Gospel was burgeoning; but Christians, absorbed in their own troubles, could not see it.

Responsiveness, to be sure, must not be overstated. Of the 160 million Americans who have little actual connection with the Church—though of these possibly eighty million have their names on a church roll somewhere—at least thirty million are hardcore pagans born of pagans. No denomination gains many of these. This block of Americans is not notably responsive.

Well over half of the rest of the world is still indifferent or even hostile to the Good News. Millions have set their faces like flint against Christ. Christian missionaries have been thrown out of Russia, China, Cuba, and other Communist lands. A few million souls in Afghanistan and Arabia are still closed to evangelization. All this and more must be taken into account. Nevertheless, many lands *are* responsive, many populations *are* receptive. Compared to a time when everyone was hostile, now only some are.

Outside the Communist blocks, it is a rare land where there is not some receptive segment of the population. The upper and middle classes in Chile are probably as scornful of Evangelical Christianity as they were in 1900, but the Chilean masses, as the rise of large Pentecostal denominations testifies, are abundantly able to hear the Good News and obey it. Most touchable castes in India have yet to ripen, but since 1947, in two Indian Methodist conferences alone, that Church has grown from 100,000 to 200,000 (Seamands, 1968:121). When the British left, many denominations in India—including the great united Churches of North India and South India—decided to lie low and not court persecution by active evangelization. These two sections of the Methodist Church, however—enduring persecution joyfully—doubled from among the lower castes. In short, the Methodist Church, rejecting the counsels of the fainthearted that the Church cannot grow in independent India, established a multitude of congregations in receptive segments of the population.

In Ethiopia (before the Communist takeover), missions which had evangelized the responsive groups saw great church growth. The Sudan Interior Mission was in 1967 assisting a Church of 100,000 baptized believers (Coxill, 1968:67) despite the fact that most of its missionaries still worked in resistant sections of the country. Had the mission concentrated its efforts on those who were responsive, it would have seen a still greater increase.

In country after country, the number of ripe or ripening sections of the population is amazing. One last illustration must suffice. In the first decades of this century, southern Brazil was flooded by hundreds of thousands of Italian immigrants. Most were cool toward the Church of Rome. They came from the laboring section of the Italian population which later became Communist. The first generation or two spoke Italian. They were highly responsive to the Evangelical message. The Methodists, Presbyterians, Lutherans, and Baptists, however, were busy among Portuguese-speaking Brazilians. The leaders of their Churches knew nothing but Portuguese and did not even glimpse the Italian opportunity.

An Italian convert from Chicago, however, totally without financial resources, moved from North America to Brazil and preached Christ. The Church he founded, which until 1936 conducted its services in Italian, by 1965 had grown to 400,000 baptized believers. Its Mother Church in Sao Paulo is a beautiful structure seating 4,000. In general it may be said that responsive segments exist in many lands, but they are not always found by missionaries or national church leaders (Read, 1965:20-44).

More winnable people live in the world today than ever before. There are far more winnable men and women in Illinois or Canada than there were a hundred years ago. The general population in many states and regions is more favorable to Christ and more open to conversion.

India has far more now than in the days of Carey or Clough. Africa has myriads who can be won. Latin America teems with opportunity. For the Gospel, never before has such a day of opportunity dawned. These populations have not become receptive by accident. In their responsiveness to the Evangel, he who has eyes to see can discern God at work. His sunshine and rain, His providence and Holy Spirit, have turned population after population responsive. One hears a great deal today about the Lord of history and His action in the affairs of men. Christians, sensitive to the oppressions of the masses by feudal lords, *hacenderos,* and *malguzars* (landowners), and longing for revolutions which will rectify age-old injustices, speak much about God at work in history. No doubt even among those who reject Him, God does work in many ways, to bring about righteousness and justice. Is it not equally reasonable to believe that He works among them to bring about a tremendous responsiveness to His Son Jesus Christ?

Since it is true that the most democratic nations today are those with the largest proportions of Evangelical Christians, may we not say that as God works to bring about the rule of justice, one of the first things He does is to touch men's ears so they can hear His apostle say, "Among those who have put on Christ, there is neither Greek nor Jew, Barbarian, Scythian, bond or free" (Col. 3:11). It takes new creatures to make democracy work. Only in Christ do men of any nation become new creatures.

This amazing responsiveness is well known. Bishop Neill, the noted authority on missions, says, "On the most sober estimate, the Christian is reasonably entitled to think that by the end of the twentieth century, Africa south of the Sahara will be in the main a Christian continent" (Neill 1964:568). If even half this forecast—with which I am in substantial agreement—comes to pass, during the next four decades we shall witness the greatest accessions to the Church that have ever taken place. The few millions who slowly became Christian in Europe in the eight hundred years between A.D. 200 and 1000 constituted, we may say, a small pilot project in God's strategy for His world. In the last third of the twentieth century He is preparing the peoples of Africa, Korea, Taiwan, Assam, and other lands to journey out of Egypt into the Promised Land. In Europe and North America, millions can be and, we are convinced, will be led to become responsible followers of Jesus Christ and members of His Church. Great movements lie ahead.

One thing can delay a vast discipling of the peoples of earth. If, in the day of harvest—the most receptive day God has yet granted His Church—His servants fail Him, then the ripened grain will not be harvested. If slight church growth persists, then the winnable will not be won. If missions and Churches continue content with little growth, God's preparations for the feast may be wasted.

The Specialist and Church Growth

The propagation of the Gospel is often hindered and often helped by the specialist. It is helped because the work of the Church is complex and men and women of different gifts are needed. It is hindered because it is so easy for specialists to forget that the central task of the Church is evangelism. As the International Congress on World Evangelization said, "*Evangelism* and the *salvation of souls* is the *vital mission* of the Church" (31). Specialist duties exempt no one from this primary thrust. All Christians should witness to Christ. They ought not take shelter in specialist roles any good humanist could play. These may never be substituted for consciously seeking to bring others into a personal relationship to Jesus Christ.

Specialist in Eurica

Christians in Europe and America, and long established Christian communities in other continents too, playing specialist roles are often tempted to neglect intentional evangelism. They neither pray that others may come to Christ nor take deliberate steps to bring this about. Such work, Satan teaches them, is what the pastor is paid to do. Specialists who teach in Sunday School, sing in the choir, usher at worship services, or cook church suppers sometimes are evangelistically influential; but often they do nothing to lead the unsaved home.

Specialists in Africasia

The great number of missionary specialists going abroad in this day of opportunity increases the danger that just this will happen there also. None can doubt the need of specialist missionaries. They are here to stay and may increase in number, if not in proportion. With added learning, life grows more and more complex, and hundreds of full-time employments undreamed of fifty years ago occupy the lives of thousands of men and women. Each specialization enriches life. For example, in medicine X-ray technique is a narrow specialization which greatly assists accurate diagnosis; today many missionaries go abroad as X-ray specialists. Hundreds of other illustrations come to mind. It is precisely the enrichment of life made possible by missionary specialization that creates the danger that such enrichment may come to take the place of strong church growth. The missionary specialist should beware lest he help church growth to remain slight. So should the specialist in American denominations.

I speak as a specialist. My professional training is in education. For many years my chief responsibility in India was schools. I approach the growth of churches not as a trained evangelist, but from the viewpoint of a missionary who was trained in and spent most of his time in an auxiliary aspect of the chief undertaking.

The great temptation of the specialist—in North American churches as well as on mission fields—is to hope that someone else will proclaim the Evangel and persuade men to become disciples of Christ. The pastor of the church should do it—he is prepared for it. Or, thinks the specialist missionary, national Christians should proclaim Christ.

"Was I right," he queries, "in allowing them to think the missionary is going to evangelize? Furthermore, if missionaries are to preach the Gospel, it should certainly not be lay missionaries. Preaching is what ordained men do. Let educators teach, medical men heal, and evangelistic missionaries evangelize."

Finally, the specialist takes refuge in theology. "I cannot win others to Christ—that is the prerogative of the Holy Spirit. I but bear witness teaching Sunday School or singing in the choir, by the service I render, the relief goods I distribute, the classes in English I teach, and the kindly acts I perform. The Holy Spirit convicts men of sin and brings them to the Savior. But not I, Lord! I am too busy. I have important assigned work to do." This is the temptation of the specialist. Since there are many specialists today, it is a widespread temptation.

The result is that, while much good work is done, there is little church growth. All sorts of useful services are performed and necessary tasks completed; but churches remain barren. One looks in vain for their daughter congregations. Barrenness was a reproach in biblical times and, despite the population explosion, still is in many parts of the world. Specialists often increase the likelihood that the congregations in which they work will be barren.

Abroad when specialist missionaries go home, small clusters of unreproductive congregations, grown accustomed to good works done by foreign helpers with large budgets from abroad, are left. These are unable to continue such works, and furthermore are quite unaccustomed to discipling their neighbors.

The specialist, however, does not need to increase barrenness. He can help make his churches fruitful, mothers of many sons and daughters. With the same eagerness with which he took up his specialty, he can learn how churches are growing in his own and other denominations in the country to which God has sent him. Educators, radio technicians, literacy experts, agricultural demonstrators, and builders can become as knowledgeable as ordained men about the processes of church growth. Several physicians and educators while on furlough have studied at the Fuller Institute of Church Growth and returned to their fields to bring added insight to bear on the communication of Christ to an entire countryside.

Perhaps the most immediately practical thing for the specialist is to devote regular time each week to church planting—proclamation and persuasion with the intent that unbelievers should accept Christ and be baptized and added to the Lord in new and old congregations. Some specialists already do this. Many more should.

In a large town in Ohio, I saw one of the most striking cases of church growth ever to come to my attention. One specialist—who earned his living selling hardware—also had a conscience on personal evangelism. Year after year, he was the chief cause for dozens of additions to his church.

The Anglican Church of Ruanda for many years owed much to several missionary physicians, who in addition to their hospital duties were fountainheads of new spiritual life for multitudes. A Baptist physician in India gave two nights a week to proclamation, often in areas where he had no former patients, and in addition commended Christ to every patient in his hospital. Because of him many on the hospital staff became active lay evangelists. A new people movement which brought a thousand a year into the Church owed much to him. Principal Miller of Madras Christian College in the early years of this century was the means under God of leading many of his upper-caste students to Christian commitment and baptism. About 1884, when the Churahs of the Punjab were coming like a flood, all the missionaries of the United Presbyterian mission, whatever their speciality, turned for a season to preaching, teaching, baptizing, and shepherding the new village congregations.

The Church expects every Christian—housewife, peasant, carpenter, mechanic, truck driver, or teacher—to do personal evangelism. How much more should she expect that every missionary of the Gospel, whatever branch of mission he may be in, to whatever special task assigned, will exercise his sacred privilege to bring men and women to the feet of the Lord. So should every ordained person and seminary professor.

THE IMPERATIVE OF MISSION TODAY

Today's task and opportunity reinforce the biblical imperative. This is the day par excellence to reconcile men to God in the Church of Jesus Christ. We must not be limited by the small expectations of our forebears, nor measure tomorrow's advances by yesterday's defeats. Modes of mission which suited a hostile population should not be continued when that population (or some other in the neighborhood) turns receptive. Concepts of what God desires our Church to do, formed during the frozen decades when our predecessor did well merely to hang on, must not deter us from planning to double the churches when, for at least some segments of the population, the climate moderates.

Verse 5 of the first chapter of the Epistle to the Romans gives direction here. One can call this the Great Commission as given to Paul. In the light of the last verses of Matthew and the redemptive purposes of God as portrayed in the entire Bible, it also speaks to the whole Church. The commission is found in three places in the epistle, but I quote it from 16:25, 26 as it appears in the New English Bible. "The Gospel I brought you . . . [is] now disclosed and . . . by Eternal God's command made known to all nations, to bring them to faith and obedience." For exact rendering of the Greek words *panta ta ethne*, "all nations" should read "all peoples." The apostle did not have in mind modern nation-states such as India or America. He had in mind families of mankind—tongues, tribes, castes, and lineages of men. That is exactly what *ta ethne* means both here and in Matthew 28:19.

In a day when few nations as wholes are turning responsive, but many segments of them are, an exact rendition is vital to understanding. When peoples are turning responsive as social classes, as peasants moving into cities, as minorities, tribes, castes, tongues, and numerous other *ethne,* the biblical mandate to bring the *ethne* to faith and obedience falls on our ears with particular force. Not only is there the command, but God has provided the opportunity. Christians might be excused for neglecting the divine directive in ages when all peoples were hostile to the Gospel; but when many segments of society at home and abroad are ready for change, can hear the Gospel, and can be won, what answer shall we give to God if we neglect the work of reconciling them to Him? What answer shall we make to men, if while providing them with all the lesser furnishings of the banquet of life, we withhold from them the bread and meat we know is true nourishment?

Thus today's paramount task, opportunity, and imperative is to multiply churches in the increasing numbers of receptive peoples of all six continents.

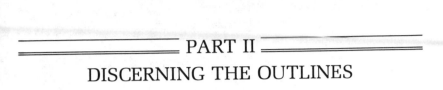

PART II
DISCERNING THE OUTLINES

4

THE MARVELOUS MOSAIC

A S WE ponder God's desire that all peoples (note the plural) everywhere hear the Gospel, have a real opportunity to set their faith
intelligently on Jesus Christ, and become members of His Body, the Church,
a shocking fact confronts us. Of the vast population of the world (four
billion in 1978) *three billion have yet to believe the Gospel*. Most of these
have yet to hear it in a way which enables them to become Christ's disciples
and responsible members of His Church. This three billion will rapidly
become four and by 2,000 A.D. *five billion*.

This shocking fact has been concealed by an understandable euphoria
which during 1920-1960 accompanied the transfer of authority from the
missionary societies to the recently founded Churches of Africasia.

THE EUPHORIA

During these years the missionary societies were broadcasting the following cheerful message:

> The heroic labors of our missionaries have borne good fruit. God has blessed
> them to the establishment of strong churches in many lands. Wonderful Chris-
> tians have been reared. We thank God for their dedication and ability. In their
> now self-governing nations, these men, not our missionaries, should be in
> control. A good missionary works himself out of a job. He prepares his
> successor and comes home. Rejoice in the successful completion of the task.

From now on mission means not world evangelization but a moderate amount of fraternal aid to our Sister Churches and the restructuring of our own society so as to bring in a just, peaceful and righteous world.

Africasian leaders, alas, rejoiced so greatly in their new responsibilities and took so seriously the kind words the missionary societies spoke of them, that they seldom, if ever, called the attention of the World Church or their founding fathers to the colossal *undone* task lying all around them. Some of them, indeed, wanting more power and more money from the West, cried, "Missionary Go Home" and demanded a moratorium on missions. They never pointed out that it was impossible for them to evangelize and church a tenth (or even a twentieth) of the enormous non-Christian population round about them—the 80 million non-Christians living in Bangladesh, 600 million in the Moslem world, 600 million in India, and 800 million in China. Africasian church leaders seldom beseeched the older Churches to "Send multitudes of missionaries on beyond us to the unreached peoples of this land."

To be fair, neither did most missionary societies and most missionaries. The promotional euphoria of "transferring authority to our sister Churches" led most mission thinkers to believe that missions in the future would be the rapid evangelization of the remaining unevangelized by "the great younger Churches," assisted prudently by the older Churches. "We must not flood them with money, or push them around. They—not we—are now in charge of missions in the Third World."

THE COMFORTABLE DOGMA

The World Council of Churches' Commission on Evangelism meeting in Mexico in 1963 declared that from now on mission was each Church in its own place proclaiming the Gospel and carrying on mission.

This comfortable dogma—which so cheerily disregarded the fact that in most places the Church in the Third World was a tiny part of the total population and confined to one or two sections of it—gave most Christians in Eurica a comfortable feeling that the main task of world evangelization was now *finished*. "The great new fact of our time" was that the Church was in every land of earth. From now on, it would grow naturally as devoted Christians of each nation evangelized their neighbors. They would be so much more effective than foreign missionaries.

THE BOMB

In 1974, into this relaxed scene Dr. Winter threw a bombshell. To understand that bomb, it will be necessary to see the background. Dr. Winter had been a Presbyterian missionary to Guatemala. In 1965 searching for faculty for the School of World Mission at Fuller, I asked him to write an article for the *Church Growth Bulletin*. His "Gimmickitis" was published in the January 1966 issue—and is still well worth reading. A striking paragraph reads:

> I used to be an expert in the gadgets and gimmicks. I was always looking for something new which would do the trick. But here in Guatemala it has become steadily clearer to me that the slickest trick of all is the planting of congregations. The care and feeding of congregations is the central strategic activity to which all gimmicks must be bent.

I decided that Winter belonged on the faculty of a School of Missions which intended above everything else to look at the *facts* of world mission in the light of Christ's mandate to disciple *panta ta ethne*—all the classes, tribes, castes, ethnic units, and economic groupings of mankind—and to devise strategies for churching them as rapidly as possible. I invited him to become a member of our faculty.

Here he became the professor responsible for the accurate portrayal of the facts of church growth for all theses and dissertations. He had of necessity to see and measure the church growth situation in hundreds of regions from which career missionaries and leading nationals came to study with us. He soon discerned that the comfortable dogma was a vast illusion.

The promotional voice of missions—which was uncritically accepted by most missionaries and Third World readers—spoke as if the population of any nation was homogeneous—made up of one kind of people, having one language and one culture, and enjoying instant communication with all other citizens. In Africa lived Africans, in China Chinese, and in Indonesia Indonesians! Promotional writing also assumed that since all the citizens were one kind of people, the Church there was of the same kind and could therefore spread the Gospel to everyone. That was the illusion. The reality was something very different.

The reality was that most nations were mosaics. In the United States, for example, as Dr. Wagner pointed out in his 1979 landmark book *Our Kind of People*, ninety million Americans arranged in eight major groups (and hundreds of minor groupings) make up the unassimilated part of the American mosaic. When educational and economic distinctions are added to ethnic divisions it is seen that even in America (where "everybody speaks English and all are Americans") the reality is hundreds of ethnic and cultural and economic segments—pieces of the mosaic. A Church strong in one piece does not spread easily to another. For example, a congregation of native-born whites in Georgia would find it very difficult to evangelize a tight-knit French Canadian or Gypsy community recently arrived in Atlanta.

To cite another example, in Mexico eighty Indian languages have survived four hundred years of Spanish domination and are spoken by eighty communities of considerable size. In India, the population is divided into more than 3000 castes and tribes, each of which is endogamous and ostracizes any of its members who marries outside it. India has thirteen major languages and hundreds of dialects. The Lutheran Church in Andhra State has arisen very largely from depressed classes converts. Ninety-eight percent of all Lutherans there are of Mala or Madiga origin. It is ludicrous to suppose that *that* Church—despite the great degree of liberation granted it by the Christian Faith—can successfully evangelize the middle and upper castes. As well imagine that renewal in England will come as Jamaican Christians in East London persuade the secular and Anglican populations of wealthy West London to become members of Jamaican congregations!

As I said in 1974 at the International Congress on World Evangelization,

> The Christian Faith flows well within each piece of the mosaic, but tends to stop at linguistic and ethnic barriers. Most congregations are shut up to one language, one ethnic unit and frequently to one social or economic class (100).

As Chapter 11 of this book insists, "Men like to become Christian without crossing racial, linguistic, or class barriers."

In short, enormous numbers of men and women belong to pieces of the mosaic from which very few have become Christians. They cannot be evangelized by their neighbors. They cannot be evangelized by any except missionaries. American Christian John Doe, who speaks English, earns $20,000 a year, lives in a middle-class home, and attends a typical congregation of about three hundred members, cannot win to Christ and bring into that congregation many Lebanese, Portuguese, Polish, French Canadian, Chinese, or Indian immigrants to the United States. Even if they were to believe on Jesus Christ and be welcomed in that congregation, converts from these and other ethnic units would not feel at home. If they came for one service, they would not likely return next Sunday. If they joined the church, they would be likely to drop out after a few months.

In other lands, the situation is even more striking. Hakka-speaking Chinese in Taiwan have the name of being very resistant to the Christian

Gospel; but Dr. David Liao maintains that the two million Hakkas have simply been neglected. They have heard the Gospel and been invited to become Christians by Minnan- or Mandarin-speaking Churches. No doubt Minnan-speaking Christians have proclaimed the Gospel within earshot of the Hakka minority, but the seed has "fallen on stony ground." To multiply churches among Hakkas, Hakka-speaking *missionaries will be required.* These may be Mandarin-speaking Chinese citizens of Taiwan—or Americans or Brazilians—*who learn Hakka, evangelize in Hakka, start congregations made up of Hakkas, and appoint Hakka deacons, elders, and pastors.*

Dr. Winter summed it up by declaring at the International Congress on World Evangelization that in the entire world perhaps three hundred million non-Christians (of cultures similar to the Christians) can be reached by near-neighbor evangelism; but that *twenty-four hundred million* (2.4 billion) *can be evangelized only by missionaries* (pp. 229, 230). That is the bombshell. Far from the age of missions being over, it is only well begun. The main task lies ahead.

QUANTIFYING WORLD EVANGELIZATION

Winter constructed many diagrams showing the situation. His most famous one is that which he used at the Lausanne Congress. (See *Let the Earth Hear His Voice*, page 229, reproduced below.)

Observe that he identifies four kinds of evangelism: E-0, E-1, E-2, and E-3. Pointing these out was his way of taking the mosaic seriously, and became one of Winter's brilliant contributions to missiology. E-0 evangelism aims to renew or reconvert existing Christians. E-1 is near-neighbor evangelism of non-Christians whose language and customs are those of the Christian who is witnessing. E-2 is evangelism across a small ethnic, cultural, or linguistic gap. E-3 is evangelism across a large linguistic, cultural, and ethnic chasm.

The whole rectangle in the accompanying diagram is the population of the world in 1974.* (It was 3,902,000,000 then. In 1980 it was 4,300,000,000. In 2000 A.D. it will be 6,000,000,000.) Above the heavy black line are all the Christians of the world—slightly more than a billion of them. Of these (at a generous estimate) 200 million (see the uppermost rectangle) are dedicated practicing Christians, while 979 million (see the next rectangle) are nominal marginal Christians. Many of these are Christo-

---

*While the present tense is used in this text, readers should remember that the figures are true for 1974, not for the year in which they read them.

pagans, secularists, positivists, Marxists, and hedonists. Note that of the 200 million dedicated Christians, 40 million are in Africa and 40 million in Asia; while of the 979 million nominals, 76 million are in Africa and 58 million in Asia.

Below the heavy black line are the 2,723,000 non-Christians: Buddhists, Moslems, Hindus, Jews, Animists, atheistic Marxists, and followers of minor religions such as Zen and Hare Krishna.

Non-Christians are divided into two major categories. The upper rectangle contains 336 million non-Christians of the same ethnic, linguistic, and cultural groupings as the Christians. They can be reached by E-1 evangelism. The lower rectangle contains 2,387 million (2.4 billion) souls of quite different languages, cultures, and ethnic make-ups. These numbers are increasing every year. They are now much larger than in 1974. These myriads can be reached only by E-2 and E-3 evangelism—across great chasms of language, economic and educational achievement, and culture. Such evangelism can be carried out only by missionaries, of course. Cross-cultural evangelists (missionaries) should be prepared and sent out by all sections of the Church in all nations.

The numbers assigned to each block in the diagram are careful estimates. Readers should not waste time debating whether they are exactly right or not. Something like this exists.

Now observe that all evangelization (portrayed by the arrows) originates in the 200 million dedicated Christians. Marginal Christians have no desire to evangelize. Observe also that the only heavy arrow—E-0—is directed at the marginal Christians. Most evangelization is of nominal marginal Christians. The thinness of the second arrow shows that proportionately only slight effort is spent on E-1 evangelism of the non-Christians who are ethnically and culturally like the evangelizer.

The second thin arrow shows that an equally small amount is spent on E-2 and E-3, i.e., on evangelizing the enormous numbers of people for whom Christ died, who are ethnically, culturally, and often economically far from existing Christians. Significantly, many of these people are geographically close to existing Christians.

Much alleged resistance to the Christian Faith proves on investigation to be resistance to allying oneself to congregations of a somewhat different community. In short, hundreds of millions *cannot* hear the Gospel from their Christian neighbors. They live in different pieces of the mosaic. Difficulty in evangelizing them rises as *cultural* distance increases.

The diagram shows the situation. It destroys the comfortable dogma that from now on mission is each denomination in its own place evangelizing its neighbors. Even if Africasian congregations and denominations

FIGURE 4.1. THE WORLD

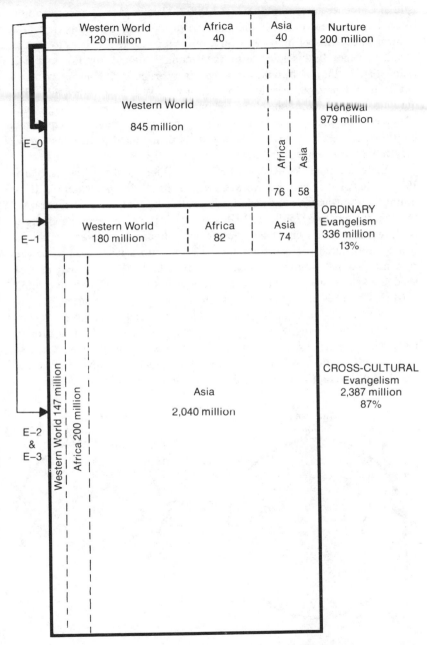

were to pour themselves out in ardent evangelism (which is not characteristic of Churches anywhere) the 2,387,000,000 souls in the lower rectangle
(who live at great cultural distance from existing Christians) would
never hear the Gospel in a way which made it possible for them to accept
it and become His disciples in existing congregations. For E-2 and E-3
evangelism of the 2.4 billion, *missionaries are required.* These may be of
any culture, language, or color—black, brown, yellow, red, or white. But
they must deculturize themselves, become fluent in another language, feel
at home in another culture, establish churches where there are none, and
build bridges to the thousands of segments of mankind from which very,
very few have become Christians.

Winter's article "Who Are The Three Billion?" in the May and July
1977 issues of the *Church Growth Bulletin,* drives this point home, illustrating it from the Chinese and Hindu worlds by two startling diagrams.
In each, the existing Church (all Christians of all Branches of the Church)
is shown as a small circle outside the main body. Those non-Christians
whom the Church can—but for the most part does not—evangelize are
shown as a small white circle inside the main body. The huge expanse of
shaded paper inside the large circle portrays the non-Christians whom
existing Churches cannot reach—except by sending missionaries.

Let us study the Chinese diagram. Note the small circle to the left of
the vertical line. It represents all Christians, Roman Catholic and Protestants. Note the tiny circle within it. That represents the dedicated Christians—the only ones who obey the Great Commission. Now observe the
small white circle inside the big shaded circle of the Chinese people. That

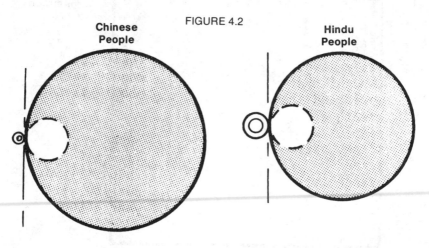

FIGURE 4.2

Chinese People   Hindu People

small circle, perhaps a twentieth of the total, represents non-Christian Chinese who are of the same linguistic, cultural, geographic, and economic groupings as the Christians. The "forty million" Chinese who are culturally like existing Christians "can" be reached by existing Christians—but are not at all likely to be. The devout Christians neither are numerous enough, nor do they have enough evangelistic passion. Most of the evangelism carried out by Chinese Christians is of existing Christians, trying to make them into better Christians. Winter writes,

> If we are sensitive at all to the heart of God, we must be stunned and crushed by the vastness of the unreached populations within this major block of mankind (*Church Growth Bulletin*, May 1977:124).

Every serious student of church growth should read the entire article, which ran for two issues. It is one of the most influential missiological writings ever published.

If in Canada and the United States, Churches are to avoid becoming enclaves of native-born middle-class whites, they must effectively evangelize (church) the 100 million and more marginal Christians and non-Christians living in the Spanish, Asian, African, and European minorities in this continent.

If world-wide, significant portions of the huge blocks of non-Christians (rapidly doubling in size) are to believe the Gospel and become members of Christ's Body, *very large numbers of missionaries,* trained in effective methods of propagating the Gospel and multiplying thousands of new congregations out beyond the existing young Churches, *must be sent out.* Europe and America, where the Church is very strong, should send out tens of thousands. Third World denominations should send out their fair share, too.

E-1 OR E-2?

In the marvelous mosaic, the "cultural distance" between the multitudinous pieces varies considerably. In the neighborhood where I live are found some of my relatives, some colleagues, both black and white, some university professors, teachers in the public schools, businessmen who are Christians, Jews, and secular materialists, some Hispanic-name Americans, some wealthy black Americans, some Armenians, and others. They all speak excellent English and live within a mile of my house; but the cultural distance between me and each of these groups varies greatly. So does the kind of evangelism which will reach each. As I evangelize these groups *am I engaging in E-1 or E-2?*

My situation is precisely that of the Christians in Palestine in the first fifteen years of the Church. Some of their neighbors were the Hebrew masses, some were Sadducees and upper-class Jews, some were Italians there as the army of occupation, some were Arabian pagan merchants, some were Greeks, some Cretans. The Church was enormously successful in winning the Hebrew masses, but not very successful in winning scribes, Pharisees, and rulers of the people. It was even less successful in reaching the non-Jews, who (while they lived in the same city and countryside and spoke Aramaic enough to get around) were at such a cultural distance from the Early Christians that they were not reached.* E-1 evangelism reached the Jewish masses, who like the apostles were "ignorant and unlearned." But E-3 or E-2 or some variant of E-1 was needed to reach the other groups.

Today variations in cultural distance surround most Christians in all continents. It is simplistic to say that all citizens of any one land can be approached by E-1 evangelism. Instead of two sharp classes, E-1 and E-2, *there are several kinds of E-1 gradually shading off into several kinds of E-2 and E-3.*

For example, as reported in the May 1974 *Church Growth Bulletin*, more than 100,000 Gypsies then lived in France. These were geographically near to millions of Christians, both Protestant and Roman Catholic. The Gypsies all spoke French—but not at home. There they spoke Romany. The Gypsies, despite living in France for hundreds of years, were culturally "far distant" from the Christians. Only after Missionary Clement le Cossec of the Assemblies of God in 1958 started multiplying congregations of Gypsies, which heard the Bible, prayed, and worshiped in Romany, did the Gypsy People Movement gather strength. In 1961 (only three years later) he appointed Gypsy leaders as pastors and colleagues. In 1974 about a third of all Gypsies in France were evangelicals. The total community numbered thirty to forty thousand. From France the Gypsy People Movement to Christ spread to many lands. In the summer of 1979 I attended a Gypsy congregation of 300 which met for worship about ten miles from my home in Pasadena. Until missionaries bridged the chasm, Gypsies never thought of becoming Christians in the churches which they passed every day as they earned their living in France, the United States,

---

* Cornelius and the Samaritans notwithstanding, the Church in Palestine remained very largely Jewish in background.

and many other lands. Were the Gypsies in France and Pasadena reached by E-2 evangelism or by a kind of E-1?

A second illustration from the United States helps clarify the situation. In 1959 I lived in West Virginia. There I observed that, though the influential denominations in the state were the Presbyterian, Disciple, Methodist, and Baptist, very few of their congregations were to be found in the many mining towns and small valleys of that mountainous state. The old, strong denominations were confined largely to the county seat towns and cities. Despite being on the ground in the early 1800s, and being mainline denominations, they had not multiplied in the *slightly different kind* of English-speaking communities which lived around the coal mines and back in the "runs and hollows." The mainline denominations were not good at the slightly different kind of evangelism needed to disciple those communities.

Illustrations from the Third World are easy to find. In Hong Kong the Chinese working classes—despite living in the same city with several hundred thousand Chinese Christians—are practically untouched by the Christian Faith. The reason is that Christians, through the extensive school system which missions have carried on, tend to be educated middle-class or upper-lower-class people. Pastors must be well-educated men. Factory laborers feel out of place in these cultured congregations. Were they to become members, they could not expect to become elders and leaders there. So very few laboring men become Christians. To persuade these factory laborers, what kind of evangelism is needed, E-1 or E-2?

There is no one *right answer* to this question. Depending on the groups involved and the stance of the person answering the question, various kinds of E-1 and E-2 can be distinguished. One missiologist might call le Cossec's evangelism a variety of E-1—he was evangelizing French citizens. Another might call it E-2—the Gypsies had a distinct sub-culture. Hunter's typology, which follows, is one good way of teaching that Christians as they evangelize people "of their own culture" *meet different groups and must therefore use different modes of evangelism.*

HUNTER'S SEVENFOLD TYPOLOGY OF EVANGELISM

The multitudinous pieces of the intricate mosaic of mankind demand many different kinds of evangelism. Lacking these, many pieces remain unevangelized. Consequently understanding the different kinds of evangelism opens up to view many hidden pieces of the mosaic.

Building on Winter's four kinds of evangelism, George Hunter, one of the creative minds in missions and evangelism, speaks effectively to the question we have been considering in the last few pages—*E-1 or E-2?* The principles he enumerates are applicable in every nation. He says:

> I have found it desirable in church growth teaching to expand the category of E-1 into four sub-categories: E-1-A, E-1-B, E-1-C, and E-1-D. For the first time, the typology Winter started can now inform evangelization within one's own culture, as well as across cultures.

> Evangelizing at an E-1-A level of difficulty engages those people of the communicator's own culture and sub-culture *who are his own intimates*—relatives, colleagues, and close friends. With these he has many natural linkages. He spends much time with them. He eats in their homes and they in his. He is one of them. What he does greatly concerns them, and what they do greatly concerns him.

> Evangelizing at an E-1-B level engages a second group of individuals. These are *very much like him,* but are not his close friends. In terms of socioeconomic class, education, vocation, needs, lifestyle, background, and aesthetic preferences they have much in common with the communicator. He can therefore speak and relate quite naturally to them. No adaptation is required. He can usually employ the very evangelistic method and motivational appeal that won him to Christian Faith.

> E-1-C engages people of the evangelizer's culture but of a *different sub-culture.* [Such as the miners in West Virginia and the factory workers in Hong Kong.] As the evangelizer and (especially) the receptor sense their differences in lifestyle, education, vocabulary, class, aesthetics, or whatever, these differences are experienced as sub-cultural barriers. The receptor, largely on a sub-conscious level, finds himself asking: "Why don't I feel comfortable with her? What did he mean by *that* word? Why is she talking to me? What is his axe to grind?" In short, it is harder for the receptor to trust and respond to an evangelizer of a different sub-culture than to one of his own. Evangelizers with cross-cultural sensitivities and communication skills can sometimes be effective, but they must *adapt* to the receptor's cultural frame of reference. In America, upper-class high-Episcopalians in Akron, Ohio, attempting visitation evangelism in a neighborhood of blue collar workers from Appalachia, will discover that E-1-C evangelism is far more demanding than E-1-A or B. They may win some—perhaps those who aspire to be upwardly mobile—but the increase will not be monumental until Episcopalian Appalachians reach out to *their* peers.

> E-1-D. Now whereas E-1-A is outreach to relatives and intimate friends of the evangelizer's own sub-culture, E-1-B is outreach to the people of his own sub-culture who are not his intimates, and E-1-C is outreach to people of an adjacent sub-culture, *E-1-D engages people of a hyphenated subculture.*

> Let us illustrate this from America. In the last three hundred years, millions have immigrated to the United States from many different lands. This nation is a rich mosaic of Afro-Americans, Mexican-Americans, Polish-

Americans, Cuban-Americans, Korean-Americans, and many other peoples of a "hyphenated" identity. Their self- and group-consciousness also become hyphenated. Some do become assimilated mainline Americans, or aspire to be—but fewer now than earlier. Most, while becoming "American" enough to make a living, bargain for a car, and otherwise cope, intentionally retain their former cultural identity, believe it to be beautiful, pass it on to their children, and socially interact chiefly with "their own people." E-1-D is not as difficult as E-2, because partial inculturation provides some ready-made bridges for the Anglo-American evangelizer to walk across. But the "how" of reaching them is more complex than E-1-C. It will require initial probing, interviewing, and experimenting to discover felt needs, points of contact, and the appropriate response pattern that will make communication with some of the receptors possible.

Two clusters of implications from this typology of evangelism demand attention.

First, a particular congregation will be easily able to expand its ranks by discipling men and women within its ministry area who are only at an E-1-A or B cultural distance from most of the congregation's members and leaders. It can win a few people from an E-1-C distance, and a very few (if any) from E-1-D, E-2, and E-3 cultural distances. The winning of *some* of these latter may be enabled by starting intentionally indigenous groups within the congregation—designed as ports of entry. But these citizens will be won in *great* numbers only through multiplying *new congregations composed of their kinds of people*. The intelligent congregation will hedge its bets both ways—winning into itself all who will come, and planting daughter-congregations for those it would like to win into itself but cannot.

Second, in order to begin a Christian *movement* among an unreached target population, the evangelizers will *begin* outreach of whatever level is necessary—from E-1-C to E-3—paying whatever price is necessary to disciple across cultural barriers. However, the sooner the new converts within each piece of the mosaic take up the task of evangelizing their kind of people into their own congregations, the sooner will the Church experience what Roland Allen called "spontaneous expansion," and what Donald McGavran calls "a people movement."

A contagious Christian movement among a people will develop best when it employs existing social networks as "the bridges of God." Over these, new Christians will reach out to their own relatives, friends, neighbors, and fellow workers.

Hunter's typology may be presented in tabular form as follows:

E-0: Evangelizing people already in the Church but not now active followers of Jesus Christ.

E-1-A: Evangelizing our intimates, of our culture, but not in the Church.

E-1-B: Evangelizing people of our culture and sub-culture, but neither our close friends nor in the Church.

E-1-C: Evangelizing people of our culture but of a different sub-culture, not in the Church.

E-1-D: Evangelizing people of a hyphenated cultural identity.
E-2:   Evangelizing people of a different culture in a different nation but within the same *continental family*.
E-3:   Evangelizing people of a different culture and of a different continental family of cultures.

The value of the sevenfold typology is that it enables us to see—for example—that a reasonably effective evangelism of secular Americans still distinctively Polish in culture will be quite different from an effective evangelism of secular Americans of German Lutheran background. Evangelism which brings in steady streams of devout biblical Christians from among the Colombians or Argentinians resident in Los Angeles is quite different from that which does the same from among new immigrants from Mexico—though both are carried on in Spanish. The type of evangelization and church planting which suited Argentinians would not suit Mexicans. To it, they would not respond. Indeed, those carrying on such evangelization would not "see" the Mexicans. To them, Mexicans would be a hidden people.

Similarly, Churches made up of Spanish-speaking Mestizos in Peru or Ecuador are not effective in winning Quechua-speaking Indians. Missions in Bangladesh creating congregations from Scheduled Caste Namashudras do not consider the sixty million Moslems in that fertile land their business at all. In a very real sense, such missions do not see the Moslems. In Kenya, hundreds of Kamba congregations seem to have little concern for the 300,000 Turkana two hundred miles to the north. They are not Kamba: they are not us. It is easy to overlook them. The sevenfold typology enables Christians to see the many "slightly different neighboring peoples."

THE HIDDEN PEOPLES OF THE MOSAIC

The illusion I have been describing (of a task which can now be carried on by Afericasian Branches of the Church) is easily believed. The tens of thousands of peoples concerned (classes, castes, segments of society) are commonly not seen. In North America eighty million have no relationship to any denomination. Yet in most churches they are seldom made the subject of prayer. Hardcore Rationalists—who loftily hold that Christianity can no longer be believed—constitute a hidden segment of society found in many parishes in the United States. We have missions to Jews, missions to Moslems, and missions to Hindus; but I know of no mission to Rationalists. Christians in Eurica, rejoicing in their Sister

Churches in Asia, it may be, or Africa, forget that those Sister Churches constitute very small parts of the total population. In Burma, for example (which in 1978 had a population of 31 million, due to be 62 million in the year 2007), Christians are a major part of the community only in the Sgaw Karen, Chin, Kachin, and Lisu tribes. In a few others—such as the Shans and Pwo Karens—Christians make up a small part of the community. In the main population—the Buddhists—Christians of Buddhist background make up less than one in five hundred. In Burma 26 million Buddhists are a hidden people.

Seeing the myriad peoples of the world as a vast mosaic, most pieces of which are hidden from the sight of both missionary societies and Churches, has vastly expanded our understanding of the task of missions. The new vision has been emphasized in various ways. Ralph Winter and the Center for World Mission focus attention on the *hidden peoples*. Peter Wagner and Edward Dayton call attention to the *unreached peoples*. Both are speaking of very large numbers of homogeneous units—ethnically, geographically, culturally, and economically separate segments of mankind. Depending on how such segments are defined, there are thousands or tens of thousands of them—the hidden peoples.

The phrase, the *hidden peoples,* is attractive. It calls attention to the huge neglected majority of mankind. Does the phrase refer to small exotic tribes hidden away behind the ranges or across the seas? Until 1935, the Stone Age tribes of high New Guinea were hidden peoples in this very limited sense. Then a man named Wissel flew over the backbone of the island and found high valleys full of men and women—a hidden people. Such hidden peoples are rare and small. Consequently, the phrase ought *not* to be used for them.

The important and very numerous hidden peoples of the world can be grouped in two sections. First, they are the hundreds of millions in the Chinese and Islamic worlds, to which Marxist and Moslem governments deny Christian missionaries access. Second, they are the peoples (note the plural) who live in great cities and in extensive countrysides *intertwined with Christians* of other linguistic, ethnic, and cultural backgrounds. For instance, scores of Brahman castes in India are well aware of Christians. They know of church buildings and sometimes walk past them every day. But between Brahmans and Christians is an enormous social and racial gulf. Consequently *to Christians,* the fifty or more Brahman castes and sub-castes are truly unreached or hidden peoples. There are thousands of Chinese in Peru. Protestant denominations and missions in Peru are made up almost exclusively of Spanish-speaking Mestizos and Aymara or Quechua-speaking Indians. Consequently to most *Protestants in Peru* the thousands of Chinese are a hidden people. Despite a small 2,000-member Japanese Free Methodist denomination in Brazil, most evangelical missions and Churches in that huge country "carry on no work among Japanese Brazilians." *To most Evangelicals in Brazil,* the Japanese are a hidden people. The two million Greek-American community in the United States is similarly a hidden people to almost all American Protestants.

Wagner and Dayton intend to publish the Unreached Peoples Survey periodically. Each volume will supplement the ones which have gone before. Each will increase the number of peoples listed. Hopefully, as the years pass, some peoples will be taken off the list. They will have been "reached." But now a nice question arises. What does it mean to reach a segment of mankind, a piece of the mosaic? When the first missionary gets there, has that segment been reached? Or shall we count it as reached only after a substantial minority in that segment has become Christian and has been incorporated in viable congregations?

In my judgment, a people has been reached only when many of its members have become disciples of Christ and responsible members of His Body. Till the Church is well rooted in that society, it has not been reached. With that definition, it is clearly seen that the remaining task is immense. Christ commanded His followers to disciple all the ethnic units of mankind. After nearly two hundred years of modern missions *only a few out of the myriad peoples of the world have been incorporated in the Church, i.e., been discipled.* In September 1979, Dr. Lal Rema, Field Secretary of the General Conference Baptists in India, was telling me that of the 600,000 Boro Kacharis in Assam, about 20,000 have become Christian. We rejoice in that beginning people movement, while noting that one can scarcely say that the Boro Kacharis have been discipled. Though more than 300 congregations are scattered through them and three mission-assisted Indian Churches carry on work among them, nearly 97% of them have yet to believe. They are still unreached, still *hidden.*

With the Mizos and Nagas the case is otherwise. Both peoples are now more than seventy-five percent Christian. Both have been discipled. They are no longer "unreached." They are no longer "hidden."

It would waste valuable time to haggle over the exact proportion of the total population of a given people which must be incorporated into ongoing congregations before it may properly be called "reached" or "discipled." Furthermore, any such discussion would miss the main point. *Whatever measure is used, it is clear that thousands and thousands of whole peoples, whole segments of society, whole classes and neighborhoods have* yet to be evangelized effectively, i.e., have yet to be "churched."

As this vision of the Undone Task spreads to more and more Branches of the Church, the significant work of Winter, Wagner, Dayton, and others will be reinforced by innumerable findings of like nature. Here in the United States, the hidden peoples (for most Protestants) are all ethnic minorities. Protestant denominations tend to be made up of and to appeal to middle-class native-born whites. Most Protestants simply do not see other segments of the American mosaic, whether of the right or the left, whether of the educated elite or the recently arrived immigrants. Both are, for Protestants, "the hidden peoples of America." In a similar way, every denomination in Asia, Africa, and Latin America is concerned chiefly with its own kind of people, and literally does not see the non-Christian masses, classes, tribes, and castes all around it. It will, no doubt, give intellectual assent to the fact that such peoples are there—who can deny it?—but will give no time to evangelizing such segments, or to praying to God for their salvation. To each Africasian denomination (as to each Eurican) the myriad unevangelized peoples remain largely hidden.

THE REMAINING TASK AND OPPORTUNITY

If God's plan for the salvation of the world is to be carried out, *a mighty multiplication of living congregations must occur in most pieces of the mosaic in most countries.* This will effect both an individual and a corporate salvation. Multitudes of men and women will find peace, joy, and power in the forgiveness of their sins and assurance of salvation. And because of the large numbers of citizens who will then be *living and voting, serving and ruling* as dedicated followers of the Lord Jesus, tremendous increase in individual and corporate righteousness will become possible. Churches are the most potent instruments of social advance known to man. They must be multiplied in every piece of the marvelous mosaic which is mankind. That is the challenge of church growth.

5

A UNIVERSAL FOG

MORE THAN 300,000 congregations dot the counties and cities of the United States. Each of them was planted and grew to its present size. Literally hundreds of millions of men and women have become members of these churches. A tremendous amount of church growth has been going on. Yet till quite recently not much was known or written about it. How churches grow and how they die remained a mystery. Did great evangelistic campaigns really increase the church? Did all Sunday Schools make churches grow or only some? Could churches survive in the inner city? How much has this congregation grown in the last decade, and what parts of it are growing most? These questions seldom received satisfactory answers. Fog enveloped the Church.

Forty-two thousand Protestant missionaries were reported in 1964, the largest number ever active in the world. Churches numbering many millions of members dot Asia, Africa, and Latin America. Many segments of society in those lands have become responsive. Hundreds of missionary societies write into their constitutions that carrying out the Great Commission is their foremost aim. Why, then, is so very little known about church growth?

Why is it so seldom even seen? Why has it not been understood long ago? We have discovered so much about how plants and animals and human beings grow—why do we know so little about how churches grow? When we devote enormous sums to teaching agriculture and to research in that field, why do we spend so little in learning about or teaching church culture—the planting and care of self-propagating churches?

Many partial answers are given to these questions. Lack of holy living militates against the spread of faith. Worldliness in all its forms is a potent enemy of the infectious Christian life. Yet these answers apply more to Christians indifferent to evangelism than to missionaries and ministers actively engaged in it, and my questions concern the latter. Why is so little known and done about church growth in Asia, Africa, and Latin America? And in Europe and America too?

Why does so much evangelism result in so little growth? What are the obstructions?

An initial obstacle which, like the cork in a bottle, must be removed first, is that *church growth is seldom seen*. Every Church and mission has its committees for education, medicine, finance, and the like; but one seldom finds one whose principal purpose is the planting of churches. Possibly leaders intend all these other activities to bring men to Christ and propagate the Gospel; but if this is so, one wonders why they do not check up on their intention now and then to see if it is being achieved. The evidence inclines one to believe that, instead, these activities become ends in themselves and shut out awareness of propagating Christianity. Few leaders of Church or mission are acutely conscious of church growth.

Missionary training schools have many good and necessary courses on the Bible, Africasian* cultures, non-Christian religions, tropical medicine, languages, and so on; little is taught of the many ways in which the Church has arisen in the lands to which missionaries go. Missionary candidates are not drilled—are not "put in the picture," are not "filled in"— as to the factors in those particular circumstances which have stimulated or suppressed church growth. Conferences of every sort are commonly held; but until very recently few have dealt with the multiplication of churches.

Should anyone object that evangelism itself is essentially concerned with church growth and has formed a substantial part of most Christian activity, it must be answered that much evangelism in both Eurica and Africasia neither results in church growth nor is expected to. When evangelism is presented, it may be assumed that renewal or seed-sowing evangelism will be meant. Searching or embarrassing questions as to how churches arise and how much they have increased will be avoided. In the literature on the theology of mission produced in the last few years, the

---

*Africasia: *Africa* plus Latin America plus *Asia*.

increase of Christians and churches is seldom mentioned. One can read literally volumes without suspecting that it is pleasing to God to have churches multiply. If theologians assume that evangelism will result in church growth, they are proceeding on a very shaky assumption. In all these manifestations of outreach, church growth remains hidden. It is seldom seen, or even focused on.

A VARIETY OF CAUSES

A strange combination of factors keeps us from perceiving church growth and church leaders from measuring what has occurred and planning for more. These factors render the phenomenon as invisible as if blotted out by a physical fog. Church leaders and missionaries, surrounded by this opaqueness, carry on programs, preach sermons, do assigned work, raise budgets, administer departments, baptize converts, teach schoolchildren, and recruit new missionaries. But only occasionally—when the cloud lifts—do they glimpse briefly the state of church growth. It is taken for granted that everyone knows about it and assumes its importance. Of course it is going on—as much as it can! Most leaders know a good deal about their own congregations, but little of the complex processes by which the Church can spread through the cultures and populations in which their denominations are at work. Very few pastors know what genuine church growth looks like or have an accurate idea of where and when it has taken place. It is seldom measured or discussed.

That Churches and missions should tolerate this obscurity is the more remarkable in view of the fact that to see, study, and understand church growth is crucially important to all pastors, missionaries, executives of mission boards, and leaders of Churches. Till the ways of growth form part of the common knowledge of all those who are engaged in the work of the Church, the reconciling of men to God-in-Christ will limp when it should run. The time has come to eliminate the sources of the fog and focus attention directly on the problem.

I am writing this chapter on a smoggy day in Los Angeles. The air stings the nose, the eyes smart, and a dull haze lies over the city. Till recently, smog was simply accepted as one of the facts of life, but better days lie ahead. It is going to be stopped at its sources. One may hope that, similarly, Christians engaged in mission will eliminate the sources of the universal fog which so effectively prevents them from seeing how well— or how poorly—they are getting on with God's mission. As a first step I shall try to point out clearly the thing itself and describe some of its causes.

As one example, note that till 1970 amazingly few books had been written on church growth. Poring over the card catalog in any seminary library one finds little listed under the growth of the Church—which is at least a major and irreplaceable purpose of every denomination and every Christian mission. If one were to classify a thousand volumes selected strictly at random from the titles in the lists periodically published by the Missionary Research Library, he would find many books on the countries of Africasia and their peoples. Tomes on history and culture abound. Biographies and autobiographies would make up about 10 per cent of the list. Promotional writings calculated to commend the missionary enterprise to supporters would comprise a larger proportion. Non-Christian religions would be extensively dealt with. Life stories of noted national Christians would not be lacking.

But books on the Churches of Eurica and Africasia—their structure, membership, rates of growth, prospects, geographical locations, aids to growth, obstacles to growth, and causes of growth—would still in 1980 be very few. On such topics one would find little, though the picture is improving.

In an interesting work, *It Began at Tranquebar,* by Lehmann the story told revolves around the first Protestant missionaries to India: Ziegenbalg and his associates. One sentence reads, ". . . the number of Christians in Tranquebar rose from 280 in 1725 to 1,321, and with the Christians in the villages, the number in 1739 totalled 3,766" (Lehmann, 1956:121). This probably means that in 1739 there were 1,321 Christians at Tranquebar, the main station, and 2,445 Christians in the villages. One additional ray of light is that annual additions of about 250 Tamils took place in 1728, 1729, and 1730 and "the number of congregation members rapidly increased in the years 1730-38." Nothing further is said about this sudden increase, which is probably the most important beginning recorded in the book. Where did this notable surge of growth take place? Were Sudras or Pariahs the chief converts? What methods brought it about? We are not told.

The Southern Baptists in the United States grew from about two million in 1900 to about thirteen million in 1980. Yet I know of no book carefully analyzing this healthy increase and telling us exactly what theological convictions fueled it, what organizational structures nurtured it, in what states the denomination prospered and in what it languished, and what were the methods which God most signally blessed.

In *Cross and Crisis in Japan* (Iglehart, 1957) Chapter I is entitled "Some Japanese Churches." One might hope for light on at least the

United Church of Christ in that land, but in vain. The chapter was written after World War II to say to American supporters that Japanese churches are just like theirs. One may applaud the friendliness that prompted these pages, while observing that, where less than one person in a hundred is a Christian and the typical congregation has less than forty worshipers on Sunday morning, saying "they are just like yours" does not help anyone to understand the churches of Japan.

Merle Davis's studies of the economic condition of younger Churches toward the end of the great depression were a step in the right direction. The missionary movement can be grateful for them, at the same time noting that even the one which promised most along church growth lines—*How the Church Grows in Brazil*—illustrates the general fog more than it illuminates the subject. On page 159, membership figures of six prominent denominations for all Brazil are lumped together—1,755 churches and 191,847 communicants. But the book gives no statistics by which one can determine how fast each denomination was growing. Though Pentecostals and Adventists are said to be growing fast, we cannot know certainly where or how much church growth was occurring. What proportion of missionary effort was serving large growth, and how much in the midst of obvious opportunity was chained to static congregations, cannot be discovered. What practices produced the evangelical wave, and through what kinds of population, remain unknown. Without the objective criterion of membership increase, all mission and church work is judged good. The eight-page description of Ponte Novo (a typical mission station with its gathered-colony congregation, where 82 per cent of the annual church income was given by missionaries) eulogizes its philanthropic services, but fails to mention that mission resources there were tied up with a static congregation in a low-potential area.

This way of dealing with the growth of the Church is typical of most missionary writing and speaking. No hint is heard that some mission work has higher priority than others. The supreme need to be appreciative of all work restrains adverse appraisal. All judgment is framed within the perspective of the kind of work described. Thus, while a writer may discuss the strengths and weaknesses of—let us say—an industrial school, it is always as an industrial school. He will never mention how far it contributes to achieving the main objective of Christian mission.

As one contemplates the consistency with which church and mission writings omit any reliable and meaningful picture of church growth, he must not imagine there has been a conspiracy of silence. Simple fog is not only a kindlier but a more correct explanation. Omission of this vital information is curious and disastrous, but it is strictly unintentional.

Since 1965 a few more books have been written which describe accurately the growth of some congregations and denominations in America and Africasia. The Church Growth Book Club carries most of these. But in thousands of regions in Africasia and in perhaps 200,000 congregations in America, visibility is still very poor. All one can say is, the fog has begun to lift.

An informational fog over an entire subject, like smog, can only be dispelled by dealing with it at its sources. It becomes important therefore to recognize the factors that produce it. Each by itself hinders the discipling of the nations. Together they could be fatal to mission. This overwhelming obscurity in a crucial area demands the immediate attention of the churches and their missionary enterprise.

Statistical Causes

Exact understanding of the increase of the Church is prevented partly by haphazard or inaccurate membership accounting. Approximations blur the picture, omissions distort it, and changed definitions mislead the unwary. As an example of the last, observe that when a Church defined members as "those who contribute to the church," the membership stood at 4,800. When it ruled that "all baptized believers in good standing" are to be counted members, without adding a single soul membership jumped to 6,000.

Accurate accounting, easy within one denomination, becomes very difficult when extended across the whole spectrum of Protestant Churches. To Baptists, members mean "baptized believers in good standing"; to Episcopalians, they mean "all the baptized, infants and adults." Community is defined so variously by different branches of the Church that figures of community are meaningless. Some report that their community is exactly the same in number as their communicants; others that it is ten times as large.

In America, the reputable *Yearbook of American Churches* solemnly publishes church memberships, some of which are baptized believers only and some the total community including baptized infants. Thus the Episcopal Church with three million members appears larger than the Churches of Christ with just under three million baptized believers, but is actually considerably smaller.

Overseas many denominations are made up of hundreds of scattered rural congregations worshiping in thatch and wattle churches. Termites eat the church records. The membership register (a cheap notebook) is used on urgent occasions as a source of writing paper, and the sheets torn out sometimes have entries on them. Village pastors are men of little education and have no idea of the importance of accuracy. They continue the names of members who move to the city, expecting them to send money to their home church while they are away and to come back soon.

City pastors and missionaries who send in reports to headquarters seldom visit the villages and almost never the homes of individual Christians, so the initial inaccuracy is built into the final total. Day school figures will be exact, for a government inspector visits the schools and checks reports; but no one checks the rolls of the congregations.

All this creates a serious fog when it comes to real numbers. Church administrators pay little attention to church statistics, partly because they doubt their accuracy.

Administrational Sources of Fog

Mission administration, at local, national, and board levels, frequently proceeds as if church growth did not matter. Budgets are distributed equally to all whether churches multiply or not. An increase of $10,000 sent out by the board is prorated to all stations. When on occasion a reduced amount is sent out, the cut is distributed proportionately to all. By its adherence to this egalitarian "democratic" procedure, administration unintentionally but effectively proclaims that what matters is faithful work; the outcome in the spread of the Gospel is immaterial.

It is easy to describe this universal phenomenon in church and mission administration and difficult to avoid it. To see the need for priorities is one thing; to put them into effect quite another.

The Gospel must be preached to every creature. "Can we leave this hundred thousand Hindus, to whom three generations of missionaries have given their lives, without any witness to Christ, simply because they will not hear?" exclaimed one missionary. To determine a true course as between "preaching to every creature" and "bringing the nations to faith and obedience" is not easy.

Even the administrator who concludes that in fidelity to the Lord Gospel acceptors have a higher priority than Gospel rejectors, and that his Church, mission, or mission board is going to plant churches that march under the Great Commission, faces difficult decisions. He must allow time for germination and growth before he expects harvest. It is hard to judge when seed is germinating and when it has rotted, and even harder to withdraw support from a weak, static congregation, for it is "our church" and all we have in that district, county, or suburb.

But acknowledging all these difficulties, mission administrators must not—dare not—act as if church growth did not matter. This is to betray the Gospel. Mere continuation of an uncritical egalitarianism is not the answer. Yet it characterizes much mission work. Itself a result of the fog that hides church growth, it generates much obscurity of its own and leads many missions to do what they earnestly do not want to do.

American church growth men can see the problem overseas easily enough; but it exists in Europe and America also. Suppose the congregation is not growing, what matter? Women's work, youth work, and stately worship services go on regularly. Colorful new robes have recently been purchased and our bell choir is the talk of the town. The bills are all paid, and are you sure we are not growing? We took in a beautiful family just last Sunday. Such administration is a potent source of fog.

Cultural Overhang Overseas

A veil which hides church growth effectively is the ethnocentricity of missionaries, or more simply: their cultural overhang. Men tend to see everything in their own cultural frame of reference.

Mission leaders know how churches grew in their own homelands. That knowledge, they think, is sufficient. "Christians preach the Gospel, bear witness to Christ, pray for God's blessing, and work hard. God gives the increase. Our denomination in this state has grown from 79 to 134 congregations in twenty-five years. That is the way the Church grows."

In any increase of the Church, the activities mentioned and God's sovereign pleasure are of immense importance. Yet if any one thing is certain, it is that churches in the varying cultures of Africasia do *not* grow in the same way as in the wealthy, educated, individualistic Protestant populations of Eurica.* The Gospel is surely one, and the Church is one; but the visible Churches which God creates in every corner of the world differ enormously one from the other. Some speak Mandarin and others Tagalog. Some exist as tiny minorities oppressed by the powerful, others as the power structure itself. Some are literate, healthy, and fat; others illiterate, sick, and hungry. Some have highly educated professional ministers; others untrained unpaid laymen. The processes of growth which cause these differences are themselves extremely different.

Strong denominationalism (which, to the surprise of some, God has blessed to great and good growth of Churches) also usually keeps Eurican missionaries from understanding the length and breadth of church growth

*Eurica: *Eu*rope and Ame*rica*.

in Afericasia. They think of their younger Churches as Episcopal, Free Methodist, Disciple, or Friends. They forget that Churches which have arisen through any given mode of growth are much more like each other than like their founding denominations in Eurica. A Lutheran Church in India, which arises by gathering in famine orphans and occasional converts, will resemble a Baptist Church there which arose in the same way much more than it will the Lutheran Church of Germany or Minnesota.

Basically different kinds of church growth are there, but denominationally loyal churchmen cannot see them. They believe they have created copies of the Churches in Eurica, which will therefore grow as those Churches do. This opinion has some substance as far as doctrine and polity are concerned; but so far as sociological structure, growth pattern, potential, and indigeneity are concerned, it could scarcely be in greater error.

Cultural overhang also veils church growth because it assumes that evangelism plants churches. Evangelism does bring in members and plant new churches in the United States. An evangelist whose preaching added no one would never be called to other churches. Indeed, ministers in America during whose regimes the membership declines are commonly asked to resign. In America evangelism often means church growth; but in Afericasia it usually does not. There it usually means seed-sowing with small expectation of actual conversions. National Christians and missionaries preach, distribute tracts and Gospels, broadcast, teach the Bible, and do many good works in Christ's name. All these activities are called evangelism—sowing the seed. Much seed—sometimes all of it—falls on the path. While the missionary enterprise includes much evangelism, it sees little church growth. Yet because evangelism is carried on, it is erroneously supposed that church growth is occurring. "Evangelism" in many cases actually diverts attention from church growth. Thus various forms of cultural overhang increase the fog that blots out the very thought of church growth.

The Semantic Cause

Vague words of many meanings are common in this field and contribute to the fog. The word *church* is an example. We read that a mission is "working with a hundred churches" in such and such a country. Does this mean a hundred churches which have an average membership of 200, permanent buildings, and trained ministers paid entirely by the churches? Or are we to understand a hundred worshiping groups of 10 to 30 illiterate members each, meeting in homes and village courtyards?

A mission reports that it is giving *evangelism* a place of first importance. This may mean it is putting most of its energies into distributing tracts to an indifferent population touring a thousand villages annually, preaching the Gospel but expecting no converts, leading 80 congregations into personal evangelism, which adds believers to half of them, or planting a dozen new churches a year. The vague word assures us that good work is going on, but tells little about what it is. Obscure approximations rather than exact understanding are precisely one trait of the fog.

In recent years the foggy word *work* has become popular. This least common denominator includes all kinds of activities. Preaching, teaching, healing, theological training, broadcasting, building, and chicken raising—all are work. Ardent church planters like the Southern Baptists, addicted to the idiom, even when they begin a church in some town in Mexico are likely to say, "We have opened a work there." Wherever used, the word hides what is being done. It says in effect: "Mission is many good works; you can never tell quite what." Where this notion of mission prevails, there church growth—if it occurs—is hidden by fog.

Witness also adds to the obscurity: "We extended our witness this year to seven new barrios," writes a missionary. Does he mean, We have planted seven new churches, or As we toured this year, we reached seven barrios which we never expect to see again and preached the Gospel at the crossroads? Usually his supporters have not the faintest notion. When a United Church wrote, "We established a witness in that province," it meant a witness to the desirability of church union, not a witness to Christ—but readers did not know it.

Similarly the words *friendly interest, response, outreach, encounter,* and the like are so vague and cover so many activities that they tell little about the increase of congregations. The more such terms are used, the less possible it is to see exact outcomes in terms of the physical increase of sound churches. Fog swirls along in the wake of these words. The semantic cause is a considerable one in America and other lands.

Psychological Causes

Of these, rationalization is the chief. Churchmen getting little church growth defensively declare they are not interested in it and do not want it. We are not afflicted by "numberitis," they retort. We would not be so earthy or hungry for quick and easy results as to seek or count conversions! We are aiming at something much higher and nobler—like building Christian character. Manufacture of high-sounding phrases *which do not involve church growth* is a specialty in some quarters. One of the best came out of China some years ago. "We are engaged," it ran, "in building Christ into the foundations of China.'' Under that broad and impressive umbrella a missionary doing almost anything could raise ample funds.

Eurican expectations of church growth comprise another psychological source of fog. In well-churched lands it is normal for a congregation of 400, let us say, to remain year after year at about that figure. Over a decade, should it increase to 500, that would be thought exceptional. The growth of the congregation in Eurica is, alas, not often thought to be its main business. Increases in Christian devotion, social action, missionary sendings, and participation in denominational activities are considered more important. These slight expectations of growth and these patterns of relative values are often carried abroad and applied unthinkingly in lands where not one in a hundred is a Christian and the chief business of congregations is precisely to grow. These Eurican standards lead us to judge slight growth excellent where great growth could be obtained, and thus again shroud churching the unchurched in fog.

Defining mission or church work so that I cannot fail often means leaving church growth out and settling for some more attainable goal. If I define my work as getting 50 per cent of the graduating class through the government examination, distributing relief to the hungry, or keeping my leading members happy and the bills paid, or preaching good sermons every Sunday, I have much greater assurance of success than if I define my work as church planting. And, when I have defined my work thus, not only am I guaranteed against failing, but I cannot see church growth. It is not my responsibility.

In North America, and around the world the excuse "I am interested in quality not quantity" must be listed chiefly as a defense mechanism, used by those not getting growth. In *Crucial Issues in Missions Tomorrow* Winter has an effective chapter dealing with this common excuse. He writes:

> Every task has dimensions of both quality and quantity. . . . All quantitative measures are measurements of certain qualities. . . . Highly important qualities have measurable dimensions. The proper way to look at quantitative measurements is to regard them—properly handled—as reliable indications of qualities (1972:178).

Anyone troubled by this psychological cause of the fog should read Winter's whole exposition. It legitimizes the use of statistics and graphs in a striking way.

Any one of these by itself may be inconsiderable, but together these and still other psychological causes account for much of the fog.

Promotional Causes

No more potent producer of confusion abroad exists than the promotional activities needed to carry on the missionary enterprise. The five hundred million dollars (and more) spent annually by foreign missionary societies in North America do not come rolling in of themselves. They must be raised. The world-wide Protestant missionary force of 42,000 must be constantly renewed from young people who hear about missions chiefly in the promotional speeches of missionaries on furlough. Promotion is absolutely essential to missions. It is an important part of what, in one way or another, most missionaries and all mission executives do.

Yet promotional writings and addresses, whose steady aims are to give satisfaction to donors past, present, and future and to present missions in a favorable light, cannot give the accurate picture of outcomes—in terms of churches planted and men reconciled to God in the Church of Jesus Christ—which mission must have. It is in the very nature of promotional speaking and writing to present an optimistic picture, packed with human interest. It inevitably creates a deluding cloudiness which prevents the multiplication of churches from being seen accurately, or even sometimes from being seen at all.

Except where missionaries work with rapidly growing Churches, their promotional speeches must necessarily recount other activities. The doctor will tell of his medical work, the educator of her school, and the literacy specialist of teaching people to read. Missionaries from nongrowing or slow-growing churches will expatiate on their labors with Christians or seeding-sowing evangelism. All are likely to maintain that their efforts are aimed toward an ultimate discipling of the nation. Of necessity most promotional speaking keeps the focus off the increase of churches and hides whatever church growth is going on.

Even when conversions and church growth are reported, a striking conversion or successful church planting made into a vivid illustration and used again and again gives the impression that it is typical—even when the speaker assures the audience that it is exceptional. For example, John Clough's 2,222 baptisms on a single day at Ongole formed a regular part of his speeches and have since been used by thousands of others. Thus the true situation is obscured by the single telling instance.

Hopes and purposes are sometimes stated as if they had been realized. "Thus," reads a communication from Japan, "through Christian bookshops and literature distribution, Japan is being led to the feet of Christ." This is hope, not accomplishment. The hope blots out the reality.

Since money must be raised for whatever is done, promotional speaking always assumes that whatever is being done—whether helping some Africasian Church, maintaining mission schools, distributing relief, or deworming a population—is *exactly what should be done to carry out the Great Commission*. But on the contrary, if the Great Commission were the clear goal and the best procedures now known were being used, "what is being done" would as a rule be considerably modified. To put it concisely, promotional speaking gives a favorably colored account of what is being done; it cannot attempt the critical evaluation essential to clear vision.*

Every pastor and missionary is both promoter and diagnostician. He occupies two chairs. Sitting in one, he is raising support for a glorious work commanded by the Lord, in which lies the surest hope for the ultimate welfare of mankind. Since he is given thirty minutes in which to present his message to his supporters, he must tell the story in dramatic pictures. He must fire men's imaginations with what he confidently expects to come about. Sitting in the other chair, however, he is a steward rendering an exact account and should present precise figures concerning what now exists by way of Church, and distinguish carefully between aims, hopes, and outcomes. He must describe what now prevents normal increase and what remedial actions should be taken, and set forth a defensible projection of what growth may be expected during the years to come.

Were the pastor or missionary to spend adequate time in each chair and never be in doubt which one he occupies when he speaks, much of today's fog would evaporate.

Theological Causes

Today's tremendous theological shifts cause uncertainty about the aim of missions, with consequent vagueness as to outcomes and goals. The reinterpretation of mission which is going on and the attempted capture of the wealthy missionary establishment by certain schools of thought deserves a volume of its own. Here only three illustrations can be given of the more common new departures.

Many Protestant leaders appear to be saying that the Church is purely instrumental: that is, it has no value in itself, but is only a means to bring in a better world. According to this viewpoint, God loves the world (John 3:16), not the Church. He is not primarily concerned with the spread of the Church. He spreads His Kingdom of justice, peace, and righteous-

---

*Pastors and lay leaders will recognize that much thinking and speaking in congregations and denominations is heavily colored by promotion.

ness among all men, whether they call themselves Christians or not. To
the extent that churches aflame with social passion are established, and
bring about changes in the direction of a more humane society, their existence is in line with God's purposes; but it is selfish to establish churches
of those who merely believe in Jesus Christ and accept the Bible as their
rule of faith and practice.

Where any such theology and philosophy prevails, interest in church
growth declines. The main task is something else. Publications and pronouncements dominated by this viewpoint add to the obscurity.

A second theological shift concerns the complex question of what
attitudes Christians should take toward non-Christian religions. Some,
heavily influenced by a pluralistic society and freeing themselves from the
authority of the Bible, opt for the view that God has revealed much in
other religions and consequently the only attitude Christians can take toward them is to learn from them. Joint search for truth through dialogue
with adherents of other faiths is, they proclaim, the contemporary mode
of "mission." That the Bible as a whole is opposed to this view does not
trouble these Christians. They rely heavily on a few verses, such as
Acts 14:17; 17:27, 28; and Romans 2:14 and 8:29, which they quote with
blithe disregard for context. They brush off Old Testament commands
concerning the religions of the land. They bypass John 14:6 and Acts 4:12
as inconvenient bits of text which cannot be taken seriously today. They
are seemingly unaware of the main teachings of the New Testament. This
school of thought considers church planting outmoded. Its words and
actions, describing mission in entirely other terms, naturally settle on the
mission scene as a dense, damp miasma.

A third common theological trend which thickens the fog is the shift
to service as sufficient witness. Missions today are engaged in an incredible
amount of service. *Diakonia* has become by all odds the chief business of
organized missions. Since, unlike mission in the New Testament, Eurican
mission today moves from wealthy nations to poor ones, it is probably in
the will of God that much service should be rendered. Most missionary
thinkers agree on this.

Where they disagree is on the questions: Is service *sufficient* witness?
Can service be substituted for church-planting evangelism? Is it maybe the
best form of evangelism? In regard to this essentially theological issue,
most Christians maintain that neither is service sufficient witness, nor does
receiving service in itself bring men to salvation. A vocal minority, however, would answer all these questions in the affirmative. For them of
course the increase of baptized believers becomes a matter of minor im-

portance. For them, it is as if church growth did not exist. The fog has swept in from the sea and blotted out the scene.

RESULTS OF THE FOG

Churches and missions which operate regularly in this complex obscurity as to church growth, and take no steps to dissipate it, find it forcing them to the decision that winning men to Christ is less important than proclaiming the Gospel. This subtle but far-reaching distinction constitutes in reality a theological decision. The question should be decided on biblical grounds; but once fog has taken over and church growth has been obliterated, what remains is proclaiming the Gospel whether men hear or not, whether they accept it or not.

A second result is that parallelism is seen as the right policy in mission. This is the doctrine, conscious or unconscious, that all the many activities carried on by missions are of equal value. They are parallel thrusts. No one of them has basic priority. Where an opaque cloudiness continually keeps the growth of the Church from being seen and valued, where figures setting forth the increase of Christians and churches are unreliable and distorted, where promotional attitudes reign supreme, what can churchmen conclude but that a dozen different works, carried on by a dozen wonderful Christians, are all of equal value. Recently parallelism is being camouflaged under the new attractive term "holism." "It would be narrow and partisan," say some influential leaders, "to hold that evangelism had the highest priority. Rather Christians should hold that all works of the Church (everything God wants done) are of equal value. This is holism." We disagree. Certainly many things should be done. The task *is* extremely complex; but this complexity must never be made to mean an aimless parallelism. World evangelization is a chief and irreplaceable work of the Church. It is the greatest and holiest work of the Church.

A third result is that fog bolsters work where no churches result, and handicaps work where many churches are resulting. Where churches multiply, there essential tasks multiply. But a firm egalitarianism caused by fog and ever producing more fog of its own, distributes resources "equally." In effect this handicaps churches which grow rapidly. *Nowhere are missionaries more burdened* than in greatly growing sections of the Church. Were it not tragic—indeed almost incredible—it would be ludicrous. For example, in two stations in Africa, manned by eight missionaries each, membership of the churches for one area was 3,000 and for the other 30,000. Egalitarian policy kept the staffs of the two stations equal for twenty years, which in effect guaranteed that the 30,000 who had flooded in would be spiritually and intellectually starved. The missionaries dealing with the 30,000 comforted themselves by believing that their churches were much more self-reliant and an outside observer agreed. He also noted that they were spiritually starved.

The fog keeps the sending Churches in the dark. They are "supporting missions" but are kept from having any idea as to the growth of the Church. One missionary society uses great church growth in a few of its stations to make all the rest look promotionally desirable. It fears to tell its supporters where growth is going on lest they withdraw support from the less productive stations. Could it be that many societies fear to give the facts of church growth to the supporting churches, lest money gravitate to where churches are multiplying?

Fog also prevents intelligent action toward discipling the nations. If Churches and missions deny themselves exact, current, and meaningful accounts of the degree of church multiplication which has—and has not—taken place, how can they take remedial action? The owners of a chain of supermarkets or any other business would think it folly not to know promptly which units are making and which are losing money. How otherwise can they rectify conditions?

Christian missions and Churches need to see steadily and accurately the Africasian Churches they are assisting. Each Church, too—American as well as Africasian—needs to see itself. The nature of each Church, its amounts and varieties of growth, should be precisely known. Only then can it devise proper care, diet, spiritual nurture, and correct assistance. Vague approximations help no one. It is inefficient to sweep disappointing facts about any Church under the rug. Furthermore, to do so is sin. Faithfulness to God in caring for His churches demands that fog be dispelled and the real situation clearly seen.

Despite the fact that in America businesses of every kind continually use charts and graphs to quantify data and present facts clearly, most congregations in America have not yet seen and studied a graph of their own growth during the preceding decade. At seminars, Drs. Arn and Wagner have shown graphs of church growth; many pastors have expressed surprise at the facts revealed.

In the Chingrai province of the Church of Christ in Thailand, congregations had been multiplying. Communicants had doubled in the previous decade and I was searching for reasons for the growth. A missionary administrator believed that the great growth (the most notable in Thailand) was due to the establishment in the province of an agricultural center, to which $50,000 worth of tractors had been given and which was asking for a further $50,000 to shift from wheeled tractors to caterpillars. The Thai moderator of the Church in that province, however, giving many illustrations assured me that the basic reason for the growth of the churches was that Christians in those rural congregations, because of their faith in Jesus Christ, did not fear the evil spirits. This one factor, he declared, brought man after man and family after family out of animistic Buddhism to Christian faith.

I do not know whether the local moderator or the missionary was right; but might it not have paid the mission to find out? And to multiply whatever was giving the Church in that province ability to double in ten years? It might also, possibly, have saved it $50,000.

Those who believe that a chief and irreplaceable purpose of Christian mission is to proclaim Christ *and to persuade men to become His disciples and responsible members of His Church* should systematically dissipate the fog that envelops the growth of the Church. It might cost 2 per cent of their annual budget to accomplish this task. Cities do not have to tolerate smog, nor do Churches have to work in frustrating uncertainty as to the degree to which they are faithful to their Master in propagating the Gospel. It is easily possible for any Branch of the Church, month by month, to see clearly the degree of church growth which has been achieved *and to feed this knowledge back into the administration of the enterprise.* It is entirely practical to understand very much more about the complex processes which God blesses to the increase of His Churches; but to do so, Christians must recognize the fog that swirls around their heads and take steps to dispel it.

6

THE FACTS NEEDED

THE NUMERICAL approach is essential to understanding church growth. The Church is made up of countable people and there is nothing particularly spiritual in not counting them. Men use the numerical approach in all worthwhile human endeavor. Industry, commerce, finance, research, government, invention, and a thousand other lines of enterprise derive great profit and much of their stability in development from continual measurement. Without it they would feel helpless and blindfolded. The vast programs of education, to which advances in every country owe so much, employ numerical procedures at every turn. The counting of pupils by sex and grade, place of residence and intellectual ability, and degree of learning and rates of progress is never questioned. Without it, effective administration and accurate forecasts would be impossible.

It is common to scorn church statistics—but this is part of the fog. This cheap scorn, casting about for biblical support, sometimes finds that God was displeased with King David for taking a census of the people (II Sam. 24:1-10), conveniently overlooking many chapters of Numbers in which God commands a meticulous numbering of all Israel and every part of every tribe. "Take ye the sum of all the congregation of the children of Israel, after their families, by the house of their fathers, with the number of their names, every male by their polls; from twenty years old and upward, all that are able to go forth to war in Israel: thou and Aaron shall number them by their armies" (Num. 1:2, 3). Also overlooked is Luke's great emphasis on numbers in the book of Acts and his careful record of the numerical increase of the Church. As A. R. Tippett points out, the motive for numbering has much to do with God's approval or disapproval (Tippett, 1965: Vol. I, No. 3). On biblical grounds one has to affirm that devout use of the numerical approach is in accord with God's wishes. On practical grounds, it is as necessary in congregations and denominations as honest financial dealing.

To be sure, no one was ever saved by statistics; but then, no one was ever cured by the thermometer to which the physician pays such close attention. X-ray pictures never knit a single broken bone, yet they are of considerable value to physicians in telling them how to put the two ends of a fractured bone together. Similarly, the facts of growth will not in themselves lead anyone to Christ. But they can be of marked value to any Church which desires to know where, when, and how to carry on its work so that maximum increase of soundly Christian churches will result.

WHAT ARE THE FACTS WE NEED?

First come *field totals* across the years. We should know the number of Christians in all congregations for our denomination in a given field. The field may be a whole nation, a state, a province, a district, or a part of a district. The number of full members for each field is almost always recorded by the denomination or missionary society. From its headquarters the annual records are easily available. As the number for each year from the beginning to the present is ascertained, part of the pattern according to which the Church has grown becomes clear. Periods of great growth, little growth, plateau, and decline will be evident. A brief inspection of the figures will tell the churchman as much about the Church as a record of daily temperatures tells the physician about his patient.

Figures, having been gathered, should be refined. In the course of years, various geographical districts are added to or taken away from ecclesiastical administrative units. For example, a congregation at Lexington, Kentucky, gives birth to several daughter congregations. At first these are counted as part of the mother church and their memberships swell hers. Then they separate. The mother church experiences a sharp drop in membership; but the field total at Lexington should show a steady rise. Church membership at the Bolenge station of the Disciples of Christ in Congo grew year after year till it reached 12,000. Then in a given year Bolenge reported only 9,000. This looked like a loss of 3,000 but was not. The Bosobele cluster of congregations, fifty miles away across the great river, which until that year had been considered part of the Bolenge Church had been constituted a church unit and reported separately. Field totals should be refined till such meaningless ups and downs are eliminated.

Grimley (1966:135) shows a graph portraying a drop from 800 to 200 in the membership of the Lutheran Church in the Languda tribe in Nigeria. But there really was no loss! In 1953 the Languda Church ruled that only those who paid a membership fee would get a membership card and be counted full members. Out of 800 baptized believers only 200 paid the fee that first year; though in other respects, Grimley says, "they were convinced Christians and were living a life in accordance with the precepts of the Church. At any rate, in 1961 there were 603 card-bearing Christians, at least 1,000 other baptized believers, and 8,108 attending church each Sunday. . . ." Grimley would have done better to refine his figures before graphing them. His graph, built on the raw figures, shows a dramatic decline, whereas the number of baptized believers was steadily increasing. Changing definitions of membership should not be allowed to confuse the picture. Refining the figures is essential to understanding.

Field totals, however, are a thin measure. They reveal little. In fact, they conceal more than they reveal. By themselves, they deceive the observer. They must be used with discretion, knowing the pitfalls that lie before the unwary. As the researcher seeks to discern church growth outlines, field totals are a good beginning, but they must be amplified by other kinds of information before safe deductions can be drawn from them.

The second fact needed is each *homogeneous unit total* across the years. The *homogeneous unit* is simply a section of society in which all the members have some characteristic in common. Thus a homogeneous unit (or HU, as it is called in church growth jargon) might be a political unit or subunit, the characteristic in common being that all the members live within certain geographical confines. For example, one could easily get a field total for the Lutheran Church in Wisconsin and a homogeneous unit total for that Church in the city of Madison. Sometimes the unit will be a county or province.

The homogeneous unit may be a segment of society whose common characteristic is a culture or a language, as in the case of Puerto Ricans in New York or Chinese in Thailand. In the island of Formosa one sees four main homogeneous units: the Taiwanese-speaking 11,000,000; the Mandarin-speaking 4,000,000 who came over from the mainland in 1948; the Hakka-speaking 2,000,000; and the 300,000 aboriginal tribesmen, the Highlanders. Seventy thousand Filipinos, mostly unchurched, lived in Chicago in 1980. The Assemblies of God in 1978 planted a church among them and can probably plant a hundred more.

The homogeneous unit might be a people or caste, as in the case of Jews in the United States, Brahmans in India, or Uhunduni in the highlands of Irian (West New Guinea). The Fomosan aboriginals mentioned above have six main tribes which together compose one homogeneous unit as regards the total population of the island; but if one were considering the Highlanders alone, each tribe would be such a unit. One might ask, How many Christians are there in each of the tribes? In answer he would be given six homogeneous unit totals.

Within a tribe subunits usually appear. These may be clans or lineages, language or dialect groups, or political or geographical units. For example we read, "As the Lord commanded Moses, so he numbered them in the wilderness of Sinai. . . . Of the children of Reuben, by their generations, after their families, by the house of their fathers . . ." (Num. 1:19, 20). Moses, by his numbering, obtained a homogeneous unit total for each clan and lineage. Similarly, within a modern city subunits appear—usually castes, tribes, or language groups. For instance, Congolese from many different tribes have flooded into Kinshasa, each speaking a different tongue. It would be profitable for the Protestant Churches to know the total Protestants from each tribe. These homogeneous unit totals would indicate to the Churches the size of their shepherding task in following up Protestants who have moved to Kinshasa. When Riddle and McGavran did this in 1977 they found that 600,000 claimed to be Protestants of whom less than 100,000 were on the rolls of all Protestant churches taken together (McGavran, 1979:145).

As these illustrations indicate, the homogeneous unit is an elastic concept, its meaning depending on the context in which it is used. However, it is a most useful tool for understanding church growth. The field total includes figures both from areas where the Church is growing and from those where it is declining. Victories and defeats are added together to make the total figure which hides all details. But when the field total is broken down into homogeneous unit totals, one sees exactly where the Church is advancing and where it is not. For example, in Latin America between 1916 and 1926 the number of Protestants doubled. This appears encouraging, but for Latin America as a whole it is falsely so, since most of the growth took place in the Baptist, Methodist, and Presbyterian Churches in one small section of Brazil. For most missionary societies in Latin America, that decade was one of slow growth; for some, of no growth at all. The general outlook was far from encouraging.

To cite a second example from Brazil: since 1946 there has been enormous growth of Evangelicals. Most of this has occurred in Pentecostal denominations, some in Baptist and Presbyterian, and very little in the conservative missions which entered Brazil after World War II. Exact and meaningful statement of the church growth situation would be concealed by any field total for all Evangelicals in Brazil. It comes to light only in the securing of homogeneous unit totals for all Churches at work there. William Read in his remarkable book, *New Patterns of Church Growth In Brazil,* has given to missions the first adequate understanding of the memberships of the larger Evangelical Churches in that big country. He shows clearly the homogeneous units which comprise the Protestant Church in Brazil.

A *Homogeneous Unit Church* may be defined as "that cluster of congregations of one denomination which is growing in a given homogeneous unit." Thus in Central Provinces (Madhya Pradesh), India, the General Conference Mennonites assist three homogeneous unit Churches. The largest is growing in the Gara caste in the southern third of the field, where the unit is a caste. The next largest is the northern Church, made up of individual converts, famine orphans, and their descendants. In this case the unit is a geographical area. The smallest Church is a cluster of congregations just starting in the Uraon caste, in the northeast corner of the field. (For this analysis I am indebted to Rev. O. A. Waltner, Executive Secretary of the General Conference, Mennonite Church; Waltner, 1962.)

Loren Noren analyzed church growth in Hong Kong between 1958 and 1962. Some of his findings are the following. During those years the Church in Hong Kong was growing at 150 per cent per decade. But:

> The Lutheran Church Missouri Synod was growing at 420 per cent per decade.
> The Evangelical Lutheran Church was growing at 400 per cent per decade.
> The Baptist Churches were growing at 120 per cent per decade.
> The Anglican Church was growing at 90 per cent per decade.

The growth in these homogeneous units is significant for understanding. Thus it is clear that, if the Anglicans and Baptists had propagated the Gospel in those sections of society where the Lutherans were multiplying churches (there was abundant room for all) and had worked in the ways in which the Lutherans were working, they would not have been limited to a mere 100 per cent or so per decade.

In America when one refines statistics using the homogeneous unit concept, he is startled to find how largely Protestants are confined to middle-class whites. Great opportunities for church growth in Hispanic and Asian and French Candian HUs are not seen by most congregations and denominations.

Three Kinds of Church Growth

Three kinds of church growth should be distinguished: biological, transfer, and conversion. Biological growth derives from those born into Christian families. Africasia is littered with tiny static denominations which obtain chiefly or solely this kind of growth. In times past by occasional converts, famine orphans, and rescued persons a small Christian community has come into existence. When the flame of evangelism burns low and "service of the whole man" comes to be the watchword, this community increases, if at all, by the excess of births over deaths. Biological growth is exceedingly slow. It often does not equal the normal population increase for the nation, for while some children become ardent Christians, some are lost to the world, or through marriage are sucked back into the other community.

In America also most denominations depend heavily on biological growth. This served them well in the past, but is a weak reed in the era of "the pill."

Biological growth is good growth. God commanded men to "be fruitful, and multiply, and replenish the earth." Christians should, truly, bring up their children in the fear and admonition of the Lord. Yet this type of growth will never "bring the nations to faith and obedience," since the non-Christian part of the world's population is growing faster than the Christian and seems destined to continue to do so. Should the Church rely on biological growth alone, the proportion of Christians in the world would grow smaller and smaller.

What a providential occurrence it was that the 120 Christians before the day of Pentecost did not rely on biological growth! One wonders whether they might not have done so, but for the intervention, entirely beyond anything they had imagined, of the Holy Spirit.

By transfer growth is meant the increase of certain congregations at the expense of others. Nazarenes or Anglicans move from the country to the city, or from overpopulated areas to new lands the government is opening up. City or "new land" congregations flourish; those from which they have come diminish. Transfer growth is important. Every Church should follow up its members and conserve as many of them as possible. But transfer growth will never extend the Church, for unavoidably many are lost along the way.

The third kind is conversion growth, in which those outside the Church come to rest their faith intelligently on Jesus Christ and are baptized and "added to the Lord" in His Church. This is the only kind of growth by which the Good News of salvation can spread to all the segments of American society and to earth's remotest bounds. The goal of mission is to have a truly indigenous congregation in every community of every culture. When that occurs, and only when that occurs, we may be sure that the Gospel has been preached to every creature. Patently, this goal requires enormous conversion growth.

In some countries a large proportion of the population has become Christian, and the distinction between the Church and the world has been blurred. In these areas a boy whose grandparents were ardent Christians, whose parents are not Christians at all, and who attends a Sunday School during his adolescent years might confess Christ, be baptized, and join the Church. It would be a nice question as to whether he added to biological growth or conversion growth. Such difficulties of classification afflict the Church in Eurica, but for the most part are unknown in the newer Churches of Africasia. There, in order to understand church expansion, it is desirable to know how much is taking place by biological, transfer, or conversion growth. A glance at the following diagram will illustrate why.

FIGURE 6.1

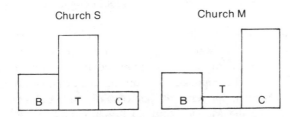

Churches *S* and *M* have about the same number of members and so have about the same biological growth (B). Here the resemblance ceases. *Church S* has a large number of accessions through transfer (T) and few conversions (C). *Church M* has few transfers but a large number of conversions. Goals for each Church, corrective action needed, the formula each ought to be fed, and distribution of the budget of each—all are different. Since both are growing equally on an equal base, they might be supposed to be very similar. Yet to treat these Churches alike because both are of one denomination, is maladministration. Until the kind of growth is distinguished, what is good for each cannot be determined. The facts help to dispel the fog.

Internal, Expansion, Extension, and Bridging Growth

Another concept, helpful in understanding church growth, sees it occurring in four ways. (1) Internal Growth: increase in sub-groups *within existing churches,* i.e., increase of competent Christians, men and women who know the Bible and practice the Christian Faith. They move from marginal to ardent belief. (2) Expansion Growth: each congregation expands as it converts non-Christians and takes more of them into itself. (3) Extension Growth: each congregation plants daughter churches among its own kind of people in its neighborhood or region. (4) Bridging Growth: congregations and denominations find bridges to other segments of the population and, crossing the bridges of God, multiply companies of the committed on the other side.

Winter and Wagner share the credit for discovering and popularizing this creative classification, which has greatly enriched the entire Church. All four ways should be familiar to and used by healthy congregations in all six continents and known by all missionaries.

Occasionally some whole population may be so thoroughly Christian that there are no non-Christians left in the vicinity. Christians in those rare parishes will then redouble their efforts at 1 and 4. But most congregations and denominations in most regions can and should engage in all four ways of growing.

Even in lands where the whole population has become Christian and almost every name is on a church roll, the number of nominal Christians, backsliders, doubting Thomases, and confessed pagans who take their infants to the church to be baptized (it is our national custom, you know) is very large. In Sweden, perhaps 90 per cent of the population falls in this category. Among the Mongo tribes in Equatorial Province in Zaire, where whole villages are Christian and most people, as boys and girls, went for years to Christian schools and were baptized after much instruction and after confessing Christ before the whole congregation, more than half the baptized seldom attend public worship. In that region in the late seventies, belief in witchcraft was reasserting itself with great power. In both Sweden and Equatorial Province, congregations of the dominant Church ought to engage in much internal and bridging growth. They should also make sure that new congregations are started in the burgeoning cities, till there is a congregation in every urban neighborhood—at least one for every thousand of the population. If the dominant Church does not do this, we may be sure that the Lord will send in other Branches of the Church—perhaps Pentecostals and perhaps Roman Catholics—to make obeying the Gospel a real option to everyone.

When one comes to those parts of the world where Christians are still a tiny part of the total population (five or two or one in a hundred or less) major emphasis should be laid on Expansion and Extension Growth. Where the Church is a tiny part of the population, Internal Growth is seldom neglected and Bridging Growth on the other side of the world is difficult to emphasize. But Expansion and Extension Growth lie close at hand and should form a major part of the work of the Church. Bridging Growth also, in segments of the population which, while near geographically are culturally at a great distance, should be a normal experience of healthy congregations.

Baptismal Figures

If baptisms from all sources—believers and infants, the Christian community and the world—are added together and recorded as a single figure, they are not helpful. But if baptisms from the Church and from the world are recorded separately, and a distinction made between the baptism of believers and that of infants, baptismal figures are well worth study. They can add a new dimension to understanding of church growth.

For example, a large Asian Church reports about 4,000 baptisms of believers a year. This is striking at first glance, but when we realize that this Church of 200,000 members, if it conserves all its own children, will baptize more than 4,000 a year as they come to the age of discretion, then the number is far from impressive. This Church, we observe, is static. She is baptizing most of her children and a few converts here and there. The missionary society assisting this Church, if it is to be truly missionary, will take all steps possible to help her regain the initiative, to begin to communicate the Christian faith in a systematic, effective way.

If the record of baptisms from the world is obtained year after year and superimposed on a graph of growth, it will be seen that growth takes place only when there are sizable numbers of baptisms from the world. Nothing produces real church growth except baptisms from the world. No baptisms: no growth! This dictum can be refined to read, "Nothing produces growth except baptism from the world provided those being baptized are properly shepherded and become vital Christians!" Aftercare is, of course, crucially important; but the refinement does not vitiate the statement: "No baptisms: no growth." The Church through baptisms must obtain new Christians before it can care for them properly. It is also true to say "No baptisms: no aftercare!"

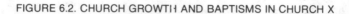

FIGURE 6.2. CHURCH GROWTH AND BAPTISMS IN CHURCH X

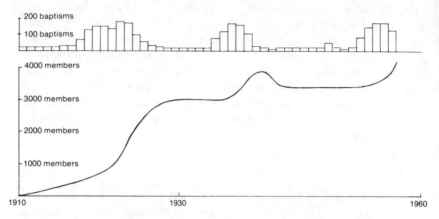

The above schematic diagram, based on many actual cases, illustrates the close relation between growth and baptisms. Note the rapidly rising line indicating three periods when *Church X* was growing normally. In each of these, annual baptisms (reported in the columns at the top) were numerous. When baptisms from the world almost ceased, though an occasional convert was won here and there, *Church X* slowed down, stopped growing, or declined.

Baptismal figures from within and without the Christian community are usually not recorded separately by most Churches and missions. To make available this dimension of understanding a minor change should be instituted in the annual statistical report required.

Ways Into and Out of the Church

There are only three ways into the Church—baptism, transfer, and restoration. (If the Church is defined as the company of baptized believers, then for paedobaptist denominations a fourth way in—namely confirmation—would have to be added.) In many Churches, very few come by the route of restoration, but some Churches excommunicate or disfellowship a considerable number of those who are baptized, and the results of this church discipline are often favorable. Many of the disciplined repent, beg forgiveness, and are restored to the Church. Bishop Azariah of Dornakal, when he first came to the diocese, excommunicated more than six hundred, chiefly for open adultery. Since the Anglicans were taking in thousands, far from stopping growth, his disciplinary action stimulated it. Many of the excommunicated repented and were restored.

Ministers, missionaries, and church leaders should know by which of these three avenues their existing members came into the Church and consequently how future members are likely to come. Is the proportion like *Church X* or *Church Y* in the following diagram, where *B* indicates those who come through baptism, *T* those through transfer, and *R* those through restoration. A Church like *Y* needs a very different prescription from that needed by *Church X*.

FIGURE 6.3

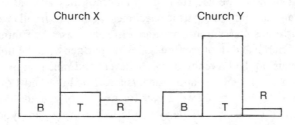

Church X   Church Y

In a similar fashion, the ways out of the Church are four: death, transfer, excommunication, and reversion. Those responsible for the congregations and the denomination should know how many are leaving by each door. In India, for example, while there is some excommunication and some lapsing to an indolent Christian position, few revert to Hinduism. In Japan, on the other hand, where there is little excommunication, many revert to the Buddhist world. Some ministers estimate that within a few years half of those baptized in Japan have ceased to count themselves Christian. Part of the reason for this difference is that in India many have been baptized *with their families and kinsmen.* They stay "Christians" even if their fervency dies down; whereas in Japan most converts come in without their families and kinfolk, so that when ardor flags they are pulled back into the non-Christian orbit.

Family Analysis

In America or any other nation a family analysis furnishes useful facts in understanding the patterns of church growth. In Thailand, an analysis revealed that in a small congregation of 49 members, 44 were women, most of whom were married to Buddhist men. In another congregation in

Thailand—this one of Chinese Christians—it became clear that if the mother alone was a Christian all the children were likely to be Christians, whereas if the father alone was a Christian none of the children was likely to be.

A family analysis of the congregation reveals the number of *full families* (where husband and wife are both Christians), *half families* (where only one partner is Christian), and *singles*. Obviously a congregation of 34 composed of four full families, seventeen half families and nine singles is much weaker than a congregation of 34 made up of twelve full families and ten of their believing children. Theoretically, the first congregation has much greater contact with the "outside," but in practice this contact leaves it much more open to erosion. How half families come about is also important and should be ascertained. Sometimes they arise as out of non-Christian families only one partner becomes a believer. In other cases they arise as Christians marry non-Christians. In some cases half families bring loss to the Church and in others the believing partner wins the unbelieving. Much depends on the fervency of the believers and much on other factors.

In Jamaica, in 1958, a family analysis revealed that most members of congregations of the masses were over forty years of age and consisted of elderly married couples and elderly single ladies. Youth and young adults of the masses, because they were living in a series of temporary unions, could not become members of the Church—though in a vague way they counted themselves Christians and brought their infants to the church to be baptized or dedicated. Congregations of the upper classes, however, consisted of a normal spread of youth, young adults, and elderly people.

Family analysis reveals the intricate network of blood and marriage relationships which tie communities together and have so much to do with the inner life of any congregation. These webs of relationship also indicate the probable modes of future growth. They are important to know as one estimates the real possibilities of church increase.

Community or Communicants

In thinking about church expansion, nothing is more confusing than the various categories, usually undefined, according to which members are recorded. For example, in 1966 Episcopalians in the United States reported 3,410,657 members, the Churches of Christ 2,350,000, Roman Catholics 46,246,175, and Protestants 69,088,183 (Jacquet, 1967:209, 201, 196). However, since Episcopalians and Roman Catholics were reporting all their baptized, including infants, and Churches of Christ and most other Protestants were reporting only baptized believers, the figures are strictly non-comparable and the proportions portrayed are entirely false. For the *Year-book of American Churches* to report these non-comparable figures year after year comes close to being fraudulent. Erroneous conclusions are annually broadcast, based on the supposedly authoritative statistics gathered by the National Council of the Churches of Christ.

If Episcopalians were to report communicants in good standing, their three million would shrink to less than the Churches of Christ figure; and if Protestants were to report the same sociological entity which the Roman Catholics do, their figure would be over a hundred and twenty million. Responsible reporting should never give community and communicant figures under the same heading.

To change the scene, when the Methodists in the Fiji and Tonga islands of the South Pacific report that in a certain island they have a community of 20,000, one can be sure that a block of humanity numbering 20,000 has declared itself Christian, destroyed its pagan places of worship, and counted the Bible as its Book. But when in Latin America a church leader affirms that the community of the Pentecostal denominations as a rule is five times their membership, while that of the Presbyterians is twice their membership, one is facing a radically different definition of community. In both the latter cases, community means "those nominal and active Roman Catholics who are so tied in with the Evangelicals that they are likely to hear and obey the Gospel."

When Queen Elizabeth visited Uganda in 1954 to open the Jinja Dam, the Anglican bishop in Ruanda, who drove up to attend the ceremony and meet the royal party, told her that the Anglican Church in Ruanda numbered "a hundred thousand souls." At the time its communicant membership stood at about 16,000. "Souls" in that parlance meant "all the baptized (infants and adults) plus all catechumens and their children."

Some conservative Latin American missions report numbers of *believers,* counting into their field total *baptized believers, unbaptized believers,* and *unbaptizable believers.* This last class of persons is fairly common in Latin America and consists of sincere men and women who as young people were married in the Roman Catholic Church, whose marriages have broken up, and who at the time they came to believe the Gospel were living with someone not their marriage partner. Divorce is difficult. Since each of the partners to the original marriage has settled down with some other person and has children by him or her, it is unthinkable for the original couple to be reunited. However, till the marriage is "regularized," the missions will not baptize these believers. They are therefore encouraged to come to church, give, pray, read the Bible, lead a Christian life, and bring others to Christ. They are "unbaptizable be-lievers"—second-class Christians. Evidence indicates that some Evangel-ical Churches have grown greatly when, free from strict supervision by Evangelical clergy, they have taken in numbers of unbaptizable believers and accorded them full status in the congregations. (Provided, of course, that they remain faithful to the partner with whom they have become Evangelicals. No Evangelical Church has allowed its members openly to break the seventh commandment and remain in the Church.)

Two other categories are commonly used: *adherents* and *sympathizers*. Horace Underwood wrote from Chung Do in Korea in 1888, before there were any Christians there at all, saying that several were asking for baptism and seventy were adherents. He meant that seventy were deeply interested in Christianity. In other cases, adherents is used in the sense of unbaptized members of a declared Christian community in which many are baptized believers. Sympathizers is a common term in Latin America, where it denotes several different kinds of people: (1) those who attend Evangelical teaching and worship but do not join the church, (2) those who are strongly anticlerical and like Protestants, and (3) those who are related to Evan-gelicals and help them out when they are persecuted.

Community, communicants, full members, members, believers, bap-tized believers, adherents, sympathizers—accurate measurement of the growth of the Church becomes impossible unless in this welter of different sociological entities, one can be found which means the same thing in all denominations and countries. Fortunately there is such an entity—the *bap-tized responsible membership*. This hard core of the Church is called by some "members" and by others "communicants," "full members," or "baptized believers." *Figures concerning this entity comprise the only re-liable comparable measure.*

To be sure, variation exists even in this category. In a few denomi-nations, "full members" are not admitted to communion; that is reserved for an inner elite who can relate a saving experience, recognized as such by the Church. Some denominations record not only communicants but "active communicants." However, by and large, full members or com-municants, defined as those who have a right to commune if they appear in church, is a category which is comparable across the length and breadth of Protestant Churches.

The compilers of world-wide mission statistics (see Bibliography, WORLD-WIDE MISSION STATISTICS)—in their volumes of the following dates: 1856, 1891, 1901, 1911, 1925, 1938, 1949, 1952, 1957, 1962, 1968—list communicants or full members. These interdenominational volumes are invaluable for study of the growth and development of the Church. Nowhere else is it possible to see the far-flung enterprise in as brief a compass on as factual a base. The varying fortunes of the Church in each country can be readily traced. Information on many aspects of missions—sending agencies, missionaries, communicants, income, total baptized, Sunday Schools, day schools, boarding schools, industrial schools, hospitals, dispensaries, numbers of workers and numerous other items— is readily available.

In this book, however, we are concerned with the growth of Churches and emphasize that, while many figures bearing on membership are kept, in any study of the growth of denominations, *only communicant figures* should be used. All others are so variously defined that to use them in cross-denominational studies is misleading.

In the future, careful definition and meticulous membership accounting should mark Christian mission. Such will assure that church statistics mirror the reality accurately.

Membership of Individual Congregations

A most useful fact in discerning the mode of growth of any denomination is the membership of its congregations across the years. Nothing grows but individual congregations. Until one knows how they are growing or not growing, reality escapes him. In Puerto Rico in 1955, I did a survey for the United Christian Missionary Society of Indianapolis. Its Church in Puerto Rico had grown vigorously for twenty years and I was sent down to understand and describe it. The reality escaped me till, almost by accident, I discovered a record of growth of every congregation. Then it became clear that the Church consisted of four kinds of congregations— big urban churches, little urban churches, small town churches, and little rural churches. During the years from 1948 to 1955, *all* the growth had been secured by the six large city churches. Industrialization of the island was proceeding apace. Rural Christians, flocking to the big cities, were making good money, and the six large city churches led by able men were getting both transfer and conversion growth. Several small beginning congregations in these same cities, on the contrary, had made little progress. The small-town congregations were (with one exception) static, with memberships around forty, and all eighteen little rural churches were static or dying (McGavran, 1956:16-20).

Membership records of individual congregations are most valuable; but unfortunately, they are usually difficult to obtain. Congregations seldom keep the annual records they make out and headquarters keeps each congregation's report only till it has added it to the field total to be published.

One of the most vigorously and steadily growing denominations of the Philippines keeps a record of every congregation and is able to tell from year to year whether it is growing or not and if so, how much. The executive secretary of the Church told me he relied heavily on this record in deciding what each congregation needed, to help it on to more Spirit-filled and victorious life.

The record of individual churches is useful in discovering causes for growth. When, for example, one sees that steadily growing Protestant congregations arose in Philippine communities where the former Aglipay-ans (now the Iglesia Filipina Independiente) were strong, he suspects that a considerable Protestant growth in those islands came from the massive Aglipayan defection from the Church of Rome. It contained so many of the nation's leaders and yet for forty-five years wandered so aimlessly in the wilderness of a sterile Unitarianism—fortunately now ended.

With the record of each congregation before him, the student of church growth can concentrate on cases of great growth and those of decline, and probe for the real reasons in each case.

The Record of Each Worker

Even more difficult to get and even more illuminating in understanding the spread of the Gospel is the record of each worker. Men are often the most influential single factor in the multiplying of churches. In one field two missionaries alternated or succeeded one another in various posts for twenty years. Whenever one came in, churches multiplied. When the other did, growth stopped. The one man was long on engine, the other on brakes. It takes courage and faith to baptize. Timid men hesitate to create new churches. We marvel at the courage of the apostles, when on a single day they baptized three thousand believers! New members bring problems which plague one during the day and dance on the pillow at night. With no baptisms, one has few problems. A friend of mine used to say that no task on the mission field is easier and more pleasant than that of being an evangelistic missionary in a field where no one accepts Christ. Day after day he preaches the glorious Gospel without ever wrestling with the heart-breaking problems which new Christians bring with them. Paul was re-ferring to this heartbreak when he wrote to the young churches in Galatia, "My little children, with whom I am again in travail until Christ be formed in you."

The man (national or missionary) often makes a difference, as can be clearly seen in the coming of John Clough to Ongole in 1865. His new policy of baptizing the Untouchables, to which he was sure God had led him, ushered in a new era for the Baptist Mission in South India. I was puzzling over a sudden rise in membership in a Church in Mexico and discovered that it was due to a worker who had been employed by the mission for a few years. He was a pearl of great price—a man through whom God was establishing new congregations in rancho after rancho— and yet twenty-five years later no one knew why he had left or where he was. From the time he left, the denomination had continued its dull way on a plateau of about 800 members. In Africa, probing the causes of a nongrowing cluster of congregations in the midst of clusters which multiplied exceedingly, I was told that night meetings were the most effective means of propagating the Gospel and the timid wife of the missionary evangelist refused to allow him to be away from the mission house at night. I am sure this was an oversimplification, but the answer was seriously given by a man who knew church growth. Men do count.

Churchmen seeking to understand church growth do well to study the records of the men who were there and see whether their policies and incumbencies have anything to do with slow or rapid increase.

KEEPING FOCUSED ON CHURCH GROWTH

It cannot be said too emphatically that the facts needed are not general facts concerning church activity. Some past studies of the Church fail at just this point. They describe what has come into being from the total church program. They relate all kinds of interesting data about numerous facets of church life. They record the number of Sunday Schools, women's societies, and youth organizations. They duly note the number, training, and salary schedules of pastors, evangelists, catechists, and workers. They set forth the number of men and women missionaries and their relation to the national leaders of the Church. They list and value church buildings, cemeteries, pastors' residences, and other property. They attempt to photograph the entire ecclesiastical enterprise, without asking whether the details presented have anything to do with the spread of the faith or not.

In sharp contrast with this process, the student of church growth is highly selective. He gathers only those facts which are needed to understand the thrusts of growth and recession. Instead of presenting a profusion of data, most of it irrelevant as concerns increase of Christians, he presents only data having something to do with his theme. To be sure, all life is such a closely woven web that every aspect and activity of the Church has at least a distant connection with her reproductive powers. Nevertheless, since many aspects and activities have very little to do with reproduction, the student of church growth concentrates on those most directly responsible for propagating the Christian religion. The facts he selects are relevant to "bringing the nations to faith and obedience." The structures he portrays will reveal growth.

Hence he avoids relating the facts of one year only. These, like a single frame from a moving picture, do not tell what is happening. The sequence across many years is of prime importance. Progress from year to year and history of growth are meat and drink to one seeking to understand how churches grow.

The Application

Every pastor should have clear, accurate knowledge of the growth patterns of his church. Every executive of a church union, conference, or presbytery, every missionary whether specialist or one with assigned church-planting responsibilities, every field director, and every executive of a mission board in Eurica or Africasia needs to build up a sharp picture of the congregations or Churches committed to him—or, in the case of lay persons or missionary specialists, "with which he works." All the kinds of information described in this chapter will go into that picture. Some will be impossible to obtain at once, but slight changes in the forms required by membership accounting will readily make it possible to obtain the essential facts. As these are added to the canvas and the picture becomes clear, one may hope that mission will cease to be "carrying on splendid work whether the churches multiply or not" and will become instead an intelligent discipling of *ta ethne*—especially the responsive *ethne* which can be found all across America and in so many countries of the world, including some long considered resistant.

RESEARCH IN CHURCH GROWTH

As the pastor or missionary sets about gathering up The Facts Needed, he is likely to conclude that a survey of the growth of his congregation, conference, or diocese must be undertaken. Not ever having done such a survey, he looks around for previous models, questionnaires, or forms which he can use. During the fifteen years 1964 to 1979, it was a rare month when I did not receive an appeal from some churchman, "Tell me how to do a survey of church growth. Send me the forms I ought to use."

Unfortunately, the varieties of Churches are so numerous, the size of the baptized membership so varied, and the reasons for growth and stagnation so different that no one set of forms can be used. Each investigator has to construct his own instruments of research. They must fit his situation. Denominational preferences and terminologies must be taken into account. Are infants counted as members, or only baptized believers? Is tithing required or not? Is record-keeping left up to the local congregation or required by the bishop?

Bearing these difficulties in mind, The School of World Mission in 1965 printed a small pamphlet called "How to Do a Survey of Church Growth." It was light enough to slip into an ordinary letter without adding to the postage. During the next fifteen years thousands of these pamphlets have been requested and sent out all over the world. They helped gather facts of growth and stimulated much interest in effective evangelism. This pamphlet is reproduced below, in the belief that it will still be of use in the beginning stages of research.

In 1972 Dr. Ebbie Smith, then a missionary in Indonesia, wrote *A Manual For Church Growth Surveys*. This excellent book gathered together the growing mass of information about how to carry out such surveys, and (perhaps more importantly) how to plan them so the Church or mission concerned would use the data dug up to make the work more effective. Any substantial survey should incorporate many of Dr. Smith's proposals.

In 1979 Robert Waymire was sent by Overseas Crusades to do a nation-wide survey of the growth of the Churches in the Philippines. He developed charts, forms, and questionnaires which—when filled in—give an accurate picture of the situation. Dr. Peter Wagner co-authored the book. In 1980 *Church Growth Bulletin* brought out this helpful volume entitled *The Church Growth Survey Manual*.

Researchers will find many models used by social scientists in the secular world helpful in obtaining meaningful pictures of the amount, quality, viability, and reproducibility of church growth in their particular parts of the harvest field.

Investigators are well advised to remember that church growth research *accomplished* (even on a small scale) is to be preferred to research *deferred* till it can be done on a more scholarly scale. Battles must be fought on what information is available.

With that by way of introduction, we turn to the brief exposition of how to do a survey of church growth, which has proved useful to many.

How to Do a Survey of Church Growth

Christian leaders in increasing numbers are realizing that the growth of the Churches, older as well as younger, must be taken with renewed seriousness. It is not sufficient to do excellent church and mission work in the hope that it will, somehow, lead to the multiplication of churches. The sheer physical expansion of sound Christian churches is a central and continuing duty of the Church. There is a rising interest in it. We must push on through promotional commendations, encouraging generalities, and the scaffolding of church and mission work to the churches actually being planted and must see them clearly.

People often ask how to discover and describe church growth. Obviously no one way will fit all Churches. Describing the growth of a Church of 1,100 members in a pagan population of 500,000 is a different task than describing one of 150,000 in a population of 280,000. Each Church grows out of its own environment. Those studying church growth will, therefore, expect to apply the procedures outlined herein to their own circumstances.

Many a pastor or missionary will want to investigate membership increase in his own *and other denominations*. It will make his work more fruitful and meaningful. It will set before him and his colleagues the real problems confronting his Church. Until Christians discern the tasks of highest priority they cannot make the most effective disposition of their resources. "Where to press for church growth and where to hold the line," a most important question, can only be answered after carefully investigating the degree and kind of growth God is granting a particular church or cluster of churches. How to do this careful investigation is described in the three steps following.

FIRST STEP: DEFINING THE STUDY

1. State carefully the purpose and scope of your study. For example:

To study the membership increase of the Churches in City X or County Y, or to study the relationship between ways of training pastors and the growth of the Church.

2. Determine the ecclesiastical bodies to be studied. It will give you more light to study several congregations working in one general kind of population than to confine yourself to your own. While you may study your own more thoroughly than you do others, comparisons with others are valuable for understanding.

3. Determine the kind of population or populations involved. Are you going to study church growth among:

Small town or large city congregations?

Indians or Mestizos?

Farmers or city workers?

The intelligentsia or the illiterate?

One caste or tribe or many?

Lowlanders or Highlanders?

How many of them are there?

What is their economic and social position?

How receptive are they?

SECOND STEP: FINDING THE MEMBERSHIP FACTS

1. Determine the *field totals* for each denomination at three- or five-year intervals from the beginning of the Church till the present. This is not easy. But by writing to your friends, consulting church histories, and reading old yearbooks you can dig up the facts. Secure as much information as you can. Sometimes there will be gaps of several years. You may get the full picture only for your own Church or mission, while information for the others will be sketchy—when they began, what their membership is now, and a few points in between.

2. Determine membership totals for each homogeneous unit in the denomination. A homogeneous unit is simply a section of society in which all the members have some characteristic in common. If Baptists in Boston number 20,000, discover how many are New Englanders and how many immigrants from the South. If the Congregationalists in Polynesia number 67,000, how many live in the Society Islands, the Cook Islands, and the Austral Islands? If the Lutherans in Taiwan number 5,000, how many speak Mandarin and how many Minnan?

3. Determine individual church totals over as many years as possible. Nothing grows but local churches. Which congregations are growing, standing still, or diminishing? You will find these figures most revealing, but sometimes difficult to get.

4. Yearbooks for each denomination give membership by regions or countries.

Field totals are compiled from annual reports from parish or diocese. Church headquarters, central mission offices, or board headquarters usually file these reports. From them you can easily compile membership totals for each homogeneous unit of the Church being studied.

Memberships of individual congregations are more difficult to find. Search church and mission records or prior studies.

5. Draw a graph for each "homogeneous unit Church." You may have several graphs for your own denomination and several for others. For example, in the diagram following, D E G H are graphs of four homogeneous unit Churches which, with several others, made up one denomination in Korea. Observe the different patterns, then draw your own.

FIGURE 6.4

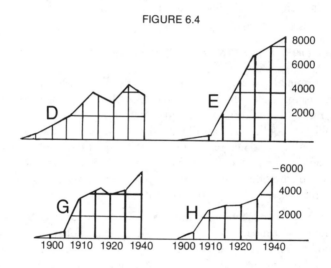

You will now have true pictures of what church growth has taken place. Keep refining these. Redraw graphs whenever you have information which leads to major corrections.

THIRD STEP: ASCERTAINING CAUSES OF GROWTH AND NON-GROWTH

1. Referring constantly to the graph, ask what caused sudden rises, long plateaus, gradual declines, little work, and much growth. What happened in 1916, for example, which arrested great growth in D, G, and H?

Look for causes—striking conversions, beliefs, and traditions of the converts, changing neighborhoods, oppressions, the work of certain men, or their death or retirement. Consider what policies the Church (or mission) has followed in times of membership increase or decrease. Did what was "adopted in hope" deliver church growth? Was evangelism stressed?

Until you complete the graphs you cannot tell what bearing a given action had on church growth. You will read an enthusiastic defense of the action—how necessary and wise it was—but you will not know whether it led to growth or decline of the church.

Learn to be ruthless with alleged reasons. You are searching for the truth. Much writing and thinking is really a defense of "whatever is." It shies away from admitting defeat. It champions "little growth" as really the best thing that could have happened. Shun such thinking.

Compare your membership increase with that enjoyed by other Churches. A church in Texas in the last ten years grew 25 per cent and felt quite gratified—but should it have been? In those circumstances some other congregations had doubled. A mission in Zaire planted a Church which by 1958 numbered 20,000—the biggest Church in that board's seven younger Churches. The Zaire mission was pleased with itself until it compared its Church with others in Zaire. Then it saw its Church was experiencing growth incommensurate with conditions.

2. Consult the three sources named below, but remember that most answers will be mistaken or partial. Some will be based on misinformation and prejudice—"the accumulated debris of defeat and resignation." Some will be genuine insights. Some will lead you to insight, though themselves faulty. You may be the first to do a serious study of your Church from the point of view of its growth. An exciting exploration in uncharted territory lies before you.

a. *The leaders who were there.* Place your graphs before them and ask particular questions. Ask those involved the following kinds of questions, which could be asked about Figure 6:5:

What caused the surge of growth in 1965 after a year of sharp decline?

What stopped growth in 1968 after three promising years?

What were we doing during this long period when our neighbor church was growing in New Testament fashion? Why did we increase only 140?

Expect to dig. Not every interview will yield information. Churchmen and missionaries, for example, who during their active lives were not interested in the growth of the Church will in retirement remember little about it. Yet their testimony has a negative value—it helps explain why

FIGURE 6.5

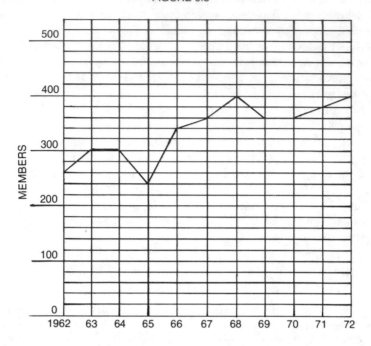

there was little growth or why there was only 100 per cent a decade growth when there might have been 500 per cent.

Beware of facile explanations. (i) "This was a very difficult field. The Church simply could not grow there." If no denomination in the country was growing, that explanation may be accurate; but frequently it is tendered when next-door Presbyterians, Adventists, or Roman Catholics are seeing increase. (ii) Or someone says, "After each surge of growth there must be time for consolidation. This is a natural rhythm of the Gospel." Is it? Or is "consolidation" an excuse for little growth? (iii) "My friend, you have no idea of the cold indifference here." Is the real trouble lack of zeal and warmth—or a ministry so highly trained (and paid) that new churches cannot start?

Consult men in their language. Talk about church growth to older members, recent converts, ministers, missionaries, and retired persons. Make "the growth of the church" a frequent topic of conversation.

b. Denominational yearbooks, church records, baptismal registers, magazine articles, mission histories, and old reports. In these is much chaff

and little information about the physical increase of the churches. But if
you will patiently winnow the chaff, you will find the wheat. Learn to
scan "inspirational" or promotional articles, written to commend the work
to supporters. Look for the sentence or phrase which tells something as
to the size, shape, or nature of the Church at a given time.

Look for information about "homogeneous units." Figures of church
growth for "all Illinois" are not nearly as revealing as those for "the rural
communities along the Mississippi" or those "in East St. Louis." Totals
for "our Church in India" will tell you far less than those pertaining to
a sudden surge of growth "in the Delhi District."

c. *Government statistics, censuses,* anthropological studies, sociological expositions, handbooks for social workers, surveys of the Church, its
medical or educational institutions, its giving, education of its pastors, and
other material. Here again you will have to pan tons of gravel to get an
ounce of gold. Do not get wrapped up in panning gravel! A book on
theological education may be interested chiefly in lifting the standard of
theological education and care nothing for the discipling of the nation. It
may be concerned entirely with perfecting rather than discipling. Even so,
it may throw both positive and negative light on church growth.

Similarly, anthropological treatises should be perused, not for intellectual interest, but to discover how the Church has grown—or has not—
and how it can grow in accordance with God's will in given populations.

3. Read all you can on how churches multiply. Since at least three
billion have yet to believe, millions of new churches will be needed. Thousands of books will be written, describing how particular pieces of the
mosaic have been or are being discipled. You cannot possibly read all of
these. First, choose the few which deal with general principles, written by
men who know the whole field. Value highly those written by authors
whose primary concern is carrying out Christ's Great Commission. Second, choose books which describe the multiplication of churches in the
kind of population to which God has sent you. If you are called to multiply
churches among the hundreds of thousands of nominal members of the
Greek Orthodox Church, now in America becoming materialists and hedonists, it will not do you much good to read about church growth among
the animistic tribes of Irian Jaya. If God has called you to disciple the
respectable castes of India, studying how churches multiply in the nominally Protestant black population of Jamaica will not be highly informative;
but accounts of how the tribes and castes of India have become Christian
will prove a gold mine of information.

RESEARCH IN GROWING CHURCHES

Research aimed to help evangelism become more effective, churches multiply, and missions become more obedient to the Great Commission, should concentrate on *growing* churches.

Numerous churches are growing healthily. Many denominations are increasing at 20, 40, or 60 per cent a decade. Some are doubling every eight years. The General Conference Baptists of the United States grew from 40,000 to 124,000 between 1940 and 1978. The Southern Baptists grew from about two million to over thirteen million between 1900 and 1978. Even in declining denominations, some congregations show vigorous increase.

Similarly in missions at home and abroad, while some labor for decades and establish only a dozen congregations, many others in a similar time span and population break through to mighty reproduction of the Christian Faith. During the sixties and seventies in the Philippines, for example, while the largest and most prestigious Protestant denomination (The United Church of Christ) was growing only slightly, several other denominations were setting challenging church growth goals, and achieving them. For example, the Christian and Missionary Alliance increased from four hundred to over a thousand congregations.

Research is carried on in order to find ways which God is currently blessing to the liberation of captives, the recovery of sight to the blind, and the acceptance of the good news by the poor. Consequently research should be *concentrated on growing churches and growing denominations to find out why they are growing.*

The point is important. Much research painstakingly finds out all the facts about some congregation or denomination. This wastes much time. Most facts have little to do with the growth of the church. The skillful researcher therefore avoids gathering information which has little bearing on growth. An able churchman came to study with me, bringing five cartons full of data which he had amassed on his own large denomination. After studying church growth for six months, he brought in the cartons one day and said wryly, "All this sheds little light on the real reasons our Church is declining. I wasted a year. What shall I do with it?" "Throw it away," I replied, "and determine never to gather any but pertinent information."

Concentrate on growing churches. Something they are doing is causing them to grow. Research should discover which among the hundreds of activities carried on, convictions held, attitudes demonstrated, and persons engaged in the work are the actual causes of church growth. As these are described and the part they played analyzed, each person reading the study will see which of them he can use in his situation, with his resources and gifts.

Let us suppose that a slow-growing denomination—it may be in Chile or Oregon—has 200 congregations. Among these, fifteen have departed from the sickly denominational pattern and grown healthily. We research the growth of these fifteen. Their growth was possibly due to intensive study of the Bible, carried on in many homes in each congregation. To be a Christian meant to be a student of the Bible. Possibly it was due to evangelizing a responsive segment of the population. Possibly these growing churches set challenging goals, directed the attention of all members to the winnable, allocated 40 per cent of the income of the church to evangelism, and preached constantly on the convictional foundations of the New Testament churches. Possibly these fifteen churches saw to it that converts very soon became parts of small groups where they rapidly came to feel a normal part of the Christian community. They joined both the church and "a sub-structure of belonging." Research will identify many such causes of growth among the fifteen growing churches. Research will therefore suggest that as the 185 non-growing congregations adopt these successful methods, they too may recover from the disease of slow growth and become radiantly Christian.

Research should make a sharp distinction between reproducible patterns of growth and those which cannot be duplicated. Some of the most striking church growth is the work of extraordinarily gifted men— geniuses. We rejoice in these men, but do not expect to find many Dwight L. Moodys or Henry Ward Beechers in our congregations. Not many congregations include a couple of earnestly Christian millionaires. Not many pastors are organizational wizards. For church growth which is de- pendent on exceptional men, we thank God; but realize that He will prob- ably not grant us that kind of growth. Research should look for *reproducible patterns of growth*, possible to ordinary congregations, ordinary pastors, and ordinary missionaries.

Stagnant congregations and denominations may, occasionally, be stud- ied with profit, but since they have *not* been growing, lessons learned from them are likely to be somewhat discouraging. It is better to commend with joy causes of accomplished growth than to point with dismay toward causes of non-growth.

Furthermore, since part of stagnancy is a sense of defeat, one of the better ways of motivating Christians to effective evangelism is to persuade them that growth is possible and to show them how the Holy Spirit has

caused it. Nothing is more potent in leading defeated pastors or missionaries to attempt church growth than to assemble illustrations of substantial
growth from their own denominations, kinds of Christians, and institutional
machinery. Illustrations of other denominations can so easily be brushed
off, saying, "That might work for Episcopalians, but we are Mennonites!"
Missionaries who have labored for long years with few congregations established, often hold that "In this country, among these people, we cannot
expect many conversions. This is a very difficult field." If they are shown
that other missionaries working in that very country with the same kind of
people are winning many to eternal life, they listen with avid interest and
make the new departures, which bring deliverance to the captives and
multiply congregations of the redeemed. *Research done among the growing
churches of any land, to discover the causes of conversion and incorporation, is a profitable use of time and money.*

SUMMARY

The importance of finding the facts cannot be overstated. There is
much lack of growth because earnest Christians, devoted pastors, and
veteran missionaries have not seen the facts concerning the growth of their
churches. Most leaders of the 300,000 churches in the United States have
never constructed, studied, or even seen graphs of the growth of the congregations they are leading. They do not know whether they are growing,
plateaued, or declining. They have no idea whether the key sector of their
congregation (the families likely to be in the community for many years)
is increasing or declining.

In 1979 Dr. Gail Law was conducting a church growth seminar in
Singapore among the Chinese Christian leaders. Because Hong Kong is
somewhat similar to Singapore, she showed a series of graphs depicting
church growth in Hong Kong. She also showed the relationship of congregations and denominations to the main sections of the urban population.
For example, the working classes in Hong Kong, who comprise 80 per
cent of the population, are almost untouched by Christianity.

At the end of the presentation, a prominent business man, an elder in
a Singapore congregation, rose to his feet and declared, "After seeing
these slides, I realize our condition. We have been like blind people groping
in the dark. But now suddenly we can see the way and know what Singapore ought to do." *He had seen the facts of growth.*

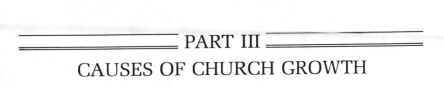

PART III
CAUSES OF CHURCH GROWTH

7

DISCOVERING THE WHY OF IT

WHEN THE STUDENT of church growth carries out the procedures described in the preceding chapter, he will obtain for a given Church, its homogeneous units, and its congregations, accurate pictures of their size; growth histories from the beginning to the present. He will also obtain sociological analyses of the membership showing where it came from, how it is composed, and what the relationships of its various parts are. The structure of the Church will become visible.

Since promotional speaking and writing properly forms such a large part of Christian work, one who would understand church growth must be particularly careful that he distinguishes between what churchmen hoped would happen, what happened in an instance or two, what ought to happen, and what in fact did happen. The picture built up by patiently assembling accurate statistics concerning the Church and its many constituent parts is the foundation of all further knowledge of church growth.

KNOWING WHY IS ESSENTIAL

Statistical knowledge is not enough. To know the structure is interesting, but is important only as it leads on to understanding *why* the Church and its homogeneous units have grown, plateaued, and occasionally diminished. The goal of church growth studies is not merely correct facts as to the quantity of growth. It is not sufficient to see the structure clearly—

though that must be done. The goal is through evaluation of the facts to understand the dynamics of church growth. Only as, on the basis of assured growth facts, we see the *reasons for increase, the factors which God used to multiply His churches,* and the conditions under which the Church has spread or remained stationary, do we understand church growth.

Understanding the times and conditions is vitally important. How multitudinous kindreds, tongues, tribes, and nations have accepted the abundant and eternal life which comes through faith in Jesus Christ and membership in His Church is the story of "opportune times."

> The phrase "in the fulness of time" has an important place in the history of salvation in the Bible. It was used by the Apostle Paul to describe the time of the birth of Christ—Galatians 4:4. In the economy, or to use more modern terminology, in the strategy of God, the coming of His Son into the world was at precisely the right time. The historical factors were right. The concept of the opportune time was so important that the Greeks had a special word for it—*kairos*. This was used in contrast with *chronos* which referred simply to clock and calendar time.
>
> As we turn to study the history of the Christian Church, especially in its expansion around the world, the concept of *kairos* again becomes very relevant. The great advances of the Church have not occurred at just any time, regardless of the historical, cultural, and social environment. The advances occurred at opportune times—at the right *kairos* (Tuggy, 1968:1).

The answer to the question "Why did church growth occur?" is complex. One reason for lack of growth in the midst of widespread receptivity is that many churchmen, not sufficiently recognizing the intricacies of propagating the Gospel, work at it along one simplistic line. The point is so important that three examples will be given here, the first from the world of radio. As the Gospel is broadcast in North America the message falls on the ears of a potential audience of at least 150,000,000 persons, to whom because they are active or nominal Christians it is more or less familiar. Contained in this multitude are literally millions of nominal Christians—the unconverted or backslidden. As these hear the unchanging, powerful Gospel, many believe, repent, and accept Christ. They find a nearby church and join it. If they are already members, they come to new life in it.

Christian broadcasting in Africasia, however, falls on the ears of Marxists, Hindus, Buddhists, Animists, and Moslems. At least half of these are illiterate. The Christian message is not familiar. On the contrary, it is totally strange. Under these conditions it is simplistic to suppose that even the unchanging Gospel, beamed over the radio waves to this audience *in substantially the same way it is in North America,* will bring non-Christians of many different cultures to Christ—especially where there are no churches with which believers can unite. Recognizing the complexity of church growth, radio should convey the message of salvation to each community *in ways which make it possible for obedience to the Gospel to become a real option to its members.*

Those who compose the programs should be well versed in how churches have multiplied in the specific populations to which they beam their broadcasts. The intricate whys of church growth are significant knowledge to all engaged in broadcasting. Christian radio, already of considerable service in Asia, Africa, and Latin America, can be made much more effective as the reasons for church growth become second nature to those preparing the messages.

Second, those who prepare and distribute Christian literature should know what factors have brought men to a saving knowledge of Jesus Christ and active membership in His Church in the specific populations where they are distributing literature. For example, in Japan because of universal literacy and advanced education, evangelism through literature should be effective in church multiplication, provided tracts and gospel messages fit the Japanese population. Of course, they must be thoroughly biblical. They must set forth Jesus Christ, the sole Savior and Lord, by whom alone men come to the Father. Yet even if the literature is biblical and sets forth Jesus Christ faithfully, if it does so in an American manner it will be read—if at all—with dull eyes. To put it positively, the more the writers of that literature are steeped in the lore of Japan, its culture, ethos, and dreams, the more eagerly will they be read. Literature which tells how typical Japanese have become disciples of Christ will be more effective than that which tells how Americans have. Writers should know thoroughly how churches have multiplied in Japan, how the patterns of growth have varied from class to class and decade to decade, and what factors in the affluent secular Japan of today are most potent in producing self-propagating congregations. The writer of literature should learn about church growth as the surgeon learns anatomy—with complete thoroughness, not by reading a book or two, but by years of study and firsthand research.

Third, one of the chief reasons why churches grow anywhere is that some person has become a flaming Christian, living his life in joyful, obedient relationship to Jesus Christ. The Holy Spirit has descended and revived men and churches. This cause of church growth is so important that it will be treated by itself in another chapter (Chapter IX). Fervent faith and ardent prayer are as necessary to growth of the Church as sunshine is to the growth of grain. Yet here again the simplistic explanation must be avoided. Sunshine, while absolutely necessary, is not the only factor in the cultivation of rice, wheat, or corn. Revival, while absolutely necessary, is not the only factor in the growth of the Church. The more the ardent Christians and the revived congregations know about what modes of growth in their populations God has blessed and which He has signally not blessed, the more likely it is that their preaching of the Word will bear fruit in the multiplication of Christian cells. Their devotion will drive them to those prepared by God to leave Egypt; the Holy Spirit will find them more amenable to His leading; and when He points out those who are now receptive to the Good News, they will obey more promptly.

One wonders, for instance, to how many revived and awakened missionaries and nationals the Holy Spirit has pointed out the receptive masses in Latin America, and one may hazard a guess that the reason why some of the revived have not gone to them is that—though revived—they did not know that, as in Corinth so in Latin America, God has called "the weak and foolish and the things which are not" and has made His Church out of them. The time has come for an extensive study of revivals in Eurican and Africasian Churches and the conditions under which these have led to great growth of the Church, as well as those under which, alas, they have led to no growth at all. Why, under the impact of revival, have some churches reproduced themselves freely through extensive populations and in other populations remained sterile and childless?

ANTHROPOLOGY HELPS UNDERSTANDING

Anthropology, one of the sciences of man, describes how men act, how they innovate, how they govern themselves, what restraints they set up for their societies, and a thousand other matters of note. Anthropology has formed the mind of America more than most pastors realize.

Should Anthropology Be Used to Further Church Growth?

Most anthropologists rigorously avoid judging whether men's actions and customs are good or bad. Some anthropologists, religiously pursuing "objectivity," believe that all cultures are equally good and each religion is simply a way of understanding reality which a given society finds agreeable or convincing. In consequence they object to changing a society in any way and particularly to Christianization. Other anthropologists, however, freely use their science to effect all kinds of change which they, their government, or their employers consider desirable. They know that a unitary world culture with a single physical base is rapidly coming about.

It will use electricity and machines. It will for the most part live in cities and towns, be literate, and follow the rules of health and sanitation. Whether the journey from the present culture to this coming world culture is a few hundred yards or a few hundred miles long, every society of man will traverse it.

The Christian missionary who believes that in Jesus Christ God has revealed a way of life rewarding for all men, also uses anthropology for directed change. He too is aware that it is impossible for various cultures to remain in their present state of development. Like other practitioners of applied anthropology, he is opposed to sacrificing the welfare of any people in order to keep it as a museum piece. He is opposed to leaving directed change in the hands of the exploiter, materialist, communist, blind chance, or selfish racism. He believes that God is calling the Church to play its part in bringing about a social order more in harmony with His will— more just, brotherly, and peaceful. In becoming Christian, increasing numbers across the nations take the most important single step in directed change. This is the humane reason why the missionary is engaged in discipling the nations. The authority for discipling the nations, seen in the Bible, fits so extraordinarily well with what his reason tells him is essential for the maximum welfare of the maximum number of men.

The Christian then turns to anthropology with a good conscience to discover why certain churches have grown and others have not, and to devise customs, institutions and other configurations which will fill the voids created by rapid social change, in a manner acceptable to the society in question and consonant with the authority of the Bible.

A. R. Tippett's *Solomon Island Christianity* is a mine of information concerning the ways in which anthropology can be used in the service of the Gospel. In relating how the various denominations in the Solomon Islands grew and stopped growing, flourished and atrophied, became really or nominally Christian, and communicated the Christian faith to others or failed to communicate it even to their own relatives, Dr. Tippett uses anthropology to cast a flood of light on the growth, in quality as well as quantity, of the various branches of the Church. For example, after describing a dramatic scene in which a taboo banyan tree was cut down by new converts and the whole population thereupon declared for Christ and put themselves under instruction, Dr. Tippett devotes two pages to an anthropological understanding of the situation. He concludes:

> (The western missionary) is working in a Melanesian world, facing a Melanesian philosophy, and will have to learn to understand Melanesian thought forms, and fight for Christianity on Melanesian levels. (The banyan tree in-

cident) is a relevant encounter and a real victory, with many scriptural prec-
edents. Western missions might do well to face up to the statistical evidence
that animists are being won today by a Bible of power encounter, not a
demythologized edition (Tippett, 1967:101).

Another recent writer, J. C. Wold, a Lutheran, in his book *God's
Impatience in Liberia* devotes a chapter to "Anthropology, A Tool for
Church Growth." In it he discusses many ways in which the church planter
finds anthropology of great value. Among his notable passages is the
following.

> The gift of the Holy Spirit makes us a new creation in Christ, and . . . gives
> us power to overcome our own sin and our own self-righteousness, and to do
> God's will. We are also given the power to discern where the Spirit is leading
> us. For the Church to grow with the Spirit, missionaries and pastors must
> discern where the Spirit is leading. A functioning knowledge of the culture
> of the people, tribe, or clan whom we hope to bring to Christ is invaluable.
> Anthropology can provide this knowledge and help us discern where the Spirit
> is moving. We must not say that with the help of anthropology we can predict
> the movement of God's Holy Spirit. He is a free agent moving when and
> where He wills; but He is just as able to help us discern His movements
> through the insights gained by a study of anthropology as to have us see a
> vision of a man saying "Come over to Macedonia and help us" (Wold,
> 1968:127).

THE WONDERFUL GRAPH OF GROWTH

Columns of figures giving the membership of any Church and its
homogeneous units contain locked-up knowledge. By careful study the
figures can be forced to reveal their secrets, but the process is tedious.
When, however, each set of figures is transformed into a graph of growth,
the secrets leap out at the reader. He who would understand church growth
should construct line graphs showing at a glance what has transpired. He
can then ask why it happened.

The process of constructing a graph is simple. On a pair of coordi-
nates—the vertical one showing membership in hundreds or thousands as
the case may be, and the horizontal showing the years—the student places
a dot above each year at the right height to show the exact number of
members. When he has entered all his annual memberships, he joins the
dots together with a line running from left to right and has an exact growth
history of that Church. See the following typical graph of growth. It shows
that after twenty years of extremely slow growth, a period of seven years
ensued when churches multiplied healthily. Then for eighteen years growth

stopped, but started up again in the late forties and, after a sharp decline, rose to new heights in 1970.

FIGURE 7.1. A TYPICAL GRAPH OF GROWTH

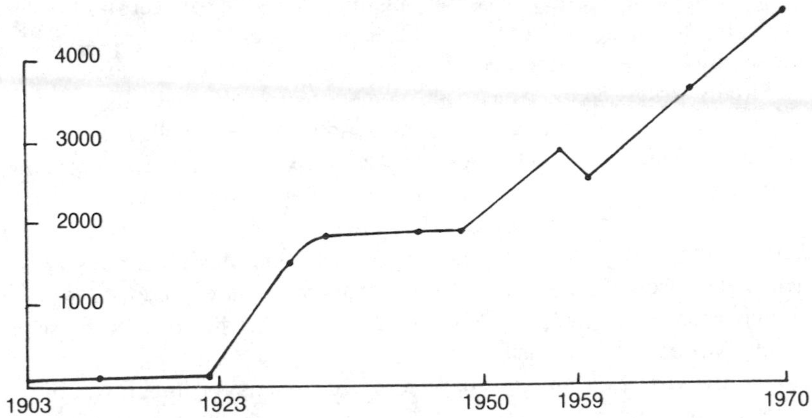

The present lack of information about the growth of the Churches may be gauged by the fact that most church leaders have never seen a graph of growth for their own denomination or for the cluster of congregations to which they are giving their lives. They no doubt have a vague idea that their own congregation is growing or standing still, but exact knowledge of their Church they have none. They work surrounded by fog.

This is unnecessary. All Churches can and should frequently see their own graphs of growth. Nothing will tell them so effectively how they are getting on with their main task. One of their chief aims is the planting of self-governing and self-propagating churches. Their intended outcome is an indigenous Church which is so natural a part of its environment that the Holy Spirit can spread it throughout the land. The graph tells them when they are and are not achieving this aim.

The typical graph of growth above should intrigue all. During the eighteen years from 1930 on, was an insurmountable obstacle encountered? Or did some errant policy, theology, or personality dominate the enterprise? What caused the sharp upturn in 1923? And the recovery of growth in 1948 and 1960? Could the twenty years of no growth at the beginning have been shortened? Most leaders neither know the answers to these questions nor, as a rule, are able to ask them. Most are not familiar enough with their own church history to know what to ask, or where in the story significant changes have taken place.

All thinking about the Church should be done against the graph of growth, because when done without exact knowledge of how the Church has and has not grown, it is likely to find itself in error. Churchmen who, without knowing the growth histories of specific Churches, make judgments about them often make wrong judgments. They substitute what ought to have happened for what did happen, ascribe wrong reasons for events, and in general indulge in wishful, inexact reconstructions.

Many writers on the American Churches have told us why they thought these have grown—frontier conditions, notable men, revivals, denominational excellencies, God's blessing, the work of "our great home missionary society," and on and on. Of course, part of this is the exact truth. Yet until the particularity of church growth is seen, and until the many parts of the total picture are described one by one against graphs of the actual increases, there is great danger that the picture presented will be simplistic. Most of the reasons for church growth will not even be seen. A few will be overly emphasized.

Many writers on missions have set forth reasons for the growth of the Church. One who roams through the volumes on the history of missions, biographies of missionaries, and records of proceedings of Churches and missions, will again and again run across statements concerning why and how the Church has grown. When these are made about growth in one homogeneous unit during a given period of time, they are usually accurate. They have been formed in view of the actual record. When, however, they are made about large units, such as field totals or "our Church in such and such a country," the complex growth history being only vaguely seen, they are apt to be faulty. It is particularly necessary for a historian to see the growth history of homogeneous units when he sets forth hypotheses as to growth. Otherwise he describes causes for growths which never took place, or relates as true for the whole what was true for only one of several parts.

A graph of the communicant membership year after year is a *sine qua non* for intelligent discussion of the progress of the Church. So much nonsense is written about the Church, so thoroughly are hopes and intentions confused with achievements, and so completely has church or mission work been substituted for church planting, that serious writing and speaking about mission must adhere to this principle.

The Graph Shows Each Plateau, Decline, or Increase

The graph of growth shows trends extending over various periods of time. If causes for church growth are to be understood, these trends must be seen. Consider the instructive graph of growth of the Church founded by the English Presbyterians in Formosa between 1865 and 1900. Without the graph if one were asked, "How did the Presbyterian Church in Formosa grow to three thousand communicant members in thirty-five years?" he would probably reply that missionaries proclaimed the Gospel, men were healed and taught, and God gave the increase. This vague reply contains elements of the truth, but is far from adequate. It actually conceals the five different kinds of church growth which occurred during these years.

On the graph one can immediately distinguish five periods of growth. The first, of about eight years, was an exploratory phase. Missionaries were learning Chinese and local geography, getting acquainted with the

FIGURE 7.2. THE PRESBYTERIAN CHURCH IN FORMOSA

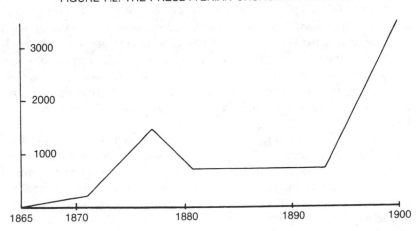

people, buying property, and winning the first few converts from among the Chinese population. During the second, a small movement brought in about 1,500 Pepohwans (see the upward swing of the line of growth). These were the aboriginal inhabitants of Formosa who were being pushed back by the Chinese settlers who had come over from the mainland after A.D. 1600. Pepohwan converts were instructed and shepherded, not in their own language, but in Chinese. Most of them, failing their baptismal examination, were not baptized. Compared with the congregations of Chinese Christians, the peasant Pepohwans did not appear promising. They were improvident and often in debt. They frequently drank to excess. The rural congregations at some distance from the main mission station were difficult to look after. The more powerful among the missionaries came out strongly for Chinese work as opposed to Pepohwan. Considerable Pepohwan reversions set in, which the mission ascribed to instability in the people. That may have had something to do with them; but a more potent cause lay in the shepherding mistakes recounted above. The reversions account for the third period—that of decline—shown on the graph.

In the fourth period—the long, low plateau—the remaining Pepohwan congregations and the station congregations made up largely of Chinese converts were cared for and evangelistic, educational, and medical work was carried on. Chinese were becoming Christians in the smallest numbers and the Pepohwan movement had been arrested. The fifth period—note the upward surge of the line of growth—followed immediately after the Japanese conquest of Formosa in 1895. Chinese culture was discredited, Chinese rulers were replaced by Japanese, and, under the impact of defeat, many Chinese became able to hear the Gospel. At just this time a remarkable missionary, Campbell Moody, toured the western part of Formosa preaching the Gospel to the Chinese with fire and persuasiveness. Hundreds turned to Christ in ones and twos, by families and kin groups. The baptism of each new person or family opened the door to others of that clan. Many small congregations were established. In 1894 the majority of Christians were Pepohwans. In 1899 the great majority of them were Chinese.

The graph by itself does not give the details which enable us to understand what really happened in the first thirty-five years of Presbyterian mission in Formosa. It cannot reveal the causes of growth and decline. Those must be dug out of histories and biographies, reports and articles. But it does clearly indicate when changes in rate and amount of growth took place and how long each phase lasted. It thus breaks the meaningless whole into its meaningful parts, enabling the student of church growth to search for causes at the right times.

Further, the graph gives substance and reality to the story. We know not merely that "some Pepohwans and Chinese were converted in the early days"; but that about 1,500 of them were. We can see not merely that "large numbers of Pepohwans reverted"; but that the numbers were not so large and that after the reversions there remained a Church of nearly 1,000 members. It becomes clear that not only was there "some growth in the nineties," but that the Church more than tripled in five years. In short the outlines of what happened stand out sharply.

Often changes in rate of growth are so sharp and dramatic that the graph presents a question which fairly begs for an answer. For instance, consider the case of the Disciples of Christ in Puerto Rico. The solid line in the following graph indicates growth of membership from zero to almost 7,000 members. The dotted line portrays schematically the mission funds spent in establishing and aiding this younger Church. The actual number of dollars spent is of no interest. The important thing is that, at the depth of the great depression, mission funds were drastically reduced and did not build back up till after World War II. The clear questions to be asked are there: After thirty-three years of slow growth, why did the Church suddenly start to expand? and did the reduction of mission funds have anything to do with the increase?

Could it be that withdrawal of support caused the sudden growth? Some might welcome an instance where a Church started to grow when it was thrown on its own resources. Unfortunately, the evidence proves

FIGURE 7.3. DISCIPLES OF CHRIST IN PUERTO RICO

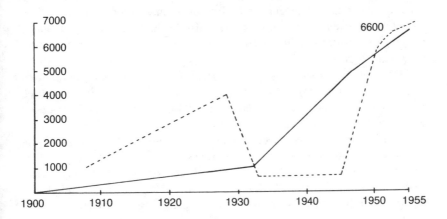

conclusively that withdrawing support had nothing to do with the growth. In Puerto Rico during the depression, financial support was withdrawn from the Baptist, Methodist, and Presbyterian missions also, and their Churches showed a marked drop in membership. But the Disciples of Christ grew vigorously. With the financial explanation ruled out, the cause or causes of growth must be sought elsewhere.

It so happened that at the depth of the depression, when financial aid had been withdrawn, this younger Church experienced a touch of Pentecostal fire. A genuine revival swept it. Its leading pastors and preachers and many others were filled with the Holy Spirit. Men and women repented of their sins, often with tears. Love, joy, peace, gentleness, and goodness, in measure pressed down and running over, were given—without any strivings to achieve them. Many experienced release from hatreds, jealousies, drunkenness, and lust. Though speaking in tongues was completely foreign to the denomination's patterns in both the United States and Puerto Rico, many spoke in tongues.

The missionaries tried to put a stop to these "goings-on" and for a time locked the Christians out of their churches; but wiser counsels prevailed and the revived churches worshiping in their own buildings and enjoying continued support from the Disciples of Christ in the United States were—like the churches mentioned in Acts 9:31—"edified and walking in the fear of the Lord and the comfort of the Holy Spirit were multiplied." News of the new power available to ordinary men through faith sped by word of mouth around the communities and out among the many relatives of the Christians. For several years, hundreds were added each year. Laymen went out regularly to preach and teach. Ordinary lay Christians carried on Sunday Schools, Bible study classes, and prayer meetings year after year in homes, sheds, and rented halls. Some of these grew into churches.

The importance of the graph of growth can be seen clearly in the light of the following incident. As in 1955 a study of this Puerto Rican Church began, a North American informant said, "You will find some Pentecostal emphasis in those churches. It came in during the depression, but fortunately is now declining." He had been scandalized at the speaking in tongues and was concerned that his churches in Puerto Rico be respectable. Though he knew the situation well, the crucial part played by the revival in the sixfold growth from 1,100 in 1933 to 6,600 in 1955 had completely escaped him. He had not seen and pondered the graph of growth.

The Extent of Gradual Slow-Downs

It often happens that after a period of rapid growth, a Church in a responsive area will slow down and become introverted, or turn its attention to cultural advance. This frequently happens in the United States. It enters a static stage of its existence. Sometimes growth stops because the kind of converts who constituted the first source of growth are no longer available, and the Church does not seek a second. Often, however, the same kind are available but the emphasis has changed—new pastors or missionaries have come who are busy perfecting the existing Christians and the absence of growth continues year after year or decade after decade.

No one is conscious of the stoppage. Good church and mission works proceed onward.

The long plateau graphically portrays stoppage and projects the question whether it was preventable. The plateau, seen in context of previous growth, encourages churchmen to believe that growth is possible and leads to a search for causes that initiated the era of slow growth and bound it on the Church.

Consider, for example, the Methodist Church in Gold Coast—Ghana. Between 1907 and 1925 (see the graph) the Cocoa Boom, the Harris movement in Apolonia, and the Ashanti ingathering under the Prophet Opong lifted the communicant membership from 6,217 to 38,941. During those eighteen years the Methodist Church increased 526 per cent, or at the rate of 292 per cent per decade. During the next thirty years, however, it plateaued, growing from 38,941 to 58,725 communicants, at a rate of only 17 per cent per decade. The graph shows the length of the stoppage and—because of the three surges of conversion growth in the preceding

FIGURE 7.4. COMMUNICANTS IN GOLD COAST METHODIST CHURCH

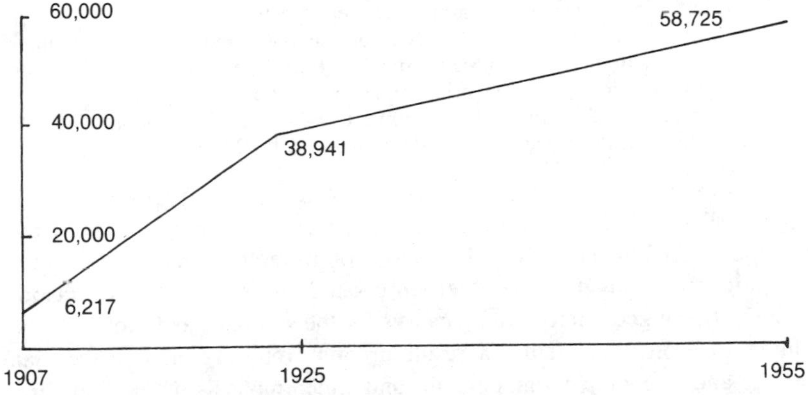

eighteen years—leads one to consider what caused it and whether it was really necessary or not.

A cause which began about 1925 and continued throughout the thirty years is required. Such a cause was the massive emphasis on education which began in the early twenties and continued throughout the period. The Methodist Church, becoming responsible for most of the education done by the British in the Methodist areas of Gold Coast, and receiving large government grants, relied more and more on converting schoolchildren through education and less and less on converting pagan adults by preaching. There were other causes for the standstill in growth, but the emphasis on education was no doubt the main one.

The near-monopoly on education held by the Churches in West Africa made this kind of growth attractive to missions—as seen earlier in the case of Rhodesia—but one wonders whether they were acutely conscious of the fact that the school approach was delivering very little church growth. It was Christianizing the leadership of the country, but it was permitting the masses to remain pagan. The theory was that once the leaders were Christian, the people would turn to Christ; but the theory was not working out—as the graph for the Methodist Church in Ghana clearly shows.

The British Methodists had planted a Church in both Ghana and Nigeria. After 1925 the policies followed in one country differed little from those followed in the other. Consequently what Deaville Walker writes in *A Hundred Years in Nigeria* (1942) has more than passing interest as we consider the slow growth that occurred in Ghana. He concludes his book with a statement which sums up Methodist mission and church policy in West Africa in 1942.

> For the present, the supreme task is that of thorough training—larger and more efficient provision for training teachers, pastors, evangelists, and ministers; the training of boys and girls in our schools, and the careful training of Christians in our churches. Until in the not distant future, the whole Methodist Church in Western Nigeria, strong and devoted to its Redeemer and Lord shall be mobilized for the supreme task—the evangelization of the yet unreached multitude within its borders (Walker, 1942:138).

Gordon Robinson in *Church Growth in Central and Southern Nigeria,* quoting Walker's conclusion, adds: "Twenty years later (in 1962) the Methodist Church has still to break out of its educational fortress in a campaign to evangelize the 'yet unreached multitude' " (Robinson, 1966:339). He goes on to sum up causes for the stoppage as follows. "The failure to grow was mainly a result of over-emphasis on humanitarian service and spreading enlightenment, and underemphasis on evangelizing. Education became the doorway to the Church, and thus limited the potential and slowed the process" (Robinson, 1966:337).

The line graph by itself does not, of course, say all this, but it does display with startling clarity the long plateau, and that in turn, illuminated by policies, actions, men, and conditions, makes possible exact thinking about growth.

Similar growth analyses need to be done in state after state in America, where similar small growth (17 per cent per decade) is accepted as normal.

Denominations who get the facts and study their little growth seriously, and change to theologies and ways which break out into growth will get growth. Others, alas, like the Methodists in West Africa, will go on doing what does *not* produce growth.

HOMOGENEOUS UNIT GROWTH

Graphs of homogeneous unit church growth contribute greatly to the understanding of causes. Since the figure easiest to obtain is the field total, copied out of the denomination's printed annual report, the most common graph is that which portrays the growth of a whole denomination in one country. Since, however, the denomination is very frequently made up of several clusters of congregations, each growing in some segment of the population, the graph of the field total is deceptive. It hides the real causes of growth. Graphs of homogeneous unit church growth are essential.

The classic example of this is given by Roy Shearer in *Wildfire: Church Growth in Korea* (1966). Shearer photographed the membership records of the Presbyterian Church in all Korean presbyteries and, carefully refining the statistics, drew nine graphs of growth, one for each presbytery. These, reproduced in Figure 7.5, show conclusively that the great growth of the Presbyterian Church in Korea took place chiefly in the two northwest provinces—North and South Pyongan.

In his fourth chapter, "Comparison of Geographical Sections of Presbyterian Church Growth," Shearer takes up the ordinary conclusions about church growth in Korea (based on the general fact that the Church there has grown greatly) and, examining them in the light of the graphs of growth in each presbytery, finds most of them wrong. His analysis is essential reading for any student of church growth. After Shearer's work, any conclusion based on a field total alone will be suspect. Time will not permit us to examine here his rich and varied argument, but two examples must be given.

A. W. Wasson (1934) did a notable pioneer study entitled *Church Growth in Korea*, which threw a flood of light on the subject, but was seriously handicapped by the fact that he studied only field totals. These showed a marked slowing down of growth from 1911 to 1919, which Wasson ascribed to loss of security of life and property under Japanese government, and to the persecution of Christians which broke out when a hundred and fifty persons, mostly Christian teachers and students, were arrested in Sunchun in North Pyongan on the charge of conspiring to kill the Japanese governor general as he passed through. After showing that

FIGURE 7.5.

COMMUNICANT MEMBERSHIP OF THE PRESBYTERIAN CHURCH IN KOREA
BY PROVINCE, 1885-1930

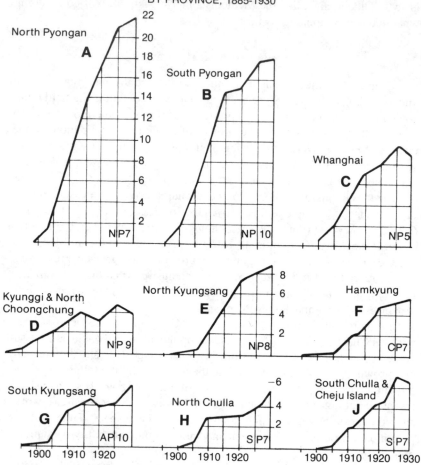

AP   Australian Presbyterian Mission
CP   Canadian Presbyterian Mission (now United Church of Canada)
SP   Southern Presbyterian Mission
NP   Northern Presbyterian Mission (now United Presb. Church USA)
     Lower right-hand corner figure is number of ordained missionaries in each
     area in 1911.

these causes did affect churches in the more southerly provinces, Shearer
says,

Had the Conspiracy Case been an important factor in the growth of the Church one would expect that the area immediately affected with the harshest persecution would have slowed in its growth. But look at Figure 11 [an enlargement of the graph of North Pyongan province]. This is the area worked from the mission station of Sunchun. One searches in vain for any slowing of communicant membership growth there . . . (Shearer, 1966:140).

Again in discussing the revival of 1907 and its outcome in church growth, Shearer addresses himself to the common opinion that the revival was *the* cause for the great growth of the Korean Church. He says,

It is true that in those areas of Korea where there had been little church growth, the rate of growth shows some increase directly following the revival. . . . However, the revival, which should have been a more important factor in the northwest because of its huge breakout there, was not. [According to the graphs] the Church shows significant growth *before* this revival and *very* little change of growth rate following the revival. Therefore, we must conclude that in the northwest the revival was not the original cause of the growth of the Presbyterian Church and probably not even a major cause (Shearer, 1966:136).

The importance of graphs of homogeneous unit Churches would become crystal clear if it were possible to take the graph of the Presbyterian Church in Taiwan during its first thirty-five years, given a few pages earlier, separate the figures for the Pepohwan Christians from those of the Chinese, and present two graphs. The first would show the growth and decline of the Pepohwan people movement to Christ and the second the growth of the Chinese membership. Unfortunately, church figures are seldom reported by ethnic or other units (unless these happen, as in Korea, to be geographical units also). Consequently, clusters of congregations growing in homogeneous units often cannot be accurately reported. Full allowance for their presence should nevertheless be made whenever possible. One can hope that, as church growth comes to be taken with greater seriousness, homogeneous unit growth will be recorded separately. This small addition to routine procedures would enable leaders of the Churches to see which clusters of congregations were growing and which were not. The reasons for growth would then become clear.

GRAPHS OF SUPPLEMENTARY FIGURES

Causes of growth will also be clearer when supplementary information is portrayed graphically, such as number of adherents who have declared themselves Christian but have not yet been baptized; gains from biological, transfer, and conversion growth; losses from deaths, transfers out, reversions, and exclusions; and data obtained from family analyses and school enrollment. Figures for these elements give depth to the reasons for growth and nongrowth. Two illustrations must suffice.

FIGURE 7.6. DANI CHURCH GROWTH — BALIEM VALLEY, PYRAMID AREA

Total population	10,000
Total adherents	8,000
Total baptized	1,122

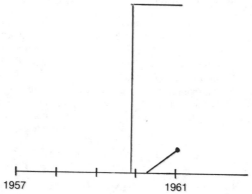

1957   1961

   In West New Guinea (now Irian) on February 14 and 15, 1960, 8,000 Dani tribesmen declared for Christ, piled their fetishes on a pyre fifty feet long and four feet wide, and burned them. Missionaries of the Christian and Missionary Alliance put the 8,000 adherents under instruction, trained indigenous leaders for them, and as men and women came to know enough about Jesus Christ to put their faith intelligently on Him, baptized them. By 1961, 1,222 had been baptized and by 1967 about 6,000 had been. The above graph of adherents and baptized believers portrays the situation in 1961 exactly. The vertical line shows 8,000 Christian adherents in 1960. The lower rising line shows the gradual increase in full members or communicant Christians (Sunda, 1963:28). The increase in baptized believers was taking place out of a community of 8,000 who had declared themselves Christian.

   The graph of membership increase in the "Church of Christ in the Sudan, Eastern" (assisted by the Church of the Brethren Mission) in northeast Nigeria shows the significant relationship of school enrollment to church growth. Observe that between 1930 and 1958 enrollment often ran ahead of membership—i.e., not all the boys in the school were baptized. After 1958 and markedly after 1960, the membership ran far ahead of

FIGURE 7.7. CHURCH OF CHRIST IN THE SUDAN, EASTERN

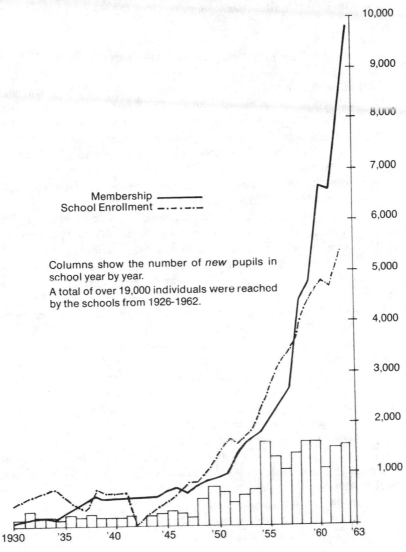

Membership ————
School Enrollment —·—·—·—

Columns show the number of *new* pupils in school year by year.
A total of over 19,000 individuals were reached by the schools from 1926-1962.

school enrollment, i.e., in addition to schoolboys, many others were accepting Christ and being added to His Church. In many lands, of course, school enrollments would have little or nothing to do with church membership, i.e., schoolboys and girls of non-Christian parents are never baptized. In Nigeria, however, during these years the graph shows enrollment was a real cause (Grimley and Robinson, 1966:122).

A WORD ON THE CONSTRUCTION OF GRAPHS

Single congregations or clusters of them in all American and European cities can easily construct meaningful graphs. So can many congregations in other continents. The following rules will be useful everywhere. Waymire and Wagner's book (see Bibliography) will prove helpful.

1. Portrayal of reality by graphs is convenient and dramatic, but it is not exact. The width of the line itself frequently covers scores or hundreds. Consequently, in exact research, tables of the figures on which the graphs are based should be carefully preserved.

2. Proportions in graphs may be managed to convey a message. The message is greatly affected by the proportion chosen, that is, by the relation of the vertical to the horizontal scale, i.e., of the number of members to the years. In the last graph, for instance, Mr. Grimley wanted to commend this growth, so he represented 10,000 members by six vertical inches. Had he considered this poor growth, he might have represented it by perhaps two inches. The impression of growth conveyed would have been much less striking.

In choosing proportions, two aims should be borne in mind. The graph should tell the truth and should tell it meaningfully. Showmanship in the construction of graphs is legitimate, but never outranks exactness.

3. In presenting a series of graphs, the proportions or relative scale in each should be kept the same. Otherwise, while the graphs may be exact and convey the truth if read separately, in sequence they mislead the reader, because he assumes a consistent scale. Even if he reads more carefully, the first impression conveyed by the general size of the increase outweighs the later exact knowledge conveyed by reading the scales. Or, on the other hand, the reader will experience annoyance at what seems almost an attempt to misrepresent.

4. If, on one sheet, Churches of great growth (above 5,000) are compared with those of a few hundreds or thousands, the lines portraying the small Churches will hug the bottom, their increases will be discerned with difficulty, and they will suffer by the comparison. Therefore, it is good procedure to use two main proportions: *(a)* for Churches above a certain figure, let us say 5,000, and *(b)* for Churches whose membership is below that—and on one sheet to present only one category of Churches. If the

first proportion is always portrayed in green and the second in red, greater clarity results.

5. In a preliminary study, or for the sake of speed, membership figures at intervals of five or ten years are sometimes gathered; but for accuracy figures should be obtained for each year. What happens during a five- or ten-year period is frequently of vital importance. Particularly as one seeks for causes, he needs to know the exact year in which the rate of growth changed.

The Eurican student of church growth, and the Africasian student too, looks behind every collection of statistics of membership increase. He has a persistent curiosity about the reasons for it. Graphs present the facts of growth dramatically, but their greatest usefulness is that they enable the student to pinpoint his investigation of trends in growth at the right moments, with accurate knowledge of their magnitude, duration, and nature.

8

SOURCES TO SEARCH FOR
CAUSES OF GROWTH

WHERE SHOULD the churchman look to find the reasons why cells of Christians (churches) have proliferated throughout a city ward, a country district, a tribe, or other segment of society?

Some may feel the question is rhetorical and the answer obvious. Evangelistic campaigns, they think, bring men to Christ and establish new churches. The churchman should find out what evangelism has been done. He need look no further. This line of thinking fails, however, to take into account the fact that evangelistic campaigns have very different results. In some places thousands are won and in others only dozens. In Africasia, many campaigns bring no one to Christ and plant not one new church. Indeed, in America, many city-wide campaigns add only a few new responsible Christians to existing congregations and not a single new congregation.

The churchman who would understand the ways in which the Holy Spirit, through establishing thousands of new communities of the redeemed, is spreading abroad the "sweet savor of Christ," must ask why evangelism issues in conversions in some populations and not in others. Why do conversions in some cases set off a chain reaction resulting in a multitude of new congregations, while in others the few scattered converts scarcely strengthen the existing ones? Why does a given Church grow vigorously during one period and stagnate in others? Why did Evangelism in Depth work so well in Guatemala and so poorly in Taiwan? What environmental and missionary factors condition church growth?

Where does the churchman look for answers to these questions? They are not rhetorical and the answers are not obvious. They must be diligently sought in the right places.

MINISTERS AND MISSIONARIES WHO WERE THERE

Unquestionably the best sources of understanding of growth are the men and women who saw it happen. They knew what was going on. They knew every inquirer and baptized every convert. They met the opposition, enjoyed the victories, and grieved over the defeats. They were part of the community in which growth was occurring. The ministers and missionaries who were there when growth, plateau, or decline was happening are the ones to ask.

They know more than other persons who were present. They are educated, accustomed to discriminating thinking, and have wide experience. They know the language spoken by the Christians and talk with them freely. Few persons are as intimately related with new churches as ministers and missionaries. They have thought much about church growth. They want it, have worked at it, and prayed for it. They have been alive to it.

They also frequently suffer from being too close to it. They are inclined to credit what they have done toward church growth with too much influence in bringing it about, and are often insufficiently aware of social structures and the considerable part they play in growth or stagnation. Fog obscures their vision just as it does that of administrators and others. Despite these handicaps, the ministers and missionaries who were on hand during the period in question are the best sources of insight. The researcher can allow for their weaknesses and help those he interviews to overcome them.

When asking for information about church growth, he should ask about specific cases and obtain light on their extent. A graph of growth of the Church in view helps to prevent irrelevant talk and elicit pertinent information. You see the sudden upturn of the line? In 1961 something happened which caused your denomination to double in six years. I am looking for the causes of that sudden surge of growth, which gradually subsided and ended about 1976. I would like to know also why it diminished. You were there during those years. Please tell me what really happened.

Retired persons are sometimes good informants, but unless they were interested in church growth while active they have little to contribute. Retired pastors whose congregations in, let us say, Vermont or Kansas, barely held their own, usually have little to contribute. They were caretakers and had no curiosity as to what makes churches grow or plateau. Retired missionaries whose work was institutional and whose talks have rehearsed again and again incidents connected with those institutions, usually know little of the growth or decline of the Church they worked with. But retired missionaries who were consciously carrying out the Great Commission are a prime source of information.

Searching for reasons for the surprising growth of the Christian Church (Disciples of Christ) in China, I interviewed two retired missionaries. The problem was this. During the years 1880 to 1940 a large number of missionaries had built up a small Church of 1,198 members, increase being at a snail's pace throughout the six decades. Why then in 1942 did this Church revive and surge forward to *add* 1,867 members in six years? (*Yearbook* 1940:624, 1948:682). Both men had been there during the critical six years.

O. J. Goulter gave two reasons. First, after the Japanese invaders had been repelled with the aid of American arms, American missionaries for the first time in sixty years appeared to the general populace as "our friends and allies." Instead of hostility, indifference, or suspicion, friendliness greeted them. The Gospel could be "heard"; it no longer appeared as itself the spearhead of a foreign invasion.[1] Second, the Bible School instituted a new form of training for evangelists. They were taught evangelism *and* agriculture. They went out able to teach peasants not only the way of salvation but also ways to increase their yields of rice and pigs. Wherever these evangelists went, small rural churches sprang up.

James McCallum, who had been the field administrator of the mission, taking one look at the figures said, "During those years several independent congregations in Nanking decided to affiliate with our Church."

The example illustrates several traits of the information to be derived from ministers and missionaries. It will usually be partial. The field administrator knew part of the reason. Living at Nanking, he had helped to

---

1. By way of contrast, consider the following reason for nongrowth in a nearby field, advanced by a competent observer. "Our missionaries went back into China after the war, but had only four years and those, in most places, were taken up with rebuilding the destroyed properties." The same people, the same environmental factors, the same years, and *no* growth, because attention centered on rebuilding properties.

unite the independent congregations with his own and remembered them. The head of the Bible School, living in a corner of the field, knew about the growth he had seen. Information from churchmen usually exhibits the enthusiasms and biases of the informant.

In most cases loyalty colors the answer. Ministers and missionaries are apt to believe that their own church or mission procedures are altogether admirable. This commendable confidence must be allowed for as the researcher evaluates the answers. In cases of slow growth or nongrowth, major allowance must be made for defensive thinking. All kinds of rationalizations are likely to be advanced. Cliches replace reasons. Thus the pastor who, confronted by thirty years of miniscule growth, exclaimed, "But the secular humanist opposition here is terrific. One simply cannot expect growth," was overlooking the fact that in an adjacent county in a similar population, churches were multiplying merrily. The real reason for nongrowth was that effective evangelism was not the highest priority of the ministers who served that church. Their top priority was carrying on a well-rounded program. When asked about church increase, he responded with a defensive cliche, not a solid reason.

Executive secretaries of missions are not likely to contribute much to an understanding of church growth. They usually administer several fields and do not become intimately acquainted with the people in any one of them. They converse with missionaries and church leaders in English, and since they are responsible for many kinds of work, automatically guard against undue interest in particular ones. Their chief duty is the recruitment of missionaries and the raising of the budget in the sending land, and for this they need and specialize in not diagnostic but promotional materials.

Nevertheless, some executives are becoming students of church growth, and more of them will. Accurate, extensive knowledge of how churches grow is essential for any administration which intends to carry out the Great Commission. The day is coming when knowledge of the natural laws—one might say the science—of church growth will be part of the qualifications for office of any church or mission administrator. As soon as this happens, executives will be a good source for learning the reasons for growth. Few others have the opportunity to know firsthand so many instances of growth, plateau, and decline.

LAY CHRISTIANS

A rewarding mine of information may be found in the laity. Church growth is the sum of many baptized believers. No one knows better what caused it than those who make it up. Granting this, it is not easy to extract the gold from this vein of quartz. Interviewing demands skill, and the interviewer needs special training. He must not suggest answers. He should be at home in the language, for interpreters retard the process and color answers with their own convictions. He should select with care those interviewed so that they constitute a random sampling of the whole unit being studied. This last point is frequently neglected, and those interviewed are apt to be the most devout, most easily reached, or most educated. Very great patience is required with rural people and illiterates. They take a long time pondering a simple question and, if one is to have a true answer, must not be hurried. They are likely to give answers they think will please their distinguished visitor.

Despite these drawbacks, lay Christians furnish a valuable source of information. They are realistic. They recount the reasons that impelled them and their intimates to become Christians. Their answers are not distorted by theological considerations and Eurican cultural overhang. If the churchman wants the whole truth, he ought to interview hundreds of laymen who have been an integral part of the growth under study. The historical treatises and statistical summaries which are all that researchers working from books can manage are good; but new light will shine on the complex processes of growth when older laymen of a Church, and the common people who make up its bulk tell why they became Christian. In both America and other lands, ordinary Christians—women as well as men—are a most rewarding source of realistic information. Let me illustrate the point first from overseas.

Two contrasting illustrations show the indigenous quality of such witness. Westerners could not invent such testimony. In the first case, a Christian family had left its village during a period of slack work to make bricks in a nearby town where there were no Christians. On their return five months later, the father of the family, after attending evening worship in the village chapel where services were held every evening, was talking to his relatives and friends in his courtyard.

"It is good to come back where we are men," he remarked contentedly. "In the brickyard we made good money, but we were like oxen, who work all day, eat the grass and straw given them, and go to sleep. Here, we eat, and then worship God in the company of all our kinfolk. Only after worship do we go to sleep. It feels good."

In the second case, a churchman was investigating a fifty-year growth which had created a remarkable Church of about 7,000, with 147 congregations, which met regularly for worship and had many educated members.

As he chatted with the older men, illiterates all, he directed the conversation to the early days when they first became Christians. Again and again they mentioned police persecution.

"We were a rough lot before we became Christians," said a grizzled old man. "Because of our bad name, the police harassed us continually, much more than we deserved. They jailed our youth. They insulted our women. They made us give them rice and vegetables and forced us to carry their burdens to the next village without any pay. We had no recourse. After we became Christians, when we were innocent our pastors spoke up for us. Even our missionary sometimes pleaded our case. Then, too, we became better people and gradually got a good name. The police do not trouble us any more" (McGavran, 1956).

The motives which lead men to become Christians are always mixed, and missionaries in recounting the beginnings of the churches are likely to omit the more selfish ones. Base motives are there nonetheless and cast much light on the factors that induce growth.

The researcher in interviewing laymen should pay close attention to homogeneous units. When he is talking to educated second-generation Christians who have grown up in mission station churches with much love and care from missionaries, he will hear one kind of answer; when talking to Christian factory workers who almost never see a missionary, he will get another; and when talking to Christian peasants in far villages still a third. The answers of Quiche Indian Christians in Guatemala will be different from those given by Tseltal Christians to the north, across the border in Mexico. High-caste converts in India who have been thrown out of house and home will give different reasons for church growth from those given by the oppressed who have turned to Christ in chains of families and have continued on in their ancestral homes doing their ancestral tasks.

The interviewer will use only some of the many lines of inquiry he knows. He approaches every new case with preconceived ideas as to why growth did or did not occur. These hypotheses form the basis of his questions. Some lines of inquiry will speedily prove useless; they do not fit the situation. They are not productive and should forthwith be dropped. Other angles of questioning, not contemplated at the beginning, will emerge and prove rewarding. These should then be continued and expanded. For example, in doing a study of the United Church of Christ in the Philippines, I interviewed lay Christians in more than a hundred congregations. I soon stumbled across the fact that some congregations consisted largely of half families in which only one partner was Christian. Compared with those consisting mostly of full families, the half-family congregations were much less vigorous. As soon as I discerned this, I made finding out the number of full and half families in each congregation a prominent part of my research. The new line of inquiry yielded much understanding of the dynamics of growth.

J. Waskom Pickett's insights into growth of the Church in India arose in large part from his systematic and extensive interviews with laymen.

> Often in our tour we heard Christians from one of these castes praying for the conversion of members of the other caste. After one such experience we asked a leading layman of the local Church, an ex-Madiga, who claimed to be eighty years old, whether he really wanted Malas to become Christians. He laughed as he replied, "Who would not want his enemies to become good men? When I was a boy we had a fight with the Malas and my arm was broken. The Madigas around here are all Christians. If the Malas, too, are converted, there'll be no more fights between us. We know that it is our duty to pray for the conversion of all castes, and we do so. We pray most for the Malas because we hear that many of them have been converted in other places" (Pickett, 1960:55).

On the basis of this and much other firsthand evidence, Pickett rightly concluded that in Christ the old enmities between castes are dissolved.

> In our Telegu tours we were deeply moved by the daily recital of evidence that Christ is dissolving these ancient enmities and uniting in one fellowship men and women who are the inheritors of prejudices, conflicts, and hatreds which have afflicted their ancestors and their villages through successive generations for centuries. The testimonies recorded in our notebooks divide into three classes according as they relate changes in feelings and attitudes (1) of the higher castes toward the Depressed Classes, (2) of the Depressed Classes toward the higher castes, and (3) of one caste toward another of comparable position (Pickett, 1960:48).

In the United States, interviewing hundreds of converts who over the last thirty years have become dependable Christians is a revealing adventure. The goal is to discover the real reasons why they first became Christians. The real reasons are usually buried deep beneath the "correct" reasons which years of Christian nurture have built up within them, but they can be unearthed.

One of my students interviewed a hundred and thirty-five new converts (not transfers) in five mainline suburban congregations. He found that the following were the most common reasons for "joining the church." (1) We felt it was a good thing to do. (2) We wanted our children to grow up in the church. (3) I wanted to become a part of a Christian community. (4) I was tired of believing nothing. (5) Living just for money and fun was not satisfying. (6) Our marriage was breaking up and we had to get a solid rule which would hold us in line.

Hundreds of other responses showed that "joining the church" is a complex matter. In a few cases the only reason given was a sudden conviction that Jesus Christ was indeed the only Savior. They insisted that this was not a later learning but a primary cause. Had the congregations concerned been more Evangelical, would the responses have been different? It would be interesting to find out. However, the interviewer must in all such inquiries make every effort to strain out his own convictions and to discover the original reasons. This is why interviewing recent converts (within the last three months) is highly desirable.

NON-CHRISTIANS

As one searches for causes of growth, non-Christians living in the neighborhood should not be neglected. In every country they are a fruitful and sometimes disturbing source of information. For instance, why does the pagan university professor think the rapidly growing church across the street is prospering? Why are some of the university community joining it?

Pickett in his classic study of the growth of great Churches in India interviewed hundreds of Hindus and Moslems who lived in the communities where churches were growing, and saw the process from a perspective which, to begin with at any rate, was highly critical. Their answers guided him to a deeper understanding of the dynamics of growth. One cannot read *Christian Mass Movements in India* or *Christ's Way to India's Heart* without sensing his debt to these non-Christian informants. One illustration must suffice. It was the Hindus who insisted that those who had become Christians had demonstrated a new scale of values for women.

These services of the Master to women have challenged many of the assumptions of Hinduism and have deeply influenced thinking in the villages. They are forcing a reconstruction of ideals and of religion. A young man, who after two years in college was back in his village home, told us of his struggle to adjust his thinking: "All that I was taught about the capacity of women for learning and culture was wrong. I want to remain a Hindu, but I want my wife to have the privileges Christian women have and to be such a woman as the pastor's wife is. But when I suggest even so small a change as that my wife learn to read, my mother becomes angry. Must my wife and I become Christian or can we change Hinduism?" (Pickett, 1960:71).

The student of church growth in America or elsewhere does well to view it also through the eyes of non-Christians or non-Evangelicals. He is seeking comprehension of the process and should look at it from many points of view.

Recent converts are a rich source of insight. Within the last few years they have turned from the world to the Savior. What brought them is vivid in their minds. Whenever possible, I ask the pastor or missionary to arrange interviews with recent converts. The ideal way is to talk to them one by one, lest what the first one says influence subsequent informants. "Tell me how you became a Christian. I want the whole story. Take your time." Or "Tell us how your people became Christians. What were the main reasons?" As the narrative unfolds, the researcher should probe likely spots and follow up promising leads. "Do you have many non-Christian relatives? Well, what do they think about your becoming Christian? And what about becoming Christians themselves?"

When interviewing recent converts in Orissa I asked a young married woman what her parents thought of her being baptized.

"Last week, before the baptismal ceremony," she replied, "my husband and I went to see my parents fifteen miles east of here to tell them we intended to become Christians and to ask their permission. They granted it readily and said, 'After you are baptized come and tell us about Christ. We are thinking of following you in this way.' "

This one remark revealed volumes concerning the attitude toward Christianity of many in the caste which God had prepared for the journey to the Promised Land.

There is no better way of judging the vitality of a congregation than to ask its members how many non-Christian relatives they have and what these relatives think of the Christian religion. On one occasion we were visiting congregations which for some eight years had shown only biological growth. We felt the Christians were cold and the churches static. Then one day we asked a group of men whether they had any non-Christian relatives.

"Many," they replied promptly.

"And what do they think about becoming Christians?" we asked.

After a moment's surprised silence, they began to tell of cousins, uncles, in-laws, and others who in the last few weeks had spoken quite favorably about seeking baptism. Finally one man jumped to his feet.

"In a village three miles from here," he said, "are a number of my relatives, who have been asking me about the Christian religion. Will you come with me and talk to them?"

On arrival we were surrounded by a crowd of about seventy-five who listened to the Gospel intently, and ended up by enrolling as inquirers. Whenever relatives of Christians are talking among themselves about becoming Christians, no matter what the past record of the Church, the harvest is ripe.

Village pastors and teachers abroad are a good source of information. They understand tables of figures and graphs of growth and should be shown them at the beginning of the interview. They can frequently give detailed accounts of the growth of the congregation where they work. They have perceptive judgment about which church and mission policies led to growth or nongrowth. If possible they should be interviewed in the absence of their supervising minister or missionary and assured that their opinions will be held in confidence; otherwise they will not feel free to utter anything except the official line of that particular area.

Since they know something about neighboring churches and denominations, a fruitful form of inquiry is to ask why others are growing while these are not, or why, when these are growing, others are static. Primary school teachers and slightly trained workers are intelligent men and have much insight. Often, too, if one says to them, "Your colleague in the other town thought churches are growing because of the following reason. What do you think?" he will receive a stream of useful answers.

In short, information about church growth is common. In every land it lies all about us in the people we meet. Any minister or missionary who makes it his business to search for the factors that caused it will find out much about it.

Scrutinize Writings

Books furnish less information about church growth than people, and different kinds of books give different yields.

History and ethnography describe the matrix in which churches grow. They inform the reader about culture, customs, racial characteristics, and governments which condition those to whom the Gospel is presented. Reading such books enables the Christian to speak intelligently to his fellows. If well written, they are fascinating; but they say little or nothing about church growth.

The follower of Christ may read them merely for intellectual interest as he would books on the birds, animals, or geology. Yet he should get much more than this from them. For they contribute to understanding of church growth if we read them asking, "What do these books mean for the propagating of the Gospel?" The growth of the Church is closely conditioned by both history and anthropology. When Japan defeated Russia in 1905 and started to take over Korea, this had a profound effect on the spread of churches there. The four-century Spanish oppression of the Indians of the high Andes is probably the greatest environmental factor faced by Evangelical missions in that region and cannot be studied too intensively. Menelik's conquest of the Gallas of Ethiopia and their forced "conversion" have constituted both an attraction to and a repulsion from the Good News. Tribal structure everywhere is the enemy of church growth—till the Church gets inside the tribe, when structure often becomes its great friend.

Church and mission history and biography yield information of a different sort. They recount what missions and leaders have done. Yet because of the promotional bias of most such books and the fact that many missions have seen little church growth and have been engaged in doing things other than planting churches, such writings are not the mine of information one might expect.

Since understanding of church growth is being sought, background books of all kinds should be read, *with graphs of growth in hand.* Only when the student has clearly in mind the real magnitude of the growth that has occurred, and its dates and changes, does he know what to look for and the times in which to search.

Unless one knows that between 1776 and, say, 1796 the enormously influential Anglican Church in the United States was suffering severe reverses because of its close connection with England it is difficult to assess aright the remarkable growth of Baptist churches in those years. However, the political factor was not the only one. During those very years the Methodists were growing tremendously, despite the fact that Asbury and Coke were English missionaries.

Unless one knows that between 1907 and 1912 the Churches in Gold Coast had a phenomenal growth, the Cocoa Boom which opened up the back country at just that time will not be seen as a likely contributing cause. Only when one sees the Pentecostal graph of growth shooting skyward for the cities of southern Brazil can he separate the great immigration into the cities of which history tells us from thousands of other occurrences, and see it as a growth factor. Only when one observes the slow growth obtained after 1916 by most old-line Evangelical missions in Latin America, does their great swing to education starting at that time and recounted in their histories take on a sharp meaning.

The student should apply his existing church growth knowledge as he reads. With its aid he will see implications he would otherwise miss. What he reads will in turn correct his existing knowledge and add to it. When he reads of the Seventh Day Adventist people movement to Christ around

1920, led by Camacho from among his fellow Aymara Indians living near Lake Titicaca in Peru, he will recognize how important it is for Aymara Indians under their own Aymara leaders to turn to Christ in social units, and will thus add to his understanding of the way in which the social situation affects growth. When he reads of the considerable initial growth of the Church which has been won by the school approach in Africa, his previous opinion, based on experience in India, that mission schools very seldom lead students to become Christians will be modified. He will conclude that under some African circumstances the Christian school is a good beginning for the Christianization of tribes.

In most writings the student will find only hints about church growth. He should learn to scan books rapidly for the occasional sentence or paragraph which throws light on how the faith has flourished and spread to new segments of society. He should expect to pan a ton of gravel to get an ounce of gold. It is helpful to keep a notebook or a card file of data on church growth and to add to this whenever reading turns up a significant fact about it or an incident relating to it.

The habit of critical, evaluative reading should be developed. Most authors recount church growth data only incidentally, and frequently in distorted form. Purely appreciative reading fails to allow for the distortions, or if it discerns them, takes them at face value. For example, *Behind the Ranges,* by Mrs. Howard Taylor (1964), a biography of John Fraser, the apostle to the Lisu in southwest China, combines adventure, devotion, and flashes of real understanding concerning the way peoples become Christian. A person without church growth eyes reading the book will see only the adventure and devotion. A person with church growth insight will see adventure, devotion, and much that is relevant to church growth. Such an individual, with training in church growth, reading critically, will wonder whether Mrs. Taylor has reported John Fraser's apostolic genius adequately and will long to study Fraser's diary and writings at firsthand.

Articles in church magazines have limited value. Their promotional bias is overwhelming, and save in reporting great growth in progress, they seldom mention the subject. Even where growth is occurring, since the articles are slanted to the supporting constituency, they furnish little understanding of the processes by which churches multiply. For instance, an article in *Christianity Today* (July 7, 1967:38) reports the conversion of thousands of Moslems in Indonesia within eighteen months—surely an epochal event—as a "revival." Revival is what occurs in cold, nominally Christian communities. When used to describe movements of non-Christians to Christ, the term conveys little understanding of what is really happening. Nevertheless, articles should be scanned. There is a small amount of gold in these sands also.

Occasionally one will find an article dealing specifically with church growth. In the October 1961 *International Review of Missions,* R. H. Drummond, summing up Hendrik Kraemer's opinions on the Japanese Church after a visit there, said:

> He tried to change the present emphasis centered almost entirely on the local congregations, to the possibility of creative effort in wider spheres that could help create more favorable conditions to the reception of the Gospel. . . . (Christians should) break out of their spiritual and sociological shell and become a light to the whole nation. . . . he appealed to Christians to express their convictions and opinions on every phase of culture . . . (and held that this) would constitute an act of evangelism of the highest significance (Drummond, 1961:455, 456).

Such articles deserve careful study; but the student of church growth must ask whether Dr. Kraemer was right or not. Was his opinion merely European cultural overhang? Does church growth in Japan and America result if the Church follows his prescription? Has this been a formula for growth in any of the great expansions of the Gospel?

Letters are an excellent source of understanding—an original source, very close to the actual happening. Their historical value is high. Some missionary societies have microfilmed all their correspondence from the field and will make it available to responsible researchers. In many cases letters show to what an extraordinary extent missionaries and field administrators deal with secondary matters—personnel problems, disagreements between staff members, finances, new buildings, repairs, and the like. Nevertheless, here and there letters yield shining nuggets and are worth careful perusal. They are our chief source for knowledge of clashes of opinion as to vital policies. Letters from Korea, for example, in the first decade of the twentieth century document the determination of missionaries in northwest Korea, when the Church was growing apace, to concentrate on church growth. They actually fought against accepting funds to build a big hospital, feeling it would shift the main emphasis from discipling Koreans to healing their diseases.

Denominational and mission minutes are readily available and furnish an impeccable source of information concerning policies and men which have affected church growth. Frequently surging growth has followed church or mission action in occupying a new area where a few hundred have already become Christian. Conversely, moving a pastor or missionary who has led hundreds to Christ to a "more important" post in administration or seminary has frequently damaged and sometimes arrested a promising movement. Commonly church and mission minutes shed dim light on the complex processes by which the Holy Spirit reconciles men to God in the Church of Jesus Christ. They show action on everything else but the increase of the Church, and thus constitute evidence as to why growth did not occur.

Budget distributions in congregations, denominations, and missions should be scrutinized. They reveal true long-range goals and indicate where the actual emphasis of the Church or mission lies. At a glance the researcher can discern both the philosophy and the main drives of the organization he is studying. The inner meanings of budget headings should be taken into account. "Student work" is commonly listed under evangelism; in some cases correctly so. In other cases, however, student work is simply shepherding Christian students and wins no one to Christ. In the seven wonderful years in Japan when the Congregational Church grew from 1,000 to 10,000, Congregational missionaries were teaching bands of ten to fifty young men. It was no doubt too early in missions in Japan for an educational department to appear; but had there been one, the budget would have shown the bulk of mission funds going into "educational work." Yet the inner meaning of *that* particular educational work was that the missionaries, with singleness of mind, were directing all their efforts to bring samurai youth to accept Jesus Christ as their Savior. The classes were merely the vehicle for an ardent, ceaseless evangelism. The "educational work" in that exceptional case was evangelism.

In short, books, articles, mission minutes, budget distributions, and letters furnish good sources in which to dig for information concerning the causes of church growth. One must know what he is looking for and search in precise years. For example, in 1936 a most promising people movement to Christ from among the Bhils was going on in what is now Rajasthan, India. It was led by an able missionary named Russell of the United Church of Canada. Waskom Pickett visited the area, toured in it extensively, and voiced the opinion that it was the most promising beginning of a people movement he had ever seen. Dr. Russell retired a year or two later, and the Bhils reverted. A careful study of mission minutes, letters, and missionary and budgetary allocations during the years 1936 to 1939 would reveal why this crushing defeat of the Christian cause occurred.

DISCOUNTING ERRONEOUS OPINIONS

Many pronouncements about church growth are rationalizations. These are normal in any walk of life (armies seldom suffer defeat—they withdraw to consolidate their lines), but should be recognized and discounted in soberly assessing the increase of the Church.

In Canada and the United States, leaders of denominations which are bending every effort to achieve structural church union, commonly stigmatize growth as partisan—one Church growing at the expense of others. Such leaders feel any expansion is bad. It produces loyalty to the denomination, not to the coming Great United Church. Theirs is not a sober scientific judgment. It is special pleading. It may in fact be justification for heavy loss of members.

In Japan in 1889 when the government, disappointed in its efforts to secure treaty revision, made an about-face and took a hard line toward the West, the wonderful Presbyterian and Congregational church growth stopped short. The communicant memberships of these two Churches remained for many years at about 10,000 each. Missionary writings after the standstill are full of defensive thinking. They see "elements of encouragement in the situation." Earlier gains were not entirely lost. The rolls were purged of the half-hearted. A higher conception of the Christian life evolved. Greater caution was exercised in admitting applicants. Missions gained a more realistic conception of the task and perceived that the Church had entered a more mature stage of its existence! (Thomas, 1959:209).

All these are rationalizations. The Christian cause had suffered a disastrous reversal and leaders were looking around for crumbs of comfort.

Methodological reasons for growth, when unduly stressed, should be questioned. For example, A. W. Wasson in the last chapter of his fine study *Church Growth in Korea* ascribed growth in the early thirties to the agricultural emphasis of Methodist missions. Yet when one observes that Methodist growth was relatively small, while Presbyterian Pyongan growth—where there was no agricultural emphasis at all—was large, he suspects that the agricultural emphasis (which, being the latest thing in missions, was sweeping around the world at the time) was at best a minor cause of whatever growth occurred among the Methodists. Similarly, when all growth in Korea is credited to the Nevius method, one must demur. Denominations and missions display a certain faddiness. At one time this method and at another that will become popular. No doubt the Nevius method is a good one, but there were other causes for church growth in Korea. When Dr. Harry A. Rhodes (1934:89) asks whether "the Church flourishes because of the system or the system is possible because of the flourishing condition of the Church," he is calling attention to the fact that ascribing church growth to a single methodological factor is one-sided. The true explanation is complex.

Theological reasons *by themselves* should often be questioned. For example, a missionary writes, "The church in that district has never flourished. Faith in Christ and willingness to stand persecution for His name seemed high in the first thousand converts, but must really have not existed at all because many reverted to their former faith." A theological reason for reversion is adduced: their faith was not deep and sincere. This may have been the case, but a conversion which separated from race and kin, lack of skill in shepherding, environmental pressures, and downright neglect have so often played dominant parts in reversions that one hesitates to believe that the theological reason was the only one.

A pastor in Texas wrote, "Among the Pentecostals, joyous abandonment to the Lord and unquestioning obedience to the Bible have been the means whereby thousands have come to a living relationship with Him." One may rejoice that these Christian graces have been found in considerable measure among Pentecostal Christians and yet observe that many environmental factors have played significant roles in their church advance.

When it comes to assessing reasons for church growth special points of view of speakers and writers should be borne in mind and allowance made for their errors. For example, an ardent "united church" man must not be expected to give an accurate account of church growth. He is likely to affirm that the separated Churches of South India were hopelessly handicapped in their evangelism by their very divisions, while the Church of South India, which unites them all into one, is much more credible. The student of church growth, however, cares little whether a Church is credible; he asks how much it has grown. He rates performance higher than promise. The following chart of growth of the Church of South India, constructed by Dr. S. N. Raju, one of its eminent lay leaders, gives the student the facts by which he can assess the truth or error of special pleading and a priori judgments concerning it. He says, "For ready visualization of the comparative magnitudes of Church Growth Indices in the Dioceses, a chart has been prepared according to linguistic States. The zero line is the datum of reference and represents the census population growths in the various dioceses. Indices above the line indicate excess of church growth over and above population growth, and indices below the line show deficits" (Raju, 1965). Thus an index of church growth of 23.74 for the Madras diocese, means that in that diocese the Church grew 23.74 per cent *more* than the population did. On the other hand in the Mysore diocese, the Church grew 6.57 per cent *less* than the population did. In the accompanying table, which I have not reproduced, Dr. Raju sums up the evidence: During the decade 1952-1962 the Church of South India increased in "total baptized Christians" by 157,218, which meant that it increased at 1.39 per cent *less* than the population did.

FIGURE 8.1. TRENDS OF CHURCH GROWTH
IN CHURCH OF SOUTH INDIA DIOCESES 1952-1962

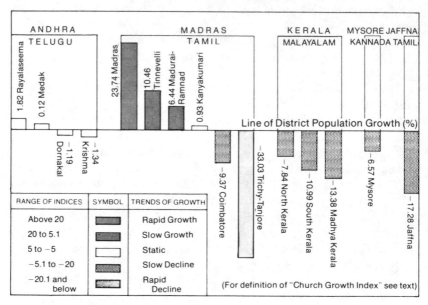

He who would understand church growth must always assume multiple causes for each spurt of growth or period of retardation. When he has discovered one cause he should search for others. That is why this chapter has described many causes and sources, each likely to add further understanding. For example, the remarkable growth of the three Philippine congregations described in the first chapter of this book was said to have seven causes. This was an oversimplification. Many other causes existed, including individuals whose conversion was so deep and whose knowledge of Christ so warm and vivid that they could not help but tell others of their Savior. Excellence in understanding church growth can be measured by consciousness of the complexity of the subject. The novice sees one cause and proclaims that he has found *the* cause for growth; the experienced student unearths a dozen causes and goes back to the sources to discover still others.

Hamilton (1963:138) points out that the reasons for church growth not only vary from case to case but are combined in different proportions in each. In the Philippine case, absence of persecution was a major cause of growth, but in other instances it is a minor one. In some, by way of contrast, persecution spurs Christians on to communicate their faith, as in the remarkable growth of the Presbyterian Church (1939 to 1944) among the Tyal and Ami tribes in the mountains near Hwaliankang on the east coast of Formosa. Despite Japanese persecution, four thousand marched down out of the hills when the Japanese left the island, to ask for baptism. Hamilton, borrowing from the art of cooking, says that ingredients of growth are mixed in different proportions in each case. This is true, and the principle applies not only to different denominations and missions, but also within the same Church or mission, to its different periods and homogeneous units.

The principle of ingredients combined in varying proportions may be clearly seen in the New Testament Church. During its first expansion—from Pentecost till about A.D. 48—it grew among Palestinian Jews. The intense people-consciousness of this population, its conviction of being "the chosen people of God," the firm belief in (Old Testament) Scripture, personal knowledge of Jesus of Nazareth, common Aramaic language, and longing for release from the Roman yoke were dominant human factors on which the Holy Spirit breathed to create, all through the hill country, a multitude of Christian congregations which continued strictly to obey the Jewish law.

During the second expansion—from about A.D. 48 to the death of the apostle Paul—the Church grew vigorously in the synagogue communities of the Diaspora. In this population, in addition to some of the factors mentioned above which operated in lesser measure, new factors came into play. For example, "devout persons" in multitudes became Christians. These synagogue-attending Gentiles were strongly attracted to the high morality and monotheism of Judaism but repelled by circumcision, food taboos, and other externals of the Law. When they learned they could be saved by faith in Jesus Christ without assuming the burden of the Law, and saw that in Christ men become new creatures who manifest the fruits of the Spirit, they became ardent members of the Church and joyfully propagated the Gospel among their non-Christian— and non-Jewish—relatives and friends. It was the same Church that was growing, but the factors in the second expansion differed from those in the first and were combined in different proportions. The source for this understanding of church growth is the New Testament itself.

SOME COMMON REASONS WHY CHURCHES
DO OR DO NOT GROW

As the student of church growth delves into the sources mentioned, he will identify dozens and then hundreds of detailed causes and come to understand church growth better and better. By way of summarizing this chapter and illustrating what he may find, I set forth below in bare outline a few common causes out of the thousands which have worked for and against growth in Churches we have studied. The student from his sources will accumulate a list like this—perhaps not quite as broad, since in an attempt to speak to churchmen in different countries I have included from Asia, Africa, and Latin America an unusually wide spread of examples. Many of these reasons, stated slightly differently, are at work in Western nations. The student of American church growth will recognize all of these and add some which operate in his particular culture. A useful exercise would be to state each of the following for *his* church.

Reasons for Growth

1. Some minister, layman, or missionary dedicated his life to planting churches.

2. The Gospel was preached to some clearly receptive part of the mosaic. Acts 2:13.

3. Some churchman recognized one of the many growing points given by God to His Church. He valued this beginning and poured his life into it.

4. Someone had a particular plan for multiplying churches which fitted his special population. He prayed for months and years that men and women would be won and churches multiplied, and worked his plan.

5. Environmental and church factors favorable to growth appeared at the same time. For example, in Korea in 1919 Christians led the freedom movement and made Christianity popular. At the same time the Methodists launched a great forward movement.

6. A Christian leader devised a broad pattern of action which multiplied congregations: Nevius in Shantung, China.

7. Some churchman refused to be tied to work which did not plant churches. Or some Christian leader discovered the difference between "good church work" and the chief purpose of Christian mission, and turned from one to the other.

8. The Christian religion became "our religion" to a sizable segment of some culture.

9. Indigenous leaders, out of the subculture being converted, were put in charge of the Church.

10. Indigenous church principles and people movement principles were used together in some prepared people.

11. The Church and mission gave prolonged postbaptismal training to Christians and to their children and grandchildren. Herbert Money of Peru notes that in 1964 Peru had 350 Evangelical missionaries. The Seventh Day Adventists had only 20, 5 per cent of the total. Nevertheless, they had more than half of the Evangelical church members in all Peru. Dr. Money credits Adventist effectiveness to systematic postbaptismal indoctrination.

12. Able leaders in the Church were converted, and praying Christians were filled with the Holy Spirit. A revival came to the Church. Examples are the Hoovers in Chile, Disciple ministers in Puerto Rico, and the Seamands of the South Indian Conference of the Methodist Church.

Reasons for Lack of Growth

1. Leaders were chained to existent maintenance work. Or, Church and mission were devoted to a nonproductive pattern, once needed but long since outmoded.

2. Church and mission were devoted to an only slightly productive pattern instead of a highly productive one. For example:

They continued the school approach when adults could be won.

They baptized no illiterates, though this limited the church largely to youth.

They required a three-year catechumenate, though few adults could last the course.

They tried to circumvent polygamy by baptizing chiefly unmarried youth and hoping they would stick to monogamy.

3. They did not learn the language of the people, worked always in English, and so established the image that the Christian religion signifies mainly cultural advance. They thus got a few of the rebel young men on their way out of the tribe, but very few older men or families.

4. Fearing the problems brought in by converts and churches made up of new Christians, they set very high standards and baptized few.

5. The ministry was too highly trained and paid, was not one with the people, and could not be supported by the churches themselves.

6. Church and mission allowed themselves to remain stuck in an area of low potential.

7. They "worked with" resistant homogeneous units, instead of baptizing the receptive units available to them:

Roman Catholic ranchos instead of revolutionary ranchos
Upper-class professional people instead of laborers
High castes instead of depressed classes
High-school youth in towns instead of peasants in the country
The "classes" instead of the masses.

8. Leaders did not learn about church growth from mistakes of the past.

9. No one checked what was being done against the degree of church growth achieved.

10. The mission faced with little growth did not seek expert opinion from the outside.

11. They accepted gradualism as a sufficient mission method.

9

HELPS AND HINDRANCES
TO UNDERSTANDING

CANADIAN, AMERICAN, and European readers should study this chapter with care. It will be most rewarding to them. They will discover many helps and hindrances to understanding which dog their footsteps and cloud their perceptions. As they read, however, they should resolve to translate these insights from the world of mission into thought forms which fit the Western scene. In this chapter all the illustrations are from Africasia. Because of this let no one say, "These have no meaning for me. I work in Chicago or Berlin."

The principles are universal. They apply in every continent and almost every culture. Take, for instance, the first illustration below. The principle there presented is that rapid growth is often considered disreputable by those not getting growth. To illustrate this I quote the remark of a missionary to China to the effect that 100 per cent growth a decade would create not a Church but a madhouse. American readers will at once recognize that such self-justifying judgments are constantly being made by "notable leaders" about their static or declining congregations and are a serious hindrance to understanding, in Europe and America as well as elsewhere.

Again the illuminating lessons illustrated by the Baptist/Mennonite case history will focus the American reader's attention on the large receptive units of society in his own city or state. A little work is being done among these. Slight growth—when worked for—is granted. More would be if his Church "counted this receptive society as a pearl of great price and . . . single-mindedly did those things which multiply churches in it."

The point need not be labored. Illustrations from the mission field may indeed help Western readers make far more applications than could possibly be printed here. This is a rich chapter for Western readers.

GROWTH-ARRESTING CONCEPTS

Many concepts current in the missionary world inhibit the discipling of the nations. They sound plausible, but they hinder and damage the only growth the Churches are achieving or are likely to achieve. They cloud the issues, sap the will to ingathering, and impose on the entire missionary enterprise methods and theology generated in static areas. As nationals and missionaries are exposed to these concepts, the passion of Christ for the salvation of the world, which once filled them and thrust them out to disciple the nations, grows cold. Resolute action gives way to debate. The will to heal is supplanted by the will to polish the surgical instruments. This noxious miasma spreads equally to Liberals and Evangelicals and weakens the ability of both to bring people to faith and obedience. To recognize these half-true and hurtful ideas and see how they have become influential is necessary if we are to break their grip on the missionary mind.

Growth-arresting concepts arise in several ways. First, Churches in their amazing spread all over the world have carried on work in many areas where men have not believed, and where inch-by-inch progress has been the only sort achieved. Mission methods congenial to slow growth have developed. Theologies have been formulated, ostensibly built on Scripture but actually arising from the debris of decades of rejection, which demand that mission be carried on in the expectation that the Church will grow very moderately. To look askance at rapid growth is orthodox in areas of inch-by-inch operation; rapid growth is regarded as more or less disreputable.

A noted leader whose experience had been in a Chinese Church growing at the rate of 13 per cent per decade exclaimed, "If growing at the sound conservative pace we are, we have such terrific difficulties developing a real Church among these people, a galloping 100 per cent a decade increase would create not a Church but a madhouse." In areas where growth has been slow, whether because of the resistance of the population or the mistakes of the Church, opinions like the following are often voiced.

1. We do sound work and are not interested in short cuts.

2. It takes decades to grow an oak. A pumpkin grows in a single summer.

3. God takes His own time to make a sound Church.

4. The field, maintained at great cost and agony over many years, often proves to be the seedbed from which a rich harvest is finally reaped.

5. Soundness of growth, not rapidity, is the criterion.

These concepts *assume* that good growth is necessarily slow and that length of labor guarantees the excellence of the product. Nothing in the Bible or the growth of the New Testament Church supports this assumption. Modern industry or education would laugh at it. That these concepts have achieved almost the sanctity of Scripture in many missionary circles may be credited to a prolonged experience of rejection—not to their truth. For it does indeed take courage to hold on in the face of rejection, a courage which instinctively needs reassurance as to its own rightness.

Sentiments such as item 4 above are frequently expressed by those Baptists whose labors have brought few to Christ. These know that their South India missionaries, whose story we told in Chapter One, after hanging on for twenty-five years during which very few believed, baptized 2,222 converts in a single day! The Church increased by 10,000 in a few months! Yet when the facts are known, this remarkable outcome does *not* support the theory that "the field maintained at great cost over many years often proves the seedbed of rich harvest." On the contrary, the Baptist "field" maintained for twenty-five years in the face of minute church growth was that of the high-caste Hindus in and around Nellore. The harvest came only when young John Clough, leaving this field in the hands of the older missionaries, pressed on to Ongole and started baptizing Madiga Untouchables.

The fallacy in the common inhibiting concept that length of occupation automatically brings growth at last is that of supposing that the Church grows in a geographical area, when as a matter of fact it always grows in people themselves—usually a homogeneous unit of society. The upper-caste unit worked by the first Baptist missionaries was precisely the one where length of labor did *not* bring forth a rich harvest, nor would it have, had they remained there a hundred years. The Madiga unit, which had not been worked for long years "at great cost and agony," was the one where Clough reaped a rich harvest.

However, a measure of truth underlies some of the opinions arising in areas of slow growth. It is true that after seed has been sown, time for germination and maturation must be allowed. In the world of farming, harvest usually comes four months after sowing. In the world of mission, it need cause no surprise that some years should elapse between sowing and harvest. But this must not be used to justify continued tiny growth in populations where other Churches are increasing by leaps and bounds, while secular ideologies and pagan religions also flourish. There is nothing biblical or spiritual about very slow progress in itself. Sometimes it must be endured, but there is no reason to canonize it.

Second, concepts inhibiting to growth arise where Christian missions have suffered not merely slow growth but decades of defeat. Failure is always difficult to bear. How can men neglect so great a salvation? How can they reject the One who died for them? When decade after decade they do, God's obedient servants, believing in His sovereignty and finding it hard to see themselves at fault, wonder whether God Himself wants church growth. In the history of Israel, they ask, do we not see again and again the crucial importance of the remnant? Was there not a time when the real "Church" was the paltry seven thousand who had not bowed the knee to Baal? Did not our Lord say that many are called but few are chosen and ask whether, when He returned, He would find faith on the earth?

Remnant theology proves attractive. A glorification of littleness prevails, in which to be small is to be holy. *Slow* growth is adjudged good growth. Concepts and slogans such as the following are born in these beleaguered outposts of the Church.

1. The tiny minority suffering for its belief is the true Church.

2. To create this minority is the highest success known to missions.

3. The persecuted Church, the Church under the cross, is the true Church.

4. The power of a small group of men, with God, must never be underestimated.

5. The creative minority is what the Church must ever strive to be.

Under some conditions, for some Churches, and in certain ways these concepts are surely true and helpful. Our Lord did say that His disciples were yeast—just a tiny pinch of yeast hidden in a large lump of dough; but the force of the metaphor is precisely that the yeast multiplies exceedingly. The virtue of the yeast lies not in its littleness but in its amazing ability to grow. The yeast cells multiply and ramify into every part of the dough. The minority, if it is to be creative, must not only generate productive ideas, but must convert the majority to them. It must grow.

Furthermore, even if we were to take the passages from the Bible to which I have alluded, without, for the time being, balancing them against many others which affirm that God desires the salvation of multitudes—still, is it not fallacious to assume that the 1,000 Christians in our congregations are exactly *the* "few" chosen? Our field has, let us say, a population of 7,000,000 souls. Out of these might not perhaps a small Church of 200,000 (only one thirty-fifth of the population!) be the "few" our Lord was referring to? If so, should we not seek the remaining 199,000 who have been chosen by the Lord, and induct them into His Church? How can we possibly maintain that our thousand constitute *all* of God's elect?

All Christians agree that they should be passionately concerned that the Church be a real Church—made up of committed Christians; but if we make a *small* company our goal, are we true to Him who preached the Gospel to multitudes? And if we make a *select* company the goal, is there not some danger that we become pharisaical and holier-than-thou? Is to be a Christian an ethical achievement—or a redemptive relationship to Jesus Christ? In view of the three billion who have yet to believe, do we do well, in unbiblical fashion, to exalt littleness?

True, when a Church is suffering for Christ's sake or is hemmed in by an overwhelming multitude of gospel-rejectors, she can correctly take comfort in the thought that, under persecution, her chief duty is to remain faithful, confident that her faithfulness is not measured by her numbers. This truth, however, ought not to be stretched to affirm that when the Lord commands sheaves to be brought out of ripe harvest fields, the chief duty of Christians is to pray in a shady corner of the field. It would have been a great pity had the Churches in Indonesia in 1966 and 1967 permitted their will to share salvation with their Moslem and pagan neighbors to be eroded by growth-arresting glorifications of littleness.

Third, antigrowth concepts arise from confusing perfecting with discipling. This confusion has been compounded by a sudden proliferation of meanings for the verb *disciple*. Standard dictionaries in 1979 do not list *disciple* as a verb; but I started using it in 1955 in *The Bridges of God*. There it meant helping a people (a segment of *non-Christian* society) turn from non-Christian Faith to Christ. Discipling was to be followed by perfecting, i.e., by the whole complex process of growth in grace, including the conversion of individuals in that first and succeeding generations.

The new English verb *to disciple* proved attractive. Shortly after 1970 it began to be used for the process by which individuals in any society (Christian or non-Christian) first became Christian. And then it was used for the entirely different process by which existing Christians become illuminated, thoroughly dedicated followers of Christ.

To clarify these three meanings the May 1979 issue of *Church Growth Bulletin* printed a lead article, entitled "How about that New Verb *To Disciple*?" In that I set forth three meanings of the verb, D 1, D 2, and D 3. D 1 would mean the turning of a non-Christian society for the first time to Christ. D 2 would mean the turning of any individual from non-faith to faith in Christ and his incorporation in a church. D 3 would mean teaching an existing Christian as much of the truths of the Bible as possible. A discipled individual in this third sense would be like a college graduate. A discipled segment of society, D 1, on the contrary would be like an illiterate village in Zaire which had resolved to build a school and send all its children to school.

Stages in the growth of a Church are as distinct as stages in the growth of a child, a fact frequently missed by those educated in the Eurican scene. They themselves see only one stage—perfecting, i.e., D 3—and advocate policies suited to it as if these were applicable at every point of the Church's development and in every society and culture. The Church which stands on the edge of a great Discipling One where tens of thousands of its kindred are friendly to the idea of becoming Christian, has a God-given duty to disciple. In such a situation, any perfecting done must above all inculcate that mind of Christ which sought—and seeks—the salvation of all men. A perfecting which lifts educational attainments, increases earning ability, heightens conscience as to social justice, and decreases concern to win kindred to eternal life, betrays the Gospel. High secular and cultural attainments must not be mistaken for dedication to Christ.

For both theological and practical reasons, the constant improvement of the existing Church—D 3—is mandatory on all Christians. God commands it and the Church will languish without it. No one should minimize the importance of perfecting. At the same time, all should be certain that undiscipled pagan multitudes must be "added to the Lord" before they can be perfected. The Church exists not for herself but for the world. She has been saved in order to save others. She always has a twofold task: winning men to Christ and growing in grace. While these tasks overlap, they are distinct. Neither should be slighted. Today's great vision, which calls the Church to rectify injustices in her neighborhoods and nations, is good; but it must not supplant the vision which calls her to disciple the nations.

Confusion at this point gives rise to many ideas which are antagonistic and stunting to growth. Let us consider a few. A missiologist writes, "A

Church may grow in numbers, and yet has the Church grown—as a Church?" Of course it has. Its churchhood arises from its relationship to Jesus Christ and does not vanish simply because it is deficient in some duty.

For many years the Church of Jesus Christ coexisted quite comfortably with slavery and addiction to alcoholic beverages. Neither of these social evils can have been pleasing to God. Both have brought incalculable sorrow and loss to mankind. Yet, despite them, the Church existed and spread abroad. Indeed, only because she spread enormously and gained tremendous political power was she able for the first time in the history of mankind to end slavery. She has been defeated, temporarily to be sure, by liquor—one of the greatest external causes of sorrow in the world; but in her defeat and even in her disgraceful decision to coexist with the liquor traffic, she yet remains the real Church. Wherever non-Christians believe on Jesus Christ, are baptized in His name, accept the Bible as their rule of faith and practice, and manifest the fruits of the Spirit, there a new branch of the real Church is born. The power of Jesus Christ becomes available to its members. They live on a higher plane. That they do not live in some respect as we think they ought—and, more importantly, do not capture the mind of Christ as greatly as they can, is regrettable, but in no way vitiates the fact that the Church *as a Church* has grown.

Or someone may say, "Baptized heathen do not make up a church at all." Of course they do not; yet perfecting does not take place except in discipled (D 1) populations. Many congregations in Eurica as well as Africasia are made up of baptized persons whose practice of the Christian virtues leaves much to be desired. Nevertheless, except in moments of petulance, Christians do not call them "baptized heathen" and throw them out of the Church. Instead Christians ceaselessly seek to bring them to fuller life in Christ and to add more of the same sort to the Church.

"Until we solve the problem of recruiting, training, and supporting a ministry and of making each lay member a functioning minister on a voluntary basis, a growth of 50 per cent a decade would be a nightmare," said one authority on missions. He was confusing growth in grace (D 3) with initial turning to Christ (D 1 or D 2). He was forgetting that D 1 or D 2 must precede D 3, and that D 3 is best carried on in growing Churches, not in static defeated ones.

"The scandal of Africasian Churches is that the lives of their members are a constant stumbling block to their non-Christian neighbors. They cannot grow in size till they grow in holiness. They cannot go further till they go deeper." There can be no question about the need of all Churches—

Eurican as well as Africasian—to "go deeper." The statement, therefore, sounds plausible, but none the less is simply not true. The least perfected Church is superior to her non-Christian origins. Congregations as they are—so imperfectly showing forth His glories—are constantly "going further." Indeed, in many cases the congregations that grow best are those which have most contact with their kindred and neighbors—are most solid with the world—though they neither have as much knowledge of the Bible nor manifest as many fruits of the Spirit as favored congregations of highly educated Christians.

It is at least equally true to say, "We cannot go deeper till we go further." Scattered little congregations cannot support a minister or assure themselves training and leadership till they grow mightily. Gathered-colony congregations at mission stations cannot get away from financial dependence on mission resources and cannot abandon the conviction that being a Christian means profiting by church or mission institutions, until some great ingathering swamps them with Christians who have never known the rich services of a founding mission. It is futile to imagine that one can build a wall around an ingrown Church, "go deeper," and *then* break out.

Neither of these cliches, however, is really true. The Church lives faithful to her Master when she disciples and perfects in a single continuous motion—the discipling helping the perfecting and the perfecting helping the discipling.

Fourth, theorists and theologians immersed in the Eurican scene inevitably favor concepts born out of the problems of Eurican Churches. These may be profitable there, yet in Africasia emasculate the will to search for the lost. For example, a noted Western leader asks, "The Church grows in numbers, yes, but has she ventured more than before into an evangelistic encounter with her environment?" He believes that growing in numbers is less important than Christianizing the environment, "evangelizing the framework of society"—in short, bringing about economic justice and the reign of brotherhood and peace. The question arises naturally where Christians constitute a majority of the population. There it is reasonable to argue that the Church which, by weight of votes, can Christianize the social order ought to do so. There a Church which grows in numbers but leaves the nation (which it *could* change for the better) as selfish, hateful, and rapacious as it was before, may indeed be derelict in its duty.

But the question simply does not arise where the Church, comprising a very small per cent of the population—and oppressed at that—has "evangelistic encounter with her environment" chiefly as she grows in numbers. Power to change the social order is closely related to the number and status of Christians, as anyone who has lived for years where one in a thousand is a Christian can testify.

The mandate and opportunity for small Churches to grow among Africasians ought not to be obscured by focusing attention on Eurican problems, nor should the Eurican proportion between social action and evangelism be considered the norm for Afericasian Churches. Churches which are one per cent of the total population have one duty. Those which are ninety per cent have another.

As the Gospel is proclaimed, men sometimes seek to become Christians from unworthy motives. Particularly when the preacher is an affluent Westerner, supposed to be making his living by getting people to become Christians, it is natural that some should confess Christ through love of money rather than love of Christ. Having no spiritual thirst, nor belief in the Savior, nor experience of sins forgiven, such "converts" get what they can from the missionary and then, when they can get no more, cease claiming to be Christians. Every churchman does well to beware of such men.

On the other hand, he who proclaims the Good News and welcomes men to salvation must also beware lest his suspicions deter those groping their way toward salvation. He is the servant of One concerning whom it is written, "A bruised reed shall he not break and smoking flax shall he not quench." Our Lord took men whose chief motivation for three years was that of sharing in His glory when He drove the Romans into the sea— and turned them into apostles. Furthermore, while the physical needs of the poor and oppressed are more clamant, their spiritual needs are more basic. The Christian dare not give rice freely for the belly and withhold the pure milk of the Gospel from the soul. It is hard to know whether to list examination of motives among would-be converts as a help or hindrance to church growth.

Waskom Pickett in *Christian Mass Movements in India* devotes a chapter to this important subject. Among many valuable emphases are these:

> The subject of motives is always difficult. . . . Its consideration encounters much prejudice and excites strong feeling. Many Christians think it necessary to examine with great care the motives of all who seek entrance to the Christian Church. . . . Others fearful of placing themselves in the position of a judge, take the attitude that whosoever will may come, and while trying to stimulate motives that they consider proper, scrupulously refrain from prying beneath the voluntary declaration of the inquirer (Pickett, 1933:155).

He goes on to point out, however, that

> the gospel often awakens in the mind of the receptive hearer a desire for self improvement and a fuller, as well as a better life, appreciation of kindnesses shown him, hope of escape from century-old wrongs previously endured without question, and ambition for his children. . . . Some of us see in the desire of Sweepers . . . to be treated like respectable people, to secure for their children some other work than the cleaning of cesspools and privies, and to obtain help against oppression, not evidence of unworthy motives, but, rather, support for their claim that they have admitted Jesus to their midst (Pickett, 1933:157).

Pickett's most startling finding about motives, however, and one which relates most to church growth, concerns the bearing which motives have on Christian achievements. He interviewed 3,947 individuals, examining them closely about their reasons for becoming Christian and ascertaining their attainments in the Christian faith. Four kinds of motives were distinguished, and respondents were placed in four groups according to their answers.

> In Group 1 (spiritual motives) are placed all those whose answers had been recorded under the heads: "seeking salvation," "convinced by the preacher," "to know God," "to find peace," "because of faith in Jesus."
>
> In Group 2 (secular motives) are placed all those giving answers such as "sought help of the missionaries," "in hope of education for children," "for improved social standing," "because landowners oppressed us," "to marry a Christian girl."
>
> In Group 3 (social reasons) we put all those giving answers such as "family was being baptized," "My people told me to do so," "I did not want to remain a Hindu when my relatives were Christian."
>
> In Group 4 (natal influences) we put those whose replies were entered as "child of Christian parents," i.e. who were brought up in the Christian faith . . . (Pickett, 1933:164).

Attainments were measured in eleven areas: Knowledge of the Lord's Prayer, Apostles' Creed and Ten Commands, Sabbath Observance, Church Membership, Church Attendance, Frequency of Services, Support of the Church, Freedom from Idolatry Charms and Sorcery, Nonparticipation in Non-Christian Festivals, Freedom from Fear of Evil Spirits, Christian Marriage, and Use of Intoxicating Beverages.

Pickett points out that, as might be expected, those who became Christians from spiritual motives had higher attainment than those who came from secular and social motives. The great surprise in his findings, however, was the small degree of difference between the Christian attainments of those who came from spiritual, secular, and social motives. Whether they had good postbaptismal training made more difference in their attainments than the motives from which they became Christian.

> Possibly the result most worthy of emphasis . . . is the encouraging attainments of converts listed in Groups 2 and 3 (those who came from secular or social motives). The smallness of the margin between Groups 1 (spiritual motives) and 2 (secular motives), we venture to say, will surprise many who have not supposed that *a purely secular motive* such as the desire for help against oppression, *may lead to conversion* and a wholesome productive religious experience. Likewise the nearness of Group 3 (social motives) in many of these tests to Group 1 (spiritual motives) will surprise people who have not discovered how *God uses social forces to bring men under the influence of the gospel.*
>
> We find that 70 per cent of the men who say they became Christian for some motive not accounted spiritual and 75 per cent of those who declare that they became Christians because others of their family or caste did so, have become regular attendants at church services. We also find that the homes of 93.2 per cent of the former and 94.8 per cent of the latter are free from all signs of idolatry; that 90.5 per cent of the former and 91.2 per cent of the latter contribute to the church . . . (Pickett, 1933:168—).

In any revival or expansion of the Church, leaders asking themselves, "Should we admit these converts who know so little of Christ and yet have determined to follow Him?" should know of Pickett's findings. The more spiritual the motive the better, but when groups of men turn to Christ, the care they receive after baptism and the excellence of the shepherding have more to do with Christian attainments than the motives which operated to bring them to follow Christ.

There Comes a Tide Which Taken at the Flood

Connected with motives is the important question when to allow the decisive act which breaks a man's connection with his former religion and admits him to the Christian community. This may be a burning of fetishes, cutting of hair, throwing away of charms, or performance of some other symbolic act. Baptism, according to the rules of the Church in that place, may take place immediately (and *it* may be the decisive act), or it may take place at the close of six months or a year after an examination testing sufficiency of knowledge.

I am not asking when baptism should take place or how long prebaptismal instruction should last. I am asking when the church planter should allow the decisive act by which a man renounces his former faith and declares for Christ. If the evangelist is indecisive at this point and does not know what to do, he may forfeit his opportunity to reconcile men to God.

We have seen (p. 140) the decisive act by which 8,000 Dani tribesmen in West New Guinea burned all their charms and decided to follow the new "Jesus Way." James Sunda in recounting it remarks that many missionaries of the four missions concerned did not know whether to permit the fetish burning or not. One in fact "tried to dispel the crowd and run off 'the false teacher.' " "Some opposed, some approved, and some did not understand fully what was going on." Fortunately the Dani knew what they were going to do! "A notable thing about the whole affair is the fact that while the missionaries debated the issue, large groups of Dani continued to burn their charms" (Sunda, 1963:31).

A different and tragic drama (for the details of which I am indebted to Bishop Pickett, who knew the persons concerned) was enacted at Mirzapur, an ancient Indian city near Benares. The London Missionary Society had maintained missionaries there from the first half of the nineteenth century, but the church had not grown. Mirzapur was a typical mission station in resistant territory; converts were few and far between, and most Christians were employed by the mission or the missionaries.

In the early years of the twentieth century, three unusual missionaries found themselves at Mirzapur. A. W. McMillan, an educator and a splendid Urdu speaker, later went to Fiji as head of the Indian Educational Service there. Robert Ashland, a physician, established clinics and dispensaries and spent himself treating malaria, smallpox, typhoid, and other diseases. John Grant, a minister, was a specialist in cooperative credit societies.

During the incumbency of these three, the notable receptivity which had enabled thousands of Indians belonging to the depressed classes to hear and obey the Gospel, reached Mirzapur district. For the first time, following Christ became a real option to the Chamars there. They had been exposed to the Gospel for years, but God had now touched their ears and they were hearing it. In short, the Holy Spirit had moved upon the *biradari* (the Chamar brotherhood).

Their leaders came to the missionaries and said, "We want to become Christians in groups, as a caste, by clusters of families, and by *mohullahs* (wards). We are tired of Hinduism. We will abandon our idols. What power is there in these stones? Christianity is the true religion. We believe on Jesus Christ. We do not know much about Him, but are willing to learn. Will you accept us as Christians, teach us, baptize us, and help us?'' These Chamars were ready for the decisive act. They wanted to declare for Christ.

The three missionaries spent hours with the leaders and satisfied themselves that these men spoke for considerable numbers of Chamars. They were leaders and would be followed. However, they knew pitifully little about Christ and were undoubtedly motivated by desire for education for their children and emancipation from their deplorably low status.

McMillan, Ashland, and Grant, talking the situation over, said to each other. "These Chamars want to become Christian because they are poor, sick, and ignorant. They are heavily in debt. Their children cannot attend the town schools. They have no hope. These are not good reasons to become Christians. Let us first minister to their needs and then let them decide for spiritual reasons to become Christians."

So they built schools to which Untouchable boys and girls could come. They established dispensaries in their midst and made them welcome at the mission hospital. They organized cooperative credit societies and redeemed many Chamars from perpetual indebtedness to the rapacious moneylenders.

After some years the lot of the Chamars improved noticeably, and the missionaries said to them, "Now you see what Christianity is and what it is doing. Now you are not driven by hunger, sickness, and debt. It is time now for us to admit you to the Christian faith. Let us talk about the next step in advance, discipleship to Jesus Christ and adherence to the true religion."

"Oh," replied the Chamar leaders, "we did not know that you knew anything about religion. You are wonderful in education, medicine, and cooperative credit societies. We are deeply indebted to you. You are our saviors; but about religion, we have our own Untouchable religious leaders, you know, and they would not be happy if we became Christians. To tell the truth, we have changed our mind about becoming Christians."

Some years after this the London Missionary Society withdrew from Mirzapur and turned the station over to the Bible Churchman's Missionary Society, which was still working there in 1960. Thus two missionary societies carried on work in that ancient city for more than a hundred years, and at the end of a century of work the congregation in Mirzapur was still a "gathered-colony church" of about two hundred, many of them employed by the Church (which used to be called the mission).

Had the decisive act been allowed, indeed encouraged, Mirzapur, like hundreds of Indian towns, might today be the headquarters of a Church numbering thousands, living in their ancestral homes in a hundred towns and villages round about. Such a Church would have continued whether the mission remained or not. If McMillan, Ashland, and Grant had allowed this numerous caste to opt for Christ, had fed the catechumens on the Word, and shepherded them in the Way, Mirzapur might have proved to be "the seedbed of a rich harvest." Church growth often depends on harvesting fields when they are ripe.

COMPARATIVE STUDY OF GROWTH ACROSS THE CHURCHES

In these days, study of the growth of Churches other than our own is not merely possible but highly desirable. No one can afford to neglect the comparative study of church growth. It uncovers a rich vein of knowledge concerning how Churches grow, and increases understanding of God's purposes for His Church and the methods He is blessing to their increase.

The basic methodology for study of other Churches is the same as that used in studying one's own. Secure accurate figures for communicant membership and other pertinent data across the years. Refine the data to eliminate statistical errors and redefinitions. Make sure all figures are for the same geographical unit. Draw accurate graphs portraying growth histories. Dig out from histories, biographies, interviews, and reports the reasons for growth or decline shown in the graph for each denomination. More accurate findings are obtained if one gets figures for the separate homogeneous units in each Church. Check all thinking about church growth against the graphs.

Compare Churches growing in the same kind of population—not those in different kinds. Churches in African Moslem tribes cannot be fruitfully compared with those growing in African pagan tribes; but Churches and their assisting missions evangelizing animist tribesmen are quite comparable. If they are evangelizing sections of the same tribe, the comparison will be even more fruitful. This principle should always be observed, but within reason, for no two populations are ever exactly the same.

For example, Loren Noren's figures for the Churches at work in Hong Kong, cited in Chapter Five, show that during the fifties, Anglicans were growing at 90 per cent, Baptists at 120, and Lutherans of the Missouri Synod at 420 per cent (Noren, 1963:6). Before this interesting information can convey much church growth meaning, we shall have to know which of the many populations in Hong Kong each denomination was working with. Were Baptists working in one or several populations? Did Anglicans grow among the middle class while Lutherans grew among refugees? Mr. Noren does not say, but when his fine beginning is carried further, the information should be given. Only for Churches working in similar populations can significant comparisons be made.

Baptist and Mennonite Growth Compared

The following comparison of Baptist and Mennonite Churches growing in the Gara caste in Orissa, India, illustrates the value of such studies. The growth took place between 1900 and 1963. Most Garas (weavers and peasants) lived in Orissa, where Baptists worked (see the shaded area of the map).

FIGURE 9.1. MAP OF THE BAPTIST-MENNONITE GARA AREA

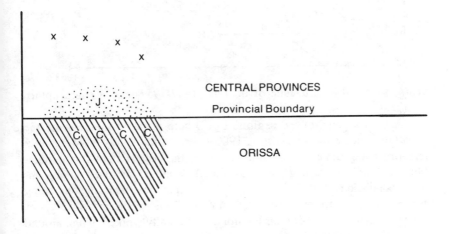

Garas also spilled over northward into Central Provinces, which was Mennonite territory. The Mennonite stations till 1924 were all in the northern part of their territory (at x x x). The Gara population was in the southern part, indicated by the dotted area. The Garas in Orissa spoke Ooriya and those in Central Provinces an Ooriya-oriented dialect of Hindi.

The following diagram portrays the growth history of each Church. Mennonite figures are from O. A. Waltner's careful study, Baptist figures from an unpublished research of my own. The Baptist line shows considerable growth till 1937, followed by a sharp decline, a ten-year plateau till 1953, and then vigorous growth for the next decade. The Mennonites did not start baptizing Garas till 1916. After nine years of small growth, they plateaued till 1935—see their line. Then they had good growth for a dozen

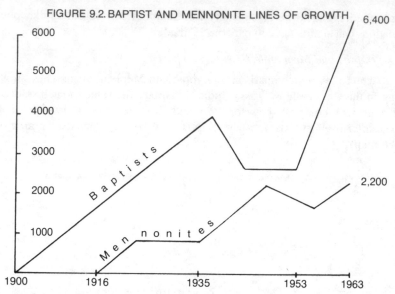

FIGURE 9.2. BAPTIST AND MENNONITE LINES OF GROWTH

years, followed by a decade of decline (1947-1957) and a slight upturn after that.

A brief account of the beginning will help readers to understand the situation. During the years from 1900 to 1916, the Garas in Mennonite territory living some twenty miles north of the nearest Baptist congregations (at CCC), knew that "we Garas are becoming Christians among our main populations to the south." But the Mennonites, their stations being forty miles away to the north, were not conscious of the receptive Garas in the southern section of their territory, so naturally worked in and around their stations, despite the fact that converts were being won there only in the smallest numbers.

In 1916 a Mennonite missionary, on a long swing south, preached from village to village in the dotted area, knowing nothing about the Garas. To his great surprise, he was sought out by a Baptist Gara, Gopal by name, who had moved across the provincial boundary to live in Mennonite territory. Gopal beseeched the missionary to come and plant a church in his village where, he said, many wished to become Christians. The missionary acceded to his request, and a small movement of Garas to Christian faith began and grew to 746 communicants by 1924. It was arrested about that time and remained stationary during the next twelve years. Pickett, who visited this area in 1935, gave the following careful estimate of the reasons for the stoppage.

The causes leading to the arrest of this movement are so evident and so instructive . . . that we relate them not to assess blame, but to illuminate the process by which Churches grow and decline.

At the outset, as was but natural at that time, there was an almost total lack of understanding of how the Church in India has grown, i.e. of how people movements have been developed into vigorous Churches. In the reports of 1924-34 there is no reference whatever to the fact that all the growth had taken place in one caste. Garas are mentioned, but not as the great open door, nor as any more hopeful than the Gonds or the Agharias. No enumeration of the unconverted Garas was attempted. Indeed, because of the problems which the Gara converts brought with them into the Church, there was some tendency to regard these people as peculiarly difficult, and to question the value of more Garas in the Church. An able and vigorous evangelistic program was carried out but on an intercaste basis. The unit to be approached was the village, not a given caste. The sociological organism of the tribe or caste was believed to be of little importance in the jungle territory around Basna, a mistake often made by missions. Church evangelistic campaigns sent Christians out to witness to all alike, rather than to the unconverted amongst their own relatives and former caste-fellows. To sum it up, the open door was not recognized and Christian forces flung themselves against the granite walls.

The second cause for stoppage was the sudden change of regime. In the beginning the mission policy was one of granting generous privileges to Christians, of treating new Christians in the same way as the older central station communities. Liberal aids to the education of the children and economic assistance of various sorts seemed reasonable. At the time of baptism a new sari or dhoti or a few annas were given to the convert. This policy was definitely altered in 1924 and many privileges were cut off. A goal was attempted which made for self-confidence and initiative. No transportation of children going to boarding school at Janjgir 60 miles away and at Mohidih 32 miles away was given. No Christmas gifts were given to employees. The change from one basis to the other is always difficult. In Basna it helped to stop growth.

Third, when a station was established at Jagdishpur in 1924 (see J on map) a large building program was necessary. Abundant work was provided for Christians. Poorer Christians moved to Jagdishpur and settled there. Although the larger number of the Christians stayed in the villages and was not directly affected by the building program, nevertheless when . . . building work ceased, Christians in and near Jagdishpur tended to feel themselves ill treated and pressure fell on the missionaries, who despite a policy which leaned the other way, felt that they really ought to do something to lift the economic status of the Christian community. A village school and dispensary were started. A "Weavers Association" was formed . . . to buy yarn and sell cloth cooperatively. This took considerable time and attention. Jagdishpur and the nearby villages became a typical mission station with the bulk of the effort being inevitably spent on the Christian community. This care (medical, educational, and economic) tended to transform the Christians into people who considered themselves the beneficiaries of the mission and to transform the mission into an organization which considered its primary function that of caring for Christians (Pickett, 1956:29f.).

Time will not permit a detailed understanding of the other movements of each Church, though these are replete with lessons. It must suffice to observe one remarkable fact which the comparative study brings out, and four lessons taught by this instance of church growth.

When we compare the two lines on the diagram, we cannot help noticing that when the Baptists were growing the Mennonites were standing still, and when the Baptists were standing still or declining, the Mennonites were growing. In three different periods this opposite movement can be seen. What shall we make of this?

First, the lines of growth in the diagram prove that the Garas were basically receptive during the entire sixty-year period. The Church was growing somewhere in their midst. They did not constitute a resistant population which steadily rejected Christ. They were winnable. In some decades they were highly winnable.

Second, when the Churches and missions did what plants churches, they were granted good growth. This is the meaning of the repeated upward turns of the lines. Anyone who worked in ways which multiplied churches, saw the Church extended. Pickett's visit in 1935 and his report, first published in 1936, helped the Mennonites to start a new surge of growth (see the diagram). In 1952 the Baptists and Disciples of Christ formed an alliance, what would today be called Joint Action for Mission, to multiply churches among the Garas. They sent in additional missionaries, and evangelized and educated *with the purpose of planting churches*. As a result, the Church doubled in the next ten years.

Third, the Gara people movements did not come with irresistible force. The winnable people did not batter down the doors of Zion. Their receptivity was mild and their growth was rather easily stopped by what the Churches and missions did or did not do. When the Christians' zeal flagged, internal frictions developed in the Church, attention focused not on church planting but on station building, persecution befell the Church, funds for evangelistic touring diminished, or perfecting took precedence over discipling, then growth faltered.

Fourth, neither mission claimed the Garas for Christ and made discipling them its main undertaking. "The Gara work" was a minor enterprise of the Orissa Baptists and the Central Provinces Mennonites. They did not see its importance. It constantly suffered by being compared with the "more rewarding" institutional work at the main mission stations. As a result, in 1963 the Christian Garas in both Churches numbered about

16,000 (total community) out of a Gara population of about 500,000. One thanks God for these two small Churches, but wonders what might have been the outcome had both missions counted this receptive people as a pearl of great price, and during the entire sixty years single-mindedly done those things that multiply churches.

Useful Information Uncovered by Comparative Study

Two very useful findings result from comparative study. First, churchmen form objective judgments about the responsiveness of populations. Estimates of responsiveness are of crucial importance to church planters. If the population to which God sends a missionary is stony hard, then the missionary should properly do those things which will enable him to hang on, bearing whatever limited witness he can. If the population is warmly responsive, it is sinful merely to hang on. His task is to disciple.

How does one know whether a population is responsive? Eventually measurements may be worked out which will tell in advance how ready for new things a given population is. The science of anthropology has learned much about societal conditions in which men are restless for change. The experience of the Church indicates that immigrants in a new country, migrants to a city, societies suffering from deprivation or shock, and the oppressed, hear and obey the Gospel more readily than contented beneficiaries of the social order.

But the surest and simplest way to know whether a population is responsive is to observe whether others working in it are enjoying church growth. Has God blessed the labors of any mission here to the growth of His Church? If so, the population in which that mission labored is responsive. In the last century Bishop Thoburn of India, observing that Baptist, Lutheran, and Anglican Churches were growing greatly from among the Untouchables, advised Methodists as he traveled among them on his episcopal duties to pay special attention to these victims of the Hindu social order. The subsequent growth of Methodist churches in several provinces of India is directly traceable to Thoburn's correct observation that the Untouchables were responsive.

To be sure, when a segment of society is large, there is no guarantee that all parts of it will be equally responsive. Degrees of responsiveness vary. For example, among the four million Hispanic immigrants to California, those recently arrived are much more responsive than those whose grandparents came here seventy years ago.

Second, comparative study tells missions what methods God is blessing to the increase of His Church. One does not have to guess. Finding a denomination or even a cluster of congregations which is growing, one observes what churchmen there are doing. Theorizing about causes of church growth can be eliminated. Estimates of what ought to work can be dismissed. One can see what has been done and measure the degree of growth which has followed.

Let it be noted that comparative study—not careless observation— reveals fruitful procedures. Some churchmen have superficial opinions, based on ignorance and denominational prejudice, about why other Churches have grown. Two churchmen in Africa were discussing a Church which had come within sixty years to number 300,000. The one who had not studied its congregations readily expressed the opinion that the wealthy mission assisting the Church, through its cooperative credit societies and liberal school policies, had "bought" Christians on a large scale. The other one, who had visited the field in question, was sure that there was much more to the long-continued growth.

Dr. Kessler in his fine study of the Protestant Churches in Chile and Peru feels that the great growth of the Adventists in Peru is in large part due to their excellent program of indoctrination of catechumens and second- and third-generation Christians (Kessler, 1967:225). Dr. Herbert Money, noted authority on Peru, agrees with him.

Many missionaries, deterred by honest reservations about the soundness of Adventist theology, might hesitate to seek growth "in the Adventist way"; but if Dr. Kessler and Dr. Money are right, and Adventist growth in Peru can be credited in large part to effective teaching of what they consider essential to salvation, why could not any Christian, copying this part of the Adventist program, *teach effectively* what *he* considered essential to salvation? It will be found that, contrary to the presuppositions of many, some causes of growth are nontheological. Anyone can use them.

Learning from others across denominational barriers is important. Consider an illustration from the Pentecostal family of Churches, whose rapid growth in Brazil and Chile has startled and encouraged the missionary world. Pentecostal growth in Latin America is complex, and many factors are involved. A missionary researcher after years of study voiced the opinion that the Pentecostals by their marchings, witnessing, praying aloud, giving testimonies in church, telling what God has done for them, gathering in large numbers, speaking in tongues, pressing into buses by the hundreds, preaching on street corners, and defying the customs of the traditional Churches are helping Christians of the "masses" to overcome their feelings of inferiority. These activities give them a taste of victory in the moral and spiritual realm. "We are sons of God. Christ has redeemed

us. We can act like men. We have rights. We can forgive our enemies. We
are freed of our sins. Praise the Lord.''

No doubt these activities are a major factor in Pentecostal growth and
would operate anywhere among victims of the social order. By contrast,
quiet, respectable congregations of traditional Protestant Churches, where
the minister, a professional, does most of the speaking, praying, and witnessing, are much less able to dissipate the social inheritance of inferiority
and the inborn conviction that ''we are little people.''

Except for speaking in tongues, none of the activities listed above runs
counter to the convictions of most Protestants. Any vital Spirit-filled Church
could use this whole gamut of activities. It would not be easy to graft
them onto the frigid procedures common to North American churches, but
no biblical or theological doctrine forbids doing so. If leaders of other
Churches can use activities like these, they can also copy effective ways
of creating a ministry, emphasizing house churches, following a kinship
web with the Gospel, and practice other methods which Pentecostals have
used to good effect.

The Nub of the Matter

Protestant diversity in all six continents constitutes a rich source of
insight. The hundreds of different missions and thousands of different
homogeneous unit Churches are in reality God's vast laboratory, in which
a man with eyes can see numerous experiments in church growth going
on. Some procedures are accompanied by no growth. Others multiply cells
of Christians under certain conditions. Still others propagate the Gospel
very satisfactorily. The churchman should train himself to see the many
different varieties of growth and the many factors which play a significant
part in each. Then he should resolutely seek for the people whom God
has prepared, and use those methods of proclaiming and persuading on
which God has put His seal of approval.

10

REVIVAL AND CHURCH GROWTH

WHAT IS REVIVAL?

REVIVAL BEARS a close relationship to church growth; yet exactly what that relationship is, particularly where the Church is growing on new ground, is often not clear. Under certain conditions revival may be said to cause growth. Under others, its relationship to church growth is so distant that apparently revival occurs without growth and growth without revival. Careful consideration of the subject is necessary if we are to understand the function of each in God's purpose of redemption.

To begin with, revival is a word used in many connotations. To the ignorant it signifies an unfortunate trait of frontier life and lower-class denominations. Some, who understand reality chiefly through their intellects, think of it as an emotional orgy stirred up by a professional, which creates an illusion of spiritual well-being and leaves congregations much as they were before. Social action partisans tend to feel that revivals are the antithesis of responsible Christian conduct. To many, the word means merely large accessions to the Church, or a period of increased interest in religion. Whenever large numbers are converted, they would say that a "revival" has occurred. To most Christians a revival means primarily purifying and vitalizing the existing Church. For certain thoughtful historians, it is God's best means for vivifying His Church and carrying out His program of justice, mercy, and world evangelization.

186

Orr's Definition

No man knows more about revivals or has studied them across the world and written more extensively about them than J. Edwin Orr. His first and best-known books are *The Second Evangelical Awakening in Britain* (1949) and *The Second Evangelical Awakening in America* (1953). He is now writing histories of revivals in Asia, Africa, and other lands. He equates revivals with evangelical awakenings and defines the latter as follows:

An Evangelical Awakening is a movement of the Holy Spirit in the Church of Christ bringing about a revival of New Testament Christianity. Such an awakening may change in a significant way an individual only; or it may affect a larger group of people; or it may move a congregation, or the churches of a city or district, or the whole body of believers throughout a country or continent; or indeed the larger body of believers throughout the world. Such an awakening may run its course briefly, or it may last a whole lifetime. Such Awakenings come about in various ways, but there is a pattern which is common to all.

The main effect of an Evangelical Awakening is always the repetition of the phenomena of the Acts of the Apostles, which narrative gives a simple account of an Evangelical Awakening, one that revived believers, then converted sinners to God.

An Evangelical Awakening may be said to effect the revitalization of the lives of nominal Christians, and the bringing of outsiders into vital touch with the divine dynamic causing every such Awakening—the Spirit of God. The surest evidence of the divine origin of any such quickening is its presentation of the evangelical message declared in the New Testament and its reenactment of the phenomena evidenced in the same Sacred Literature. . . .

A student of Church History in general and of the Great Awakening in particular must surely be impressed with the remarkable continuity of doctrine as well as the continuity of action. Any one could begin reading the story of the Gospels, continue on into the narrative of the Acts of the Apostles, and then without any sense of interruption begin reading the story of Wycliffe's preachers, or the Covenanters, or Wesleyan circuit riders, or Hans Nielson Hauge in Norway, or Judson in Burma. It is the same kind of Christianity.

Not only so, but the student of such movements would find in the preaching of the Awakenings and Revivals the same message preached and the same doctrines taught in the days of the apostles. Non-evangelical Christianity, with its accretions of dogma and use of worldly power, would seem to be a system utterly alien to that of the Church of the Apostles, resembling much more the forces both ecclesiastical and secular that opposed New Testament Christianity.

The reader of the Acts of the Apostles must surely notice that the Church began to spread by extraordinary praying and preaching. So too the "upper room" type of praying and pentecostal sort of preaching together with the irrepressible kind of personal witness find their place in the Great Awakenings rather than in less evangelical patterns (Orr, 1965:265-66).

Prayer Brings Revival

While "an Evangelical Awakening is a movement of the Holy Spirit in the Church of Christ" and thus depends on the initiative of Almighty God, it is usually granted to those who pray earnestly for it. In hundreds of instances, prayer has brought revival. The pattern is the same: first intense prayer, often long continued, then revival. Three typical quotations will suffice to illustrate the point.

> Early in the year 1858 the wave of revival (which originated in the east) passed over the crest of the Appalachian system of mountains and poured down the Ohio Valley following the line of settlements established by the pioneers. . . . Union prayer meetings were soon launched in Kentucky's big city [Louisville], secular journalists observing that the meetings were growing so that it was impossible for the Y.M.C.A. premises to accommodate the crowds. . . . In early April, four popular prayer meetings attracted the crowds to the Masonic Temple, the Mechanics Library, the Key Engine House, and the Relief Engine House. A reporter on April 5th stated that "an immense concourse" had entirely filled the Masonic Temple. . . . Revival had already commenced in Lexington, Covington, Frankfort, and other towns throughout the state. . . .

> . . . In Cincinnati, attendance at the daily prayer meeting became so large that the venue chosen was unable to accommodate the crowds. . . . In Cleveland, in population forty thousand, the attendance at the early morning prayer meetings throughout the city churches was two thousand. . . . Noonday prayer meetings were begun in Indianapolis. . . .

> There was a striking instance of the power of prayer in Kalamazoo in Michigan. Episcopalians, Baptists, Methodists, Presbyterians, and Congregationalists united in announcing a prayer meeting. The ecumenical effort was begun in fear and trembling, and many wondered if the public would consider attending.

> At the very first meeting a request was read: "A praying wife requests the prayers of this meeting for her unconverted husband." All at once a burly man arose and said, "I am that man; I have a praying wife, and this request must be for me. I want you to pray for me!"

> As soon as he was seated, another man arose, ignoring his predecessor, to say with tears: "I am that man; I have a praying wife. She prays for me. And now she asks you to pray for me. I am sure I am that man. I want you to pray for me!"

> Five other convicted husbands requested prayer and a spirit of conviction moved that assembly. Before long there were between four and five hundred conversions in the town (Orr, 1965:119ff.).

Prayer for revival is no mere American phenomenon. All through the British Isles on numerous occasions prayer has brought revival. I present but one illustration, and that from staid Scotland.

In the middle of August 1859, the Revival became news in Glasgow with all the suddenness of a summer thunderstorm. . . . The *Scottish Guardian* of 2nd August 1959 claimed that:

The Holy Spirit has been manifesting his gracious power in a remarkable manner in this neighborhood during the last few days. Our readers are aware that ever since the news of the Great Revival in America reached Scotland, prayer meetings for the special purpose of imploring a similar blessing have been held in Glasgow as well as in other places. The intelligence which has reached us recently leaves no room to doubt that these prayers have been heard. . . .

The noon prayer meetings gave rise to prayer meetings and preaching services in the various evangelical churches on week nights, and in these meetings there were scores of reported conversions. After a year of the movement, Glasgow was still enjoying "times of refreshing" (Orr, 1965:134).

Prayer for revival is the essential first step not only in Eurica but also in Africasia. Time would fail were examples from country after country to be presented. Two quotations from Goforth relating events of the great revival of 1907 in Korea effectively state the case for revival everywhere.

It paid well to have spent several months in prayer, for when God the Holy Spirit came, He accomplished more in half a day than all of us missionaries could have accomplished in half a year. In less than two months more than two thousand heathen were converted. It is always so as soon as God gets first place; but, as a rule, the Church which professes to be Christ's, will not cease her busy round of activities and give God a chance by waiting on Him in prayer.

A Bible colporteur from Kang Kai among the pine forests along the Yalu (who heard Dr. Howard Agnew Johnston tell how the Holy Spirit was poured out upon the Kassians in India) went home and told the Kang Kai church of 250 believers that the Holy Spirit alone could make effective the finished work of the Lord Jesus Christ, and that He was promised them as freely as any other gift from God. The church members honored God and appreciated the gift of the Holy Spirit by meeting in the church for prayer at five o'clock— not five o'clock every evening but every morning—through the fall and winter of 1906-7. They honored God by six months of prayer; and *then He came as a flood.* Since then their numbers have increased manyfold. Do we really believe in God the Holy Spirit? Let us be honest. Not to the extent of getting up at five o'clock through six months of cold weather to seek Him (Goforth, 1943:12,16).

Revival is God's gift. Man can neither command it nor make God grant it. God sovereignly gives revival when and where He wills. It "breaks out," "strikes," "quickens a church," "comes with the suddenness of a summer storm," "makes its appearance," "inaugurates a work of grace," and "blesses His people." But God responds to sincere continued prayer.

Prayer is what God wants His people to offer. "Ask and ye shall receive, seek and ye shall find, knock and it shall be opened to you."

Feeding on God's Word Is a Precondition of Revival

Knowledge of the Bible is necessary. It does not invariably lead to revival; but unless it is there, revival in the classic sense does not occur. Revivals in the Churches of Europe and America were preceded by long years of careful reading of the Bible in homes and churches. The Korean revival owed much of its power to the thorough Bible study which formed an integral part of the Presbyterian Church's regimen from the days of its inception in 1895. Elder Keel, whose story is related in the next paragraph, would not have known that he was Achan, nor would the congregation have felt the impact of his confession, if both had not been familiar with the biblical account. The God of righteousness and love, prayer for revival, ethical heights reached by the revived, concern to share salvation with those for whom Christ died, reality of the Holy Spirit, and many other aspects of Christian revival would be impossible without knowledge of the Christian Scriptures.

Revival Leads to Holy Living

Though it is often accompanied by powerful emotions—trembling, weeping, agonizing prayer, and feelings of great joy and peace—revival is no mere emotional binge. It is restoration of New Testament Christianity. Humility, "brokenness," and yielding of self to God our righteous heavenly Father result in confession of sin and restitution to those sinned against. An Evangelical Awakening results in holy living. The following from Korea is a typical happening in revivals.

It had now come to the first week of January 1907. All expected that God would signally bless them during the week of universal prayer. But they came to the last day, the eighth day, and yet there was no special manifestation of the power of God. That Sabbath evening about fifteen hundred people were assembled in the Central Presbyterian Church. The heavens over them seemed as brass. Was it possible that God was going to deny them the prayed for outpouring? Then all were startled as Elder Keel, the leading man in the church, stood up and said, "I am Achan. God cannot bless because of me. About a year ago a friend of mine, when dying, called me to his house and said, 'Elder, I am about to pass away; I want you to manage my affairs; my wife is unable,' I said 'Rest your heart; I will do it.' I did manage that widow's estate, but I managed to put one hundred dollars into my own pocket. I have hindered God, I am going to give that one hundred dollars back to that widow tomorrow morning."

Instantly it was realized that the barriers had fallen, and that God, the

Holy One, had come. Conviction of sin swept the audience. The service commenced at seven o'clock Sunday evening and did not end until two o'clock Monday morning, yet during all that time dozens were standing, weeping, awaiting their turn to confess. Day after day the people assembled now, and always it was manifest that the Refiner was in His temple. . . . [Sin] hindered the Almighty God while it remained covered and it glorified Him as soon as it was uncovered; and so with rare emotions did all the confessions in Korea that year (Goforth, 1943:8).

Confession and restitution is sometimes the key to revival, sometimes the result of it. Often the first initiative seems to rest with man. Until Elder Keel determined to confess his sin, "the heavens seemed as brass." But when revival comes and the Holy Spirit is outpoured, then conviction of sin sweeps the audience and men and women accomplish what, of themselves, they would be powerless even to attempt.

Revival Gives Tremendous Power

The supreme good of an Evangelical Awakening is that it gives tremendous power to do Christ's will. Thoroughly Christian conduct becomes practical for ordinary men when they earnestly seek and God graciously grants revival. When the Holy Spirit comes, He accomplishes the impossible in the lives of believers. Sins which a person hides as if his life depended on it are openly confessed and renounced. Evil habits of mind and body—covetousness, hate, lust, addiction to drink, idolatry, race prejudice—which had for years enslaved men are broken. The Holy Spirit gives new standards of justice and mercy to the revived, and they begin to advocate advanced social righteousness which may take a hundred years to become common practice in their nations. Thus have been born most social advances of Christendom.

Christ's will for the world covers all spheres, individual and corporate. Body, mind, and spirit; political, economic, social, and intellectual life; interpersonal, interracial, and international relationships; black, brown, yellow, and white races—Christ's will concerns all these. All of a Christian's activities in any of these spheres—worshiping, learning, working, playing, holy living, and evangelizing—have some relationship to the growth of His Church; but only evangelizing or mission intends to communicate Christ and multiply His churches. The intent of worship, for example, is to adore and glorify God; yet when unbelievers see Christians joyfully worshiping, some may—without the Christians intending conversion—be influenced to seek the Lord. One chief intent of holy living is to eradicate race hatred and establish brotherhood among all men; yet when unbelievers living among Christians experience heightened brotherhood, some may—

again without the Christians intending it—become disciples of Christ. We rejoice in these unplanned outcomes. However, since church growth is the chief intent only of mission and evangelism, I shall devote no further time here to those activities of the revived which issue in social righteousness, devotion to the Bible, and adoration of God. I must confine what follows to the remarkable power of the revived to preach the Gospel and give men, near and far, a chance to share in the glorious new life.

Revival Drives Men to Proclaim the Gospel

Revival implants Christ's Spirit in men and forthwith they, like their Master, make bringing salvation to men a chief purpose of their lives. A holy anxiety that their neighbors and loved ones share the redeeming power of the Gospel seizes the revived. Like those indwelt at Pentecost, they go everywhere preaching the Word. They seek to win men to Christ. The good life they now enjoy they ardently wish others to experience.

A missionary in Manchuria sent two evangelists to Ping Yang, Korea, to find out all about the revival. When they returned he asked if the missionaries had opened many street chapels. The evangelist replied, "None at all. They do not need them because every Christian is a street chapel." Christian workmen have been known to spend a summer in a country where there were no Christians in order to evangelize it. Merchants as they travel from place to place are always telling the wonderful story. A hat merchant, converted in a revival on the east coast, when we were there, had within a year afterwards started up little Christian communities in about a dozen places. . . . A student spent a month's holiday in an unevangelized district and won a hundred souls for God. Another resolved to speak each day to at least six persons about their soul's salvation. At the end of nine months he had spoken to three thousand (Goforth, 1943:24).

[In the United States] the last decade before the turn of the [nineteenth] century began in discouragement. Bishop Madison in the diocese of Virginia, shared the conviction of Chief Justice Marshall, a devout layman, that the church was too far gone ever to be revived. Bishop Provost of New York felt that the situation was hopeless and simply ceased functioning. . . . Colleges in the longest settled parts of the country were hotbeds of infidelity and immorality. Interest in things spiritual had ebbed away. When the tide turned, it did so imperceptibly at first in scarcely noticeable gatherings of just a handful of students for prayer. . . .

[At Yale College] in 1802, however, one-third of the total student body made public profession of conversion in a revival that moved the halls of ivy. In succeeding years, the student revivals at Yale were repeated.

On a summer afternoon in 1806, five students of Williams College were driven from a grove of maples where they were accustomed to meet for prayer. They sheltered from the thunderstorm under a haystack, and there prayed about a plan to reach the unevangelized heathen for Christ. . . . Out of the Haystack compact grew the whole modern American missionary movement.

Revivals of religion followed in Andover, Princeton, Washington, and Amherst and other university colleges, producing not only the modern American missionary movement but a generation of evangelistic ministers to serve the opening western states. . . . The spread of infidelity was effectively halted and out of the movement came not only the home and foreign missionary societies, but also the foundation of numerous academies and colleges, theological seminaries, religious societies, and philanthropic organizations (Orr, 1965:22f.).

In summary we may say that when, driven by their own powerlessness, men turn to God and devote themselves to prayer, He pours out the Holy Spirit on them. Filled with the Holy Spirit, men sometimes experience feelings of great joy and exaltation. Sometimes the chief effect appears to be in mind and conscience. Without emotional accompaniments, the revived dedicate themselves to *be* Christ's people and *do* His will. The gift of the Holy Spirit enables men to confess sin, make restitution, break evil habits, lead victorious lives, persuade others of the available Power, bring multitudes to Christ and cause the Church to grow mightily.

WHAT DOES REVIVAL MEAN TO CHURCH GROWTH IN AFERICASIA?

Church growth in Africasia is different from that in Eurica. Revival in Eurica means the growth of the Church from among highly individualized populations which consider themselves, not Confucians, Marxists, Hindus, or animists, but Christians. They may not be members of any Church, but their parents, grandparents, and uncles or aunts were. Most of them "have a church preference" and perhaps send their children to Sunday School. In Africasia, however, to obtain church growth of any kind, adherents of a non-Christian religion, complete with cult, priests, and often scriptures and temples, must renounce their ancestral religion and accept Christ and His cult, priests, scriptures, and church buildings. Furthermore, populations are not highly individualized, but group conscious. Individuals seldom act alone, and do so with difficulty.

To call ingathering in both areas of the world "revival" prevents understanding. To make possible clear thought we must distinguish between the various kinds of growth which the Churches in Africasia are experiencing. Otherwise those seeking to propagate the Christian faith there will use unmodified Eurican techniques and prove themselves poor harvesters of ripe fields. The evidence demands certain distinctions.

In Africasia Revivals Occur After Populations Become Christian

By the very structure of the word, revival means revivification of an existing Church or existing Christians. There must first be tired believers before they can be revived. All accounts tell of cold, indifferent, or sinful congregations which, by revival, are kindled to new consecration. For instance, the American colleges in which revival took place were founded by Churches and manned chiefly by minister-teachers. The president of the college was almost always a minister. Students were frequently sons of church members, and the little bands who gathered to pray were composed of Christians. In Europe the Irish, Welsh, Norwegians, and others whose revivals have been recounted were mostly baptized persons. Such as were not would nevertheless have called themselves Christians rather than pagans. As Orr says, "It can be clearly demonstrated that great numbers of actual church members are professedly converted in every Revival movement" (Orr, 1964:51).

In the Fiji Islands, where practically all the original population became Christians in a series of people movements, the early missionaries distinguished two stages in Christian growth. In the first—a most meaningful stage which cost many converts their lives—whole communities declared for Christ, destroyed their fetishes, were instructed and baptized, built churches, heard the Bible several times a week, learned hymns and Scripture portions, and sent their children to Christian schools. After several years of this, deeper consecration became possible and the second stage began. Revivals broke out in the churches. Old cannibals who had been Christian for some time broke down and wept bitterly at the thought of their sinful, cruel, and fear-ridden lives. They had been nourished on the Bible for years and had learned how to pray; a revival which lifted the churches to new heights became possible. Revival generally takes place in existing churches.

The Ruanda revival brought great blessing to East Africa. It took place some sixty years after Uganda was discipled and about thirty years after Ruanda tribesmen became Christian. "Multitudes of pagans becoming Christian long ago" was not revival. Revival came in a Christianized body of people.

It is essential to avoid calling every turning to Christ, every ingathering, and every accession to the Church a revival. If the significant meaning of the word—vitalizing an existing Church—is to be preserved, it must not be used for the original turnings of non-Christians to Christ. And indeed, these disciplings seldom partake of the nature of revival. Non-Christians do not ardently pray God to revive them. They do not have the biblical background to make dedication result in ethical conduct. The Holy Spirit certainly moves them, but He moves them to take the steps which at that time are most essential to them—to renounce all other gods, believe on Jesus Christ as Savior, and accept the Bible as sole Scripture. Once these fundamental steps have been taken and converts have been baptized and organized into churches, other advances will follow as the day the night.

Discipling (D1) on New Ground Is Not "Revival"

The revival I have been describing has a distinct pattern.

1. Prolonged exposure to the Bible and knowledge of its teachings;

2. Persistent prayer for revival on the part of a group or congregation whose members are in kin-contact with a generally Christian population;

3. Descent of the Holy Spirit on that group or congregation;

4. Confession of sin and restitution in open meeting under circumstances where these acts can be seen and known by many nominal Christians and unbelieving relatives and friends;

5. Vital, convincing witness and consequent inflooding of converts from among the homogeneous unit of which the Christians are an integral part.

In contrast with these, conversion on new ground follows radically different patterns, of which we will describe three.

1. The very first spread of the Gospel in a new non-Christian population frequently brings individuals one by one, against the will of their kindred, into conglomerate congregation at or near the mission station. The congregation consists of rescued persons and orphans, converted schoolboys and girls, and an occasional adult convert. All these are uniquely dependent on the churchmen, missionaries, and teachers at the station for spiritual guidance and schooling. Sometimes, in addition, they depend on them for food, clothing, and shelter. Laborious formation of such congregations over a period of several decades is a far cry from revived persons winning multitudes of their fellows to Christ; but it is often a prerequisite. It painstakingly gathers Christians who will later be revived.

2. The spread of the Gospel on new ground frequently occurs through people movements to Christ. The causes, nature, and cultivation of this important means of communicating Christ will be taken up in a later chapter. Here it is sufficient to point out that, though these are often called revivals, since they involve the turning of multitudes of non-Christians to Christ, they *should not be*.

People movements have some superficial resemblance to revivals. They bring in large numbers. Converts are enthusiastic Christians with deep conviction of the truth of Christianity and the benefits of becoming Christian. They seek out relatives and friends (within their own homogeneous unit) and persuade them to become Christians. They receive Bible teaching and, though often illiterate, learn the key stories of the drama of salvation and commit to memory sections of Scripture such as the Ten Commandments and the Lord's Prayer. They are usually not baptized till they pass an examination proving that they grasp a minimum of Christian truth.

Yet people movements have great dissimilarities to revivals. They begin on their own timetable. Unlike European revivals, they are not triggered by news of revivals in other lands. Among the means God uses to ripen a given population, news of distant revivals plays a minor part. Local cultural influences of all sorts—dissatisfactions, wars, oppression, deprivation, shock, hostility, erosion of belief in the old gods, and a thousand others—bring a given population into a condition where it can "hear" the Good News. Information that whites in Baltimore, Edinburgh, or Stockholm are being greatly blessed by God does not affect them in the least. Since they care nothing for what another caste or tribe of their own color a hundred miles away is doing, why should they care what whites on the other side of the globe are doing?

But, it will be protested, did not the revival in Wales trigger that in the Khassi Hills in Assam? And did not news of the Khassi Hills ingathering set off the great Korean revival?

To understand what happened, one must recognize that in 1905 hundreds of bands of missionaries were working in thousands of populations. It is a safe assumption that most missionaries heard about the Wales revival and many besought the Lord to grant them similar blessing and power. In the Khassi Hills and Korea (and a few other places) God had ripened populations. In *them*, when the missionaries and congregations they had raised up heard the news from Wales and asked God's blessing and turned single-mindedly to reaping, great church growth followed. We hear about such instances. But in hundreds of mission stations whose populations were not ripe, the news of distant Wales did not lead to ingathering. We do not hear about these. News of revivals activates church leaders. It does not and cannot activate non-Christians who are not in kin-contact with Christians.

Eurican revivals operate in nontribal societies, which are not split up into language and caste and race units. They spread throughout a city or a country. In Africasia each people movement spreads almost exclusively among its own folk. For example, a Yoruba people movement of great power brought tens of thousands of Yorubas in Nigeria to Christ, but it left the Egons west of Badagri solidly pagan. Much later, in the early 1950's a people movement started among the Egons.

Eurican revivals seem good to the substantial Christians of the land. Leading businessmen and professionals are pleased to hear of revivals, which are often favorably reported by the secular press. New Christians are seldom persecuted, nor do they feel they are leaving their own folk or doing something unpatriotic. People movements in Africasia, on the contrary, often experience great hostility and active persecution.

Literate Protestants when "revived" or converted join existing churches or are assisted to establish new congregations in which there are multitudes of former Christians. In Africasia, on the other hand, as the Church advances on new ground by way of a people movement involving illiterate Moslems, Hindus, Animists, or Buddhists, there are few existing churches to join. Most church growth means planting new congregations in new populations.

All of these factors and many others—language, culture, economic status, inevitable tension between missionaries of one land and Christians of another, idolatrous festivals, drunken fiestas—make people movements so different from classic Christian revivals that it is misleading and really confusing to Christian thought to use the same word for both.

The complex nature of the subject is indicated by the fact that, while a people movement as such should not be called a revival, it establishes churches which are parts of a world-wide fellowship. These can be influenced by accounts of revival in other lands and, when in kin-contact with unconverted relatives, can start new people movements. The colporteur from Kang Kai mentioned earlier is a case in point. When he heard from Mr. Johnston about the Khassi Hills revival, he went back and told his church of 250 members along the Yalu in North Korea. Those members prayed for six months for revival and then, when the Spirit came like a flood, went out to win their relatives and friends. Yet even here, Dr. Goforth's concise account oversimplifies what really happened. The congregation of 250 had reached that size in a very short time in the vital, expanding people movement of Ping Yang province. Before the special six months of prayer, it was already praying and growing and winning its relatives and friends. The news from the Khassi Hills simply nudged it along in the direction it was already traveling.

3. "Web movements" to Christ (that is, movements through extensive family or class relationships) are common in Latin America, where great numbers of unshepherded Roman Catholics hear the Gospel, read the Bible, and come to Christian faith. The Evangelical position has a self-

authenticating quality among Roman Catholics. Evangelicals do without circumlocution what the Bible says. This appeals to Roman Catholics. Simple reading of the Scriptures has led many to the biblical faith. Faith has flowed along kin lines. Extended families, compadres and comadres (god-parents) have been converted. There is no tribalism among the Spanish- and Portuguese-speaking multitudes in Latin America, but there are close family ties. There is also the powerful opposition of the Church of Rome—though this is diminishing as she gradually comes to recognize the validity of Evangelical Churches. All this, while bringing many to Christ and causing church growth, is very different from Eurican revival.

In the big cities of Latin America, however, revival is beginning to occur and will no doubt occur more and more frequently. Churchmen in Latin America should study Eurican revivals, work and pray for them, and learn how to modify them for Latin America and extend them. If members of existing congregations are in living kin-contact with thousands of their own folk, and congregations are revived in the classic sense, the biblical faith will spread among their relatives and friends.

Revivals, conglomerate congregations, people movements, and web movements to Christ are all the doing of God. So is any conversion whatsoever. Men cannot make the Church grow—only God's Holy Spirit can do that. I am not trying, here, to contrast a godly manner of church growth—revivals—with men's ways. I want to emphasize, rather, that revivals among Christians are one specific kind of church growth, while the various patterns by which the Church grows among non-Christian populations are other kinds. All are brought about by the Holy Spirit.

Revival in Mission-Station Churches

Most mission stations are manned by dedicated churchmen who are frequently in prayer and are frequently revived. Weekly prayer meetings of church leaders and missionaries, periodic special meetings for deepening the spiritual life, carefully planned annual and other meetings where leaders from several areas gather, much private prayer, and many retreats mark the normal life of the mission station. Yet frequently little church growth is seen.

It will be argued that, while there is some prayer, in view of the difficulties between younger Churches and missions and the friction between missionary and missionary, and between nationals and missionaries, there should be *much more*. Pride, ambition, selfishness, and laziness afflict all men, including missionaries and churchmen. If there were only *enough* consecration and prayer, it is said, God would grant His Holy

Spirit. He would solve all problems, and the Church would grow. What shall we say to this?

Two answers are called for. First, brokenness, humility, love, forgiveness, brotherhood, and justice are usually in short supply. The enabling presence of the Holy Spirit is desperately needed. Truly, He does more in a half-day than we can do in half a lifetime. No one can have too much of God's presence. If there were only more consecration and prayer, God would grant more revival. His resources are unlimited. Our petty expectations and failure to ask are commonly where the fault lies.

Second, in mission-station churches revival *in itself* often does not issue in growth. God's obedient servants need to learn much more about the condition under which revivals lead to victorious growth and then meet those conditions. Revivals frequently occur in sealed-off congregations, boarding schools, and orphanages. One can thank God for them, while recognizing that *by themselves in such circumstances,* they seldom lead to great growth in the outside world. The point is so important that I pause to illustrate it.

In 1935, in the Free Methodist Church in Yeotmal, India, the Holy Spirit came and a genuine revival took place. Sins were confessed and restitutions made. Cold, nominal Christians were reborn. In the warmth of Christ's love, old animosities were melted and old offenses forgiven. Relationships between missionaries and nationals became most cordial. The worship of God became sweeter and dearer, and prayer more natural and meaningful. A tremendous concern came on the congregation to tell others what God had done for them. They resolved to meet on the courthouse steps at five each evening (when several hundred government employees ended their day's work) to bear witness to the wonderful things God had done for them.

Since the Christians were mostly of low-caste origin and the judges, lawyers, and clerks in the courthouse were mostly high-caste people, to speak and sing there took courage; but God gave the Christians strength and the Holy Spirit told them what to say. Their testimony was well received. Lawyers, clerks, and judges went home impressed, to meditate on what they had heard, ponder the Gospel, and read the tracts they had bought. Some wished to know more about the Savior and thought longingly of the power available. But none became Christian and none joined the church. The social distance between them and the Christians was too great.

After some months, the revival died down and became a fragrant memory. Joy of sins forgiven, benefits of the holy life, good relationships between persons, and freedom from evil habits—these and other blessings continued in the Yeotmal congregation. Gradually the courthouse meetings were discontinued.

Yet Free Methodists say that all their later growth stemmed from that revival. The story is this. Two men who were revived broke out of the encircled church and started congregations on new ground. One, a Moslem convert of many years' standing, was an evangelist on mission salary. With the approval of the missionary in charge of evangelism, he started preaching from village to village, telling the story to high and low. He traveled barefoot and lived a life of great simplicity. In most places he was heard with courtesy. When interest flagged, he went to another village. Thus, wandering across the Yeotmal plains, he came to the town of Rajur, in one of whose wards lived a small community of immigrant Madigas from Hyderabad State, attracted there by employment in the mines. These knew that thousands upon thousands of their caste fellows in Hyderabad had become Christians. It may be that some of them had Christian relatives. They not only listened courteously, but declared for Christ and asked for baptism. After they became Christians, they evangelized their relatives in nearby towns. A number of small Madiga churches (groups, they were called) came into being.

The second man was a cook in a missionary's home, who came from an aboriginal tribe, the Pardhans. He carried the message to his relatives and some of them became Christians. Three little churches of his caste people were started.

Mahars are the laborers, the largest of the many depressed classes in the Yeotmal district, comprising about 10 per cent of the population. The revived Christian community and the Spirit-filled missionaries found themselves among a large, receptive Mahar population. Mahars were willing to talk favorably about becoming Christian, though for actually taking the final step they wanted to wait till Dr. Ambedkar (the greatest Mahar of all time) should lead them all out, for they intended to follow him. (He became a Buddhist shortly before he died, about 1956, and more than two million Mahars followed him into that faith.)

As the revived Church met the awakened Mahars, a few small Mahar churches were established in Free Methodist territory. It must be added that other missions in that area which had not been blessed by a revival in 1935 also won Mahars to the Christian faith, and perhaps a hundred village congregations of three or four families each dotted the plains of South Central Provinces, Berar, and East Maharashtra.

This instance of revival is replete with lessons concerning how churches grow Since the church at Yeotmal lacked kin-contact with unconverted thousands of her own folk, her truly revived members, despite glorious efforts among the upper-caste people at the courthouse and in the town, were unable to spread their faith. Marginal efforts of single individuals, however, did start a few little churches.

Would the outcome have been different if the revived had known more about how churches grow? Suppose, instead of going to the courthouse steps, they had fanned out all across the Yeotmal area, seeking receptive groups? Suppose they had concentrated on the Mahars? Suppose they had found *all* the Malas and Madigas who had moved north from Hyderabad— where hundreds of thousands of them had become Christians—and tirelessly told *them* of the wonderful things God had done "for us who like you are peoples of the lower castes"? Suppose they had concentrated missionaries and nationals on communicating new life to each Madiga hamlet as it came in—teaching each to read the Bible, pray for revival, and go out among its own folk to witness to its faith? Would the outcome have been different? One cannot say for certain, but since churches did arise when these receptive groups were discovered in groping, blindfold fashion, the answer should probably be Yes.

We cannot help but remember that our Lord sent His disciples specifically to the very receptive "lost sheep of the house of Israel," and that after the great revival at Pentecost, *under the leading of the Holy Spirit,* "they spake the word to none but [the receptive] Jews," and later to the receptive (John 4:35) Samaritans. The revived must see the hand of God creating receptive peoples and seek these out, if the divine purpose of revival in Africasia is to be achieved.

Seven Bearings of Revival on Church Growth

The dynamic of revival is so great and the potential for church growth so tremendous that all concerned with mission must be deeply interested in it. The more ministers and missionaries know about the growth of Africasian Churches, the better stewards of God's purposes in revival they will be. The same God brings both revival and great church growth. It must grieve Him when a revival in the midst of receptive peoples remains shut up among a few churches. He has given His people power, and they have not used it to reap the harvest He has ripened. With this in mind, I shall venture to set forth seven basic ways in which revival bears on church growth. These are not exhaustive but will, I hope, prove suggestive.

1. Revival in the Church can bring great ingathering if Christians are

in living kin-contact with a non-Christian population, provided that the spiritual power is channeled into witness with the purpose of winning to Christ. If activity is directed toward other members of the homogeneous unit in which the revival has broken out, greater growth will occur than if it is diverted to other peoples.

2. Revival in the Church brings growth when a constant stream of converts is flowing into her. It is many times more likely to lead to great growth in an already growing congregation than in a blocked church which is doing many good deeds in the non-Christian community.

3. Revivals in conglomerate congregations at towns have more chance of issuing in reproductive conversions outside the existing church if

    a. Individual churchmen have church growth eyes—that is, if they know which are the receptive units in their general population; which congregations are growing greatly and why; that group conversion is a valid form of conversion; and that the rich services rendered by Church and mission are no substitute for Christ.

    b. Individual churchmen carry out a consistent program over the years, single-mindedly dedicated to church growth. Mr. Krass of the Evangelical Presbyterian Church in northern Ghana is a splendid example. He turned from the sealed-off town churches to the deliberate proclamation of the Gospel to whole villages, expecting them to accept the Lord as units. Continuing this policy for several years, in 1968 he was well on the way to the discipling of the Chokosi tribe. One wonders why a hundred missionaries, using this program, are not sent to the Northern Territories in Ghana at once.

    c. Churches and missions form their policies in the light of whatever means the Holy Spirit has already used to multiply churches in their kind of societies.

4. Revivals within people movements and web movements have far more chance of issuing in great church growth if

    a. Focused on the winnable elements of their own population.

    b. Leaders from among the new converts are discovered and trained.

    c. As much biblical training as possible is given to entire congregations, as well as to leaders.

5. Revivals issue in church growth when leaders of revival are taught all now known about how God has brought about great ingatherings:

a. The various kinds of readiness and how to discover and serve them.

b. Right methods, which do not hinder the Holy Spirit and do not put a ceiling on church growth.

c. Known revivals which have led to great church growth.

d. The priorities in mission and church work which help or frustrate, respectively, the spread of churches throughout the world.

6. Revivals issue in church growth when revival is counted of great importance. If the choice has to be between revival and knowledge, Christians should choose revival.

7. Revivals issue in great church growth when *revival plus knowledge* is counted of even greater importance. Christians should learn all God has to teach us about church growth, and pray without ceasing for revival.

Revival is like a head of steam in a railway engine. Without it the engine remains motionless. With it, plus rails, pistons, water, oil, timetables, engineer, and other elements, the engine travels widely and fast. Great growth of the Church following revival will come where all the conditions are *right*. So right, in fact, that people are not conscious of them. This was the case at Pentecost, which is the prime example of the bearing of revival on church growth.

PART IV
THE SOCIOLOGICAL FOUNDATION

11

SOCIAL STRUCTURE
AND CHURCH GROWTH

S INCE CHURCH growth takes place in the multitudinous societies of mankind, essential to understanding it is an understanding of their structure. Men exist not as discrete individuals, but as interconnected members of some society. Innovation and social change, operating in particular structures, play a significant part in determining the direction, speed, and size of the move to the Christian religion. This is as true in America as in Asia or Africa.

The normal man is not an isolated unit but part of a whole which makes him what he is. For instance, the individual does not choose what language he will speak. The society in which he is born, the mother who nurses him, and the children with whom he plays determine it. Moreover, society either determines or strongly influences every aspect of what he says, thinks, and does. Consequently when we comprehend the social structure of a particular segment of the total population, we know better how churches are likely to increase and ramify through it.

SOME COMPONENTS OF SOCIAL STRUCTURE

Social structure is a broad reality comprising many factors, each of which has bearing on how the Church can reconcile men to God among

207

the three billion who have yet yielded no allegiance to Jesus Christ. A few typical elements of social structure will be considered.

The Unique Self-Image

Each society, finding itself in certain physical, economic, and political circumstances, develops a characteristic culture and self-image, as Ruth Benedict has pointed out, which makes it different from every other society. The physical base has much to do with this. All rice-planting societies which depend on hand labor share a complex of customs which arise from working barefoot in rice paddies. Since the culture of each society, however, is the combined outcome of many different forces—racial, military, religious, climatic, and other—rice planters in coastal valleys of Buddhist Japan will have a different self-image from Christian rice planters in the mountainous country between India and Burma.

The rugged individualism of the American people a hundred years ago was developed by the frontier. Baptist, Methodist, and Christian Churches, because their system of creating leaders and certain other traits fitted the frontier temperament, grew better than Episcopal and Presbyterian Churches. The highly regimented mentality of Americans today has been developed by a number of years of compulsory schooling, intricate traffic regulations, national press and television networks, and other similar influences. American denominations are trying out many different activities and methods to find those which, in this particular culture with its particular self-image, really communicate Christ and build up the Church.

In Latin America, the structure of society among hacienda owners is radically different from that of hacienda serfs. The former think of themselves as the conquerors, the latter know they are the conquered. The first not only own vast estates, but until recent times held the power of life and death within them; the second lead a safe life only if they obey the master of the big house and his overseers. If the peon works five days on his master's thousand acres, he is allowed to work two days on his own few. He can keep five sheep—if he gives their dung to the fields of the *hacendero*. The structure of both societies differs again from those of independent mestizo peasants and free Indians who own a few acres of their own. The Church grows differently in each of these four Latin American structures.

Marriage Customs

Where men get their wives is an important element in social structure. In rural Mexico men find wives within their own rancho (village) or those immediately adjacent. In the Gangetic valley of India, each caste is made up of many *gotr* (exogamous clans). A man must get his wife outside his *gotr* but inside his caste. All girls of his own *gotr* are his sisters even if there is no blood connection for ten generations. Some castes take daughters-in-law from the east, give daughters to the west. Where men get their wives determines where their maternal uncles, fathers-in-law, and sisters' sons live. This, in turn, influences where the Christian will normally visit, in which villages his intimates will be found, and consequently where the Gospel will spread.

The Chinese kinship system, illustrated in the following diagram, not only defined degrees of consanguinity within which marriage was incestuous, but determined the mourning obligations of each generation and each degree of collateral relationship. The reader should study it carefully but need not master the intricacies of the system to realize how thoroughly it organized life. Some relatives would be tremendously impressed by Ego's becoming a Christian, but others would care little for it. Were some to become Christians, all their kin might notice it, but their action would commend Christ only to some. Blood and marriage lines are of great significance for the growth of the Church. For the missionary to China to know the web of relationship, he needs to know about 75 words which name 75 different relationships. This small, specialized vocabulary must be learned—if God's messenger is to present the Gospel and help churches form in the kinship web with maximum effectiveness.

The Elite, or Power Structure

I am not speaking now of the elite of a whole country or city, but of those in a given *ethnos* or homogeneous unit. Every university faculty has its power structure—its elite, whose opinions have great weight. So does every labor union.

Each segment of society has its own power structure or aristocracy, as I found to my great surprise when I discovered that among the latrine-cleaning caste of Jubbulpore there were certain elite families. The Dumars of that city were organized into twenty-nine associations, each of which was ruled by a *chaudhari* and his assistant, the *sakidar*. Thus the Sweepers—the lowest of low castes—had an aristocracy of these fifty-eight families and their relatives.

The power structure of a community sometimes consists exclusively of men born in the right families. Often wealth has something to do with it. In many societies in Africasia a light skin gives prestige. Religious talents, too, such as shamans, sorcerers, and priests are supposed to pos-

FIGURE 11.1. THE CHINESE KINSHIP SYSTEM

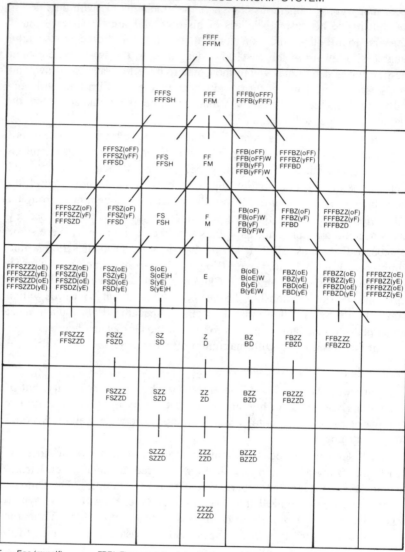

E = Ego (myself)
F = Father
M = Mother
B = Brother
S = Sister
Z = Son
D = Daughter
H = Husband
W = Wife

FBZ(oE) means father's brother's son who is older than I.
FFB(yFF)W means the wife of "father's father's brother who is younger than father's father."
SZZ means sister's son's son.
ZZZZ means son's son's son's son, i.e., great-great grandson.

Chinese has at least *one distinct word* for each of these 41 squares. For some squares they have 4 distinct words!

sess, elevate their owners to the elite. In the villages where I worked, the wise man *jis ki baat nahin kut-thi* ("whose decision cannot be controverted") was part of the power structure. He knew village and caste law by long observation, had a judicious mind, and patiently listened to the ins and outs of each dispute till, sensing an unspoken consensus, he would announce a decision which carried the day. The wise man has been a part of the power structure from time immemorial. In the saga of Iceland from A.D. 1000 we read:

> Nyal was so great a lawyer, that his match was not to be found—wise, foreknowing, and far sighted. Good counsel and ready to give it. All that he advised men was sure to be the best for them to do. Gentle and generous, he unravelled every man's knotty points, who came to see him about them (Dasent, 1960:34).

When one of the elite becomes a Christian, the faith is likely to spread among his blood and marriage relations.

Land Rights

Land-owning rights are complex and a most important aspect of social structure. In Madhya Pradesh, India, most peasants own merely the cultivating rights to land. They can neither buy nor sell the land itself, which belongs to the feudal lord of the village. If he permits them to sell it, he does so after "graciously accepting as a gift" a third of the price at which it is sold. If he does not like the person wanting to buy, or wishes to prevent his becoming part of the village, he simply refuses "the gift," i.e. refuses to sell. Some peasants, however, have a few fields of a second land right. These they can sell to whomever they like, but still have to pay a proportion of the sale price to the feudal lord. The third kind of land is that owned outright, which can be sold without asking permission of anyone. If the feudal lord is hostile to Christianity, and Christians own only cultivating rights, it is impossible to get land for a church building.

In Puerto Rico the low fertile coastal lands belong to the sugar barons, but in the interior, coffee growers own their own patches of the hillside. These independents can become Evangelicals if they want to, whereas landless labor on the sugar estates can be ordered off if by becoming Evangelicals, or in any other way, they displease the owner.

In some areas, land formerly owned by common people is fast gravitating into the hands of moneylenders. The peasant borrows money at 75 per cent interest for a yoke of oxen or a big wedding, intending to pay it back when harvest comes. That year the harvest is poor, or he is negligent.

By the next year he has twice as much to pay back. Soon he surrenders the land to the moneylender. One Church took up the cudgels for the peasants, loaned them money at a fair percentage, and reversed the flow of land. When, after this display of social justice, she proclaimed the Gospel, many heard and followed in the Way. Land rights influence church growth. Then, too, land-owning Christians make solider churches. Wherever land is disappearing into the control of city moneylenders, the ability of peasant Christians to support their pastors diminishes.

Congregations made up of renters and sharecroppers differ from those made up of landowners, as any pastor in rural Texas or Virginia will tell you.

Sex Mores

The degree to which sex mores affect the growth of the Church has not commonly been recognized in Eurica. There, because for long centuries the state enforced the sex code taught by the Church, ideals of monogamy and faithfulness until recently have been part of the common life of the people. Since practically no divorce was permitted, lifelong marriages became the rule. Among the truly converted, faithfulness was commonplace. Adultery, mistresses, premarital sexual intercourse, and the like were, of course, found but were recognized as sin. To be converted meant leaving the abnormal for the normal, the illegal for the legal.

In some countries, however, non-Christian sex mores are the dominant variety and militate heavily against the growth of the Church. For example, in Jamaica, where the great bulk of the population is descended from slaves freed in 1838, two patterns of marriage obtain. Marriage Pattern I—Christian marriage—is that used by the higher classes: the wealthy, educated leaders of Jamaica. The masses, however, who comprise more than 85 per cent of the population, practice Marriage Pattern II. In this, temporary unions outside of marriage are formed from middle adolescence on. Some last a week, many a few months, and some for years. Either party is free to leave when he or she tires of the other. A succession of temporary unions is the rule.

As long as couples are living together out of wedlock, no Church will accept them as members. However, they count themselves as, in a vague way, belonging to the community of this or that Church and bring their babies to the ministers to be baptized or dedicated. If, in a revival meeting, fifty such persons were converted, the first question asked them in the after-meeting would be, "Are you married or willing to be?" If the answer were No, then they could not be baptized or added to the Church. Many ministers, sure that adolescents of the masses will "fall away" and have to be removed from the roll, do not encourage them to join the church.

After the age of forty, many women and some men, through with sex, decide to live alone. They become eligible for church membership. Older men of the masses who have made money and want to step up in the world get married. Their children and grandchildren attend the wedding, which— a costly affair with suitable clothes, rings, wedding feast, and the like— is a status symbol and proclaims that this man and wife, who have been living together for years, have now "arrived." They have also become eligible for church membership.

Consequently the Church in Jamaica is comprised mostly of members of the upper classes and some of the elderly among the masses. In research done there in 1957, I came to the conclusion that fourteen out of fifteen adults of the masses between the ages of sixteen and forty could not join the Church (McGavran, 1962). They were living in Marriage Pattern II, which they called "our Jamaican way," and intended to continue in it. The slow growth of the four Churches in Jamaica mentioned earlier (Chap. III) is largely due to the adverse effect which sex mores have had on growth.

Pattern II is found throughout the Caribbean and in some countries of Latin America. A period of sexual experimentation increasingly affects church membership in North America also.

In Africa, the system of polygamy keeps very large numbers from confessing Christ. Churches rule that men who have married two or more women according to tribal custom must give up all but one on becoming Christians. For several reasons, Churches are not happy with this rule and are discussing whether it is really Christian. All branches of the Church agree that polygamy cannot be allowed in the Church for those who have been brought up as Christians or who come in with one wife. That is not the issue. The issue is whether converts with two or more wives whom, while pagans, they have married according to tribal law, may be baptized with their wives and continue living with them, on the clear understanding that (1) while they will be members in good standing, they may not be deacons or elders, and (2) they will cleave strictly to monogamy as a system. If a wife dies they will not replace her, and they will arrange monogamous marriages for their sons and daughters.

A few Eurica-connected denominations have ruled that, on this understanding, they may be baptized. Most Eurica-connected denominations have ruled they may not. Many independent African denominations not only allow men and wives to become Christian but permit polygamy to those reared in the Church. Their great growth of recent years is at least partly due to their open attitude toward polygamy.

Some churchmen maintain that the most certain way to *perpetuate* polygamy is to keep the wealthy, influential members of a tribe out of the Church. Since these are the ones who have plural wives, the policy of exclusion builds up a wealthy polygamous society at the heart of each Christian community. These churchmen argue that the correct procedure is (1) to induct polygamous families as *families* on the understanding that from baptism on they will adhere to monogamy *as a system* and (2) to trust that the Holy Spirit will do His work of grace in their hearts. Unless perpetuated by unwise church policy, polygamy as a system, they declare, is likely to decline. It was viable in a slave-owning society, where the more laborers a man had, the wealthier he was. In today's free, urban society, the more wives a man has, the poorer he becomes.

The full argument pro and con cannot be given here, but it is surely clear that this aspect of social structure vitally affects the Christianization of all Africa south of the Sahara.

People Consciousness

A homogeneous unit of society may be said to have "people consciousness" when its members think of themselves as a separate tribe, caste, or class. Thus the Orthodox Jews in Eurica have high people consciousness, as do the castes in India, the Indian tribes in Ecuador, and many other societies in many lands.

The degree of people consciousness is an aspect of social structure which greatly influences when, how, and to what extent the Gospel will flow through that segment of the social order. Castes or tribes with high people consciousness will resist the Gospel primarily because to them becoming a Christian means "joining another people." They refuse Christ not for religious reasons, not because they love their sins, but precisely because they love their brethren.

The degree of people consciousness is an aspect of social structure which determines or greatly influences the ability of the people concerned to discipline members who marry outsiders. In "melting pots" or highly individualistic societies, no one cares who marries whom, and therefore these societies are universally those of low people consciousness. One thinks immediately of middle-class mobile society in North America. Yet even there, marriages out of "our kind of people" encounter considerable difficulty. Norwegian-Italian marriages are the exception not the rule. The more fiercely Norwegian or Italian the family is, the less chance of such a marriage taking place. People consciousness counts everywhere—even in melting pots.

In India, Brahmans and many others whose people consciousness is very high, discipline their members rigorously. They ostracize those who marry non-Brahmans and read the funeral ceremony over them. They have debased the blood and must be excluded.

It may be taken as axiomatic that whenever becoming a Christian is considered a racial rather than a religious decision, there the growth of the Church will be exceedingly slow. As the Church faces the evangelization of the world, perhaps her main problem is how to present Christ so that men can truly follow Him without traitorously leaving their kindred.

The only solutions to this problem to date are: (1) to wait till the society disintegrates, people consciousness grows low, a melting pot develops, or the military might of a conqueror destroys pride of peoplehood; and (2) to enable men and women to become Christians in groups while still remaining members of their tribe, caste, or people. Where Christians can continue marrying among their own kind, attending each other's weddings and funerals, and maintaining close connection with their non-Christian brethren, there the Church can grow both fast and soundly.

The resistance of Hindus, Buddhists, Confucianists, and Moslems to the Christian faith does not arise primarily from theological considerations. Most of the adherents of these faiths do not prefer their religion as religion to Christianity. Most of them, being illiterate, know very little about their religious system. Most Hindus are more animist than Hindu, and the same may be said for each of the other religions. Their resistance arises primarily from fear that "becoming a Christian will separate me from my people."

It is often affirmed that primitive peoples and low-caste folk become Christians easily, whereas Christianity has not appealed to followers of the great ethnic religions; but this is to distort the truth. In many cases, tribes resist Christianity quite as effectively as advanced peoples. The Egons of Badagri in the southwest corner of Nigeria solidly refused the Gospel for a hundred and fifteen years, though it was ably presented first by the Methodists and then, when these retired from the area, by the Roman Catholics. The Masai of Kenya—a primitive tribe if there ever was one—have been entirely indifferent to Christianity. Most of the low castes of India have proved just as resistant to Christ's appeal as the high castes. The fact is that men and women, high and low, advanced and primitive, usually turn to Christian faith in numbers only when some way is found for them to become Christian without leaving their kith and kin.

The great obstacles to conversion are social, not theological. Great turning of Moslems and Hindus can be expected as soon as ways are found for them to become Christian without renouncing their brethren, which seems to them a betrayal. Confirmation of this can be seen in the 1966 and 1967 turning to Christ of perhaps fifty thousand Moslems in Indonesia. Whole communities became Christians together. It was reported that in one place twenty-five mosques became twenty-five churches. The principle need not be labored. It is patently true that among societies with high people consciousness those methods of propagating the Gospel which enable men to accept Christ without renouncing their peoples are blessed of God to the growth of His Church.

Where People Live

Where people live, their geographical location, is an obvious part of the social structure and greatly affects church growth. Throughout Hindu India, the depressed-class ward has been separated from the rest of the village by physical distance—often a hundred yards or more. As people of these wards became Christian and pastors were appointed to shepherd them, the separate location posed a problem to missions. Should the pastor— an educated, respectable Christian—live in the Untouchable ward or seek quarters in the upper-caste section of the village? Arguing that it would help Christians more if their pastor lived in a respectable part of the town, missions in North India located their pastors there. Arguing that the pastor's place was with his people, missions in South India located him in the Untouchable ward itself. Pickett observes that the South India procedure (its use of the social structure) was much more successful in terms of creating a genuine Christian Church (1933:228).

Floyd Filson calls attention to the influence of house churches in ancient Corinth. After setting forth the fact that the Early Church, once the split with the synagogue was complete, ordinarily met in the homes of wealthy members, as the Christians multiplied in number, he says,

> It became increasingly difficult for all the believers in the city to meet in one house. For all ordinary occasions, at least, the total body would split into smaller groups which could be housed in private homes . . . the house church dominated the situation . . . the regular setting for both Christian meetings and evangelistic preaching was found in the homes of believers . . . a study of home churches furthers understanding of the apostolic church [in five ways].

> The house churches enabled the followers of Jesus to have a distinctively Christian worship and fellowship from the very first days of the apostolic age. . . . [They] afford a partial explanation of the great attention paid to family life in the letters of Paul. . . . The existence of several house churches [con-

gregations] in one city goes far to explain the tendency to party strife in the apostolic age. . . . A study of the house church . . . also throws light on the social status of the early Christians. . . . The development of church polity can never be understood without reference to the house churches. . . . (Filson, 1939:105ff.)

Lacking church growth insight, Filson misses the most important influence of house churches: that they enabled the tiny Church to grow mightily. At one stroke they overcame four obstacles to growth which the Church met as it liberated new populations. (1) The cost of a church building. Without any cash outlay at all, house churches provided as many places to worship as there were groups of Christians. This first common obstacle to multiplying churches never appeared. (2) The obstacle of the Jewish connection. House churches pushed the Church away from the synagogue into the Gentile population. (3) The obstacle of introversion. Each new house church exposed a new section of society—a new set of intimates and relatives—to close contact with ardent Christians. (4) The obstacle of a limited leadership. Each house church thrust the responsibilities and prestige of leadership on able men of the new congregation. These, within the elastic bonds of the Old Testament, oral tradition of the life of the Lord, and a letter or two of Paul's were free to follow the leading of the Holy Spirit. The physical fact of the house churches should be taken into consideration in any assessment of the causes of the growth of the Early Church. In modern times, these four factors still retain their importance.

Language

Hundreds of millions of men live in two worlds. The first, of great importance to them, is that of "our intimates who speak our own language"; the second, of relatively slight importance, is that world of a strange tongue in which we trade and work with outsiders. In the first the "medium of communication" is the language of the heart; in the second, the "medium of confusion" is a trade language or standard language, good enough for buying and selling, taking orders and finding one's way, but pitifully inadequate for the things that really matter. Men fight, make love, and mourn in their mother tongue.

Because the only way modern nation-states can function is to create a citizenry all of whose members speak one language, governments and education departments work ceaselessly to propagate standard languages and to eliminate what they call dialects (some of which are languages in their own right). The standard language is the key to unity. Nevertheless, the language of the heart is difficult to stamp out. It is learned from the mother's lips and spoken in the home. It is an inner sanctuary where the outside world cannot penetrate. It is jealously guarded because it enhances a sense of peoplehood. In Mexico, eighty-eight Indian languages have survived four hundred years of Spanish dominance and are heart-languages for hundreds of thousands today. Even when a land has gone over to a standard tongue, leaders sometimes insist, as they did in Ireland, that "our own language" must be relearned.

The United States and Canada offer a startlingly clear illustration of how language conditions the spread of Churches. Protestant denominations, chained by English, have established sweeping movements to Christ in no other language group—Hispanics, Greeks, Italians, French Canadians, Portuguese, Chinese, Poles, or others. For citizens of these heart languages, becoming a Protestant means joining an English-speaking body—even when, as is often the case, the first generation worships in the language of the new converts.

As the Church spreads throughout the earth, she is constantly dealing with hundreds of millions who live in these two worlds. In some cases she speaks the heart language and flourishes, in others she presents the Gospel in a standard language and languishes. Where it appears that the "dialect" is going to die out and the standard language is the one in which Bible and hymnbook are available, government carries on its business, and schools do their work, there it seems reasonable for the Church to preach, pray, sing, and read the Bible, not in the potent language of the heart but in the important language of the future. It may be reasonable and cheap, but it is seldom effective. However, it must be said that such is the power of the Gospel and so many are the other factors that impel men to become disciples of Christ, that frequently the Church grows despite this handicap. That it is a handicap should never be forgotten.

Examples of this aspect of social structure and its bearing on church growth could be given from almost every country. The great turning of the Lisu in southwest China to Christ was unquestionably made possible by John Fraser's mastery of the Lisu language. It is impossible to imagine him reaching the hearts of these people, had he spoken Mandarin to them. Those missionaries who started the Bataks in Sumatra on the road to Christ—over a million Bataks are now Christians—spoke Batak freely. They did not try to work in Indonesian.

Rural Japan well illustrates this component of social structure. Japan is a land of many islands, mountain ranges, remote valleys, and geographically isolated sections. Till the modern era dawned, this meant that the

Japanese spoke many dialects. Even today, though compulsory education and a national press have made standard Japanese universally known, dialects are commonly spoken by the country people. In their homes, among themselves, when they are at ease, rural Japanese fall back on the sweet familiar language of the heart. One cannot help but wonder whether one reason the Church has not prospered in rural Japan is that churchmen (nationals and missionaries) have learned only standard Japanese and have not preached the Gospel in any of the heart languages of the common people. That the government and intelligentsia are engaged in wiping out the dialects (and will eventually succeed) encourages the Church—to her loss—to bypass them.

The use of the standard language in proclaiming Christ and persuading men to become His disciples is, alas, normal procedure in Christian missions. It is hard enough to master one language, let alone two. Efficient administration seems to require transferring missionaries freely as needs arise throughout an area. If a missionary located in one district learns the heart language of a hundred thousand persons there, and on return from furlough is located in another district where the people speak another language, the learning will have seemed a waste of time. This is specially true if the standard language would have served, after a fashion at least, in both districts. Not four hundred miles from where I am writing, for instance, many missionaries from half a dozen boards of missions are working among the Navaho Indians, but winning few to Christ. In Arizona and New Mexico, English is the standard language and Navaho the "dialect." A knowledgeable informant assured me that of all the missionaries in Navaholand he knew, only one was fluent in the Indian tongue. On the entirely untenable assumption that "the Navahos all know English," most missionaries had not even tried to learn it.

Today educated nationals who lead the Churches of Afericasia know and love the standard languages of their nations and scorn languages spoken by small segments of the population as "dying vernaculars" or "corrupt forms of the national language." They usually believe that the welfare of the nation demands eradication of the dialects. They are not sympathetic with the argument that the people could hear the Gospel better and obey it more readily if it were presented in their heart language, and insist that "everyone understands our national language." They also feel that the best interests of existing Christians demand getting them away from the dialects and making them proficient in the national language. Hence church services, they think, should be in Spanish, Hindi, Swahili, Amharic, or other national language. Probably unconsciously, they subordinate discipling to a cosmopolitan civilizing process.

Governments usually require that all schooling be done in the standard language. This invests it with prestige and makes it difficult to use the vernacular for propagating the Gospel. In Ethiopia for example, the government requires all schools to use Amharic as the medium of instruction and all missionaries to learn Amharic. Many naturally never go on to learn the tribal language of the people with whom they seek to share the inestimable benefits of the Christian religion.

Sometimes the only practical course is to work in the *lingua franca*. Thomas Birch Freeman, one of the great missionaries of all time, never learned any of the many tribal languages of West Africa. He always spoke English and depended on interpreters to convey his message. In 1838, speaking to many tribes, and under the conditions of that era, he was effective, led many to Christian commitment, and established many churches. Nevertheless, the man speaking to people who speak something else in their homes should never deceive himself that the standard language is "just as good" as the heart language as a vehicle for the Gospel.

The basic reform needed in those fields where missions are evangelizing speakers of dialect is to cease spreading one team of workers over several dialects or languages and to begin assigning single teams to one homogeneous unit only—preferably one believed to be responsive. Each member of the team would then learn the heart language of that people. Transfers could be made *within the one language area* as the good of the young Church required. The Wycliffe Bible Translators have demonstrated that as a mission procedure this is quite feasible.

The language aspect of social structure is specially important because the Good News of God's acts must be told in words. Biblical instruction has to be in words. Worship, prayer, and singing the praise of God all use words. Transmitting the faith takes place in words. Missionaries who skillfully use social structure at this point, are intelligent stewards of God's grace.

THE INFLUENCE OF SOCIAL STRUCTURE: TWO ILLUSTRATIONS

In 1820, the population of Jamaica was composed of three homogeneous units. (1) The English and Scotch estate owners were members of the Anglican and Presbyterian Churches. (2) A considerable mulatto population, which had arisen in towns and estates through miscegenation, was culturally somewhat advanced. Some mulattoes had been educated by their natural fathers. Some had been freed. Many were foremen of the sugar plantations. (3) The black slaves formed by far the largest part of the population.

Till the early 1800's, Anglicans and Presbyterians, fearing unrest among the slaves if they permitted them to become Christians, had discouraged Christianization. True, some Baptist slaves of Tory planters, who left the thirteen states after the Revolutionary War, had before 1800 started a few churches among the slaves in Jamaica. Though "Baptist sectarians" were in great disfavor with the plantation owners, who often burned down the slave chapels, Baptist churches began to increase among the third homogeneous unit.

Then about 1800, Baptists and Methodists from England, in the first flush of their missionary zeal, came to Jamaica and a tremendous turning to Christ took place among the slaves. Baptist churches multiplied among the blacks and the Methodist churches among the browns. Not that no mulatto ever became a Baptist or that Methodists resolutely refused to admit blacks, but rather each Church prospered in its own segment of the social order.

Baptists found it hard to extend their churches among the mulattoes. Their Gospel was sound, but their congregations, made up very largely of the blacks, did not attract the mulattoes. These said to themselves, "Our friends are in the mulatto community. We want our children to marry people of their own color, and these Baptist services are not up to the standard of language or thought which we like." Methodists could have extended their churches among the blacks, but the existing brown Methodists did not encourage it. They did not want too many black men and women and black boys and girls in their churches. They did not want black leaders and ministers. The Methodists had some right on their side. The brown community was relatively more cultured, educated, and free of voodoo. It formed a separate subculture. Methodists did not want to debase their Church by bringing in lower-class people. They wanted churches which appealed to their kind of people and in which they felt at home.

By way of a second illustration from the same area: the Christian Churches (Disciples of Christ) sent missionaries to Jamaica in 1868 and established a small denomination there, mostly among the dark-skinned. In the early 1950's a gifted minister of this Church, while pastoring the King's Gate Christian Church, a congregation composed largely of the servant class in Kingston, carried on a most interesting and vital young people's society. Middle- and lower-class youth from that section of the city flocked to join it. In the course of his work, he sought to lead the young people to decide for Christ and join the church. Most of them did decide for Christ, but only the young of the masses joined the King's Gate Church. Parents of middle-class youth saw to it that their sons and daughters joined Presbyterian and Methodist churches. In North America, youth work leads those it touches into the congregation which carries it on. In Jamaica, since society exists as the upper classes and the masses, upper-class youth when converted join upper-class congregations.

Summary

The influence of social structure on church growth is great. It can hardly be overestimated. Americans will find social structure influencing the growth of their churches in every segment of the vast American mosaic from Maine to California. Africans, Asians, Latin Americans, and Europeans can readily see that social structure has a profound effect on the growth of the churches in their countries. A prominent Anglican recently said to me, "In England the Church has lost the working classes. If a person of the working classes is truly converted, he seldom joins the Anglican Church. That to him is a Church of the upper classes."

The case must not be overstated. The Bible tells us that in Christ the two are made one. That blessed movement has been seen again and again. Yet the Bible also tells us that the Church was composed of the common people. It was notably unsuccessful in winning the scribes and Pharisees, the doctors of the law and the rulers of the people. The strategy of evangelism must take serious account of social structure and find ways to repeat the break out which the eleventh chapter of Acts so vividly relates.

12

WITHOUT CROSSING BARRIERS

MEN LIKE to become Christians without crossing racial, linguistic, or class barriers.

This principle states an undeniable fact. Human beings do build barriers around their own societies. More exactly we may say that the ways in which each society lives and speaks, dresses and works, of necessity set it off from other societies. Mankind is a mosaic and each piece has a separate life of its own which seems strange and often unlovely to men and women of other pieces.

Novak in his perceptive book *The Rise of the Unmeltable Ethnics* ably defends the right of each ethnic group to remain itself. He sees the barriers each group builds around itself as normal and desirable parts of the human scene. His list of "ethnics" in the United States shatters the notion of "one American people."

> When I say "ethnics" . . . I am speaking mainly of the descendants of the immigrants of southern and eastern Europe: Poles, Italians, Greeks and Slavs . . . Armenians, Lebanese, Slovenes, Ruthenians, Croats, Serbs, Czechs (Bohemians and Moravians), Slovaks, Lithuanians, Estonians, Russians, Spanish, and Portuguese (46).

He does not deal with the English, Scotch, Irish, Danish, Norwegians, Swedes, Germans and French, the Chinese, Japanese, Filipinos, Pakistanis, Indians, Arabs, Africans, and Vietnamese.

Like the United States, most nations are composed of many unmeltable

223

ethnics. India, for example, has more than 3,000 ethnic units (castes and tribes) each of which practices endogamy.* Highly educated and politically powerful Indians are members of tightly structured segments of humanity, each of which has a stout wall built around it. Afghanistan, often thought of as one country and one people, is, in fact, composed of many different peoples, with different languages and customs.

In this vast mosaic, how does the Christian Faith spread from piece to piece? Does it invite members of all pieces to leave their own people and become parts of the people of God? Or does the Church form inside each piece?

The mosaic is a useful figure of speech but can easily convey an untruth. The many colored pieces of the mosaics in the beautiful renaissance buildings in Italy have changed neither shape nor color in four hundred years. The human mosaic is not like that. Its pieces are constantly changing, merging with, swallowing, and being swallowed by other pieces. The languages they speak change. The clothes they wear change. They used to walk; now they ride cycles or drive cars. They were solidly illiterate; now they are highly educated. Their cultures change radically. In view of this great readiness to change should we think of the propagation of the Gospel as a process of change by which all peoples and cultures are gradually transformed into a new and beautiful Christian culture? Or, does the Christian Faith enter each changing, yeasting culture and transform it from within while it yet remains itself, and separate from other cultures which have become Christian?

The biblical teaching is plain that in Christ two peoples become one. Christian Jews and Gentiles become one new people of God, parts of the One Body of Christ. But the One Body is complex. Since both peoples continue to speak separate languages, does not the oneness cover a vast and continuing diversity?

This chapter describes the obvious fact that human beings are born into thousands of very different societies, separated from each other by many barriers. It also explores the ways in which the Christian Faith, while building the Una Sancta and making all Christians one in Christ Jesus, can

*See my *Ethnic Realities and the Church: Lessons from India* which discusses at length the effect which unmeltable ethnic units have on the structure of Churches and on the propagation of the Gospel. Each piece of the mosaic is seen to present a different evangelistic opportunity. All the pieces taken together add a new dimension to the concept of world evangelization and the proper extension of the Church.

be communicated across the barriers, over the ditches, and thus built into the other societies, classes, castes, tongues, and segments of humanity.

For the sake of convenience, we talk about these as homogeneous units or HUs. Some are linguistically, some ethnically, some economically, and some educationally different from the others. The term homogeneous unit is very elastic. Scandinavian Americans might be considered a homogeneous unit; but since there are many kinds of Scandinavians, so might the Swedish Baptist denomination in 1930. The Brahmans in India are a homogeneous unit, but so is each of the scores of Brahman castes.

James C. Smith, impressed by the universal applicability of the HU principle, in 1976 wrote his doctoral dissertation on "Without Crossing Barriers, The Homogeneous Unit Concept in the Writings of Donald McGavran." He discovered that this aspect of human society had intrigued me from the beginning, noting that in *The Bridges of God* (1955) I had written, "Peoples become Christian fastest when least change of race or clan is involved" (23). After that I had very frequently called attention to ethnicity as a significant factor in propagating and arresting the flow of the Gospel.

During the seventies, church growth thinking has been enriched by the writings of Lyle C. Schaller, who has explored thoroughly the part played in growth and decline by diversities (different groups) within seemingly homogeneous congregations.

Schaller, more than anyone else, has studied the various parts of congregations and denominations. For example, on the basis of face to face conversations with thousands of Christians and extensive returns on questionnaires, he explored questions such as this: Why did those who have joined the church during the past ten years take that step? He found that

3 to 8% walked in on their own initiative

4 to 10% came because they liked the program

10 to 20% joined because they liked the pastor

10 to 25% joined in response to visitation evangelism

3 to 6% came because of the Sunday School

60 to 90% were brought by some friend or relative.

Then he explored reasons as to why those who have left the church did so. Again he identified a number of groups of people. Those who moved away numbered 30 to 40 per cent. Those unhappy with the congregation numbered 20 to 35 per cent. Those who left for personal or family reasons were 20 to 30 per cent and those dissatisfied with the pastor 15 to 25 per cent. Those dissatisfied with the denomination numbered only 5 per cent.

In many congregations, Schaller found two main groups which he calls the "pioneers" and "homesteaders." The former are the founding members, the old timers who by virtue of fighting the early battles formed a tightly knit fellowship; the latter are those who joined a growing congregation and thus automatically were not a part of the pioneers. A vivid paragraph reads as follows:

> As the years go by, an ever decreasing proportion of the members have first-hand recollection of those adventures of pioneering days when the new parish was being developed. . . . The pioneers sit around the campfire before, during and after committee meetings and social events. They exchange stories, refresh memories, and tell tales about how it used to be. . . . A few home-steaders listen attentively . . . others go home feeling they have been excluded (The Costs of Rapid Growth, *Church Administration,* Sunday School Board of the Southern Baptist Convention, May 1976, p. 12).

Two of his most telling illustrations of homogeneous units *within* seemingly homogeneous wholes are these. 1. Young marrieds looked at one way are a single group. They are quite different from the senior citizens or the high schoolers. Looked at from a different angle, the young marrieds themselves have several groups within them. There are significant differences among the members of this one group which older members refer to simply as "the young married couples." Each of the following sub-groups has different needs and schedules. *(a)* Many 22-year-old couples with no children feel nearly a generation younger than the 28-year-old husband with the 26-year-old wife and two children; *(b)* the couple with both husband and wife employed outside the home and the couple with only the husband employed; and *(c)* the couple born and reared in this community and the couple living 1,000 miles from "back home." 2. As the congregation assembles, the casual visitor will see all as very much alike. The perceptive pastor, however, knows there are two major groups concerned—*(a)* those who play an active part in the congregation and feel a part of the inner group; and *(b)* those who have no special role, are part of no small group, and are, in fact, just spectators. The others run the show.

Schaller's writings are much richer than these few excerpts indicate. His books, mentioned in the bibliography, should be consulted; but here the point is that none of these American homogeneous units on which

Schaller focuses our attention is an ethnic or linguistic group. Yet they are important for church growth. The same kind of sub-groupings affect the growth of churches in all continents. In many countries of Africa, for example, the early growth of the Church has come from older school boys; but the *great* growth did not come until the mature started becoming Christian in groups of like-minded persons.

Men and women do like to become Christian without crossing barriers. This universal principle is readily seen when we think of the linguistic barrier mentioned in the last chapter. In Los Angeles or San Francisco, English-speaking Americans are not likely to become Christians in Spanish- or Japanese-speaking congregations. When they become Christians it will be in English-speaking churches. American Protestants living for a short time overseas seldom worship in the Protestant churches there, partly because the service in Urdu, Mandarin, or Portuguese is unintelligible to them. How much more difficult it would be to leave one's ancestral faith and *join* a congregation whose members spoke a different tongue. In the 1870's hundreds of Pepohwans in Formosa were burning their memorial tablets and fetishes and declaring for Christ. They built chapels and were put under instruction by the English Presbyterians. Those who passed the examination were baptized. But the instructors spoke only Chinese, and while some Pepohwan men knew a little Chinese, the women and children knew practically none. The result was that out of a whole village which declared for Christ, only a few would be judged eligible for baptism. The movement eventually failed. It was hard for Pepohwans to become Christian across the linguistic barrier.

The principle is also readily discerned when it comes to pronounced class and racial barriers. It takes no great acumen to see that when marked differences of color, stature, income, cleanliness, and education are present, men understand the Gospel better when expounded by their own kind of people. They prefer to join churches whose members look, talk, and act like themselves. Although apartheid laws in the Union of South Africa apply to Indians as well as Africans, the differences between these dark-skinned peoples are so great that it is difficult for Indians to join African Churches. The Africans would be glad to have them, but the Indians do not want to identify with them. Once a Church made up of Indians started to grow, however (so that Indians could become Christians without having to cross a pronounced race barrier), thousands of Indians became Christian in one denomination.

In the case of inconspicuous racial and class differences or minor dialect differences, the operation of this principle is harder to perceive.

Christian mission—to its great loss—commonly ignores it. In 1979 some pastors in Indiana, the heartland of North America, told me that their rural congregations made up largely of landowning farmers were declining. As the farms grew larger and larger the number of landowners grew smaller. "But," I interjected, "the renters, tenants, and mechanics are there in ever larger numbers." "True," they replied, "but they are not quite the same people as the landowners and do not join our churches."

In Denver, Colorado, a Presbyterian congregation was declining because its members were moving out to the suburbs. The new whites moving into that part of the city did not join this congregation in any but the smallest numbers. The class barrier (which would have been vehemently denied by the congregation), while not high, was there. It was inconspicuous but effective.

During 1966 in West Africa, a Christian movement among the country people started as soon as the missionaries who lived in the town realized that the inconspicuous difference between Africans of the towns and Africans of the countryside had great meaning for church growth. Futile attempts to win the townsmen were replaced by systematic attempts to win the countrymen village by village. The missionaries had been ignoring the principle. When they saw it and acted on it, growth of the Church began (Krass 1967:1).

In the nineteenth century, the high, cool plateau of Mexico was the site of many haciendas which originated in sixteenth-century land grants given by the king of Spain and therefore ultimately by the Pope himself. In each hacienda, villages—called ranchos—had grown up where water and arable land lay close at hand. The Spanish-speaking population was at least nominally Roman Catholic and was composed of the exploited masses and the upper classes. The latter—beneficiaries of the social order—lived chiefly in the towns and were close allies of the Roman Catholic Church (McGavran 1963:38).

The revolutions of the early twentieth century—and in particular that of 1927, when the central government was breaking up the haciendas and giving the land to the peasants—divided the peasantry into two parties: *agraristas* who were ready to fight for land distribution, and *cristeros* who had been persuaded that, since the land had been given to the hacienda owners by the Pope, taking it away from them was stealing and would be punished by God. *Cristeros* fought to keep the feudal lords in power.

The peasants of both parties looked very much the same. All spoke Spanish, counted themselves Roman Catholics, had the same culture, cultivated the same kind of land, and wore the same kind of clothing. Yet for the propagation of the Gospel the difference between the two had crucial significance. For the establishment of Evangelical congregations, the *agrarista* ranchos were of great importance and the *cristero* ranchos of none. True, *agraristas* did not rush to become Evangelicals, but, freed from the control of the feudal lords, thinking of the Church of Rome as an ally of their oppressors, and having divided up the land despite the fact that it was given to the feudal lords by the Pope, they could "hear" the Gospel. For the first time becoming Evangelicals became a live option to them.

Yet this minor difference was not seen by most Evangelical ministers and missionaries working in the high, dry heart of Mexico. To them, the people of the ranchos were all rural Mexicans, poor, illiterate, and indifferent to the Evangelical. Suspicious of revolution and cultivating friendly relations with the business and professional leaders of the towns, Evangelical leaders did not concentrate on planting churches in the revolutionary ranchos. A few churches did arise there—eloquent testimony to a crucially important "minor" difference. Had a movement been begun which gave agrarian reform a biblical base and thus enabled *agraristas*, while remaining ardent *agraristas*, to become Evangelicals, it might have swept the revolutionary ranchos of the plateau.

One of the most difficult minor differences for the outsider to discern is that which arises from kinship webs. The city ward or country village appears to be full of one kind of people. These, the missionary or minister is inclined to say, are all Japanese, Congolese, Chileans, or Americans, and that is true. But it is also true that in that ward or village are several webs of relationship, which may overlap but are nevertheless distinct. Not everyone in the village will be equally affected when a family becomes Christian. Those in its kinship web, since they can become Christian while remaining within their subgroup, are much more likely to consider following Christ than are members of other kinship webs. Robert Redfield, the anthropologist, tells of a village in Mexico where the kinship webs of two leading men became Evangelicals and those of two others remained Roman Catholic (Redfield, 1950:92).

CHURCH PLANTERS WHO ENABLE MEN . . .

Church planters who enable men to become Christians without crossing *such* barriers are much more effective than those who place them in men's way. But biblical barriers must not be removed.

The offense of the cross is one basic barrier to becoming Christian.

To accept the truth that one is a sinner whose salvation depends not at all on what he does but entirely on his accepting what Jesus Christ has done for him on the cross, affronts his ego. To repent of one's sins and turn from them is another basic barrier to discipleship. Openly to confess Christ before men, be baptized in His name, and join the Church is a third obstacle. To those who accept the authority of the Scriptures, these barriers must remain, to be accepted and surmounted as part of the test of a Christian.

But the Church and her emissaries are constantly tempted to add others. In most cases of arrested growth of the Church, men are deterred not so much by the offense of the cross as by nonbiblical offenses. Nothing in the Bible, for instance, requires that *in becoming a Christian* a believer must cross linguistic, racial, and class barriers. To require that he do so is to take the spotlight off the three essential biblical acts and focus it on the requirements of men. The Scriptures affirm that in Christ there is "neither Jew nor Greek, there is neither bond nor free, there is neither male nor female" (Gal. 3:28); but this is true only for those who, being baptized into Christ, have put on Christ. It is a fruit of the Spirit.

During the first fifteen years of the Church's history, almost all believers became Christians *while remaining members of the Jewish community.* Unless we are foolhardy enough to say that members of the Early Church, because they "preached the Word to none but Jews" and maintained intact most of their Jewish antipathy to Gentiles, were not really Christians at all, we must go on to add that fruit often takes a long time to mature. Furthermore, the last phrase in the text (that in Christ "there is neither male nor female") must be taken into account. It certainly does not mean that in order to become a Christian one must adopt a manner of life as if sex differences did not exist, or that Churches which deny ordination to women are no part of the true Church. Nor must the first phrase be made to mean that, to become a Christian, one must act as if class and race differences do not exist.

The New Testament Church

Nineteen hundred years ago the Church found that the Jews liked to become Christians without crossing racial barriers. The Jewish caste was a tightly knit society. It had effective control. It insisted that Jews marry Jews. It ostracized women who "went wrong" with men of other races. It took seriously the command not to take women of the land to wife.

And Shechaniah . . . said to Ezra, We have trespassed against our God and have taken strange wives of the people of the land. . . . Now, therefore, let us make a covenant with our God to put away all the wives and such as are born of them. . . . And Ezra said, Ye have transgressed, and have taken strange wives to increase the trespass of Israel. Now therefore . . . separate yourselves from the people of the land and from strange wives. Then all the congregation answered and said with a loud voice, As thou hast said so must we do (Ezra 10:2, 3, 10-12).

The Jewish caste had no dealings with the half-breed Samaritans. In foreign cities, Jews lived in their own wards. Distant Jews sometimes married back into Jerusalem families, as in the case of Paul's sister. This gave the community marked commercial advantages. Jewish families became banking families and money could be transmitted by letter and a double-entry system of bookkeeping.

All this provided a broad avenue for the expansion of a *Jewish* Church. As long as Jews could become Christians within Judaism, the Church could and did grow amazingly among Jews, filling Jerusalem, Judea, and Galilee. (When she broke over into the half-breed Samaritans, there is no reasons to believe that Christian Jews started to interdine and intermarry with them.) When the Church began to grow in the synagogue communities around the Mediterranean, the first to become disciples of Christ were devout Jews who had been eagerly expecting the Messiah. These, becoming Christians within the synagogue, could do so without crossing racial and class barriers.

As soon as numerous Gentiles had become Christians, however, to be a Christian involved for a Jew leaving the Jewish people and joining a conglomerate society. Admitting Gentiles created a racial barrier for Jews. Indeed, it is a reasonable conjecture that as soon as becoming a Christian meant joining a house church full of Gentiles and sitting down to agape feasts where on occasion pork was served, would-be Jewish converts found the racial and cultural barriers too high and turned sorrowfully away.

The Conversion of Europe

It is difficult to comprehend that it took a thousand years to win the peoples of Europe to the Christian faith. Two hundred years passed during which Ireland was Christian and England pagan. The British Isles were Christian for a hundred years before that great Englishman, Boniface, led North Germany to turn from her pagan gods. France was Christian for at least six hundred years before Sweden was baptized. During each of these long periods, the natives of the pagan country knew something about Christianity. Travelers and tradesmen passed to and fro. An occasional missionary labored in the land. Northern mercenaries in southern armies became Christian and returned home. Christian women were carried off by pagan marauders and became parts of their harems or households or communities. Yet during this two hundred years, or that five hundred, the natives of the adjoining pagan land did not become Christian. They were highly resistant. This resistance consisted chiefly of linguistic and racial barriers.

The time came when some military change, political realignment, conquest, or Spirit-filled missionary of genius opened up a way for the pagans of a given territory to become Christian without crossing these barriers. Then pagans flooded in. Since Church and state were one, Christian law became the law of the land, the monastic system of education and the holy life were established, churches were built, and the land became "Christian."

When Gathered Churches arose, they insisted that only the intelligently committed person, consciously subordinating his will to that of the Lord Jesus and deliberately feeding on God's Word, could rightly be called a Christian. It then became popular to decry the initial turning from paganism to the Church. Yet had it not occurred, the Gathered Churches would never have been born.

In the initial turnings to Christian faith in northern Europe, the principle that men like to become Christians without crossing barriers kept whole countries out of eternal life for *centuries,* and then when a way to become Christian within the social unit was found, a whole country would speedily declare for Christ.

India

The principle is well illustrated in the growth of the Baptist Church among the Panos and Kuingas in the Kond Hills of India. From 1918 to 1957, British Baptists carried on work at Udaigiri in the hills. Two-thirds of the hill population was made up of the aboriginal Kuingas and one-third of the low-caste Hindu Panos. The Kuingas considered themselves superior.

The goal of the mission was the conversion of the land-owning Kuingas. But soon after 1918, the Panos began to turn to Christian faith. The more they turned, the more others of them wanted to turn. By 1956, 1,700 were communicants in good standing. They liked to become Christians without crossing caste (racial) barriers. They continued to interdine and have marriage relationships with non-Christian Panos, and lived on in the Pano section of the villages.

About a hundred Kuingas—the steady objects of mission work—by ones and twos became Christians, mostly around the big mission station of Udaigiri, where the schools and the hospital were located and all the missionaries lived. Many of the Kuinga converts, alas, had married Christian Pano women. To Kuingas in general, becoming Christian began increasingly to look like becoming Pano. Thus, since Kuingas could not choose Christ without crossing racial lines, very few followed Him.

Then, about 1955, about thirty miles from Udaigiri in a little-worked section of the hills, a series of group conversions brought in hundreds of Kuingas, who became Christian while remaining Kuinga. As conversions continued enough came in so that Christian Kuinga youth could marry within their own race. When village congregations met for worship, Kuingas met with other Kuingas. At meetings of all Christians in that section, thousands of Kuingas looked around and saw their own people. Between 1955 and 1961 ten new churches a year were established and in 1962 twenty were (Boals, 1963:67).

In Andhra Pradesh in India, hundreds of thousands of Malas and Madigas (depressed classes) became Christian between 1860 and 1920. Immediately above them in the social order were the Shudra castes. According to the laws of Manu, the Shudras are the laborers, the fourth or lowest division in the quartet of caste divisions. They are touchable and consider themselves much superior to the Depressed Classes or Untouchables. During the sixty years when multitudes of Untouchables were becoming Christian, the Shudras remained resolutely aloof. That large numbers of their Mala and Madiga neighbors were becoming Christian did not in the least affect them. Indeed, it may have stiffened their opposition to the Evangel. For any of them to become Christian would have meant instant exclusion from his own caste and consequent joining of the Christian Malas and Madigas. When, to become a Christian, Shudras had to cross a caste line and join Christians from the Untouchables, very, very few became Christians. Then a change occurred.

Between 1927 and 1932, in forty Shudra castes, more than 15,000 persons acting in small groups sought instruction and became baptized believers. They continued social contact with their castes. They remained in their ancestral homes. There was little social fraternizing between converts of different castes, outside the worship service at the church. They did not intermarry or interdine with Mala and Madiga Christians. They attended existing churches, though in a few cases the older Christians, in order to make further turning of Shudras easier, built a new church either in the Shudra ward or midway between it and the Untouchable ward. Despite strong taboos against receiving food from the hand of a person of another caste, Shudra converts in most cases triumphed over their feelings to the extent of receiving bread and wine from Mala or Madiga ministers. The common cup, however, raised some difficulty, and in some areas Shudra Christians drank first.

Pickett devotes an entire chapter to the Shudra movements to Christ (1933:294ff.), the significant point of which is that until Shudras could become Christians without crossing caste lines, very few were baptized. When they could become Christians within their own people, many were baptized.

Some thinkers on mission have assumed that this principle holds only among primitives and Untouchables; but there is no reason to believe that this assumption is true. The principle was true with the Jews, who were among the most able races of the Roman world. It was true with the European tribes, who were far from primitive. It has enormous applicability today in Canada and the United States. It was true among the Shudras of Andrha Pradesh. It was true among the Moslems in Indonesia. Is it not a very human trait? May we not assume that the great turnings still to come in the years ahead will be among men who become Christian without renouncing their culture and kindred?

A Case from Brazil

Around the turn of the century, great waves of Italian immigrants were flooding into Brazil. These

> settled in certain districts of Sao Paulo, being attracted to their fellow countrymen already "in transition" into the Brazilian culture and national life. The barrio of the Bras was an Italian colony in the growing city of Sao Paulo. The adults spoke Italian exclusively while the children quickly picked up Portuguese. . . . The process of integration took two or three generations and the arrival of Louis Francescon (the Italian immigrant to Chicago who, converted there, went to Brazil as a lay missionary) was timely. He was able to enter, move, and work in a community of Italians that was in evolution into the new culture, but at the same time was receiving new immigrants regularly from the old country (Read, 1965:23f.).

For the first twenty years or more, the churches Louis Francescon started grew entirely among the Italians, because the only language known to the founder and the first Christians was Italian. Starting from no members at all in 1910, the Congregacao Cristan—for such is the name of the denomination—grew till by 1962 it numbered 260,000 full members. From zero to over a quarter million members in fifty-two years is unusual growth for any Church. Most Italians in Brazil are now in comfortable circumstances and some have become citizens of wealth and position.

When I visited the Mother Church of the Congregacao in 1965, the streets were lined with cars in which members had come to the service

None can imagine that the Congregacao has grown among a primitive people. Yet here, too, the principle that men like to become Christians without crossing class and language barriers is clearly a factor in the amazing growth. It must be emphasized that in Sao Paulo, during the years 1910 to 1962, the Methodists, Baptists, Lutherans, and Presbyterians were strong. Only a very small number of the responsive Italians, however, became Evangelicals in these well-established, Portuguese-speaking denominations, each with notable mission schools and colleges buttressing it. Among other reasons, unquestionably one was this: that to become Evangelicals in any of these four Churches, Italians would have had to cross linguistic and class barriers and leave their own community. This Brazilian illustration has great meaning in the United States, where until indigenous movements within each minority surge ahead, great growth is unlikely.

It is instructive to note that, though there are large numbers of Indians in Mexico and the high Andes, not many of these have become Evangelicals. The first few converts won from among the Indians were inevitably integrated into the Spanish-speaking congregations connected with and often dependent on the missionary. To become an Evangelical seemed to the Indian to be one way of becoming Spanish—and for four hundred years the Indian community had resisted becoming Spanish. Indians think of Spanish culture as the conquering culture. Dr. Dilworth, veteran missionary to Ecuador, in his "Historical, Ethnological and Sociological Factors in the Evangelization of the Quechuas of Ecuador," says (1967:74):

> If (believers) are joined by sufficient of the family they can resist the pressure of society. . . . Every time a man takes a stand alone, he imperils the group movement . . . which alone can bring great additions to the Quechua Evangelical Church. . . . (The missionary's) biggest problem . . . will be holding back the desire to separate the first one or two into an isolated Christian society. [Isolated from the Indian, i.e. a mestizo Christian society.]

At least, it is easily proved that where significant numbers of Indians have turned to Evangelical faith, it is because a way has been found whereby they can become Evangelicals without leaving their own people. The Tseltals, Chols, and Otomis in Mexico, and the Adventist Aymaras in Peru immediately come to mind.

OTHER ESSENTIAL FACTORS

Mere ability to become Christian without crossing linguistic, racial, and class barriers never made anyone Christian. By itself it provides no incentive to follow Christ. To realize this, one has only to look at middle-class white Americans in any university community. In them anyone can confess Christ without this deterrent; yet large numbers remain outside the Church. Other factors are essential to the growth of the Church: the Bible must be taught (and often translated), the Word must be proclaimed, and—constrained by love—Christians must seek to persuade their intimates and relatives that it is a wonderful thing to become a follower of the Lord of Life.

How Does the Process Begin?

Right at the beginning, when there is no church in the new segment of society, when no one from that segment has ever become a Christian, the principle I have been setting forth would seem to inhibit all movement. When each would-be convert says to himself, "Becoming a Christian means leaving all my kith and kin," how do enough converts act together so that they do come in without crossing class and linguistic barriers? The hard fact of history is that most sizable movements to Christ have begun with the conversion of an individual—or at most a few families. How then can he—or they—avoid being ostracized? How can he avoid feeling that he is leaving his own folk to join another people? The answer is that right from the beginning the lone convert who starts large group decisions deliberately continues on as one of his own folk. He refuses to be ostracized. He may be physically excluded, but he refuses to be mentally excluded. He continues to love his people, identify with them, serve them, spend as much time with them as possible, proving to them that though he has become a Christian he is still a good member of his society—indeed, a better member than he was before.

Difficult to See

Each nation of Europe and America is accustomed to think of itself as a unified people. Everyone speaks the standard language. Compulsory education has put a single stamp on all. A large majority of citizens consider themselves Christians in some sense, and many who do not nevertheless draw heavily on a Christian heritage. At least in Protestant lands, freedom of conscience allows every individual to follow the religion or ideology he desires. In these countries, therefore, becoming a Christian is a religious rather than a racial decision. It carries no stigma of "betraying and abandoning our people" or "acting in an unpatriotic way."

Consequently Eurican Christians are apt to think that others become Christian for rational, denominational, or theological reasons only. When a person hears the Gospel, finds it reasonable, and is convinced of its truth, he becomes a Christian. He has heard and seen many ideologies, and finally, like Simon Peter, says, "Lord, to whom shall we go? You have the words of eternal life" (John 6:68).

Denominational reasons, too, seem of paramount importance. Each Christian knows his own Branch of the Church well and likes to think that men become Christians for the reasons that led him and his fellows to that particular denomination. On my return from an investigation in Puerto Rico concerning the growth of the Churches there, I was chatting with Dr. Jesse Bader, then Secretary for Evangelism of the National Council of the Churches of Christ. Dr. Bader belonged to the Christian Churches (Disciples of Christ), and when I reported that between 1933 and 1956, the Christian Churches in Puerto Rico had grown from 1,100 to 6,600 while the Lutherans had plateaued at 1,200, Dr. Bader commented, "One would scarcely expect the Lutherans to grow. They are not an evangelistic Church. The Christian Churches, on the contrary, have always been intensely evangelistic." He was surprised when I told him that Lutherans in Africasia have grown far better than the Christian Churches, and that this denomination distinction was not responsible for the outcome in Puerto Rico.

American Christians are accustomed to give theological reasons for church characteristics and growth patterns. They believe that those who like a closely reasoned theological position become Presbyterians, those who like beautiful liturgy and ceremony become Episcopalians, and those to whom a clear New Testament position appeals become Baptists. Or, they say, when a man accepts Christ's sacrifice for him on the cross and rests his faith on Him, he seeks baptism. Men called by God and elected to salvation become Christians. When the Gospel is preached, then the Holy Spirit convicts men "of sin, and of righteousness, and of judgment" (John 16:8), and brings them to repentance and eternal life.

Rational, denominational, and theological factors certainly play a large part in the conversion of men everywhere, but so do environmental factors, of which an important instance is this one that Eurican Christians see with such difficulty: that men like to become Christians while remaining within their own people, without crossing social barriers.

Brotherhood-Oriented Christians

Another reason the element of peoplehood is commonly ignored by Christians is that today the Church in America is fighting a great battle for *brotherhood*. To many Christians, the establishment of brotherhood among the races is the supreme goal of the Church. They are opposed to segregation in any form. They doubt the validity of any principle which encourages Christians of one class or race to worship together or form congregations for their particular kind of people only. In 1976, an eminent white Christian, on reading for the first time the sentence which heads this chapter, wrote me indignantly saying, "Of course they like to, and must not be permitted to." Let us consider their position.

The dedicated Christian in discipled populations, where most persons consider themselves in some way Christian, for the most part thinks exclusively in terms of "What should Christians do?" rather than "How do non-Christian populations accept Christ?" He is particularly critical of allowing one kind of people (one subculture) to form congregations of its own. He erroneously calls this segregation, and says Christian mission should never promote or condone it. It is better, he thinks, to have a slowgrowing or nongrowing Church which is really brotherly, integrated, and hence "really Christian," than a rapidly growing one-people Church.

Such a position is natural for light-skinned Christians today engaged in the battle for brotherhood. When they see the injustices perpetrated on Negroes in the United States and ethnic minorities in many lands, what other position can they take? Furthermore, dark-skinned Christians in Africasia, revolting against white imperialism, add a powerful voice to this demand that the American Church in no way countenance discrimination against dark-skinned citizens. In 1963 a Church in India wrote its sister denomination in America, saying,

> In such a time as this the Church must become afresh the tangible living embodiment of the Gospel of reconciliation in its own fellowship and demonstrate to the world with unmistakable clarity its unequivocal stand on the side of freedom from discrimination, injustice, and intolerance of any kind, whether racial, cultural, or national. We commend every effort being made to lead our Church to assume its proper Christian role in every peaceful struggle to secure full moral and civil rights for all American citizens (Masih, 1964:6).

One must, of course, cordially endorse these sentiments. The principle I am setting forth, which plays such a large part in the growth of the Church, should not be understood as condoning white race pride. Nothing I have said justifies injustice and intolerance, or the strong enforcing segregation against the weak. My own considered opinion is that, in the United States, the refusal of any congregation to admit blacks as members is sin. The Church, I hold, is rightly engaged in a great battle for brotherhood against all such non-Christian behavior. In the battle, she is ranged on God's side.

Part of that battle, however, is to lead non-Christians to Christ. Simply becoming Christian is the greatest step toward brotherhood which it is possible for most people to take. All nations have their classes. Human pride encourages the formation of exclusive groupings. Many religions encourage their adherents to feel that they alone are the superior people. Hinduism gives its caste system not merely legal but religious sanctions. When men become Christians they adopt a faith which teaches the fatherhood of God and the universal brotherhood of man. They espouse a religion whose Scriptures demand brotherhood. If class distinctions continue, they do so in spite of the Christian faith, not because of it. Brotherhood is part of the basic theology of the Christian Church.

The Christian in whose heart Christ dwells inclines toward brotherhood as water runs down a valley. True, Satan occasionally throws some great dam across the valley and the water does not flow. Such a dam is the iniquitous system of slavery which intertribal warfare in Africa and plantations in the Americas made possible. The tearing down of such dams requires, in addition to the natural inclination of the Christian heart, special action on the part of the Church, and this social action is part of the Church's work. But it must never be considered the whole work. If Christ in the heart did not impel toward brotherhood, no amount of social action would help the situation. The Church's real business is the proclamation of the Gospel. Her real business is also to obey her Lord's command to love one another. The Church needs to get on with both.

While the Church is properly engaged in the battle for brotherhood, she must always remember that the rules for that battle are not the rules for a prior discipling which brings men and women of various sub-cultures, minorities, tongues, and ethnic units into the Church and makes the growth of brotherhood possible. Christ is indeed "our peace, who has made us both one, and has broken down the dividing wall of hostility, by abolishing in his flesh the law of commandments, that he might create in himself one new man in the place of the two" (Eph. 3:14). But it must be noted that He creates one new man in place of the two *"in himself."* Jews and Gentiles—or other classes and races who scorn and hate one another— must be discipled before they can be made really one.

As the debate in America raged concerning the rightness of the Homogeneous Unit, C. Peter Wagner determined to write his doctoral dissertation at the University of Southern California, maintaining that properly understood the concept is thoroughly Christian and very helpful in that discipling of *panta ta ethne* commanded in the New Testament. His dissertation was published in 1979 by John Knox Press—a landmark book entitled *Our Kind of People*. Anyone who wants to probe the depths of the radical turnaround in theory of evangelism and mission which the concept has caused must read this book.

Two Examples of This Doubt

A few years ago Puerto Ricans, among them many Protestants, were migrating to Bridgeport, Connecticut, for work. The churches there said, "We shall not establish segregated Puerto Rican churches. That would be wrong. We shall open our churches to these brothers and sisters, make them welcome, and count ourselves fortunate to have our fellowship broadened and enriched by their coming." The Puerto Ricans were invited, came a few times, and were treated most cordially. But they felt more at home in their own Spanish worship services. More importantly, unconverted relatives and friends came more readily to those than to the stately New England churches where the services were so orderly and no one shouted *Amen!* or *Gloria a Deo!* when he approved of something in prayer or sermon. So the Puerto Rican Protestants established congregations of their own in rented halls and vacant stores, and grew. They wisely avoided premature integration.

In the Yakima Valley of the state of Washington is an Indian reservation. Between 1860 and 1880 many Yakima Indians became Christians and members of the Methodist church at White Swan. In the nineties, the government allowed Indians to sell their land, and white settlers bought up farms throughout the reservation. To protect the Indians, the government then forbade Indians to sell their land. This left many whites within driving distance of the Methodist church. They joined it, making it an integrated congregation. Soon leadership drifted into white hands. They sang better, read the Bible more, came more regularly, gave more, and knew more about how churches operate. The Indians found themselves attending a church run by whites. At just that time a nativistic movement called the Shakers began to spread among the Indians, and many Indian Methodists, wanting a church of their own where they would function under their own leaders and in their own way, became Shakers. The Shaker church which Yakimas could join without crossing racial and cultural lines prospered, while the Methodist (unquestionably the more Christian and orthodox congregation) became less and less Indian. Integration, before both groups of Christians are ready for it, is often the kiss of death to the weaker party.

In other words, segregation is sin because it is an exclusion enforced by one group on another. "One-people" churches are righteous, since they are the choice of a group as to language and customs and do not come about through a desire to exclude "inferiors"—quite the contrary.

Many large Africasian denominations are conglomerate Churches, composed of several "homogeneous unit branches"—clusters of city or country congregations, or clusters which have arisen in various castes, tribes, and classes. In these denominations, leadership gravitates to the racially or culturally advanced segment—to whites rather than to Yakima Indians, Chinese rather than Thais, or Syrian Christians rather than Nadars. Whenever this happens, it is difficult for the culturally retarded homogeneous unit branches to grow. Being members of a conglomerate Church, where the pace is set and the coloration and tone determined by leaders of the advanced culture, the Christians of retarded branches find it difficult to remain solid enough with their erstwhile fellows to be able to communicate Christ. They could persuade them to become Christians in a Church "of our people"; but when they urge them to become disciples of Christ in a Church which is obviously "not of our people," they have little power to persuade.

DISCIPLING OUT TO THE FRINGES

Whenever people-consciousness is high—when classes and races think of themselves as distinct, and Christian churches are starting to multiply in one or two of them—correct policy of evangelism is to *disciple each unit out to its fringes*. To attempt to plant congregations in several units at once, arguing that brotherhood demands this, and insisting on integration *first*, whether the Church grows or not, is a self-defeating policy and contrary to the will of God.

The first fifteen years of the history of the Church abundantly illustrate this point. Despite the later struggle with the Judaizers, the emphasis on discipling the receptive Jews cannot be dismissed as an unfortunate error of the Holy Spirit. The risen Lord made no mistake when He commanded His disciples to begin in Jerusalem and proceed to Judea. In both places, as we have seen, the Holy Spirit led the Christians to witness exclusively to Jews. Only after the one-people Church grew strong among the Jews did He lead it out to win the Gentiles. By that time, through the conversion of the proselytes and devout persons, tens of thousands of Jewish Christians had multitudes of Gentile intimates and relatives to whom they could witness effectively.

When the Christian religion is beginning in certain pieces of the mosaic of mankind (often only in one small piece of it), Churches and missions should base their policies on the principle that people like to become Christian without leaving their own folk. When Christian cells are starting to spread through a suburb, a new development, tribe, caste, or other segment of society, the rule should be: disciple that unit out to its fringes.

In many places of the world, notably Africa south of the Sahara, the Church has disregarded this principle and now finds herself with a few congregations of educated Christians of several different tribes. The period of responsiveness has passed and only small, walled-off Christian enclaves remain. In several cases, tribes which were once responsive have become Moslem. No practical priority on earth is higher than that of discipling *out to its fringes* a people which under the leading of the Holy Spirit turns responsive. The "pigmy complex" that afflicts certain Churches—that the true Church is necessarily a tiny Church—must be resolutely rejected in favor of claiming that whole society for Christ. When a population of 900,000 ripens, the people of God must not be content with a Church of 10,000. This is as true in America as in Asia or Africa.

When several units of a society turn responsive at the same time, policy should be to disciple each out to its fringes. In these societies, "loyalty to our people" becomes the chariot in which Christ rides to the hearts of men. If the units are completely discipled, nothing can prevent Him from merging them into one fellowship; but if, before 2 per cent of each unit has become Christian, Churches and missions devote their energies to building up *one* "Christian brotherhood," then most non-Christians (98 per cent, to be exact) will have to leave their own folk and cross class and race barriers to become disciples of Christ. If this stumbling block is put in their way, the movement to Christian faith will usually falter and stop. Christian brotherhood is a *result* of the operation of the Holy Spirit in the lives of Christians—not a prerequisite for baptism.

Common Sense Assumed

In applying this principle, common sense must be assumed. The creation of narrow Churches, selfishly centered on the salvation of their own kith and kin only, is never the goal. Becoming Christian should never enhance animosities or the arrogance which is so common to all human associations. As men of one class, tribe, or society come to Christ, the

Church will seek to moderate their ethnocentrism in many ways. She will teach them that persons from other segments of society are also God's children. God so loved the world, she will say, that He gave His only Son that *whosoever* believes in Him might have eternal life. She will educate leaders of several homogeneous unit Churches in one training school. She will work with the great current in human affairs which is leading on to a universal culture. She will make sure that her people are in the vanguard of brotherly practices. The one thing she will *not* do—on the basis that it is self-defeating—is to substitute kindness and friendliness for the Gospel. She knows that the first is the fruit and the second the root.

And the Church, I am sure, will not deify the principle I am describing in this chapter, whether it brings men into the Way or not. Knowing that growth is a most complex process, she will humbly recognize that God uses many factors as yet not understood by us, and will not insist that He use just this one. If in a given instance, congregations which neglect this principle grow better than those which observe it, she will not blindly follow the principle. She will be open to the leading of the Holy Spirit.

The Church will remember that many factors contribute to church growth and a suitable combination is more important than any one factor. She will not press the factor emphasized in this chapter disproportionately nor allow it to obscure others. Good judgment and a humble dependence on God who alone gives growth is assumed in this discussion.

The Homogeneous Unit Principle is certainly not the heart of church growth, but has nevertheless great applicability to many situations in America and other lands all around the world. Apply with common sense is the rule.

An Urban Exception

In true melting pots, the fact that the Church is a unifying society, different from any of the disappearing clans, classes, or castes, and seems likely to supersede them, draws men to the Christian faith. As their great growth in the cities of Brazil testifies, Pentecostal Churches provide a fellowship which migrants fail to find among members of their own subcultures or homogeneous units. The Christian Church in the cities of the Roman Empire flourished in just such melting pots. She provided a supraracial community or ecumenical fellowship to which city dwellers, emancipated from their provincial and tribal bonds, flocked in great numbers.

The educated Christian today, forgetting the immigrant group, clan, tribe, or caste from which he was digged, and emancipated from his parents' subculture, thinks of cities as just such melting pots. Eagerly looking forward to "one world," he imagines it has arrived. He finds it easy to believe that men—Jews and Arabs to the contrary notwithstanding—long for tribe-transcending fellowships. He finds it difficult to believe that "people-consciousness" is still so high among most homogeneous units that even when their members migrate to the city they like to become Christians within their own particular social class.

In a few metropolitan centers, the fire under the pot has grown hot enough so that homogeneous units *are* disintegrating, many cross-class marriages *are* taking place, and migrants from various parts of the country *are* becoming one new people. A true melting pot has developed. In such cities, some conglomerate Churches are growing rapidly by conversion. Congregations which worship in a standard language and disregard class differences multiply. In such cities the unifying brotherhood should be stressed and worship in the standard language should become the rule.

In most cities, however, conglomerate Churches are not growing rapidly by conversion. If congregations increase, they do so by transfer growth. Non-Christians are not becoming Christians in numbers. Brotherhood ought to attract these urbanites—but does not. Congregations made up of "Jews and Gentiles," Thais, Chinese, and Europeans, French and English, university professors and dock laborers do *not* multiply. In such cities it is good stewardship to remember that human beings like to become Christians without crossing linguistic, class, or racial barriers.

13

THE RECEPTIVITY OF
MEN AND SOCIETIES

The Fact of Varying Receptivity

OUR LORD spoke of fields in which the seed had just been sown and those ripe to harvest. Sometimes men hearing the Word do nothing. The field appears no nearer harvest after receiving the seed than it did before. Sometimes, however, men hearing the Word leap to obey it. They receive it with joy, go down into the waters of baptism, and come up to Spirit-filled lives in self-propagating congregations.

Our Lord took account of the varying ability of individuals and societies to hear and obey the Gospel. Fluctuating receptivity is a most prominent aspect of human nature and society. It marks the urban and the rural, advanced and primitive, educated and illiterate. It vitally affects every aspect of missions, and must be studied extensively if church growth is to be understood. I turn, therefore, to consider the fact of receptivity, its common causes, and its bearing on church growth in every country. Dr. Arthur Glasser explains that

> there is a time when God's Spirit is peculiarly active in the hearts of men. They become ripe unto harvest. . . . When this empirical factor has been deliberately made determinative of strategy, God has abundantly confirmed with good harvests. . . . In seeking to win those whom God has made winnable, we have not unnaturally gained new insight into what it means to be co-laborers with God in the building of His Church (38).

The receptivity or responsiveness of individuals waxes and wanes. No

245

person is equally ready at all times to follow "the Way." The young person reared in a Christian home is usually more ready to accept Jesus Christ at twelve than at twenty. The sceptic is often more willing to become a disciple after serious illness or loss than he was before. This variability of persons is so well known that it needs no further exposition.

Peoples and societies also vary in responsiveness. Whole segments of mankind resist the Gospel for periods—often very long periods—and then ripen to the Good News. In resistant populations, single congregations only, and those small, can be created and kept alive, whereas in responsive ones many congregations which freely reproduce others can be established.

Unevenness of growth has marked the Church from the beginning. The common people, the Gospels tell us, received our Lord's message better than the Pharisees and Sadducees. For the first three decades of the Christian era, the Jews responded far more than the Gentiles. When Judea had been Christian for a hundred years, Philistia on one side and Arabia on the other still remained solidly pagan.

Western nations display the fact that segments of the population ripen to the Gospel at various times. Following the Revolutionary War, as immigrants kept pouring into the United States, the population was remarkably responsive. The Episcopal Church failed to see this and would have denied it. Heavily handicapped by its connection with the English State Church, it declined. Its system of creating ministers (priests) did not fit the free scattered settlements of the frontier. Baptist and Methodist churches, however, multiplied exceedingly. The immigrant population, when approached the right way, was remarkably responsive.

Today's inflooding immigrant populations also are notably responsive; but neither Roman Catholic nor Protestant denominations have been successful in altering their ministerial systems to multiply thousands of congregations among them.

The old white population too, becoming mobile and educated, has been much more responsive than commonly thought. At the very time that many denominations were growing slowly or even declining, other denominations increased rapidly. The Nazarenes grew from nothing to 600,000 in seventy years. The Southern Baptists in the same decades increased from two to thirteen million communicants or a total community of at least twenty million.

Missions in Asia, Africa, and Latin America also abundantly illustrate the fact that societies ripen to the Gospel at different times. During the century 1850-1950 at least 500,000 in the Chota Nagpur area in India became Christian, whereas in nearby Mirzapur the century ended with less than 300 in the Church. The aboriginal tribes of the first area were much more responsive to the Gospel than the castes of the second. The sharp contrast must be softened by remembering that in Mirzapur the Church had mishandled at least one budding receptivity (as related in Chapter Nine). Nevertheless, since the Church in Chota Nagpur had no doubt mishandled some receptivities there, the great difference in outcome can safely be ascribed to a basic readiness in one and its absence in the other.

Southern Baptists between 1950 and 1960 maintained major missionary forces in Thailand and Hong Kong. In 1960 they had 42 missionaries in Thailand and 38 in Hong Kong. The outcome in terms of people "added to the Lord," to use the Lukan phrase, varied enormously. At the close of the decade, in Thailand the membership of churches planted by Southern Baptists was 355; in Hong Kong it was 12,527.

About 1949, the province of Apayao in the extreme north of Luzon in the Philippine Islands was largely occupied by the Isnegs—a pagan aboriginal tribe. The country is exceedingly mountainous and they lived by the slash-and-burn method of cultivation. A few had become Christians in the small town which was the capital of the province and very difficult of access. The United Christian Missionary Society sent an agricultural missionary and his wife to teach this one congregation of Isnegs the cultivation of irrigated rice. Just as the couple, which had no children, arrived, pagan Isnegs all across the province turned highly responsive. They were not interested in growing more rice. They wanted baptism. The missionary was called to villages all through the mountains whose inhabitants had decided to become Evangelical Christians and wanted instruction. He would scramble up a two-thousand-foot ridge and down the other side, slosh up a creek bottom for five miles, and spend two weeks instructing one group. In his absence, a call would often come from some other hamlet and his wife would hike off in the other direction to instruct its residents. In four years several thousand became Christians in the United Church of Christ.

The Roman Catholic Church, hearing of the great turning, sent in its missionaries and also won several thousand. The Evangelical missionary told me that if the United Church had sent in three more couples in 1952, Apayao could have become an Evangelical province, the only one in the Philippines.

Sudden ripenings, far from being unusual, are common. No one knows or has counted the ripenings of the last decade, but it is safe to say that they total hundreds. Those which have been effectively harvested are, alas, smaller in number. One wonders why a single one of them should have been lost!

One of the most remarkable instances of receptivity in the sixties was that manifested by the Tiv in central Nigeria. This tribe of a million souls was occupied by the Christian Reformed Mission. In 1960 the Church consisted of 7,352 communicant Christians, in and around the several mission stations. Out among the Tiv villages the mission had instituted hundreds of CRI's (classes of religious instruction), which were in effect small schools, too elementary to receive grants in aid. In these, slightly educated and slightly paid workers taught the Bible, reading, writing, and arithmetic, and held worship services on Sunday for schoolchildren and interested adults. In 1963, the Sunday church attendance of the Tiv at station churches and CRI's was 105,242 (Grimley, 1966:103, 104)—testimony to tremendous receptivity.

Will this receptivity survive political turmoil and military action? It is impossible to foretell. One thing is clear—receptivity wanes as often as it waxes. Like the tide, it comes in and goes out. Unlike the tide, no one can guarantee when it goes out that it will soon come back again.

In short, uneven response has marked church growth for nineteen hundred years and must be studied carefully if growth is to be understood, and if evangelism is to issue in growth.

COMMON CAUSES FOR FLUCTUATION IN RECEPTIVITY

Myriads of factors affect responsiveness; I cannot attempt to list them all. A few, however, are so common and influential that they should be set forth.

New Settlements

When Bishop Rodrigues of the United Church of Christ in the Philippines was conducting me through Mindanao in my 1956 study of church growth, we came to a well-watered plain cut up into sections by dusty roads. Everywhere palm trees eight to ten feet tall were visible.

"See these small palms?" he said, pointing them out. "Churches can grow here."

I replied, "I see the palms, but what do they have to do with church growth?"

"Everything," he answered. "These young palms proclaim that this is a new population, recently moved in, broken loose from old associations, and not yet hardened into new patterns. These settlers are making new friends, entertaining new ideas, and are free from the social and religious bondages of the old barrios. They can become Evangelicals."

A Methodist minister in Lima, Peru, bore similar testimony when he said that country folk who moved to the shack-towns of that great city remained winnable for a decade or so; but when they began to earn well, built a brick house, and educated their sons and daughters, they grew hard of heart and dull of hearing. The nub of the matter is that immigrants and migrants have been so pounded by circumstances that they are receptive to all sorts of innovations, among which is the Gospel. They are in a phase of insecurity, capable of reaching out for what will stabilize them and raise their spirits. It is no accident that the tremendous growth of Pentecostals in Brazil has taken place largely among the migrants flooding down from the northeast to the great cities of the south.

There is no need to labor the point. Every American pastor is well aware of the fact that new suburbs in which are no churches whatever are an excellent field in which to plant congregations. And new arrivals in any community yield a much higher proportion of new Christians than old inhabitants. Newcomers are looking for community and are open to new decisions; but they must be purposefully evangelized.

Returned Travelers

Travel sometimes turns people responsive. Soldiers in World War II who had seen the world came back to resistant tribal areas of Africa and sparked movements to the Christian faith. The bleak paucity of pagan life repelled them. Since they had prestige and were "of our people," their revulsion against paganism spread. When they told of the outside world, they were believed. The climate became more favorable for change. Becoming Christian became a real option for many.

Mexican laborers, during the years 1940-64, flooded into the United States for six months each year, worked on Protestant farms, and frequently were invited to attend church with their employers. They were sometimes—not often, alas—given Spanish Bibles and New Testaments, and took these back with them to their fanatical ranchos in Mexico. Years later Evangelical missionaries commonly found that braceros (returned laborers) were remarkably open to the Gospel. Numerous beginnings of congregations can be credited to the bracero movement. In at least one case (the Otomi Church) a man converted in the United States founded a whole denomination. Had Evangelical mission in 1944 sensed the importance of braceros, the presence of 300,000 Mexicans on the Protestant farms of the United States each subsequent year could have had tremendous effect in spreading the biblical faith. Unfortunately, only in 1962 and thereafter was the importance of the bracero as a carrier of the Gospel widely realized—

and by then the arrangements between the Mexican and American governments which made the bracero movement possible were being terminated (Taylor, 1962).

Conquest Affects Responsiveness

Since they have not been invaded and defeated, Englishmen and Americans do not realize the shattering effect of being conquered. Defeat means not merely deaths, brutalities, and hostile armies marching across the motherland, but also terrific shock to the entire culture of the conquered. Their pride is humbled, their values trampled underfoot, their institutions abolished, and their gods dethroned. Five hundred years ago, when Moslems conquered Hindu states, they defaced Hindu idols, knocking noses and breasts off gods and goddesses. Though physical insult is frowned upon today, conquest defaces the national image just as effectively. Brutalities characterize every war, and though rape, pillage, arson, and murder among civilian populations are no longer the automatic accompaniment of victory—still, to be conquered is a traumatic experience, which has great meaning for church growth.

Sometimes the conquered are bitter against the victors, and evangelization meets implacable rejection. This is likely to be true among the ruling classes. The steady resistance of the intelligentsia of India to the Christian faith may be credited partly to this cause.

Sometimes the conquered are favorable toward the conquerors, and evangelization meets with cordial acceptance. This is likely to be the reaction of the ruled. They have new masters and are disposed to learn from them. Sometimes conditions attending defeat conduce toward acceptance. For example, Japan's defeat in 1945 coupled with her amazement at the decency and humaneness of the occupation produced seven years of wonderful receptivity toward the Christian religion.

In general, that nation which is seen as "the enemy of our conquerors" will be favorably regarded by the conquered, and missionaries from that nation will be heard with sympathy. It was clear that in 1967 the conquered Arabs were very favorably disposed toward Russia, which was posing as the enemy of Israel. The religion of communism received a good hearing among some Moslems in the following years. If some African Islamic power were to conquer the United States today, the Caucasian population would probably be resistant to Islam, while large numbers of the Negro population—regarding the Islamic power as "the enemy of our enemies, the whites"—would be responsive.

Sometimes a population is not conquered but merely comes within the influence of some expanding power and is rendered receptive. For instance, Latin Rite Roman Catholics in the province of Kerala (southwest India) number about 900,000 and are composed chiefly of the fishing castes along the coast. Their conversion dates from the time the Portuguese ruled Goa, five hundred miles to the north, and were the sea power in all that part of the world. A remarkable Indian Christian named De Cruz championed the fishermen against oppression by Arab Moslem traders, and about 20,000 became Roman Catholics within a few years. That community has grown, by further conversion of members of the fisher castes and by the excess of births over deaths, to its present large size (Gamaliel, 1967:39).

Nationalism

Nationalism exerts a profound influence, both for and against the growth of the Church. In Korea, after nine years of small growth in most provinces (1910-18), there came five years of great receptivity (1919-24). The circumstances were these. Following World War I and the proclamation of the Wilsonian doctrine of self-determination for small nations, Korean patriots in 1919 launched a movement of nonviolent noncooperation against the Japanese with the purpose of forcing Japan to grant self-government to Korea. "Of the thirty-three Korean signers of the Declaration of Independence, fifteen were Christians, some of whom were prominent Protestant ministers" (Shearer, 1966:64). The Church became the rallying point for the oppressed Korean people. Evangelism building on the pronational stance of the Church produced a significant surge of growth in most provinces. Nationalism aided church growth.

By strange coincidence, Gandhi launched a "nonviolent noncooperation" movement against the British in India in the same year; but his movement was led almost exclusively by non-Christians. Indian Christians, fearing that in a self-governing state Hindus and Moslems would persecute them, did not join the fight for freedom. Nationalism in India, therefore, retarded the growth of the Church.

In Mexico, in 1857 at the height of the Juarez revolution a great company of priests walked out of the Roman Catholic Church. Finding no guidance and no allies, some married and became secularized, some sought pardon and went back into the Church, and a handful became Protestants. Had Evangelical missions in North America been afire to extend the biblical faith in Latin America, the Mexican revolution might have been given a sound New Testament base, with incalculable consequences. But in those days missions were just beginning, and were convinced that Latin American countries were tight shut. American Churches had very few Spanish-speaking ministers and no idea at all of the speed with which nationalism turns populations responsive.

Erosion of belief in religion and the general secularization of man do not in themselves lead people to accept Jesus Christ as Lord and Savior. Some think that these trends make men indifferent to all religion. A theme which recurred again and again after the 1928 meeting of the International Missionary Council at Jerusalem was that, because of erosion of "faith" in all religions, Christianity should form an alliance with non-Christian religions to combat the spread of secularism. Such thinking misses the main point, which is that continuing erosion of belief in religions creates a vacuum of faith. Whether in St. Paul, Minnesota, or Sao Paulo, Brazil, atheistic communism and other materialistic ideologies will do their best to fill the vacuum; but the way to prevent that happening is not to join hands with fading religions in an alliance against irreligion. The suggestion would be amusing if it were not so tragic. The way is to proclaim the truest faith we know with the greatest ardor of which we are capable, and ask God's richest blessing on the enterprise to which He sets our hands. Christians who believe that there is "no other name" (Acts 4:12) and that Jesus Christ is the Savior of the world, can meet the vacuum of faith only by steady church-planting mission, century after century.

> The function of the universal Church is to be the messenger of God's universal offer of reconciliation. The "all" who are one in Christ exist for the sake of the "all" for whom Christ died, but who do not know or acknowledge him. The appeal which God makes to humanity is made through ambassadors. . . . They are to make disciples of all nations. . . . The Church does not apologize for the fact that it wants all men to know Jesus Christ and to follow him. Its very calling is to proclaim the Gospel to the ends of the earth. It cannot make any restrictions in this respect ('t Hooft, 1963:101, 116).

Man is a believer by nature. If faith in old religions fades, he becomes responsive to some new religion—of science, communism, or an updated version of his ancestral cult. He may deify a new leader, his secular civilization, a political party, or Man—but worship he will.

Theologically minded Euricans are inclined to weigh erosion of belief as an agent of change more heavily than they should. Believing Christ and accepting Christianity are only partially an intellectual exercise. The growth of the Church depends on other factors besides right belief. Apologetics, or what Bavinck calls *elenctics* (the presentation of the Christian faith to adherents of non-Christian religions, in such a fashion as to persuade them to believe on Jesus Christ), must never be regarded as the sole or even the chief knowledge needed by Christians as they woo non-Christians. Nevertheless, the vacuum is one important cause of a rise in receptivity and should be discerned with precision.

It is quite possible for the Church to see a vacuum of faith and fail to fill it. Since to lead men into life-giving relationship to God in the Church of Jesus Christ so many factors must converge and must have the express blessing of God, it is possible for erosion of faith to be followed by no growth of the Church. For example, all other factors favorable to conversion may have been assembled by God, and then the disobedience of a Church, a congregation, or a Christian prevents church growth. Or, those who have lost all faith in their own religion may hate and fear Eurica so greatly that they cannot hear the Gospel, which in a given case happens to be proclaimed by Euricans. It is highly unlikely, for instance, that those few Arab Moslems today who are complete sceptics concerning the truth of Islam and the Koran could hear the Gospel proclaimed by missionaries of any nation remotely connected with Zionism or Israel. English and American missionaries are particularly impotent. Indonesian Moslems, however, in 1965 were quite favorably disposed to hear the Gospel from Americans. They would not listen to Russian missionaries, proclaiming the gospel of Marx; they hated and feared the communists. The erosion of faith in non-Christian religions is correctly seen in the total context, as one among many factors which turn populations responsive.

An extraordinary happening has gone almost unmarked in the world of missions. One of the four great non-Christian religions has died during the last fifty years. In 1920 Confucianism, the religion of four hundred million Chinese, was a most powerful faith. The communist conquest of China has radically altered the situation. The whole family system, so basic to Confucianism, has been liquidated, Inside mainland China, Confucianism has lost its power. True, it is still practiced by some Chinese of the dispersion and may continue in vestigial form for decades or centuries; but as a great faith, Confucianism is finished. Buddhism in China is greatly weakened, too. As in 1980 China opens to freer interchange of thought, the Church will face at least eight hundred million who live in a faith vacuum. Some, of course, are convinced Marxists and many will be in love with the world, but many more will be hungry for sure belief. To be sure, any communist government can heavily handicap and persecute Christians. The Church always evangelizes within the limits of the possible. But nevertheless Christians all around the world should be expecting a new and remarkable receptivity of the Chinese toward Christ. An unbelievable desire to learn English is sweeping mainland China. This would seem to offer considerable openings for sensitive and sensible evangelism.

Adherents of polytheistic religions with millions of gods are particularly likely to experience growing vacuums of faith. Current cults may continue, but without conviction. The Church in Africasia will face these in the twenty-first century as she did in the Roman Empire in the second and third. It took three hundred years for the cultured people of Greece and Rome to move from gods and goddesses in whom they could not believe, and whose immorality degraded them, to God the righteous Father Almighty, Maker of Heaven and Earth, and Jesus Christ His Son. Gnosticism, Mithraism, and many other religions furnished half-way stations and for a time challenged Christianity. But in the end the polytheists of Rome and Greece accepted baptism in the Church of Christ.

What will happen in Islam, when Moslem scholars subject the Koran to the same intense examination to which Christian scholars have subjected the Bible? And when Moselm archaeologists share the generally accepted findings of Jewish and Christian archaeologists? When the Koranic versions of biblical events are seen—as they certainly will be—to be garbled reproductions of Old and New Testament records, what will Moslems do? The faith of Islam is uniquely dependent on the claim that the Koran is the true and the Bible the corrupt version. When the acids of modernity eat away the protective layers of ignorance and the light of learning exposes the falsehood in this claim, faith in Islam is likely to wane. After Moslems have tried substitutes of various sorts, they will become responsive—to communism or to Christianity—in very large numbers. They, too, are men and cannot live in a faith vacuum.

Freedom from Control

Control inhibits responsiveness to the Christian Gospel. Relaxing of controls encourages it. Most of the three billion who yield no allegiance to Jesus Christ live under rigid controls. When these disintegrate, men become free to consider the claims of Christ.

Controls are of several varieties. The most intimate is that exercised by the family and immediate relatives. Persons do not exist as independent entities who make decisions entirely on their own, but as parts of a social whole. Their thoughts and feelings are conditioned and determined to a very large extent by the control of the family. The elaborate mourning, with loud wailing and repeated address to the dead, common in the villages of India is carried on as much for the observer as to express the bereaved's own sorrow. Villagers are not conscious of the control which dictates their form of mourning, but it is real nevertheless. "What will others think of my conduct?'' is a serious consideration in all societies where each member is truly dependent on the family for almost every aspect of life.

The control of the village, the rancho, the tribe, and the caste is also an objective fact of life. The welfare of the village requires that all sacrifice to the god who is causing cattle disease. Failure to sacrifice draws down the wrath of the whole village.

"Ah," they exclaim, "so you are no longer one of us. You want our cattle to die. You refuse to share in our sacrifice to the god who brings the hoof-and-mouth disease? We shall deal with you."

The tribe believes that those who become Christian anger its gods and thus destroy the fertility of the fields for the whole village. The tribe has effective controls which vary all the way from beating the innovator and grazing his fields to putting a hex on him.

The ecclesiastical organization, the hierarchy, also exerts control. As pastors and missionaries on furlough compare notes at the School of Missions at Fuller Seminary, they find that whether the ecclesiastical machine be that of one religion or another makes little practical difference. In some territories, an illiterate leader of the pagan religion will visit villages which are considering becoming Christian to dissuade or threaten them. In other territories, a well-educated priest will do the same.

Freedom from these controls is also of various kinds. The most obvious sort is that which emerges when the state guarantees real freedom of conscience. When the national constitution declares that all citizens have freedom to worship, proclaim their faith, and persuade others to follow it, ecclesiastical control is greatly relaxed. The constitution of Puerto Rico guarantees religious freedom, but the executive secretary of the Puerto Rican Federation of Churches in 1956 told me that each year he instituted many civil suits against priests and others who denied Protestants the rights granted them in the constitution. He felt that this enforcement of freedom was essential to its real presence in the island.

A less obvious sort of freedom is that which arrives with the spread of religious pluralism and the disintegration of the power of peoples to ostracize. When the general population feels that what men believe is strictly their own business and interference with such belief is frowned upon, then the controls of the tribe and the village are diminished. Control is less in the city than in remote rural areas, and less in mobile than in stationary populations.

Each degree of control or freedom from control in each kind of pressure system affects receptivity. The increase of religious pluralism throughout the earth and the spread of the ideal of religious liberty are bringing about an era in missions when resistance due to controls will grow less and less, and receptivity due to freedom will grow more and more.

Acculturation

Acculturation is the dynamic process by which a society in contact with other societies changes its culture, adapts to the new situation, accepts some innovations, and modifies its system. A. P. Elkin, Professor of Anthropology in the University of Sydney, Australia, says:

> From the viewpoint of the native race, three stages can frequently be distinguished in the history of its contact with the dominant immigrant white people. The first . . . is one of bewilderment, opposition, resentment, and a sense of loss; the adults can find life and hope only in and through their own customs, traditions, and beliefs; they can see nothing of value for them in the culture of the white man except perhaps in some of his material goods and tools . . . they may deem it wise to pay lip-service to those Whites who are zealous in religious endeavor, and they very often entrust their children to missionaries for education; but their closing days are saddened by the spectacle of the young men and women being attracted to the ways and delights of the white man. . . .
>
> In the meantime, members of the next generation, being influenced by the white man and his culture before they had really been gripped by the spirit of their own faith, become scornful of the old ways and superstitions, at least outwardly, and feel that they must rise above it. This attitude of scorn of the past and a feeling of inferiority with regard to their native culture are characteristic of the second stage of contact. . . .
>
> [The third stage] is the reaction from the feeling of worthlessness regarding native culture in general . . . which is usually held for a generation or so after the initial stage of contact . . . they tend to revert to the old or what they can recapture of the old; they make what adjustments they can apart from the white organization of social and economic life and in some cases become leaders of discontent, though not necessarily of a revolutionary nativistic movement . . . what we see in the third stage of culture contact is a return [to the old culture] and to a sense of worth regarding native arts, crafts, literature, law, and custom . . . the return to faith [which marks the third stage] should be to a Christian faith in which the most valuable features of native belief were gathered up (Elkin, 1937:537-45).

Although Elkin was writing about Australian aborigines and the duty of the dominant whites toward them, the stages in acculturation he describes can be observed in many places—including American and Canadian cities. Variations occur, but the stages can usually be distinguished. Resistance in stage one, wide acceptance in stage two, and—where in stage two the Christian faith has not been made fully their own—reaction in stage three is quite common. Acculturation in stage two produces scorn of the old ways which is the reverse side of the coin of receptivity.

THE BEARING OF RECEPTIVITY ON OUTREACH

I have been analyzing receptivity not as an intellectual exercise but to obtain light on the complex process of church growth. The correct response to this chapter is not mental pleasure in understanding how receptivity fluctuates, but rather joy that through knowing these variations we may be more faithful in the discharge of our stewardship and commission.

Ministers and missionaries often ask, Are the factors which create receptivity measurable, so that with proper techniques of appraisal we can know that such and such a population is ready for the Gospel or is on the way to becoming ready? One keen churchman asked, Could measurements be fed into a computer so that the Church would know exactly the degree of receptivity and whether it was increasing or decreasing? The answers to these questions are "in the distant affirmative." Someday this will become possible. Indeed, today a trained observer can judge with a fair degree of accuracy that a given homogeneous unit is in a state where its members will welcome change. But in practice, rather than carry on an elaborate program of measurement, the Church or mission has at hand a quicker and more reliable method of ascertaining receptivity.

Are groups of persons becoming Christians? As Jesus Christ is proclaimed to this population and His obedient servants witness to Him, do individuals, families, and chains of families come to faith in Him? Are churches being formed? Is any denomination working in similar peoples planting self-propagating congregations? If the answers are in the affirmative, the homogeneous unit concerned is receptive.

Once receptivity is proved in any one segment of society, it is reasonable to assume that other similar segments will prove receptive. Evangelism can be and ought to be directed to responsive persons, groups, and segments of society.

Two creative thinkers have written influentially on the bearing of receptivity on church and mission policies. George Hunter has described how receptivity ought to guide the outreach of North American congregations and denominations. Peter Wagner discusses how it ought to guide missions and churches in the Third World.

In *Frontiers of Missionary Strategy,* Wagner entitles Chapter Six "Anticipatory Strategy." He declares, "To a large extent, missionary strategy must be based on predictions or at least on some intelligent anticipation of the future" (106). This immediately raises the question as to whether in Christian work predictions should be made at all. Are they biblically justifiable? After examining the Scriptures, he concludes that while pre-

dictions are human wisdom and must be used with caution, they are nevertheless required of one who would be a good steward of God's grace. With
that matter settled, Wagner goes on to explore how reliable predictions of
church growth may be made. He points out that

> Nongrowth is just as important to discover as growth. If no churches are
> growing in a given area, anticipatory strategy might lead to another more
> promising area (111).

The central question is:

> Where is the church most likely to grow? Which countries have the greatest
> potential and which particular groups of people within those countries show
> signs of being receptive to the gospel? . . . by careful soil tests, missionary
> strategists should be able to advise sowers where they should plant the seed
> first (115).

Wagner was for years field secretary of the Andes Evangelical Mission. As such he naturally thought in terms of getting the right resources
to the right places. Receptivity demands strategic action and the rearrange-
ment of priorities.

> What resources are needed for an efficient job? If the university student com-
> munity in a socialist country turns ripe, one kind of worker will be needed.
> If a group of animistic peasants turns ripe, someone with different qualifi-
> cations is needed. Part of good management is to look ahead and . . . deter-
> mine where the needs will be and what kind of missionary should be recruited
> or reassigned (116).

George Hunter in "The Grand Strategy" (Chapter V in *The Contagious Congregation*) discusses receptivity in the North American setting.
He considers it enormously important and counts it "the greatest contribution of the church growth movement to this generation's world evangelization" (104). The chapter is full of insights for American churches
which, with rather small adjustments, would apply equally well to churches
in other continents.

A particularly helpful section deals with guidelines for discovering
receptive mainline Americans. Hunter lists indicators of receptivity and
urges that congregational and denominational policy be set in the light of
these. These, he says, have "a special potency for the Christian mission
to America."

> . . . Pray to be led to receptive people. God . . . is preparing people to
> hear the gospel . . . and to accept reconciliation with Him and to become
> followers of Christ.

. . . The people visiting and wanting to join your church are receptive people . . . their receptivity is frequently short lived, and wanes rather quickly. Dr. Larry Lacour of the First United Methodist Church of Colorado Springs has fashioned a strategy for reaching visitors. (Each is invited to) join a four session orientation class. . . . When invited immediately some 90 percent join the class, when invited a week later 50 percent join, and if a month later 10 percent.

People who have recently lost faith (in anything) are very receptive.
. . .

. . . People among whom any church or religion is growing are receptive.
. . . In the O'Hare airport I was encountered by a pretty devotee of the Hare Krishna cult. She said, "Excuse me, sir, but all of the handsome gentlemen are wearing carnations today. May I give you one?" . . . We briefly conversed and I remember saying, "Look, I know you are into this now, but it will leave you hollow and let down later on. Whenever that happens telephone me collect anytime day or night." I gave her my card. She looked to see if her partners were busy elsewhere, her eyes teared, and her voice trembled as she almost whispered, "Thank you, Mr. Hunter, I just might do that."

. . . People of the same homogeneous unit as your members will be more receptive to the outreach of your church.

. . . People with conscious needs that your ministries can help will be receptive.

. . . Be prepared to start ministries to reach populations with special needs. Such groups are: undiscipled young couples with small children; mature adults fifty-five years and above; men with a 'shop' interest who would gather for an evening in "The Carpenter Shop" in the church's educational plant; Koreans or French Canadians or Arabs or Vietnamese who need classes in English. . . . The possibilities of growth through relevant ministries are almost boundless for congregations that can spot such populations and create special ministries for them.

. . . Reach out to persons in transition. These are much more likely to be receptive than during periods of relative stability. Such transitions include: adolescence, going off to college, or armed forces, first job, getting married, first child, last child leaving home . . . menopause, retirement, loss of a loved one, sickness, getting fired, job advancement, second marriage. . . .

The whole chapter is stimulating reading for pastors anywhere.

The *Church Growth Bulletin* for many years has been describing the receptivity of various populations in all six continents. One vast population very much on the hearts of Christians is the 700 million Moslems. This group is made up of thousands of separate pieces, each one varying in receptivity from the next. The general opinion that all Moslems are highly resistant is not true. Large communist blocks which arise in Moslem countries bear witness that Moslems in considerable numbers are turning from the worship of Allah to an atheistic understanding of reality. If they can do that, they can turn to the Christian Faith. The September 1979 issue of *Church Growth Bulletin* has a perceptive article by Dr. McCurry on receptivity as it bears on the evangelization of the huge Moslem mosaic. He says,

> We need to use all the skills available to us in church growth thinking to find the responsive Muslim units scattered all over the world and then move in with sufficient force to disciple those subgroups (220).

Distribution of Receptivity

As a churchman regards the people with whom he works, he often asks, To what degree is becoming a Christian a real option to members of this homogeneous unit? How receptive is it? In answering these questions or estimating the receptivity of any population it is helpful to locate it on a receptivity axis. If a line is drawn, such as that in the following figure from A to Z, every population can be located at the letter which corresponds to its likelihood to become Christian. At A would be placed those peoples who solidly resist Christianity. At Z would be placed those whose members break down all barriers in order to become Christian. In between, all other populations would be distributed according to their degree of responsiveness.

FIGURE 13.1. DISTRIBUTION OF RECEPTIVITY

A B C	J	S	X	Z

Populations at A would be pre-evangelized in a manner suitable to the highly resistant. Those at Z would be harvested. At A the task of the Church or mission is chiefly to hang on sowing the seed and practicing the kind of mission Charles de Foucauld of North Africa, a Roman Catholic missionary, has made famous. Mission, he said, is a Christian simply being there with a presence willed and determined as a witness to the love of God in Christ. In populations near Z, on the other hand, Foucauldian mission would be criminal. When the Holy Spirit has so moved on men that, resolved to become Christians, they press in to take the kingdom by violence, it is the height of unfaithfulness for the missionary simply to remain there as a Christian. Mere witness to the love of God is not what is demanded. At Z, the obedient Christian must baptize multitudes in the name of the Father, Son, and Holy Spirit.

Two illustrations from the United States will help us see the situation. In the multitudinous new suburbs—which must surely be grouped at the Z end of the scale—the speedy establishment of adequate numbers of new congregations is clearly God's will. Also a much greater attention to first generation immigrants is surely God's command. These fine people are intensely interested in becoming Americans and we should make sure that they do not become pagan Americans. The difficulty is that the first generation, for economic reasons, cannot become the same kind of affluent congregations which they see about them. To recreate that kind of Christianity would be to require them to fight in Saul's armor. Nevertheless they should be discipled into a form of church which is culturally agreeable and economically possible to them. They are Z populations.

Most populations today fall neither at A nor Z, but in between. To some degree they are winnable, but they are not storming the gates of Zion. In the mid-ranges of the axis, method is of supreme importance. Winnable men may be lost by one method and gained by another. For instance, heavy subsidy may give a rapid start but impose an intolerable burden on the fathering mission and set a low ceiling to growth. No subsidy, suitable for populations at the right end of the distribution, if woodenly enforced in populations toward the left end, may prevent any congregations at all from forming except at mission stations where the presence of missionaries and the rich services of the mission furnish hidden but effective subsidy. Heavy dependence on the school approach in Africa, south of the Sahara, makes possible the Christianization of 1 to 5 per cent of populations left of center; but when these grow receptive and move to the right of center, excessive reliance on the school approach dooms the Church to very slow advance. Proclaiming Christ to individuals only and taking them out of their society into Christian colonies may be the only mode of mission which will win any to Christ for populations grouped around B and C on the receptivity axis; but when increased responsiveness places these populations at J, S, or other positions toward the right, it is fatal to continue the "one-by-one against their kindred" method of mission.

One of the most wealthy missions in Colombia, South America, formed its habits of work during the nineteenth century, when its principal task was simply to survive as a Protestant mission in that very Roman Catholic land. It developed its institutional pattern when Colombia would have had to be located at the extreme left of the axis. Today, when men in Colombia are freer to accept the biblical faith, the same methods, suitable to a resistant population, are unfortunately continued.

No Receptivity, No Mission?

Recognition of variations in receptivity is resisted by some mission thinkers because they fear that, if they accept it, they will be forced to abandon resistant fields. Abandonment is not called for. Fields must be sown. Stony fields must be plowed before they are sown. No one should conclude that if receptivity is low, the Church should withdraw mission.

Correct policy is to occupy fields of low receptivity lightly. They will turn receptive some day. They also have children of God living in them. Their populations are made up of men and women for whom Christ died. While they continue in their rebellious and resistant state, they should be given the opportunity to hear the Gospel in as courteous a way as possible. But they should not be heavily occupied lest, fearing that they will be swamped by Christians, they become even more resistant.

They should not be bothered and badgered. Generations should not be reared in schools where—receiving small doses of the Gospel which they successfully reject—they are in effect innoculated against the Christian religion. Resistant lands should be held lightly.

While holding them lightly, Christian mission should perfect organizational arrangements so that when these lands turn responsive, missionary resources can be sent in quickly. The Church today is hearing a great deal about the sudden new receptivity among Moslems in Indonesia. It is devoutly to be hoped that missionaries to Moslems in great numbers will be transferred to that part of the world. Reinforcing receptive areas is the only mode of mission by which resistant populations *which become receptive* may be led to responsible membership in ongoing churches of Christ.

The ways in which highly receptive populations may be filled with Christian congregations should be a subject of study in every seminary and theological training school. True, not every pastor will encounter a highly receptive population, but some of them will. Every minister in training therefore ought to have instruction as to how churches may be *multiplied* in the great receptive populations of Canada and the United States. The same is even more true of theological training schools in Asia, Africa, and Latin America. In Europe, however, with its intrenched State Churches, what church growth means is not yet clear. The State Churches appear to believe that nothing more than renewal is called for. The population is already "Christian," i.e., baptized. I myself am inclined to believe that renewal is not enough. Only the creation of multitudes of new vital congregations (either within or without the State denominations) will reconvert the myriads of European Christo-pagans. Much thought should be given to this.

Every missionary candidate also in schools of mission ought to have instruction in how churches may be multiplied among populations which show great response to the Gospel. No single method will fit all populations. A primitive tribe needs one method, urban masses of Brazil another, and rural Filipinos in the barrios of Mindanao a third. Africans welcome one kind of congregation, Latin Americans a second, and men out of the tightly closed caste system of India still another.

Particularity of Church Growth

Church growth in receptive populations is marked by particularity. Much confusion and loss are caused by forgetting this. Each population is a separate case, more different from other populations than one person is from another. Its nature conditions church growth; so do the previous history and the unique characteristics of the mother and daughter Church there. The kind of missionaries and mission policies has vast influence on growth potential and pattern.

The accredited seminaries of the West will not produce the kind of Hispanic, black, French Canadian, and Navaho pastors who will multiply viable and reproductive congregations in the huge minorities concerned— 25 million Hispanics, 25 million blacks, 6 million French Canadians, and on and on. Present seminaries are almost exclusively concerned with turning out care-taker ministers to look after existing congregations. Most seminaries have no idea as to how to start a movement like that of George Fox or John Wesley or Louis Francescon. The Pentecostals have some insight in these matters, but we need much more light on the subject.

Each population, therefore, must have its own formula. Whole milk, so to speak, must be modified by the addition of different ingredients in different proportions. The essentials of the Gospel, the authoritative Bible, and the unchanging Christ remain the same for all populations. But the accompaniments can and must be changed freely to suit each particular case. This principle is well illustrated by the institutions of mission— hospitals, schools, agricultural demonstration centers, literacy drives, radio stations, orphanages, leprosy homes, and theological seminaries. Are these, one might ask, good for reconciling men to God and multiplying cells of the Church? Under some circumstances the answer is an emphatic *Yes*. Some burgeoning Afericasian Churches can scarcely have too many institutions. Under other circumstances, the answer must be an emphatic *No*.

In most circumstances, however, the answer is *Yes, if . . . if,* in the schools, many are "added to the Lord"; *if* church expansion is demonstrably aided; *if* the splendid institutions do not overbalance the little, pitiful church; *if* the multiplying churches can build similar institutions of their own; *if* the seminary or theological training school trains church planters as well as caretakers; *if* church growth is enhanced and not eclipsed; *if* the medical institutions stimulate reproduction of churches; *if,* rather than create a small community of cultured, middle-class, sealed-off Christians, mission institutions lead the churches out to multiply—then the answer must be *Yes, Yes, Yes!*

Similarly when a mundane matter such as the scale of pay of ordained ministers is considered, or when we ask, "What proportion of ministers should be tentmakers?"—answers depend, not on immutable general principles, but on conditions in a particular population such as its social structure, the stage in which its Church finds itself, and the nature of its aid from abroad. Church growth in receptive populations is always particular. Nothing grows but individual churches, and the growing Church can always be seen best in single homogeneous units.

FITTING METHOD TO RECEPTIVITY IN VIEW OF THE CHIEF END

That receptivity should determine effective evangelistic methods is obvious. When, about 1840, in Bombay female education was a revolutionary idea, the Scotch Presbyterian mission paid little Parsee girls a few annas a day to get them to attend. A hundred and twenty years later, prestigious mission schools charged substantial fees and took only a few out of many applicants. Adjustment of mission methods to the desire of people for Western medicine, education, production, and the like is easy and universally practiced. The missionary is a hardheaded realist in such matters.

But readjustment of the total program of a Church in America or a mission in Africa to enable it to fit a greatly increased responsiveness is difficult and rare. Few large populations change as a whole. When a community of 100,000 develops a mild degree of receptivity, moving let us say from *D* to *P* on the axis of receptivity, this never means that all 100,000 have suddenly become winnable, but rather that among the total population *a few thousand* persons belonging to some homogeneous unit have become winnnable, and then *only if approached in the right way.* If they hear the Gospel from their own folk, they are winnable; but from strangers they are as resistant as ever. If they recognize the Christian messenger as "a man who is on our side," they are winnable; but if those proclaiming Christ appear to them as disinterested professionals, they remain resistant. If those who become Christian are really changed, the few thousand become winnable; but if the new Christians are as unhappy as ever, non-Christians remain indifferent to the Gospel.

Unless churchmen in all six continents are on the lookout for changes in receptivity of homogeneous units within the general population, and are prepared to seek and bring persons and groups *belonging to these units* into the fold, they will not even discern what needs to be done. They will continue generalized "church and mission work" which, shrouded in fog as to the chief end of mission, cannot fit outreach to increasing receptivity. An essential task is to discern receptivity and—when this is seen—to adjust methods, institutions, and personnel until the receptive are becoming Christians and reaching out to win their fellows to eternal life. *Effective* evangelism is demanded. It finds the lost, folds those found, feeds them on the Word of God, and incorporates them in multitudes of new and old congregations. That is why it is called effective evangelism.

PART V
SPECIAL KINDS OF
CHURCH GROWTH

14

THE MASSES, THE CLASSES, AND CHURCH GROWTH

MORE THAN any previous century, ours is conscious of "the masses" and their claim to justice and equality of opportunity. The burden-bearers have always comprised the major part of society, but in the twentieth century they have gained more and more power. Industrialism has created a huge proletariat in our ever enlarging cities. Labor organizations have achieved tremendous strength. The Churches have called for social justice. An awakened conscience among national leaders has changed our tax structure in the direction of a more just distribution of wealth. Communism has established dictatorships of the proletariat in many nations, defending these as a necessary step toward a just society.

Scores of millions, through reading, study, lectures, the mass media, and indoctrination, have learned of both the needs of the masses and their might when organized and armed. Perhaps more powerful than books and speeches, however, managed events such as elections, victories at the Olympic Games, space explorations, summit meetings, riots, and wars have strikingly focused attention on the masses and their right to education, health, leisure, and power. That mankind should be divided into beneficiaries and victims of the social order no longer seems right to thoughtful men. The condition of the disinherited has become a matter of profound concern to the state. Those who oppose communism do so not on the basis that its championing of the masses is wrong, but that it is ineffective, its means and consequences are self-defeating.

What does this radically new element in human thinking, which dominates the world scene as the Himalayas dominate the plains of North India, signify for bringing nations to faith in Jesus Christ and obedience to the Gospel?

CLASS/MASS SOCIETY DESCRIBED

While most Americans will agree with the first paragraph above, they understand it with their heads rather than their hearts. Though they have their poor, Americans are accustomed to a unified society and do not like to speak of "the classes and the masses." The carpenter earns as much as the college teacher and the millworker drives a better car than the minister. The idea of a privileged aristocracy is alien to our national ethos. So while they sometimes talk about the masses, Americans do not really know what it is to live as victims of the social order. In fact we are apt to think "victims of the social order" too barbed a phrase to describe any portion of our own society.

Notwithstanding this, America has her exploited masses. In his State of the Union address in 1968 President Johnson dwelt on the five hundred thousand "hard core unemployed." Vice President Humphrey has said, "The consequences of being poor and hopeless in a society where most are not produces a deep sense of alienation. This feeling is nowhere more fully expressed than in the attitudes of some ghetto dwellers toward the law. . . . In the eyes of the impoverished, it is the law which garnishes the poor man's salary . . . evicts him from his home . . . binds him to usury . . . cancels his welfare payments . . . and seizes his children" (Humphrey, 1967).

In Africasia outside the strictly tribal societies, the (upper) classes and the masses are a vivid part of the scene. Economies, power structures, and religions are so arranged that the more comfortable classes remain high above the great mass of people. The distance can be measured in many areas of life. In income, the classes average 200 a month, the masses 20. In language, the classes speak the national language fluently and correctly. The masses speak many dialects and express themselves clumsily in the standard languages. In housing, the classes live in comfortable and permanent homes, with all modern conveniences. The masses live in shacks made of thatch and wattle, adobe and crude tile, odds and ends of lumber, and tin cans. As to health, the classes obtain competent medical service, buy sufficient food to keep well, rear their children to maturity, and enjoy old age. The masses depend on herbalists and medicine men of one sort or another, eat chiefly corn or manioc or rice, meal after meal, day after day, and year after year. True, their diet is fortified by a few beans, vegetables in season, and very occasionally meat or fish. Men of the masses are lean. They do not count calories, their infant mortality is high, and they seldom live to have grey hair.

In Africasia, in the political arena, the classes are intimately related to the men who run the country. The masses have little to do with those who rule them and care less. In religion, the classes are assured that they are God's special creation—recall the Hindu doctrine of castes. The masses are assured, in effect, that God created them "little people"—Shudras or inferiors in India, Indians in Bolivia and Peru, Negroes in North America—to be laborers forever.

Brazil is one of the advanced nations of Africasia. It has a superabundance of land and is installing great power dams and industrial complexes. Yet the following quotations indicate that even in Brazil the masses are a prominent feature of the demographic landscape.

> Brazil's Negroes (38 per cent of the population versus 10 per cent in the United States) have never feared a Ku Klux Klan, never fought in a race riot, never staged a sit-in. Indeed, President Janio Quadros was expressing a common opinion of Brazilians when he once said, "We have become the most successful example of racial co-existence and integration known in history."
>
> But the facts suggest otherwise. Brazil's colored people are the nation's dispossessed and, in many respects, race prejudice in Brazil matches anything to be found in the Deep South. Even the Portuguese word for people—gente—has racial overtones in Brazil. "Whites," runs a bitter Negro saying, "are gente, blacks are beasts." . . . On a visit to Sao Paulo, Louis Armstrong exclaimed, "They told me this place had no discrimination, and all I see is my color pushing the broom." . . . Many white Brazilians have a superiority complex which staggers the wildest Yankee imagination. "According to Brazilian stereotypes," a Negro lawyer in Sao Paulo said to a North American newspaper reporter, "you are now talking to a man who is shiftless, lazy, irresponsible, lawless, stupid, drunk, immoral, and oversexed." In Sao Paulo police training classes, only Negroes are used to simulate crooks. . . . Most colored Brazilians accept these white stereotypes without question. . . . until Brazil's Negroes climb off the bottom rung of the ladder, no one expects any pressure for change. Most of Brazil's struggling Negro millions are still too busy trying to get enough to eat to worry overly much about discrimination (*Newsweek*, September 7, 1964:47).

"The masses" in Brazil in 1964 included almost all the Negroes, and millions of mestizos as well. In 1942, Merle Davis of the International Missionary Council estimated the situation as follows.

A wayside house. One backless bench, a hammock and a broken chair were the only items of furniture. The other room had a table, a bed with rags covering rusted springs, and a bench. In one corner hung a small mirror, and on a kerosene box beneath were a powder puff, a spool of thread, and a thimble. Two naked children played about on the dirt floor with chickens and a small pig. Food was cooked in a kettle over a fire of sticks, kindled on a mud-covered shelf. The home and equipment were typical of many of the rural houses we entered.

Approximately ten million workers with their families comprise the bulk of the nation. They are the *fazenda* workers, the small farmers, the share-croppers, the forest and stock men, the mill hands, and the common laborers. This great group of workers who comprise between 96 and 97 per cent of the population earn an average wage of $10 (U.S.) per month, with a spread of from $15 for skilled labor to $5 or even less for the unskilled worker of the north.

The North American thinks of food in terms of bread, butter, milk, eggs, meat, cheese, and vegetables. The Brazilian worker can afford but tiny amounts of these food staples; to him they are luxuries; he lives on starchy roots, potatoes, black beans, manioc, and occasionally salt fish and bananas (Davis, 1942:19, 35-36).

Brazil has made progress since 1942, but it was then and is in 1980 definitely ahead of many nations in Africasia.

In India the masses include not only 99 per cent of the untouchable Shudras but most of the touchables, and great numbers of the upper castes also. In manufacturing cities and villages, the hungry are to be found in all castes, though the proportion grows less as one approaches the upper-most. In China, Japan, the Philippines, Indonesia, Africa, and all the countries of Latin America, as one adds disinherited, shirtless ones, share-croppers, landless labor, and illiterates together, a vivid picture of the huge size of the masses and the depth of their misery emerges.

FIGURE 14.1

Landowners
Business Community
Professionals
Artisans and Mechanics
Peasants
Unskilled Laborers

"There are various classes in society" is not an accurate statement; it conveys falsehood rather than truth. A missionary communication recently said, "We are reaching all classes of society with the Gospel," and then, to give point to the words, appended the misleading diagram shown on page 272.

There are these classes, true; but the landowners, business community, and professionals are emphatically not as large a part of society as the artisans, mechanics, peasants, and unskilled labor.

The world of mission is indebted to Eugene Nida for popularizing a much more accurate diagram of the social order. The three pear-shaped figures below show proportions and classes much more truly.

FIGURE 14.2. THE SHAPE OF CLASS/MASS SOCIETY

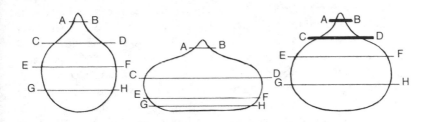

Any analysis to be meaningful must define accurately the terms used. Exactly who comprise the classes and masses? *Until sharp definition has been made of each segment of a given society, precise thinking about it is impossible.* Since society in each country, however, differs from that in other countries, and in a given country the definitions of thirty years ago will not fit society as it exists today, I shall not attempt precise definitions. Those made for Mexico would not fit Korea in 1980, those for Canada would not fit England.

Instead, for the sake of the illustration, I shall count the landed aristocracy as the upper classes (above *AB* in the left pear-shaped diagram), the business community and professionals as middle classes (above *CD*), artisans, mechanics, mill foremen, and truck drivers as upper-lower classes (above *EF*), peasants and unskilled labor as middle-lower classes (above *GH*); and the unemployed, unemployable, serfs, drifters, and diseased as the lower-lower classes (below *GH*). Note the extremely small proportion the upper classes form of the whole—perhaps 1 per cent of the total population. Note the small size of the middle classes, perhaps 6 per cent of the population. The place of line *CD* varies up and down depending on what country and what decade in that country is being considered. Note also how words mislead the mind. The middle classes are "middle" in no real sense at all; it is more realistic to call the "middle" and "upper" classes together "the classes." They are the beneficiaries of the social order. In many places they are the exploiters and the lower classes could more exactly be called the exploited. Consequently in this chapter I speak of only two main divisions: the classes and the masses. Any true picture of mankind in Africasia must portray the small numbers in the tip and the very large numbers in the swelling bulb of the pear-shaped figure— everything below the line *CD*. Tiny classes and tremendous masses characterize most countries of Africasia today.

In North America and increasingly in Europe, the middle figure more truly represents the population of each nation. The flattened pear shows that the distance between the classes and the masses is not so great. The middle class is more truly middle and is much larger. The "upper-lower classes" form a large section of the whole and the lower-lower classes comprise a smaller segment of the whole than in the typical Africasian land.

In the right-hand figure, the heavy black bars *AB* and *CD* represent breaks between the three segments. The upper classes are not only far above the middle classes but compose a different breed of men. The middle classes, too, are so far removed from the lower classes that intermarriage and interdining are rare. Such caste—or perhaps one should say space— lines are demanded by human pride and mark most societies, but are institutionalized in some. Hindu India with its caste system is the most obvious illustration of institutionalized race pride, though for four hundred years the old white families of Latin America have run the twice-born of India a close second.

Rev. Oscar Maldonado (1966:43) writes,

> Colombian society, seen as a whole, seems to be more of a caste society than a class society. There is an abyss between "the social classes which direct society" and the masses. The latter still have not acquired the nature of a class since they lack an awareness [of their situation] and will continue to remain in this condition given the high rate of illiteracy, low quality of instruction in the primary schools, and the past experience of labor movements.

Tribal societies, where every member of the tribe has an equal right to the land, present an exception to class/mass society; but the exception will not be long-lived. As tribal societies break down, emerge into the common life of the world, and flood into cities they become the masses.

In ages past, despite the fact that their aristocracy became Kshatriyas (ruling castes), the great mass of tribesmen in India became Shudras (inferior castes).

As industrialization and education progress, the middle classes, particularly in favored nations, increase in size. Observe the shift in per cent of the total population which each class is undergoing in Brazil as described by Havighurst and Moreira (1964:99). Let the eye follow the "lower-middle" class from 1870 to 1955. The growth of "middle classes" may be observed in most lands; more in the industrialized, less in others. See how the slaves in 1870 melted into the "lower-lower" class in 1920.

SOCIAL CLASS DISTRIBUTION IN BRAZIL BY
PER CENT OF TOTAL POPULATION

Class	1870	1920	1950	1955
Upper Upper	1	1.5	2	2
Lower Upper	1	1.5	2	2
Upper Middle	5	2	3	4
Lower Middle	6	9.5	12	16
Upper Lower	73	10	33	36
Lower Lower		70	50	42
Slaves	15			
	100	100	100	100

Middle-class growth does not decrease the tremendous numbers in the masses. For example, in Brazil in 1955, the lower classes (masses) comprised 78 per cent of the total population, and, since the population had grown so greatly, 78 per cent in 1955 meant millions more than 80 per cent in 1920. In other countries, the masses might comprise 70 to 95 per cent of the total population, but their exact numbers in each country do not concern us here. In Africasian lands, on the most favorable estimates, the masses (the disinherited, the burden-bearers, the one- and two-acre men, and the landless) still comprise the vast majority of the human race.

One rejoices in the increase of the middle classes, in land reform and other moves in the direction of justice, but one cannot help noting that by comparison with the size of the problem, these changes are small. There is not much to rejoice about. For instance, the February 1962 *Viewpoints* carried a brave headline: SYRIA MAINTAINS LAND REFORM OFFENSIVE. The story underneath was this. In 1957, Syria passed a law to distribute land which enabled each owner of a large estate to keep for himself and for each person in his family 160 acres of land. Which parts he kept were determined by himself. Only the balance of his estate was to be distributed. After three years, only 6,000 families (out of a total population of 3,000,000) had been given an average of ten acres of irrigated or fifty acres of unirrigated land! The headline might better have read: SYRIA FIDDLES WHILE THE FUZE SIZZLES.

Christians must not imagine that these moves toward justice, in which they rejoice, materially affect the discipling of nations. The glowering masses still remain. Their numbers grow with every passing year. The middle classes are still small and will remain small, if not proportionately smaller. Christians today should address themselves to the current problem. Fifty years hence our grandsons will no doubt address themselves to the situation they face.

The masses in the past have been resigned. They thought the kind of life they lived was the only kind possible. Wise men simply accepted life the way it had to be. But resignation or what passes for contentment is disappearing. One should not overestimate the rate of its going, but it *is* retreating. The masses are learning that they do not have to live in perpetual poverty. Educated men inform them that they have a right to plenty, and organize and arm them to wrest a large share of this world's goods from the privileged. This is the revolution which seethes in every land.

The Marxists are determined to ride this revolution to world domination. They believe communism offers the only way by which the masses, through class struggle and the dictatorship of the proletariat, can wring justice out of the reluctant classes. Idealists among the students, groaning at the rank oppression which present systems impose on the multitudes, demand change. Patriots, seeing that nations composed of hereditary elites battening on a vast illiterate peasantry are weak, seek to enfranchise the latter so that their countries may become powerful. Whoever does it— Marxists, idealists, or patriots—the masses are being roused, organized, and pushed into the battle for more of the good things of life.

Their temper is well illustrated by a letter which the Student Federation of Chile addressed to President Eisenhower on the occasion of his visit to South America in 1959. It reads in part:

> In the United States, it makes sense to fight to defend the prevailing order. . . . In Latin America, to defend the prevailing order means maintaining the privilege of a thin layer of the population surrounded by an ocean of poor people for whom the social order means little or nothing. . . . If the injustices of today are all Christianity or democracy can offer this continent, no one should be surprised if the best children of these nations turn toward communism.

These few pages describing so briefly today's class/mass society will recall to most readers a familiar picture. The existence of the classes and masses need not be labored. We press on to ask what is the meaning of the masses to the mission of God.

THE BIBLE AND THE MASSES

The Bible shows a steady preference for the common man. It begins by declaring that all men are sons of Adam and hence brothers and equal. It ends by affirming that all men, "great and small alike," will stand before the great white throne and be judged. Wealth, learning, blue blood, power, and thrones count for nothing as men are judged. The sole criterion, equally possible to the masses and the classes, is: Have they washed their robes? Are their names written in the book of life? Have they confessed Christ before the world and, abandoning all sin and other allegiance, been faithful unto death?

To Christians of the masses in India, the biblical account—that God created one man and one woman and all men are their descendants—is particularly dear. It contrasts sharply with the Hindu account that the great god Brahm created the Brahmans from his head, the warrior castes from his shoulders, the merchant castes from his thighs, and the masses from his feet.

When God selected a people in Egypt and made a covenant with it, he chose not the learned, not the princes, not the aristocrats, not the students—but the slaves.

> The Lord said, "I have seen the affliction of my people who are in Egypt and have heard their cry because of their taskmasters; I know their sufferings, and I have come down to deliver them out of the hand of the Egyptians, and to bring them up out of that land to a good and broad land, a land flowing with milk and honey" (Ex. 3:7, 8). . . . The people of Israel . . . came to the wilderness of Sinai . . . and Moses went up and the Lord called to him out of the mountain saying, "You have seen what I did to the Egyptians, and how I bore you on eagles' wings and brought you to myself. Now therefore, if you will obey my voice and keep my covenant, you shall be my own possession among all people; for all the earth is mine, and you shall be to me a kingdom of priests and a holy nation." . . . And the people answered and said, "All that the Lord has spoken we will do."

Later when the Hebrews were settled in Canaan and wanted a king, the Bible records that God was not pleased with their thirsting after a more efficient aristocratic structuring of their society. In a remarkable passage He foretold the oppressions which the classes have always inflicted on the masses. The forms vary from age to age and land to land, but the oppression remains.

> These will be the ways of the king who will rule over you: he will take your sons and appoint them to his chariots and to be his horsemen, and to run before his chariots; and he will appoint himself commanders of thousands and commanders of fifties, and some to plow his ground and to reap his harvest, and to make his implements of war. . . . He will take your daughters to be his perfumers and cooks and bakers. He will take the best of your fields and vineyards and olive orchards. . . . He will take your manservants and maidservants, and the best of your cattle. He will take a tenth of your flocks and you shall be his slaves (I Sam. 8:11f.).

When the aristocratic order flowered and came to fruit, and all these prophecies and more had come to pass, God sent His prophets to plead the cause of the poor and to demand justice for the common man.

> The Lord has taken his place to contend, he stands to judge his people. The Lord enters into judgment with the elders and princes of his people: It is you who have devoured the vineyard, the spoil of the poor is in your houses. What do you mean by crushing my people, by grinding the face of the poor, says the Lord God of hosts. . . .
>
> Woe to those who add field to field and house to house, until there is no more room and you are made to dwell alone in the midst of the land. Woe to those who rise early in the morning that they may run after strong drink. They have lyre and harp, timbrel and flute and wine at their feasts. . . .
> Woe to those who decree iniquitous decrees, and the writers who keep writing oppressions.
>
> To turn aside the needy from justice and to rob the poor of my people of their right,
>
> That widows may be their spoil and that they may make the fatherless their prey (Isa. Chaps. 5 and 10).
>
> Hear, you heads of Jacob and rulers of the house of Israel!
> Is it not for you to know justice?—you who hate the good and love the evil, Who tear the skin from off my people, and their flesh from off their bones: Who break their bones in pieces and chop them up like meat in a kettle....
>
> He has showed you, O man, what is good; and what does the Lord require of you but to do justice, and to love kindness, and to walk humbly with your God? (Mic. 3:1-3; 6:8).

Nathan, Jeremiah, Amos, and other prophets immediately come to mind when we focus attention on the rights of the common man and the oppression meted out to him by the upper classes. It is no accident that communism arose in Christendom. The communist ethical passion, so strangely distorted by its metaphysical framework, arises straight out of the biblical insistence that God is a God of righteousness and *will not have the poor oppressed*.

New Testament Emphasis

The New Testament tells us that, when it pleased God that the Word should become flesh and dwell among us, Jesus was born to a peasant girl of Nazareth and grew up in the home of a carpenter. The Son of God learned the carpenter's trade and carried heavy planks and beams on His head and shoulders. Like the masses everywhere, He ate His bread "in the sweat of his face."

When at Nazareth our Lord announced the purpose of His coming, He said,

> The Spirit of the Lord is upon me, because he has anointed me to preach good news to the poor.
> He has sent me to proclaim release to the captives and recovery of sight to the blind, to set at liberty those who are oppressed, to proclaim the acceptable year of the Lord (Luke 4:18).

No one can miss His marked emphasis on God's will for the masses, a point which received added confirmation when later He included in the signs of the coming of the Kingdom the significant one that "the poor have the good news preached to them" (Matt. 11:5).

Of the twelve apostles, eleven were Galileans—country people who spoke with an accent. The rulers, elders, scribes, and high priests scorned them as "uneducated common men." The Book of Acts tells us that the Christian religion spread through the masses in Jerusalem and Judea. The common people heard the apostles gladly. The rulers of the Jews were afraid to act against the apostles because they feared the people. "The people," we are told, held the apostles in high esteem and when the captain with the officers went and brought the apostles (Acts 5:18) to the high priest, they did so without violence "for they were afraid of bein stoned by the people." It is no wonder that the masses were solidly behind the Early Church. She was made up largely of the common people and had common people for leaders. All the common people in Jerusalem must have had Christian relatives. The Church had only a few of the intelligentsia, and the great company of priests who later became obedient to the faith were perhaps those who were dependent on the masses who had become Christian.

When the Church grew in the synagogue communities of the Roman Empire, she took in large numbers of the underprivileged, as is amply

attested by the famous passage in I Corinthians—the only breakdown of
the social standing of church members that we have.

> For consider your call, brethren; not many of you were wise according to
> worldly standards, not many were powerful, not many were of noble birth;
> but God chose what is foolish in the world to shame the wise. God chose
> what is weak in the world to shame the strong. God chose what is low and
> despised in the world, even things that are not, to bring to nothing things that
> are . . . (I Cor. 1:26f.).

There were, to be sure, men of wealth and learning in the Church. Only
the well-to-do had houses large enough to serve as places of assembly, and
the Jews were not a poverty-stricken community. Still, as one reads the
passage he is confident that in social structure the Early Church resembles
the Afericasian Churches which are rising out of the masses more than she
does the middle- and upper-class congregations which assemble in taste-
fully-appointed, air-conditioned churches all across Eurica.

The Masses Are Dear to God

These selected passages must not be distorted to mean that God loves
the poor and not the rich. God is no respecter of persons, and the wealthy
sinner is just as lost as the poor one. While the Old Testament prophets
inveigh against the rich who sell the needy for a pair of shoes, the great
weight of their judgment falls not on the rich but on those, rich and poor,
who abandon God for idols. Wealthy women were disciples of our Lord,
and Nicodemus and Zacchaeus were far from poor. All this must be held
steadily in view. Nevertheless, it remains true that the common people are
dear to God. The fundamental thrust of God's revelation demands a high
valuation of the masses.

The infinite value of a single soul, the doctrine that God judges the
heart, and the clear directive that the commandment of God is to believe
on His Son, Jesus Christ—all proclaim that structuring society into the
classes and the masses is displeasing to God. Any such division—whether
intentional or not—is man's device, which like divorce may be allowed
by God because of the hardness of men's hearts, but is no part of God's
intention for man. His ideal is a society in which all men, because each
is of infinite worth, are judged by the same standards and saved by the
same faith in the same Savior, receiving equal opportunity and equal
justice.

Facing the classes and the masses, the Church and her emissaries may
well pray the following missionary prayer:

Almighty God our heavenly Father, Who didst make of one blood all that dwell on the face of the earth, we worship Thee, we adore Thee, we bow in reverence before Thee. We yield ourselves to Thee and implore Thee to be born in us, take command of our wills and make us Thine in truth.

O Lord Jesus Christ, we remember that Thou wast born of a peasant mother in a poor carpenter's home and didst surround Thyself with disciples and apostles whom the educated of that day called "ignorant and unlearned." Thou didst tell men that a sign of the coming of Thy Kingdom was that the Gospel was proclaimed to the poor

The common people heard Thee, Lord, gladly. Thy blessed Mother sang, My soul doth magnify the Lord and my spirit hath rejoiced in God my Saviour, for he hath scattered the proud in the imagination of their hearts, he hath put down the mighty from their seats, and exalted them of low degree. He hath filled the hungry with good things, and the rich hath he sent empty away. And didst not Thou, O Lord, invite all those who labor and are heavy laden to come to Thee and find rest?

O Holy Christ, we lift up before Thee the poor of earth, the masses of mankind, the rural multitudes whose backs are bent with toil, the urban proletariat who live in tenements, and shacks, and favellas, and barrios, and zongoes. The illiterate, the oppressed, the disinherited, the fishermen and the carpenters, the landless labor, the unskilled. . . . The poor, Lord, the poor for whom Thou didst shed Thy precious blood and on whom Thou didst look with compassion, for they were as sheep without a shepherd. Grant us, Lord, Thy compassion, that we too may see the great masses of mankind as Thy lost children, and like Thee spend ourselves for them. In Thy blessed name, Amen.

MISSIONS FAVOR THE CLASSES

Missions from the wealthy West usually overlook the Bible at this point. Missionaries customarily place a high value on the educated, the wealthy, the cultured—in a word, the middle and upper classes. This is dictated and inspired, not by the Bible but, unconsciously, no doubt, by the extraordinarily affluent society of which most missionaries are a part. They thus devote themselves to "maintaining cordial relationships with the business and professional leaders," seek to win the leaders of the coming generation, and believe one Brahman convert is worth a thousand Untouchable Christians. In a given congregation of 200 communicants there may be 10 from the middle classes and 190 from the lower classes; but if asked, "What classes are you reaching?" a typical churchman will reply, "Middle and high—and some low, of course." Part of the scorn which has, in days past, been poured on the Pentecostals in Latin America is due to the fact that Pentecostals are frankly churches of the masses.

From the human point of view, preference for the middle and upper classes is eminently reasonable. The masses, as Moses and Paul could testify, bring problems with them when they become the people of God. The wealthy can support a paid ministry much more easily than the poor. Having grown up with more to manage, they are much more experienced in managing things.

Eurican Churches are middle-class Churches. Anglicans, Lutherans, Presbyterians, and Catholics in Europe have largely lost the working classes. An Anglican clergyman remarked to me, "After the industrial revolution started, we never had the working classes, and the Methodists got only a small part of them." In the United States, where all segments of the body politic are relatively affluent, many laboring men and women are Christians; but here, too, redemption and lift make many congregations and denominations middle-class organisms and rather pleased at being such. Most missionaries are middle-class people. They have grown up with interior plumbing, electric light, and plenty of books. They ride in cars and travel to the lands of their work in jet planes. Really, in relation to the masses of the lands to which they go, they are not middle-, but upper-class people.

Naturally they create middle-class Churches. There is nothing surprising in this, for the middle-class congregations in which they grew up have formed their standards. What is reverent worship, good singing, Christian treatment of wives, and proper use of leisure? What are efficient ways of conducting church business and educating one's children? Answers to these questions, given by Eurican missionaries and Africasian leaders trained by them, cannot but be middle-class answers, unless churchmen, recognizing this part of their cultural overhang, steel themselves against it.

Occasionally they create small middle-class churches by converting middle-class non-Christians; but more frequently they plant churches among the peasantry or lower classes and then over a period of decades educate the youth of the Church. These then, in lands where education is the key to the middle classes, find themselves middle-class people. The older the Africasian Church, provided it has had Eurican assistance through the years, the more middle-class are its controlling members. Not everyone becomes educated and middle-class, but those who do, control the Church. They are the ministers, elders, deacons, church school teachers, and heavy givers. The smaller the number of communicants in relation to the mission resources, the more rapidly does a Church become middle-class. A mission which stresses education, builds schools and possibly a college, and engages Christians as teachers, will build up an educated community. As we have amply seen, this may not grow much, but its members will assure you that they are not interested in numerical expansion. They want quality Christians, by which they mean middle-class Christians. They disdain unwashed congregations of the masses.

By contrast the large Africasian Churches—such as those built up by Lutherans, Baptists, Anglicans, Methodists, Presbyterians, and Pentecostals among the Bataks, Karens, Malas, and Madigas, Formosan Highlanders, and Chileans—are composed of the masses. Their members are poor (peasants, landless labor, urban proletariat) and commonly illiterate. Having many members and small mission resources they remain Churches of the masses.

Missionaries identify with the leaders of younger Churches, who by virtue of their education are middle-class, and thus reinforce the image of the Church as a middle-class organization. They tend to press middle-class clothes on a Church made up of the masses. They give middle-class armor to the Davids of the masses to fight in. Then growth stops.

First the Upper Classes in Africasia?

One of the key questions on which mission policy hinges is this: Should we seek to win the upper classes first, confident that if we do they will win the lower classes? Many missionaries and nationals, living in cities, working with students and maintaining schools, believe the question should be answered in the affirmative. In part their answer is dictated by their own middle-class standing, but in part it is based on what seems a reasonable assumption: that the middle classes are the leaders and the masses are the followers.

Striking instances of the lower classes following the upper into the Church can be found. The slaves in the United States unquestionably became Christian because their masters were Christians—and would have become Moslems had their masters been Moslems. In the Philippines, the feudal lords of a large estate in Negros Oriental became Evangelicals, and most of their peons followed them. A church of several thousand resulted, made up of many small congregations scattered over the vast holding.

But for the most part, the strategy of winning the upper classes first has not worked. They will not be won. The middle classes "have it too good." Why should they risk losing it all to become Christians? For when they do, they are often disinherited and lose their position of leadership. No one has made a more careful study of this issue than Waskom Pickett. His findings should be carefully pondered before answering the question.

Movements to Christ, he says, "have not generally developed where missionaries were most closely associated with the Government" and hence with the rulers of the people, nor "in areas where Western influence has been most strongly felt" through schools and colleges where the upper and middle classes were educated. "Nor have movements developed in areas where missionary forces have been most numerous or longest at work. . . ." Where movements did begin, they began almost in spite of the missionaries, for "the missionaries in practically every area were working primarily for the high castes hoping that they might first be won and might then take over the winning of the lower castes."

> The fear that reception of large numbers of the depressed classes into the Church would interfere with the winning of the upper classes seems to have restrained a section, at least, of the missionaries in every area when movements were beginning. . . . But it is a matter of record that the great harvest expected of the upper classes and the subsequent conversion, through their efforts, of those lower in the social scale, have not occurred (Pickett, 1933:55f.).
> Our first recommendation is that every possible effort be made to win all the remaining groups of the Depressed Classes to Christ. Although the case for this recommendation is clear and compelling . . . there is grave danger it will not be implemented. There is a disposition to neglect the Depressed Classes whenever hope is entertained that the higher castes may be induced to respond. To neglect them now would be both a capital folly and a grievous wrong. There is strong reason to believe that the surest way of multiplying conversions of higher caste Hindus is to increase the scale on which the transforming, enriching and uplifting grace of Christ is demonstrated in the Depressed Classes. And one certain way to arrest the movements of the higher castes to Christ is to turn away from the poor and the despised (Pickett, 1960:96, 95).

Pickett's findings in India in 1933 can be duplicated in Brazil and Chile in 1979. Far greater numbers of middle-class people are being won for Christ in those two lands where hundreds of thousands of poor people have become Evangelicals in Baptist, Pentecostal, and other Churches than are being won in Colombia, Costa Rica, and other lands where the chief effort has been to win the middle classes to Christ.

Arnold Toynbee has pointed out that, far from a new religion first being accepted by the classes and then by the masses, it is usually first accepted by the proletariat. Later, of course, as in the case of Christianity in the Roman Empire, the classes accepted it. He says, "Higher religions make their entry into Society from below upwards and the dominant minority [the classes] is either unaware of these new religious movements or . . . is hostile to them. . . . [In the Roman Empire] the philosophies appealed to the middle class. . . . Christianity appealed to the masses" (Toynbee, 1956:37, 99).

First the Upper Classes in North America?

Americans should not imagine that the winning of the masses is of concern only in Africa and other far-off places. It is also of great concern in the United States and Canada. Since God blesses Christians, they soon come to be comfortably fixed people. It is easy for them to believe that if they evangelize their own kind of people, the task will be done. This is disastrously not true. If the denominations of North America are to break out of their present middle-class encirclement, they must very soon establish thousands of congregations of factory laborers, mechanics, members of labor unions, dock hands, mill workers, and the like. The pastors of these congregations also must be of the same socio-economic level. "The people" do not obediently follow the middle and upper classes in any but a feudalistic society.

The Masses Are Increasingly Responsive Today

Often the masses, groaning under centuries of oppression by the classes, regard their old religion as the instrument of their enslavement. Thus Ambedkar used to exclaim, "When I read the New Testament I find the very antidote my people need for the poison of Hinduism which they have been drinking for three thousand years." Emilio Willems, the Brazilian sociologist, says (1964:103):

> Revolutionary changes . . . are related to and perhaps reinforced by a steadily growing desire on the part of the lower classes, to overthrow the traditional social order. The main target of a generalized and intense hostility is . . . the conservative, landholding upper class, and all those institutions (including the Roman Catholic Church) perceived as its allies. . . . conversion to Protestantism . . . constitutes one of many ways in which hostility and rebellion against a decaying social structure may be expressed. . . . The Catholic Church is often perceived by the masses as a symbol of the traditional order or as an ally of its supreme exponent, the landed aristocracy. . . . The farther removed the ideology and structure of a particular denomination are from those of traditional society, the stronger the appeal it holds for the common people.

"Steadily growing desire"—these words of Willems, penned in regard to Brazil, have a very much wider bearing. The next fifty or a hundred years are certain to see the masses everywhere in the grip of a "steadily growing desire" to get the good things of life—and to overthrow the traditional social order, if necessary, to get them.

The landless in the Philippines are desperately unhappy with the large landed estates and the holdings of the Church of Rome—witness the Huk revival of the late sixties. The depressed classes in India are temporarily comforted by concessions of various sorts given them by the upper classes; but nothing will fully satisfy them now except complete equality, which the upper castes will not give them. No thirty million in Africa have made the advances that thirty million Negroes have made in the United States, yet the Detroit and Newark riots of 1967 bear powerful witness to the fact that even that great degree of progress is not enough.

Decades of struggle lie ahead, with victory now in the hands of the proletariat and now in the hands of the bourgeoisie. The form of the struggle will vary from country to country and decade to decade, but it will rage ceaselessly. And it will continually turn the masses responsive. Christians should realize that this is the kind of world in which they are called to proclaim the Gospel, find the lost, and multiply cells of *the redeemed*—the most potent ingredient of the righteous order God is creating.

The Good News and Its Corollary

The Christian Church has good news for the awakening masses—first that God the Father Almighty is just, and second will give those who love and obey Him power to treat other men justly. Let us consider both parts of this Gospel.

That God is just—the revolutionary impact of this simple statement should be grasped. It affirms that the very structure of the universe favors the common man. It proclaims that the vast mysterious Personal Power, whom we call God the Father Almighty, intends an order of society in which each man can and will receive justice. Consider this ultimate fact in the light of the needs of the masses. Contrary to much superficial thinking, the greatest need of the masses and their leaders is neither aid nor kindness. Their greatest need is not handouts, but a world view, a religion, which gives them bedrock on which to stand as they battle for justice.

What attracted Ambedkar to Christianity was the New Testament, which gave his people the antidote against the poisons of Hinduism. These latter were not the particular disabilities under which the Untouchables labored in the thirties and forties, but rather *the ultimate religious sanctions of the caste system.*

Although the Bhagavad Gita is commonly regarded as the highest Hindu scripture and has passages of profound beauty and wisdom, it must be recognized that it consciously sanctifies the caste system. It declares that the superiority of the classes and the inferiority of the masses are rooted in the divine order. The Gita, some scholars think, rose when Hinduism was battling Buddhism—that almost-successful revolt against caste. It teaches throughout that men according to their *karma* (deeds in a former life) are born into specific castes and each must carry out his own *caste dharma*, i.e. the "duties" or "law" suited to his caste and hence required of him as part of the immutable order of things. The argument underlies much of the conversation between Arjuna and Krishna and becomes explicit in several passages, among which is the following from the eighteenth book or lesson.

41. Of *brāhmins*, of *kṣatriyas*, and *vaiśyas*, as also of *śūdras*, O Conqueror of the foe (Arjuna), the activities are distinguished, in accordance with the qualities born of their nature.

42. Serenity, self-control, austerity, purity, forbearance and uprightness, wisdom, knowledge, and faith in religion—these are the duties of the *brāhmin*, born of his nature.

43. Heroism, vigour, steadiness, resourcefulness, not fleeing even in battle, generosity, and leadership—these are the duties of a *kṣatriya*, born of his nature.

44. Agriculture, tending cattle, and trade are the duties of a *vaiśya*, born of his nature; work of the character of service is the duty of a *śūdra*, born of his nature.

45. Devoted each to his own duty, man attains perfection. How one devoted to his own duty attains perfection, that do thou hear.

46. He from whom all beings arise and by whom all this is pervaded—by worshipping Him through the performance of his own duty does man attain perfection.

47. Better is one's own law though imperfectly carried out than the law of another carried out perfectly. One does not incur sin when one does the duty ordained by one's own nature.

48. One should not give up the work suited to one's nature, O Son of Kunti (Arjuna) though it may be defective.

(Radhakrishnan, 1957:161)

If this view of human relations is correct, then all efforts to change the social order and to elevate the masses are both wicked and futile. For a Shudra (or Śudra) to become an excellent teacher brings him less happiness and keeps him farther from "consummation" or "perfection" than to be an indifferent ditch digger. No wonder Ambedkar felt he had to find some antidote to these poisonous concepts.

By contrast, the highly valuable gifts of the Christian religion are:

God the Father Almighty who hates injustice, God the Son who died for each man of the masses, the Bible, and a world view which requires justice for the common man, thus endowing every human being with infinite value. "Making people Christian," along with other things, means giving them a world view which irresistibly, though often slowly, creates equality of opportunity and undergirds all strivings against entrenched privilege. With this wealth in hand, the man of the masses can conquer all secondary poverties.

The second aspect of the Good News is this: God gives those who love and obey Him power to treat other men justly. Those who accept Jesus Christ as God and Savior receive the Holy Spirit and His gifts—love, joy, peace, patience, goodness, faithfulness, gentleness, and self-control. They receive power to live the good life. They are able to live justly whatever the framework of their society.

The Good News has a powerful corollary which appeals greatly to the masses today: that just men can build a just society. This just society must be clearly differentiated from the ultimate Kingdom of God—that reign of perfect goodness when death itself shall have been abolished, which comes as God's gift. Man can do nothing to bring that in. The just society of which I speak, however, is the kindlier, more humane order which by God's grace arises within family, neighborhood, city, or state as the number of Christians multiply. Since a just society must be built, not by, but *out of* men who are profoundly interested in the welfare of others, and determined to devise structures which provide justice for them; as such men and their churches multiply, the structures of society will become more and more righteous.

Because God is just, His mission maintains that every move toward justice is pleasing to Him. It assures men that when they are fighting for justice He is on their side. Even more truly, in working for justice and brotherhood they are on God's side, and God will win.

Because man is a sinner and cannot of himself do justly, God's mission maintains that man's chief need is not justice but forgiveness and a clean heart within. The just order he strives for will disappear as he fashions it, unless he strives as a godly person. He is to be more concerned with *being just* than receiving justice. Patriots and guerrillas, partisans and revolutionaries, can drive foreign imperialists from the soil of the motherland with hunger strikes, marches, bombs, and terror; they can seize power, burn cities, and shoot alike domestic aristocrats and foreign oppressors. But these tactics will not drive evil from the hearts of their people or themselves. Only another society of new pressures and tensions—another sinful society—can arise as men set up new frameworks supposed to guarantee the people justice. The old competitions between men in high places (as well as low), the raw struggles between those of opposing views are not laid to rest by revolutions, however far reaching.

A peaceful and righteous society—and till the millennium this only in muted measure—can come only from redeemed men seeking to implement what they conceive to be God's will. Therefore Christ's mission, confident that there is no more effective service it can render the masses, will press ahead, bringing men to Christ, that He may redeem them in His Body, the Church, which at the right times and in all places where she has arrived and achieved at least a little influence, will Christianize the framework of her societies.

In October 1978, Pope John Paul II in his first encyclical *Redemptor Hominis,* again and again underscored the fact that universal evangelization *was the ground work for the new righteous order.* On page 33 we read that all Christians should "consciously join in the great mission of revealing Christ to the world, helping . . . the contemporary generations of our brothers and sisters, the peoples, nations, States, mankind, developing countries and countries of opulence . . . to know 'the unsearchable riches of Christ' " (John Paul, 1978).

Fluctuating Responsiveness

For years, I worked with the Satnamis of Central Provinces, India. These oppressed people were beginning to turn to Christ when, in 1947, with the arrival of self-government, their community of half a million received four seats in the provincial legislative assembly. Satnamis flocked to election rallies and began to idolize political power. This became their new savior. They believed their representatives in the legislature would give them prestige, power, education, and a higher standard of living. They neither knew, nor would have believed, that the good life does not consist in the abundance of things a man has. Their interest in the Gospel waned sharply.

Over the next twenty years, however, they began to realize that seats in the assembly, help in getting an education, a share of jobs, and other exterior changes, while good, do not constitute a long step in the direction of justice. These things do not rebuke sin nor call sinners to repentance. They do not make bad men into good men. They neither increase kindness, gentleness, goodness, and self-control nor hold out promise of eternal life. The Satnamis began to see the contrast of which Isaiah sings (55:1-3):

> Ho, everyone who thirsts, come to the waters;
>   and he who has no money, come, buy and eat!
> Come, buy wine and milk without money and without price.
> Why do you spend your money for that which is not bread,
>   and your labor for that which does not satisfy?
> Hearken diligently to me, eat what is good,
>   and delight yourself in fatness.
> Incline your ear and come to me; hear that your soul may live.

Perhaps they saw more clearly that minor concessions would not give their people equality with the real rulers of the province, who still believe that the lower castes are inferior breeds of men. The illusion of progress is beginning to wear off. The Satnamis will have a steadily growing desire for *more,* which will enable large numbers of them to "hear" the Gospel. Some who hear will obey.

In the next hundred years—and no doubt longer—the masses, like my Satnami friends, will time and again put their trust in kings, elected officials, alliances, horses, chariots, walled cities, urban renewal, million-dollar schools, and fertilizer factories. But when they discover that these are not bread and cannot satisfy, and that the new elites are as rapacious and corrupt as the old, they will again be able to hear the Gospel. Like the Israelites, when masses get possession of vineyards which they did not plant, and cisterns which they did not dig, and walled cities which they did not build, they will conclude that they have arrived in the land of milk and honey. But again and again they will realize that the essential nourishment and sweetness are within, and that there is salvation in none else but God and Jesus Christ His Son. Then they will listen.

For the foreseeable future, the masses will be substantially responsive. Their responsiveness will fluctuate, but just because they are the victims of the social order, they will listen to the Good News. Like the Jews of our Lord's day, they are looking for a deliverer. Like those who joined themselves to Jesus of Nazareth, they may come looking for a worldly kingdom; but those who tarry with Him will find the Kingdom of God.

POLICY TOWARD MASSES AND CLASSES

As the Church faces the three billion who know little or nothing about Jesus Christ, what should be her policy toward the classes and the masses?

Winning the Winnable

Policy should be formed on two assumptions: (1) that the masses are growing increasingly responsive and will continue to listen to the Good

News, just because every influence bearing on their lives will make them increasingly dissatisfied with their present status; (2) that particular masses in certain countries and sections of countries fluctuate in response as they are played upon by military fortune, economic forces, victories and defeats. In some places they will temporarily become highly resistant, in others highly receptive. Non-Christian classes, on the other hand, may be counted on to be generally resistant to the Gospel, though their attitude also will fluctuate. Some sections may for brief periods become significantly responsive, and should be effectively evangelized.

Since the Gospel is to be preached to all creation, no Christian will doubt but that both the receptive and the resistant should hear it. And since gospel acceptors have an inherently higher priority than gospel rejectors, no one should doubt that, whenever it comes to a choice between reaping ripe fields or seeding others, the former is commanded by God.

Winning the winnable while they are winnable seems sound procedure. This is the strategic meaning of our Lord's words "beginning at Jerusalem." While the Palestinian Jews were responsive, the Holy Spirit led the Church to focus upon them. The first twenty years saw a powerful, one-race Church built up among the residents of Jerusalem and Judea. When either masses or classes are winnable, they should hear the Gospel, be baptized, and added to churches which immediately, without pause to consolidate, go out to win their still receptive fellows.

The Rev. A. C. Krass, writing from northern Ghana in 1967 about the Chokosi tribe (from which in the previous three years about 800 had accepted Christ and been baptized), said it is reasonable to believe that in about ten years "the whole Chokosi tribe will have become Christian." Christian mission on a very wide scale needs not only to see these potentials, but to master such modes of proclaiming the Gospel and discipling the peoples that hopeful possibilities become actualities. Whole populations should be claimed for Christ. This is the highest priority in evangelism.

If in any given sector the masses turn indifferent or hostile, then efforts to win them should be transferred to other sectors where men will hear and obey. When our Lord gave directions to the twelve (Luke 9:5), He said, "Wherever they do not receive you, when you leave that town shake off the dust from your feet as a testimony against them." When He instructed the seventy (Luke 10:10), He gave them precisely the same instructions. The indifferent of the masses have no more right to coddling efforts at persuasion than other men. Those who stand with arms outstretched, whether of the classes or the masses, have a higher right to hear than those who stop their ears and turn away.

It should not be evangelistic policy to besiege indifferent and resistant or even rebellious segments of any type because they are children of Abraham (prestige-laden elements of their societies). God is able to raise up men of prestige from the very stones—the rejected, the disinherited, and the things which are not—provided they become members of His household.

Social Action and Church Growth

It should not be *mission* policy to foment rebellions among the masses and thus help them to achieve political, economic, and cultural goals. Mission (which proceeds from one country to another—from India, let us say, to Africa, from Korea to Thailand, or from America to China) is always a guest in the country to which it goes. Its emissaries are there by permission of the government. They can be ejected at an hour's notice. The function of the missionary and his institutions is to reconcile men to God in the Church of Jesus Christ. It is not his business to lead Christians to the barricades and teach them to make Molotov cocktails or seize power. On the contrary, the missionary teaches submission to existing governments as ordained by God. For this he has abundant scriptural warrant and churchly precedent.

With *the Church* it is otherwise. The Church is made up of citizens of the country. They are part and parcel of the oppressed and the oppressors. The Church cannot avoid the ceaseless struggle going on between the classes and the masses. Its members cannot be repatriated to some other land at a moment's notice. They cannot be accused of being outside agitators. They speak from within by right, and what they say, they alone must decide in the light of God's will for them.

On occasion He will direct them, as He did the Church during the days when the New Testament was being written, quietly to bear great injustices, such as slavery.

> Slaves, be obedient to those who are your earthly masters, with fear and trembling, in singleness of heart, as to Christ; not in the way of eye service, as men-pleasers, but as servants of Christ, doing the will of God from the heart, rendering service (which if they did not render they were beaten) with a good will as to the Lord (Eph. 6:5-7).

On occasion God will direct them as He did Moses, to defy the oppressor, in rebellion, confident that the Lord marches on before.

I have seen the affliction of my people who are in Egypt . . . and have come down to deliver them out of the hand of the Egyptians. . . . I will send you to Pharaoh that you may bring forth my people, the sons of Israel, out of Egypt. . . . The king will not let you go unless compelled by a mighty hand. So I will stretch out my hand and smite Egypt . . . after that he will let you go. . . . When you go, you shall not go empty . . . you shall despoil the Egyptians (Ex. 3:7ff.).

When churches multiply in a non Christian population, they will bring God's purposes for His children to bear on the particular part of the social order which they can influence. The village which becomes Christian among the Higi of northeast Nigeria will forbid parents to scarify their daughters. The county in the United States, a majority of whose citizens are evangelical Christians, may vote—as hundreds of counties already have—to forbid the manufacture and sale of alcoholic beverages. The nation most of whose citizens become Christian will pass fair employment acts and fair housing laws—and enforce them. Not only will individual Christians take part in such social action, but again and again whole congregations and denominations, as in the days of Abolition and Prohibition, will act for righteousness.

There should be no tension between mission and the advocates of social action. There is the most urgent need for *both* extension of the benefits of the Gospel to all communities and countrysides where there are no Evangelical Christians at all, *and,* where Christians are found, the application of Christian principles to all of life.

Time Is Short

This is not only the age of the common man, but the future belongs to him. Evangelistic policies should not be determined on the basis of the aristocratic feudal order which dominated the world a few years ago. What God requires of His Church is based upon the forms that society is going to take, not those that flourished a hundred years ago. Christian mission stands at one of the turning points of history. A new order is being born. Its exact form is hidden from us; the forces which combine to make the new world are far too complex to allow anyone a clear view of the outcome. Yet it seems reasonably certain that, whatever else happens, the common man is going to have a great deal more to say in the future than he has in the past.

Mgr. Cardijn, founder of the Young Christian Workers, recently wrote, "These proletarian masses, which today are powerless, will tomorrow become the arbiters of order, progress, and peace. Only the blind are unaware of this. No technological power can prevent these Asiatic populations from deciding tomorrow the future of the world" (Retif, 1962:154). There is no good reason to limit the power of the masses to Asia. Each continent contributes hundreds of millions to earth's masses.

It may be that the most significant movement in Christian mission is the discipling of the advance elements of the masses to the Christian faith—the people movements of India, the tribal movements of Indonesia, the hundred and fifty million and more who have become Christians in Africa, and the Pentecostal Churches of some countries in Latin America. To win the winnable while they are winnable would, indeed, seem to be an urgent priority. The evangelization and incorporation of the receptive sections of the masses is the best gift we can give to them.

15

HALTING DUE TO
REDEMPTION AND LIFT

OUT OF the class/mass situation just described arises the crucial question: How can mission avoid the halting of growth essentially due to the effect of redemption plus the "lift" of a program of educational, medical, and perhaps agricultural aid? As the Church is established among the masses in the world, again and again it is stopped dead in its tracks. A Baptist Church of 3,000 members has remained at about that figure for thirty years. A Lutheran cluster of 1,000 has "grown" at 1 per cent for fourteen years. An Evangelical Church of seven congregations, planted by an interdenominational mission, has "climbed" from 400 to 500 in twelve years!

Many static denominations in America and Europe are classic cases of stoppage due to redemption and lift. They have benefitted so greatly from obeying Christ and having "all these things" added to them that they are gravely handicapped in propagating the Gospel among their fellows. This is why the best denominations in America and other lands are so frequently the least growing. While many illustrations in this chapter will be from the developing nations, the problem we are exploring is universal. It is well known in the West.

Africasia has so many arrested Churches that churchmen commonly think of mission as aid in perpetuity to stopped little denominations on the other side of the world. A large per cent of the resources of missions is

295

poured into these clusters of non-growing congregations. They receive the rich services of a permanent staff of fraternal workers or missionaries and much mission money; yet they remain encircled enclaves of a few hundred or a few thousand communicants.

For example, a mission with a college, high school, hospital, ten missionaries, budget of £30,000 or $80,000, and seven congregations whose aggregate membership remains less than a thousand year after year is no rare sight. It does not intend or expect to grow into a Church of even twenty thousand. Its small size and stagnant condition are concealed in some cases by the fact that it has become part of a "large, united Church"; but behind the facade, the fact is inescapable that this cluster of congregations continues to be aided and continues stopped. Clarity—facing reality—is so important here that again I ask the reader's patience for what may seem a blunt or staccato use of terms. Such a mission is typical of hundreds of others in and out of the united Churches. Its problem—stoppage due to redemption plus "lift" which results in sealed-offness—is a major problem in missions today. Let us see how it arises and examine some suggestions for its solution.

The Redemption of Christ

Every true Church observes among its members a redemption due to Christ's saving activity in the human heart. When Christ comes in, man becomes a new creation. He repents and turns from his sins. He gains victory over pride, greed, laziness, drink, hate, and envy. He ceases quarreling with his neighbors and chasing women. He turns from litigation to constructive activity. He educates his children. He learns what God requires of him, and worships regularly. He becomes a more effective human being.

The fellowship of the Church buoys him up. The brethren gather at his bedside to pray for him in sickness. He reads or hears the Bible and realizes that God is for him and is available to him. He realizes he is a son of God and begins to act as such—begins to live for others. His community, in which many others have accepted Christ, becomes a better and better place to live. All these redemptions occur in imperfect measure, to be sure, but they occur. The churchman from abroad may see much less advance than he hoped for, but then he is probably measuring converts against his background, not theirs.

Redemption, depending solely on the Bible, the Church, the Savior, the Holy Spirit, and prayer, is indefinitely reproducible. Wherever men trust Christ, read His Word, obey Him, and gather round His table they are redeemed in this way, even when wholly independent of any aid from abroad.

Lift Due to Mission and Church Activity

A second kind of improvement, which I am calling "lift," is due to church and mission activities. The congregation and its members have the great benefit of medicine, education, loving friendship, and protection. The founding mission or Church establishes schools, hospitals, agricultural centers, literacy classes, and many other institutions to serve and help the general public and specially the new brothers in Christ. If these are illiterate, they are taught to read. Their children, attending church and mission schools—or, increasingly, tax-supported schools—become grade-school, high-school, and college graduates. Perhaps they go to Christian vocational schools and become mechanics, radio technicians, or artisans. Girls, sent to nurses' or teachers' training schools, are snapped up by the rapidly expanding government health and education programs and get good salaries. Able men and women rise to positions of international note in the Churches. A few or many, depending on the country, enter government service and hold positions of influence. The wealth of Christians rises. They become middle-class people. Members of the Christian community who have not personally done so well, nevertheless share in the general sense of well-being. All this I am calling "lift."

Lift is reproducible only to the limits of mission budget and staff. The whole institutional thrust of Africasian Churches still depends heavily on Eurican aid. True, where Christian institutions can get government grants-in-aid, it is possible for a national Church to parlay a small amount of aid from abroad into a substantial sum. Given good buildings, a first-class high school in India charges enough fees and gets enough grants-in-aid to maintain itself with very little mission money. Many a mission hospital receives a couple of thousand from abroad, adds to it twenty thousand from local receipts, and runs a sizable medical work. But all this notwithstanding, the institutional complex and its lift are not indefinitely reproducible. The "self-supporting" institutions which run at central stations with a modicum of mission aid (now called church aid) cannot be duplicated for each of a thousand congregations out across a countryside.

To the aid received from abroad (from sister churches in other lands and from missionary societies) may be added lift received from the denomination, the institutional complex built up across the decades and the centuries by Christians other than ourselves. The colleges and seminaries and orphanages and retirement homes must be counted as "foreign" aid.

So must publication houses, Bible Societies, Christian Women's Temperance Unions, Societies of Christian Endeavor, and great numbers of para church organizations. No single Christian and no single congregation could possibly create these. The good life which these make possible, the social reform which these institute, the more intelligent, sweeter, juster social order which they foster, are all "foreign" aid. All result in lift rather than redemption. The line between these two is, of course, a thin one, and the separation must not be too rigorously interpreted.

Christians Become Separated

The "redeemed and lifted" become separated from their former associates. Often, especially in mission lands the blame is not theirs. They are pushed out, ostracized, disinherited, and neglected. They are told never to show their faces in their ancestral homes. They take employment in the Church (or mission) because nothing else is available for them.

Often, however, in America and abroad, the process is intensified by the Church itself, which insists that Christians must live separate from the world. Sometimes there is no other way for converts to survive. Bitter experience has indicated that those who remain in the midst of their former associates find the pressures too heavy and revert to their former faith. Where resistance and hostility to the Christian religion are high, the lone Christian is terribly exposed. Moreover, most Churches and missions stress education and encourage Christians to send their children to school. This furthers the separation process. When Christian youth, educated in Christian schools, marry in the Christian community as Churches insist they do, even if the first generation lives out among non-Christians, the second generation comes to think of itself as different from its relatives.

So, pushed out by their own people and pulled out and transformed by the Church, educated and redeemed Christians form a separated community. They begin to move in new circles. They cease to use the dialect and start using the standard language. Crude or obscene talk is repellent to them; they do not want their children to hear it. They no longer like the old life. They are earning more and saving more; they come to have a higher standard of living; among primitive people they are personally cleaner. They imbibe from medical staffs a new attitude toward germs and dirt, flies and disposal of waste. The gulf between them and their old associates grows deeper year by year.

Because of this separation they often cease to be effective communicators among their former intimates and have no kin-contact with non-

Christians at their new level. The congregation lives in a refined type of ghetto, as it were. Physical separation may or may not be a factor, but social separation is marked. Christians have a different marriage market. Their web of relationships comes to be radically different. They have little part in civic affairs or tribal business. They worship in churches, not temples. They do not observe the non-Christian festivals. Sometimes social separation is masked, for they work with non-Christian associates, enjoy fellowship with the non-Christian teachers in the school or college, or get elected to the town council and share in its deliberations. Yet underneath the surface unity, separation is there. Non-Christians have a keen awareness that "the Christians are not our people."

The hope is always expressed that when the children of humble Christians rise in the world, they will prove to be a doorway to the middle classes. This hope seldom materializes. Non-Christians of the classes remember the humble origin of the Christians and do not propose to join such a community. The congregation remains lower-class even if a third of its members rise into the middle classes. If one whole congregation becomes middle-class, its sister congregations proclaim that not many wise or noble have become Christians. Indeed, elevation to the middle classes for any congregation usually diminishes ability to communicate the Gospel. The congregation cannot spread the faith among the resistant non-Christian middle classes, and it has departed so far from its simple origins that it does not want to bring the receptive lower class into itself. Nor would they feel at home there.

This separateness (described above in terms which fit Hong Kong, Madras, Lusaka, or Manila) can be observed in Oslo or Texas. In Europe and America, it would appear in slightly different garb—but as our Lord said clearly, Christians are and must be different. "The men whom Thou gavest me . . . are not of the world, even as I am not of the world . . . and the world has hated them because they are not of the world" (John 17:6, 16, 14).

How then can the Church lift and redeem Christians and yet have them remain in effective contact with receptive sections of society which they *can* influence? How can we keep goodness and educational advance from creating separation? How can the Church maintain solidarity with the world and yet remain Church? How can we establish churches which grow among the masses and keep on reproducing themselves without too much aid from the mothering Church or mission? In short, how can the Church avoid this kind of stoppage? This is the problem.

SOME WRONG METHODS

1. Nominal conversion of great numbers of the masses might appear to be a solution. It certainly maintains "faithful solidarity with the world." Christians remain little different from non-Christians. Since there is very little redemption and lift in this case, there is very little separation. The non-Christian feels quite at home socially, culturally, and religiously with the Christian. Connections remain excellent. Webs of relationship are preserved intact. The faith can flow over them to the unconverted.

Nevertheless this method is unacceptable. It creates great hordes of pseudo-Christians. It accepts ignorant, unspiritual multitudes as permanent parts of the Church of Christ. In winning men into a human organization it destroys the Church, the Bride of Christ. A religious form holds the people in the Church's orbit, but does not lead them on to Christ. Winning the masses but failing to redeem and lift them is the method which the Roman Catholic Church has used in certain stretches of Latin America and the Philippines, where one finds many Christo-pagans. Yet today thoughtful Roman Catholics themselves proclaim that such Christo-pagans are not really Christian. Certain Protestant people movements also have resulted in such very nominal Christians that the label Christo-pagan ought to be attached to them also.

2. Another method is the planting of small clusters of non-growing congregations which strive to be middle-class and form tiny enclaves in huge populations. Far from preventing stoppage, this "solution" requires it. A ghetto Church of four thousand in a population of a half million "solves" the problem by ignoring it. In making these few Christians, the Church has so elevated and separated them from their folk that the salvation of multitudes is effectively prevented. If the first wrong method has been favored by the Roman Catholics, the second has been favored by the Protestants. It also is no solution. It bypasses the masses by going above them and contents itself with "carrying on a work" instead of bringing nations to faith and obedience. The Church may be there as a vaguely Christian "presence," but she effectively denies the power of Christ to multitudes who need Him and would become His disciples if they could.

Since this "Protestant method" absorbs great mission resources and claims the lives of thousands of missionaries (in the little-growing Churches I have been speaking of), it deserves careful attention. These congregations are not only introverted, but are tied to foreign money and assistance. What they unconsciously proclaim is not the redemption of Christ, but the advantage of cultural lift. When they seek to relate Christianity to all of life, they do so with foreign capital through "church" financed and staffed institutions.

None of this is in any way to contradict or depreciate the solidly Christian character of little-growing Africasian Churches which are holding high the banner of Christ in difficult circumstances. They have their fair share of earnest Christians who live holy lives and preach the Gospel in street and marketplace in a manner which puts many Eurican Christians to shame. Some of them have borne persecution manfully. Nevertheless, *(a)* what non-Christians see as they look at these arrested Churches is communities which enjoy the rich services of a foreign connection; and *(b)* these clusters of congregations are growing so slowly that they themselves have no expectation of discipling their peoples. They have no solution to the problem: How can redeemed and lifted Churches maintain such solidarity with their segments of humanity that *they liberate community after community and multiply cell after cell of the redeemed?* Most of them never see the problem.

It will aid understanding of church growth, if we see this aspect of the whole picture against the stark economic reality posed by the Christianization of the masses. When the masses become Christian, their income does not suddenly quadruple. Christian peasants do not, following baptism, start earning ten times as much as their Buddhist relatives. After becoming Christian, people of the masses will continue to spend 80 per cent of their earnings of, let us say, fifty cents a day, for grain to eat. Their margin will continue to be only 20 per cent of their daily income, i.e. ten cents a day must cover clothes, taxes, education for children, and support of the Church! This slim base is all that is available to the Church when the masses become Christian. Among the poor of earth it will supply only a very simple kind of Christianity, which affluent Churches constantly judge inadequate. They may even say it is no Christianity at all! It certainly is not what they themselves can afford.

The crux of this disturbing situation is this: which is more pleasing to God—that the receptive masses become Christians according to a pattern possible to *masses who remain masses,* or that the middle-class Churches should rule—however unconsciously—that until the masses become wealthy enough to support a middle-class type of Christianity, they shall not become Christians?

THE RIGHT SOLUTION

The right solution to the problem of stoppage due to redemption and lift lies in a combination of the following two emphases.

First, members of the stopped Church should see redemption as the supreme blessing of the Christian religion. Redemption is defined as what God makes available to men in unaided churches, simply by virtue of sincere belief in Jesus Christ and unwavering dedication to Him. It is the kind of redemption we read about in the New Testament. Its enormous potential should be clearly recognized and constantly stressed. Let us consider several points.

The open Bible should be made available as an essential part of redemption. Since so many of the masses are illiterate—as they were in Europe and America in 1700 and earlier—this involves teaching Christians to read the Bible as a *religious duty,* an inalienable part of church life. Making provision for the Lord's Supper is no more sacred a part of Christian activity than making provision for believers to partake of the Lord's Word. Ordinary Christians should teach other ordinary Christians to read the Bible. The omission of this duty, as of giving to the Church, attending worship, or holy living, is sin. Christians of the masses, not by foreign-financed campaigns conducted by missionaries but by the spiritual dynamic available to every congregation, should become Bible-reading communities.

That fringe of the intelligentsia among Western Christians which will immediately warn against bibliolatry should be disregarded. How ironic it is (and how blind we often are to it) that as Christianity spreads among the masses, the danger is not bibliolatry but spiritual starvation. Ivory tower specialists, who have no conception of what it means to have a Church of a hundred thousand illiterates, must not set the rules for those whose task is to lead the hundred thousand to victorious Christian living.

Literacy classes should be in church buildings, closely tied to church programs, and built around a sharply worded doctrine which demands Bible reading as a normal Christian duty. Wherever there are significant numbers of illiterates in the membership, to invoke God's blessing on the Church teaching its members to read the Bible and to ask His grace for the learners should form a regular part of Christian worship and be built into the liturgy.

Teaching non-Christian illiterates to read as a philanthropic activity or evangelistic strategy is an entirely different matter, of which I do not speak here.

The presence of the living Christ, the empowering of the Holy Spirit, the guidance and protecting providence of God should be taught as open to ordinary Christians. For this the New Testament gives abundant illumination, which, however, is hard to realize in the climate of modern thought. The first congregations had neither printed Bibles nor manuscript

Gospels. Though they had Old Testament scrolls, they depended heavily on oral traditions concerning the teaching of Jesus their Lord, and on the leading of the Holy Spirit. They knew the loving heavenly Father as immediately available to each believer. They taught that the power of Christ drove away evil spirits, the Word of God dwelt in the heart, the mighty hand of God averted disaster and the touch of the Lord cured sickness.

Today also, Emmanuel is what every deep revival etches on the minds of Christians God with us, marvelously present. The baptism of the Holy Spirit confers upon very humble people the unshakable conviction that He is standing at their elbow to deliver them from danger, comfort them in sorrow, and enable them to praise, witness, and live as children of God.

This power is available in congregations made up of the very poorest people. Our Lord does not require literacy, wealth, or a cosmopolitan outlook before He will bring blessing. He requires only burning faith. He requires that men believe utterly in the authority of Christ and the Spirit. Churches where the real faith of the church leaders is in secular education and medicine cannot make redemption appear as the supreme blessing. A traditional Church which has—quite properly—placed great emphasis on education and medicine, may find it has unintentionally been saying also, "What really counts is secular education and closeness to the hospital. We go through the motions in our churches, but prayer and worship are of little value without our technology." To make Christ's redemption the supreme blessing in any congregation or Church may require revising instruction, liturgy, preaching, and perhaps most of all the casual conversation of Christian leaders.

It is impossible to exaggerate the importance of this first emphasis. The Bible-obeying, Spirit-filled life cannot be stressed too much.

Second, the lift made available by Christ's people through modern education, medicine, and technology should be seen by the stopped Church as a derivative part of Christian redemption, particularly valuable when rising out of the unaided efforts of Africasian Churches. The more abundant physical life (which can be made available by non-Christian governments quite as readily as by Christian missions) should be proclaimed also as part of Christ's blessing—a secondary part, to be sure, but still a part.

Since the power of scientific medicine and agriculture is so clearly observable, Christians and non-Christians do not require persuasion to believe in them. Emphasis will need to be placed on seeing them also as gifts of God. Since secondary gifts may easily be overemphasized, perhaps what is needed is quietly to provide lift, while laying tremendous emphasis on redemption. As states take over education and medicine, the Church is freed to take lift for granted and emphasize only redemption. The difficulty, of course, occurs where a large proportion of the missionary and national staff is continually employed in medicine, education, and agriculture. In such places, even when churchmen proclaim with their lips the primacy of the redemption of Christ, what they do speaks so loudly that what they *say* is hardly heard.

The lift due to mission aid (schools, agriculture, medicine, care), must in the minds of the people, Christian and non-Christian alike, *neither displace the redemption due to the Holy Spirit nor even bulk larger*. No churchman wants it to seem more important, but unless lift is consciously balanced by unusual stress on redemption as the great good, the wrong impression will be given.

Missionaries and ministers themselves must believe in the sufficiency of Christ and the Bible—that is, the sufficiency of the unaided Church to meet life's deepest needs. At this point, the work of churchmen who have given their lives for prayer, revival, and the infilling of the Holy Spirit takes on great significance. A minister may have spent years working with a congregation, educating it, caring for it, counseling it, preaching the Word to it, teaching Bible classes to its youth and adults, and may have seen it full of frailties, sins, tensions, and tears. When revival comes, these ugly manifestations of the old Adam disappear. Men and women, boys and girls, are transformed—some for a week and some for life—but changed as the minister found he could not change them. He then realizes how much greater God Himself, who unquestionably creates and uses good human institutions, is than His creations. He has His own pace and way of tilling the ground of human experience. Then, when He comes directly into men's lives, He does in a day what His servants cannot do in a decade.

Each churchman should think his way through the crucial case: If you had opportunity to found a church in a village or urban ward in which you could establish no school and no hospital, would you do it? Or still more sharply: If you had church, school, and hospital in some town and had to take away two of them, which would it be? Of the three, which helps men more fundamentally to live as children of God? Which is generically more important—which will give birth to the others?

SEVEN PRINCIPLES BEARING ON THE CORRECT SOLUTION

1. Real redemption results in great efforts to *grow*. This is a rather simple fact. If a person really shares the mind of Christ, he will be tremendously in earnest about persuading others to become disciples. At the

Communion table he hears the Savior say, I went to the cross for the salvation of all men. How far have you gone? The person who walks with the *Savior,* will devote himself to the spread of the Gospel. It is no accident, as J. Edwin Orr points out, that revivals, where the processes of redemption reach a peak, have initiated advances in the missionary movement.

To see this clearly, it is necessary to resist the temptation, so constantly before modern Christians, to appraise redemption in cultural terms. This is to confuse it with lift. On the contrary, we must estimate it in strictly Christian terms. Redemption is that which is as available to believers today as it was on the day of Pentecost. Those who are truly redeemed, like the Jerusalem refugees, go everywhere preaching the Gospel and planting churches.

2. Real growth results in great efforts to *lift.* Growth is not mere sociological accretion. Church growth, the conversion of men and multiplication of churches, is God's work. There is no such thing in church growth as "mere numerical increase." The increase is always of baptized believers, new members in the household of God and new churches. The new creature in Christ Jesus will face and journey toward goodness—he may take detours, but in general this is his direction. Indwelt by the Spirit, he will welcome moves toward love, peace, and justice. He is hungry to learn of God's will. In West New Guinea, missionaries found that

> until the people burned their charms, they were not—as a simple matter of fact—interested in the Word of God. They did not care to hear or obey it. After they burned their charms, however, they were eager and hungry to hear and obey the Gospel. Dani believers felt strongly that charm burnings were a necessary step in understanding the Gospel (Sunda, 1963:30).

A few months later these new creatures in Christ, striding toward goodness, decided to burn most of their weapons as a sign to all that they were through with fighting and killing.

Growth and redemption are intertwined. There is no such thing as redemption which opposes growth or growth which manifests no redemption. With lift the case is otherwise. Lift *can* be a thoroughly Christian elevation of body, mind, and spirit. It can also, alas, be an entirely secular matter. For example, teachers in Protestant parochial schools in Africa can cause a Church to ramify throughout a tribe. A congregation can grow up around each teacher. They can also take the position that, since they are paid for teaching school and not for creating churches, they will not do the latter.

3. When lift is so rapid that it breaks social contact between Christians and their non-Christian relatives, it ceases to be an unqualified good. Change of language, style of living, clothing, and occupation may appear desirable. These Christians are making great progress, churchmen say. But if these same changes tear the Christians away from their communities, they are dubious blessings. The Christian must, of course, break contact with all idolatrous ceremonies and those binding him to the non-Christian religion whether that be atheistic communism, animism, or some other system; but those who guide him would do well to insist that he redouble his connections at all other points. His Church, instead of dwelling on activities which he cannot share with others in his original background, should look for those which he can. A rejection of the deep sense of brotherhood must not be a part of his first step into Christianity. The educated Christian's constant emphasis should be, I am still one of you. You are my people, bone of my bone. The differences which have come through education and other factors do not erase my essential oneness with you. Hispanic converts in Chicago must become better connected with the Spanish-speaking community, not less.

Lift must not separate and isolate Christians—that is, must not lead to social dislocation. Whenever this occurs, the individual may be won, but at fearful cost, for the social unit from which he came will be lost. In the pluralistic society that marks our modern world, the existing Church should plan to start congregations in various subcultures, encouraging them to take on the tone of the subculture and to cater specially to persons and family units of it. Men can then follow Christ while remaining within their people.

Creating multiracial congregations (churches of all peoples) which pride themselves on being a foretaste of the time to come when all men will have one language and one culture, may be suitable in parts of cities like London or Los Angeles, where the races are already largely Christian. But when the races, tribes, or castes are substantially non-Christian, multiracial congregations are a poor pattern. Far from assisting the spread of the Church into those races, tribes, and castes, they prevent it. It is foolish to add racial and linguistic barriers to the essential religious and moral hurdles which converts must surmount. Men do not join churches where services are conducted in a language they do not understand, or where members have a noticeably higher degree of education, wear better clothes, and are obviously of a different sort.

To be sure, the Scriptures command us to come out and be separate. Our Lord called James and John as they were mending their nets and immediately "they left their father Zebedee in the boat with the hired servants and followed him." In directions concerning marriage, Christians are told not to be unequally yoked with unbelievers. Nevertheless, it is noteworthy that while the apostles did leave their father and mother and follow Jesus, they did so within the Jewish culture. It was customary for disciples to follow their teachers, while remaining good Jews. In doing so they did not leave the Jewish nation. Together with these words of our Lord must be put those of the apostle Paul, who, when advising Christians in the thorny matter of eating meats sacrificed to idols, said, "If one of the unbelievers invites you to dinner and you are disposed to go, eat whatever is set before you without raising any question on the ground of conscience. But if someone says to you, 'This has been offered in sacrifice,' then . . . do not eat it" (I Cor. 10:27ff.). St Paul was advising Christians as far as possible to maintain solidarity with their non-Christian comrades.

New Christians must fight both to be really Christian *and* to maintain unbroken contact with their kin. This is their task. On its successful completion depends their effectiveness as witnesses. They must be both solid with and separate from their people. Slowness of lift helps win this fight.

4. Efforts toward lift and growth must be proportioned in view of how much lift and how much growth are actually going on. Lift should be maintained in proportion to the growth of the Church. Confined to a nongrowing group of richly served Christians, it soon ceases to be productive of the life of the lowly Nazarene. The Church must fear too much lift coupled with too little growth. She should not rejoice in producing prideful little groups of spiritual athletes or, better, cultural elites.

The schematic diagram on p. 308 illustrates the problem and fruitful procedure.

Church A is already greatly growing. She is giving much effort to growth and little to lift. She should devote more to lift, but should continue enough emphasis on growth to insure that it does not stop or even slow down. Stopping growth to stress lift is always an error.

Church B is a stopped Church, heavily institutionalized and growing at only a few per cent per decade. She now devotes very little effort to growth and very great effort to lift. It is difficult, perhaps impossible, for her to grow from among her present neighbors. Further lifting and polishing of the existing Christians will set them off still more. With her assisting mission, she should reduce emphasis on lift and devote much more to effective evangelism and growth.

She could probably find a receptive population in her district. As she

FIGURE 15.1. PROPORTIONING EFFORTS CORRECTLY

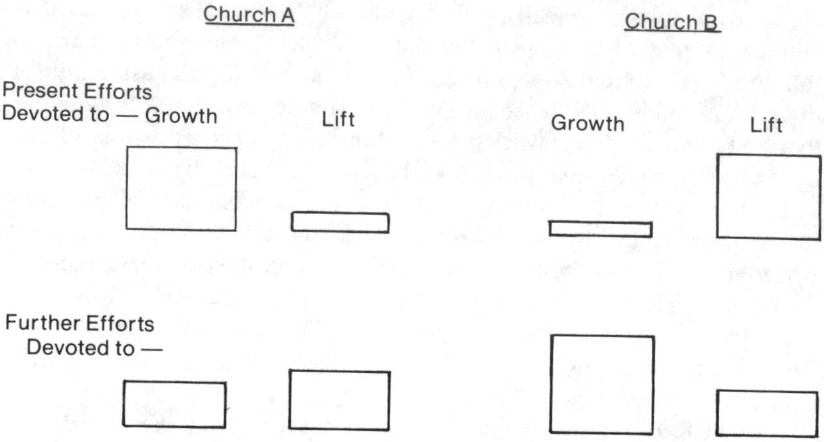

Church A   Church B

Present Efforts
Devoted to — Growth Lift   Growth   Lift

Further Efforts
Devoted to —

awakens to mission, therefore, she should search for the most receptive segment of the general population—very likely a group other than her own—and make every effort to start congregations in it. Such congregations at the beginning might have only token contact with their originator, *Church B*. If started along their own lines, they will grow in their own homogeneous unit and in time merge with other Christians in the district to form the multifaceted and variegated Church.

The diagram is, of course, an oversimplification. Constant tension exists in allocating resources between the needs for lift and for growth—at least partly because each reacts on the other. The very process of becoming Christian lifts men, and lifted Christians can be a powerful argument for others accepting the Savior, if acute separation from kindred is not involved.

5. It is absolutely necessary, in order to determine the amount of lift, to step resolutely outside one's own cultural heritage or overhang. Much lift has little to do with essential Christianity. It is instituted by Euricans to help men forward into the general culture of the world and thus tends (as we have seen before) toward civilizing rather than evangelizing. Lift wants to break down tribalism rather than to build up the Church. It glories in preparing rural Christians to earn good salaries in cities. It cooperates with governments in creating clerks, accountants, policemen, machinists, engineers, nurses, and teachers—all of whom play an important part in the new states which are arising. These are all good activities, and missions

and Churches should be fostering them. In fact, Christian missions are good for a nation wholly aside from the growth of the Church.

Nevertheless, churchmen should discern what part of the total expenditure of effort is devoted to civilizing and what to Christianizing. Good questions to ask oneself are: Did the early Christians in the Judean hills have this amount of lift? Did my own Christian ancestors? Are efforts toward education and other Western advantages keeping a respectful distance behind efforts to multiply congregations?

6. It is of particular importance not to try to resolve the tension by *reducing* the energy put into lift until it achieves parity with a small effort at growth. Rather the rule should be: *increase efforts at growth till they surpass the efforts at lift.*

Nor (again as we have seen earlier) is it fruitful to increase cultural efforts expecting that they will result in the growth of the Church. In *Church B* no increase of medical aid, schooling, or other philanthropy is likely to overcome the encirclement that shuts this Church up to small growth. *Only a stream of converts entering the Church will bring her into living contact with her environment.* It is fallacious to assume that all an introverted Church has to do is to "become interested in civic life, put up candidates for office, make pronouncements about national affairs, or undertake more helpful acts." These are small steps in the right direction; but something much more organic is needed. I have discussed this problem at length in *Church Growth in Mexico* and must content myself with a brief quotation from that source.

> How shall we establish living connections? How shall we achieve the involvement of a Church with her community? The fundamental answer is by continuous and costly and Spirit-directed finding of the lost. Churches with rapid growth have good connections. They have inevitable, unsought involvement with their communities. . . . They break out of every encirclement before it can become binding. . . . Before a convert is transformed so far that he is separated, he has led several others to Christ and they, in turn, are leading still others (McGavran, 1963:110).

It is erroneous to advocate *only* the lifting of a limited group, or only multiplication of sound Christian churches. Both are needed. As both develop, balance should be maintained between lift and growth. The right policy sets high value on lift—education, physical and spiritual health, production, and technology. These are gifts from God for men's use and enjoyment. But it ceaselessly seeks for much growth and believes that the physical increase of the Church is pleasing to God. A Church stressing uplift and cultural improvement is in for trouble unless she is effectively communicating the Gospel and multiplying churches. As a result of re-demption and lift enormous numbers of congregations in Europe and America have become so permanently middle-class or even upper-class that they have closed the door to most growth from the working classes. They should devote proportionately very large resources to purposeful evangelism. Let them stop everything else they are doing till they get a steady stream of converts entering the church.

7. Stoppage is avoided by using a pattern of church growth which is indefinitely reproducible *with the resources available to a given Church.* The following common overseas patterns violate this principle and increase stoppage.

a. Each congregation has its full complement of missionaries, school, hospital, agricultural center, and evangelistic department. This pattern is good for a mission station or church headquarters, but poor for a Church which is expected to arise in village after village across a countryside. It is not indefinitely reproducible on the resources available in villages. What is possible to the richly served congregation, many of whose members are employed in church institutions, is impossible to the village congregations. The center church is not a better church than the village congregation— it is simply one of a different pattern. Real redemption is just as possible in a village church as in a congregation at headquarters, though singing will be less tuneful, Bible knowledge less exact and abundant, services less regular, and sermons will be teaching rather than preaching sessions. If spread among the masses is the end sought, the central station pattern must not be used. It violates this principle.

b. Each congregation has an ordained minister paid largely with mis-sion funds or the contributions of mission-employed Christians or mis-sionaries. He has full seminary training and is married to a lady whose gifts and education are comparable to his own. This pattern of ministry, which at first blush seems so desirable, is as a matter of fact undesirable because it cannot be reproduced indefinitely on the resources of the small congregations so typical of the Church growing on new ground.

c. Each church building is paid for largely by mission funds. This gives small congregations permanent and fitting places of worship, but since building them requires subsidy they are not the indefinitely repro-ducible pattern of church house. They lead Christians and non-Christians to expect church buildings beyond what can be constructed by local congregations.

The following common patterns observe the principle. (i) The con-gregation normally has no missionary living within its boundaries or mission institution located there. Any educating is done in the church building. "Being Christian" means being "people of the church" not "people of the school-hospital-church complex." (ii) The congregation either depends on unpaid or part-time leaders or has a pastor of such education and pay that it can support him. (iii) The church building is one the congregation can erect and keep in repair by itself. For example, the Pentecostals in Brazil meet in house churches, rented halls, and cheap small chapels in their own neighborhoods. When they grow numerous enough, they pool their resources and erect a large central building. A church ranging from one to five thousand members results, which may have two hundred branch congregations. This is a pattern which can be repeated over and over again.

In short, the congregation should be of such structure and pattern that *common people* can operate it and *multiply it indefinitely* among the masses.

In North America, the indefinitely reproducible pattern is not the hugely successful church, led by a very exceptional preacher, which erects a set of buildings covering a city block and counts its members in the thousands. That is one good pattern in certain situations, but it is impossible in most places. In North America there are many indefinitely reproducible patterns. Each one will fit one of the socio-economic segments of the pluralistic population. A good rule to follow is: "Observe what patterns of church life are being blessed by God to the growth of His churches in the population which you are evangelizing. Use the one which best fits your gifts and those of your people."

QUESTIONS AND OBJECTIONS PRO AND CON

Some might object to this whole argument, which subordinates lift to redemption, on the grounds that the Church must lift people up. She must not teach them to be content with unjust poverty. Part of the Church's task is to create divine discontent with soul-eroding and unnecessary poverty.

The answer to the objection is simple. Nothing in this chapter should be construed as leading Christians to be content with poverty. I thoroughly agree that the Church must lift. One wants her to lift far more widely than she is now doing. One wants a congregation to exist in every section of every city and in every village and hamlet throughout the earth, for only then will the passion of God for righteousness and justice working through men dedicated to His will and feeding on His Word be applied to every community.

But one must point out that uplift paid for by Churches not of that area often prevents a vast extension of the redemption-cum-lift that characterizes Christianity. This thought will be driven home as we consider the following difficult questions.

Dare the Church take in only those it can lift to middle-class status?

Are the masses doomed to remain outside the Church because they are poor and probably will continue to be poor?

Has the Church no Gospel for carpenters, fishermen, and burden-bearers—the masses of mankind?

Must not the Church, to be truly the Church, take people at whatever level of economic ability they now find themselves?

Is Christ's redemption really limited to the amount of education at mission expense that the Church can give to new Christians? Is the Gospel of itself impotent?

Does any Church dare, in this day of the common man, when control is rapidly passing out of the hands of the middle classes, limit itself to the upper or middle classes, or—worse—take pride in being a middle-class Church?

What should we think of a Eurican Church which gauged its success by the number of members it was able to lift to twice their present income? Why, then, count increase in standard of living as so valuable a part of the Church's faithfulness in Africasia?

SUMMARY

It can now be seen that the wrong methods, mentioned on pages 300-301, are not entirely wrong. They are merely beginnings. If taken as points from which to carry forward thorough and widespread Christianization of the masses, both are defensible.

The great people movement Churches need perfecting. They should fear—as they would death itself—to accept a permanently depressed spiritual condition as normal for their members. They should continually devise ways by which their multitudinous members, on their own resources, hear, read, and learn the Bible. They should devise indigenous systems of revival and direct the resulting zeal to further learning of the Bible and extending of the Church. The people movement is an excellent place to begin, but a poor place to end.

As Dr. Tippett insists, people movements should be consummated in revival. If one-tenth of the creative effort spent on missions were to be devoted to devising a mode of revival-cum-evangelism which large Asian and African Churches could institute on their own and carry forward on a really indigenous basis, they would become fountains of spiritual life and foci of explosive spread throughout the three billion non-Christians of the earth. The world is waiting for the large Churches of Africasia to burst into missions *on their own patterns*. The methods of missions from

Eurica will not fit missions from Africasia to their own or other lands. But something really vital and really indigenous will.

God has granted His Africasian Churches men filled with His Spirit and gifted in bringing Christians of the masses to deeper dedication; but these men are not being used by the Church as they could be. They are often not known outside their own denominations, and sometimes work in opposition to the Churches arising out of missionary efforts from the West.

Existing stopped Churches—in Eurica fully as much as in Africasia, in Canada fully as much as in Karnataka—need great growth. They should fear, as a debilitating disease, accepting as a permanent thing the role of little-growing, middle-class Churches. They should regard themselves as God's pilot projects, dedicated to liberating the multitudes of their lands. They need to understand church growth. Among the many factors of growth, they should see the one dealt with in this chapter: the difference between the redemption offered by essential Christianity and the lift offered by its middle-class cultural accompaniments. The stopped Churches have been greatly blessed by the Christian faith. They must now break out of their middle-class encirclements, seek receptive peoples in their neighborhoods, and establish constellations of living congregations among the masses. These will be different from themselves yet thoroughly Christian, for they will have the Bible and Christ.

16

DISCIPLING URBAN POPULATIONS

T HE CHRISTIAN religion was born in the city of David and grew to manhood in the great cities of Caesar. Unlike Islam, which became powerful in the small towns and oases of the Arabian hinterland, the expansion of Christianity is inextricably associated with centers of power in the ancient world: Antioch, Ephesus, Corinth, Alexandria, Carthage, and Rome. St. Paul, evangelizing a receptive population—the synagogue communities, which lived by commerce in the cities—traveled from urban center to urban center. Eight of his epistles are titled by the names of the urban centers to which they were directed. Cities and larger towns had great meaning for the Early Church and have even more significance for Christian missions in the next half century.

THE GROWING CITIES

The importance of cities for church growth increases when we see that larger and larger proportions of earth's population are living in them. The rush to the cities is on, and within the next few decades perhaps three-fourths of the human race will be born, live, and die in urban rather than rural areas.

In making this statement, I classify as rural all those who earn their living from the soil, dwell in villages, and eat largely what they raise. All those who live in market centers and live by trade or manufacture, I classify

314

as urban. Some will live in towns of less than ten thousand, others in towns of ten to ninety thousand, and still others in great manufacturing cities of a hundred thousand and up. The huge metropolises—Tokyo, Toronto, Calcutta, Atlanta, Kinshasa, Berlin, Sao Paulo, and others—present special problems, but for the time being we shall consider them also simply as urban populations.

Good reasons exist for men to flock to the cities. Cultivating two acres by hand wastes manpower. With machines, fewer and fewer men can farm more and more land and raise more and more food. Farms are becoming huge food factories. Even a 160-acre farm is not economical to run. Machines can handle hundreds of acres and cost more to buy and replace than a man who owns only 160 acres can afford to pay. Cotton, which used to be picked by hand, requiring thousands of laborers, is now picked by machines requiring only a few. Even vegetables and fruit are being harvested with machines.

Huge populations in Africasia will be thrown out of work when men there are replaced by machines. Fear of this dislocation restrains Third World mechanization of farms and temporarily holds enormous numbers on the soil, tilling two or three acres per family; but the mere fact that hand labor is the most expensive way to grow food will eventually force adjustment in these overpopulated lands, too. Their cities are growing apace and will grow more and more in the future.

City living has great benefits. Backbreaking toil in hot sun and deep mud is replaced by work in which machines provide the muscle. In cities men can be organized for much greater production. Arrangements for sanitation, clean water, and education are more readily made. City dwellers earn more money and buy more things. More amusements and excitements are available. Paved streets banish mud and dust. Medical services are more readily at hand.

For the time being, large numbers of city dwellers in Africasia are at heart villagers. They keep one foot in their ancestral homes, and marry in the correct community. During periods of unemployment, they return to their own people. In Liberia they are called target workers—when they have made their target, they return to their forest hamlets to spend it. Such city dwellers dream of earning enough to go back and be "big shots" in the little village. But this come-and-go business is a transitional phenomenon. Larger and larger numbers are becoming permanent residents of the city—as in the West, they never return to the rural solitudes.

Dispersion of industries will not reverse the rush to the cities. On the contrary, since it will scatter cities throughout a nation, exodus from the villages will become easier and easier. Planned cities, created from scratch, being better places in which to live than those which have grown up by themselves, will accelerate the irreversible trend toward urbanization.

The Church faces huge city populations growing still more enormous. Her task is to disciple, baptize, and teach these urban multitudes. It was urban multitudes that the Lord would have gathered as a hen gathers her brood under her wings; and His Church, indwelt by Him, longs to do the same. Yet the Church is not growing in most cities in both Eurica and Africasia.

After a hundred and fifty years of modern missions, the plain fact is that Churches have not done well in most cities of Africasia. The great movements to Christ have taken place among country people. In the South Pacific, for example, where four of the five million island inhabitants have become Christians, practically all were converted in their ancestral village homes. The 800,000 Baptists in Burma (total community) were not baptized in Rangoon and Mandalay; they became Christian in ten thousand little communities scattered through the rice paddies and forests of Burma. The towns and cities of India have not been the scene of the great turnings to Christ by which about 16,000,000 Indians were Christians in 1980. The turnings took place in castewise movements to Christ in India's myriad villages. In African countries, even greater movements to Christian faith, which by 1980 had brought at least 100,000,000 into the Christian fold, were almost without exception rural movements. Much of the significant growth in Latin America has taken place in rural areas. For example, the growth of the Presbyterian Church in the provinces of Tabasco and Chiapas, Mexico, took place among the peasants of that land. Most towns have been shut tight against the Evangelical Church. However, in Brazil, Chile, and a few other lands we find notable exceptions to this rule. After 1970 urban proletariats have been increasingly responsive to surging national evangelistic movements. Roger Greenway, in *Apostles to the City* (1978), calls attention to the striking growth of the Luz del Mundo Movement in the great city of Guadalajara, Mexico. So emphatic is this Church about the importance of learning to read the Bible and practicing the Christian life that

> theirs is the only municipal district in the state of Jalisco that has no illiterates. . . . There are no taverns, saloons or houses of prostitution in the area. Brawling, fighting between families, and drunkenness are virtually unknown . . . streets are safe and clean. . . . Women dress modestly and children are well behaved. Men are known for industriousness and honesty in their work (52-53).

In Africasian cities and towns, congregations have, to be sure, been established, but for the most part these have grown up around mission stations and their related institutions and have formed introverted, static, "gathered-colony" congregations. Their members were heavily dependent on the missions for employment and have shown inability to multiply themselves across the urban scene. Were it not for the great country movements, church growth in the cities would by this time have created Christian communities of less than one tenth of 1 per cent of the total population.

Multiplying congregations in countrysides and static congregations in cities have characterized Christianity in Africasia for the last 150 years.

The general statement should, however, be qualified in several ways. Some city congregations have grown greatly—but by transfer growth. Christians whose ancestors were converted in the country have moved to town and now make up 50, 60, or even 95 per cent of the church members there. In some cities, huge churches are found. In Kinshasa in 1977 I saw several of two or three thousand members; but these had become Christian in the tribal areas and had moved to the city looking for work. In Kinshasa in 1977 about 600,000 of the city's population of two and a half million claimed to be Protestants, but less than 100,000 were members of any Protestant congregation. Even in a hugely receptive population like that the Churches and missions had failed to do significant discipling (McGavran-Riddle, 1979:145). As Barrett says of the African situation in general, the "ponderous machinery of initiation cannot let in fast enough those who ask for instruction and baptism" (1973:175).

In a few countries, growth has been largely urban. In Japan, for example, the Church has grown scarcely at all in the villages. What growth has occurred has come from converted city dwellers. Nevertheless, Japan has seen no great urban movements to Christ. Making the statement for total community, less than 1 per cent of the population of Japan is Christian, despite much missionary work and two periods of extraordinary openness to the Christian faith.

In 1965 in the towns and cities of Indonesia, 7 per cent of the Chinese were Christian (Haines, 1966:35). In Hong Kong in 1968 10 per cent were (Coxill, 1968:150, 222). However, the ways in which these congregations have been established have yet to be described, and with the influx from the mainland, the percentages have declined.

Of all the countries of Africasia, in Brazil and Chile alone the general picture of much growth in the countrysides and little growth in the cities has been reversed. The great growth of Evangelical Churches in Chile and Brazil—particularly the Pentecostal Churches—has been in the cities. A map of Evangelical congregations shows them thickly clustered in the great urban complexes. In Chile, churches have multiplied among the urban proletariat. In Brazil great migrations from the drought-plagued northeast to the cites of the south have been rich sources of church growth. Some of the migrants were already believers (*crentes*) when they came south; hundreds of thousands more joined them in the factory communities. The significant Latin American Church Growth Research of 1965-68 has light for Christian mission at this point. Its chapters on urbanization and church growth are essential reading for churchmen anywhere in the world concerned with the Christianization of tomorrow's cities (Read, Monterroso, Johnson, 1969).

Failure of the Church to grow in most cities is not due to lack of effort. Most missionaries live and work in cities. These centers of population and communication are well supplied with postal and telegraphic services and are natural sites for mission stations. Headquarters of almost all missions and Churches are located in cities, and the larger institutions are there also. Tremendous amounts of Christian treasure and life have been poured out in "city work in Africasia."

But, whether in North America or elsewhere, city work is not the task. The assignment is not "to reach the cities." The Church has already done that. Her task is to bring urban multitudes to faith and obedience. The goal to be constantly held in mind is so to preach and live the Gospel that baptized believers in increasing numbers flow into existing congregations, and form themselves into new congregations which ramify and branch out through the suburbs, new towns, wards, *barrios, colonias, mohullas,* and other sections of urbania, soon to be occupied by 2,500,000,000 human beings. Success in churching the cities, which is beginning to characterize urban mission here and there, points in the right direction. In *Urban Strategy for Latin America* Greenway writes,

> If revitalized churches whose leaders have been trained in church growth-oriented schools can be turned loose in the burgeoning cities, then a multiplication of churches will occur such as the world has not seen since the first century (236).

URGENT NEED FOR RESEARCH

Many conditions conducive to church growth are found in cities in North America and other continents. Uprooted and transplanted immigrants, starting life anew in strange surroundings and needing community and friendship, flood into cities. These newcomers are away from the close control of family and intimates. Their priests and religious leaders do not know where they are. The old gods of hearth, field, and forest and the evil spirits whom they feared have been left behind. American and European cities are full of lonely people looking for community. Like the city-dwellers in the ancient world, they should be receptive to the Gospel. They are easily reached. They have come out of a thousand far-off valleys, mountain ridges, distant plains, or deep forests and now live within an hour's walk or drive from where able national ministers or missionaries live. They are also very open to the mass media.

True, many conditions in cities militate against church growth. The population is extremely mobile. It is here today and gone tomorrow— sometimes back to its ancestral villages, sometimes on to other wards of the same city or to other cities. People are tied by hours of work and close schedules. There are no seasons when, because of dryness or heat, field work is at a standstill. The 1905 Korean system of month-long Bible study for laymen would not work in most urban centers. City dwellers are apt to become sophisticated and indifferent to religion. They have movies, radio, and other entertainment. Preaching has to be very dramatic or insistent to catch their attention. After they have lived in a given city for a while, they have rebuilt their circle of friends and do not feel the need for community. They have fitted into the religious activities—secular, Hindu, Buddhist, Moslem, or other—which have grown up in the city. The oppressions of the village and its feudal lord do not touch them in the city, and they are not looking for a liberator.

The urban puzzle facing the Christian Church consists in just this open-shut nature of the cities. In urban areas, where some conditions favor church growth and others inhibit it, sometimes churches multiply but mostly they do not. One cannot help asking why. Indeed, Christians have the most weighty reasons to find out what makes churches grow or stop growing in cities. If all denominations witnessing in cities were in a state of non-growth, the Church could conclude that the city presents a climate so hostile to the Gospel that evangelism there is simply bearing witness to Christ, providing a genial Christian presence, and leaving the rest to God's inscrutable purposes. But in face of the fact that some denominations are growing well, the Church dare not come to any such cheap conclusion. She should instead go through the difficult process of discovering under which conditions multitudes will believe and under which they will not; in which homogeneous units, cells of Christians will proliferate and in which they will not; and what modes of evangelism God is currently blessing to the increase of His congregations, and what He is not. Let us look at a few growing urban Churches.

In the United States and Canada, churches have multiplied in new suburbs among native-born white Protestant populations, but have declined in inner cities and in "changing neighborhoods." The notion that the Church cannot grow in these last two areas is erroneous. It can grow there, but new methods and strong biblical convictions will be required. Old strong congregations and denominations should set goals for multiplying new congregations in these precise areas. In 1979 in Southern California when Hispanic churches resolved to multiply new churches among their own people and to use all the insights of church growth theory and theology to assist such expansion, the rate of establishing new congregations shot up. American cities are full of winnable men and women.

In Mexico, a certain indigenous denomination, the Iglesia Apostolica de la Fe en Cristo Jesus, has without any missionary assistance grown well. In 1967 it numbered about 16,000 communicants, most of whom lived and worshiped in towns and cities. While this was happening in Mexico, this same communion was establishing over fifty congregations among the Latins living in the metropolitan area of Los Angeles. When large North American missionary societies plant few congregations among this piece of the Californian urban mosaic, how does the Iglesia Apostolica plant so many? What is she doing that effectively communicates the faith?

In Japan, the Spirit of Jesus Church has—again without any mission assistance—multiplied congregations in many urban areas. What is it doing that the traditional Churches could not do if they tried?

In Brazil, the six major Protestant denominations have thousands of city churches—some with memberships of several thousand each. In 1978, according to the estimate of Dale McAfee, Presbyterians had 252,516 members, Seventh-Day Adventists 263,533 baptized believers, Brasil Para Cristo 405,000, Baptists 441,062 baptized believers, Congregacao Cristan 717,873, and the Assemblies of God 3,200,000. *Most members lived in the cities.* What are the secrets of this tremendous increase? It would be revealing to contrast the methods which bring in these numbers with those which have resulted in the very small growth of the denominations planted by thirty or more small missions which went to Brazil after World War II.

Large-scale research is needed in every major country—West as well as East—to reveal what activities, modes of life, and kinds of proclamation communicate the Christian faith in cities and which do not. Many illustrations of the latter and some of the former can be readily obtained; they would cast invaluable light on this urban field in which the Churches will spend many billion dollars in the next thirty years.

Wide surveys of whole countries are proving valuable at the present time and will probably continue to do so for several years. But together with these should go studies of limited but significant portions of the total problem of growth. The exploration of crucial problems should comprise a larger and larger proportion of all church growth research.

For instance, many American denominations are composed of middle-class citizens. Of these some are very largely of Dutch, German, Mennonite, or Swedish background. They find it "almost impossible" to grow in other segments of the populations. They are sealed off to their own little fragment. *How do such Churches break out of their ethnic/class encirclement?* Fortunately some breakouts have occurred. Research in this field will cast significant light on church growth everywhere. What is learned in North America will help sealed off denominations in Asia, Europe, and other continents also.

Or again, is it true that in the cities of Brazil 70 per cent of Presbyterian increase comes from the Christians moving to town and 30 per cent from "conversions in the cities," while the corresponding figures for Baptists are 50-50 and for Pentecostals 30-70? This is the opinion of some perceptive churchmen in Brazil. If it be so, what can Baptists, Presbyterians, Methodists, Lutherans, and others do to find the lost as effectively as the Pentecostals? Information about this limited aspect of evangelism would be well worth securing. It is only one of dozens of facts the Church needs if she is to be faithful to God in her stewardship of the Gospel in the cities. She must avoid squandering a billion dollars in "urban work" which repeats the mistakes of the last fifteen decades and is granted only small church increase.

It would be very useful indeed to know what kinds of literature distribution and radio broadcasting are sowing seed on the path, to be devoured by birds, and which are sowing it on good soils, some of which may produce a hundred, some sixty, and some thirty congregations. Such matters can be discovered, to the great benefit of mankind.

The real tasks of research will not be done by some missionary or minister released from his regular duties for six months to make a quick swing around the cities, talk to a few people, and write up his impressions. Denominations and boards should train able and devout men—preferably those who have spent some years planting churches in cities—in the best techniques of social and religous research. The more than two hundred missionary societies of North America, either singly or together, could easily create a small, highly trained corps of missionaries and ministers (citizens of all six continents) who would make research in church growth their life work. A missionary society entirely devoted to studying church growth might be organized. Social scientists in the service of urban evangelism should have no difficulty in raising support.

Such church growth researches over the next fifteen years should cost many million dollars. Since they will illuminate, guide, and fructify evangelistic endeavor costing hundreds of millions, this should be considered a small and essential expense. The Church cannot afford to blunder ahead evangelizing the cities with her eyes closed. To throw as much light as possible on what evangelism is effective and what is not is good stewardship. Failure to acquire light would in these days be called, in the business world, criminal negligence. Our Lord would regard it no less seriously. Research in urban church growth demands immediate development by all who take evangelism seriously. It surely would be pleasing to God were His servants to obtain the best guidance possible on the task He has given them to do—reconciling men of all nations to Himself.

EIGHT KEYS TO CHURCH GROWTH IN CITIES

Since the meticulous research described in the previous paragraphs has not been done, no one yet knows what modes of mission promise most for communicating the Christian faith to urban man. The eight keys I am about to mention, however, are not mere guesses. They describe principles about which church growth men are agreed. As stated here, they are much too general to describe what needs to be done in specific cities, for which the formula will vary from country to country and culture to culture. Yet these "keys" are in the neighborhood of the truth. Anyone who would use them must modify them to fit specific homogeneous units and sponsoring Churches. They are offered in the hope that church growth thinkers in America and all over the globe will carry the process further, and describe more exactly the keys which will unlock specific conurbations in which the Church is commanded to bring many sons to glory.

1. *Emphasize house churches.* When the Church begins to grow in cities among new segments of the population, each congregation must soon find a place to assemble. The obvious way to do that is for the founding Church or mission to buy a small plot and put up a meeting house. In cities, the cost of land is usually quite beyond the purse of a new little cell of Christians. The obvious way may be the only way in areas of great hostility, but it is contraindicated in responsive areas.

The congregations should meet in the most natural surroundings, to which unbelievers can come with the greatest ease and where the converts themselves carry on the services. Where non-Christian leaders are antagonistic, the meeting place should neither attract attention nor throw out a challenge to them. Obtaining a place to assemble should not lay a financial burden on the little congregation. The house church meets all these requirements.

The Disciples of Christ in Puerto Rico enjoyed vigorous growth in a multitude of house churches. These began as Bible study groups, when one neighbor would call in others to share in his new-found light; as prayer meetings when several families of believers would gather together in a convenient house; as branch Sunday Schools to which laymen from the fathering churches devoted a night a week; or as branch congregations which met on Sunday. Many house churches carried on with no financial outlay at all. Those that prospered under the lay leaders (and an occasional visit by the pastor) built little shacks, entirely on their own initiative, ten by twenty feet in size perhaps, and began to hold preaching services there, first on Sunday evening and later on Sunday morning. Some of these prospered and grew into strong congregations.

The house church has drawbacks. If believers do not increase fast so that at least some house churches rent halls or build "meeting houses," worship year after year in someone's home gets wearisome. Only those friendly to the householder will go to church in his house. Chickens, dogs, and cows strolling among the worshipers distract their attention. Wear and tear on the house is considerable. Nevertheless, so much urban growth has begun in house churches that they should always be seriously considered, both for initial planting and for later extension. Eurican patterns of worship should be adjusted till ordinary Christians in ordinary homes can lead them. It should be remembered that the Early Church met almost entirely in houses for at least the first seventy years of her life.

2. *Develop unpaid lay leaders.* Laymen have played a great part in urban expansions of the Church. One secret of growth in the cities of Latin America has been that, from the beginning, unpaid common men led the congregations, which therefore appeared to the masses to be truly Chilean or Brazilian affairs.

In any land, when laborers, mechanics, clerks, or truck drivers teach the Bible, lead in prayer, tell what God has done for them, or exhort the brethren, the Christian religion looks and sounds natural to ordinary men. Whatever unpaid laymen—earning their living as others do, subject to the same hazards and bound by the same work schedules—lack in correctness of Bible teaching or beauty of prayers, they more than make up for by their intimate contact with their own people. No paid worker from the outside can know as much about a neighborhood as someone who has dozens of relatives and intimates all about him. True, on new ground the outsider has to start new expansions—no one else can—but the sooner he turns the churches over to local men the better.

Some new converts have leadership ability. Discovering these, laying the responsibility of the prayer meeting, Bible class, branch congregation, or house church on them, and getting out of the way so that they can function without embarrassment is close to the essence of the matter. From then on, they lead the churchlet, win new men to Christ, and instruct them in the faith. Enough contact should be maintained and enough encouragement given to sustain them in crisis; but they should realize that the enterprise is theirs under the Holy Spirit.

Lay leaders need much training whether in town or village. Nevius trained his unpaid leaders for a whole month each year, bringing them from their villages to his station two hundred miles away. He fed them for the month and gave them financial help to get back home. During the month he instructed them intensively in the Bible in the mornings, sent them out two by two to witness and preach in the afternoons, and had a rousing revival service with them in the evenings.

The four-month sessions of the Assemblies Bible School in El Salvador train mostly unpaid lay leaders. Only a few, after coming back for training over a period of six or eight years, become paid preachers. Elsewhere, once churches get under way, an apprentice system trains men. However it is done, motivating laymen to learn and providing ways to learn are essential. It is here that the battle is won or lost.

3. *Recognize resistant homogeneous units.* The city is not a homogeneous whole, but rather a mosaic made up of hundreds of segments of society, a few responsive, many indifferent, and a few highly resistant. The obedient and intelligent steward of God's grace recognizes this and plans his work in the light of it.

Frend, in describing the growth of the Donatist Church of North Africa, says that, while all the country people (and responsive units among the city dwellers also) became Christians between A.D. 250-300, the government officials and large landowners in the cities of Libya remained pagan, worshiping the gods and goddesses of Rome for another seventy-five years (Frend, 1952:108). The officials and owners had a vested interest in paganism and were highly resistant. They instituted the great persecution of 305. Had Christian missionaries to Libya between the years A.D. 100

to 300 spent their time presenting the Gospel to them and bypassing those who were responsive, very little church growth would have resulted.

Some new missionaries to Sao Paulo, Brazil, asked whether I would advise them to concentrate on neighborhood evangelism (by which they meant presenting the Gospel in a natural fasion to immediate neighbors in their section of the metropolis). In reply, I pointed out that since they were car owners and rented houses with garages, this guaranteed that their neighbors would be car owners—people of the classes, beneficiaries of the social order, and likely to be resistant. I counseled them to try neighborhood evangelism for a year, and if at the end of that time they had not assembled a church of at least five *converted* families, to seek a more receptive section of the city. I said "converted families" because it was quite possible to pick up a few second- or third-generation middle-class Protestants and form them into a new congregation.

Every minister hesitates to judge that "the people in this section cannot be won." All of us want to believe that those with whom we have established cordial relations are the people to whom God has sent us. Yet surely God expects us to use our common sense. Indeed, may we not be confident that the Holy Spirit Himself leads us away from gospel-rejectors to gospel-acceptors? This is the clear testimony of the New Testament.

In California an experienced pastor pointed out that fourth generation Hispanics were much more resistant to the Gospel than new immigrants. He was correct, even though among the former are some highly responsive individuals. University chaplains know that some kinds of students are harder to reach than others. The wise pastor does not spend most of his time on the men and women least likely to join his church.

A Presbyterian layman of Recife, Brazil, observed that incoming migrants were receptive for a number of years; but when they had prospered and moved out of the *favella,* they became deaf to the Gospel. He felt that Christians should not walk past the responsive to those resistant on the dubious plea that the Holy Spirit was leading them precisely to those who had stopped their ears against the Gospel. Believing in the sovereignty of God, the Christian must grant that the Holy Spirit may on occasion lead a Christian to resistant populations. If He does, the Christian should certainly obey. Yet the Christian should beware lest his own class pride or love of ease rather than the Holy Spirit is what is leading him to neglect the receptive and spend himself on the resistant.

Resistance often arises because of land ownership. For example, a missionary in generally receptive Sao Paulo evangelized a certain section of the city fruitlessly for five years, only to discover that the houses in that section were built on land belonging to the Roman Catholic Church! Becoming an Evangelical there entailed sharp economic loss. When he began evangelizing in another district his labors began to bear fruit. Congregations arose.

Resistance fluctuates, and sometimes units supposed to be responsive turn out resistant—sometimes, for example, recent immigrants. They intend to return to their villages, and think to themselves, How will it go with us if we should go back Christians? J. C. Wold observes that in Liberia the young single men working on the Firestone rubber plantations are not as likely to become Christians as they are back in their forest villages with their families (Wold, 1968:45).

4. *Focus on the responsive.* The city mosaic has responsive units. Which units are receptive will differ from city to city. The receptive units in Vancouver differ from those in Nashville. Responsive units in Bangkok will not be the same as those in Tokyo or Hong Kong—though all three are mainly Buddhist Asian cities. Both the degree of receptivity and the ability of the Churches and missions to harvest will fluctuate. There are thousands of responsive units, of which only a few can be mentioned.

One group which should normally prove receptive is that made up of recent rural immigrants who have come permanently to the city—especially if they have come from overseas. For a generation or so these are villagers at heart. Unless they live in unusually tight ghettos, they are hungry for community and are forming all kinds of new associations. Their basic receptivity can be frustrated, however, if the first congregations receive extensive aid from outside churches. Then becoming Christian means being richly served by a wealthy foreign organization called "the Church," an understanding which is fatal to healthy growth. Furthermore, the foreign organization, though wealthy, never has unlimited funds, and if every new congregation means an additional five or ten thousand added to the budget, its interest in church growth diminishes rapidly.

City congregations that multiply establish a personal and corporate life that satisfies far better than the old cults and rituals did, and it can be carried on by the congregations themselves.

5. *Multiply tribe, caste, and language churches.* In some circumstances building homogeneous unit congregations is a key to growth. Part of the feeling of lostness in responsive homogeneous units in cities comes from the fact that the immigrants are not at home in the standard language used in the city. Even when they learn to speak it after a fashion, it never sounds as sweet in their ears as their mother tongue. They like to get together with those who worship in their own language.

At just this point, however, missions and Churches, under pressure to care for congregations in the most economical way, and antagonistic toward dialects and tribal languages, set up congregations where the praying, preaching, and singing are all done in the "national language." Where the city is made up of many peoples and many languages, this is a dubious procedure. It means that many, if not most Christians have to worship God and hear His Word in a language which they imperfectly understand. Even worse, they have to try to bring their non-Christian friends to hear the Gospel proclaimed in a strange tongue.

In 1954, in Leopoldville, I witnessed a still more dubious procedure. In one large building, services were held for two or three tribes in two or three languages *simultaneously*. The singing went well—the tune drowned out the words. But the praying, Bible reading, and preaching (two leaders at once, each in a different language) were bedlam. This device, no doubt, served the more devout among the existing Christians, but non-Christians would scarcely be attracted to it. Such a device could never help the urban congregations to win every non-Christian of every tribe flooding into the city. In Calcutta, for example, Telegu, Ooriya, Uraon, Chhattisgarhi, Hindi, and Santal congregations are essential if congregations are to multiply in these linguistic units of the city.

When the Church forms a tiny minority in any city, its first business is not to assist assimilation or—in some countries—detribalization, but to disciple all who can be persuaded to believe on Jesus Christ. The first business of the Church is not to fuse the various populations of the metropolis into one people. The establishment, *in* each linguistic and ethnic group, of congregations whose members worship God with delight in their own mother tongue should be the aim. If any disagree with this principle, I suggest that he go and "worship" with a congregation of whose services he understands only one word in three! When city churches set themselves the task of discipling out to its fringes each ethnic unit in which there are already some Christians, and multiplying ethnic churches as the best means of accomplishing the task, discipling the cities will become much more possible than it is today.

When discipling of the responsive homogeneous units is advanced, shifting into the national language and broadening the base to appeal to "the Gentiles also," is desirable and, indeed, inevitable.

In a few cases, the melting-pot aspect of cities brings it about that large numbers in each ethnic or linguistic unit *truly want* to leave their past and join the dominant culture. Under such circumstances, multitudes will flock into congregations which worship in the standard language, encourage intermarriage, and demonstrate the melting pot at its hottest. But in most cases the melting-pot aspect has been grossly overestimated.

How can the Church know when the melting pot is hot enough to make it advantageous to feature an "all-peoples church?" To worship in the standard language? To shift out of ethnic congregations? There is only one sure test: Do congregations which play up "one great brotherhood of all tribes and castes" multiply like yeast cells throughout the city? If they do, that is the time to shift out of ethnic churches.

6. *Surmount the property barrier.* Congregations must have places to meet, and house churches (as we have seen) furnish an excellent pattern to begin with. But house churches among common people under the very crowded conditions of modern cities have great handicaps. A whole family may be living in one or two rooms and sharing a tiny courtyard with two other families. In some high-rise apartment houses, such as have been built in Hong Kong, each family has only one room and no courtyard. In *favellas* in Brazil a half-dozen adults can with difficulty crowd into one dwelling. Inner cities are congested.

Unless some way is found for new congregations to get a place to worship, the multiplication of Christian cells becomes increasingly difficult. Various means have been devised to meet the problem. The commonest among indigenous denominations is for the little congregation to obtain marginal land—an unused corner of a back lot, for example—and build a shack on it. Such a shack, made of odds and ends of lumber and roofed over with flattened tin cans, is the first chapel. As the congregation grows, better and better shacks are built, until at last a permanent church building goes up.

Renting a hall, saloon, store, or storage shed is another expedient. In 1965, the 3,000-member Mother Church of the Brasil Para Cristo denomination met in a huge Quonset hut which was once a storage shed. Store front churches are common in New York.

A combination of many house churches, rented halls, and shack churches, with a "respectable" mother-church building seems to work well for the Assemblies of God in Brazil. In El Salvador, however, where the average congregation of the Assemblies numbers twelve baptized believers, about as many unbaptized believers, and their children, heavy dependence is placed on house churches.

One longs to discover a way in which the enormously wealthy world Church can help multiply congregations in Afericasian cities, eliminate the bottleneck of high-priced land, and get suitable meeting houses. It is easy enough to buy a suitable site and help the congregation erect a good building on it; but unless the world Church is prepared to continue such aid indefinitely, this only teaches young congregations that being Christian involves accepting a church building from overseas friends. The Southern Baptists, investing about $15,000 in each site plus building, have put a solid Baptist church in the capital city of every prefecture (province or state) in Japan. As long as the missionary society is willing to invest $100,000 a year in Japan, it can build six or seven new churches annually. Till 1960, these new churches, using their own resources only, had not in turn planted other congregations (Wright, 1961).

All kinds of proposals to solve the property problem have been advanced. Some suggest that the mission buy a suitable site, erect a basement on it, and give land and building to the Church when the congregation adds a top story. Others propose loans in which the congregations put up part, the mission gives part, and a part is loaned to the congregation to be repaid over twenty years. Others put a good roof on a building when the congregation buys the land and puts up the walls. Others have the mission buy a whole floor in an apartment house and use it as a pastor's home and congregational meeting place. Each scheme has its drawbacks and solves the property problem only under special circumstances.

The index of growth has a great deal to do with the matter. A Church which has found a way to communicate the Gospel, where the number of baptized believers is constantly increasing and the smell of victory is in the air, eliminates the building bottleneck in cities much better than a Church which is not growing. A Church which grows greatly often thereby solves its building problem.

The building bottleneck cannot be eliminated by concentrating on it alone. What must be found is a more effective way of winning men and women to Christ in the city. As soon as this is done, the building problem will be more than half-solved.

7. *Communicate intense belief in Christ.* The prime ingredient in the patristic capture of the great cities of the ancient world was an intense, fervent faith. This shines through the pages of the New Testament and was manifested by all the planters of the Early Church. The Jerusalem Church was born in persecution. The first great explosion of the faith was sparked by an oppression so great that it drove all but the apostles out of the city. Paul and Barnabas were beaten again and again as they established congregations in synagogue communities. Reliable tradition has it that Paul was beheaded, Peter crucified, and every other apostle martyred—Thomas dying in far-off India—in the cities of the ancient world.

Unshakable faith in Christ, fervent enough to withstand flame and wild beasts, fanned the spread of the Early Church in the urban proletariat of those days. While of major eschatological importance, the Revelation of John is at the same time convincing evidence of the climate of faith in that city-conquering Church.

> Do not fear what you are about to suffer. Behold, the devil is about to throw some of you into prison, that you may be tested, and for ten days you will have tribulation. Be faithful to death and I will give you the crown of life. . . . He who conquers shall not be hurt by the second death. . . (Rev. 2:10, 11).

> After this behold a great multitude which no man could number, from every nation, from all tribes, and peoples, and tongues, standing before the throne and before the Lamb . . . and one of the elders said . . . "These are those who have come out of the great tribulation" (Rev. 7:9).

The spread of Christianity throughout urban populations is due to no mere human appeal to dissatisfied groups of men. It is rather that believers submit themselves to God, believe His revelation, accept His Son as Savior, receive the Holy Spirit, and press forward as new creatures, earnests of the New Heaven and the New Earth in which shall be no more anything accursed, but the throne of God and of the Lamb shall be in it, and His servants shall worship Him, and the Lord God will be their light, and they shall reign for ever and ever.

8. *Provide the theological base for an egalitarian society.* Egalitarian society arises from a theological foundation and must have a theological framework to spread and endure. Men will live and die for what they know is the will of God—for what is eternal truth. Christianity provides the perfect base for the emerging masses of the world. Indeed, the only place where the common man has even dared hope for justice has been Christendom. Marxism did not arise in animist, Hindu, Buddhist, or Moslem societies, despite all their excellences. It arose in Christian society, and would hardly have been thought of except for the soaring hopes for the common man which the Christian faith has engendered, even when the Church has failed to embody them in the social structures of mankind.

The Christian faith as it spreads in all six continents has not usually *consciously* provided a theological base for that new world of the common man whose dim outlines loom through the mist. Yet everywhere, though in varying degrees, it has done so unconsciously. The Afericasian revolutions of the twentieth century have many causes. One of the more influential has been the concepts of self-government and justice which arose in Eurica. After ten million Untouchables turned Christian, and many among them became teachers, preachers, and educated men and women, the ancient myth that they were inferior souls born in permanently inferior castes was badly shaken. Untouchables themselves began to disbelieve it. A Hindu scholar said to me, "This is indeed the Kaliyug (the last and worst age of man), because we see some untouchables becoming good and learned men while many Brahmans remain ignorant and wicked men." After ten million had become Christian, and Hindu India feared lest they all might, thus changing the political weight of Hindus, Moslems, and Christians, major changes in basic Indian law concerning the masses became possible.

K. M. Panikker (1963:50) has borne eloquent testimony to this point, when he said,

> where large numbers of the same community (caste) had been converted, the difference in social conditions was sufficiently glaring to create widespread discontent among the depressed classes who had remained within the Hindu fold. . . . (This) led to the upsurge of the depressed classes . . . one of the most significant movements of the two decades preceding the establishment of independence. . . . Gandhi's flaming zeal . . . contributed greatly to the success of the movement for the uplift of the untouchables. But its original source was the preaching of the Christian missionary.

The charter of rights which the United Nations has enacted and which is invoked by nation after nation bears a close relationship to what many Churches have fought for and many congregations have embodied in their day-by-day living.

Suppose now in North America and every other land, it became the conscious goal of the Church to combine redoubled proclamation on the one hand with the provision of a theological base for an egalitarian society on the other? Such a theological base is clearly biblical. It is congruous with the mind of Christ. It has already been put into practice by those bodies of Christians which have set out to live thoroughly Christian lives, whether these were the post-Pentecost Church in Jerusalem, the monastic orders before wealth corrupted them, or the gathered Churches in the first flush of their dedication.

Such a combination would undergird the social order-to-be with an unshakable belief that justice and mercy are incarnate in God Himself, and that God's good hand is upon all those who believe in His Son, guiding and directing them to just, peaceful, and merciful solutions to the complex problems of human life in this most changeable of all ages.

The Christian base for a just social order is enormously superior to all atheistic ideologies, which of necessity advocate justice on the shaky ground that—fortunately—it is not only a good but an eternally valid invention of man, and pays off in this life.

The Christian base is desperately needed by the proletariat in a secular age. The revolution to establish the rights of man will be lost in area after area simply because those into whose hands power falls will themselves be sinful men who have no belief in a righteous and almighty God, who has shown the way in which they and other men can become inwardly righteous.

Provision of a sound theological base for an egalitarian society should aid the multiplication of Christ's churches in towns and cities. Christianity would be recognized as the religion which provides bedrock for urban civilization.

Discipling urban populations is perhaps the most urgent task confronting the Church. Bright hope gleams that now is precisely the time to learn how it may be done and to surge forward actually doing it.

17

PEOPLE MOVEMENTS

THIS AND THE next chapter on people movements apply fully to tight ethnic societies such as tribes or castes, and describe aspects of the *first movements out of non-Christian Faith.* They apply less to highly individualized societies in both the East and the West and to populations which already count themselves as "Christian."

Nevertheless, because all human beings tend to act together, and because—in a revival, for instance—when a wave of conviction sweeps a town or city, many take action which they would never have taken alone, *people movements should be studied by leaders in North America and Europe.* This revision of 1980 leaves the two people movement chapters very much as they were in the 1970 edition; but Euricans should read them carefully. Many insights concerning church growth in the West may be garnered from them.

As denominations enter new ethnic and social units to propagate the Gospel and multiply churches they will achieve their goal much more readily if they work along people movement lines. The goal should be to start some variation of the people movement to Christ. Any congregation composed of individuals who confess Christ one by one and who come from different social units inevitably becomes a conglomerate organization and tends to be slow growing. It easily becomes a sealed-off enclave.

Adequate understanding of church growth in any continent calls for thorough comprehension of people movements. These play such a large part in the expansion of Christianity that understanding of both church history and history of missionary expansion is seriously jeopardized unless one sees clearly this pattern which God has so abundantly blessed to the discipling of the nations. People movements are important both quantitatively and qualitatively and merit the closest attention.

PEOPLE MOVEMENTS DEFINED

Despite its importance, the concept "people movement" is relatively new and needs precise definition. Much objection to the thing itself arises from a misunderstanding of the term, which identifies it with undesirable methods. First, then, let us ask, What is a "people"? The word has three meanings. It may mean individuals or persons, as in the sentence, "I met several people today." It may mean the public, the masses, or the common people, as in "The People's Republic" or the phrase "the will of the people." It may also mean a tribe, a caste, or any homogeneous unit where marriage and intimate life take place only within the society. The term "people movement" uses the word exclusively in this third sense. A people is a tribe or caste, a clan or lineage, or a tightly knit segment of any society.

A tribal movement is always a people movement, that is, it is the movement of one single people or society. The term "tribal movement" is not used here, however, because a tribe is only one of many societies which can move to Christian faith. The society moving may be a caste, a clan, some extended families, or a linguistic group which would resent being called a tribe or caste. Only the word "people" describes these various kinds of societies which may move into the Church.

The Jews in the United States are a people. One could have a people movement to Christ from among the Jews. They might then become Christians while maintaining their taboo against pork and their strong desire to marry only within their own community. The first large Japanese movement to Christ (1882-87) was probably a people movement of the warriors of Japan, the Samurai. A small Brahman people movement to Christianity occurred in Orissa, India. It is not necessary for the people to be primitive, though for understandable reasons most successful people movements have been from among underprivileged masses.

It is helpful to observe what a people movement is *not*. It is not *large numbers* becoming Christians. Most people movements consist of a series of small groups coming to decision. At any one time only one group makes the decision, is instructed, and is baptized. A people movement does not involve careless accessions or hurried baptizing.

> It is a mistake to assume that People Movement Christians, merely because they have come to Christian faith in chains of families, must inevitably be nominal Christians. Such an assumption is usually based on prejudice, not fact. . . . People movements in themselves do not [produce] nominal Christians (McGavran, 1955:74).

Neither does a people movement involve neglect of quality and postbaptismal care. Such neglect will, in fact, guarantee the failure of any people movement. Nor are people movements caused by the missionary's hunger for numbers or haste to baptize, so that he can report large accessions to his supporters. Many of them start in the face of doubt on the part of the missionary that they are a good thing.

A people movement is *not* a mass movement. This unfortunate term, which should never be used, gives an entirely erroneous idea that large, undigested masses of human beings are moving into the Church. On the contrary, what really happens in people movements is that relatively small, well-instructed groups—one this month and one several months later—become Christians. Numbers are achieved to be sure; but usually only with the passage of the years.

What Is a People Movement?

Bearing these things in mind, a definition of this type of movement can now be given. "A people movement results from the joint decision of a number of individuals—whether five or five hundred—all from the same people, which enables them to become Christians without social dislocation, while remaining in full contact with their non-Christian relatives, thus enabling other groups of that people, across the years, after suitable instruction, to come to similar decisions and form Christian churches made up exclusively of members of that people." Each phrase of this description adds a needed dimension of meaning, and the complete definition helps one to understand the people-movement type of church growth.

Waskom Pickett says of people movements that they

> constitute for many the most natural way of approach to Christ. The more individualistic way preferred in Western countries is not favored by peoples trained from early childhood to group action. To object to [people] movements is to place obstacles in the path along which an overwhelming proportion of Indian Christians have come to profess faith in Christ Jesus. We see no reason to believe that any considerable proportion of [people] movement converts could have been brought to Christ along any other path. Nor do we see any reason to wish that they had been led by any other way (1933:330).

K. S. Latourette was speaking of people movements when he wrote:

More and more we must dream in terms of winning groups, not merely individuals. Too often, with our Protestant, nineteenth century individualism, we have torn men and women, one by one, out of the family, village, or clan, with the result that they have been permanently de-racinated and maladjusted. To be sure, in its last analysis, conversion must result in a new relationship between the individual and his Maker, in radiant transformed lives. Experience, however, shows that it is much better if an entire natural group—a family, village, caste, or tribe—can come rapidly over into the faith. That gives reinforcement to the individual Christian and makes easier the Christianization of the entire life of the community (Latourette, 1936:159).

The Numerical Importance of People Movements

At least two-thirds of all converts in Asia, Africa, and Oceania have come to Christian faith through people movements. In many provinces, nine-tenths of all those who first moved out of non-Christian faiths to Christianity came in people movements. Most Christians in Asia and Africa today are descendants of people-movement converts. But for people movements, the Churches on those continents would be very different and very much weaker than they are. People-movement growth has accounted for considerable ingathering in Latin America also.

It cannot be forgotten that great movements to Christ were the normal way in which the peoples of Europe, Asia Minor, and North Africa became Christian. The Reformation faith also spread across Germany, Switzerland, Scotland, England, Scandinavia, and other lands in a special variety of people movements, very different from the growth of congregations and Churches in Eurica today.

But much more than this can be said. The great growth of the future is likely to be by people movements. It is inconceivable that any other pattern will bring the nations to faith and obedience. The great ingatherings from Islam, for example, will come by people movements to Christ. This has been abundantly illustrated by the tens of thousands of Moslems who have become Christian in Indonesia between 1966 and 1980. These multitudes did not drip into the Church drop by drop; they came in by communities. Whole extended families, minor lineages, and villages moved in together. Indeed, it is defensible to affirm that the chief resistance of Islam and other religions is social, not theological. If social resistance can be overcome, the Gospel can be heard. The people movement is the God-given way by which social resistance to the Gospel can be surmounted.

The Qualitative Importance of People Movements

People movements convey a quality to the Christian Church which individual action seldom does. In considering quality, one must not compare people movements in pagan areas with the mode of increase of congregations in Eurican towns and cities. These are gatherings of persons who are already Christian in some sense. They certainly are not Moslems, Hindus, Confucians, or animists. Most have grown up in Christian homes and are part of a social web made up of the baptized. "Converts" join wealthy, adequately housed congregations and are skillfully shepherded by a host of lay persons and a highly trained, paid staff. People movements must be contrasted with the other main mode of increase from among non-Christians—i.e. with the "one-by-one against the social tide" pattern of growth so commonly seen among Churches advancing on new ground. As soon as this is done, it is clear that people movements bring in qualitatively superior churches.

Communities move in without much social dislocation, without searing wounds between members of the same family, and with their normal relationships intact. The resulting congregations have a social structure complete with leaders and family loyalties. Instead of a conglomerate of converts from many different backgrounds who must learn to get along together, people-movement congregations are comprised of one kind of people accustomed to working and living together. People-movement churches are therefore more stable, less dependent on minister and missionary, and more likely to bear up well under persecution. Conviction is buttressed by social cohesion. When all my relatives are Christian and renouncing the Christian faith means breaking with my dearest, my love of the Lord is reinforced by my love for my brethren.

Discipline, too, can be more effective and more indigenous. What leader of a gathered-colony congregation does not know the difficulty of devising discipline which expresses the church's displeasure rather than the foreigner's? The people-movement congregation knows how to keep its members in line. It will enforce whatever it really believes in.

When men come to Christian faith by group decision, community sins and weaknesses can be given up. When the new Christians rule that there must be no more liquor at "our weddings," they have no difficulty in enforcing the ban. When, in New Guinea, clans which had become Christian decided to give up feuds, they ruled that half their weapons should be burned, despite the fact that the non-Christian clans were still fully armed. All the Christians burned half their weapons—not because the missionaries said so, but because the converted villagers thought it a good thing to do.

Seen Against the One-by-One Mode

For full understanding, as noted above, the people movement should be seen against the common one-by-one mode of spreading the Gospel. The latter can be called Christianization by abstraction and is the second major way in which the Church has grown. The people movement is the first.

In the one-by-one mode, leaders *expect* only individual converts. This is how each of them was converted. This is the manner of becoming Christian each has known in his years of experience. It is the way in which the few persons they have seen won to Christian decision have come.

As the Gospel is preached, the Bible is studied in school, and men are exposed to Christian influences, now and then some individual is attracted to the Christian faith. Maybe the patience of his Christian teacher intrigues him, as in the case of young Rodrigues of the Philippines, who many years later became a bishop of the United Church of Christ. Maybe he is healed in the hospital or helped through some difficulty. Maybe the straight preaching of the Gospel touches him. He attends meetings, reads the Bible, and, fearing that his family will object, becomes a secret believer. Gathering courage he declares his faith, and against family opposition and threats accepts baptism. He is ostracized and persecuted, but remains firm and thus is added to the Lord.

Ministers, workers, and missionaries often believe that this is the New Testament way. "If a man love father or mother more than me . . ." is often quoted. Many similar passages come to mind. Churchmen conclude that "one by one against the tide" is not only the way conversion happens in this land, but is the right and biblical way for it to happen. Men must expect to suffer for their Lord.

When leaders preach the Gospel and talk with seekers they unconsciously present this one-by-one pattern. What *they* expect, inquirers come to regard as the normal pattern and correct way in which to become Christian. When inquirers become Christian, they in turn expect this pattern and unconsciously proclaim it.

The non-Christian community, too, seeing that men become Christians in the face of family disapproval and community sentiment, conclude that Christians are always rebels against the community. The later educational advance of Christians reinforces that impression. The image gets fixed in the mind of the public that to become Christian is an antisocial act. Once this conviction has seized the minds of church leaders, Christians, and public a people movement is very unlikely, even in circumstances where it might normally occur.

One of the factors which turned the great Ambedkar away from the Christian faith was this image of what it meant to become a Christian. He said,

> When I read the Gospels, the Acts of the Apostles and certain passages of St. Paul's epistles I feel that I and my people must all be Christians, for in them I find a perfect antidote to the poison Hinduism has injected into our souls and a dynamic strong enough to lift us out of our present degraded position; but when I look at the Church produced by Christian Missions in the districts around Bombay I have quite a different feeling. Many members of my own caste have become Christians and most of them do not commend Christianity to the rest of us. Some have gone to boarding schools and have enjoyed high privilege. We think of them as finished products of your missionary effort, and what sort of people are they? Selfish and self-centered. They do not care a snap of their finger what becomes of their former caste associates so long as they and their families, or they and the little group who have become Christians get ahead. Indeed, their chief concern with reference to their old caste associates is to hide the fact that they were ever in the same community. I don't want to add to the number of such Christians.

To his quotation of Ambedkar, Pickett adds,

> This is a terrible indictment. We would like to believe that it is not deserved. But there is in it a considerable measure of truth. Christian missionaries from the West are the product of a social order in which rugged individualism is highly esteemed. . . . They tend to assume that the relation of the individual to the community with which they have been familiar since childhood is the Christian norm and to commend it to the converts with whom they may be associated. . . . So a boy of Dr. Ambedkar's caste may be consciously taught in school and Church to follow the Christ who said, "If any man come after me, let him deny himself and take his cross and follow me" . . . and yet what the boy really learns may be to stand on his rights as an individual, disown all obligations to the group in which he was born, and pursue a strictly selfish programme of personal enrichment (Pickett, 1938:29f.).

It is against the background of this configuration, this image, and this popular idea of what it means to become a Christian that the people-movement mode of Christianization should be seen.

MULTI-INDIVIDUAL, MUTUALLY INTERDEPENDENT CONVERSION

Some churchmen turn from people movements on theological grounds. They feel that the very idea of group conversion is contrary to the individual faith which leads to salvation. Men followed the Lord Jesus one by one. He called them out singly from among the multitude. Mere going along with the crowd, these churchmen argue, is not conversion and can never save anyone. This real stumbling block must be squarely faced.

The kind of conversion on which people movements are based is the root of the difficulty. The crucial question is: Do people movements rest on "group conversion"? The answer is No. There is no such thing as group conversion. A group has no body and no mind. It cannot *decide* anything whatever. The phrase "group conversion" is simply an easy, inexact description of what really happens.

What really happens is *multi-individual, mutually interdependent* conversion, which is a very different thing. These exact terms are important. One should learn to use them correctly and easily. Just as in atomic science *fusion* and *fission,* or in electrical science *direct* and *alternating current,* are terms essential to exact thought, so in missionary science the words "multi-individual" and "mutually interdependent" are necessary to understanding.

What I am affirming is that conversion does not have to be the decision of a solitary individual taken in the face of family disapproval. On the contrary, it is better conversion when it is the decision of many individuals taken in mutual affection. *Multi-individual* means that many people *participate* in the act. Each individual makes up his mind. He hears about Jesus Christ. He debates with himself and others whether it is a good thing to become a Christian. He believes or does not believe. If he believes, he joins those who are becoming Christian. If he does not believe, he joins those who are not becoming Christian. When in a minor matter, none participate except those who have decided that they will help, how much more will only those abandon their old gods and become Christian who have individually and personally decided that they will do so?

Mutually interdependent means that all those taking the decision are intimately known to each other and *take the step in view of what the other is going to do.* This is not only natural; it is moral. Indeed, it is immoral, as a rule, to decide what one is going to do regardless of what others do. Churchmen ought frequently to say to inquirers, "Since Jesus Christ is the Savior, the pearl of great price which you have found, and since you are a loyal member of your family, you do not want to enjoy salvation secretly all by yourself. The first thing you want to do is to share your new-found treasure with your loved ones. The person who loves the Lord most will try most to bring his intimates to Him. Andrew went and found his brother Simon. You do the same."

In a people movement—whether in Berlin or Bombay—members of the close-knit group seek to persuade their loved ones of the great desirability of believing on Jesus Christ and becoming Christians. Often they will defer their own decision in order to be baptized together. A husband waits six months for an unbelieving wife. A brother labors for two years so that his other three brothers and their wives will all confess Christ together—the conversion made sweeter because it is shared with the people who supremely matter to him. A wise man deciding to become Christian leads many of his fellows to promise that they will accept Christ the same day he does.

Conversion means participation in a genuine decision for Christ, a sincere turning from the old gods and evil spirits, and a determined purpose to live as Christ would have men live. The individual decisions within a people movement exhibit all these marks. It is *a series of multi-individual, mutually interdependent conversions.*

The great awakenings of the late eighteenth and nineteenth centuries brought large numbers of nominal Christians to purposeful dedication to Christ. While the converts were not of any one tribe, they were generally of one class of society. While usually they did not decide together to confess Christ and be baptized, their changed lives certainly influenced their fellows. Because of the large numbers of consciously Christian converts (whose conversion had taken place in a short time and a distinct neighborhood), action against sinful social conditions became possible and was common throughout populations touched by these awakenings. Tremendous movements against slavery, for prison reform, organization of labor unions, and spread of schools and colleges came out of these Western forms of the people movement.

Near the city of Raichur in South India, about 120 Madigas were making up their mind to follow Christ. They had considered the step for years. Many of their relatives were Christians. They believed becoming disciples of Christ was a good thing to do. During the year of decision, the question came up as to what they would do with their temple—a small dark room with an idol on a cylindrical stone. After weeks of discussion, all participated in the decision that on the day of baptism they would throw the idol into the village pond, make the cylindrical stone their pulpit, place the Bible on it, and hear what God really had to say. This was a multi-individual, mutually interdependent decision and part of their conversion. Had any of them decided to remain an idol-worshiper, the rest could not have used the temple for Christian worship; but when the group acted as a unit, the change presented no problem.

When the 8,000 Dani tribesmen in West New Guinea declared for Christ in a multi-individual fashion, they resolved to burn their fetishes on a certain day. This symbolic act destroyed their former fears and allegiances and opened the way for them to learn biblical truth. When, in one of the Indonesian islands recently, twenty Moslem communities decided to accept Christ and turn their mosques into churches, the very grave decision entailed participation by each person concerned. Each was saved, not by going along with the crowd, but *by his participation in the decision.* Multi-individual conversion is not a light matter. It, too, can result in persecution or death. Feared fetishes or remaining Moslems might take a terrible revenge. Participating in such a decision requires genuine personal faith.

What is inexactly known as "group conversion" resembles a prolonged vote-taking in which all participate. For months and maybe years, each member of the group is expressing himself again and again on the issue: Shall we believe in Jesus Christ? As votes pile up in favor, group action becomes more and more possible.

There is usually room for "stay-outers." Most groups are fissured internally. They are full of subgroups. If a person has no faith, he simply stays out in company with those who do not wish to become disciples of Christ. This helps guarantee that the decision is meaningful for those who come in.

Multi-individual decisions achieve great power. They enable individuals to do together what they could never do alone. Grains of gunpowder burning one by one have no power, but when they all burn together in a confined space they can blast granite rock to pieces. Similarly, while one woman all by herself finds it difficult to leave father and mother, it is no uncommon sight to see ten women together accept baptism which cuts them off from their twenty parents. The women are parts of multi-individual conversion. Their husbands and children are becoming Christians. They believe that some day their parents, too, will follow. In joint action ten women are granted power to do the impossible.

EDUCATION AND ENLIGHTENMENT IN A PEOPLE MOVEMENT

People movements depend on extensive prior education. Now and again one occurs in which there is little antecedent knowledge of the Gospel. One thinks at once of the Harris movement in Ivory Coast and Apolonia. Yet the fact of the matter is that plenty of prior education existed in Ivory Coast and Apolonia. Without prior education it is truly impossible for society to move.

People movements require years—in some case decades—of enlightenment and gospel impact before they begin. In 1950 a great Methodist missionary, Andrew Mellor of southwest Nigeria, decided that in the last few years of his career he would attempt the conversion of the Egons, a very resistant tribe whose headquarters were at Badagri—a coastal town, and during the eighteenth and early nineteenth century a noted slaveport. By 1954 this headquarters of fanatical resistance had yielded to the Gospel and about two thousand had become Christian. Andrew Mellor set off the decision, but the hundred and ten years of Christian work, the great turnings of the Yorubas to the north, the educated Christian Nigerians who had come to Badagri as government servants, and many other factors had been educating the Egons.

Much popular education is constantly going on. This is why today is full of promise for the spread of the Church. Never in the history of the world have so many non-Christians observed Christian worship and been so powerfully attracted by it. Never has there been as much comment on the new religion as there is today. True, some comment is unfavorable or even hostile; but much of it—how could it be otherwise?—agrees that the Christian religion is good, Jesus Christ is the Savior, and "we are all going to be Christians someday."

Many popular images are abroad of what it means to be a Christian. Some contain elements which do not bulk large to the Christian leader. Some elements which he thinks vital are not there at all. But the images *are* of what it means to be a Christian and in many populations they are favorable. Christians are educated people, worship God more, do not get drunk, do not fear the evil spirits, and do not work on Sunday. They are more dependable and face death with peace of mind. They treat their women better and know God's commands more. In a wayside restaurant near Campinas, Brazil, I asked the waiter what he thought of *crentes* (believers).

"Ah," he replied, "they are good people. My sister is one. They worship God all the time and save their money. I am going to become a *crente* myself one day."

From those hostile to Christianity different views are heard. Christians are traitors to their people, paid to defect, meat-eaters, and no better than we are. If one is an orphan, it is a good thing perhaps to become a Christian, but not for people who are respected in their communities.

Endless debate rages in many populations between those who think it would be well to become Christian and those who do not. The startling conversion of Moslems in Indonesia, just mentioned, was preceded by just that kind of debate, certainly for months, possibly for years. Non-Christians receive much teaching and hear much preaching. Some read the Gospels and tracts. Returned travelers tell of countries where Christians are numerous and being Christian has been good for them. All this is *preparatio evangelica*—education for conversion.

Verbalized theological education, of course, is largely absent. In a population trembling on the edge of a people movement, thousands may believe firmly that Christianity is a good religion, without being able to tell a single fact about the life or death of Jesus Christ. We should not scorn this condition. Acts 9 records that after Aeneas, bedridden for eight years, had been cured by Peter, all they that "dwelt at Lydda and Sharon . . . turned to the Lord." While a few Christians lived there before Peter's visit, it would be too much to suppose that all the residents of those two villages had exact theological knowledge of the Lord Jesus. Yet they certainly had much popular education of the kind I have been describing. They turned to the Lord in a multi-individual, mutually interdependent conversion.

Immediately following such conversion, much verbalized theological education should be provided in prebaptismal and post-baptismal courses. The original decision is made more meaningful by conscious instruction in the Bible. This is already common practice among all Churches and missions. Hundreds of thousands of converts who come to Christ each year by group decisions are enrolled as catechumens (inquirers, seekers, probationers), and are instructed, baptized, and instructed still further.

The kind of verbalization correctly expected of catechumens and baptized believers after instruction must not be expected before multi-individual decisions are made. At that early stage, convictions strong enough to risk death for are common, but nicely phrased theological and biblical reasons for the action are rare. Are we then to despise the little-educated forms of courage and devotion that constitute their starting point?

GOOD DEEDS AND PEOPLE MOVEMENTS

As churches multiply across the face of a land, the Christian finds many occasions to do helpful things. Unpremeditated overflow of kindness, just because the messenger is a Christian, is unavoidable. Like his Master, he does good. With the Holy Spirit in his heart, how can he avoid it? At the beginning of the people movement, when numbers are small, nothing but praise to God redounds from this person-to-person service.

When the movement continues, however, and thousands have become

Christians in far-flung villages or towns, for a Church or mission to do good deeds to all about it in any practical way very soon becomes prohibitively expensive and unnecessary. If well-integrated groups become Christian, the resulting community includes men of substance and responsibility who are accustomed to looking after their own poor. In hard times, the poor are accustomed either to working or to pulling in their belts a few notches and weathering the storm. As soon as relief begins to be handed out, however, a new situation arises in which it is extraordinarily difficult for an outside organization to distribute money, clothing, or food justly. Help given to a few individuals face to face is one thing; given to a whole countryside in the process of becoming Christian, it is something entirely different.

During the 1930-36 Christward surge into the Baptist Church in West Utkul, Orissa, two years of scarcity occurred. When famine relief was given, some villages whose residents felt they ought to get it, did not. Others did not get as much as they felt they deserved.

"Why did we old Christians not get any when the new Christians got so much?" "Why did we new Christians get none while the old Christians got plenty?" were some of the questions asked. The Gospel was negated and the movement to Christian faith stopped (McGavran 1956:17).

Many promising beginnings of people movements are stopped. Small, arrested people movements form a typical part of the picture in most Africasian countries. Often arrest is due to ill-timed or ill-advised good deeds. The process operates in somewhat the following fashion. Christians and missionaries too think of their work in terms of good deeds. We are here to serve these poor people, they say. Christian nationals soon come to think they have a right to receive education, medicine, money, and goods. Non-Christians begin to think that becoming a Christian means getting something done for you. As numbers grow or Eurican funds decrease, benefits decline. Then Christians and non-Christians alike think they have been tricked and deceived.

This difficulty does not at all indicate that Christ's ambassador with a beginning Church of 200 should shut up his heart and dry up his compassion. Indeed, he should continue his help, but he should deliberately shift over to a pattern possible for a Church of 2,000, and from that to a pattern possible for a Church of 10,000. Rev. P. W. Major wrote me in 1963, saying,

> We have some two hundred converts scattered out in thirty villages. To teach them to read and write, encourage them to educate their children, help them in their sicknesses, and get them to conferences and lay training institutes,

takes men and money. Yet I do not want these Christians to get the habit of expecting aid. Is there some magic way they can be properly shepherded without doing these things?

This is precisely the problem churchmen shepherding beginning people movements face. How can Christ's ambassador help his fellow Christians without spoiling them?

I answered Mr. Major as follows.

> There is no magic way. Press on helping your brothers in Christ. But, together with literacy, education of children, and medical aid, teach them the Bible, teach them to give, involve them in much liturgical worship, and lead them out into witness which intends to persuade others to accept the Savior. Physical aid should be balanced with spiritual aid. Benefits paid for from abroad should be exceeded by benefits paid for from India. It is very easy to let physical aid from abroad become the chief kind of aid. Do not cut back such aid however, but rather quadruple spiritual aid. Give them abundant opportunity to learn the Bible and teach what they have learned to their intimates and kinsmen. As your churches multiply, lay more and more emphasis on the indefinitely reproducible spiritual benefits of the Christian life and less and less on those which require mission subsidy.

Personal good works soon escalate into organized institutional philanthropy at central stations—schools, hospitals, nurses and teachers, training institutions, and the like. These are useful adjuncts to any Church. Many more people are served. Much greater good is done. Many nationals are employed in the ventures—and, also, many detrimental marginal learnings begin to appear. The large staff employed regard institutionalized philanthropy as their means of livelihood—which it is; and their continued support as the reason for the institutions—which it is not. "The Church" appears to be the institutional complex at the big central station rather than the multitude of congregations in the towns of the land. The focus is taken away from discipling the peoples and fixed on "maintaining institutions of excellent quality."

As churchmen managing a movement so that the whole people is brought to faith and obedience try to balance institutionalized good works and maximum growth of the churches, what principles should guide them? I suggest three.

1. Those institutionalized good deeds are more valuable to the Christian movement which can be reproduced out as far as the fringes of the receptive people. For example, in the Tiv tribe in Nigeria, the CRI's (classes in religious instruction) in 1966 were very simple village schools, run by Christians of little education who could not demand anything like the salary qualified teachers in government-recognized and aided primary

schools could expect. The CRI's could be reproduced out as far as the Tiv villages ran. Primary schools with their required buildings and scale of pay for teachers could not be. For the expansion of the Church, the CRI's had much more immediate value than the central primary schools. This does not in any way diminish the value of primary and secondary schools in the training of an adequate ministry, but it does warn against a disproportionate evaluation of them in the early stages of such an immense task as discipling the million tribesmen who comprise the Tiv.

2. The institutions should serve the Church adequately. Institutionalized philanthropy, serving chiefly the state, commercial interests, or resistant segments of the non-Christian public, is a luxury Christian mission cannot afford. It diverts Christians from reconciling men to God. It is a civilizing, not a Christianizing, activity. It is education of resistant oppressors rather than the Church growing among the receptive oppressed. Granted that one should not interpret the grace of "loving the brethren" too narrowly, nevertheless the scriptural injunction is to do good to all men, *especially those of the household of faith.*

3. Institutionalized good works should be oriented to the local situation. Are they such that the churches can eventually take them over? Do they meet a felt local need? Will nationals start them if they are not already in operation? Do they meet current need, or has government in fact moved into this field and—so to speak—released the Church to attend to other, more pressing matters?

People-movement Churches should be particularly alert to these questions, for if the main thrust of the Church-cum-mission is in organized good deeds at central stations, care of far-flung churches and their extension to still further areas adjoining them is inevitably neglected. The chief purpose of organized philanthropy should be to help the Church disciple receptive peoples—not simply to help the existing Church build up showcases at centers of population.

ARE PEOPLE MOVEMENTS SOUNDLY CHRISTIAN?

The student of church growth (heir to generations of evangelistic efforts which have usually operated with little understanding of people movements, no intention to claim whole populations for Christ, and no idea of how to do so) raises the question as to whether people movements are Christian. Are we not promulgating something which is not biblical? Is there not grave danger that the high standards our denomination has set as it separated itself from nominal Christians will be betrayed in people movements?

These are fair questions. In answer, one should turn directly to the Bible and observe its authority for discipling tribes. At the outset, the whole Old Testament is the story of God's dealing with peoples. God called the Hebrew *people*, the children of Israel, the twelve tribes, out of Egypt. Again and again He disciplined them *as peoples*. Again and again they made group decisions, repented of their sins, and covenanted with God to walk in His ways.

Coming to the New Testament, we note that Matthew 28:19 instructs Christians to *disciple the tribes*. In Hindi, the national language of India, the words read *jatiyon ko chela karo,* i.e. "disciple the castes"—a much more accurate rendering of the Greek than the common English version "make disciples of the nations." What our Lord said was precisely "disciple the tribes," the castes and families of mankind. Just as the Jewish tribes were the people of God, so the multitudinous peoples of the Gentiles should become God's household.

The first ten chapters of Acts make numerous mention of multitudes becoming Christian. In the New Testament we repeatedly come upon the conversion of households—*eikoi* in Greek. The *eicos* pattern, once seen, is a noteworthy feature of New Testament church growth. Christians of the Baptist persuasion have been slow to recognize this, lest it endanger their position that *believers only* should be immersed. Yet the *eicos* pattern really has nothing to do with who is baptized. Family by family, men became Christian—this is what is affirmed. At what stage they are baptized is another question. The truer we are to the New Testament, the more we shall welcome *eicos* and other multi-individual conversions. Both East and West, winning families is a good goal.

The Mighty People Movement in the New Testament

Most Euricans, reading their New Testaments through the eyes of highly individualized congregations and interpreters, see a pattern of conversion and Christian decision which closely resembles their own in Chicago or Toronto or Berlin. Yet it is most unlikely that the growth of the Church in the highly specialized populations of the Roman Empire would resemble church growth in Eurica today. For one thing, those converted were mostly illiterate, while today most Euricans are high-school graduates. Those then coming to Christian faith previously knew nothing about Christ; most of those who join churches in the West are children of existing Christians. During the writing of the entire New Testament, it is doubtful whether any congregations built meeting houses. In Eurica, ecclesiastical buildings—called churches—are invariably found. In that early period, women had very few rights and fathers decided matters for their families; today in the West women have equal rights, and children do as they wish. Then, each ethnic unit thought of itself as a special race and had its own language or dialect. Timothy, no doubt, spoke the local Galatian dialect more fluently than he did Koine Greek. It is doubtful that he spoke Aramaic at all. Today everyone in Germany speaks German; in England, English; and in the United States (so the English say), American.

In my earlier volume, *The Bridges of God,* Chapter III illustrated the people movement from the New Testament. I wrote that chapter not to prove from the Bible that people movements are right, but simply because the New Testament affords a good example of a people movement. The document is open to all and can be studied at leisure. When once the tight caste structure of the Jewish community of our Lord's day has been realized, it is impossible to miss the people-movement nature of New Testament church growth. The journeys of St. Paul also, far from being like those of the modern missionary, are typical of the way in which a movement expanding in a single urban caste or rural tribe follows the line of relations and the natural connections of one family with another.

The fact that the New Testament describes a people movement, however, has weight when we are considering whether people movements are right or not. If it was right for the synagogue community at Beroea, for example, to decide for Christ and form itself into a congregation in a very few days, surely community action is one acceptable way into the Church. The account of this rapid decision of a considerable number of families to become Christians (Acts 17:10-14), condensed though it is, looks amazingly like a multi-individual, mutually interdependent conversion. Not only did they accept that the Messiah was Jesus but also that Greeks could become Christians without being circumcised. They resolved to form themselves into a congregation despite the hardcore Jews who came down upon them from Thessalonica. And all this took place in the few days necessary for word to get from Beroea to Thessalonica and for the Jews there to send down their emissaries.

In *The Bridges of God* I have argued the case at length—there is no need to go into it again. Here it is sufficient to call attention to the fact that if the Holy Spirit guided the Early Church to grow in people-movement fashion, there cannot be any inherent wrong in it. Here my plea is simply that a kind of church growth which occurs in people-conscious societies is right and biblical. The Holy Spirit used it in the Early Church. He can and does use it today.

STARVED AND WELL-FED PEOPLE MOVEMENTS

Most objections to people movements come from those who have seen them starved and neglected. Mishandling of these God-given movements is easy—particularly when one comes from the highly individualized countries of Eurica—and results in a caricature of the Christian Church.

God sometimes gives the precious beginnings of a people movement to His servants working ahead in the exploratory phase of missions. If they continue patterns of action suitable to that phase—i.e. if they continue doing what they were doing before the fire of faith started running through a prepared homogeneous unit—then it is likely that the new churches will be confirmed, not in the faith, but in ignorance and nominalism. This is not the fault of the way in which non-Christians turned to Christ, but a failure of shepherding. People movements to Christ require special care. The more socially and intellectually removed the Eurican missionary is from the Afericasian people he serves (or the more removed the educated national is from the masses flooding into the churches), the more danger there is of his mishandling God's gift.

All this merely underlines the important and cheering fact that a *well-shepherded people movement has a soundly Christian character*. Let us observe four characteristics of a well-nurtured movement to Christian faith.

First, at the beginning converts corporately renounce loyalty to "other gods": their worship, their houses, their priests, and their rituals. Renunciation usually takes the form of destroying the religious objects or symbols. Fetishes are burned. Idols are thrown into the pond. Sacred turtles are killed and eaten. Amulets and charms are taken off and thrown away. Thus their hold on the believer is broken and he becomes free to follow his conscience.

George Vicedom in his important little book *Church and People in New Guinea* describes vividly a formal service of renunciation. The following few lines do not do justice to him, but do convey the depth of the corporate turning.

> The various clans were represented by their chiefs. . . . Each had small pieces of wood in his hand and said, "The name of this piece of wood is war. We used to fight . . . and kill each other. Since the Word of God has come, peace has arrived. . . . Now what is your choice? Shall we go back to fighting

. . . or live in peace?'' The people answered, "We choose peace." The chief continued, "See now, as I throw away this piece of wood, we all throw away war." The people responded, "We will not kill any more."

In the same way, sorcery, infanticide, theft, adultery, the worship of ancestors and so on were one by one renounced and thrown away forever (Vicedom, 1962:19).

Second, converts corporately accept Christ as Lord and Savior, enroll among His people, and identify themselves with His Church. Often they eat openly with Christians. In well-cared-for movements, new Christians build a meeting house and covenant to assemble there, hear and learn the Bible, send their children for regular instruction, commit hymns and Scripture passages to memory, and give to the Church.

Third, leaders from among the new converts are trained so that, at the earliest possible moment, the new congregations assemble under their own deacons, elders, and teachers. J. T. Seamands credits the recent healthy expansion of the Methodist Church in South India (From 95,000 to 190,000 in twenty years) to a thorough system of training lay leaders. A. C. Krass in his remarkable description of the beginning of a people movement among the Chokosi in northeast Ghana says,

> Concurrently with this work [teaching the whole village], we began a leadership training program in Bible and literacy for young men from the villages in which we were working. This has provided leaders in weekly worship for the new churches, some able men who served in the evangelization of other villages, and has educated one segment of the church membership in depth. Two trainees have now become assistant evangelists, six others have become literacy instructors, and one has gone out to serve as a missionary among Chokosis and Konkombas in an area a hundred miles away . . . a most important aspect of our work has been immediate training of indigenous leaders out of the people being converted (*Church Growth Bulletin*, September, 1967).

Fourth, the regular worship of God, not only on Sunday but during the week as often as possible, is instituted. In India those people movements where the worship of God was a *daily* occurrence showed much more growth in grace than those where Christians assembled only on Sunday. Congregations which worshiped morning and evening showed more Christian achievement than those who worshiped only in the evenings. Since liturgical worship requires repeated use of Scripture passages, it is specially suited for illiterate congregations. As part of catechetical instruction, all Christians commit the passages to memory. Repeated use inscribes these on the tablets of their hearts. Christian virtues begin to form part of their character. Regular giving also can be taught. It is part of this fourth step.

Since the movement brings eager congregations into existence, these four steps become immediately practical. During the first months after conversion, Christians are highly teachable. They eagerly learn the Christian way. Of course, if neglected for the first few years, they become accustomed to a mere nominal Christianity. It is then more difficult to ingrain these highly desirable habits of attending, learning, worshiping, and giving.

THE FIRST DEDICATION AND MORAL REFORM

Liquor, race pride, and exclusiveness; smoking, dancing, polygamy, and gambling may be renounced at the very beginning of the Christian life; or they may not. In any case these actions should be regarded as the fruit of the Spirit. They are not legalistic requirements which must be met *before* men can become Christians. The Gospel is the good news of God's free grace. It is not a legal and moral barrier which must be surmounted before one dare present himself before the Savior. It is noteworthy that New Testament Christians did not renounce plural wives, liquor, or race pride before becoming disciples of Christ.

One of the mistakes churchmen make who desire moral purity in Christians is to demand that seekers out of paganism, before they receive the Holy Spirit or are baptized, demonstrate conduct which millions of good Christians in Eurica do not demonstrate after twenty generations in the Church. It is no mistake to desire moral purity. There can scarcely be too much of it. And the Holy Spirit *will bring purity* when He indwells God's people. The mistake is in demanding fruits the Spirit has given in old Christian communities as prerequisites to becoming disciples.

However, it should immediately be added that as a Christward movement advances among a receptive people, each new group is more than ready for new standards of conduct. If the new congregations wish, or can be persuaded, to ban liquor, make an advance in brotherhood, give up gambling, outlaw tobacco, or burn weapons while the movement goes victoriously forward, it would be sinful and foolish not to require these good actions. It would be equally sinful and foolish, however, to refuse baptism to groups who are prepared to carry out all four steps mentioned above, but want to continue eating pork and smoking tobacco. The general rule should be to load on all the moral reforms possible but, remembering that these are not essential to beginning life with Christ, never to stop a sound movement with legalistic demands. The Holy Spirit—as Roland Allen has said—must be trusted more than most of us have been willing to trust Him.

18

KINDS OF PEOPLE MOVEMENTS
AND THEIR CARE

A COMMON ERROR in understanding people movements is to assume that they are all of one variety and occur only among primitive
tribes. The people movement is understood as the way in which the pariahs
of South India, the Wallamos of Ethiopia, or the Tseltals of Mexico turned
to Christ. Once this stereotype has seized the imagination, it is easily
argued that the movement described in the New Testament was not a people
movement and that, since the number of primitive tribes is limited, the
people movement is of little importance as Christians face winnable peoples
in all six continents.

If we are to understand people movements, however, we must see that
there are many varieties, each fitted to and conditioned by the particular
society in which a given Church is growing. We have already seen that
men like to become Christians without crossing tribal, racial, class, or
linguistic barriers—i.e. human beings like to become Christian with their
own kind of folk. In receptive populations, people movements result when
adequate account is taken of this principle and provision is made for multi-
individual accessions. Men and women of any society, advanced or primitive, urban or rural, literate or illiterate, can come to Christian decision by
the people-movement route, though the pattern of movement in each society
will differ from that in any other.

A strong, proud people's movement will be unlike that of a weak,

354

submissive people. A people in contact with the modern world in a thousand places will not turn to Christian faith in the same way as the tribes of high New Guinea. It would be quite conceivable for the Jews of America—surely a most advanced and cultured race—to decide that they would become Christians while maintaining their identity as Israelites. (No people has—so it would say—to mongrelize itself in order to become Christian. Cross-racial marriage is not one of the marks of a Christian!) But in order to do so, Jews would have to adopt the Christian religion in a people movement. Such a movement would be very different from that of the Malas and Madigas of Andhra Pradesh, but it would nevertheless be a people movement to Christ.

At this point it is interesting to observe that most opposition to the Christian religion arises not from theological but from sociological causes. Men hate to separate themselves from their own people and join another. This rouses their emotions. They then look around for reasons to back up their feelings of fear and disgust and announce that they reject Christianity because of some theological weakness in it. For example, Moslems say it is blasphemous to affirm that God has a Son; but for tens of thousands of Indonesian Moslems this theological objection vanished like the morning mist as soon as they found they could become Trinitarian Christians without abandoning their people. One should not affirm that theological objections are mere rationalizations, but it can scarcely be doubted that they have been greatly overrated. If Jews could come to Christ without losing their identity as Jews, most of their theological difficulties would—to say the least—be greatly reduced.

The degree of dissatisfaction, disintegration, oppression, and tension in any society also affects the kind of movement possible to it. A society in the last stages of disintegration, for example, could not move as the Icelanders did whose trek to Christ is recounted in the first chapter of this book. Members of an oppressed people, such as the Chamars of India, are powerfully impelled toward Christianity, but extreme economic and social dependence on the higher castes handicaps their ability to act. Chamar movements of North India have manifested a different pattern from those of independent animistic tribes of Assam. A people which forms but 5 per cent of the total population cannot move in the same way as one which forms 95 per cent. When a receptive caste lives in large settlements (40 to 100 houses per village), its members move to Christian faith more easily and can be formed into better churches than when the caste lives in small settlements. The people are less afraid of their overlords and, once Christian, form larger congregations which can be instructed more easily and support an indigenous ministry better than small scattered churchlets of three or four families to a village.

In North America the many strata of society are satisfied or dissatisfied with themselves in different degrees. Each has a different degree of winnability. First generation immigrants as a rule are much more winnable than third or fourth generation. Each segment of society (including the many segments of the old white population) poses its own problems and offers its own opportunities to multi-individual conversion. Web movements in different homogeneous units are quite dissimilar.

In understanding people movements, it is helpful to arrange segments of society along an axis of distribution such as the following. All peoples in the world can be located on this line, each at the point where its characteristics place it. At the left end of the axis would be grouped tight, closed societies, powerful and satisfied peoples, and well-disciplined tribes with high people-consciousness. The more political and military power a people has, the closer to the left end of the line it would be placed.

1	2	3	4	5	6	7	8	9	10

Tight, closed, powerful, satisfied, well-disciplined, proud peoples

Loose, open, weak, dissatisfied, ill-disciplined, humble peoples

At the right end of the axis would be grouped loose, open, dissatisfied, ill-disciplined populations. Humble and submissive tribes and disintegrating peoples would be placed at the far right. All other peoples would be placed in between, at 3, 7, or some other number.

A different kind of people movement will occur at each of the ten major locations. Puerto Ricans flooding into Chicago, Buffalo, and other cities would be located in the middle of the axis. The tribes of New Guinea described by James Sunda would be located at the far left. They were well integrated, had military and political power, formed tight, cohesive social units, and always acted as units in marriages, funerals, work, and war. Since the Dutch had no police in the highlands, each tribe and each clan possessed the power of life and death. No wonder Sunda says, "In these tightly knit clans, either all burn their charms and declare for Christ, or no one does."

The significant turnings to Christian faith yet to occur among the great populations of Asia, Africa, and Latin America will come by people movements. It is inconceivable that any extension of the "one-by-one against the social tide" pattern could be great enough to bring to the castes of India and the city masses of China and Japan the blessings of reconciliation with God in Christ. In years to come, whole families and groups of families, without social dislocation, without deracination, within their culture, and carrying on their accustomed means of livelihood, are going to become Christian. They will be well instructed and will commend the Christian faith to others. That is, they will come to faith and obedience by the people-movement route. This is what people movements are. Future movements of great peoples, however, will be different from those among the Uraons and Mundas near Calcutta or the Masai movements starting in Kenya in 1980.

One of the great advances in evangelism urgently awaited is the working out of patterns by which it is possible for advanced peoples—West as well as East—to become disciples of Christ. Canjanam Gamaliel, a third-generation Lutheran minister in Kerala, maintains that in India caste should be recognized as one of "God's orders of preservation." He insists that breaking this social structure, this order of preservation, is no necessary part of becoming Christian and proposes that Churches and missions boldly plant churches in all castes, which for some time would remain one-caste denominations or sections of the Church Universal (Gamaliel, 1967).

His proposal is in line with missionary practice in India between 1705 and 1820, but contrary to practice from that time to the present. The proposal would make possible caste-wise movements to Christ in the great Indian social structures. He is confident that becoming Christian and accepting the Bible as the only Scripture will destroy the religious sanctions which reinforce Hindu caste; and that with religious sanctions gone, the sense of separateness and class distinction will gradually disappear while conserving the riches of Indian culture. The growing unity of mankind, the fellowship of the world Church, and the indwelling Holy Spirit who is given to all Christians who seek Him will hasten its disappearance. Canjanam Gamaliel's proposal, if put into practice, would give rise to new and interesting forms of people movements. Whether existing Churches and missions follow his proposal or not, it is very likely that truly indigenous Churches of this pattern will arise of themselves in Indian castes, as the Independent African Churches have arisen in Africa.

Some Types of Movement

Classification of people movements has not yet been attempted, but soon should be. The scores, and possibly hundreds, of varieties of movements would then be clearly seen. Merely naming the different kinds of movements would help churchmen to understand their task and reveal both its complexity and its promise. Classification should help discipling in a major way. A few years ago I distinguished four kinds of people movements, based on the kind of Church that resulted. I name these four here merely to indicate that adequate classification has yet to be made.

Lyddic movements: the entire community becomes Christian. (All they that dwelt at Lydda turned to the Lord.) The United Presbyterians in the Punjab experienced a Lyddic movement among the Chuhras. Within half a century hundreds of Chuhra communities became Christian. Sunda calls this kind of movement the "clean sweep," and under that heading describes a Uhunduni movement thus, "One thousand four hundred Uhundunis live in the Ilaga and three thousand one hundred live in the Beoga Valley. Nearly all adults in both valleys have been baptized" (Sunda, 1963:18).

Lystran movements: a part of the people become Christian and the balance become hostile to the Christian religion. (Some of the synagogue community at Lystra turned to the Lord, while the rest drove Barnabas and Paul out of town.) The people movement, by virtue of resistance, opposition, or mishandling by the founding Christians in establishing congregations, splits the existing people. Lystran movements are much more common than Lyddic, though over the decades they can *become* Lyddic— and this should always be the end sought.

Laodicean movements: a movement slows down and stagnates. It becomes full of nominal Christians. It loses its first love and is the caricature of what a Christian Church should be. This is usually the outcome of a failure to shepherd. A starved and neglected people movement generally becomes Laodicean.

Ephesian movements: Paul found a small church at Ephesus, composed of "disciples" of Christ who knew little about Him, had not been baptized in His name, and had not received the Holy Spirit. Twelve men and their families were the beginning of a major extension of the Church.

Irregular forms of the Church are often established in advance of the arrival of traditional Churches. Autonomous Churches arise which to the traditional Churches seem to have grave deficiencies. We may confidently expect many more of these in the future. The six thousand Independent African denominations, the Congregacao Cristan and other indigenous Churches in Brazil, the Spirit of Jesus Church in Japan, and many others come to mind. All are forms of people movements—some quite orthodox and some heretical—and present Christian mission with both a challenge and a problem.

WEB MOVEMENTS

Notable web movements have occurred all across the United States and Canada as the faith spread among relatives of existing Christians. The spread was seldom confined to relatives, but the Scotch, Irish, Swedish, German, and Welsh communities were the seedbeds of certain denominations.

In Latin America among the Portuguese- and Spanish speaking populations there are no castes or tribes, but tightly knit webs of relationship and many extended families are the rule. As tribal society breaks down all around the world, its place is taken not by highly individualized men but by communities with a strong family life. A close blood and marriage web is clearly discernible long after tribe and caste have ceased to exist.

Some Eurican families value their relationships very highly; but for the most part man in Eurican society does not know his own second and third cousins. He may see his nieces and nephews and immediate in-laws now and then, but what they do is of little moment to him. In individualistic, mobile societies one's intimates are not likely to be those of his own household. The web does not count for much.

In Africasia, the web counts tremendously. Every man has, knows, and is intimate with not merely brothers, sisters, parents, and grandparents, but also with cousins, uncles, aunts, great-uncles, sisters-in-law, mothers-in-law, godfathers and godmothers, grandnieces and grandnephews, and many others. In his world, these are the people who count. He can expect a night's hospitality in any of these houses. He belongs. Relatives will shield him from the law, try to get him a job, or help him select a wife or an ox in case he should need either. News of deaths and marriages within the web passes through the family like lightning, and relatives drop all other duties to go to the funerals or weddings. Members of other clans of families can become Christian and he remains unmoved; but let "one of us" become Christian and he is deeply stirred.

"One-by-one against the tide" is a mode of conversion that pries a single person out of this social matrix and leads him to become a Christian or an Evangelical. It encourages him to renounce his people. It assumes— often with good reason—that the tribe, the family, will be hard against the Christian religion. The family gathers on the tenth day to eat the funeral feast and "feed the ancestors." Since this is forbidden to the Christian (on the ground that the ancestors are godlings and hence "feeding them" is "worship of other gods"), he is conspicuous by his absence. Frequently the very people who will not hear his testimony are "those of his own household." They regard him as a traitor and the evangelist as one who goes about snatching individuals out of families. Once this image has been firmly planted in any population, the Church grows very slowly. Rajago-palacharya, an eminent Brahman and the first Indian Governor-General of India, had the one-by-one pattern in mind when he inveighed strongly against missionary work and wrote that "efforts for proselytization . . . tend to disturb family and social harmony, which is not a good thing to do" (Levai, 1957:6).

Against this one-by-one mode we must see the web movement to Christian faith, which may be thought of as a somewhat disconnected and long-drawn-out people movement. A diagram will illustrate the point. (The web is always more complex than any diagram. To be accurate, many more lines of relationship should run between the individuals shown. Hundreds of lines should also be shown running to very numerous relatives.) Despite its oversimplification, however, the diagram will help us to see the real situation in community after community in most countries.

Even in North America and Europe many communities have webs of relatives. The population is not composed of entirely unrelated individuals. The faith often flows along family lines. Prayer focused on relations is more effective than that for the general public.

In every *rancho* in Mexico, *barrio* in the Philippines, *gaon* in India, or compound in Africa, the ambassador of Christ should see not simply Mexicans, Filipinos, Indians, or Africans, but webs of relationship—that is, organisms composed of individuals closely and permanently linked together. The evangelist should memorize the two or three dozen technical words which describe the common relationships. He can then learn the names of the yet-to-be-won relations in each group of new Christians. He will thus become aware of the extensive nature of the web and see the true dimensions of his task. He soon comes to see that faith can flow through the lines of relationship which comprise the web—or, not using these, can be effectively halted.

In Figure 18.1, the numerals indicate the order in which these individuals became Christian. The circular lines include all the individuals who acted together at one time to become Christian.

The first to become an Evangelical was Martin Perez (1). His action was shocking to everyone else in the rancho. His wife and children drew back in fear and disgust. His father-in-law, old man Fernandez, was incensed at his son-in-law's infidelity to the Virgin Mary. After some months, however, his wife Maria and his son Leon with his own young wife (2), observing what it meant to be an Evangelical, hearing the Bible, and

FIGURE 18.1. THE WEB MOVEMENT

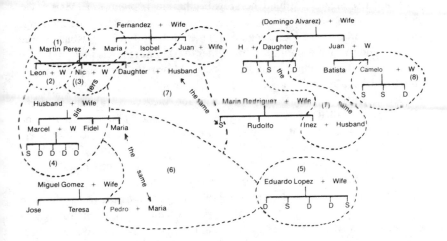

impressed by Martin's witness, decided to become Evangelicals and were instructed and baptized. The four assembled together for Bible study and prayer, walked to a nearby Evangelical churchlet for worship, and behaved like good Christians. Leon's brother Nic and his wife and Maria's younger brother Juan and his wife (3) used to attend these meetings, and within the year became believers themselves.

All this had not been going on in a corner. Everyone else in the rancho was deeply stirred. Some would curse the Evangelicals. Others would drop in to see them worship or pray. Nic's wife had a sister whose husband Marcel was a good friend of both Leon and Nic. They often worked together. Marcel said to his wife, "Why not let us become Evangelicals. My father and mother are willing and so is Fidel (4). The Evangelicals are good people. They do what the Bible says to do. I like their worship." All these decisions, however, hardened Isobel, who withdrew from association with her brothers and lived more and more with her old parents.

Eduardo Lopez and wife (5), newcomers to the rancho, had no close relatives, though both were distantly related to almost everyone there. After attending an occasional meeting for two years, they decided to accept the Lord. And very shortly afterward Maria (sister of Fidel and Marcel) persuaded her husband to become a believer (6). She liked to sing and invariably attended the worship services.

The only daughter of Martin and Maria, with her husband (7), followed suit—persuaded by the visiting pastor on the one hand and Maria and Martin on the other. At the same time Marin Rodriguez' daughter Inez and her husband joined her big brother in baptism (7). Marin was not hostile to the act. He was, in fact, a frequent attendant at the meetings of the church, but was by no means a believer. Inez and her husband cared for his widowed grandmother (daughter of Domingo Alvarez, a famed character in the rancho, long since dead). Carmelo, a cousin-in-law of Inez, had been a chief opponent of the Evangelicals and at first laughed loudly when he was told that his cousin and Inez were praying for him. But when he fell ill, and they prayed at his bedside and he got well, he bought a New Testament and read it carefully. When he found no prayers to the Virgin Mary in the New Testament and no mention of Purgatory, he concluded that the Evangelical religion was the true faith and confessed Christ with his wife and three children (8).

This highly simplified account merely suggests the part which the web of relationships plays in the spread of the Church. It is instructive to consider each of the eight accessions and to name the relatives who preceded them into the Baptist church. Thus Leon could have said, as he was being baptized, "I am joining my father in the true faith." Juan could have said, "I am joining my sister Maria and my brother-in-law and my nephew Leon." But by the time Inez was baptized, the rest of this page would scarcely suffice to name the relatives whom she was joining in baptism.

The diagram also indicates those members of the web who would most likely have the prayers of many loved ones focused on them. After the eighth group was baptized, Marin Rodriguez and Isobel would be particularly moved by the prayers of all their relatives—so might old man Fernandez and wife, particularly if his Evangelical children and grandchildren were affectionate and helpful.

No one should conclude that web ingathering is a method of evangelism which will invariably sweep in whole communities. People do not "sweep in." They become suspicious if made the special objects of a sales campaign. Instead, the evangelist should say to himself, "I must remember that whole families make stronger, better Christians than lone rebels, and congregations built of interrelated persons have more endurance and communicative ability than those built of disparate individuals. Hence I shall seek to rebuild the web inside the church. To be sure, since 'it is better to enter life lame than with two feet to be thrown into hell' (Mark 9:45), I shall accept single individuals when they cannot persuade their relatives; and single families when, after effort, their relatives refuse to come with them. I shall press on steadily, seeking lost men and women. I shall learn the web in each community so that I know who belongs to whom. I shall carry good news from one section of the web to others and constantly teach that in Christ family webs are stronger and family joys are greater than in the world." Any evangelist who says this opens himself to the leading of the Holy Spirit as He inclines natural groupings—families, minor lineages, major lineages, and clans—to accept the Savior.

A further consideration is now possible. The foregoing sequence of baptisms took place in a denomination and a country dominated by the North American individualistic pattern. It took more than four years for eight small groups to decide to become Evangelicals. Each made a decision against the total group that surrounded them—though as the number of Evangelicals increased, each decision more and more meant "joining my people who are now Evangelicals." Suppose a multi-individual pattern had been dominant. Suppose Martin's baptism had been deliberately delayed so that he could, while still entirely solid with his relatives, communicate his new-found convictions to them. Suppose he had proposed to all his relatives—both those who later gradually believed and those who later turned stiffly away—that they become biblical Christians as a whole, build a meeting house, and continue on in the new faith with relationships intact. Instead of a series of decisions *against* the group, might not the unity of the group have been preserved and enhanced? Within that unity, a prolonged vote-taking would have occurred and common sins would have been renounced. Much teaching would have been received and much Bible study done. A multi-individual, mutually interdependent decision would have been made.

Had this been the pattern of church growth in that land, the outcome might have been a larger *and better* congregation than the one that was established. It would have come into existence with a great feeling of unity. Of course, the relatives might have counterpersuaded Martin, in which case no congregation at all would have been the result. This puts one issue concretely: Is it better to seek larger units which have more strength and cohesiveness, or to seize each person as he comes, conscious that the churchlet may stop growing after a few are baptized?

When members dribble in as they did in this case, the dribbling pattern is what both Christians and non-Christians see. In consequence they imagine that men ought to become believers one by one in an extended sequence. Conversely, if multi-individual conversions take place, there is considerable likelihood that throughout that countryside these will become the accepted way in which men become disciples of Christ.

CARE OF PEOPLE MOVEMENTS

Postbaptismal Care

The quality of people-movement Churches is uniquely dependent on postbaptismal care. In these movements relatively large numbers of converts form new churches quickly. If they are neglected, or if it is assumed that the same amount and kind of care that new Christians received back in California will be sufficient for them here, a starved and nominal membership can be confidently expected. If, on the contrary, new congregations are nurtured with imagination and faithfulness, in ways which lead their members to a genuine advance in Christian living, solid congregations of sound Christians will result. Much of the failure in people movements is wrongly ascribed to the multi-individual way in which they have decided for Christ. It should be ascribed rather to the poor shepherding they have received, both before and after baptism.

Pickett's studies published in 1933 show conclusively that the motives with which men turn to Christian faith play a smaller part in developing Christian character than good postbaptismal care. Converts who came for rather secular or social motives became good Christians when they became parts of congregations which faithfully worshiped God. Converts who came for spiritual motives and became parts of poorly led and scandalously neglected congregations became weak Christians.

Postbaptismal care involves a whole complex of activities. Prominent among these are instituting regular worship and securing a place of meeting. For congregations to continue for long with no place to meet is to court disaster. House churches, rented halls, or other provision if the congregations arise in towns and cities, or buildings of light materials easily erected if they arise in the country, are an early necessity. Together with this, the systematic worship of God is essential. For literate Christians, regular study of the Bible at home and regular teaching on Sundays is valuable. For illiterates living in barrios or villages, daily worship after the evening meal is highly beneficial. At no place does the Eurican pattern damage new movements more than in the assumption that because good Christians in Edinburgh or Nashville meet only on Sunday morning at eleven, therefore it would be burdensome for new Christians in Peru or Peking to assemble each evening. On the contrary, regular evening worship for the whole new Christian community (which in any village lives within a hundred yards of the meeting place) is not only feasible, but soon comes to be a cherished experience and is influential in developing a truly Christian character.

For illiterates and semiliterates liturgical worship using memorized passages such as the Lord's Prayer, the Ten Commandments, the Twenty-third Psalm, Romans 12:9-16, the Apostles' Creed, and a few hymns is specially valuable. If a passage from the Bible is worth commiting to memory at all, it should be repeatedly used in worship. To commit a passage to memory and then not use it regularly is to waste the time spent in learning it, for it is soon forgotten. What is used a hundred times a year, on the contrary, becomes part of the spiritual equipment of the Christian. He can quote it at any time, night or day. He leans on it in hours of stress and teaches it to new converts. It becomes dear and meaningful to him. Liturgical worship, contrary to the expectation of missionaries from the Free Churches of Eurica, does not get tiresome to village Christians. They rejoice in its familiarity, comfort, and certainty.

Lay training is essential in postbaptismal care. The daily worship and memory work required of all catechumens train at the first level; but a goodly number of the community should be led on to higher things. Younger men welcome such training. Unpaid leaders are needed in every congregation. *As soon as they learn anything they should teach it to catechumens and others.* This provision of a body of essential Christian knowledge, the same for all in that denomination or cluster of congregations, helps insure that learning is meaningful and ties the new Church together. In young Churches much emphasis should be laid on teaching laymen and laywomen the way of salvation—the kind of knowledge they need to meet common objections to Christian truth and to persuade others of the value of the Christian religion.

Family and tribal ties should be strengthened in postbaptismal care. Jacob Loewen has enumerated several "satisfactions" which the Choco Indians in Panama derive from the Gospel. Among these a prominent one is that fellowship is enhanced among new Christians by strengthened family, group, lineage, and other ties. Meaningful worship and communal working bees on each other's land, plus deliberate building up and idealizing of family and tribal ties, gives new Christians a heightened sense of community which they find delightful (Loewen, 1967:20).

When possible, postbaptismal care should provide day-school education of Christian children. In some countries this means maintaining mission or church schools. If the state provides schools, it means seeing that Christian children go to school. In order to be a Bible-reading and Bible-obeying fellowship, the Church should also teach illiterate Christian adults to read the Bible and hymnbook. The duty of every Christian to teach illiterate Christians to read God's Word cannot be overemphasized. As stated in Chapter XIV it should be counted as important as observing the Lord's Supper.

Revival in a Few Years

As non-Christians are reconciled to God, their first understanding of the Christian life is unavoidably thin. They have no biblical background. They have never worshiped on Sunday. The rich biblical material which forms the mind of all residents of an old Christian community is completely absent.

Adequate postbaptismal care makes good this deficiency. Conscious learning, regular worship, instruction by sermon, crises met under guidance of older Christians, living in the presence of the righteous God and feeding systematically on His Word, all lift the community to a place where revival—an entirely new level of Christian commitment and experience—becomes possible for large numbers. Some, to be sure, have been granted a deep blessing in the early months or years of the new Church's life, but most have not. Deliberate prayer and planning for large numbers of Christians through revival to face the blackness of their sins and the availability of the Holy Spirit, is a desirable part of the care of people movements. Unless the Church is to sink into apathy, it needs continual revival everywhere. Continual rededication is the secret of spiritual life. Cold, formal churches do not grow. People-movement churches need revival as much as any others—perhaps more.

It is no accident that, in the one Methodist Conference in India which has been granted large growth since India became a republic in 1947 (from 95,000 to 190,000 in twenty years), annual "camp meetings" were a regular part of the church year. Programs were planned to keep before all who attended both the rigor of biblical demands and God's grace and power to help believers meet these demands. Whether in America or Asia, a program of secular education for youth in Christian day schools, with an hour a day given to instruction in the Bible, is no substitute for revival in the congregations; but it does prepare the way. Africasia is full of younger Churches which have their own extensive day schools. While the spiritual climate is often chilly in the Churches, through the schools an excellent foundation of biblical knowledge has been laid on which an extensive and beautiful structure of revival and renewal can be built.

The people movement which gets good postbaptismal care in at least some of the ways I have described becomes ripe for revivals and further advance in Christian living. Praying for revivals, expecting them, and providing for them should be a regular part of Church and mission programs. Churchmen should not be deterred by those current ecclesiastical fashions in Eurica which are emotionally biased against revivals and fervent prayer.

In Korea, Kenya, and other lands, inflooding of converts has been followed by revival to the great benefit of the Christian cause. In some other places, however, people movements after hopeful beginnings have been allowed to stagnate. As larger and larger numbers of slightly educated or even illiterate men become Christians, the Church and its assisting missions have a serious problem in providing, generation after generation, for deepening dedication. Maintaining the original freshness and wonder of the Christian life is easy neither for Churches which arise by the one-by-one method nor for those arising through group decisions; but keeping the Church in touch with her Head is part of the perpetual task. Keeping her blessed and renewed is completely in accord with God's will and forms the second part of the Great Commission.

STARTING PEOPLE MOVEMENTS FROM SCRATCH

Hundreds of millions of men live in communities and social structures where the Church has not yet arrived. Thousands of clans, tribes, and castes have never seen Christianity as a real option.* In a typical one of these, a congregation of Christians may have existed in some central town,

---

*Some theorists in mission will gasp at the suggestion that they should. These, pursuing the point that a deep difference exists between essential Christianity and the Eurican Churches or, as they like to say, between Christ and the empirical Church, affirm that the Christian mission never propagates Christianity. To do so is mere proselytizing. Properly Christian missions simply proclaim Christ, who then forms the Church as He pleases. There is a modicum of truth in this puristic contention, but it is readily exaggerated to the point where it becomes error. The fact of the matter is that the empirical Church is the visible Body of Christ. Christianity is the religion which Christ creates among those who believe in Him, obey Him, are baptized in His name, and form themselves into Christian cells—His Church.

Since Jesus Christ is not some vague spirit of cosmic truth who in one place affirms that God is impersonal and in another that He is personal—in one place decrees that His followers accept the Bible and in another that they accept the Rig-Veda as their rule of faith and practice—the religion He creates will everywhere have basic similarities. It will be Christianity. The truth is that to accept Christ is to accept Christianity—not Christianity arrayed in its Western garbs, but Christ embodied in His Church, His Word, and His sacraments. He is, to be sure, greater than these; but these are invariable accompaniments of His presence. So I repeat: Many populations have never known Christianity as a real option.

or a missionary who garbled the language may have talked about his Savior in the villages now and then, and yet the Christian faith has never appeared to the people of that segment as something *for them*. They have looked at Christianity as Americans look at Marxism. Millions of Americans have read extensively about Marxism. Headlines constantly tell about the social revolution and what Communists claim it will do for the oppressed; yet to become practicing Marxists never occurs to these Americans. In the same way, a Methodist congregation of Fantis existed at the port of Axim in Apolonia for many decades without the Nzima of the nearby countryside having the faintest idea that they might become Christians. Then in 1914 Prophet Harris, having baptized perhaps ninety thousand in Ivory Coast, came east into Apolonia. To the Nzima tribesmen there, who knew that their kinsmen in Ivory Coast had become Christians by the thousand while remaining in their ancestral culture, becoming Christian suddenly appeared as a real possibility. Within a few weeks, 10,000 Nzima had declared for Christ. Prophet Harris baptized them, told them to build churches, buy Bibles, and wait for the coming of Christian teachers.

As we consider the possibilities of starting people movements from nothing we must ask, Can Churches start movements in the receptive populations round about themselves? Because of the tremendously important place which Afericasian Churches occupy in mission, this is one of the key questions in modern missions. During the years 1928 to 1968, because of the attention focused on turning authority over to Afericasian Churches, it has been assumed that the answer was an unqualified Yes. It was taken for granted that if there were one Christian congregation of any kind in the midst of a non-Christian population of a hundred thousand or more, the task of the foreign mission was largely over. Nationals would evangelize their own people. The best the foreign missionary could do was meekly to assist the national Church. Of course national Churches could start people movements!

This assumption was correct in some cases. In growing people-movements Churches, where every congregation was in kin-contact with non-Christians and the top churchmen were ethnically one with the rank and file, there Churches have extended existing people movements and started new ones. There missionaries have, to advantage, simply assisted the rapidly growing Church. One may generalize by saying that in *growing* people movements, the missionary should simply assist the Church to grow more.

In great reaches of the world, however, the assumption was gravely in error. In most districts of practically all countries, the true answer to the question was No. Where local congregations were made up of un-typical people, or where redemption plus lift had changed the Christian community so greatly that it ceased to maintain living contact with its relatives, there local churches were markedly unable to spread the faith to their own countrymen. And there cessation of missionary work guaranteed that stopped little congregations remained stopped. There, for the missionary meekly to assist the Church was to squander his gifts. The more he served the introverted churches, the more introverted they became. The more he taught them to do good to all men, the more separate they became. The more he induced them to make pronouncements on national and international issues, the farther they separated themselves from their kith and kin. No amount of such missionary assistance is likely to start new people movements.

Missionaries can, however, start people movements among receptive populations, both on radically new ground and in the neighborhood of sealed-off churches. When church growth insights are shared with leaders of the introverted and arrested Churches, even they can start people movements. The work of Pastors Currens and Wold among the Loma and kindred tribes in northwest Liberia is a notable example of such well-planned action. Pastor Wold's last chapter in *God's Impatience in Liberia* devotes itself entirely to the question: How can little-growing culture-bound Churches and their assisting missions begin people movements among tribesmen? It is essential reading for evangelists, mission executives, missionaries, and church leaders.

An Illuminating Account

A. C. Krass's beautifully clear account of the small beginning of the Church among the Chokosi (Tschokosi) tribe of northeast Ghana touches so many crucial issues in starting people movements from the beginning that it is reproduced here in full. The differences between it and the methods advocated by J. C. Wold indicate that, even in rather similar populations, people movements usually follow different patterns. The similarities in the methods described indicate also the great gulf between "normal expansion of congregations by the one-by-one method of growth" and people movements. Mr. Krass (1967) says:

> In 1964, in the extreme northeast part of Ghana, the congregation at Chereponi consisted of about forty communicant and noncommunicant members. Slightly more than half of these were Southern Ghanaian Christians in government service, teaching, or trading. The remainder were young Chokosi men who had become Christians while at middle school in the town of Yendi, 56 miles away, and some of their wives and acquaintances.

Prior to my coming, Chereponi area had been part of the large pastoral district of Yendi, and the pastor stationed at Yendi, sixty miles away, usually a Southern Ghanaian, visited here once a quarter for a few days. The general work of the area was in the hands of an evangelist at Chereponi, a native Chokosi.

The evangelist regarded his work as ministering to the town congregation, recruiting additional members, and teaching the children in the local primary and middle schools. Occasionally a foray was made into the villages, but without much regularity. The purpose of such visits was that of recruiting additional members for the town congregation. The evangelist, though a Chokosi himself, did not anticipate the development of Chokosi congregations in the villages.

Chereponi District had a population of about 20,000 people, in 122 villages, and Chereponi town had 1,300 inhabitants. Socially and economically, Chereponi was far from representative of the area as a whole. The townspeople were traders, government workers, craftsmen and teachers of many Ghanaian tribes, whereas the village population was almost one hundred percent agrarian, and solidly Chokosi. The townspeople were either Christian or Muslim, whereas the local people were almost all animists. Many in the towns were literate, but illiteracy was the general rule in the villages.

As I surveyed the situation, it seemed to me that the concentration of evangelistic effort on the town and the town congregation was too one-sided and, in addition, too likely to be sterile as an approach to the village population. It did not seem likely that illiterate Chokosi villagers would feel happy in a town congregation whose members—even the Chokosi members—sang European hymns in Southern Ghanaian vernaculars, dressed in a foreign style, and worshipped in English, Ewe, or Twi. The tribesmen needed biblical instruction in their own tongue. Nor did it seem likely that the town congregations would be happy to worship in the Chokosi language or use African-type hymns.

It therefore seemed best to continue the Chereponi worship services and church work much as they were, with some minor cultural adaptation (such as the regular inclusion of a good Chokosi summary of the sermon), and *to run concurrently* a vital program of evangelism in the villages aiming at the formation of Chokosi congregations *wholly independent of the town congregations.*

At this point I may be accused of an unwillingness to take seriously the possible role of the town congregations in the evangelization of the villages. I was unwilling. I had well-founded doubts as to whether the town congregation was ready to embark on such a program. No barrier is greater in the northern tier of West Africa, and perhaps farther south as well, than that between the educated and the illiterate. The townspeople are not spiritually or emotionally equipped to make the identification across cultural barriers necessary for real evangelism. This has been the failure of the Muslims in their attempts to convert the village animists: they looked down upon them as "uncivilized" and "pagan." Whatever efforts they made were made with a sneer, with a deprecation of the native culture and its values, or with a sense of paternalistic condescension.

So we embarked on a weekday program of village evangelism. We made introductory visits to a number of villages, asking the chiefs or headmen to gather their people for a meeting early in the morning on an appointed day. Usually our services were held about 6:30, before the men had gone off to their farms. In the first meeting we would preach a sermon, sometimes in the form of a dialogue with the villagers, setting forth the whole of the Gospel from creation to the coming of the Kingdom. We would ask whether they were interested in hearing more and, if so, set a regular date once a week on which we would come and preach. Soon we had six villages, one for each day of the week. Generally, at the first meeting all the people of the village would attend, and attendance would drop off to half of the people in a few weeks.

We would always speak to the village as a whole. We never made an approach merely to individuals. We never referred to "those who might accept our teachings." We never, in fact, raised the question of acceptance or rejection. We simply said, in effect, "This is the gospel. This is how God has acted on your behalf. This is how God is speaking to the people of Famisa. This is what God wants the people of Famisa (or any other village in which we might be preaching) to do." Prior to our coming, the village had always acted as a village, and we assumed it would act as a unit with respect to our preaching.

The Evangelical Presbyterian Church has a rule that inquirers shall receive regular Christian teaching for a period of at least one year before baptism. Therefore, we did not have to raise the question of acceptance or rejection, or of baptism, the sign of such acceptance, until at least one year had passed. By that time many of the villages had sufficiently understood our teaching and we assumed they would accept it. By hearing the Word, by participating in prayer, and singing simple hymns they were already taking part in the redemptive community.

Our preaching was always positive, setting forth the drama of salvation, the work and teachings of Christ, and the revealed will of God for man. Only by presenting Christ as the all-sufficient Lord could we later make clear that animistic observances were superfluous and unnecessary for the Christian. We did not start by saying "All these observances are fruitless and blasphemous." We let them draw their own conclusions.

Well, what happened? At the end of the first year of preaching we raised the question of baptism and church membership in the three villages which we felt were most ready for it. They accepted our invitation in quite a natural fashion. Then we began catechetical instruction. At first we tried to limit catechetical teaching to two to three months, in order to avoid the impression that baptism was a graduation from Christian teaching. We taught the people that they would continue to learn Christian truth after they were baptized. All that we felt necessary in the pre-baptismal instruction was to make clear the nature of baptism as the enlistment as disciples, and to outline the basic nature of Christian practice. If the catechumens could demonstrate their understanding of the fundamentals of the faith and we could insure that they knew what the consequences of Christian faith were, then we felt we had discharged our obligations to them. Subsequently, we would regard them as full brothers and sisters in the faith, learning with us at the foot of the cross.

It turned out that many of the catechumens were not, in fact, ready to make the decisive break with animism on the basis of such short instruction. More detailed discussion was necessary, more consideration of the issues they would confront, more time to learn a catechism. We have now composed a catechism in Chokosi, which catechumens are expected to learn, and we take about six months for catechetical training.

At any rate, two whole villages and the majority of the third were baptized and took their place on the Sunday congregation-oriented program. This left three gaps in our weekday program, and we were able to begin work at first in three other villages and later, when a new evangelist had been assigned to our area, in six other villages.

Concurrently with this work, we began a leadership training program in Bible and literacy for young men from the villages in which we were working. This has provided leaders in weekly worship for the new churches, some able men who served in the evangelization of other villages, and has educated one segment of the church membership in depth. Two of the trainees have now become assistant evangelists, six others have become literacy instructors, and one has gone out to serve as a missionary among Chokosis and Konkombas in an area 100 miles away.

We now have work in thirty-five villages out of the Chokosi area, have six congregations, with 689 baptized persons, and are progressing rapidly. There will be two pastors this October, in addition to the four evangelists, and we will also be getting an agriculturalist to do village extension work, and hopefully, a nurse.

It would not be too much to expect that, in ten years or so, the entire Chokosi nation will have been discipled for Christ.

We cannot claim to be without problems, nor can we present the Chokosi Church as faultless. What we can say is that many Chokosi villagers have now come to regard themselves as Christians, and that they continue to learn day by day, through their experiences in the light of their study of the Word, what it means to be disciples of Christ.

In summary, we can say that the most important aspects of our work have been:

(1) an approach to the village as a social unit, trying to claim the village as a unit for Christ,

(2) positive preaching of the good news of God's love for man in Christ,

(3) immediate training of indigenous leaders,

(4) weekly preaching and teaching on a set day,

(5) a short catechumenate.

10

INDIGENOUS CHURCH PRINCIPLES
AND GROWING CHURCHES

INDIGENOUS CHURCH principles are very popular. Properly understood, they have great value for the propagation of the Gospel. They are
just as useful in Texas as in Tanzania and should be taken seriously by all
students of church growth. A considerable body of writings in regard to
them exists. Books by Nevius, Clark, Allen, Ritchie, and Hodges are
essential reading to all missionaries and to many pastors.

Unfortunately, these principles are sometimes loosely defined. In the
revolution in missions that marks our day, almost anything which is against
the old order and uses the word "indigenous" becomes in itself a part of
indigenous church principles! This is regrettable, since much for which
the old order is criticized is ephemeral, mere froth on the waves, and will
vanish in a few years.

Indigenous church principles are often confused with nationalization.
They should not be, for they deal with the way in which self-propagating
churches are planted, whereas nationalization has to do with turning authority over to Africasian church leaders. It is quite possible for a na-
tionalized Church to be completely static and to plant no further
congregations at all. Many Africasian Churches operating under their own
leaders are consumed with domestic difficulties. They devote all their spare
energies to church mergers and social ventures, and have no intention of
taking the Great Commission seriously. Some Africasian Churches led

completely by nationals and having a program of evangelization and mission, far from using indigenous church principles in the program, run it according to paternalistic patterns.

Indigenous church principles have theological and ecclesiological overtones. Thus today the Church, goaded by nationalism and the passion for Christian unity, is insisting that mission is not duplicating European or American denominations abroad. One hears that "indigenous church principles" have to do with the way in which Jesus Christ the Lord plants His churches. Churches of Jesus Christ are neither branches of American Churches nor dependencies of American missions. They are *His* Churches. The indigenous Church results, it is said, when Jesus Christ the Lord calls men out of the world and sends them back into the world to do His work. He is not Eurican. He is the Lord. He is not dependent on Eurican budgets or missionaries. He is the Lord. He makes His servants self-reliant, not dependent. If the new little band of Christians is a real Church (an *indigenous* Church) it will survive and flourish without depending on the founding congregation, the Mother Church, the missionary, or mission budget. It will have springs of power within itself. The Lord Himself will defend and extend it.

Since the Church in every land ought to be a Church of that land and that culture, and since our Lord uses missionaries from one land to plant the Gospel in others, the essential question is this: How can a foreign missionary multiply churches of Jesus Christ rather than pale copies of the ones that sent him out? How can missionaries multiply churches which are Spirit-filled and thoroughly of the people? In China, truly Chinese? In Bolivia, thoroughly Bolivian? Among the upper classes, genuinely upper-class, and among the masses genuinely of the masses? How can new Presbyterian churches, in mining communities in West Virginia or new Italian settlements in Toronto, remain truly mining communities or truly Italian?

The whole indigenous-church school of thought has pragmatic overtones. Missionaries and missiologists have been concerned with the same problem that animates this book: namely, that much proclamation of the Gospel does not get through to non-Christians. Groping for reasons why this should be so, and devising remedial action so that proclamation will communicate the Gospel more effectively, they have advocated indigenous church principles. They claim that indigenous principles "work" better, and mission methods which contravene them are a chief cause of non-growth. The whole subject is of absorbing interest and great importance.

INDIGENOUS CHURCH PRINCIPLES

Henry Venn of the English Church Missionary Society and Rufus Anderson of the American Board of Commissioners for Foreign Missions both advocated what would today be called indigenous church principles. Anderson wrote, "The grand object of foreign missions is to plant and multiply churches, composed of native converts, each church complete in itself, with presbyters of the same race, left to determine their ecclesiastical relations for themselves, with the aid of judicious advice from their missionary fathers" (Beaver, 1967:107). The nub of the matter is contained in this single sentence. With the "grand object" so defined, indigenous church principles which will achieve that object can readily be sought.

While our first illustrations are taken from the world of missions overseas, indigenous principles can be profitably applied to church planting in many parts of America. Existing denominations arose in particular parts of the national mosaic and soon developed their own particular lifestyle. When they now approach new pieces of the mosaic, this looks foreign to those being evangelized. Such denominations should use indigenous methods, i.e., such methods as allow their new congregations to fit the social units of which they are parts.

To John Nevius in the 1880's fell the opportunity to work out what indigenous church principles meant in practice and to publicize these through writing and speaking. He was fortunate enough to have his system adopted *in toto* by the Presbyterian Mission in Korea in 1894. When the churches of that mission multiplied exceedingly, and the system to which the multiplication was credited was explained, indigenous church principles as expounded by John Nevius became well known all around the world. His original book, first published in 1888, is so important that I recapitulate it here. Nevius says that:

The old or traditional method of mission is to hire paid agents from among the converts. To those chosen this is very welcome. They need the money. They speak the language fluently. They can go anywhere. They know the region. They live on small wages. When trained and tested, they do well as evangelists and village pastors. The method appears to be sound and advantageous to both missions and converts.

But the old method has grave defects hidden under the surface. It harms the convert who becomes an evangelist, for now he witnesses for money. Sincere though he doubtless is, he has become a paid agent. This method renders it impossible to distinguish true believers, because noting that some believers are put on salary, each inquirer—specially the more able—is tempted to become Christian in the expectation that in due time he will qualify for a job. Thus the method stirs a mercenary interest in all believers. Further, since proclaiming the Gospel, teaching inquirers, conducting worship services, distributing tracts, and selling Gospels is something done for pay by the village pastors or catechists, the method stops ordinary Christians from unpaid evangelizing and unpaid shepherding of the flock. Finally, it lowers the whole evangelistic enterprise in the eyes of the public. As tea planters send out agents (commonly called coolie-catchers) to recruit labor for the tea plantations, so missionaries send out agents to persuade men to become Christians. It is quite commonly believed that evangelists are paid at so much a head for each man they persuade to become Christian.

John Nevius then describes the indigenous church method, setting it forth under six principles. First, let each convert abide in the calling wherein he was called (I Cor. 7:20). Each continues to earn his living as he did before he became Christian and to live where he did before he was baptized. Christianity is seen as a new way of life for ordinary men.

Second, trust unpaid lay leaders—elders and teachers—to shepherd the little flock. "The characteristic feature of our churches is that the principal care of them is entrusted not to paid preachers set over them and resident among them, but to unpaid leaders belonging to the churches." These elders and teachers are to be chosen slowly and wisely.

Third, let the church meet in the homes of the members, or let them build a meeting house on their level, belonging to them. If some member wishes to build a large room in which the church can meet on his land, owned entirely by him, this is agreeable.

Fourth, let the churches be supervised by paid evangelists or helpers and by the missionary himself. Nevius baptized about 1,000 persons and lost (by reversion? excommunication?) about 200. The remaining 800 constituted sixty churches, i.e. there were about a dozen members to a church. One *paid* worker supervised forty churchlets, another supervised ten, and Nevius himself still another ten in addition to having general direction of the whole.

Fifth, give extensive training. (1) The Sunday service is chiefly teaching, not sermonizing. Teaching consists in telling the Bible story, having the congregation memorize it, explaining the catechism, and having the Christians memorize it item by item. Worship uses the memorized materials. (2) Instruction of catechumens is done by the unpaid local leaders. They are better than paid agents. Catechumens get from three to twenty-four months of instruction, according to a *Manual for Inquirers*.

This and Scripture question books are invaluable parts of the training system. Without them the lay leaders would be helpless. (3) A month-long Bible training class at the mission station (two hundred miles distant from the churchlets) gives intensive training to the leaders. (Nevius fed and housed all who came and paid their return fare. He tried to get the more advanced converts to attend.)

Sixth, new churches are planted by existing churches. As Christians earn their living and visit their friends and kinsmen in a web of relationship and acquaintance, they find new groups which are considering becoming Christians. Existing Christians teach these inquirers, the supervisor also instructs them occasionally, and when they are ready for examination and baptism, the missionary first sees them. Thus churches multiply in a normal way.

As may be seen, Nevius advocated indigenous church principles as pragmatically sound. This system worked. It was in line with psychology. It kept missions from seeming foreign. It was capable of indefinite expansion, and it presented the Gospel in a true light. It multiplied sound, self-propagating congregations.

Roland Allen

In the first two decades of the twentieth century Roland Allen, an Anglican missionary to China, probably influenced by Nevius' insights, developed a biblical base for indigenous church principles. He pointed out that top-heavy modern missionary practice was very unlike the missionary methods of Paul the apostle. Paul used indigenous church methods. He never appointed paid agents. He always appointed unpaid elders from among the new Christians. He left all matters of discipline to the local churches, under the guidance of the Holy Spirit. Allen's great book, *Missionary Methods: St. Paul's or Ours?*, kept in print by World Dominion Press for fifty years, has been one of the most influential documents on mission methods ever written. Its great contribution was that it anchored indigenous principles to the Early Church and thus implied that they were not only pragmatically sound but also scripturally correct. At the latter point, I shall have some comments to make.

It is worth noting that many denominations in North America, which have grown exceedingly, have used the Allen/Nevius systems for creating churches —and did so long before these men were born—simply on the basis that the New Testament knows nothing of a highly trained corps of ministers, appointed to their places by some central authority. Many denominations in North America *started* on the assumption that those God called to lead the flocks should remain in the calling wherein they were called.

Postwar Popularity

Following World War II, indigenous church principles came into their own. (1) Lack of success in long battles to get Africasian Churches to pay their own ministers and village pastors, inclined many missions to believe that there must be some better way to launch congregations. What better way could there be than to make them independent of mission support from the beginning? (2) Lack of success in planting churches led many to suspect that when foreign missions paid evangelists and pastors, they heavily handicapped the Gospel. If, from the beginning, the Gospel was seen to be a matter of obedience to God with no cash consideration at all, the whole atmosphere would be conducive to growth. (3) Friction between nationals and missionaries who paid them rose sharply after World War II as 700,000,000 ruled people became citizens of independent nations. A good way to end the friction was to cease paying mission agents at all. Indigenous church principles seemed to be a good solution for all these difficulties.

Several missions and boards swung wholeheartedly behind indigenous church principles. In field after field, all mission-paid evangelists and village pastors were dismissed. The little congregations were told that they had the Bible and the Holy Spirit and the means of grace and would no longer receive the paid services of a pastor. Melvin Hodges' book *The Indigenous Church,* which describes how the Assemblies of God put indigenous church principles into operation in Central America, sold far and wide. Several professors of missions taught indigenous church principles to all who passed through their classes as the bright new hope for successful missions. These principles held out the best hope of getting missions out of the doldrums. St. Paul's method would keep the enterprise from getting bogged down. The frightening expense of institutional missions would be checked and, above all, churches would grow and multiply. The power of the Gospel would be seen as indigenous churches, loosed from their foreign bonds, ramified throughout the nations, bringing the blessings of the abundant life to the entire world.

Good reasons, which can be summarized under eight heads, thus lay behind the postwar popularity of indigenous church methods.

Eight Reasons Why Indigenous Churches Grow Better Than Others

1. The missionary who follows indigenous church principles intelligently, interprets mission primarily as church planting. The heart of these

principles is a passion to advance the Gospel and multiply churches. Nevius was primarily a church planter; his system describes what he felt was the most effective way of carrying out his task.

Simply to omit paying pastors and evangelists from mission funds is not, however, following indigenous church policy. A mission spending 80 per cent on education, 15 per cent on medicine, and 5 per cent on caring for existing congregations is *not* following indigenous church principles. If a mission neither subsidizes pastors nor pays evangelists, while spending most of its time and resources on philanthropic activities, it is not using indigenous principles.

2. Non-Christians see unpaid leaders of indigenous churches as people like themselves—indeed, for the most part, their own relatives. In rural areas, Christian leaders are also peasants, planting and harvesting rice in season, walking to the weekly market, buying oxen, selling baskets, weaving cloth, hunting game, and doing a thousand and one other things exactly like their non-Christian neighbors. In urban areas, they are laborers, servants, factory workers, taxi drivers, or plumbers, earning their own living as everyone else does and subject to the same hazards and working conditions. Both urban and rural Christians have innumerable opportunities to bear their own quiet witness. Non-Christians have many chances to see their changed lives. The Christian is one of them. Consequently such indigenous churches grow.

3. Leaders of local churches learn by doing. When they teach others, they learn doubly well themselves. Their convictions grow continually stronger. Their satisfaction comes *(a)* in being leaders of well-knit groups earnestly engaged in doing the will of God, and *(b)* in reading and expounding His Word.

4. It costs the founding mission no money paid to pastors to establish a new church. Each local church grows according to a pattern which others can follow. The best person in the local church (though he may be quite ignorant compared with the lesser members of educated congregations) becomes the teacher, leader, or elder and serves without pay. When a new group is deciding to become Christian, its members do not expect the mission to give them a resident paid worker. They expect that one of their number will become the unpaid shepherd and elder. They do not expect a meeting house built with mission money; they expect to worship in some home or to build a church house with their own labor and cash.

If each new group to become Christian is given a pastor paid by the Church or mission, then the number of groups formed is determined by the amount of the mission budget; but when each new cell provides its own leaders, then there is no financial ceiling on expansion.

The burden of training leaders and supervising the cluster of church-lets remains, however, the responsibility of the founding Church. Indigenous church principles should not be seen as a cheap way of evangelizing. Fully as much should be spent training the volunteer leaders of the Christian cells and paying those who give full time to supervising each cluster as was formerly spent on paying evangelists.

5. Natural witness by the whole membership becomes more possible. The naturalness of Christian life and worship, witness and learning, is what tells. "Unconscious" witness is perhaps the most potent element in growing churches. Indigenous church principles, when successful, create congregations in which Christians tell of a good life possible to them and their listeners. When they explain biblical truth, they do so in thought forms and illustrations meaningful to them at their state of culture. To the people in high New Guinea, the pig is the supreme sacrificial animal. The Eurican missionary, though he may agree that it would be meaningful to say "Jesus is our pig-sacrifice," can scarcely bring himself to do so. The Westernized New Guinea preacher, too, who reads his Bible, knows that John the Baptist said, "Behold the *lamb* of God." But the lay Christian, without any effort and with complete reverence, speaks to his fellows—Christians and non-Christians—about Jesus as the pig of God. Often the idea communicated may not be entirely biblical according to Western notions, but it will commend the Savior to those who have not yet believed, *in terms they understand.*

I once pitched my tent under a fine shade tree on the outskirts of a village in which lived several Christian families. Putting the tent there evidently created consternation among the non-Christians, for a deputation soon came to see me, asking that I shift it to some other place. The village idol was on the other side of the tree trunk and would be defiled by such near presence of Christians! I was about to agree to their request when a village Christian spoke up.

"Why all the fuss, my brothers? Don't you know that as long as the missionary's tent is here, the village dogs won't urinate on your god?" This argument, of which I would never have dreamed, proved most effective.

"Ah, well," they replied, "that is true. There is no need to shift the tent. We shall come and listen here to the Good News."

In truly indigenous congregations ordinary Christians speak openly about the advantages and blessings of being Christian. The Bhil movement of 1935 began with a lay Christian telling his relatives one evening about the power of Christ. Long after the meeting broke up, in the middle of the night a cousin whose water buffalo had suddenly become very sick called the layman. He rose, went to the man's house, laid his hand on the buffalo's flank, prayed to God to restore it to health, and confidently told them all to go back to sleep. In the morning, the buffalo was perfectly well and the whole village listened to the Good News with the deepest respect.

6. When ordinary Christians witness for Christ and persuade others to become His disciples and responsible members of His Church, then churches multiply in extraordinary places—from family to family, village to village, clan to clan, and across the mountain range and down the next valley. An instructive instance of such establishment took place when the Tyal movement to Christ was beginning during the last years of the Japanese occupation of Taiwan during World War II. The Japanese military, getting word of a growing interest in Christianity among the Tyal, had strictly forbidden Bible study or Christian preaching. Then, in an attempt to divert and entertain the Tyal, they took a team of athletes around the villages, putting on games and a show in each. Among the athletes was a Tyal wrestler who was an unbaptized Christian. As the troupe went from village to village, up one remote valley and down the next, the wrestler after his demonstration bouts would quietly meet with his people and encourage them in their secret Bible study and gatherings of unbaptized Christians and friends. After the war a series of congregations arose where the wrestler had made his rounds. There is no defense against this natural witness so characteristic of indigenous churches. A Bible study group grows into a church without arousing any opposition from non-Christian "headquarters."

7. As congregations grow in size and increase in number, indigenous church principles teach that Christians should call full-time pastors paid by the congregation, not by the founding Church or mission. Church buildings too should be constructed as soon as possible, but by the Christians themselves, not by outside aid. In the Kond Hills in India, a visiting Indian Christian doctor attended a meeting in a church house in which a rafter had broken, the thatch sagged, and a pool of water was standing on the floor.

"How much would it cost to fix that roof?" he asked.

"About five rupees," the supervising minister replied. The doctor reached for his wallet, only to be stopped by the remark, "Please, no. We appreciate your willingness to help; but we have a strict rule here that each congregation keeps its own church building in good repair."

That constellation of congregations was following indigenous church principles.

8. Indigenous church principles stress that discipline should be left to the local churches. They are Christ's churches, not the missionary's. What Christian conduct *is* under Greek circumstances should be decided by Greek Christians—not Jewish. What Christian conduct *is* in Kikongo tribes which have become Christian should be settled by Kikongo Christians subject to the Scriptures and the Holy Spirit.

This principle has much to do with church growth. It removes at one stroke the irritation of being judged by foreigners and allows considerable latitude for cultural adjustments of all sorts. It is difficult for any foreigner to separate truly biblical requirements from those which to him, reared in Germany it may be, or some other land, *appear* to be biblical. Canjanam Gamaliel feels that "breaking caste" as a first step in becoming Christian is no essential part of the Gospel—but few American missionaries yet agree with him. One reason why truly indigenous churches grow so much better than missionary-planted churches, even after the latter have been indigenized, is that they are free to follow what the Holy Spirit and the Scriptures direct them to do.

Some Reservations

During the last fifty years, the proposals put forward by Nevius and Allen have been vigorously debated by staunch advocates and opponents. In certain lands indigenous principles seemed the right way to work, likely to produce sound vigorous churches. In other regions, nationals and missionaries looked at the principles longingly, but concluded that "under our circumstances, they simply will not work." Many leaders have reservations such as the following.

Most great Churches in Africasia started and grew for years manned by teacher-preachers, catechists, and village pastors (names vary) who were paid at first entirely by the mission, for many years partly by Church and partly by mission, and finally—after the Church had grown greatly—entirely by the Church. Churches of fifty thousand, a hundred thousand, and a million members arose under the old method. If it was so blessed of God, these leaders argue, it cannot be entirely wrong. Furthermore, as one calmly surveys the entire field, they say it simply is not true that when workers are paid with foreign funds Churches cannot grow. On the contrary, church leaders paid by a national or missionary who trains them, transfers them, recruits them, advances the best to heavier responsibilities, and manages the entire enterprise, is the only system which will advance the Gospel under some circumstances.

According to indigenous church principles, the Church or mission can properly pay missionaries, teachers, medics, and agriculturists, but not shepherds of the flock. Therefore in a Church or mission with the ordinary institutions, these principles handicap congregations by curtailing funds to pay church workers, which funds are then turned over to pay schoolteachers, car drivers, and other helpers. When this occurs, no matter what the real aim may be, it appears to everyone as if the Church or mission were saying, "Our institutional program is of paramount importance; our church program is of none."

Indigenous church principles work well where many are won *soon,* but are not effective where few are. Nevius' thousand converts came rapidly in a rural population where large famine relief had been distributed in the previous decade. The movement to Christ created sixty churches in a short time. St. Paul also went to synagogue communities where congregations were rapidly established. Had he been evangelizing resistant populations, where converts were gathered one by one over many years and churches arose from these occasional converts, famine orphans, rescued persons, and converted schoolchildren, would he have been able to depend on an unpaid local leadership? Particularly if he had been maintaining schools and hospitals?

It is not true that "indigenous church principles make churches grow anywhere." Rather it is true that rapidly growing churches become able to use indigenous church principles. Since this is the case, the correct procedure is to use indigenous principles where they promise to yield good results and not use them in other circumstances.

There is grave danger that indigenous principles will become a new idol, and God's servants will say, "Whether the Church grows or not, whether churches multiply or not, we will adhere strictly to indigenous church principles. These are biblically based. We cannot be good Christians and use anything else. We can pay teachers, servants, missionaries, radio technicians, and nurses, but it is mortal sin to pay evangelists."

Indigenous church principles are good, but it is a serious oversimplification to imagine that they are the only factor or even the chief factor in growth or nongrowth. The tremendous role played by revival should not be overlooked. Nor can the weaknesses of the "one-by-one against the social tide" mode of conversion in tightly organized societies be forgotten. Many other factors also affect growth.

Reconciling These Positions

The cause of world evangelization will not be advanced by dividing into camps for and against indigenous church principles, but rather by understanding when and how these exceedingly useful tools can be used in discipling the nations. The following few rules, tendered in the hope that they will help to reconcile the two positions, are by no means exhaustive. The populations of mankind are so varied that an exhaustive statement doing justice to each would be difficult to make. Readers who know well a cluster of congregations in one homogeneous unit will probably not find these rules, framed with a thousand units in mind, entirely to their liking. But perhaps they will agree that any attempt to describe the circumstances under which indigenous church principles work best is a step in the right direction. And perhaps they will be able to draw up a set of rules which will more adequately meet their specific needs.

1. The true goal of evangelistic effort is independent congregations and Churches, and usually the best way to reach the goal is to plant the first churches according to indigenous church principles. These are much wider in scope than the rather limited question as to who pays the pastor or whether dependence is placed entirely on unpaid local leaders.

2. When establishing churches in a population where older denominations are not subsidizing pastors, and have been growing, never subsidize. Giving subsidy will damage the older Churches, and any temporary advantage gained will be more than lost in the years ahead.

3. In greatly growing Churches, there is no need to subsidize. New congregations are prospering with unpaid leaders or with leaders paid by themselves. To introduce subsidy would be foolish.

4. When establishing churches in populations where previous Churches are subsidizing, the new mission is limited to three options: subsidize; put forty miles between itself and the older churches and try to start without subsidy; or create congregations with a tremendous sense of separateness. The Seventh Day Adventists follow the third option in most places. The Congregacao Cristan of Brazil began in 1916 with a completely unpaid leadership right in the city of Sao Paulo, in the presence of paid ministers of Methodist, Baptist, Lutheran, Presbyterian, and other denominations. It grew in fifty years to be a Church of 400,000 baptized believers. This was possible only because the Congregacao was growing in a separate homogeneous unit (the Italian-speaking immigrants) and had a vivid consciousness of its own separateness.

5. When establishing churches in resistant populations, try to start on indigenous church principles. The naturalness of these sometimes overcomes resistance. Do not, however, dully continue indigenous church principles for decades whether churches multiply or not. In a country like Nigeria or Brazil, a mission which with great indigenous church zeal has spent thirty years and two million dollars and has a total present membership of less than 400 baptized believers, is a poor steward of God's grace. It should have shifted to a limited subsidy plan, or otherwise adjusted its policies, many years ago. There is no merit in sticking to indigenous church principles whether churches are established or not. The basic purpose of Allen's and Nevius' proposals is to plant churches more effectively than the "old method." Nevius would have been the first to modify indigenous church principles—or even discard them—if they had not planted growing, multiplying churches.

6. If a mission subsidizes in part or in whole, it should constantly seek to start other congregations on new ground with unpaid leaders. Sometimes at the very beginning priming the pump is necessary, but it must never be forgotten that the goal is to get an abundant flow without pouring in a stream of subsidy. No truly great growth will occur till the Church is going forward on an indefinitely reproducible pattern in which new churchlets are begun with no expense to the central treasury. This is what spontaneous expansion means.

7. Train unpaid leaders vigorously in all congregations, even where the pastor gets a subsidy. Put more and more responsibility on laymen, whatever the present system. Few Churches are in such a desperate plight that the only move left to the assisting mission is to dismiss all mission-paid evangelists and *then* start to train laymen. Teach the whole national leadership the advantages of indigenous church principles.

8. Work constantly for church multiplication. When churches grow, subsidy to the pastors and workers can be much more readily ended or diminished. When new small congregations are formed, let them be led by unpaid men. When old congregations increase in size, let each take a larger and larger share of its pastor's salary. Place several small congregations under one "circle" pastor, like Nevius' supervising worker who had ten churchlets under him. Stopping church multiplication till an indigenous unpaid leadership has been created is a counsel of despair.

9. Make provision for paid leaders at the supervisory level. Sometimes direct payment from mission funds is necessary. It is no sin. It is not the best and most permanent arrangement, but it has produced good churches in hundreds of cases. Sometimes it is well to establish a church fund

administered by the Church into which contributions from the congregations and the mission go, and from which workers and pastors are paid. The ultimate goal is for the national Church to pay local pastors, circle pastors, and all other staff entirely from its own funds, but few Africasian Churches have yet reached the place where this goal is in sight.

PEOPLE MOVEMENTS AND INDIGENOUS CHURCH PRINCIPLES

Understanding people movements helps us to understand indigenous church principles and the circumstances under which they are effective in reconciling men to God. It is well worth noting that Roland Allen took his telling biblical example of indigenous church methods from the flourishing people movement which began among the common people in Jerusalem and Judea and later expanded in the synagogue communities around the Mediterranean. His genius and contribution to missions are in no way diminished by recognizing that his insights were somewhat distorted because he did not—at that time could not—understand the people-movement nature of New Testament church growth. For example, he imagined that Paul (like a modern missionary pioneer) went to the great cities of the ancient world because they were centers of commerce, government, communications, and culture. Allen missed the fact that Paul went to the great cities only because the Jews lived there. Only in the cities could he find large synagogue communities and hundreds of relatives and business associates of existing Christians. These were the stuff of which his movement to Christian faith consisted. His churches were growing in a web of relationship which happened to be based in the cities. Hence he went to the cities. Had it been based in rural areas, he would have followed it to rural areas.

Allen did not see the people movement at all. Hence he could not see that indigenous principles describe the ways in which people movements progress in receptive populations. People movements, in fact, *are* indigenous churches *par excellence*. They are not the only indigenous churches, by any means; that is, some indigenous churches are not parts of people movements. But a properly shepherded people movement is a cluster of thoroughly indigenous congregations.

We have no example in the Bible of indigenous principles being used in a resistant population, where the task is to hang on and proclaim decade after decade while nurturing small dependent congregations. It is foolish to assume that the Acts pattern will work equally well in resistant populations, and even more foolish to imagine it will turn resistant populations receptive. St. Paul devised and practiced his missionary methods in a population where sizable congregations came into being rapidly, often after only a week or two of preaching. It is in such populations that his methods are most fruitful.

One may conclude that missions evangelizing receptive homogeneous units should use indigenous church principles. In those units, they are markedly superior to the paid worker system. If two missions are working in a notably receptive population, the first using indigenous principles and the second the old system, growth in the second will grind to a halt while it continues in the first. The enormous growth of the Pentecostals in Chile and Brazil is due in considerable part to the fact that, without being conscious of the fact, their churches have followed indigenous church principles on a vast scale. In markedly resistant populations, however, the paid mission agent still has a place of importance. He has contributed splendidly to the growth of Churches in the past and will play an important role in the future.

Here again, it will be useful to think in terms of an axis of receptivity. At the left end—highly resistant populations—the founding Church will probably have to depend on missionaries and nationals paid by itself. At the extreme left there is no Church, or existing congregations are weak and dependent and likely to remain so. At the right end—highly responsive populations—congregations will form ahead of mission effort under their own unpaid leaders. Here it would be the height of foolishness to institute a system of subsidy. In between, however, in the midreaches of the distribution, are populations where it will not be clear whether strict indigenous principles are advantageous or not. Here giving indigenous principles a thorough tryout first is wise. If subsidy has to be used, regard it as detrimental to the best interests of the growing Church and try to shift out of it as rapidly as possible, especially in all new areas.

How to terminate the old method and get onto an indigenous church basis is a thorny question. If all missionaries are banished from a land, or war and revolution throw the Church entirely on its own for a while, chances for churches to develop unpaid leaders are good. But when the missionaries are not banished and institutions continue paying their staffs, when the mission can readily pay evangelists and pastors and yet wickedly and stubbornly refuses to do so (as it appears to the pastors who are dismissed and to their relatives), drastic action seldom brings good results. It is better to promote abler paid workers to supervisory positions, pour funds into training lay leaders, give generous severance allowances to such catechists as are released and help them to get land or employment, and step up efforts to plant new churches. The shift to indigenous principles should never be made as a part of retrenchment. Otherwise at the very time that mission-paid workers are dismissed and form an aggrieved element in the small congregations, less and less attention is paid to those very congregations.

Indigenous and People Movement Principles Buttress Each Other

1. *Indigenous principles aid greatly in establishing healthy people movements.* They do this for several reasons. First, they lead Christians to go to their own folk, to their kith and kin, and thus to grow among their own kind of people. Peasants win other peasants. Tiv tribesmen win Tiv. Displaced northeasterners flooding into south Brazilian cities evangelize other displaced northeasterners. Aymara immigrants in northwest Argentina on becoming Evangelicals win other Aymaras; they do not win old Argentinians. Hence indigenous principles make it possible for congregations and missionaries to get group action in like-minded units.

Second, they lead Christians and churches to choose the national patterns which feel good to them. Indigenous churches are free to act. The missionary sees them but seldom.* Their leaders are accustomed to doing what seems good to them. If they want to have guitar music in their churches they do. If they want to dance at the communion table they can

---

*This is true only after church planting has been going on for some time. Where there are either no churches at all or only a few beginning congregations, the missionary must play a much more vigorous role. He must be seen all the time. He is the church planter God has sent there. He cannot be too active. One of the unfortunate effects of some training in indigenous methods is that it sends missionaries to the field afraid to do *anything,* lest they take initiative away from nationals. Quite the contrary, according to indigenous church principles, the role of the missionary at the beginning of church planting is to be a chief church planter. We may be sure that Nevius' sixty churches did not just happen while Nevius stayed nervously in the background, letting them be born and meekly permitting indigenous leaders to grope their way into Bible study, regular worship, and the whole carefully planned sequence he insisted was essential.

A. C. Krass's church planting in Ghana, reported in the previous chapter, is a model which new missionaries may study to advantage. Seeing what needed to be done, he did not hesitate to bypass national leaders in the existing town congregation and to direct church planting according to a program *he* designed and controlled in the villages. True, when he gets sixty churches, he will seldom be seen in any one of them; but till the Presbyterian Church of Ghana appoints some able Ghanaian to direct Operation Discipling effectively, Mr. Krass (like Dr. Nevius) should be seen a great deal. He should actively direct the entire enterprise. Part of his job is to develop leaders of the village churches. They will not pop up of themselves.

do so. Such churches inevitably are and remain indigenous in their customs. The customs feel good to non-Christian relatives. When these contemplate becoming Christians they are attracted, not repelled, by the church practices. Hence groups, large and small, find it agreeable and possible to visit, learn, and discuss becoming Christian, and finally make multi-individual decisions for Christ.

Third, indigenous churches and their members use arguments which appeal to their kind of people. In Chile, one reason for great Pentecostal growth is that the common people believe it is patriotic to become an Evangelical. A man becomes a better Chilean by becoming a Pentecostal. The average missionary would neither think of this argument nor judge it a worthy reason for becoming an Evangelical—but the indigenous churches of Chile find it effective. Persuaded by arguments that appeal, large numbers of their kind of people turn to the Lord.

The Lord Jesus frequently used arguments which appealed to the common people. Between Luke 19:48 and 22:6, the Evangelist records eight occasions when Jesus' words appealed to "the people," but so angered the ruling classes that they resolved to put Him to death.

Without effort indigenous churches appear more reasonable and sensible to men of whatever homogeneous unit the churches are part of, and hence get group action without specially trying for it.

Fourth, the meetings are held in places which fit the segment of society concerned—in houses of friends, or rented halls in humble sections of the city, or thatch-roofed chapels in the country districts. The doorsill in these places is the right height for non-Christian intimates of the Christians. They are not awed by the "grandeur" of the house or place of worship. Hence more of them assemble there and, feeling at ease, make group decisions for Christ more readily.

Fifth, indigenous churches are led by local men, who speak with the right accent, know the people intimately, do intuitively what is understood and appeals, and are, in brief, as comfortable as an old shoe. Hence these leaders get group action from those to whom they commend the Gospel.

2. *People movements aid greatly in establishing indigenous churches.* People-movement congregations irresistibly seek their own folk and proliferate among their own kinsmen—and hence cannot help but be thoroughly indigenous. People-movement churches choose national patterns. To be exact, they choose patterns of their own subculture. Consequently, without making the slightest effort to be, they are thoroughly indigenous. People-movement Christians know what brought them to Christ and simply repeat these arguments. These are all they know. Such arguments are not likely

to impress men of other classes, languages, or cultures, but they do impress members of their own kinship web. Thus without effort those who come to Christian commitment continue and add to the indigenous quality of the Church.

In the same way, people-movement churches are led by their own natural leaders, are out away from central towns and Western-educated nationals, run on their own power, are not assisted much by the missionary or educated national, are thrown back on their own resources, and are free to be led by the Holy Spirit. Consequently they look, sound, and smell indigenous.

About 25,000 non-Christians had become Christian in the famed Dornakal diocese in South India in a rather successful people movement. In the forties, I visited the diocese in company with an Anglican minister named Elliott who was Bishop Azariah's chief assistant. Our first stop was a church on the west bank of a large river where about a thousand people had gathered for baptism. It was the dry season and a small stream two feet deep and ten wide flowed down the west edge of a dry, sandy bed about half a mile in width. A party of young Christian men were waiting on the east bank to welcome us. They were bare from the waist up, lean as whips, and wore flowing white dhotis to their ankles. Long black hair hung about their shoulders. After greeting the bishop, they formed a circle around a man who played a local tune on a hand-pumped organ slung around his neck. As they led us across the sand they danced and sang, circling round the organ and staying a few steps ahead of our party. The words, I was told, were Christian, but the tunes were those sung by Hindus all across that part of the land. The welcome given us was thoroughly indigenous. Villagers had been welcoming honored guests in this fashion from time immemorial.

As non-Christians viewed the performance, they thought of the Christians assembled there, including the white men, not as adherents of some foreign religion, but as followers of an Indian religion—different from their own to be sure, but still Indian to the core.

This illustration focuses attention on the externals of life—music, dancing, long hair, and bare bodies—and thus exposes only the tip of the indigenous iceberg to view. The indigenous externals are not important. They could be imitated by Westernized Christians resolved to "become indigenous." Underneath these externals are indigenous ways of thinking, loving, hating, working, spending leisure, earning a living, and obeying orders. The value system of these 25,000 Christians was just as indigenous as their flowing white dhotis, dark skins, and local music. The truly important indigenous characteristics of the Dornakal Christians are the inner aspects of life. These unseen qualities came into the Church as, over several decades, a thousand groups of four castes declared for Christ in people-movement fashion.

Indigenous church principles encourage group action and make it both easier and more permanent. Group action brings an indigenous way of life with it. The indigeneity which sensitive leaders in large towns labor to achieve arrives without effort where people movements to Christ surge through any population.

The more churchmen know about people movements, the better indigenous churches they can build. The more they know about indigenous church principles the better people movements they can create. Those occurring in London, Paris, Boston, or other Western city will, to be sure, be somewhat different from those established in Kinshasa, Belo Horizonte, Lima, or Hong Kong. But they will be indigenous and will be movements of the people or peoples concerned. The more indigenous the type of evangelism used, the more likely it is that many will respond. And when many respond, particularly if they respond in people-movement fashion, the resulting cluster of congregations is very likely to be an indigenous Church. It is particularly urgent that "following indigenous church principles" not be used as an excuse for non-growing churches and non-effective evangelism, whether this is carried out in New York or the New Hebrides.

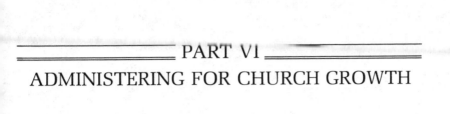

PART VI
ADMINISTERING FOR CHURCH GROWTH

20
STREAM ACROSS THE BRIDGES

EVERY HUMAN society is like a town on one side of a river over which at convenient places bridges have been built. Citizens can cross the river at other places, but it is much easier to go across the bridges. People near the bridges are better connected than those far from them. Ideas, foodstuffs, processions, and convictions flow to and fro across the bridges.

As congregations administer for church growth, they ought to discover and use these bridges to the unreached. Good stewards of the grace of God should remember the bridges and stream across them. "Find the bridges and use them" is excellent strategy for all who are impelled by the Holy Spirit to share the Good News.

During the years of research which led to writing *The Bridges of God* I was constantly impressed by the crucial role played in the expansion of the Christian Faith by the relatives of Christians. Again and again I observed that though Christians are surrounded by thousands of fellow citizens, the Christian Faith flows best from relative to relative or close friend to close friend. This was true whatever the nationality or language. It was as true in the heartland of America as in Uganda or the High Andes.

In 1955, in *The Bridges of God* I wrote,

> Every nation is made up of various layers or strata of society. In many nations each stratum is clearly separated from every other. The individuals in each stratum marry chiefly, if not solely, with each other. Their intimate life is

therefore limited to their own society, that is, to their own people. They may work with others, buy from and sell to individuals of other societies; but their intimate life is wrapped up with the individuals of their own people. . . . When (these) start becoming Christian, this touches their very lives (p. 1).

In 1979 George Hunter wrote,

A strategic American church will continually work to locate and reach out to kinsmen, and especially to the friends of active Christians and new converts. The church will also encourage its members to make new friends in the community continually. People are more receptive when they are approached by authentic Christians *from within their own social network* (p. 126, emphasis added).

BRIDGES HAVE ALWAYS BEEN IMPORTANT

The Early Church used its bridges to good effect. It started among the common people of Jerusalem. Their bridges were to the common people—their relatives and intimates. While a few of the scribes and Pharisees did become Christian (Nicodemus, Joseph of Arimathea, and Saul come immediately to mind), most Christians were not of that high stratum of society. When persecution drove Christians from the city, they went of necessity to their relatives in the villages of Judea for shelter. There they "preached the Gospel," that is, they told their intimates about the Lord Jesus and the way of salvation opened for all who believe. The Church grew greatly among the peasants of Judea. Two whole villages, Lydda and Sharon, became Christian, together, we may be sure, with many other groups in many other villages.

Barnabas was a Levite of Cyprus. How natural that the first missionary journey was to Cyprus, where his family lived. How natural also that on his first missionary journey Paul visited Derbe, Iconium, and Antioch. These towns were only 125, 150, and 200 miles west of Tarsus on the main Roman road. It is highly likely that Saul's father had commercial dealings with many of the Jews in those towns. Saul was probably known by them as a brilliant young rabbi of Tarsus, who had studied under Gamaliel in Jerusalem. He was always invited to speak in the synagogues.

The last chapter of the Epistle to the Romans gives vivid evidence of the bridges Paul habitually used. He mentions 26 Christians in Rome by name, and knew of several others—though he had never been in Rome. Some of these were his own relatives. One—Rufus' mother—may have been his own *mother*, though it seems more likely that Paul meant "she has been like a mother to me." All of the twenty-six had relatives and intimates in the Jewish community in Rome. So while Paul considered himself a special messenger of Christ to the Gentiles, he streamed out to them across his bridges in the Jewish community and their bridges to others. One can rejoice in the bridge which Roman Christians had to Caesar's household (Phil. 4:22). It may have been built after Paul arrived.

Down through the centuries the great expansions of the Faith have commonly been along lines of relationship. Latourette tells us that the conversion of the Anglo-Saxons in England around the year 600 A D began and continued along lines of relationship. Gregory the Great in Rome had sent Augustine the missionary to England. His party landed on the island of Thanet at the mouth of the Thames River, and proceeded to contact Ethelbert, King of Kent—the southeasternmost kingdom of England which had

> already been . . . touched by influences from the mainland. Its ruler, Ethelbert, had for wife a Christian Frankish princess, Bertha. As a condition of the marriage, Ethelbert had promised that she would be allowed to observe her religion, and a bishop Luidhard had accompanied her. She worshipped at Canterbury, the capital of Kent (45 miles southeast of modern London), in a church dedicated to St. Martin which is said to have been built in Roman times. . . . Augustine and his party were established in Canterbury . . . Presently Ethelbert himself was baptized . . . accessions rapidly increased. . . . A letter of Gregory, undated, speaks of ten thousand having been baptized by Augustine on one Christmas (*The Thousand Years of Uncertainty*, p. 66).

In the nineteenth century the great turnings in Burma took place along lines of relationship. An early convert of Adoniram Judson was a Karen, Ko Tha Byu. Judson considered his main work to lie with the Buddhist Burmese, but Ko Tha Byu went to his relatives among the Karens and from these, groups became Christian. The Karen People Movement had begun. It spread almost exclusively from contact to contact, relative to relative until today more than half a million Karens are Christians and the Karen Church is one of the strongest in all Asia.

In the United States in the late seventies, under the impact of the church growth movement and the researches of Lyle Schaller recounted in Chapter 12 which showed that most accessions to churches came through the efforts of friends and relatives, many congregations resolved to discover and befriend the relatives and close friends of families from which one person was an active member. Sometimes this was a husband or wife, sometimes a son or daughter, and sometimes a brother or sister. In every case from one to ten other people immediately came within the circle of congregational concern. "Befriending" meant much more than inviting them to church. On occasion it meant having them over for a meal or to a neighborhood party. On occasion it meant loaning them a lawn mower or joining their car pool. Several times it led to playing golf together.

One congregation had in it several ardent professional football fans. These bought season tickets to the series and invited an equal number of unbelieving husbands (whose wives were already active Christians) to go with them to the games. Going there, coming back, and the intermissions offered many opportunities for natural conversation about the Church and Christ. The unchurched husbands soon came to think of Christian men as normal human beings who rooted for the right teams and knew the right players by name. They went with their new-found friends (and their own long-time wives) to church and became active Christians themselves.

"Streaming across the bridges" works equally well among primitive tribesmen. James Sunda tells of the beginning of the remarkable ingathering among the West Danis in the Baliem Valley in Irian. The great ingathering there has been briefly touched on in Chapter 7; but the important part played by relatives in beginning the movement is well worth recounting. Until 1954, the West Danis were a Stone Age tribe with very few contacts with the outside world. Christian Missions in April 1954 flew into the high valley (5000 feet), landing on the Baliem River. Perhaps a dozen mission stations were established, the language was learned, medical relief was given, evangelism was carried on. But no one became Christian! The West Dani whose villages dotted the valley were indifferent and even resistant. It looked as if decades of seed sowing lay ahead.

Then, from November 1958 to February 1959 in the Ilaga Valley, four days' march to the west across a high, cold 11,000-foot plateau, 2,000 West Danis burned their fetishes and became Christian. They were well instructed by Missionary Donald Gibbons at a Witness School to which specially intelligent married couples were sent by the converted tribesmen. These remembered the main tribe four days' march away, "who know nothing of Christ, though many missionaries work in their midst." The Ilaga Valley Dani Christians resolved to send their best Christians to the Baliem Valley. Since they had to travel through enemy territory, they took their white missionary along with them. His presence guaranteed them safe passage on that historic journey of February 1960.

Arriving among their relatives they told them, "Become Christians like we did. Hold village meetings and as a group resolve to burn your fetishes at the mission station. Get all your fetishes, carry in wood and make a long funeral pyre, put your fetishes on it, and burn them all. Declare for Christ. Appoint the men you desire to be your teachers and pastors. The missionaries will instruct them. You will give them food so they will have time to teach you. God will bless you. That is the way you become Christians."

Within a very short time 8,000 West Danis in the Baliem Valley had come to group decisions and marched in to the mission stations. Faced with this novel way of becoming Christian, the missionaries scarcely knew what to do. Some opposed any such decision for Christ; but most accepted it as a first step. As related in Chapter 7, by 1967 most of the 8,000 had been baptized.

By 1980 more than 30,000 West Danis and thousands of men and women of other tribes had been baptized. The highlands of Irian have become substantially Christian, though outlying tribes are still being evangelized, baptized, and incorporated in Christian churches.

Until approached by *their own people*, relatives and friends, the Danis were indifferent or hostile. When they heard the Word from those from within their own social network they proved exceedingly responsive.

Many indifferent or resistant segments of society in Canada and the United States would similarly become responsive were they to be approached by their relatives, their own people. As long as becoming a biblical Christian appears to mean joining "those other people," they are cool to the idea; but when they can remain themselves, and all their precious contacts not only remain but become more precious, they make haste to become followers of Jesus.

The remarkable multiplication of Chinese Alliance churches across Canada in the late seventies beautifully illustrates the principle. When to become a Christian meant to leave the community and join a Caucasian congregation, then few Chinese became Christians, but when Chinese from Hong Kong, who had become Christians there in Alliance congregations, immigrated to Canada, and settlements of Cantonese-speaking Chinese were evangelized by Chinese Alliance pastors from Hong Kong, new Chinese congregations sprang up in many cities.

In North America the large ethnic minorities, which to date have been solidly resistant to earnest Protestant denominations, are like the West Danis and the Chinese in Canada. Each awaits the creation of apostolic teams *of their own relatives and close friends*.

It is not too much to say that around each of the 300,000 and more congregations in the United States there is a population which appears indifferent to the Gospel. It is being approached by Christians who are usually strangers and at best are acquaintances. That is one factor which makes us think these populations are unresponsive. If each congregation were to discover and list the multitude of relatives, contacts, and close friends, and were to befriend them and witness to them in natural ways, many of these very populations would become highly responsive.

Norman Piersman relates an attractive instance of the principle at work in Colombia, that great nation of 25 million souls just 1,500 miles south of Miami.

> Jose was saved a year ago in Blas De Lezo and was baptized with his wife and three oldest children on Palm Sunday, 1970. At four months in the Lord, he made a long trip back to his home village. There he gave his testimony to his many relatives and left a Bible. In November 1970, the Lord in a dream showed him his people coming out of the river after being baptized. This spurred him on to plan another trip.
>
> On Saturday, January 2, 1971, he and I reached this village and presented the plan of salvation, intimating that the next day would be the "day of decision." Sunday morning Jose preached and I asked for decisions. Nineteen received Christ. At the evening gathering, thirty more responded to the invitation. After further biblical teaching we asked people to gather for the special orientation classes to be held the next day. Wednesday many villagers were present to see their first Protestant baptismal service. We gathered at the banks of the Sinu River. Twenty-four of Jose's relatives—his mother, brothers, sisters, cousins, brothers-in-law, nephews and nieces—testified to their new faith in Christ and obeyed the Word in baptism. How true the Word is— "believe on the Lord Jesus Christ and you shall be saved, *and your household*" (*Church Growth Bulletin,* March 1971).

Bridges Not Always Relatives

The bridges of God are not always relatives. Often good friends serve Christians as natural avenues of communication. Campus Crusade for Christ built its vast para church organization on the fact that college students can speak normally and effectively to other collegians.

In this connection it is interesting to remember that Patrick, who is credited with the conversion of the Irish tribes, was not an Irishman. He had no relatives in that land. He, an English youth, was captured by a band of Irish raiders and carried off to many years of servitude in Ireland. He fled Ireland and went to France. As his Christian conviction grew, he believed God was calling him to go back to Ireland and tell the Good News to his captors and multitudes of other Irish. Most missionaries, by definition, are not of the people they evangelize. Missionaries find bridges (or make them) and carry on cross-cultural evangelism across these.

A very nice example of making bridges occurred in England in the years 1975 and 1976. A dying congregation, which had once filled its sanctuary with 300 worshipers, was reduced to 27 persons, all fifty years of age and above. A couple of young American missionaries threw in their lot with this congregation. They made it their special purpose to dress as young people of the factory town dressed, to frequent the places they frequented, and to be interested in the sports and entertainments which drew their attention. Thus they manufactured a bridge. In the course of the next two years, the attendance at that church mounted to 230 and its baptized membership to 119. To be sure, the style of the service was fitted to the newcomers' needs and many other steps were taken; but without building that bridge none of the later steps would have led to church growth—or indeed, to have been possible at all.

Robert Bolton in Taiwan studied a remarkable instance of growth and charted carefully how the faith had flowed from one relative to another. A lay leader in Philadelphia on seeing the following chart exclaimed, "Something very like that has happened in our congregation. Perhaps they are not all relatives, but they are all from the same social network."

The T'ung-hwa Church began when Mr. Hwang, a very sick patient, was treated at a Christian hospital in Shi-lin. He was so moved by the tender heart of the Chinese Christian doctor that he accepted Christ as his Saviour and requested baptism.

After his baptism a very strange thing happened. Mr. Hwang said he had seen the Lord and that in three days the Lord would receive him to Himself. He arranged for his return to Keelung and told his wife that at 4:00 p.m. on the third day he would be received into heaven. Precisely as he had predicted, Mr. Hwang died at 4:00 p.m. on the third day, just after he had entered his house.

Through visitation and teaching the Word in homes, the Gospel began to flow along the natural family and friendship lines. The following chart and text developed by Allen Swanson explains the network of relationships along which the Gospel flowed in the next few months.

1. Mr. Hwang died three days after his conversion.

2. Mrs. Hwang, the widow, and all her children were led to Christ by Brother Lee.

3. A close friend attended Mr. Hwang's funeral. His whole family was converted.

4. A close friend attended Mr. Hwang's funeral. He influenced his entire family to the Christian faith.

5. An old grandmother heard the Gospel in #4's home. She suffered from a serious internal bleeding. Brother Lee prayed for her and she was

FIGURE 20.1

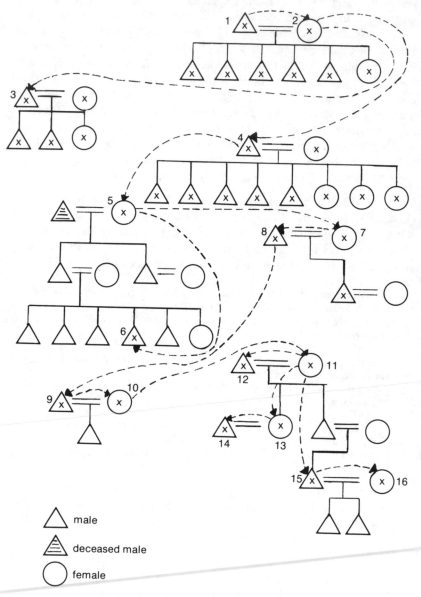

△ male

△ deceased male

◯ female

x   Christian believer

healed. After her conversion at the age of 72 she was baptized. She lives with her older son and his children.

    6. She is close to one grandson who has become a Christian.

    7. A former neighbor of #5 heard the Gospel. Although she was mentally ill for seven years, she, too, was prayed for by Brother Lee and was healed as well as converted.

    8. She then led her husband, a police officer, to the Lord.

    9. A fellow policeman was led to Christ by #8.

    10. Wife of #9 was led to Christ by him.

    11. A neighbor was won by the wife of #9.

    12. The husband of #11 was converted to Christ.

    13. The daughter of #11 and #12 was converted to Christ.

    14. She won her husband to Christ, and also,

    15. A grandson of #11 whom she brings to church.

    16. The wife of #15 also believes.

Readers should trace the flow of the gospel within the intricate network of familial and neighborhood associations. The following connections are discernible.

Parent to child	19 cases
Husband to wife	4 cases
Co-worker to co-worker	3 cases
Woman to woman (neighbor)	3 cases
Wife to husband	3 cases

    Through the conversion of Mr. Hwang, therefore, 34 members of families, neighbors and friends were brought to conversion and into fellowship of the T'ung-hwa Church within a relatively short period of time (*Church Growth Bulletin*, Jan. 1977).

BRIDGES ARE MORE INFLUENTIAL IN TIGHTLY STRUCTURED SOCIETIES

    In tightly knit societies, where people consciousness is high, and all marriages take place within the segment of society concerned, the chain of relationship is particularly strong. Once Christianity has been established, once a couple of thousand have become Christian, tens of thousands of bridges become available. The potential for explosive growth is high, because across all such bridges the faith may flow. In times of revival when large numbers of Christians are acutely conscious of the power of God in their lives, they stream out across many bridges.

    In loosely knit societies, however, where individuals from many segments of society are living together, coming to speak a common language, *there* while bridges exist they are not so influential. More exactly, there the weak, narrow bridges of casual contact are numerous. These do not carry Christian conviction so well. When the Gospel flows across such bridges it does not carry as much power. Individuals are won, but not groups. And, those won are not so likely to go on and win others.

Nevertheless, since more and more people live in loosely knit societies, Christians should stream across the numerous bridges there—narrow and weak though they may be. They are God's bridges. He wants us to use them.

Bridges Are Frequently Neglected

In pluralistic societies, the feeling grows that what individuals believe is their own business. Others should not interfere. We should simply accept persons as they are, recognizing that within the nation are many different lifestyles and many different scales of values. All are equally citizens of the state. Provided that a citizen does not hurt other people, he ought to be free to believe and do whatever he wishes. We are not commending this point of view, but merely noting that it is prevalent.

In such a climate of belief, many congregations perhaps unconsciously act as if their main duty was to live as Christians, worship God, feed on His Word, and be friendly toward those who seek them out. "Our door is always open to those who come to worship with us. We are very warm and cordial. But quite frankly, we do not think it our duty to speak about our faith to others—perhaps specially not to those near and dear to us. They may believe something quite different and we might find their religious beliefs separate us." Thus spoke an elder of an influential church— which had been static for many years. It was not only neglecting its bridges, but had formed a philosophy of life which denied their importance.

Many congregations—at least a hundred thousand in the United States—never consciously seek for bridges nor instruct their members in how to find and use them. Their evangelistic opportunities are limited to making their church attractive, locating it on a much traveled street, and providing facilities such that visitors who have already decided to choose a church home will conclude that this is the church of which they would like to become members.

In India the first generation of Christians was very conscious of its non-Christian relatives. But second and third generation Christians, most of whom have not come to Christ by conversion from non-Christian religions, but by biological church growth, know few if any non-Christian relatives. They do not attend their weddings or funerals. Each group of relatives has shut the other out of its life. The bridges long neglected have fallen into disrepair. Some have been swept away by floods. Such churches, having no bridges, have become ethnic enclaves or, in plain words, ghettos. Neglect of bridges leads to that dismal outcome.

"Use bridges before they disappear" should be ordinary procedure for congregations and Christians everywhere. The January 1977 issue of *Church Growth Bulletin*, in discussing reasons why Pentecostal Churches grow, carried the following paragraph,

> Common Christians—soon after they become disciples of the Lord—have multitudinous good connections with friends and relatives among Secularists, Buddhists, Hindus, Jews, Materialists, Agnostics, and other worldly people. It is along these connections, these bridges of God, that the Gospel flows. Those who have been Christian for many years, or who grew up in Christian homes and have married Christians and thus have few intimates among the worldly, do not have such bridges. They have few intimates among the worldly and so are not evangelistically as potent. Old Pentecostal congregations find the same thing operative among them. It is the new congregations which are potent. Pentecostals have more new congregations than most denominations— and trust them more.

Any denomination—Pentecostal or other—which uses its bridges (evangelizes its relatives and friends) is likely to grow.

Danger of Segregation?

Does streaming across bridges produce segregated congregations? Are such congregations likely to be racist or at least introverted and concerned chiefly about themselves? Is going to one's own relatives and intimates dangerous advice to give to churches as they become concerned about effective evangelization? These questions deserve careful answers.

As a result of such evangelism, one-segment congregations do arise. This is beyond question. When university professors evangelize people of their own kind, with whom they have normal intimate fellowship, the resulting church is likely to be largely composed of members of the university community. When Rev. Argos Zodiates evangelizes Greek Americans in Boston, he builds up a 300-member evangelical church made up almost exclusively of Greeks living in New England.

Overseas monoethnic congregations and clusters of congregations certainly do arise. In Northeast India, when the first Mizo converts in the Lushai Hills streamed out across their bridges, they had to go to their own tribesmen. As a result, of the 400,000 Christians in the new Indian state of Mizoram in 1980, more than 90% are Mizos. The mature denomination is sending Mizo missionaries to other peoples in Tripura, Korkuland, and Arunachal.

When in the first decade of the twentieth century the Mono tribes living in Equatorial Province of Belgian Congo started turning to Christ, they went exclusively to their own fellows. They had been at war with surrounding tribes for hundreds of years. Their obvious first duty was to Christianize their own relatives. By 1969, the official statistics recorded 229,856 baptized believers. Practically all of these belonged to Mono tribes (*Zaire: Midday in Missions,* Valley Forge, Judson: 113). If this Church is to evangelize other peoples it will have to send Mono missionaries and keep them at work in cross-cultural evangelism.

In Guatemala, the first few Aguacatec Indians to become Christians thought of joining the Mestizo congregations of the Central American Mission. Then, realizing that other Aguacatecs would feel no urge to join Mestizo Spanish-speaking congregations, the converts formed an Aguacatec cluster of congregations. Soon Evangelical Aguacatecs numbered a tenth of the tribe. Monoethnic congregations do tend—like the Early Church for fifteen years—to be largely confined to one people.

Must we, therefore, conclude that multiplying congregations largely of one kind of people in Boston, university campuses, or Burma is a step backward? Must we resist it and declare that we want *real* Christians, who feel brotherly to all peoples, and who in their congregational structure and worship demonstrate that the two peoples concerned have actually become "one in Christ Jesus?" The answers to these questions must be a firm, though qualified, No. Multiplying churches largely of one kind of people is *not* a step backward. It is an essential step forward. *There is no other way in which the multitudinous pieces of the human mosaic can become Christian.* Such churches are Christ's way to the hearts of those pieces. Requiring converts to join conglomerate congregations will hinder the Church from rapidly spreading to *panta ta ethne.*

Using the natural bridges of "our kind of people" is common sense. Whose salvation are new Christians most concerned about? Their own loved ones and intimates. Who will hear them most gladly? Who will be most likely to respond? Their own loved ones and intimates. Who, upon conversion and incorporation in the congregation, will feel most at home? Who will participate most gladly? Again the answer is clearly men and women of that particular network of society. Finally, who will be able to reach out to others and bring them into that church? Without doubt new Christians can reach their intimates and kinsmen much more effectively than they can anyone else.

The options then are: (1) building conglomerate congregations which from the beginning bring men and women of many different ethnic, linguistic, and educational backgrounds into one new family of God; and (2) rapidly building up congregations of one kind of people. In many populations (1) is a small option. Only in true melting pots is it a big option. There old segments of society are in fact breaking down. Many mixed marriages are taking place. Children growing up together in school regard each other as essentially one people. *There conglomerate congregations are both possible and desirable.* There the best opportunity for growth may truly be that of bringing into one congregation converts of the new-people-being-formed. Elsewhere the Church of God should press ahead making sure that congregations arise *within each segment of society.* These will be led by elders and deacons of that segment and will ordain ministers of that segment, too.

If some segment is being omitted, left unchurched, prayer and labor for its evangelization should be mounted in many congregations. As this is done, the Holy Spirit will call "men of Cyprus and Cyrene" (laymen) and send them to many an "Antioch."

I said that the answers to these questions must be a firm but qualified, No. Let us consider four qualifications. *First, most segments of humanity are themselves mosaics. Each segment includes individuals who belong to other segments.* The university community includes some who live in the country and are gardeners or small farmers as well as teachers. Many white congregations have black members whose place of residence, education, and income make them feel at home in such churches. Hispanic Americans include fourth-generation citizens who may speak no Spanish at all, immigrants from Argentina who arrived six months ago, and every shade in between. Every congregation, therefore, is likely to have a wide spread of members. Going to relatives and friends does not mean going to an increasingly narrow segment of society. "Friends" often come from other sections of society, and increasingly "relatives" do too. A Thorwaldson marries a Gonzales, a Chen marries a McDonald, Mrs. Kennedy marries Aristotle Onassis. Consequently each congregation as it follows its relatives and friends disciples many kinds of peoples.

Qualification two is that every large congregation has many small groups meeting around different interests. The choir draws in those of musical ability and obviously will welcome a rich tenor and a lyric soprano, whatever classes or ethnic backgrounds they come from. The leaders of the scout troop and the sewing circle eagerly look for those who want to engage in these activities. Streaming across the bridges must not be distorted to mean limiting a congregation to the relatives of its dominant group. All the data indicate that in urban society using the bridges leads to the inclusion in many small groups of many different kinds of people.

Qualification three is that many congregations already have won most of their own narrowly conceived connections. Thus an Episcopalian congregation in a typical town already has those who are Episcopalian by upbringing or inclination. A Mennonite congregation already includes in its oversight all Mennonites in its parish area. Streaming across the bridges certainly does not mean limiting oneself to such little enclaves.

Common sense is assumed. *Christians*—just because they are one in Christ—in an open-ended society welcome every opportunity to expand the fellowship. They make strangers welcome in the church. They demonstrate inclusiveness. At the same time, Christians should start new congregations in largely unchurched populations. Roman Catholics in France and the Church of England will find that new congregations of working-class men and women, in which leaders of labor unions are the elders or influential members, will evangelize this important segment of French and British society more effectively than bringing a few working-class people into existing middle- and upper-class congregations. The latter, of course, is being and should be done; but it would not be wise to depend exclusively on it.

Streaming across the bridges of friendship and relationship will not normally lead to segregation. If any tendency in that direction is discerned, the principle is being misused.

Qualification four is that congregations and denominations of similar people should recognize that they are tempted to become exclusive and sub-Christian. The very fact that most of their members are of one cut of society makes it easy for them to object to apartheid in far-off lands and to talk about brotherhood while they themselves are not practicing it. It is easy to overlook the Gentiles and Samaritans in their neighborhood. Each "one-class" congregation and denomination, therefore, should lay great stress on the unity of all Christians. All are *one people in Christ.* The missionary obligation of each segmental Church to evangelize across the linguistic, class, and race gulfs which surround it should be heartily emphasized. Black congregations and denominations in the United States, for example, should send out large numbers of missionaries to unevangelized hidden peoples in Asia, Africa, Europe, and other lands. It is high time that the concern blacks feel that other segments of the Church treat *them* fairly be powerfully reinforced by *their* concern *for thousands of other peoples far more deprived than they.* The Mizo Church does well to send out scores of missionaries to other castes and tribes in India. Every Christian is saved to serve.

Furthermore, denominations of the middle class or of the working class should train their ministers together with candidates from denominations which have arisen in other segments of humanity. Often young people's conferences can be planned for Christians of several cultural or racial backgrounds. The youth camp draws together high schoolers or collegians from as many racial groups as possible. It invites speakers from those sections of the Church Universal which are socially farthest away. It continually says, "Remember, we are all children of Adam and therefore brothers and sisters. We are all alike sinners. All alike are saved not by our wisdom or wealth, but by the grace of God. All have equal access to the throne of God. Sensible Christians allow temporary differences to keep the door open to the unconverted; but we reject as heresy any thought that God has made men and women of different materials, and that in consequence there are superior and inferior races. We are one in Christ and we intend to grow more and more obviously one."

The attention of every denomination and every congregation (whether multiethnic or monoethnic) should be riveted on the unreached peoples, on the three billion who have yet to believe, the three billion who "have not Christ," and who therefore do "*not* have eternal life" (I John 5:12). The most helpful activity in bringing about the unity of mankind will be a never ceasing manufacture of bridges to those pieces of the mosaic to which a given congregation has none. *Continuous* crossing of such bridges, praying for those on the other side, sending of missionaries, and cross-cultural evangelism are the most effective ways of building brotherhood and encouraging justice.

The heart of the matter therefore is this: *Multiply congregations of the redeemed inside every piece of the mosaic; create in all congregations a vivid consciousness of oneness in Christ.*

DEFINITE PLANNING TO USE THE BRIDGES

The tendency of churches to devote themselves to maintenance rather than evangelism is strong. Water runs downhill. Intellectual assent to the principle that we should use our bridges will help, but of itself seldom produces ongoing expansion. For that to happen, leaders will have to plan continuous use of the bridges. In a letter to me, Dr. Met Castillo of the Philippine Alliance Church declares,

Adequate plans intended to multiply churches in rural and urban centers of population are urgently needed if we are to fulfil the mandate of the Lord of the Church. . . . Good planning minimizes waste of time, resources and personnel. It insures continuous growth.

His statement is particularly impressive in view of the fact that in the five years after 1975, his denomination planted 339 new churches and increased the membership from 26,830 to 51,629.

One of the most effective plans to come to my attention, and one which could be used in congregations in the United States and every other nation, was the focusing of prayer by every member of the congregation on carefully chosen individuals. The story is this. In twenty-three small-town congregations of one denomination all but one were static. They had stopped growing at about forty members. *They believed that in their circumstances, they could not grow more.* One, however, had grown from the typical forty members to two hundred and twenty! What had caused this phenomenal increase? The town had grown no more than the other twenty-two. Of the several factors which had influenced growth, one was, by the people themselves, called the chief factor.

Each year in January that growing congregation had led every member to select from among his or her relatives and intimates that one person who appeared most winnable. "I like him very much." "We spend much time together." "She thinks a great deal of me." Each member then covenanted to pray daily by name for the salvation of that person. The pastor in the course of the weeks often prayed publicly for "our friends for whom each of us is praying." The whole congregation had a keen consciousness of being God's instrument in the salvation of scores of their own best friends and loved ones. The outcome was summarized by one of the leading women, "We pray and every year God gives us those we pray for—some years ten, and some years twenty, and one year sixty new members." Such focused prayer could be used in all six continents.

CONCLUSION

Of all the factors which influence church growth, none is more immediately available to all Christians than to evangelize the natural fringes of the existing church. This is where most growth occurs. These are the nearest of the fields white to harvest. These are the people who already have some knowledge of Christ and the Christian life. Evangelizing each network of social connection out to its fringes is always sound procedure. True, it must always be supplemented by deliberate attempts to go to the

Samaritans among whom Jews have no relatives and few friends. The huge numbers of unreached peoples of the world warn us not to limit evangelism to networks of friends. New congregations in every *ethnos* on earth are essential strategy if Christians are to obey the Great Commission. Nevertheless, once the new start has been made, *its* network of relatives and intimates is very likely to be its best avenue for expansion. *Use the bridges.*

21

SET GOALS

NOTHING FOCUSES effort like setting a goal. As Christians seek to do effective evangelism, they need to set membership goals. This focuses their efforts on the main task.

Goal setting requires securing needed facts. It reminds pastors and missionaries of their basic responsibilities and available resources. It forces them to arrange their priorities aright. It locks them onto their polestar.

It is essential that Christian leaders align their basic purposes with the eternal purpose of God to save men through faith on Jesus Christ. This is the first step in the consequent growth and development of the Church. Goal setting helps implement such alignment.

World evangelization is a very wide enterprise. It runs *from* pre-evangelism through proclamation, persuasion, baptism or incorporation, growth in grace and knowledge of the Lord, *to* men and women mature in Christ. It inevitably includes corporate aspects of life. Social structures must be Christianized more and more thoroughly. In the academic field, both evangelism in one's own culture and missiology in other cultures are concerned. Both must harness many disciplines and sciences to the one goal of discipling *panta ta ethne*. Sociology, the science of communication, elenctics, anthropology, theory and practice of education, ecumenical relationships, history of evangelism and mission, biblical studies all have substantial contributions to make.

This very wide enterprise, however, must always remember its center—God's unswerving purpose that every knee shall bow. Goal setting helps it to do so. Missiology is not a mishmash of many different ingredients. Rather it is that science whose steady aim is world evangelization in all six continents, Europe as well as Asia, America as well as Africa. The Savior is its center and driveshaft. Evangelization and mission are not a hundred good enterprises all of equal value, it making no difference which gets done and which is omitted. Holistic mission/evangelism must not mean that; instead it must be carried out to the specific end that *all peoples shall*, in accordance with the Master's express command, *be discipled*. The thousands of unreached peoples, the three billion who have yet to believe, stand as rebuke and challenge to all teachers of evangelism and missiology.

Goal setting helps pastors and missionaries keep their priorities pleasing to God. It keeps them from getting lost in a jungle of maintenance jobs and good works. It helps missiologists remember that unless the discipling of *panta ta ethne* is the steady aim, they are, perhaps against their wills, engaged in vague humanitarianism or intellectual exploration, not world evangelization. Whatever Christians do or teach in America or any other land, goal setting helps them remember that their great Head ever leads them and the Holy Spirit ever impels them to world evangelization.

WALKING PAST THE LIONS

Setting membership goals has only recently become popular. Lions have stood in the way. The situation in 1980 and the notable service Peter Wagner and Vergil Gerber have rendered in applying this principle to evangelism and church growth must be seen against the long years when growth goals were neither set nor considered proper.

Churches in North America

Churches in Canada and the United States have seldom set membership goals. Indeed, most of them have never seen a line graph of their past growth or made an estimate of what future growth might be. Were one to ask what the rate of growth of his church was, the average pastor would not know.

American congregations have set goals neither for their total membership, nor for its various parts such as young adults, seniors, middle-aged, and college contingent. The question, "Is the number of your communicant members who are permanent residents of this community decreasing?" would not likely get a firm answer.

Setting goals for membership increase is beyond the thinking of most Christians. They set goals for their business activities, the number of cars they will sell, the amount of steel they will produce, or the number of new buildings they will erect; but not for the number of converts their church will win.

To be sure, evangelistic campaigns are mounted and pastors call on prospects who visit the church or move into the neighborhood, but before 1972 it was a rare congregation or denomination which had studied its past growth and made faith projections as to future growth.

Home mission boards, which had the specific duty of multiplying new congregations in developing parts of the United States—the Midwest, the Southwest, and the Far West—did, of course, do some planning. However, even home mission boards were more likely to do the work and let the results be what they might be, than to set goals. Some home mission boards turned from evangelism and church planting to good works among some minority as their main task. Mission work became not propagating the Gospel and multiplying indigenous churches, but serving depressed sections of the body politic. Home mission boards seldom set goals in regard to the increase of members or congregations.

Missions Overseas

Missions overseas also traditionally have *not* set membership goals. As missionaries arrived in some new land, they faced years of exploratory activities—learning the language, finding a place to stay, overcoming indifference or hostility, maintaining health under difficult conditions, and on and on. Often it was many years before the first converts were won. Sometimes famines, epidemics, revolutions, and the like prevented systematic work. The population had never heard of Christianity or of Christ. In that language the Bible was not available. Under such circumstances, to set a membership goal would have been foolish. Such missionaries did well simply to hang on.

Even after a settled mode of work and a firm base of operations had been established, converts were so slow in appearing that the goal rightly was considered to be "mission work" rather than membership increase. Much opposition to church growth arises precisely because even today missions under such circumstances, feeling that membership increase is chancy and the real task is proclamation of Christ and service of the people, reject the very idea that membership increase should be the criterion. Setting a goal, such as doubling membership in the next ten years, would be considered unwise.

During the early stages of mission in most populations of Planet Earth the task is commending the Gospel by good works, learning the language, translating the Scriptures, producing and distributing Christian literature, and serving the people with medicine, agriculture, education, development, or other tools.

Missionaries tend to say, "As far as members are concerned, let us take what God brings to us, love them and rear them as good Christians. Let us teach them the Bible, habituate them to weekly worship, and train indigenous leaders for them. The tithe must be taught, congregations organized, problems of the new churches solved, and Christians made into good Christians. We must establish a form of Christianity which fits the existing economic level, and the dominant culture. While some noxious elements of the culture (such as idol worship) must be purged, most elements can be brought into the church, which will increasingly take on a thoroughly indigenous hue. The task is not setting membership goals but laboriously and lovingly forming the kind of Christian community which is thoroughly Christian and which feels thoroughly at home in its culture."

Furthermore, promotional concerns weigh heavily in the minds of missionaries and executive secretaries of supporting boards. Where the growth of the Church looks difficult, what will happen if great goals are set and then few are baptized? Will this not discourage supporters? An executive of mission once said to me, "The most dangerous thing I could do, would be to allow the supporters of our mission in Pakistan to think that the Church there could and ought to grow. When they learned that it had not been growing, their giving would drastically decline."

These lions have stood in the way of setting membership goals in America and overseas.

Even more threatening are the theological lions. Because slow growth or no growth has been common, the task has seemed to be that of caring for existing members and their children. A maintenance mentality characterized most congregations and denominations *and was defended on biblical grounds.* Caring for those in the fold was deified and searching for lost sheep was denigrated. Some went so far as to suggest that evangelism was an imperialistic imposing of one's own beliefs on others. Some called all evangelism "self-aggrandisement." Goal setting was viewed as abhorrent to God and contrary to the spirit of Christian kindliness.

It is surprising to what degree the Bible has been read in this light. To sealed-off and declining denominations, the Bible appeared to be speaking exclusively to Christians. For example, in Ephesians the third chapter and the eighteenth verse, Paul, kneeling in prayer, asks God to grant the Ephesian Christians strength "to grasp what is the breadth and length and height and depth of the love of Christ" (NEB). In view of the fact that Paul's prayer begins reminding his readers that "every family on earth" takes its name from the Father, and concludes "from generation to generation evermore," it is clear that the inspired Word is here referring to a love which extends to all mankind throughout all generations. The prayer is that Christ may so dwell in the hearts of Christians that, overcoming their provincialism and tendency to think only of themselves, they will be strong to grasp Christ's purpose that the Gospel be preached to all mankind. Of Christ's love, they are to know its *length* (to earth's remotest bounds), *breadth* (to the myriad societies of mankind), *height* (up through all principalities and powers), and *depth* (to the most desperate needs of the unsaved). Instead of this missionary interpretation of the passage, Christians in static churches take the four words to mean exclusively qualities of Christ's love for Christians and the Church.

The correct interpretation includes both emphases. It is wrong to hold that this Scripture refers exclusively to the unsaved in faraway lands or exclusively to existing Christians. Not only must both emphases be seen in the words, but their outward thrust must be seen to be as fully potent as their inward. Congregations and denominations dominated by a maintenance mentality seldom see this.

With such a defective ethnocentric view of Scripture, it is not surprising that theological lions such as the following should stand, growling at goal setting.

We do not convert. The Holy Spirit does. Consequently it would be impious for us to set goals or to assume that we shall win such and such numbers to Christian faith.

We are commanded to preach the Gospel to the whole creation (Mark 16; Acts 1). We are to let the earth hear His Voice. But we are not commanded to church the nations. God gives the increase as He sees fit.

We are to expect few Christians. The gate is narrow. Many are not going to be saved (Mt. 22:14; Lk. 18:8, etc.).

The task is to make real Christians. To be avoided at all costs is cheap grace. We ought not to rush out and increase our membership. A large number of baptized heathen is not the goal. Care for the flock has abundant biblical support, but we find no impassioned pleas for Christians to surge out in evangelistic efforts. In the July 1979 *International Review of Missions* Lesslie Newbigin wrote:

You cannot find in Paul's letters a single passage where he urges his readers to be more active in evangelism. There is absolutely nothing in the New Testament corresponding to the almost frantic appeals for missionary activity which has been common in Protestant missionary practice (308).

The Lions Are Chained

As Bunyan noted in *Pilgrim's Progress*, lions deter only the fainthearted. As courageous Christians carry out God's will, they find the lions just described securely chained.

The Scriptures must be used intelligently. When the whole inspired Word is read, we find that while the Holy Spirit converts, He operates in most instances through Christians. The Holy Spirit said, "Set apart for me Barnabas and Saul." The Lord said, "Go, disciple *panta ta ethne.*" Paul said, "Imitate me in this tremendous concern I have by all means to win some."

When the Lord said to His disciples, "Whatever you bind on earth will be bound in heaven and whatever you loose on earth will be loosed in heaven," it is difficult to hold that evangelism is mere proclamation. The Lord committed to His followers the duty of persuading men to believe and then purposefully completing the complex tasks of incorporating believers in visible, countable congregations and denominations. The Holy Spirit was certainly at work in all this, *through men and women filled with the Holy Spirit.*

In Acts the eighteenth chapter we read,

He (Paul) argued in the synagogue every Sabbath and persuaded Jews and Greeks. When Silas and Timothy arrived from Macedonia, Paul was occupied with preaching, testifying to the Jews that the Messiah was Jesus. . . . The Lord said to Paul one night, "Speak and do not be silent."

When the Jews dragged Paul before Gallio, the proconsul, they charged him with "persuading men." In view of these passages it is difficult to hold that deliberate plans for persuading men to become followers of Jesus and for incorporating them in churches are in any sense impious. Setting membership goals is in accordance with God's eternal purpose. Goal setting in the service of the Great Commission is pleasing to God. The lions may growl, but they are chained. Scripture is solidly on the side of careful planning for church growth.

THE HISTORY OF GOAL SETTING

Against this background we briefly consider the three thrusts which in the last fifteen years have made the setting of church growth goals such a helpful part of the Christian movement.

Laying the Foundations for Goal Setting

The Bridges of God (1955), in a time of missionary retreat, maintained that great growth of the Church was what God desired. The book compared growth by the mission-station approach to that by the people movement and maintained that God granted both. Sentences such as the following sum up the book.

> In this day the Christian churches can win their most notable victories. Out of imminent disaster . . . they can contribute the only enduring bases of national well-being—great numbers of living churches which fear and love and worship the true and ever-living God (155).

> The peoples who can today be discipled consist of millions of individuals whose salvation *God wills* (156).

> George Fox, at the beginning of that great People Movement which soon brought one in a hundred of the population of England into the Society of Friends, had a vision in which he saw "an innumerable company, as many as motes in the sun which shall come to the One Shepherd and the One Fold." It is given to all of us to see that same vision (157).

No wonder Kenneth Scott Latourette, in the Introduction to the *Bridges of God,* called this one of "the most important books on missionary methods which has appeared in many years."

The first edition of *Understanding Church Growth* (1970) printed what had formed the substance of church growth seminars, classes, lectures, and articles in the preceding fifteen years. From beginning to end it assumed that quantitative growth of the Church was God's will and ought to be measured, depicted, discussed, and made the basis for evangelistic and missionary labors.

Chapter One declared that quantitative church growth was faithfulness to God. Chapter Two explained that search theology (which required no growth at all) was unbiblical and that harvest theology (which required objective finding and folding of the lost) was thoroughly biblical. Chapter Four stressed the utter necessity of recognizing and dispersing the fog which so effectively obscured the real shape and size of Churches. Diagrams in chapter after chapter portrayed amounts of church growth, rates of growth, and history of membership increase. The whole book accustomed readers to the explosive idea that the goal was discipling of all classes and conditions of men, and that such discipling should be measured and charted. Other chapters set forth the main activities of mission—from revivals to social improvements—in terms of their effect on the increase of countable followers of Jesus Christ. The concluding chapter declared that hard, bold plans for membership increase were biblical, respectable, and practicable.

Between 1955 and 1965 these and other church growth concepts burst on the scene. Some Churches and missions welcomed them and found in them new courage and new direction. Some resisted them. In both cases, the growth concepts prepared the ground for goal setting. Had these concepts not ploughed the soil for more than a decade, goal setting anywhere would have been difficult, if not impossible.

At the Institute of Church Growth in Oregon (1961-65) and the School of World Mission in California (1965-70) scores of career missionaries studied a missiology of which the Great Commission was the dynamic center. Missiology included more than Christ's command to disciple all nations. It included comparative religion, sociology and anthropology, missionary methods, biblical studies, theologies of mission, and ecumenical endeavors, but no one of these was its center. None could have created the world mission of the Church. That is uniquely dependent on God's eternal purpose to save people through belief in Jesus Christ, the Savior. God's purpose being to save countable persons, the vast mission enterprise and the foundational concepts of church growth necessarily follow.

Those who studied here went back to their countries resolved to do theology and mission in the light of the clear biblical directives to advance the Gospel and spread the Faith.

In 1963 the Director of the Institute of Church Growth in Eugene, Oregon, applied to many foundations for a substantial grant for a continent-wide survey of church growth in Latin America. In January 1965, he received a grant from Lilly Endowment of $54,000, and by May had secured Messrs. Read, Monterroso, and Johnson as researchers. For the next three years these men (operating out of Pasadena, California, where I had gone as founding dean of the School of Missions) carried on the study of church growth in 17 nations. Carrying out such a survey furnishes innumerable opportunities for impressing on denominations, congregations, mission boards, and missionaries the fact that they are working at an enterprise which can be and ought to be measured and charted.

When *Latin American Church Growth* was published in 1969, its findings fell like a bombshell on the missionary societies at work in Latin America—particularly on the Conservative Evangelical boards, grouped under the EFMA/IFMA standards, whose labors were resulting in relatively little church growth. They believed themselves to be theologically sound, and knew they were working hard, yet they were experiencing less growth than the mainline missionary societies and the Pentecostal Churches. They were troubled.

Consequently, they called a consultation in Elburn, Illinois, in September 1970. More than 50 executives of mission appeared and spent two days discussing ways and means of getting on with their main task. They had never seen an authoritative, quantitative analysis of their labors before. They had been carrying on splendid mission and drinking satisfying draughts of promotional presentations. The landmark book, *Latin American Church Growth*, with its 174 pages of pictorial representations of growth and 209 pages of convincing analysis of the factors governing growth drove them to devise a new vehicle for spreading the eminently useful church growth way of thinking. They asked, "How can we get our missionaries and the pastors of churches in Latin America to see that their basic task is communicating the Gospel to more and more people?" (II Cor. 4:15). Church growth dynamics were leavening the whole lump.

As other researches in church growth were published, they too awakened leaders in many lands. Read's *New Patterns of Church Growth in Brazil* and Shearer's *Wildfire: The Growth of the Church in Korea* had profound influence, Grimley and Robinson's *Nigeria*, Wold's *God's Impatience in Liberia*, Montgomery's *New Testament Fire in the Philippines*, McGavran's *Church Growth in Jamaica*, and Hamilton's *Church Growth in the High Andes* roused mission leaders in many nations to the actual state of the Church. Granting that it is important to know whether the Church is soundly Christian or nominal, it is also important to know whether it is one-tenth of one per cent of the population or half of it; and whether it is growing vigorously or declining.

In 1970 Alan Tippett decided that the constant attack on church growth was sub-biblical and must be ended. He consequently wrote a most influential book, *Church Growth and the Word of God*. The biblical base proved in that and other books freed pastors and leaders from the burden of guilt— that growth was somehow sinful. It proved that the Word of God authorizes church growth.

By 1970 the stage had been set for systematic goal setting as essential missionary strategy. The ground had been plowed and sown. The foundation for the edifice had been laid.

The last step in laying the foundation was taken by Leonard Tuggy. The story is worth telling. He had studied here in 1967-68 and was appointed by the Conservative Baptist Board to the all-Philippine Survey Team. With Ralph Tolliver, he put in more than two years charting the growth of the many denominations which make up the Evangelical Church in the Philippines. The Tuggy-Tolliver research was published in 1971 under the title *Seeing the Church in the Philippines*. Believing ardently in church growth and seeing the great growth possible, in 1971 Tuggy proposed to his Baptist colleagues that they (who at the time had about thirty congregations and 2,000 members) set a 1981 goal of 200 congregations and 10,000 baptized believers! Thus "Operation 200" was born.

While many graduates of this school were working for church growth, and while researches, charts, and revolutionary concepts were stimulating large numbers of pastors and missionaries to communicate the Gospel more effectively, Tuggy's was the first deliberately to set goals. Furthermore, he followed up his goal with a well-thought plan, revised annually. In the light of what growth had been granted, resources were allocated. The goal became the guiding star of the Conservative Baptist Church and its assisting mission. The foundation was now complete. Goal setting was about to become popular. Walls would soon be erected. The strategy of mission would be strengthened by a most effective tool.

Building Walls or Setting Goals Overseas

Walls were about to be built on the theoretical and theological foundations which required open acknowledgment of countable Christians as a legitimate indication of faithfulness in Christian Mission. Peter Wagner and Vergil Gerber played the key role in building those walls—seeing goal setting as a necessary strategy of evangelization and demonstrating how to carry it out.

Wagner had just pointed out the urgency of strategy in his influential book, *Frontiers of Missionary Strategy* (1971), and had trumpeted: "Strategy cannot be accurately planned or effectively evaluated without measurable goals" (132). He further declared that the *ultimate objective* of all evangelistic goals must be increase in the numbers of faithful followers of Jesus Christ. "The inexorable goals of any evangelistic program should be the making of disciples" (145).

In late 1971 the Evangelical Committee on Latin America (ECLA) named Wagner, ably assisted by Vergil Gerber and Edward Murphy, to conduct a pilot workshop in Venezuela. The purpose was to lay heavily on the hearts of the participating pastors that *making disciples* was a necessary and measurable objective of their labors. The workshop was held in June 1972 and 47 pastors attended. In the July 1972 issue of Church Growth Bulletin, Wagner tells the story of that historic venture.

In November 1973 *Church Growth Bulletin* published the following summary of the Venezuela workshop program, which by that time had become standard for workshops in many other countries.

Spanish speaking pastors of ordinary churches brought records (some woefully inadequate) of their membership during the past ten years. Workshop leaders taught them how to analyze, chart, and understand the growth which had taken place and was taking place. That provided a background of reality. The pastors were talking about their own problems, tasks and opportunities. They were not reacting against new North American schemes! In that setting it became fruitful to set forth church growth principles—they could then be seen as "something *we* need." The third step was to ask the participants, on the basis of their past experience (in faith and after prayer), to project the growth they believed God was calling on them to attempt. The fourth step was to calculate what the average rates of growth during the last ten years had been, and during the coming five years would be. The last step was to plan for another workshop a year later, attended by these same men, to see what in fact had happened.

The Venezuelan experience furnished a base for a significant advance in church multiplying evangelism. Dr. Gerber prepared a small book, *A Manual For Evangelism/Church Growth,* which told how any group of pastors and/ or missionaries could hold a church growth workshop.

All around the world Christian leaders, who had been imbibing church growth ideas and who believed that the first business of the Church was to lead men and women to Christ, were looking for a tool they could use to get pastors thinking about the vast opportunities for the spread of the Christian religion. The Gerber manual (soon to be republished as *God's Way to Keep a Church Going and Growing*) was that tool. As soon as leaders discovered it, they held similar workshops and planned for others. Dr. Gerber was flooded with invitations from many nations to hold demonstration workshops there. In August 1973 he took a team with him to Kenya, Nigeria, and Ivory Coast and, similarly, year after year to many lands of earth. By 1978 he had been in 48 different countries. *God's Way* had been published in 32 languages and translated into several more. After a pause in 1978-79 for health reasons, he was again stimulating the Churches in every corner of the globe to set growth goals and showing them how to do so. His influence has been world-wide.

One of the basic emphases of the church growth movement is that methods should be evaluated in the light of whether they actually produce growth. Methods which have worked somewhere else or "ought to work," but which add few if any to Christ's Body are, alas, all too common. One of the gratifying features of the Wagner-Gerber thrust around the world is that in many regions, after goal setting in seminars and workshops, congregations and denominations have shown marked growth. In the Philippine Islands, for example, from 1964-1974, the organized churches of four denominations (Conservative Baptist, Alliance, Southern Baptist, and Foursquare) increased from 1,148 to 1,331—a net increase of 183 congregations. Then after the 1974 Church Growth Workshop, called and sponsored by James Montgomery and led by Drs. Gerber and McGavran, the same denominations in only four years planted 879 new churches. The Decadal Growth Rate (how *fast* new churches were being established) for the ten-year period was 16 per cent, and for the four-year period 255 per cent. Membership also increased significantly. The careful 1980 research of Robert Waymire sets forth the facts in clear detail. Of course, a large part of the credit for this explosive growth must be given to the foundations laid between 1964 and 1974 by Montgomery, Tuggy, Tolliver, Castillo, Arthur, and many other participants in the evangelistic campaigns and church growth thinking of that decade. The goal-setting walls were built on those foundations.

It must not be supposed that explosive growth everywhere follows goal setting. Where there has been no prior laying of the foundations and little follow-up, goal setting often results only in a short spurt of growth. In a highly resistant population, it may result in no growth at all.

Nevertheless, across the world, the outcome of goal setting has been gratifying. Where goals have been set, most churches have grown. Goal setting is a most rewarding step in carrying out the Great Commission.

Setting Goals in America

In 1971, the need for church growth thinking in Canada and the United States was enormous. Out of a combined population of about 221,000,000 only 65 million, at a generous estimate, were committed Christians. About 90 million were nominal Christians, and about 66 million were either lapsed Christians or purposefully non-Christian men and women. Most denominations (Protestant and Roman Catholic alike) were either plateaued or declining and most Christian leaders were saying that they wanted quality not quantity. The Church apparently would soon follow Europe's lead and enter a post-Christian era. The attention of the Church was on other things. Indeed, the stage was set against acknowledging church growth as a desirable goal. While the church growth movement had achieved considerable acceptance overseas, in 1971 it still elicited smiles when mentioned in America.

The awaking of America to church growth owes a great deal to two men—Peter Wagner and Winfield Arn. In 1971 Professor Wagner, convinced that America needed church growth, enrolled prominent pastors and lay leaders living in and around Pasadena in a regular seminary course in church growth. He asked me to team teach it with him. We met in the Lake Avenue Congregational Church every Tuesday morning from seven to ten. Tuition was charged and seminary credit given.

After the various rationalizations of defeat which were common coin in ministerial circles had been examined, held up to the light, gently laughed at, and laid to rest, the pastors ate up church growth. It was thoroughly germane to their deepest convictions. They began to chart the past growth of their congregations and to envisage future growth. Of course they were interested in more Christians! In this they were unconsciously demonstrating the way thousands of other gatherings of pastors and people in the seventies and eighties would feel.

Dr. Winfield Arn was a member of that famous class. At the time he was Director of Christian Education for the Pacific Southwest Conference of the Evangelical Covenant Church in America. As he saw the critical need for growth and the potential of the church growth movement, he determined to resign as Director and start the Institute for American Church Growth. He would gather ministers into seminars, give them two or three days of concentrated study of church growth, and send them back to turn their churches around. He would publish a paper called "Church Growth: America." He would make sound-and-color films preaching church growth. His only source of income would be the registration fees which those attending the seminars would pay. His program, starting from zero in 1972, in 1980 was training twenty thousand pastors and key lay leaders each year, and spending over $300,000 a year doing it. His films "How to Grow a Church," "Reach Out and Grow," "They Said it Couldn't Be Done," and "Planned Parenthood" have been seen in tens of thousands of congregations. In all of these, recognizing the biblical imperative to make disciples, charting past growth, and setting realistic and devout goals for future membership increase became acceptable procedure.

Dr. Wagner, too, in addition to his duties as professor of Church Growth at Fuller Seminary's School of Missions, turned the Fuller Evangelistic Association into another seminar-holding organization and reached other hundreds of congregations. Often Arn and Wagner spoke from the same platform in the same seminars. Naturally Wagner, whose main thrust was strategy of evangelism, emphasized setting goals.

The denominations started catching fire. For example, in the decade preceding 1975, the United Methodist Church had declined from eleven to under ten million. Its main emphasis was social action, brotherhood, peace, and other such causes. Evangelism was at a low ebb. It became obvious that unless the decline was reversed, the denomination would grow less and less influential. The Methodists appointed Dr. George Hunter, Professor of Evangelism at Perkins Theological Seminary in Texas, as Executive for Evangelism of the United Methodist Board of Discipleship, and gave him a quarter million dollars a year budget and a mandate to reverse the downward trend. He, like Wagner and Arn, started holding church growth seminars, writing church growth books, promoting the reading of church growth books, and producing a church growth film for Methodists. He studied every aspect of Methodist increase and decline. Under his guidance Methodists started to see the quantitative dimensions of their denomination. They, too, began to set goals.

The Nazarene Church, which began in 1906, had grown very vigorously in the early years but started slowing down in the fifties. By 1970, with a membership of 600,000, it showed signs of plateauing. In 1974, it threw itself into the recovery of growth. Its national leaders called meetings of all pastors. Dr. Raymond Hurn, head of the Home Mission Board, committed his board to planting many new churches and allocated men and money to that goal.

As I am writing this chapter, the September 1979 issue of *Hot Line*, the news sheet of the prestigious Reformed Church in America, is before me. On the first page it declares, "Church growth is marching on all across the country."

Many other denominations and thousands of individual congregations to varying degrees began to think quantitatively about church growth.

None of the denominations turned away from qualitative to quantitative growth. Rather they saw that any true qualitative growth would of necessity be concerned that the lost be found and brought to the fold. They recognized that a quality unconcerned with the salvation of multitudes would be doubtfully Christian.

All these activities of congregations, denominations, and church leaders threw the spotlight of truth on the growth and decline of Churches. All necessitated counting Christians and setting goals for increase of members. By 1980 it had become commonplace in thousands of congregations to see the complex subject of church growth in scientific detail. Various strands of growth had been charted, analyzed, graphed, discussed, and viewed in time perspective. Goal setting had become thoroughly at home in the American Church on both sides of the Canadian border.

However, much remained to be done. Of the more than 300,000 American congregations, only a fraction had been aroused to church growth.

Great segments of the Church slept on. Even some of those who had drawn up church growth goals, failing to allocate resources to growth, had sadly concluded that this latest fad had not worked. At the beginning of the eighties, great growth of the Church was still not assured. But goal setting was helping churches evaluate what they had done and set forth clearly what they intended to do.

How to Set Goals

1. Three Essential Steps

The first step is to emphasize that evangelism is a thoroughly biblical activity. In the midst of hundreds of good things to do, Christians should be clear that a chief and irreplaceable task is always that of bringing unbelievers to saving faith in Christ and membership in his Church. Finding the lost, bringing them back to the fold, "teaching them all things," and sending them out to find others, is a main thrust, perhaps *the* main thrust of the New Testament. Goal setting should start by teaching that measurable church growth is biblically required.

The second step is to chart past growth. Occasionally the chart will go back fifty years; but more often ten years is sufficient—and much easier to do.

Total membership of the congregation or the cluster of congregations concerned for each year should be ascertained and a simple line graph constructed which will show the rises, plateaus, and declines which have occurred.

In the total membership there are various strands—the settled members and the transients, the landowners and the renters, the college students and the business community, the young adults and the senior citizens. In Southern Baptist congregations on the West Coast, between 1935 and 1965 there tended to be Southerners-who-had-moved-west and others. Charts showing how much of the congregation each group made up were revealing. In Nairobi, charting showed that congregations worshiping in Swahili and composed of Christians from several different tribes did not grow as well as congregations composed very largely of one tribe and worshiping in that tribal language. Missionaries and pastors will find charting the more important strands in their membership rewarding.

As indicated in Chapter Five, it is desirable to know where the members come from. Are they children of existing members? Or Christians transferring in as they move to this locality? Or converts from the world? Realistic goals must be set in the light of such facts.

Charting past growth involves calculating the rate of growth. If a church has been growing at 2 per cent a year without any special attention to evangelism, it is reasonable to judge that as the congregation emphasizes evangelism a much higher rate will be possible.

Pastors and missionaries often ask whether the memberships of daughter congregations should be included when the growth of the mother church is being calculated. The answer is both yes and no. Certainly, the mother church is entitled to credit for the new congregations and their initial growth. At the same time, since they are now separate congregations the chart should make that clear.

The third step is to make faith projections. These are considered estimates as to what growth God is going to grant this congregation, or denomination, facing these circumstances and made up of these strands of members. Are we going to grow more from the Appalachian factory workers or the business community? Does membership increase more from university students or people who buy houses in this suburb? In Madras City, will congregations increase more from Mala or Madiga background converts? In Mindanao, will our denomination increase more rapidly from the Christian immigrants or the tribal populations? In Guatemala—on the basis of the charts of past growth and other pertinent facts—should we anticipate more growth from the Quiches or the Mams?

In making projections we are confident that the present rate of biological growth will continue. It requires no faith to assume that. So the faith projection should be on top of an assured biological growth. Similarly, if in the past ten years three-fourths of all growth has come from country Christians pouring into our factory town, faith projections should be calculated on top of a large transfer growth. If a people movement is in full swing, the faith projection will be much larger than if the congregation faces continuation of the one-by-one-against-the-current pattern of growth.

Faith projections are made in prayer and confident assumption of the continued presence of the Holy Spirit. Faith projections are what we ask God to grant us. As responsible stewards of His grace we ask what we believe is in accordance with His will.

2. Adjusting to Specific Situations

The discipling of *panta ta ethne* goes forward in the midst of rapid social change. Huge urbanizations are changing the nature of whole populations. Printing, universal literacy, radio, and television give wings to radically new ideas. Expectations rise. Demands increase. Marxists teach that capitalistic nations are sucking the blood of the developing world.

Cuban troops "liberate" African countries. Half the population of Cambodia is wiped out. Two million Chinese are hounded out of Vietnam. An "amoral society" develops in great areas of the inner cities of America. Secularism and materialism become the religions of hundreds of millions. One land opens and another closes to missionaries.

Missions and evangelization proceed in this kind of world. It is in this milieu that congregations and denominations grow and decline. Each one, therefore, must set its growth goals in the light of its own specific situation. All these factors and many more have influenced the past growth and will influence future growth.

Each occasion of goal setting is unique. When, after the death of Stephen, a great persecution befell the Church and forced most Christians to flee Jerusalem, great growth in the villages of Judea became immediately possible. There is no indication that the apostles set growth goals; but when they heard that the refugee Christians went everywhere preaching the Good News of God's message (Acts 8:4), they surely realized they stood on the edge of great growth. A pastor in a county whose population is rapidly increasing from inward migration will set larger goals than a pastor in one from which multitudes are moving away.

3. Calculating the Average Annual Growth Rate

A most useful instrument in estimating future growth is the Average Annual Growth Rate (AAGR). In addition to knowing the absolute numbers (this church grew from 149 to 191 in two years) leaders ought to know how *fast* it was growing. What was its AAGR? It is possible for it *to continue to grow at that rate*. If a car is going at thirty miles an hour, it is reasonable to assume that it can continue at that speed.

The AAGR is especially useful in freeing Christian leaders from illusions generated by absolute numbers. For example, if Church H of one hundred grows to two hundred in five years, it has grown much faster than Church S of six hundred which has grown to seven hundred in the same time. Both have added 100 members, but the first has an average annual growth *rate* of 15 while the second has one of only 3.

Dr. Winter is the missiologist who has emphasized the concept and the methods essential for computing the AAGR. The process is the same as computing interest compounded annually. Just as the interest in a savings account is reinvested to draw further interest, so in churches new converts can be led to effective evangelism by which new members (which the old Christians would not have won) are added to the Church. The congregation which keeps up a high rate of growth year after year obeys the Great Commission better than one which slows down in the rate of growth.

The formula for figuring the Average Annual Growth Rate is as follows:

1. Divide ending membership by starting membership.
2. Multiply the resulting quotient by 100, i.e., move the decimal point two spaces to the right.
3. Subtract 100. The result is the Basic Percent—BP in the following Table of Average Annual Growth Rates, made available by Dr. Winter.
4. In the lefthand column (BP) of the table look for the Basic Percent you have obtained. Read across to the figure under the number of years involved. That is the AAGR you are seeking.

For example, we use the formula and the table to calculate the AAGR for Church S above.

1. Divide 700 by 600. Resulting Quotient: *1.1666*
2. Move decimal point two spaces to the right: *116.66*
3. Subtract 100: *16* (i.e., 16%)
4. At 16% in the left column read across to the five-year column. The number there is 3.01%. Church S is growing at the rate of 3% per year, or has an AAGR of 3.

The Table of Average Annual Growth Rates can be used in magical ways. It is not necessary to know why the procedures described give these results. Just follow the directions. Round off figures to the nearest whole number. If the figure lies between two lines or columns, make the approximation needed. The memberships you are dealing with are not exact. This makes it permissible to use such approximations. Vertical Column 10 and the Horizontal Line at 100% are particularly useful.

For example, we have just calculated that Church S has an Average Annual Growth Rate of 3. *What is its Decadal Growth Rate?*

Directions: Find 3.01 in Column 10 . . . 3.05
On *that line,* read back to column BP . . . 35
Church S has a Decadal Growth Rate of 35%. It is growing at 35% per decade.

Assuming that Church S continues to grow at an AAGR of 3 or a DGR of 35, *how many years will it take it to double?*

Directions: On the 100% Horizontal Line, between 3.53 and 2.81, place this AAGR—3.01
Look *up* at the number of years heading these columns— 20 and 25
It will take Church S approximately 23 years to double.

TABLE OF AVERAGE ANNUAL GROWTH RATES

Years / BP	1	2	3	4	5	6	7	8	9	10	15	20	25	50	75
1%	1.00%	0.50%	0.33%	0.25%	0.20%	0.17%	0.14%	0.12%	0.11%	0.10%	0.07%	0.05%	0.04%	0.02%	0.01%
2%	2.00%	1.00%	0.66%	0.50%	0.40%	0.33%	0.28%	0.25%	0.22%	0.20%	0.13%	0.10%	0.08%	0.04%	0.03%
4%	4.00%	1.98%	1.32%	0.99%	0.79%	0.66%	0.56%	0.49%	0.44%	0.39%	0.26%	0.20%	0.16%	0.08%	0.05%
6%	6.00%	2.96%	1.96%	1.47%	1.17%	0.98%	0.84%	0.73%	0.65%	0.58%	0.39%	0.29%	0.23%	0.12%	0.08%
8%	8.00%	3.92%	2.60%	1.94%	1.55%	1.29%	1.11%	0.97%	0.86%	0.77%	0.51%	0.39%	0.31%	0.15%	0.10%
10%	10.00%	4.88%	3.23%	2.41%	1.92%	1.60%	1.37%	1.20%	1.06%	0.96%	0.64%	0.48%	0.38%	0.19%	0.13%
12%	12.00%	5.83%	3.85%	2.87%	2.29%	1.91%	1.63%	1.43%	1.27%	1.14%	0.76%	0.57%	0.45%	0.23%	0.15%
14%	14.00%	6.77%	4.46%	3.33%	2.66%	2.21%	1.89%	1.65%	1.47%	1.32%	0.88%	0.66%	0.53%	0.26%	0.17%
16%	16.00%	7.70%	5.07%	3.78%	3.01%	2.50%	2.14%	1.87%	1.66%	1.50%	0.99%	0.74%	0.60%	0.30%	0.20%
18%	18.00%	8.63%	5.67%	4.22%	3.37%	2.80%	2.39%	2.09%	1.86%	1.67%	1.11%	0.83%	0.66%	0.33%	0.22%
20%	20.00%	9.54%	6.27%	4.66%	3.71%	3.09%	2.64%	2.31%	2.05%	1.84%	1.22%	0.92%	0.73%	0.37%	0.24%
25%	25.00%	11.80%	7.72%	5.74%	4.56%	3.79%	3.24%	2.83%	2.51%	2.26%	1.50%	1.12%	0.90%	0.45%	0.30%
30%	30.00%	14.02%	9.14%	6.78%	5.39%	4.47%	3.82%	3.33%	2.96%	2.66%	1.76%	1.32%	1.05%	0.53%	0.35%
35%	35.00%	16.19%	10.52%	7.79%	6.19%	5.13%	4.38%	3.82%	3.39%	3.05%	2.02%	1.51%	1.21%	0.60%	0.40%
40%	40.00%	18.32%	11.87%	8.78%	6.96%	5.77%	4.92%	4.30%	3.81%	3.42%	2.27%	1.70%	1.35%	0.68%	0.45%
45%	45.00%	20.42%	13.19%	9.73%	7.71%	6.39%	5.45%	4.75%	4.21%	3.79%	2.51%	1.88%	1.50%	0.75%	0.50%
50%	50.00%	22.47%	14.47%	10.67%	8.45%	6.99%	5.96%	5.20%	4.61%	4.14%	2.74%	2.05%	1.64%	0.81%	0.54%
60%	60.00%	26.49%	16.96%	12.47%	9.86%	8.15%	6.94%	6.05%	5.36%	4.81%	3.18%	2.38%	1.90%	0.94%	0.63%
80%	80.00%	34.16%	21.64%	15.83%	12.47%	10.29%	8.76%	7.62%	6.75%	6.05%	4.00%	2.98%	2.38%	1.18%	0.79%
100%	100.00%	41.42%	25.99%	18.92%	14.87%	12.25%	10.41%	9.05%	8.01%	7.18%	4.73%	3.53%	2.81%	1.40%	0.93%
120%	120.00%	48.32%	30.06%	21.79%	17.08%	14.04%	11.92%	10.36%	9.16%	8.20%	5.40%	4.02%	3.20%	1.59%	1.06%
140%	140.00%	54.92%	33.89%	24.47%	19.14%	15.71%	13.32%	11.56%	10.22%	9.15%	6.01%	4.47%	3.56%	1.77%	1.17%
160%	160.00%	61.25%	37.51%	26.98%	21.06%	17.26%	14.63%	12.69%	11.20%	10.03%	6.58%	4.89%	3.90%	1.93%	1.28%
180%	180.00%	67.33%	40.95%	29.36%	22.87%	18.72%	15.85%	13.74%	12.12%	10.84%	7.11%	5.28%	4.20%	2.08%	1.38%

200%	200.00%	73.21%	44.22%	31.61%	24.57%	20.09%	16.99%	14.72%	12.98%	11.61%	7.60%	5.65%	4.49%	2.22%	1.48%
220%	220.00%	78.89%	47.36%	33.75%	26.19%	21.39%	18.08%	15.65%	13.80%	12.33%	8.06%	5.99%	4.76%	2.35%	1.56%
240%	240.00%	84.39%	50.37%	35.79%	27.73%	22.63%	19.10%	16.53%	14.57%	13.02%	8.50%	6.31%	5.02%	2.43%	1.65%
260%	260.00%	89.74%	53.26%	37.74%	29.20%	23.80%	20.08%	17.36%	15.30%	13.67%	8.91%	6.61%	5.26%	2.59%	1.72%
280%	280.00%	94.94%	56.05%	39.62%	30.60%	24.92%	21.01%	18.16%	15.99%	14.28%	9.31%	6.90%	5.49%	2.71%	1.80%
300%	300.00%	100.00%	58.74%	41.42%	31.95%	25.99%	21.90%	18.92%	16.65%	14.87%	9.68%	7.18%	5.70%	2.81%	1.87%
320%	320.00%	104.94%	61.34%	43.16%	33.24%	27.02%	22.75%	19.65%	17.29%	15.43%	10.04%	7.44%	5.91%	2.91%	1.93%
340%	340.00%	109.76%	63.86%	44.83%	34.49%	28.01%	23.57%	20.35%	17.89%	15.97%	10.38%	7.69%	6.11%	3.01%	2.00%
360%	360.00%	114.48%	66.31%	46.45%	35.69%	28.96%	24.36%	21.02%	18.48%	16.49%	10.71%	7.93%	6.29%	3.10%	2.06%
380%	380.00%	119.09%	68.69%	48.02%	36.85%	29.88%	25.12%	21.66%	19.04%	16.98%	11.02%	8.16%	6.48%	3.19%	2.11%
400%	400.00%	123.61%	71.00%	49.53%	37.97%	30.77%	25.85%	22.28%	19.58%	17.46%	11.33%	8.38%	6.65%	3.27%	2.17%
450%	450.00%	134.52%	76.52%	53.14%	40.63%	32.86%	27.58%	23.75%	20.85%	18.59%	12.04%	8.90%	7.06%	3.47%	2.30%
500%	500.00%	144.95%	81.71%	56.51%	43.10%	34.80%	29.17%	25.10%	22.03%	19.62%	12.69%	9.37%	7.43%	3.65%	2.42%
600%	600.00%	164.58%	91.29%	62.66%	47.58%	38.31%	32.05%	27.54%	24.14%	21.48%	13.85%	10.22%	8.09%	3.97%	2.63%
700%	700.00%	182.84%	100.00%	68.18%	51.57%	41.42%	34.59%	29.68%	25.99%	23.11%	14.87%	10.96%	8.67%	4.25%	2.81%
800%	800.00%	200.00%	108.01%	73.21%	55.18%	44.22%	36.87%	31.61%	27.65%	24.57%	15.78%	11.61%	9.19%	4.49%	2.97%
900%	900.00%	216.23%	115.44%	77.83%	58.49%	46.78%	38.95%	33.35%	29.15%	25.89%	16.59%	12.20%	9.65%	4.71%	3.12%
1000%	1000.00%	231.66%	122.40%	82.12%	61.54%	49.13%	40.85%	34.95%	30.53%	27.10%	17.33%	12.74%	10.07%	4.91%	3.25%
1500%	1500.00%	300.00%	151.98%	100.00%	74.11%	58.74%	48.60%	41.42%	36.08%	31.95%	20.30%	14.87%	11.73%	5.70%	3.77%
2000%	2000.00%	358.26%	175.89%	114.07%	83.84%	66.10%	54.49%	46.31%	40.25%	35.59%	22.50%	16.44%	12.95%	6.28%	4.14%
2500%	2500.00%	409.90%	196.25%	125.81%	91.86%	72.12%	59.27%	50.27%	43.62%	38.52%	24.26%	17.69%	13.92%	6.73%	4.44%
3000%	3000.00%	456.78%	214.14%	135.96%	98.73%	77.24%	63.32%	53.61%	46.46%	40.97%	25.73%	18.73%	14.72%	7.11%	4.69%
3500%	3500.00%	500.00%	230.19%	144.95%	104.77%	81.71%	66.85%	56.51%	48.91%	43.10%	26.99%	19.62%	15.41%	7.43%	4.89%
4000%	4000.00%	540.31%	244.82%	153.04%	110.16%	85.69%	69.98%	59.07%	51.08%	44.97%	28.09%	20.40%	16.01%	7.71%	5.08%
4500%	4500.00%	578.23%	258.30%	160.43%	115.06%	89.29%	72.80%	61.38%	53.02%	46.65%	29.08%	21.10%	16.55%	7.96%	5.24%
5000%	5000.00%	614.14%	270.84%	167.23%	119.54%	92.57%	75.36%	63.47%	54.79%	48.17%	29.97%	21.72%	17.03%	8.18%	5.38%
6000%	6000.00%	681.02%	293.65%	179.47%	127.54%	98.41%	79.91%	67.17%	57.90%	50.85%	31.53%	22.82%	17.87%	8.57%	5.63%
7000%	7000.00%	742.61%	314.08%	190.28%	134.56%	103.49%	83.85%	70.38%	60.58%	53.15%	32.87%	23.76%	18.59%	8.90%	5.85%
8000%	8000.00%	800.00%	332.67%	200.00%	140.82%	108.01%	87.34%	73.21%	62.95%	55.18%	34.04%	24.57%	19.22%	9.19%	6.03%
9000%	9000.00%	853.94%	349.79%	208.86%	146.50%	112.08%	90.49%	75.74%	65.07%	57.00%	35.08%	25.30%	19.77%	9.44%	6.20%
10000%	******* %	904.99%	365.70%	217.02%	151.69%	115.80%	93.34%	78.05%	66.99%	58.65%	36.03%	25.96%	20.27%	9.67%	6.35%

Suppose a congregation or denomination faces an important date seven years away. It would like to increase its membership toward a target of a 50% increase. What is the necessary Average Annual Growth Rate?

Directions: Find 50% in the BP column.
Run over to the 7 year column.
5.96% is the AAGR needed to reach that target in 7 years.

We suggest that the reader, following the formula and the directions, calculate the Average Annual Growth Rate, the Decadal Growth Rate, and "the number of years it will take to double" for each of the following churches. The correct answers are given in the parentheses following.

Church H grew from 100 to 200 in five years. (14.87, 300, 5 years)

Church D grew from 40 to 90 in four years. (22.50, 750, 3½ years)

Church J grew from 200 to 220 in eight years. (1.20, 13, 60 years)

Use the Average Annual Growth Rate Table with cases of growth you know until you can easily find AAGR, DGR, and years to double.

Cautions

The likelihood that the Decadal Growth Rate really represents what the congregation or denomination can do, is much greater if the membership figures for *ten years* are used. If on the basis of two years' actual experience one calculates a Decadal Growth Rate, it is an unreliable indicator. The congregation concerned may have been enjoying a spurt of growth or suffering a brief period of decline. Neither will necessarily continue. But if one can honestly say, "During the past ten years this congregation grew from 112 to 336," then, other things being equal, it would be fair to assume that it could continue at that rate.

Similarly, if a cluster of congregations has been part of a people movement to Christ and has in consequence been experiencing rapid growth, its rate of growth can be projected only if it is assumed that the people movement will continue, supported by increased resources.

In the two or three years following goal setting and church growth seminars, when the attention of the leaders concerned is focused on church growth and they know that they will be reporting their growth at the next annual meeting, the AAGR is likely to be high. It will likely continue at that rate *if the same motivation is continued.*

In 1972 Quentin Nordyke of the Oregon Friends researched growth from the Aymara tribes in Bolivia. He noted that if the Friends Church continued to grow at 13.6 per cent (which had been its growth rate for the last 13 years), by 1980 the Church would number 40,000 and by 1990 it would number 220,000 (Nordyke, 1972:140, 145).

He pointed out that this was not a prediction, but *was* possible. He might have said that it was possible, provided that the Aymara Church continued vital and evangelistic, and that the Oregon Friends continued to pour in resources which bore the same relationship to the power and size of the Church that their missionaries and money had borne during the years 1959 1972.

Factors affecting church growth are so many that long-range predictions are at best approximations. Nevertheless, it is reasonable to assume: 1) that, given the same motivation and resources, what has taken place by way of growth in the past ten years will continue; and 2) that, given greatly increased motivation and resources, growth can be significantly increased. Goal setting assumes that motivation and resources will be not only continued but increased. Methods will be improved. Priorities will be rectified in the light of Scripture and focused on carrying out the Great Commission and reaching the 3 billion who have yet to believe.

22

MAKE HARD, BOLD PLANS

IN MUCH evangelism, it is common to assume that church growth will take place without planning, i.e. that church planting (proclamation of the Gospel by word and deed resulting in conversions and a banding together of converts into congregations) is an indirect outcome. Evangelism, it is frequently believed, consists of many preparatory activities, many ancillary enterprises, many years of seed-sowing, many decades of shepherding, educating, and developing a few congregations, and many attempts to help churches apply Christianity to all of life. As the whole intricate operation is carried forward, church growth will take place, it is held, in whatever degree is pleasing to God and according to His timetable. After many years' labor, the church starts growing in a way no one could have foretold. Church growth is after a fashion, the main aim, but it takes place chiefly as leaders do sound Christian work and do not fret about whether the church is growing or not.

During the last thirty years a growing body of ministers and missionaries, and perhaps a majority of those who direct old-line missions, would modify the sentence above which reads: Church growth is, after a fashion, the main aim. Their modifications would be many, but a typical one would read as follows: "Carrying on the whole program of God in the world is the mission of the Church. While winning men to Christian faith is undoubtedly part of the program, it is by no means the chief part. In places church-planting evangelism must be muted, so that other instruments in the orchestra may be heard. Christian unity, racial harmony, economic justice, service of the poor and ignorant, education of the existing churches, and many other emphases—all are parts of mission." Leaders of these convictions assume that church growth may or may not take place as the vast general program is quietly carried forward; but since *mission* is being carried on, church growth really does not matter.

In line with this assumption, pastors, lay leaders, and even some missionaries do their assigned work whether churches grow or not. Sometimes duties are assigned by the mission, sometimes by the Church. This pastor concentrates on exegetical preaching, that one on shepherding the flock. This missionary teaches in a theological training school, that one runs a hospital and the third "does student work" or evangelistic touring. All carry out their assignments on the unformulated assumption that *as each does his work men will be reconciled to God in Jesus Christ, to the extent that they can be.*

The growing tendency of Africasian Churches to request specialist missionaries ("who can do things our national leaders cannot") and of boards to send out builders, radio technicians, trained nurses, physicians, agricultural experts, accountants, translators, and teachers in theological training schools greatly increases the number of missionaries who say, "I am not responsible for propagating the Gospel. I do part of the total task. Others do their parts. The national Church plays her part. No one is responsible to see that the whole effort does multiply churches, but I hope that is the outcome. I serve men, proclaim the Gospel, witness to Jesus Christ by word and kindly deed, and church growth takes place (or does not) according to circumstances." Others say briefly, "I am friendly to church growth, but it is not my job."

In North America and Europe, many congregations believe substantially this same doctrine but phrase it in ways fitting to local churches. "We carry on our program, worship God regularly, have a good Sunday School, keep the building neat and beautiful, and are friendly to visitors. We have a remarkable choir and a good kindergarten. But despite all this effort, like many other congregations, this one has been declining. We face a very indifferent population."

Theological rationalization of this position is very common. Some lean heavily on verses like Mark 16:15 and believe that the task is done when the Gospel is proclaimed by literature, radio, voice, or kindly act—whether any believe or not, whether any churches are established or not. Others argue, with less biblical justification, that the era of planting churches is over . . . still others, that planting churches is not the chief purpose of missions in any case. Thus J. C. Hoekendijk, arguing that real evangelism must seek to create (not churches but) outposts of the Kingdom of God in all its perfect purity, love, and power, most vigorously rejects "the misconception" that evangelism is

> the planting of the Church (or even the extension of the Church). This (misconception) has a respectable past. In the seventeenth century Voetius defined as the aim of missions the *plantatio ecclesiae* . . . (but) . . . planting the Church in this institutional way of thinking cannot be the aim of missions. Evangelism and churchification are not identical and very often they are each other's bitterest enemies . . . it is impossible to think of *plantatio ecclesiae* as the end of evangelism (1963:7, 8).

The ease with which Dr. Hoekendijk dismisses church planting as an aim of mission, despite the fact that it was what the apostle Paul devoted himself to and what the founders of the modern missionary enterprise unitedly proclaimed, indicates the strength of the pernicious modern tendency to regard the main task as something else. Church growth will take place, and should take place, if at all, without special effort, as a by-product of the Christian life. Hoekendijk seems to argue that if the *shalom* of God is there, the institutional form of the Church will, of course, appear. If one could disregard biological reality, he might similarly argue that if the living germ is present in an egg, no shell is needed. Sooner or later the living germ will create its own shell.

Fear of ecclesiastical aggrandizement, failure of nerve in postwar Europe, shock of loss of empire, jealousy for the position of Christ rather than the Church, defensive thinking induced by lack of church planting, and other factors all tempt churchmen to play down plans for the actual communication of the Gospel, i.e. the establishment of cells of believing, baptized Christians open to the irradiation of the Holy Spirit and alive to the clamant needs of men and societies.

The documents of Vatican II on mission indicate that the Church of Rome is much closer to the New Testament Church in its concept of mission than some Protestant leaders who have captured the mainline missionary societies and in the sixties and seventies were defining mission to mean everything but the communication of the Gospel and the increase of believers. Harvey Hoekstra's *The WCC and the Demise of Evangelism* is a sober and well-documented account of how this happened. In some reaches of the Church to aim for growth has become a sin. Correct procedure—they think—is to live as socially concerned Christians, assuming that evangelism will occur, as much as it should, without special effort.

THIS ASSUMPTION A SERIOUS ERROR

As we seek to understand church growth we should recognize that this common assumption is a serious mistake. Church growth seldom comes without bold plans for it. Only those who disregard the evidence can believe that church growth is a by-product of multifaceted Christian activity. The assumption is contrary to the New Testament practice. We do not see the apostles carrying out a genial program of koinonia, diakonia, and kerygma and the churches happily rising here and there like dandelions in a well-watered lawn. There we see Paul and Barnabas throwing their lives into a tremendous program of church planting, racing against time to reach as many as possible with the message of salvation before the Lord returned. There we have the picture of Paul in Corinth arguing in the synagogue every sabbath and persuading Jews and Greeks. The record is careful to point out that Paul "was occupied with preaching, testifying to the Jews (with abundant proofs from the Law, Psalms, and Prophets) that the Christ was Jesus." When the Jews opposed and reviled him, he shook out his garments and said to them, "Your blood be upon your heads. I am innocent. From now on I will go to the Gentiles" (Acts 18:4-11). But he did not go empty-handed. He took Crispus, the ruler of the synagogue, and all his household, a near proselyte who had been attending the synagogue, Titius Justus, and all his household, and many others *into the new church which he established.*

Before Paul arrived at Corinth, he had been practicing his bold plan for planting churches, and after he left he continued using the same effective plan. He would have been amazed at any idea that the Church grows as an unplanned by-product of the full Christian life or that the true end is a just society to which the Church is strictly instrumental.

This modern assumption, held chiefly by liberals (but sometimes by conservatives, though for different reasons), is contrary to the missionary practice of the Church for nineteen centuries. It is contrary to the universal practice of the last 150 years of modern missions. It is contrary to the passion of Christ for the redemption of the world. It is contrary to common sense.

The only way in which the Good News of Jesus Christ can possibly reach the myriads of earth is for fantastic church planting to take place. . . . The only way in which Christian values, economic justice, racial brotherhood, social betterment or democracy can spread is for multitudinous cells of baptized believers to be formed in which the Word is preached and the Sacraments are observed. It is inconceivable that the Spirit of God will so operate on men in these tumultuous and revolutionary times that some new religion which knows nothing of Jesus Christ and the Bible will arise and sweep all men into itself. It would be the height of foolishness to opt for such a religion before it has even appeared.

One can well believe that, under the guidance of the Holy Spirit and the Bible, devoted Christians from the churches of Africasia will develop new forms of the Church which are loyal to Jesus Christ as God and Savior and believe in the Bible as their sole rule of faith and practice. But if such forms do arise, they will not happen by themselves. They will come as the result of careful planning on the part of consecrated Africasian Christians and Churches, assisted often by their Eurican friends.

One can also believe that as larger and larger proportions of the great minorities in America are discipled, the form of the Church will be enriched by their contributions—Chinese, Cuban, Hispanic, Vietnamese, French Canadian, and on and on. But winning these to Christ and incorporating them into a hundred thousand congregations will not happen by accident. It will take careful planning and a deliberate resolve to align our purposes with the unswerving purpose of God to disciple *panta ta ethne in every nation,* including the United States.

EVERY GREAT FORWARD MOVEMENT HAS PLANNED FOR CHURCH GROWTH

As we consider the place of planning in church growth, we recall the great growth of the Methodist Church around the world. Wesley's class meetings did not arise by chance as he led a devout Christian life. He created them. He standardized them. He required new believers to form themselves into them. As long as he hoped that through them the Anglican Church might be renewed, he called them class meetings. When that hope faded, or in countries where the Anglican Church was merely one of many denominations, class meetings became Methodist churches and continued to be planted according to plan. Revival meetings on a grand scale were held in order to save men, whose salvation was not complete till they were firm members of Methodist churches. Wesley, Asbury, Coke, and others would have laughed at any idea that church growth took place by itself without any planning.

Time would fail me were I to recount the bold plans which undergirded the great extension of Churches in all six continents. Even the spread of Pentecostal congregations in Brazil from none in 1916 to thousands in 1980—as unstructured a spread as can be found on earth—was certainly not an unintentional by-product of full-orbed mission touching all of life. Some famous leaders of the Assemblies of God in Brazil have baptized ten, twenty, and thirty thousand people. These baptisms did not happen by accident. They were planned. The great growth of the Assemblies in Brazil came as a result of bold plans for church growth carried out by the common people. An essential element of these plans was the conviction that wherever a *crente* (believer) went, it was his duty and privilege to win his fellows to similar belief in the Lord and to bind them together in a regularly worshiping, praying, praising, and evangelizing congregation.

The sentimental supposition of some that "Christian presence," "working for secularization," "witnessing to Christ by kindly deeds," "industrial evangelism which seeks to improve laboring conditions," "discerning God in the revolution and lining up with Him" will through some mysterious process result in as much communication of the Gospel as they should, hangs in mid-air without a shred of biblical or rational evidence to support it. World evangelization is concerned with the three billion men (fifteen times the population of the United States in 1980) who are yet completely unchurched, completely under the domination of sub-Christian or anti-Christian ideologies, value systems, and religions. Churching these billions will never happen of itself as an unplanned by-product of kindly Christian activity.

It must immediately be added, however, that planting churches is only the first half of the Great Commission. The second half is to "teach them all things whatsoever I have commanded you." All must applaud the Church pressing ahead to perfect those who have become disciples of Christ and these in turn applying Christ's principles to the social, economic, and political structures of their neighborhoods and nations. The program of perfecting those of the billions who become disciples of Christ is entirely praiseworthy. Leading them on to more and more appropriation of the mind of Christ, more and more infilling of the Holy Spirit, and more and more ethical and aesthetic advance, is unqualifiedly good. On this point most Christians will agree.

Nevertheless, if men are to understand the place of the Church in the real world confronting them, they must see that before the great ethical goals can be achieved, *first there must be many churches*. Only churches which exist can be perfected. Only babies who have been born can be educated. Only where practicing Christians form sizable minorities of their societies can they expect their presence seriously to influence the social, economic, and political structures. The Church must, indeed, "teach them all things," but first she must have at least some Christians and some congregations. What she must totally reject is the naive idea that God will act in and through those who reject His Son and His revelation so much better than He will through those who accept His Son and His revelation, that she should cease at once from planned church planting and try to create a vague community of justice and goodwill among all men.

WHAT DO WE MEAN BY BOLD PLANS FOR CHURCH ESTABLISHMENT?

Vague general work and shifting emphasis from discipling to some form of perfecting is not what we mean. Neither emphasis will liberate men from bondage to evil nor "spread the fragrance of the knowledge of him everywhere" (II Cor. 2:14). Bold plans mean something far more positive. In understanding church growth it is not enough to see the faulty assumptions which prevent maximum multiplication of sound churches. We must go on to devise and operate intelligent and adequate plans for establishing church after church throughout whole populations.

Reading a book or two on the dynamics of mission and the growth of Christ's churches is merely a glance in the right direction. Stating a church growth concept of mission is not enough. Espousing a purpose to plant churches is only a beginning. Copying a plan by which the Lord has multiplied churches somewhere else is merely a part of the preliminary exploration. Knowing enough about a piece of the mosaic to hazard a guess as to what might win its men to Christ and His Church is one of the bricks in the foundation—no more. God's obedient servant should not deceive himself that any of these introductory activities is his goal.

His goal is to devise an intelligent plan for establishing churches— one which fits his population, is similar to plans which have multiplied churches in other populations of this sort, and can be carried out with the resources which God has put into his hand. The plan should be adequate. If his piece of the mosaic contains fifty thousand people, his plan should be large enough to disciple the whole piece. No one expects that all fifty thousand will become and remain devout Christians—but because the compassionate Lord holds the door open for every one and the faithful ambassador beseeches each to be reconciled to God, an adequate plan should make becoming a disciple of Christ a real option to every one of the fifty thousand. No plan is adequate which *aims* at creating a tiny enclave of two hundred and so elevating its members by lift and redemption that they are unable to communicate Christ to their kinsmen. Church leaders should beware of petty plans. Plans for establishing "power centers of liberated and liberating persons" (churches) should, then, be both intelligent and *adequate*.

Putting such plans into operation is the true goal. A good plan on paper does nothing. Only as it becomes incarnate in flesh and blood does it achieve anything. It may be born in imagination or given to the Christian in dreams, but until it is drenched in sweat and sprinkled with blood it remains the talent laid away in a napkin. It is better to put an imperfect plan into operation than to carry on splendid church and mission work while waiting for the perfect plan to appear. Many a time the specialist will have to strike out on his own because the denomination or the evangelist has no intelligent plan and does not intend to get one. Plans in operation are the only things which count.

In this day, each Africasian and Eurican Church should prepare a hard, bold plan for discipling its receptive populations. Sharing with the splendid leaders of these Churches an adequate evangelistic attitude toward the receptive populations of their lands is urgent, even when the internal needs of the Churches are great. Plans for multiplying cells of the liberated and redeemed must not be postponed till all domestic problems have been solved. Many a Church, thrown on its own after years of tender loving care by its founders is—not unnaturally—engaged in domestic power struggles. For example, L. Clayton Kitchen after a visit to India writes sadly,

> I found church after church torn by factionalism and dissension. In some, litigation has replaced the love feast. Koinonia has been fractured by strife due to desire for personal aggrandizement and the lust for power. In place of diakonia, frequently there appeared a woeful unconcern for the needs of . . . Christian and Non-Christian alike (Kitchen, 1965:2ff.).

It is erroneous to suggest that this carnality (and there is much of it in America and other countries) must be eradicated *before* church-planting mission can be carried out. The Churches of the West (from the Roman Catholics to the Quakers) were far from perfect, were indeed squabbling competitive sects filled with worldly Christians, when the devoted among them organized missionary societies and commenced the greatest expansion of the Church ever to take place.

True, the devoted among them were (to an extent not ordinarily realized) the products of the revivals and awakenings which marked the nineteenth century. George E. Morgan says, surveying the vast growth of Home Missions, the conviction gains force that the period following the Revival of 1859 was one of the most fruitful in the annals of Christianity in this country; and also that . . . the *entire Home Missions Movement was not only inaugurated and manned but also financed* by Revival converts and sympathizers (quoted by Orr, *The Second Evangelical Awakening:* 1964:91).

This fact, however, must not be distorted to mean that the revived must make their own churches perfectly just and loving before sharing the Good News abroad. The revived did not do this in 1870 and should not do it today. Had the Church at Jerusalem waited till she had conquered her "castiness" before trying to bring the Gentiles to faith and obedience, she would have waited a very long time. Church-planting, revival, and perfecting the saints normally go forward together, each buttressing the other.

There is good reason to believe that as Asian Churches get their minds off themselves and rear a generation of Asian missionaries (to peoples other than their own) whose consecration will challenge "churches torn by factionalism and dissension," they will discover (as thousands of churches in Eurica have) that the missionary church is the best local church. As denominations begin in earnest to church receptive populations they will heal the wounds of God's households. The devout in the Churches of Asia, Africa, and Latin America ought to be drawing up intelligent, adequate plans for the evangelization of the winnable peoples in their neighborhoods. So ought the devout in North America.

It is a sound principle that "each national Church evangelizes its neighborhood and missionaries residing there help the Church do so"; but in case some national Church sits calmly by, neglecting a homogeneous unit prepared to accept the Gospel, God will not hold the mission guiltless which also sits calmly by, sharing the neglect. If the mission cannot inspire the Church to action, it should draw a circle around each moribund congregation and in the vast territory outside the circles put into operation an intelligent and adequate plan for multiplying churches. The work is urgent, the day is far spent, and God wants His lost children found. No Church—Africasian or Eurican—has the right to cordon off populations hungry for the Word, neither feeding them herself nor permitting other Churches to do so. "Dog in the manger" comity is displeasing to God. The sovereignty of each Church should not be inflated to mean that its indifference to the salvation of the peoples of its land binds the hands of God's people elsewhere. When the Holy Spirit sends Paul to Rome, if he finds the Church already there made up of Judaizers who resist his message, he should not argue that the missionary must subordinate himself and his convictions to "the great national Church in Italy."

The Christian and Missionary Alliance, a Church of 192,000 members in North America in 1977, has shown the way to other denominations. It resolved to double this membership, reaching 384,000 by 1987. It then added in its members overseas and found it had 952,000. It resolved to double this also, reaching the high total of 1,904,000 by 1987. Then Louis L. King, the President of the whole Church, penned these significant words:

> To reach these goals we are calling the Church to a renewed emphasis on evangelism, to maximum participation, to planning at every level, to teaching and training for outreach, to accurate reporting, to sacrificial giving, and to much intercessory prayer.

The whole story is told in the *Church Growth Bulletin* for September 1979. I know of no better example of hard, bold plans.

Operating intelligent, adequate plans for seeding a countryside with congregations necessarily involves adjusting these plans in view of the outcomes. Certain aspects of the plan do not work, others produce far better than anticipated, still others give promise of improved performance if modified and regulated. Adjustment, modification, and regulation are not New Testament words, but they describe a New Testament reality. In Luke's account of the first thirty years of church planting he indicates again and again modification of the plan to fit changed circumstances. When the *ecclesiae* began to include not only born Jews, but also uncircumcised God-fearers, new departures in the kerygma were made by the apostle Paul. When the synagogue was no longer available as a place to argue, testify, and prove that according to the Law, the Psalms, and the Prophets the Messiah was Jesus of Nazareth, new evangelistic and worship centers had to be found. When the poor of the Greek Christians were neglected, deacons had to be appointed to wait on tables. When the initial thrust of spontaneous expansion through the Jerusalem refugees slowed down, a new form of propagation through church representatives sent out by a church was instituted.

SUITED TO THE STAGE OF MISSION

Christian mission may be regarded as the process through which God makes known to all peoples His plan of salvation and calls them from death to life and responsible membership in His Church.

Looked at from the viewpoint of the agents of reproduction, one may say that in most regions of earth, Christian mission passes through four stages—exploration, pioneer labors, scattered successes, and substantial Christianization. Plans must fit each stage. Looked at from the viewpoint of the reproduction achieved, one may say that the Church passes through four stages. *Exploration* becomes "resolve of missionaries to evangelize a new population." *Pioneer labors* become "well supported outposts of the Church." *Scattered successes* become "strong clusters of congregations organized into beginning presbyteries, conventions, conferences, and dioceses rooted in a few of the populations." *Substantial Christianization* becomes "The Church organized into permanent unions, conferences, conventions, presbyterians, dioceses and synods, well rooted in most pieces of the marvelous mosaic which makes up the national population."

Adequate plans for the propagation of the Gospel must recognize these stages and fit each. For example, in North America as a whole Christian mission is in stage four. The plans suited to *this* stage are quite different from those employed by the North American Church as it carries on mission in Palestine or Kalimantan.

To be realistic one must at once add that North America as a whole is far from a homogeneous whole. The situation in Canada is different from that in Florida. A well-rooted Church comprising a fifth of the total population in British Columbia, for example, will at one and the same time carry on Stage One Mission among the new immigrants to Canada from Hong Kong and Uganda and Stage Four Mission among those who have been in Canada for several generations. Similarly in Java, as the Church impelled by the Holy Spirit carries on its work of proper expansion, it will at one and the same time do Stage Four Mission in some sections of the population, Stage Three in others, and Stage Two or One in others. In Andhra State in South India, the Convention of Telegu Baptist Churches among unbelieving Malas and Madigas will be carrying on Stage Four Mission, but among the Brahman and Kshatriya castes will be carrying on Stage One—Exploration. This is true even though the latter live within the ministry area of the Baptist congregations. The new population which a given Church has resolved to evangelize may live in the same city but, because it is at a considerable linguistic and/or cultural distance away, may for some years require *exploration* or the establishment of *well-supported outposts.*

Having placed the four stages of church expansion (mission) in proper perspective, let us consider each.

First comes that of *Exploration*. The Church (or more commonly, some churchly sodality or modality) has resolved to evangelize a new segment of the human race. Quite properly it sets about discovering everything possible about this homogeneous unit which may be composed of hardcore rationalists of the universities, French Canadians in upper New York, the sixty thousand Korean miners at work in Germany, the Nishis in Northeast India, or unchurched multitudes in South Central Zaire. It will not only learn about this segment of society, but will also explore how to evangelize it and how the evangelizers will continue evangelizing till churches start multiplying in it.

For missionaries overseas, this will mean finding a place to live, learning the language, being misunderstood, persecuted, banished, or killed, establishing beachheads of one sort or another, commending themselves by good works and holy lives, winning the first converts, and founding the first few congregations. For evangelists operating in their own nations at an E-1-A, B, C, or D level, this will mean learning a sub-culture and establishing ways of living which enable maximum communications and are acceptable to each new population.

Because the first congregations are started by outsiders they will inevitably have a foreign flavor. Despite the best efforts of the advocates, the population being evangelized will think that to become Christian is "to leave our community." If the expansion is into a new language area, the first translations of the Gospels or other portions of Scripture tend to be awkward. First congregations everywhere tend to be made up of those who before their conversion were already at outs with their own people. Nevertheless, these first congregations *are a great triumph*. Hundreds of that culture or sub-culture are now living as Christians. Christ has His way in their lives. They believe in Him, and have become new creations in Him. They feed on His Word and are being transformed into His likeness. They are having a beneficial effect on their societies.

The second era of mission is that of *Well-Supported Outposts*. In a scattered but systematic way the whole population has been exposed to the Gospel and outposts established throughout it. If the population is—let us say—Mexican Americans in Texas and the Evangelizers the Southern Baptists—then Baptist strategists, having found out where the Mexican Americans are numerous and how receptive different sections of that community are, have planted a network of Baptist churches in every county of the state. Churches are most numerous where there are concentrations of Hispanic-name Americans. Special attention is paid to recent arrivals, because these are usually responsive to the Gospel.

During the second era of missions, the congregations still have a somewhat foreign flavor. To become Christian, to join these new congregations
is still regarded by the great majority of the population as "leaving our
people." So becoming a Christian tends to be more a social than a religious
step. When, for example, a son in a strong Lutheran family becomes a
Roman Catholic, his parents feel he has betrayed them. When a Moslem
moves to Christian Faith all the members of his family feel he has "left
us." So a sweeping movement is not likely. Second Stage congregations
(well-supported outposts) grow slowly. Nevertheless, if the founding Church
or Mission continues to support and buttress these outposts, they increase
steadily. *Because they are there, Stage Three becomes possible.*

In Stage Three, *strong clusters* of congregations arise in various
places. The third stage begins as here and there in the target population
responsive segments, moved by cultural compulsion or other action of the
Holy Spirit, begin to turn to Christ in a multi-individual way. Enough of
them become followers of Jesus Christ so that Christians become numerous. Converts feel, "We are not leaving our people. We are charting a
way which all of them sooner or later will follow." Congregations begin
to think of themselves as advance guards of their people. Among the
hundreds of thousands of Koreans in the United States, the feeling is quite
common that "All of us are going to become Christians. Most Koreans in
South Korea also are soon going to be Christians." Among the hundreds
of thousands of Brazilians moving into Casas Populares (government housing developments which ring all burgeoning industrial cities) becoming
members of Baptist, Pentecostal, Presbyterian, and other congregations is
considered a step upward. Mission in such industrial complexes is therefore
in Stage Three.

During this era the Church grows strong. Denominations come to
number fifty thousand, a hundred thousand, or half a million communicants. Schools and seminaries prepare leaders. Hymnbooks, prayer books,
and good translations of the Bible are printed. Regular worship in well-
built churches becomes common. Christian ways of burying the dead,
marrying, and celebrating festivals are developed and become precious to
Christians. Pastors, elders, deacons, teachers, district superintendents,
evangelists, and seminary professors are trained to function *in an indigenous
way.* The institutional Church, while faithful to God and the Bible, takes
on a thoroughly national hue.

The good lives of Christians, the good deeds they do, their labors for
justice and the public good, and the transformations of life which faith in
Christ brings are noted by neighbors. The persecution and ostracism which

plagued the early stages of the Church die down. The Church (as *strong clusters* of congregations scattered in receptive segments of the population throughout the region) prospers and appears likely to survive. It becomes strong in more and more communities throughout the nation.

During Stage Three, transition to national leaders is very largely completed. Outside leaders, noticeable in Stages One and Two, have turned over to local leaders. In Stage Three, missionaries should not go home but turn over authority and *go on* to yet unconverted populations. Contrary to much popular opinion, missionaries are sent *not* to help younger Churches, but to multiply churches in new segments of the population. Nevertheless, because the turnover usually occupies several decades, many missionaries are temporarily helping young denominations; but that is *not* their permanent task. They are missionaries, not fraternal workers. Failure to appreciate this basic distinction often brings about a situation in which the mission stays on "helping" the young Church when it should be evangelizing sections of the population which have yet to hear.

In Stage Four of the expansion of the Church, *substantial Christianization* of the population has taken place. A third, a half, two-thirds, or nine-tenths of the population has become Christian.

It must be remembered that a Church may be at Stage Four in regard to one homogeneous unit, and at Stage One in regard to another. Thus the Church in Jerusalem in the year A.D. 45 was at Stage Four in regard to the Jewish masses, and at Stage One in regard to the Italian Army of occupation. Thus the Reformed Church in America is at Stage Four in regard to the well-to-do whites in scores of suburban areas of the United States, but has yet to enter Stage One in regard to the Puerto Rican multitudes in New York, Buffalo, Cleveland, Detroit, and Chicago. Thus the Episcopal Church of North India, with 600,000 members, may be considered a Stage Four denomination, yet in regard to *more than a thousand castes* which live all around its congregations, it has *yet to enter Stage One.*

What does this mean in regard to hard, bold plans for church growth? This, that an essential duty of each congregation and denomination is to ponder the stage of mission in which it finds itself and to devise adequate plans which fit that stage. In addition, it will no doubt feel called to play its proper part in the ongoing task of *world* evangelization. This may mean additional plans for Stage One, Two, or Three evangelization in adjoining populations.

Especially during Stage Four, the Church ought to surge out in ceaseless ardent evangelism which proceeds on two tracks, bringing back two kinds of fruit. Along track one it will conduct near-neighbor evangelism irrespective of homogeneous units or different kinds of people. If a Syro-Phoenician child needs healing, it will heal her. It will invite all sinners to repent and become members of a congregation in which all Christians are accepted as equally people of God, having equal access to the Throne. Congregations will arise in which "There is no such thing as Jew and Greek, slave and freeman, male and female" (Gal. 3:28 NEB). These may be called conglomerate or multi-ethnic congregations. In tightly knit societies, this will mean that—one by one—converts leave—or more likely are forced out of—their families, and consequently chances for great growth are dim. In loosely knit societies, converts are not ostracized and considerable growth may occur. In short, God has blessed this kind of church growth and is continuing to bless it, but not to the discipling of whole societies.

Along the second track, evangelism will seek to bring those who believe into congregations made up of their own kith and kin, their own kind of people, in India of their own caste fellows. This may sound impossible to Christians who have been reared in conglomerate congregations where all growth has taken place from a dribble of converts from many different backgrounds. To some who are fighting the battle for brotherhood, the very idea of track two evangelism, which brings in congregations composed of one kind of people, smacks of segregation. Its theological validity is questioned. Churchmen have doubts whether this second track is really Christian. However, when it is remembered that the rapid spread of congregations through one homogeneous unit, through one segment of society is a mode of growth which God has abundantly blessed, doubts will be resolved. Through the ages, as men and women have left non-Christian faiths for Christ, *most of them have come along track two.* God blesses track one. He also blesses track two. Rather than attack either of these ways of coming to Christ, the task is to understand them and use both.

But now a question arises. Does not the Bible say, "Many are called but few are chosen"? Is there any biblical authority for supposing that all mankind will hear the Gospel, believe, and be saved? Should we labor to disciple every segment of humanity, every piece of the marvelous mosaic? The questions are fair and must be answered.

The Bible teaches and Christians consequently believe that Christ will be Lord in every segment of mankind. (See Matthew 28:19; Luke 24:47; John 1:29; 3:16; Romans 16:26; II Corinthians 4:15; Philippians 2:9-11; Revelation 5:9, 10; 7:9; and many other passages.) In every piece of the complex mosaic, Jesus Christ will be acknowledged as Lord to the glory of God the Father. Every tribe and tongue and kindred and nation, every class and economic level, every community rural and urban, will come to its true fulfilment in Him.

However, the Scriptures do not support the notion that all this will happen before the Lord returns. Before His Second Coming, on the contrary, much rejection of the Good News and much rebellion against God may be expected. But nothing in Scripture supports the curious ethnocentric idea that during the time of natural man, in Europe and North America hundreds of millions will be among the saved, but in other continents only a tiny sliver of humanity (and that from a very small number of ethnic units) will accept the Savior. The reasonable position is that the exact proportion in each piece of the mosaic which will believe can safely be left in the hands of a just Judge. In the meantime, the duty of every Christian is to press forward fervently proclaiming Jesus Christ as God and only Savior, and persuading men and women to become His disciples and responsible members of His Church. We should be confident that in God's good time, every knee will bow and every tongue will confess.

As we rejoice in the transient triumphs of technology, science, space travel, public health, and brotherhood, we rejoice in the eternal triumphs of the Gospel. We are unashamed triumphalists. Error, we are sure, will give place to Truth. Cruelty will give way to kindness. False and inadequate ideas of God and man will give way to the revelation which it has pleased God to give to all human beings through the Bible and His Son, our Savior.

Does this mean that the rich cultural diversity of the pluralistic world will be wiped out and replaced by a dull uniformity? By no means. The Bible is very clear on that point. Nothing good will be lost, all the jewels of the world will adorn the foundation of the City. All the glory, all the honor, all the true and beautiful will remain. Just listen to the Word. It speaks directly to pluralistic society. This is what the Lordship of Christ in a pluralistic world means.

> And I saw no temple in the city, for its temple is the Lord God the Almighty and the Lamb. The city has no need of sun or moon to shine upon it, for the glory of God is its light, and its lamp is the Lamb. By its light shall the nations walk; and *the kings* [the civilizations, the cultures, and the sciences] *of the earth shall bring their glory into it,* and its gates shall never be shut by day—and there shall be no night there; *they shall bring into it the glory and honor of the nations. But nothing unclean shall enter it, nor anyone who practices abominations or falsehood* (Rev. 21:22-27).

Christ will be Lord in a pluralistic society. In every segment of society His will will be done. *His* will be the final Word as to what is glorious and honorable, and what is unclean, false, and abominable. Consequently perfect beauty, perfect justice, perfect peace, and perfect truth will cause every facet of every culture to blaze with everlasting glory.

Every plan requires continual adjustment to make it deliver continuous church multiplication. What should be done at the beginning when a denomination is planting the first congregation in a suburb which may grow to be a city of a hundred thousand is very different from what needs to be done thirty years later when there are twenty congregations there of many denominations. The first plan must be majorly modified to fit the new opportunities. What should be done at the very beginning when the missionary (who may be an Asian or African just as readily as a European) and a few nationals comprise both Church and mission is very different from what the bold plan should entail when a Church of half the receptive population has been established and a major task is near-neighbor evangelism.

SOME SPECIFIC PLANS EXAMINED

Most instances of church growth recounted in this book were the outcome of bold planning. If each of the eight examples mentioned in Chapter One is analyzed, the deliberate effort to plant churches will be seen. Mr. Dia's church planting in the Philippines during the Japanese occupation is a beautiful example of a bold plan. Consider the alternatives. It was wartime and the safest thing for any patriotic Filipino to do was to lie low. Mr. Dia might have argued that what the Church in the mountains needed was shepherding, Bible teaching, quiet service of men and women in need, patriotic efforts to repel the Japanese, or merely Christian presence. To stay Christian in those difficult circumstances was enough. Why call attention to oneself by leading three congregations to quadruple in size, win many outsiders to Evangelical faith, and antagonize parents, relatives, and priests? The Japanese were not far away. Instead of this easy rationalization, Mr. Dia formulated and operated an aggressive plan for church multiplication.

The remarkable multiplication of congregations among the Madigas of Ongole District was not a function of "dialogue" or an overflow of "the servant church." It did not happen by itself. From the moment John Clough turned away from the futile preaching of the Gospel to the upper castes and turned to the receptive Madigas, through every month of the next ten years the unfolding of a bold plan is clearly evident. He was not tied by his plan. He changed it to fit circumstances; but every circumstance was laid under tribute to church planting. Hiring non-Christian Madigas to work on the canal began as a humane action to save the relatives of Christians from starvation, but when Clough saw that these attended Christian worship gladly and learned well, he built their interest into his plan— first by not baptizing them as long as he paid them, and second by evangelizing their villages and kin webs when the famine was over. Even the three days of baptism when over three thousand were immersed were a part of the plan—a dramatic way of proclaiming the Gospel to multitudes who did not yet believe. No wonder that ten thousand in one year were added to the Lord.

So we might go through case after case recounted in Chapter One, pointing out what the plan consisted in, confident that, had we reported each instance in full, the size and conscious intention of the plan would have been enhanced.

CONTEMPORARY PLANS FOR CHURCH GROWTH

The contemporary plans for church growth which follow are replete with lessons for any who wish to understand the dynamics of mission. They fit different populations, missions, and Churches. None is set forth as *the* right plan for planting churches everywhere. Each suggests how one Church or mission, facing a specific homogeneous unit at a specific degree of responsiveness, goes about propagating the Gospel. All agree in one respect—they are focused on church growth. They intend to multiply churches throughout an unchurched population. Their goal is to establish a multitude of congregations and each is reaching its goal.

A Bold Plan in the Philippines

The Association of Baptists for World Evangelism, a missionary society with headquarters in Philadelphia, started work in the Philippines in 1927 and in 1962 had 215 churches with about 12,000 faithful members. At first it heavily subsidized the pastors of new churches, but since World War II it has given no subsidy. Its stated purpose is to establish indigenous churches, and the plan by which it carries out its purpose is as follows.

A theological training school closely cooperating with existing churches and field missionaries is the heart of the plan. The process can best be seen by following out a typical case. The field missionary with intimate knowledge of many surrounding towns consults with the practical work department of the school as to where to start a new church. As a first step toward that end, students are assigned to a given town or ward of a town to begin and develop a Sunday School, i.e. Evangelicals and sympathizers are gathered who wish to study the Bible regularly, sing and pray together, and function as a rudimentary church.

In due time, the Sunday School community invites the missionary to come and hold a campaign. A Filipino evangelist, student workers, and the missionary, together comprising a tent team, then hold a six- to twelve-week intensive evangelistic campaign, using every means to attract people to the meetings. Converts won are added to the Sunday School community, which gradually becomes a new church and goes forward under the student pastor. The church pays his transportation to and from the school and at least fifteen pesos toward his school expenses. The student gives more and more time to the church. Thus a new church is planted.

Not every attempt is successful. Some students have more ability than others. Some new converts are more potent in winning their fellows than others. Enough plantings survive and grow so that a constant succession of churches arises and a constant stream of theological school students are trained in church planting and development.

The field missionary helps each new church with an annual evangelistic campaign of several weeks' duration. New Sunday Schools are planted at a rate which keeps just ahead of the number of graduates coming out of the theological training school. When a student graduates, he usually has several calls to serve small churches.

Each December during the vacation a conference is held for the youth of all churches. Some young people from the new churches respond to the call for full-time service. So within a year or two of their birth, new churches are sending students to the school, that is, new converts are being transformed into future pastors. The youth conference, while deepening the spiritual life of all who attend, aims specifically at recruiting future church planters.

First-year students at the school are not allowed to work. Their parents and local churches are encouraged to pay their tuition, board, and room. Second- and third-year students may apply to the mission for work scholarships. Income from the small new churches is also available to those who work in them. The more any new church grows, the more support it can give its student pastor.

This plan assumes that the first business of the mission, the theological school, and the churches is establishing more and more churches. The plan would not work if the faculty of the "seminary" were primarily interested in academic excellence or looked on "field work" merely as a means of getting funds to see poor students through school. The plan does work because each man on the faculty is primarily a church planter. Those in charge of the youth conference hold as their primary aim leading the best of the conferees to give their lives to a church-planting ministry. The field missionary, moreover, is not engaged in any vague evangelism or philanthropic or educational enterprise which may sometime, somewhere, make people willing to listen to the Gospel. The field missionary evangelizes populations in which he believes are men who will accept Christ and out of which he expects new churches to be formed. In short, this plan intends to plant congregations in as many towns and cities of the Islands as possible and measures success by the degree to which any Branch of the Church or mission contributes to that specific aim.

The Chokosi Plan

Rev. A. C. Krass's plan for church planting among the Chokosi tribe of Ghana, reported in Chapter Seventeen, speaks plainly to the modern situation. To appreciate its boldness, one has only to imagine what many missionaries, facing those circumstances, would have done. There in the Moslem town of Chereponi was a little congregation made up of educated Christians from which an occasional foray had been made out into the Chokosi villages. How natural to begin with the national church, work and pray with the Christians, create an aura of helpfulness around the church and its missionary, spend much time with the Moslem neighbors in literacy efforts, personal evangelism, sale of literature, discussing Islam with the mullah, touring among the Chokosi villages in good weather, showing stereoptican slides on malaria, flies, and the life of Christ, and getting Chokosi youth to play volleyball. Out of such a varied program one would hope that some would turn to the Lord, but would scarcely expect it in a people as difficult and resistant as the Chokosi.

Instead of this generally good work, Mr. Krass, concluding that the town congregation was culturally too far removed from the Chokosi tribesmen to be able to disciple them, made provision for its spiritual care, and then devoted himself to a well-laid plan for multiplying congregations in the Chokosi villages. He stuck to this plan for three years, adjusted it from time to time as villages became Christian and freed his evangelistic team to go to non-Christian villages, and at the close of the three years in 1967 had several congregations totaling about 800 members. With the experience gained, he expected to work forward according to his plan till, in about a decade, the entire Chokosi "nation" of twenty-two thousand souls had been discipled.

Missionaries in fields where the Church is not growing, would do well to ponder the fact that many missionaries, sent to Chereponi with the assignment Mr. Krass had, would come away three years later without seeing any church growth. Lack of church growth in truly resistant populations is one thing. It should not be confused with the common practice of coming empty-handed out of a ripe field for lack of an intelligent, adequate plan of church growth.

The Sevav Plan

Nigeria is the scene of a remarkable contrast between an effective plan for winning men to Christian faith and a splendid piece of mission work. The mission concerned is the Christian Reformed, whose headquarters in the United States is in Grand Rapids, Michigan. The American Church is a small one, soundly conservative in the Calvinistic tradition, and composed chiefly of descendants of immigrants from the Reformed Church of Holland during the nineteenth century. When the Nigerian mission of the Dutch Reformed of South Africa began to experience hostility as a result of the apartheid policies of the Union of South Africa, the Christian Reformed of Michigan took over. The field worked in Nigeria was the Tiv tribe of about a million members located about the center of the country. The sound Nigerian Church, made up of Tiv tribesmen who had passed through mission schools and the stiff three-year catechumenate of the Dutch Reformed Church, numbered a couple of thousand members in 1956.

At Sevav, Rev. Eugene Rubingh found that, because many men had come to Christ one by one against the social tide mostly via the school route, most Christians were concentrated at the central station and the rest were scattered out across the area. He discovered that the smallest unit of the tribe, called *ipaven,* was an extended family made up of about ten compounds (hamlets) with about twenty souls in each. As he visited the villages, he found that outside the station itself Christians existed as lone persons in scattered ipaven. In a given unit (ipaven) of 200 souls living in eight or ten compounds there would be one Christian. In several adjacent ipavens there would be no Christians at all, and then several miles farther on another Christian.

He concluded that the school approach plus evangelistic touring through the villages (the old method of mission work) won an occasional Christian here and there but never gave the rest of the extended family a real chance to decide for Christ. The theory that the one Christian would evangelize the rest of his ipaven had not worked out, probably because to become a Christian involved long schooling or a long catechumenate in which the person walked in to some center regularly for instruction. Most villagers were not going to spend that much effort or give that much time to hearing about a new religion.

He then devised the hard, bold mode of evangelism called The Sevav Plan. He selected an ipaven, called on the chief, and arranged that on a certain day each week for twelve weeks a team of ten Christians would arrive in the ipaven. One Christian would go to each hamlet and assemble all the people for a well-planned three-hour teaching session. The program was interesting, doctrinal, and punctuated by much singing and learning. The twelve-week presentation took the people of each ipaven through a course on man's lost condition, God's plan of salvation, the birth of the Savior, His mighty works of healing the sick and casting out devils, His sacrificial death, and His Resurrection. At the closing session, all were invited to a conference at the head man's hamlet and given a chance to declare for Christ and become catechumens. About 20 per cent of the adults of the ipaven decided for Christ. Arrangements were made for them to be instructed. A year later most of these were still faithful learners.

This plan suffered from the previous pattern and the strict rules of the Tiv Church that no illiterate could be baptized and no polygamist could even be instructed. Nevertheless, that out of one cluster of ten interrelated hamlets twenty closely interrelated individuals decided to become Christians and were taking instruction regularly was highly significant. After baptism they formed the church in that ipaven. Mr. Rubingh had swung away from good mission work to a bold plan for planting churches.

Mr. Krass's plan has some advantages. It wins to Christ a larger proportion of the souls in the village and creates a stronger, more cohesive church; but the Christian Reformed on doctrinal grounds or because they allow themselves to be bound by the Tiv Church may have to stick to the Sevav Plan. I am not concerned to praise one above the other, but to point out that both have the great merit of being courageous plans for planting churches.

THE CENTRAL TASK

Nothing will advance the cause of world evangelization more than for church leaders and missionaries to cease thinking exclusively in terms of good work of one kind or another and begin thinking *of the central task* in terms of incorporating responsible converts in ongoing congregations and multiplying these in natural social units. The goal is to multiply sound churches in every people, every homogeneous unit, on earth. The central task is the communication of the Gospel to the billions who have yet to believe. The degree to which that is being accomplished can be measured in terms of countable disciples of Christ assembling under the Word of God in His churches to praise Him and to do His work. Hard, bold plans to carry out this central task can be made. Resources of men, women, money, prayer, and sacrifice can be allocated. It is time to focus on the chief purpose of mission and to make effective use of the science of management in achieving that godly end.

The Roman Catholic Church has spoken clearly on the point. In 1964, Vatican II called evangelization "the greatest and holiest work of the Church." In 1975, Pope Paul VI addressed to "all the faithful of the entire world" an apostolic exhortation entitled *Evangelii Nuntiandi* (Evangelization in the Modern World). This authoritative statement could be read by all Christians with profit. He says,

> The presentation of the Gospel is not an optional contribution for the Church. It is the duty incumbent on her by the command of the Lord Jesus so that people can believe and be saved . . . (8). There is no new humanity if there are not first of all new persons. The purpose of evangelization is therefore precisely this interior change . . . (16).

In 1979, John Paul II in *Redemptor Hominis* declared,

> We must all share in this mission and concentrate all our forces on it, since it is more necessary than ever for modern mankind. [He urged that Christians] consciously join in the great mission of revealing Christ to the world, helping each person to find himself in Christ. . . .

Numerous Protestants take this same strong stand in regard to world evangelization. The missionary movement, decade after decade, continues to send out more than 30,000 missionaries from North America alone. The rapidly expanding missionary movement from Asia, Africa, and Latin America is adding its thousands of missionaries to the global army of liberators. The Church Growth Movement, now strong in America and many other countries, emphasizes the conversion of millions of nominal and lapsed Christians and of hundreds of millions of secularists, Marxists, humanists, hedonists, and pagans who make up such a prominent part of most modern societies.

In all six continents, world evangelization—Christian mission—is well begun. The Church does *not* stand in the sunset of the Christian mission to the world. Rather, the missionary movement stands at midmorning. The era of greatest advance lies ahead. A mighty stream of witnesses and lay evangelists will stream out, across the bridges of God, to the hundreds of millions living in darkness. Some of these are our neighbors and relatives. Many are unreached peoples in our own and other lands. God intends for them all to hear. The Apostle Paul in the closing verses of the Epistle to the Romans declares that the Gospel was revealed by command of the Eternal God Himself precisely to bring these myriad peoples (ethnic units) to the obedience of the faith. Christ commands His followers to go into all the world and disciple *panta ta ethne*—all the classes, castes, and other segments of mankind—in all six continents.

Hard, bold plans to carry out this unswerving purpose of God are demanded. The Holy Spirit impels the Church to this central task and reveals what plans, allocations of resources, and petitions to God He wishes Christians to make. Understanding church growth begins in obedient enlistment in this cause of Christ, continues through intellectual discernment of the many factors which affect growth, and ends in great joy as Christians come bearing many sheaves and hear their Lord say, "Well done, good and faithful servant."

EPILOGUE

Let us, then, lay down that defeatist attitude which keeps us convinced that the Church is not only at a standstill but in retreat. Let us lay aside our contentment in changing a few aspects of non-Christian thinking for the better. Let us brush aside the cobwebs of opinion which obstruct our vision and lead us to believe that the morality and concern for others which rises from a Christian base may equally well rise from a non-Christian base.

Let us realize that all we desire and hope for in the world can come only from peoples who acknowledge God as Lord and Christ as Savior and the Holy Spirit as Faithful Guide.

Let us face the fact that the world is open to belief in Christ as widespread as is our obedience to proclaim Him. The Church can move forward mightily. It is God's will that she do so. His power will bless us as we devote ourselves with heart, mind, and will to the multiplying of churches from earth's one end to the other.

> Your young men will see visions
> And your old men dream dreams.

Visions of a world that will be when its peoples are following Christ! Dreams of a God-centered community of nations in which true brotherhood will be found in Christ.

> "Dreams are they?
> But they are God's dreams!"

458

cries the poet.

        "Go ye into all the world . . . the harvest is ripe!"

cries the Lord.

           "Who will go?
            And whom shall I send?"

A new vision of what mission can be opens out before us. The vision of a discipled, working, and worshiping world appears before our eyes.

May we, O Lord, be faithful to Thy dreams and make Thy commands the working rule of our lives.

BIBLIOGRAPHY

ALLEN, Roland
  1962 *Mission Methods: St. Paul's or Ours?* Grand Rapids, Eerdmans. (First published 1912, London, World Dominion).
ANDERSON, Gerald H. (Ed.)
  1961 *The Theology of Christian Mission.* New York and London, McGraw-Hill.
ANDERSON, Rufus
  1967 "The Value of Native Churches," pp. 107-119 in R. Pierce Beaver, *To Advance the Gospel.* Grand Rapids, Eerdmans. (Chapter VIII of *Foreign Missions: Their Relations and Claims*, New York, Scribner, 1869).
ARN, Winfield and McGAVRAN, Donald
  1973 *How to Grow a Church.* Glendale, Regal Books.
  1977 *Ten Steps to Church Growth.* New York, Harper & Row.

BARRETT, David B.
  1975 *Kenya Churches Handbook.* Kenya, Evangelical Publishing House.
BEAVER, R. Pierce
  1967 *To Advance the Gospel: Selections From the Writings of Rufus Anderson.* Grand Rapids, Eerdmans.
BOALS, Barbara M.
  1961 *The Church in the Kond Hills — An Encounter with Animism.* Nagpur, National Christian Council of India.
BOLTON, Robert
  1977 "Gathering a People in Taiwan" in *Church Growth Bulletin.*

CASTILLO, Met
  1979 "Alliance Plants 339 Churches" in *Mindanao Church Growth Bulletin*, September 1979.
CHURCH GROWTH BULLETIN
  1964- Edited by McGavran, Wagner, and Montgomery. Bimonthly. From Box 66,

460

Santa Clara, CA 95052. Consolidated Five Year Volumes: 1964-69, 1969-75, 1975-80 from William Carey Library, Pasadena, CA 91104.

CLOUGH, John E.
1915 *Social Christianity in the Orient: The Story of a Man, a Mission, and a Movement.* Philadelphia, American Baptist Publication Society.

COXILL, H. Wakelin, and GRUBB, Kenneth (Eds.)
1968 *World Christian Handbook.* London, Lutterworth.

CULLMANN, Oscar
1961 "Eschatology and Missions in the New Testament" (An essay in Anderson, Gerald H.).

D'ANTONIO, William V. and PIKE, Frederick B. (Eds.)
1964 *Religion, Revolution, and Reform: New Forces for Change in Latin America.* New York, Praeger (Chapter 5, "Protestantism and Culture Change" by Emilio Willems).

DASENT, G. W.
1960 *The Story of Burnt Nyal.* London, Dent & Sons; New York, E. P. Dutton. First published 1861.

DAVIS, John Merle
1943 *How the Church Grows in Brazil.* New York, London, Dept. of Social & Economic Research and Counsel, International Missionary Council.

DILWORTH, Donald
1967 "Historical, Ethnological, and Sociological Factors in the Evangelization of the Quechuas of Ecuador." A Master of Arts Thesis in the School of Missions and Institute of Church Growth, Fuller Theological Seminary, Pasadena.

DRUMMOND, Richard H.
1961 "Hendrik Kraemer in Japan," *International Review of Missions*, pp. 453-459.

ELKIN, A. P.
1937 "The Reaction of Primitive Races to the White Man's Culture: A Study in Culture Contact," *Hibbert Journal*, July 1937, XXXV, 4, pp. 537-545.

FILSON, Floyd V.
1919 "House Churches," in the *Journal of Biblical Literature*, Vol. 58, pp. 105-112.

FREND, W. H. C.
1952 *The Donatist Church.* Oxford, Oxford University.

GAMALIEL, James Canjanam
1967 "The Church in Kerala: A People Movement Study." A Master of Arts Thesis in the School of Missions and Institute of Church Growth, Fuller Theological Seminary, Pasadena.

GERBER, Vergil
1973 *God's Way to Keep a Church Going and Growing.* Pasadena, William Carey Library.

GLASSER, Arthur F.
1976 "An Introduction to the Church Growth Perspective of Donald Anderson McGavran" in *Theological Perspectives on Church Growth*, ed. H. M. Conn, Den Dulk Foundation.

GOFORTH, Jonathan
1943 *When the Spirit's Fire Swept Korea.* Grand Rapids, Zondervan.

GRAHAM, Billy
1975 "Why Lausanne?" in *Let The Earth Hear His Voice.* Minneapolis, World Wide Publications.

GREENWAY, Roger
1971 *Urban Strategy for Latin America*. Grand Rapids, Baker.
1978 *Apostles to the City*. Grand Rapids, Baker.
GRIMLEY, John B., and ROBINSON, Gordon E.
1966 *Church Growth in Central and Southern Nigeria*. Grand Rapids, Eerdmans.

HAINES, J. Harry
1966 *The Chinese of the Diaspora*. London, Edinburgh House.
HAMILTON, Keith E.
1963 *Church Growth in the High Andes*. Lucknow, Lucknow Publishing House.
HAVIGHURST, Robert J., and MOREIRA, J. Roberto
1964 *Society and Education in Brazil*. Pittsburgh, University of Pittsburgh.
HOEKENDIJK, J. C.
1963 "The Call to Evangelism." Occasional Papers, WCC, Geneva.
HOEKSTRA, Harvey
1979 *The World Council of Churches and the Demise of Evangelism*. Wheaton, Tyndale House.
HUMPHREY, Hubert H.
1967 "Partnership With the Poor," *Los Angeles Times*, August 8, 1967.
HUNTER, George G.
1979 *The Contagious Congregation*. Nashville, Abingdon.
1979 *Finding the Way Forward*. Nashville, Discipleship Resources.
1980 *Church Growth: Strategies That Work*. Co-authored with Donald McGavran. Nashville, Abingdon.

IGLEHART, Charles
1957 *Cross and Crisis in Japan*. New York, Friendship.
INTERNATIONAL CONGRESS ON WORLD EVANGELIZATION.
1975 *Let the Earth Hear His Voice*. Minneapolis, World Wide Publications.

JACQUET, Constant H. (Ed.)
1967 *Yearbook of American Churches*. New York, National Council of the Churches of Christ.
JOHN PAUL II
1978 *Redemptor Hominis*. Rome, Libreria Editrice Vaticana.

KESSLER, J. B. A.
1967 *A Study of the Older Protestant Missions and Churches in Peru and Chile, with Special Reference to the Problems of Division Nationalism and Native Ministry*. Goes, Netherlands, Oosterbaan & Le Cointre, N.V.
KING, Louis L.
1979 "A Rising Tide of Expectation," *Church Growth Bulletin*, September Issue, Santa Clara, CA.
KITCHEN, L. Clayton
1965 "Discussion on Evangelism," *Occasional Papers*. Division of Studies, World Council of Churches, Geneva.
KRASS, A. C.
1967 "A Case Study in Effective Evangelism in West Africa," *Church Growth Bulletin*, Vol. IV, No. 1, Pasadena.

LATOURETTE, Kenneth S.
1936 *Missions Tomorrow*. New York, Harper.
1938 *The Thousand Years of Uncertainty*. New York, Harper.

LEHMANN, E. Arno
    1956   *It Began at Tranquebar*. Madras, The Christian Literature Society.
LEVAI, Blaise (Ed.)
    1957   *Revolution in Missions*. Vellore, South India, The Popular Press.
LOEWEN, Jacob
    1967   "The Christian Encounter with Culture," *World Vision*, Vol. 11, No. 1, Monrovia,
            CA.

MACNICOL, N.
    1948   *Hindu Scriptures*. London, J. M. Dent; New York, Dutton.
MALDONADO, Oscar
    1966   "Camillo Torres," *CIF Reports*, Vol. V, No. 6, Cuernavaca, Mexico, Center of
            Intercultural Formations.
MASIH, Samuel M.
    1964   "Civil Rights and the World Mission of the Church." Social Action Letter, February
            1964, Indianapolis, United Christian Missionary Society.
McGAVRAN, Donald A.
    1955   *The Bridges of God*. London, World Dominion; New York, Friendship.
    1955   "The Church in a Revolutionary Age." St. Louis, Christian Board of Publication,
            mimeographed book.
    1956   "A Study of the Life and Growth of the Disciples of Christ in Puerto Rico."
            Indianapolis, United Christian Missionary Society, mimeographed book.
    1956   "Church Growth in West Utkul, Orissa, India." Indianapolis, United Christian
            Missionary Society, mimeographed book.
    1958   *Multiplying Churches in the Philippines*. Manila, United Church of Christ in the
            Philippines. Republished in 1980 by O. C. Ministries in the Philippines.
    1959   *How Churches Grow*. London, World Dominion; New York, Friendship.
    1962   *Church Growth in Jamaica*. Lucknow, Lucknow Publishing House.
    1963   *Church Growth in Mexico*. Grand Rapids, Eerdmans.
    1965-1976   *Church Growth and Christian Mission*. McGavran (Ed.). New York, Harper
            and Row. Pasadena, William Carey Library.
    1965   "Wrong Strategy: The Real Crisis in Missions," *International Review of Missions*,
            Vol. LIV, No. 216, Geneva.
    1966   "The Church Growth Point of View and Christian Mission," *The Journal of the
            Christian Brethren Research Fellowship*, October 1966, 60 Park Street, Bristol,
            England.
    1967   "Contemporary Arguments Against the Missionary Society." "What About Non-
            Muslim Resistant Peoples?" "The National Church and Resistant Peoples." *IFMA
            Study Papers*. Interdenominational Foreign Mission Association, Ridgefield Park,
            NJ.
    1967   "Kann Man Das Wachstum Der Kirche Planen?" *Das Word in Der Welt*, No. 1,
            1967, Hamburg, Germany.
    1968   "Church Growth in Japan." *Japan Harvest*, Vol. 18, No. 1, Tokyo.
    1970   *Understanding Church Growth*. Grand Rapids, Eerdmans Publishing Company.
    1972   *Crucial Issues in Missions Tomorrow*. McGavran (Ed.). Chicago, Moody.
    1973   *How to Grow a Church*. With Winfield Arn. Glendale, Regal Books.
    1974   *The Clash Between Christianity and Cultures*. Grand Rapids, Baker.
    1976   *Church Growth and Group Conversion*. With J. W. Pickett. First printed 1956,
            Pasadena, William Carey Library.
    1977   *Ten Steps to Church Growth*. With Winfield Arn. New York, Harper and Row.
    1977   *Conciliar Evangelical Debate: The Crucial Documents 1964-1976*. Pasadena,
            William Carey Library.
    1979   *Zaire: Midday in Missions*. With Norman Riddle. Valley Forge, Judson Press.

1979   *Ethnic Realities and the Church: Lessons From India*. Pasadena, William Carey
       Library.
1980   *Church Growth Strategies That Work*. Co-authored with G. G. Hunter. Nashville,
       Abingdon.
MONTGOMERY, James.
1978   *Fire in the Philippines*. Wheaton, Creation House.

NEILL, Stephen
1964   *A History of Christian Missions*. Baltimore, Penguin Books.
NORDYKE, Quentin
1972   *Animistic Aymaras and Church Growth*. Newberg, Oregon, Barclay Press.
NOREN, Loren E.
c. 1963   *Urban Church Growth in Hong Kong* 1958-1962: Third Hong Kong Study, 3
       Lancashire Rd., Kowloon, Hong Kong, privately produced.
NOVAK, Michael
1971   *The Rise of the Unmeltable Ethnics*. New York, Macmillan.

ORR, J. Edwin
1949   *The Second Evangelical Awakening in Britain*. London, Marshall.
1953   *The Second Evangelical Awakening in America*. London, Marshall.
1964   *The Second Evangelical Awakening: An Account of the Second Worldwide Evan-
       gelical Revival Beginning in the Mid-Nineteenth Century*. Fort Washington, Chris-
       tian Literature Crusade.
1965   *The Light of the Nations: Evangelical Renewal and Advance in the Nineteenth
       Century*. Grand Rapids, Eerdmans.

PANIKKER, K. M.
1963   *The Foundations of New India*. London, Allen and Unwin.
PICKETT, Jarrell Waskom
1933   *Christian Mass Movements in India*. Lucknow, Lucknow Publishing House.
1956   *Church Growth and Group Conversion*. Lucknow, Lucknow Publishing House.
1960   *Christ's Way to India's Heart*. Lucknow, Lucknow Publishing House, Third Edition.
POPE PAUL VI
1975   *On Evangelization in the Modern World*. Washington, U.S. Catholic Conference.

RADHAKRISHNAN, Sarvepalli, and MOORE, C. A. (Eds.)
1957   A Source Book in Indian Philosophy. Princeton, Princeton University.
RAJU, S. P.
c. 1965   *Are the CSI Churches Growing — A Study of Trends and Growth*. Madras,
       privately printed.
READ, William R.
1965   *New Patterns of Church Growth in Brazil*. Grand Rapids, Eerdmans.
READ, Wm. R., MONTERROSO, Victor and JOHNSON, Harmon A.
1969   *Latin American Church Growth*. Grand Rapids, Eerdmans.
REDFIELD, Robert
1950   *The Village That Chose Progress*. Chicago, University of Chicago.
RETIF, Louis and Andre
1962   *The Church's Mission in the World*. New York, Hawthorn Books.
RHODES, Harry A.
1934   *History of the Korea Mission, Presbyterian Church U.S.A.* Vol. 1. Seoul, Korea,
       Chosen Mission of the Presbyterian Church U.S.A.

ROBINSON, Gordon E.
1966 *Church Growth in Southern Nigeria (Part II of Church Growth in Central and Southern Nigeria by Grimley and Robinson).* Grand Rapids, Eerdmans.
RYCROFT, W. Stanley (Ed.)
1946 *Indians of the High Andes.* New York, Committee on Cooperation in Latin America.

SCHALLER, Lyle C.
1975 *Hey, That's Our Church.* Nashville, Abingdon.
1975 "Where Are the Young Marrieds," in the February issue of *Survey.* Presbyterian Church in the United States.
1976 "The Costs of Rapid Growth" in *Church Administration,* Sunday School Board of the Southern Baptist Convention, May issue.
1977 *Survival Tactics in the Parish.* Nashville, Abingdon.
1979 *Assimilating New Members.* Nashville, Abingdon.
SEAMANDS, J. T.
1968 "Growth of the Methodist Church in South India." Unpublished dissertation, Asbury Theological Seminary, Wilmore, KY.
SHEARER, Roy E.
1966 *Wildfire: The Growth of the Church in Korea.* Grand Rapids, Eerdmans.
SMITH, Ebbie C.
1976 *A Manual for Church Growth Surveys.* Pasadena, William Carey Library.
SMITH, James C.
1976 "Without Crossing Barriers: The Homogeneous Unit Principle in the Writings of Donald McGavran." Unpublished doctoral dissertation at The School of Missions, Fuller Theological Seminary, Pasadena.
SUNDA, James
1963 *Church Growth in West New Guinea.* Lucknow, Lucknow Publishing House.

TAIWAN PRESBYTERIANS SYNODICAL OFFICE
c. 1966 *Announcing the Second Century — Basic Facts and Discussion Materials.* (Title translated from the Chinese). Taipei, Taiwan Presbyterian Synodical Office.
TAYLOR, Jack E.
1962 *God's Messengers to Mexico's Masses: A Study in the Religious Significance of the Braceros.* Privately printed, Eugene, OR.
TAYLOR, Mrs. Howard
1964 *Behind the Ranges.* Chicago, Moody.
THOMAS, Winburn
1959 *Protestant Beginnings in Japan.* Rutland, VT, Tuttle and Company.
't HOOFT, Visser
1963 *No Other Name: The Choice Between Syncretism and Christian Universalism.* Philadelphia, Westminster.
TIPPETT, Alan R.
1965 "Numbering: Right or Wrong." *Church Growth Bulletin,* Vol. I, No. 3
1967 *Solomon Island Christianity: A Study in Growth and Obstruction.* London, Lutterworth. One of the World Studies of Churches in Mission, edited by Victor E. W. Hayward.
1970 *Church Growth and the Word of God.* Grand Rapids, Eerdmans.
TOYNBEE, Arnold
1956 *An Historian's Approach to Religion.* London, New York, Oxford University.
TUGGY, A. Leonard
1968 "Philippine Society and Church Growth in Historical Perspective." A Master of Arts Thesis in the School of Missions and Institute of Church Growth, Fuller Theological Seminary, Pasadena.

TUGGY, A. Leonard and TOLLIVER, Ralph
  1971 *Seeing the Church in the Philippines*. Manila, O.M.F. Publishing Company.

VICEDOM, G. F.
  1962 *Church and People in New Guinea*. London, Lutterworth, World Christian Books No. 38.
VIEWPOINTS
  1962 "Syria Maintains Land Reform Offensive," Washington, D.C., American Friends of the Middle East.

WAGNER, C. Peter
  1971 *Frontiers of Missionary Strategy*. Chicago, Moody.
  1972 *Church/Mission Tensions Today*. Chicago, Moody.
  1972 *Stop The World—I Want To Get On*. Glendale, Regal.
  1973 *Look Out—The Pentecostals Are Coming*. Glendale, Regal.
  1976 *Your Church Can Grow*. Glendale, Regal.
  1978 *What Are We Missing?* Carol Stream, Creation House. (First published as *Look Out—The Pentecostals Are Coming*.)
  1979 *Your Spiritual Gifts Can Help Your Church Grow*. Glendale, Regal.
  1979 *Our Kind of People*. Atlanta, John Knox.
WALKER, F. Deaville
  1942 *A Hundred Years in Nigeria*. London, Cargate Press.
WALTNER, Orlando A.
  1962 "The General Conference Mennonite Church in India." An unpublished manuscript resulting from research done at the Institute of Church Growth, Eugene, OR.
WASSON, Alfred W.
  1934 *Church Growth in Korea*. New York, International Missionary Council.
WAYMIRE, Robert and WAGNER, Peter
  1980 *The Church Growth Survey Manual*. Santa Clara, Church Growth Bulletin.
WILLCUTS, J. L.
  1979 *Friends in the Soaring Seventies*. Newberg, OR, Oregon Yearly Meeting of Friends.
WILLEMS, Emilio
  1964 See D'Antonio.
WINTER, Ralph D.
  1966 "Gimmickitis" in *Church Growth Bulletin*, January Issue.
  1971 "The New Missions and the Mission of the Church" in *International Review of Missions*, January issue.
  1972 "The Planting of Younger Missions" in Wagner, *Church/Mission Tensions Today*.
  1972 "Quality or Quantity" in McGavran, *Crucial Issues in Missions Tomorrow*.
  1974 "The Highest Priority: Cross Cultural Evangelism" in *Let the Earth Hear His Voice*, International Congress on World Evangelization, Minneapolis, World Wide Publications.
  1974 "Seeing the Task Graphically" in *Evangelical Missions Quarterly*, January issue.
  1977 "The Grounds for a New Thrust in World Mission" in *Evangelical Missions Tomorrow*, edited by Coggins and Frizen, Pasadena, William Carey Library.
  1978 *Six Essential Components for World Evangelization: Goals for 1984*. Pasadena, William Carey Library.
  1979 *Penetrating the Last Frontiers*. Pasadena, William Carey Library.
WOLD, J. C.
  1966 "Liberia, Land of Startling Change." *World Encounter*, Vol. 4, No. 1, New York.
  1968 *God's Impatience in Liberia*. Grand Rapids, Eerdmans.

WORLD-WIDE MISSION STATISTICS

1856   Newcomb, Harvey (Ed.), *A Cyclopedia of Missions — containing a comprehensive view of missionary operations throughout the world*. New York, Scribner.

1891   Bliss, Edward Munsell, *Encylopaedia of Missions*. Vols. I & II. New York, London, Funk and Wagnalls.

1901   Beach, Harlan Page, *A Geography and Atlas of Protestant Missions*. New York, Student Volunteer Movement. Two volumes.

1911   Dennis, James S., Beach, Harlan P., Fahs, Charles H. (Eds.), *World Atlas of Christian Missions*. New York, Student Volunteer Movement for Foreign Missions.

1925   Beach, Harlan P. and Fahs, Charles H. (Eds.), *World Missionary Atlas*. New York, Institute of Social and Religious Research.

1938   Parker, Joseph I. (Ed.), *Interpretive Statistical Survey of the World Mission of the Christian Church*. New York, London, International Missionary Council.

1949   Grubb, Kenneth and Bingle, E. J. (Eds.), *World Christian Handbook*. London, World Dominion.

1952   Grubb, Kenneth and Bingle, E. J. (Eds.), *World Christian Handbook*.

1957   Bingle, E. J. and Grubb, Kenneth (Eds.), *World Christian Handbook*.

1962   Coxill, H. Wakelin and Grubb, Kenneth (Eds.), *World Christian Handbook*.

1968   Coxill, H. Wakelin and Grubb, Kenneth (Eds.), *World Christian Handbook*.

WRIGHT, Morris

1961   "Survey and Growth Evaluation of the Japan Baptist Convention." Unpublished thesis at Southwestern Baptist Theological Seminary, Fort Worth.

YEARBOOK OF AMERICAN CHURCHES, Jacquet (Ed).
YEARBOOK OF CONVENTION OF CHURCHES

1940 and 1948   Indianapolis, IN, *The International Convention of Churches of Christ*.

INDEX

accurate accounting 81, 88, 91, 107, 123

adherents 106

administration 82, 83, 157

administrator 91, 92, 147

Adventists 116, 154f, 184, 320

Africasia xiv, 21, 172, 173

Afghanistan 50

Africa 52

Aglipayan 108

agraristas 228

Aguacatec 406

Allen, Roland 377f

Ambedkar 286, 339

America 47, 75, 81, 83, 85, 91, 97, 103, 135, 142, 144, 148, 151

American denominations 321, 333, 375

Americans 50, 53, 61, 130, 165, 188, 207, 222, 223, 264, 270, 396, 413

Amos 278

Anderson, Rufus 375

Andes 154

Andhra 62

Anglican 55, 62, 97, 102, 154, 220, 282, 438

Anglo-Saxons 397

Animists 22, 92, 124, 128

anthropology ix, 126-128, 153

Apayao 247

Apolonia 368

Arn, Winfield 91, 423-424

arrested church growth 195-213, 301

Asbury 438

Assam 52, 74

Assemblies of God 68, 320

Association of Baptists for World Evangelism 451

Atlanta 62

Average Annual Growth Rate 428-432

awakenings, Evangelical 185, 203

468

Aymara Indians   155
Azariah, Bishop   102

Baliem Valley   398
Bangladesh   60, 72
baptism from church   101
baptism from world   101
baptism, when allow   175
Baptist Church   97
Baptists, American   10, 321
Baptists, British   46, 55, 179, 183, 320
baptized responsible membership 108
Barnabas   396
Barrett, David   317
barriers   61, 223-244
Bataks   216
believers   105
Bhagavad Gita   286, 287
Bible and the masses   277-281
Bible, the open   302
Bible—teaching Christians to read   302, 316
biblical barriers   229f
biological church growth   98, 99
Black Americans   67, 407
Bolenge   94
Bolton, Robert   401-403
Boro Kacharis   74
Boston   406
braceros   24
Brahman   73, 287, 334
Brasil para Cristo   320
Brazil   17-19, 51, 74, 80, 96, 97, 271, 318, 343
Bridgeport   240
bridges of God   71, 395
   neglecting bridges   404
bridging growth   100-101, 395-411

brotherhood   44, 45, 238-242
Buddhists   4, 22, 92, 124
budget distributions   157
Burma   73, 397

California   10, 20, 320
Campus Crusade   400
Canada   57, 67, 157, 158, 165, 263, 313, 320, 399, 413
Cardign, Mgr.   293
Carey, Wm. 51
castes   224, 232-234, 241, 274
caste system   286-287, 357
Castillo, Met   409
causes of growth   123-143
Chile   46, 50, 317
Chin   73
China   49, 50, 146
Chokosi   291, 351, 453f
Chota Nagpur   246
Christianization
   by abstraction   338f
   people movement mode of   333-372
Christian and Missionary Alliance   118, 140, 410, 443
Christian Reformed Church   248
Church Growth Bulletin   vi, 66, 111, 170, 260, 400, 405, 421f, 443
Church Growth Movement   vi
church growth
   a by-product   435f
   and revival   185-203
   and social structure   207-222
   as faithfulness   3-21, 91
Church of South India   50, 159, 160
Church extension   5
Church history   154
Church multiplication   455
Church statistics   81, 82, 83, 94

Church union 158
Church work 86
Churches of Christ 81, 104
city/cities
  churching the 318
  discipling urban populations 314-331
  dwellers 315
  flood into 318
  great church growth in 317, 320
  populations 315
  reaching the 318
  rush to 315
classes, the 269-294
class barrier 228
class/mass society 270
Clough, John 11, 51, 87, 167, 450
Colombia 400
communicants 104f, 130, 320, 413
communicate Christian Faith 299f, 321, 372
communicators 298
Communism 269-293
community 104f
community of nations 459
comparative study of church growth 178f
Conciliar Churches 43
conglomerate congregations 407
Congo 94, 406
Congregacao Cristan 320
conversion,
  individual 338f
  interdependent 340f
  multi-individual 339f
  work of Holy Spirit (see Holy Spirit)
conversion church growth 98, 99
corporate righteousness 75, 191
corporate salvation 75

Cullmann, Oscar 7
cultural advance 163
cultural distance 67, 68
cultural diversity 449
cultural overhang 83, 148, 156, 185
culture 126, 153, 163, 415

Dani 140, 342, 398
Davis, Merle 80, 272
Dayton, Edward 74f
decisive act 174-176
decline in growth 147
defeat 168
defeated Christians, pastors, bishops 119, 459
defensive thinking 415
de Foucauld, Charles 260
denominationalism 83
Denver 228
depressed classes 285
development 309f
Dia, Leonardo G. 8
diakonia 89
dialects 270
discipled 74
discipled (D-1, D-2, D-3) 169f
Disciples of Christ 46, 94, 133, 134, 146
discipling vii, 85, 91, 92, 127, 294, 301, 418, 421
discipling urbanites 314-332
discrimination 238
diversities in homogeneous units 225-227
D-1 not revival 195-198
doctrine 84
domestic aristocrats 288
Dornakal diocese 390
Double the Church Plan 443
Dumars 209

E-1, E-2, E-3, 63-70
E-1-A to D 70-71
Early Church and bridges 396
Ecuador 72
education 44, 54, 135f, 154, 157,
   311
EFMA/IFMA 419
egalitarianism 90
eicos pattern 348
Eisenhower, President 276
endogamy 224
England 47, 62, 220, 397, 400
environmental factors in church
   growth 159, 162
Episcopal Church 81, 104f, 246,
   282
equal justice 280f
equality of opportunity 269f, 280
Equatorial Province 100
Ethiopia 4, 51, 154
ethnic/class encirclement 321
ethnicity 225
ethnic minorities 238, 399, 438
ethnic realities 224
ethnic segments/units 62, 72, 75,
   223, 224, 333-372, 457
ethnic unmeltables 223
ethnocentricity 83
ethnography 153
Eurican xiv, 21, 172-173, 313, 374
Europe 3, 83, 142, 165, 263,
   360-362
Evangelical 43, 166
evangelism 25, 43, 55, 60, 77f, 84,
   144, 157
   effective evangelism 72, 307,
      410, 412
   essentially biblical 426
   resulting in monoethnic churches
      448

resulting in multiethnic churches
   448
seed sowing 77
typology of 69
evil spirits 92
excommunication 103
executive 110, 147
expansion growth 100-101
extension growth 100-101

facts and figures needed
   baptismal figures 101
   biological growth 98
   bridging growth 100
   communicant growth 104
   community growth 104f
   conversion growth 98
   extension growth 100
   external growth 100
   family analysis 103
   field totals 94f
   homogeneous unit totals 95f
   record/workers 108
   transfer growth 98
   ways in 102
   ways out 102
faithfulness 3-22, 257
faith projections of membership
   414, 427
family analysis 103-104
fetish burning 398
field totals 94, 95, 96, 113, 137
Filson, Floyd 216
finding 27-39
fog 76-92
foggy words 84, 85
folding 6
foreign oppressors 288
forgiveness 288
Formosa, see Taiwan

Foursquare Gospel 48
France 68
Fraser, John 155, 216
Freeman, Thomas B. 220
French Canadian 62, 98
friends as bridges of God 395-411
Friends (Church) 4, 45
full families 104, 149f
Fuller Evangelistic Association 424

Gamaliel, Canjanam 357
Garas 179-183
General Conference Baptists 118
Georgia 10, 62
Gerber, Vergil 421-423
Gerber workshops on church growth 422
Gibbons, Donald 398
Glasser, A. F. 245
glorification of littleness 168
goal setting 412-433
    chart past growth 426
    essential strategy of evangelism 420-423
    executives and 415
    foundations of hard bold plans for 419
    in United States 423f
    keeps priorities straight 413
    not often done 413-416
    pleases God 418f
    Scripture supports 417
    secures needed facts 412
    ultimate objective 421
    widely accepted now 425
Gold Coast 135
good works 24, 44, 47, 54, 344f
Gospel
    unchanging 124

a real option 125
graph of growth 91, 114, 128, 142, 145, 182
Great Commission 56, 66, 88
Greek Americans 74, 405
Greenway, Roger 316
Gregory the Great 397
growing churches 110-120, 410
growth-arresting concepts 166
growth histories 130
Guadalajara 316
Guatemala 145, 406
Gypsies 68

Hakka 63, 95
half-families 104, 149
halting 295-313
Harda 46
Harris, Prophet 342, 368
harvest 25f
heart language 217-219
hidden peoples 72f
high-rise apartments 328
Hindus/Hinduism 22, 82, 124, 151, 215, 239, 250, 277, 286, 331, 390
Hispanic Americans 67, 407
history 153, 154, 155
Hoekendijk, J. C. 436
holism 90
holy living/holiness 76, 190-191
Holy Spirit, 126, 144, 157, 161, 163, 178, 186-206, 241, 304, 395, 413, 457
    baptism of 303
homogeneous 61
homogeneous unit 73, 95, 97, 113, 117, 130, 148, 223f
homogeneous unit Churches 97
homogeneous unit principle 223-243

homogeneous unit totals   95-97
Hong Kong   68, 97, 120, 247, 317
house churches   216f
household conversion   348
humane order   288
humanitarianism   413
Hunter, George   69, 258, 396, 425
Hurn, Raymond   425
Hwang   401f

Iceland   16-17, 355
Ilaga Valley   398
Illinois   51
illiterates   365
immigrants   10, 62, 72, 246, 318
increase in members   93-119, 130
indefinitely reproducible   296f,
   310, 346
India   11, 49, 50, 103, 199, 209,
   232-234, 274, 366, 404
indigenous   18, 415
indigenous church principles   373-
   391
   defined   373f
   essentially New Testament   377
   external indigeneity   390
   Nevius statement of   375-377
   people movements and   386-391
   pragmatically useful   374
   reasons for   378-382
   reservations concerning   382f
   rules governing   384-386
   value systems   390
indoctrinating catechumens   184
Indonesia   317, 343
industrialism   269, 275
inferior breeds of men   290
ingathering   193
injustice   43, 238, 275, 288
inner city   75

Institute of American Church Growth
   424
Institute of Church Growth   vi, 54
institutionalized philanthropy   347
internal church growth   100-101
International Congress on Evangelism   62
interviewing in church growth research   149f
intolerance   238
Ireland   400
Italians   51
Ivory Coast   342f

Jamaica   46, 47, 62, 104, 212, 220
Japan   46, 80, 103, 156, 317
Japanese   74
Jews   72, 96, 246, 334, 355
Jubbulpore   209
justice   v, 44, 89, 186, 191, 276,
   286f, 311
just society   288

Kachin   72
Kamba   72
Kansas   146
Karen   72
Kentucky   94
Kenya   72, 367
Kessler, J. B. A.   184
kin-contact   298, 368
King, Louis L.   443
Kingdom of God   288
Kinshasa   96, 317
kinship system, Chinese   209
Korea   52, 137, 153, 156, 367
Ko Tha Byu   397
Krass, A. C.   228, 291, 351, 369f,
   388, 453, 455

labor unions   269f
laity, laymen   147
landed aristocracy   273
landless   275, 285
landowners   273
land reform   275
land rights and church growth   211
language and church growth   217,
    227, 270
Latin America Church Growth
    419
Latin American   276
Latourette, K. S.   397, 418
Lausanne   62, 63
Law, Dr. Gail   120
le Cossec   67, 69
letters and church growth   156
Liao, David   63
liberals   166
liberation   44
Liberia   369
lift   295-313
lift and church growth   305-307
Lisu   72, 155, 216
literature distribution   125, 321
littleness   169
liturgy   365
Loewen, J.   365
London   22, 62
London Missionary Society   176f
Los Angeles   72
lower classes   273
Lutherans   10, 62, 72, 95, 97, 128,
    282, 321

Madigas   11, 62, 167
maintenance   30, 34, 163, 410
Major, Pat   345
Maldonado, Oscar   274

Mandarin   63, 95
marriage   customs and church
    growth   208-209
Marxists   4, 73, 273
masses   269-294
Mellor, Andrew   343
melting pots   214, 243f
memorized passages in worship
    365
Mennonite   179-183
Methodists   4, 10, 12, 46, 50, 135,
    240, 282, 343, 366, 425, 438
methods God blesses   183, 185
Mexicans   72
Mexico   62, 228, 320, 359-363
Micah   278
middle-class churches   282f, 312f,
    321, 409
middle-class Christianity   301
middle classes   273f, 299f
migration to city   318, 428
millennium   30
ministers   145, 152
Minnan   63
minorities   67, 83, 438
Mirzapur story   176f, 246
mission
    a divine finding   24
    history   154
    is God's   23
    minutes   156
    social reconstruction   25
    "work" vs. church growth   80,
        85, 414
missionaries   67, 75, 145
missionary societies   75, 87, 321
Mizos   74, 405f, 408
Montgomery, James   420
mosaic   vii, 59-75, 223f, 375, 407,
    409

Moslems 60, 72, 73, 124, 151, 259, 262

motives, mixed 149, 173-175

movements out of non-Christian Faith 333-353

multiply causes of church growth 160-164

multiplication of churches 44, 75, 77, 91, 117, 124, 293, 309, 317, 406, 409, 455f

multi-racial churches 306-310

Nagas 74

Nazarenes vii, 4, 98, 246, 425

near-neighbor evangelism 63

Neill, Stephen 52

Nevius method 158, 375-377

Newbigin, Lesslie 416f

New England 406

New Guinea 73

new settlements 248f

new suburbs 249

New Testament church growth 161

New York 95

Nida, Eugene 273

Nigeria 95, 136, 140, 343, 346, 454

nominal Christians 124

non-Christian religions 27, 28, 79, 89

Nordyke, Quentin 432

North America 3, 48, 49, 72, 86, 87, 124, 221, 318, 333, 360, 377

Northeast India 405

Norway 15

numbering 93, 96

numbers
mere 36, 37
of the redeemed 38

numerical approach 93, 94

Nyal 16-17

Nzima 368

Ohio 55

one-by-one out of 338f, 359, 363

one-class congregation 409

one-in-Christ 230, 238-242

one-people church 241, 406

Ongole 20, 87

open-ended society 408

"Operation 200" 421

oppression 269-294, 319

ordained minister 310

Oregon Friends 432

Orissa 345

Orr, J. Edwin 185-206, 442

"our kind of people" 240, 406

panta ta ethne vii, 22, 56, 240, 413, 427

parallelism 90

Pariahs 79

particularity of growth 130, 263-264

Pasadena 68

pastor 88, 110, 112, 134, 147, 159, 249

Patrick 400

peace 89

Pentecostal 3, 101, 133, 154, 316, 405

people/peoples v, 56, 59, 60, 72, 73, 155, 167, 224-267

people consciousness and church growth 214, 241, 403

people movements
care of people movements 364-372
corporate decision for Christ 341f, 351
defined 334-336
education and 342-344
good deeds and 344f
group conversion 340, 342

Holy Spirit-guided 349
indigenous principles and 388-391
managing a people movement 346
many kinds of 354-363
mode of Christianization 339f
moral reform and 352f
multi-individual
    conversion 340, 342, 344
New Testament people movements 348f
qualitative importance of 337
quantitative importance 336
soundly Christian? 347-349
starting a people movement 367-372
starved people movements 350
web movements 359-363
well-fed people movements 350
worship of God essential 351
people movements, care of
assemble each evening 364
day-school education 365f
post-baptismal care 364-372
regular worship 364f
revival soon 366
strengthen family ties 365
systematic shepherding 366-372
teach much Bible truth 365f
Pepohwan 131, 132, 194
perfecting 134, 312
persuasion 34, 35, 38, 92, 219, 341, 417
Peru 73, 74, 155
Philippines 8-9, 118, 410, 420, 451, 452
Pickett, J. W. 46, 284, 339
Piersman, N. 400
planning for church growth 434-457

adequate plans needed 440f
adjust in light of outcome 443
assumed unnecessary 434
biblically based 437
operate plans 441
plans God has blessed 451-455
prerequisite for just world 437
suit to stage of mission 443-448
plateau 130f, 135, 147
pluralistic 49, 89, 404, 449f
Polish 62, 72
polygamy 163, 213f
poor, the 280, 281
post-baptismal training 163
poverty 311
power by revival 191-193
power structure and church growth 209
Pope John Paul II 289, 456
Pope Paul VI 456
prayer 125, 410
prayer for revival 186-206
prayer meetings 188f
Presbyterian 3, 4, 9, 45, 46, 116, 220, 282, 320
presence, Christian 260, 319
proclaim the Gospel 192, 219
productive patterns 163
proletariat 269f, 276, 293
promotion 87-88, 147, 154f
Protestants 104, 300
psychology 31
Puerto Rico 132-134

qualitative growth 425
quality not quantity 86
quantifying evangelism 63
quantitative growth 418, 426
Quechuas 72
questionnaires 110

race pride 44, 191, 235
radio broadcasting 321
Raichur 4, 341
Raju, S. N. 159
random sampling 148
rationalists 72
rationalization 85, 86, 157f, 167, 415
reached 72-73
Read, Wm. R. 420
reasons for growth 123-143, 151, 159, 161-164
receptive 162, 164, 165, 245-268
receptivity and strategy 257-260
its distribution 260
receptivity axis 260-261
receptivity in USA 261-262
receptivity and mission 262-263, 264, 265
reconciliation 27-39, 43, 87
redemption 295-313
redemption and church growth 304f
Reformed Church in America 43, 425
reinterpretation of mission vii
relatives are bridges of God 395-411
relativism 27, 28
renewal 77
reproducible patterns of church growth 119
research 110, 111, 117, 118, 120, 144, 164, 395
in urban church growth 318-322
researchers 156f, 183, 322
resistant/resistance 48, 63, 163, 215, 245f, 298, 324f, 399
responsive 33, 37, 48, 50, 52, 56, 85, 183, 245-267, 399

responsiveness/receptivity, factors affecting:
acculturation 256
conquest 250
erosion of belief 252
freedom from control 254
new settlements 248
retired travellers 249
vacuum of faith 253
responsiveness fluctuates 291
results 29, 30, 31
reversion 103
revitalization vii, 187
revival 133-134, 139, 186-203, 312
revival and church growth 201-203
revivals differ from people movements 192-306
revolution 276
revolutionary ranchos 228f
Rhodesia 12, 20f
righteousness v, 311
righteous world order 289
ripe fields 178
ripen to Gospel 246
ripenings, sudden 247
Rodriguez, Bishop 248
Roman Catholic 4, 101, 104, 116, 247, 282, 300, 436
Ruanda 105
Rubingh, Eugene 454

salvation of multitudes 300
Sao Paulo 51
Satnamis 289-290
Schaller, Lyle 225-227, 397
school approach 11-15, 135f, 140-141, 155, 163, 261
Seamands, J. T. 50
search 25-40

secular Americans 72, 147
secular education 303
secularists 4, 22, 50
segments of society 407
self-image and church growth 208
seminaries 263, 264
service as sufficient 89
Sevav plan 454
sex mores and church growth 212
Shakers 240
shake off dust 291
Shearer, Roy 137, 420
Shudras 271, 272, 288
Sinaloa 45
Singapore 120
singles 104
slaves 275, 277, 292
slow-growing denomination 119
slow growth 167
Smith, E. 111
social
  action 25, 26, 43, 86, 88, 89, 191, 292-293
  advance 75
  dislocation 306
  justice 269f
  network 396
  obstacles to conversion 215f
  order 25, 127
  realities 15
  sciences vii
  structure 84, 207-222
  units 333-372
sociological foundation 208-222
sociology 6
solidarity with the world 300, 307
Southern Baptists vii, 10, 46, 79, 118, 246
sovereignty of God 37, 38
specialists 52-53

Spirit-filled churches 374
spiritual hunger 50
spiritual motives 174-175
spiritual reasons 177
stages of mission 443-448
  exploration 445
  firm outposts 445
  strong clusters of churches 446
  substantial
    Christianization 447-448
stagnant churches 119
State Churches (European) 263
static churches v, vi, 49, 415-416
statistics 81, 86, 94
stoppage 180, 295-313
stopped churches 135, 136, 295, 313
structure of church 123
substituted for evangelism 89, 243
suburban 150
Sudan Interior Mission 51
Sudras 79
Sunda, J. 398
Sunday Schools 75
survey of church growth 111-117
Sweden 100
Syria 275
Syrian Orthodox 4
sympathizers 106

Taiwan 46, 52, 63, 95, 131f, 139, 161, 227, 401-403
Thailand 91
theological causes of fog 88-90
theological factors in church growth 159, 237
  rationalization of no growth 435f
theology vii, 54, 88, 89, 129
  of egalitarian society 330-332
  of harvest 27-40

of indigenous church 374
of maintenance 415
of mission ix, x, 77
of new mission 43
of remnant 168
of search 26-40
to be done 419
Texas 159, 212
Thoburn, Bishop 183
three billion 41, 44, 59, 63-66, 208, 439
Tippett, A. R. 93, 127, 312, 420
Tiv (Nigeria) 248, 346
Tolliver, Ralph 420
tongues, speaking in 134
Toynbee, Arnold 284
transfer church growth 97-99, 103
transfer of authority 59, 60
Tranquebar 79
triumphalism 449
truth 7
Tuggy, Leonard 124, 420

Uganda 105
undiscipled vi, x
United Church 159
United Church of Christ 45, 118
United Presbyterians 45
United States 8, 10, 67, 68, 72, 76, 79, 96, 104, 118, 133, 134, 150, 154, 158, 210f, 246, 261, 263, 282, 293, 320, 397, 399, 413
unity of the group 363
unpaid leaders 311
unreached peoples 73, 74
Untouchables 12, 281, 286
urban areas 319f
urban churches 100, 120
urban church growth
    focus on responsive 326

house churches 322
intense faith in Christ 329
keys to 332
lay leaders 323
movements 317
multiply homogeneous unit churches 326
populations 314-322, 427
recognize resistant units 324
research 318-322
wards 303

varieties of church growth 185
Venn, Henry 335
Venezuela 422f
victim of the social order 183, 269f
village 303, 310
Virginia 212

Wagner, Peter 62, 74, 91, 100, 111, 240, 257f, 421, 424
Waltner, O. A. 179
Wasson, A. W. 137, 158
Waymire, Robert 111
ways into church 102, 103
ways out of church 102, 103
webs of relationship 360-362
Wesley, John 438
West New Guinea 140, 342
West Virginia 60
White Americans 407
Willems, Emelio 285
winnable 33, 37, 290f, 410
winning upper classes first 283-285
Winter, R. D. 61-66, 75, 100, 428
    Winter's diagram 63-68
witness 84
Wold, J. C. 128, 369
work 80, 85, 414

working classes   120, 222, 269-293
working-class denominations   409
World Council of Churches   60

Yakima Indians   240
Yeotmal   199-201

younger Churches   59, 60, 84, 99

Zaire   100, 406
Zambia   12
Zodiates, Argos   405f